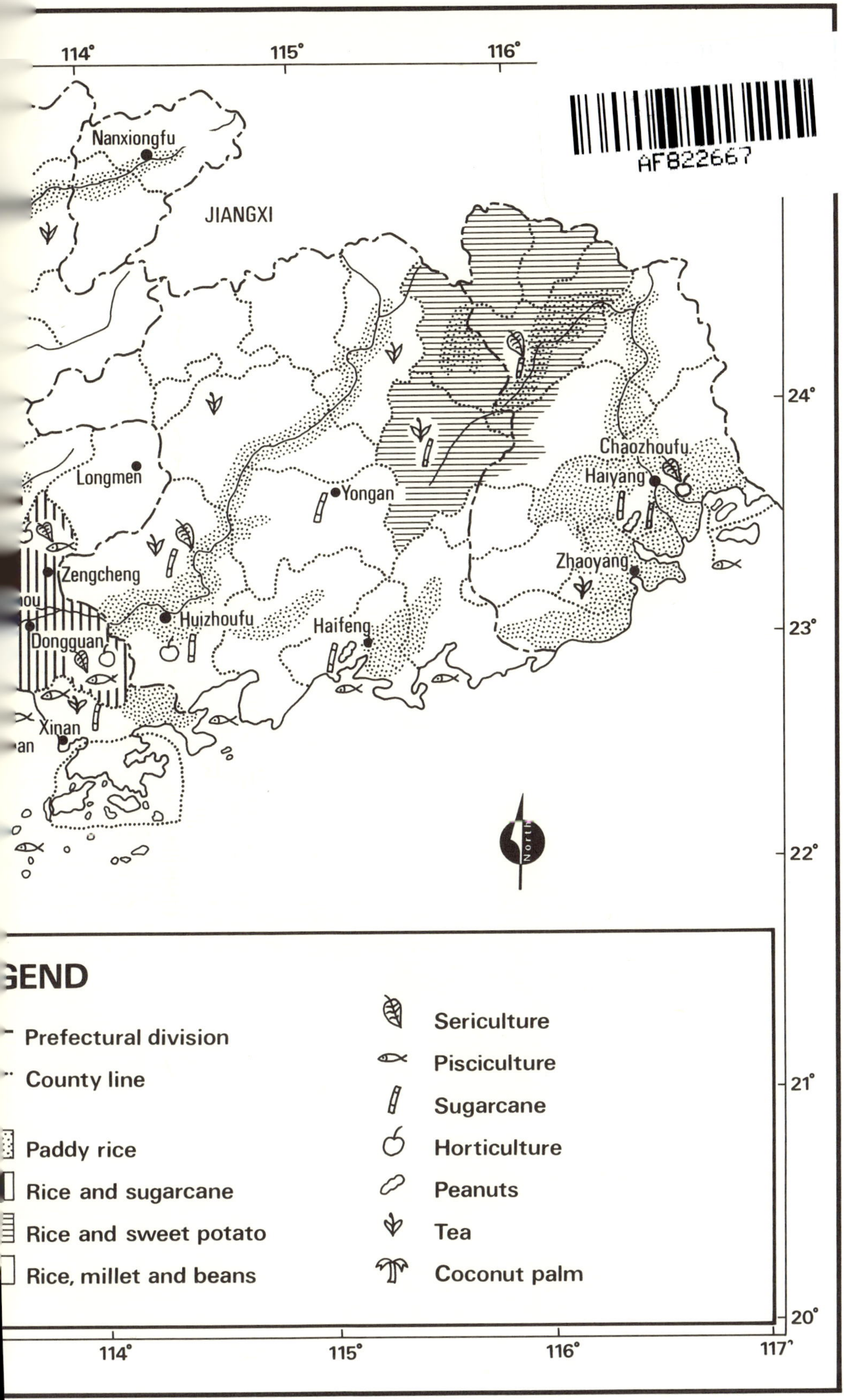
114°
115°
116°
117°
24°
23°
22°
21°
20°
Nanxiongfu
JIANGXI
Longmen
Yongan
Chaozhoufu
Haiyang
Zengcheng
Zhaoyang
Huizhoufu
Haifeng
Dongguan
Xinan
North
GEND
Prefectural division
County line
Paddy rice
Rice and sugarcane
Rice and sweet potato
Rice, millet and beans
Sericulture
Pisciculture
Sugarcane
Horticulture
Peanuts
Tea
Coconut palm

To Bill,
with warm regards.
Sucheta

SUGAR AND SOCIETY IN CHINA

Harvard-Yenching Institute Monograph Series 45

SUGAR AND SOCIETY IN CHINA

PEASANTS, TECHNOLOGY, AND THE WORLD MARKET

Sucheta Mazumdar

Published by the Harvard University Asia Center
and distributed by Harvard University Press
Cambridge (Massachusetts) and London
1998

Printed in the United States of America

The Harvard-Yenching Institute, founded in 1928 and headquartered at Harvard University, is a foundation dedicated to the advancement of higher education in the humanities and social sciences in East and Southeast Asia. The Institute supports advanced research at Harvard by faculty members of certain Asian universities and doctoral studies at Harvard and other universities by junior faculty at the same universities. It also supports East Asian studies at Harvard through contributions to the Harvard-Yenching Library and publication of the *Harvard Journal of Asiatic Studies* and books on premodern East Asian history and literature.

Mazumdar, Sucheta, 1948–
Sugar and society in China : peasants, technology, and the world market / Sucheta Mazumdar
p. cm. -- (Harvard-Yenching Institute monograph series : 45)
Includes bibliographic references and index.
ISBN 0-674-85408-X
1. Sugar trade--China--History. 2. China--Economic conditions.
3. China--Social conditions. I. Title. II. Series.
HD9116.C62M39 1998
338.1'7361'0951--dc21 98-4763
CIP

Index by Mary Mortensen

♾ Printed on acid-free paper

07 06 05 04 03 02 01 00 99 98

Endpaper map based on Situ Xiangji, "Mingdai Guangdong jingji dili qutan," appendix; and *Guangdong xinyu*, pp. 371–460, 683–729

David M. Farquhar

1927–1985

in memoriam

ACKNOWLEDGMENTS

DAVID FARQUHAR INTRODUCED ME to Chinese history in my sophomore year at UCLA and saw me through my Ph.D. dissertation. An encyclopaedic scholar and caring and challenging teacher, David's extended seminars on Tang to Qing history on topics ranging from serfdom to commercial crops have found their way into many parts of this book. I was privileged to study with him and shall always be grateful for the many hours he spent reading texts with me in spite of his failing health.

I would also like to acknowledge my intellectual debt to my other teachers at UCLA. Lao Kan and Shirleen Wong shared with me their vast knowledge of history and classical Chinese; Fred Notehelfer encouraged my interests in comparative history, and seminars with Robert Brenner helped me begin exploring theoretical concerns. Undergraduate seminars with Philip Huang introduced me to studies of rural China.

The UCLA exchange program made it possible for me to study at Zhongshan University and the Hua'nan Nongxue Yuan in 1981. Professor Liang Jiamian and the staff of the library at Hua'nan Nongxue Yuan were most generous with archival material and their insights into the history of agriculture in Guangdong. I want to thank the many members of the Zhongda faculty who patiently set about teaching me Guangdong history. In particular, I want to thank Ye Xian'en for his warm collegiality and steady support for my projects. Without Professor Ye's guidance and continued kindness in sharing materials, arranging forays into libraries and collections, and long hours of conversation on Qing history, this would have been a far poorer book.

I have enjoyed the help of many individuals and institutions and it is a pleasure to have this opportunity to express my appreciation. A fellowship at the Center for Chinese Studies and the Asian American Studies Program at the University of California Berkeley helped me begin the difficult process of translating the dissertation into a book. Discussions with Frederic Wakeman while at Berkeley helped me begin this reconceptualization, and I am very grateful to him for the many discussions that we have continued to have. The encouragement and repeated readings of my work by Evelyn S. Rawski and Susan Naquin have been crucial, and I am indebted to both of them for not letting me go under and drop out of the field when David Farquhar died. James Watson and Rubie Watson helped me discover the intricacies of Guangdong society; their comments on my work have been invaluable. I sincerely appreciate the close and critical readings of both my dissertation and the manuscript by Nathan Sivin. His probing comments forced me to confront difficult questions in my writing; his generosity and his wit made the process less painful. A postdoctoral fellowship in 1987 at the Fairbank Center, Harvard University, allowed me to attend Philip A. Kuhn's seminar on Qing documents; the seminar proved fundamental to my own understanding of the period, and his support has been pivotal to the completion of this project.

I cannot adequately acknowledge the valuable suggestions and comments on my written work and presentations that have been given so generously by so many scholars over the past decade. In particular I would like to thank Eugene Anderson, Ben Barker Benfield, Loren Brandt, Anita Chan, Kent Guy, Steve Harrell, Joyce Kallgren, Richard Lachmann, Nicholas Lardy, Daniel Little, Robert Marks, Seymour Mauskopf, Ramon Myers, Dwight Perkins, Elizabeth Perry, Thomas Rawski, Alex Roland, Françoise Sabban, Jonathan Unger, R. Bin Wong and Madeline Zelin. I benefited immensely from the opportunity to exchange ideas with economists at the workshop on Economic Methods for Chinese Historical Research, held in Honolulu in 1987, and the comments of Peter Lindert on my work. The substantive help and feedback I received on my chapter on overseas trade from participants at the ACLS-SSRC conference on East Asian trade in 1988, particularly William Atwell, Leonard Bluss, Kawakatsu Heita, Mio Kishimoto, Oba Osamu, Geoffrey Parker, Ronald Toby, Jack Wills, and Shiba Yoshinobu is much appreciated. A postdoctoral award in 1985 from the Jackson School of International Studies, University of Washington, allowed me the time to continue my training in comparative history; the Nuala Drescher Award from the New York State United University Professionals at SUNY Albany in 1990 provided me with the resources necessary to learn to work with Dutch materials.

Several scholars have sent me materials I would not have otherwise located, shared bibliographic sources, photocopied, and graciously accommodated my many demands; I especially want to thank Chen Chunsheng, Mark Chan, Myron Cohen, Robert Eng, Janet Ewald, Michael Finnegan, Robert Gardella, Atsuko Kanazawa, Kuan Manbun, Harry Lambley, Si-tu Xiangji, John Shepherd, Carl Smith, Alvin So, John TePaske, Tan Dihua, Kären Wigen, Wing-ho Wong, Eri Yasuhara, and Yip Hon-ming. The collegial environment of the History Department at Duke has made the final process of revisions less onerous.

I am grateful to Tomohisa Ando, Hwang Dong Youn, Hope O'Neill, and Sophia Ling for their help at critical junctures with reading, editing, and tracking down materials; Huang Ling-kuan tackled my messy references and glossary with outstanding good cheer. My experiences at Zhongda as a graduate student were rendered infinitely more pleasant with the help and hospitality of Liu Yueling and Ou Hong. I am grateful to the Overseas Chinese Bureau and particularly Him Mark Lai and Russell Leong for enabling me to travel to various villages in the Pearl River Delta in 1986. Marlon Hom and Raymond Lum generously shared their family genealogies; I thank Min Zhou and her parents for their hospitality in Zhongshan county in 1993.

The staff of various libraries have cheerfully acceded to my many requests and queries; in particular I want to thank the librarians at Duke University Special Collections, Baker Library, Feng Jintang Tushuguan, Feng Pingshan Tushuguan, Perkins Library, Harvard Yenching, Hoover East Asia Collection, Hua'nan Nongxue Yuan,

UCLA, UC Berkeley, Widener Library, and Zhongshan Tushuguan. I want to acknowledge especially the help of Timothy Connor, Evelyn Himler, Karl Lo, Raymond Lum, Edward Martinique, Peng Shijiang, and Kristina K. Troost.

Katherine Keenum and Patricia Ruprecht guided me through the first stage of the editorial process. David Glenn made comprehensible my sketches of technical machinery, and Jim Robb painstakingly designed the maps. Grants from the Trent Foundation, Asia Pacific Studies Institute, and the Mary Biddle Duke Foundation at Duke University have crucially helped with subventions for the production of maps, illustrations, and the index.

Finally, it is a great pleasure to acknowledge with deep appreciation that this book could not have been conceived or completed without the loving support and constant intellectual partnership of my husband, Vasant Kaiwar.

CONTENTS

TABLES, MAPS, AND FIGURES

Tables

Maps

Figures

NOTE ON TRANSLITERATION, NAMES, AND CONVERSIONS

CHINESE TERMS AND NAMES ARE rendered in pinyin, except when individuals have published using other forms of romanization. For personal names, normal Chinese and Japanese word order is used, with the surname first, with the exception of those Chinese or Japanese authors who have published in English and have selected to state their personal name first followed by the surname. Place-names are given in contemporary international postal spellings.

Weights and money. Tons refer to British long tons, 2240 pounds. Hundredweights are British 112 pounds.

The dollar sign ($), unless otherwise specified, is used for money amounts in China denoting either the Spanish or Mexican dollar coin that was used as bullion and currency of account in much of South China by the nineteenth century.

Principal weights and land measures used in the text. The following short table of standardized conversion rates is offered as a convenience to readers. For a more extensive discussion of the complicated equivalencies and variations over time and locality among Asian and European weights, measures, and currencies found in the sources fot his book, see the Appendix.

Weight
1 tael = 1 *liang* = approx. 1 oz. avoirdupois
1 *jin* = 1 catty = 16 taels = 1.32 lbs avoirdupois
1 picul = 100 *jin* = 133.3 lbs avoirdupois

1 long/short ton = 2,240/2,000 lbs avoirdupois
1 *dan* = 185 lbs avoirdupois
1 Dutch pound = 1.1 lb avoirdupois

Land

1 *jia* = 1 hectare = 2.47 acres
1 *mu* = 0.1647 acre

SUGAR AND SOCIETY IN CHINA

INTRODUCTION

Like amber presented on a crystal plate,
Is there anything more beautiful than crystallized sugar?
—Su Shi, 1074

THE FAMOUS POET WROTE THE ODE as he said goodbye to a friend setting off for Sichuan, an area then noted for its cane sugar.[1] How was the sticky, brown-green juice of a grass transformed into the golden crystals inspiring the poet's eulogy? As the title suggests, this book is concerned with the answer to that question and the history and technology of cane-sugar manufacture in China.

But the book embraces more than this; it is a study of long-term agrarian change. I have sought to place the story of sugar in China in a broader perspective. Sugarcane, its cultivation, and the technology of its manufacture provide convenient focal points for asking questions about aspects of the Chinese economy and society over a period of three hundred years. In some of the chapters that follow, sugar melts into the background as I grapple with the local social and economic formation in the Qing period. These two projects are linked by my attempt to explain the ways in which certain property structures, such as peasant possession of land and the means of subsistence, may have shaped the specific historical trajectory of development in Qing China and molded the market demand for commodities, including sugar.

There are two distinct chapters in the history of cane-sugar manufacturing in the pre-industrial world. Only one is well recognized; its elements include, in Fernand Braudel's words, "the black slaves, the planters, the production techniques, the refining of raw sugar, the cheap food supplies for the plantations which were unable to feed themselves; the shipping routes, the warehouses and the retailers in Europe."[2] But the drama of the New World sugar plantations, and their intimate relationship with the development of capitalism,[3] has overshadowed the quiet history of small-scale sugar cultivation and manufacture in the rest of the world. This book will take up that neglected story.

China, for long one of the largest producers of cane sugar, did not develop plantations in the seventeenth, eighteenth, and nineteenth centuries. Cane cultivation continued to be integrated into the multicrop economy of provinces such as Guangdong, Fujian, Taiwan, and Sichuan. Sugarcane was grown on thousands of small landholdings by producers who owned some, if not all, of the land on which they cultivated cane. The output was significant. A conservative estimate, based on the scattered figures we have, suggests that China produced approximately 10–15 million pounds of sugar for export annually in the 1630s. By way of comparison, the total output of Brazilian sugar in 1630, when the Portuguese supplied nearly all of Europe with sugar from Brazil, was around 45 million pounds. In the following centuries, Chinese output increased as world market demand accelerated. Until the end of the nineteenth century, sugar was the third most important item of export from China, next to tea and silk in volume and value.[4]

Sugarcane was introduced into southernmost China sometime in the third century B.C. After a long hiatus, its cultivation started spreading in the sixth and seventh centuries. How do we explain the seeming conjuncture of increased sugar consumption and the expansion of Buddhism? Was there a connection? Eleventh- and twelfth-century urban China seems to have developed quite a taste for sugar; the night markets of Kaifeng sold scores of varieties of candies, cakes, fruit preserves, flavored powdered sugars, brown sugars, white sugars, and sugar syrups. Chapter One discusses this history of consumption of cane sugar, its various uses from medicine to the delicate pastries eaten by the elite. Although the Chinese liked sweets and sweeteners, as I will show they did, after the sudden increase in the uses of sugar in the eleventh and twelfth centuries why was there was no renewed burst in the level of consumption? Even by the end of the nineteenth century, most Chinese continued to use only very modest amounts of sugar. Many scholars consider trade and the corresponding increase in the size of the market fundamental factors propelling the transition from the premodern economy to the modern economic system.[5] It has been argued that the competition brought about by trade leads to improvements in technology and consequently specialization. Over time, as a result of specialization and better technology, production and distribution are rationalized, leading to further development of the market, and so on. Was the domestic market limited in China? What were the factors affecting the development of the technology of manufacture and specialization in China? Since the direct producers did not manufacture cane sugar for personal use, but always for sale, the level of sugar consumption is a convenient avenue for entering into a discussion of the potentialities of the domestic market as a whole in late imperial China.

In contrast to China, the world market was undergoing a dramatic expansion, not least because of the economic transformation already under way in parts of Europe from the sixteenth century. The consumption of sugar, for example, multiplied many times. By 1800, the British consumed twenty-six times as much sugar as they did in 1650. China was linked to this world market through sugar exports to the Netherlands starting as early as the 1620s, when events in distant Brazil reduced supplies to the Amsterdam refineries and led to a demand for Chinese sugar. In addition, China also had an expanding commodity trade of its own in the Pacific, particularly Japan. Chapter Two traces the patterns of Chinese involvement in world trade before the nineteenth century and investigates whether Chinese shipping and mercantile capital could have profited from this more intimate nexus with the world market prior to the full thrust of colonialism in Asia. Could these profits then have been productively deployed by using available technology to improve output?

In the worldwide transformation of cane sugar–manufacturing technology that took place in the seventeenth century, Chinese innovations were significant, possibly even fundamental. Chapter Three looks closely at the technologies of manufacture from the twelfth century to the seventeenth and places Chinese manufacturing techniques in a broad comparative framework alongside Indian, Mediterranean, and Japanese techniques. This comparison hopes to show that there was no "technological standstill" in China innovations continued well into the seventeenth century and later.[6] But what direction did these innovations take? Did they strengthen certain social property structures, such as the small-holder economy in South China?[7] Did the small units of production establish a baseline, as it were, for innovations and the adoption of new technologies?

Interest in the manufacturing and handicraft sector of premodern rural China was stimulated by two major debates in the immediate post–World War II period; one a critique of theories of Asiatic stagnation,[8] and the other a hypothesis of incipient capitalism in China. Initially, these debates primarily involved scholars coming from a Marxist tradition of historiography engaged in understanding the impact of colonialism.[9] The origins of these debates go back to discussions initiated in the late 1920s and 1930s among Chinese and Soviet Marxist historians regarding the potential of commerce to effect structural transformation, the feudal nature of Chinese society and the Asiatic mode of production. Criticism of theories positing divergent routes of evolution in Europe and Asia had already begun in 1929; Stalin's formal exclusion of the Asiatic mode of production from the list of accepted social formations in 1938 gave the five-stage model of history the status of an orthodoxy. Agricultural technologies, rural manufacturing, and the economic history of indigenous firms were closely investigated; the findings documented the existence of extensive commodity production. In the late 1940s, Nishijima Sadao's study of the Chinese cotton industry furthered the debate by attacking the dominant theories of Asian stagnation as mere apologia for Western and Japanese imperialism and demonstrating that important changes in production and marketing structures during the Ming-Qing period had been ignored.[10] Yet, Nishijima did not interpret the impressive expansion of cotton handicraft production and the technological developments in manufacture as indicators of incipient capitalism.

Scholars working in China differed sharply from Nishijima and his colleagues such as Fujii Hiroshi, Imahori Seiji, Hirase Minokichi,

Suzuki Shun, and Tanaka Masatoshi[11] and viewed the expansion of commodity production in the Ming-Qing period as "the sprouts of capitalism" or indicators of incipient capitalism (*ziben zhuyi mengya*).[12] A vast body of source materials compiled in the 1950s and early 1960s by scholars such as Fu Yiling, Fu Zhufu, Li Wenzhi, Peng Zeyi, Shang Yue, Zhang Youyi, and others provided the basic resources for this analysis.[13] The fundamental query posed by this debate was why incipient capitalism failed to develop into mature capitalism in China. Formulated within the framework of a Stalinist five-stage development model, most of these scholars suggested China was on the verge of a capitalist transformation that was dislocated and then terminated by the intrusion of imperialism in the nineteenth century.

More critically nuanced Chinese studies followed in the 1970s and 1980s dealing with the local social structures of production. Fu Yiling, Jing Su, Luo Lun, Li Wenzhi, Wei Jinyu and Jing Junjian, Ye Xian-en, Li Longqian, Huang Qichen, and Tan Dihua among others have investigated intra-elite differentiation in economic behavior rather than overly simplified delineations of exploiter and exploited.[14] Li Wenzhi's findings are representative of this approach. In a recent work, Li richly documents the rise of commoner landlords, entrepreneurial owner-operators, and wealthy tenants in the Qing. He links the expansion of commodity production to the changes in legal statutes that upheld the independent status of wage-laborers and agricultural workers. Li argues that one result of these social and economic changes was the gradual emergence, over a three-hundred-year period, of capitalist tendencies among a new class of landlords, which nonetheless failed to culminate in a capitalist transformation. Attributing this thwarted development to the pervasiveness and tenacity of feudal relations of production, in particular the institution of landlordism in rural China, Li concludes that Chinese development continued but was unable to transform the relations of production.[15]

Li Wenzhi's focus on feudal landlordism fails to explain why production structures in rural China remained dominated by small-peasants. What prevented the "new" landlords, these putative yeomen, from undermining the small-scale peasantry completely, driving them off the land, taking over, and reorganizing production for the market? What were the sociopolitical barriers that forced the "managerial landlords" back to the status of rentiers?

The relationship between peasants and landlords and this one set of class relations have received the most attention from scholars seeking to explain why, despite the impressive levels of commercial manufacture, capitalism did not develop in China. But that clearly has not led to fully explaining the dynamics of economic behavior among the peasants themselves. Instead of isolating one set of inter-class relationships, I seek to examine the totality of the social formation of South China, in which all the actors on the scene—peasants, gentry and commoner landlords, not to mention merchants—sought to maintain or improve the class positions they *already* held by choosing the most rational options. I suggest it was the sum total of these intersecting actions, both inter-class and intra-class relationships, that molded the specific pattern of economic development.

The social upheavals that marked the transition of political power from the Ming to the Qing were accompanied by peasant rebellions and tenant uprisings in Guangdong as in other parts of the empire. In the Guangdong Delta and in Taiwan, strongholds of Ming loyalists and Zheng Chenggong (Koxinga) sympathizers, the dislocations accompanying this political transition lasted longer and were more severe than in the northern provinces. Though the Qing came to power in Beijing in 1644, the South was not pacified until 1683, when Taiwan was finally conquered. Did this long drawn-out contest for Qing hegemony have substantial effects on the relations of production?

Chapter Four examines the social outcome of these struggles, the emergence of small property holders whose property rights now received support from the state. Many of those who became full possessors of land and other means of subsistence had earlier been customary or unfree tenants, such as the *nupu*.[16] What were the consequences of these newly won rights, and how did peasants organize to protect them? Did these rights, while preventing complete proletarianization of the peasantry, also slow down the entry of outside capital by denying potential investors rights to land? How did these interests of the direct producers affect their relationship with the "lineage," a fundamental social organization in South China?[17] And how did the gentry and other propertied elites deal with the new economic rights gained by the direct producers?

In developing this framework, I have drawn on Robert Brenner's concept of social property relations, a concept encompassing the totality of relationships among the direct producers, among the surplus extractors, and between this "class" and the producers.[18] Social property relations determine the regular and systematic access of all the economic actors to the means of production and to the economic product, and most relevantly, enable the direct producers and the propertied elites to maintain themselves in the class position they already hold. What I find most useful is Brenner's insight that these property relations, once established, will determine the economic course of action which is most rational for the direct producers as well as the surplus extractors.[19] Brenner argues that given a particular form of property relations (systemically imposed or regulated) there is a *best strategy* for individuals or groups of social actors, be they peasants, landlords, merchants, or others seeking to reproduce their material interests, and that though the strategy appears to be subjectively driven, the logic of its reproduction is given by the existing system of property relations. Once a pattern of social and economic reproduction is set in motion it will tend to reproduce itself, as alternatives will not be readily apparent to the actors involved. Brenner's interpretation provides a framework for understanding the opportunities and constraints confronting all the various actors in a given social environment. Examined in the context of Qing China, peasants emerge not as irrational participants or as helpless victims but as active agents who, in pursuing their material interests, may ally with gentry and landlords. This, in turn, may leave room for understanding why poor peasants from a lineage in Guangdong and Taiwan often allied with wealthy landlords from their own lineages against poor peasants of another lineage, thereby going beyond what a simplified, and economistic, interpretation of "class" would have predicted. Is this what happened?

Chapter Five turns to agricultural practices in a smallholder economy. The rapid expansion of the commercial agricultural and manufacturing economy from the seventeenth century onwards, as a result of increased involvement with the world market and the growth of the domestic market, was based largely on decentralized small-scale peasant household production. This did not mean that peasant households stopped cultivating their own food such as sweet potatoes. But they also produced an astonishing variety of things for sale: salt, rice, sugar, silk, cotton and ramie cloths, fish, fruits, tobacco, tea, bamboo and palm-leaf products, and dozens of other items. Was the diversified production by the peasants driven by the profit motive or by the need for cash to meet obligations to the state, landlords, and moneylenders and to round out their own subsistence needs? How were the subsistence and commercial sectors of the agrarian economy linked, and what were the long-term implications of such links? Chapter Five explores these questions. In addition, it investigates the role of merchant loans for cash crop cultivation. Did merchants promote increased cultivation for the market and technical transformation, or were the loans merely a form of advance purchase of commercial products at below-market prices, with no further involvement in production?

Chapter Six brings us back to the market. I examine the market not just as the economic sphere of circulation of commodities and capital where the buyer and seller met and where prices were determined but as a spatial and temporal entity shaped by specific socio-historical realities. Were the lowest-level markets—the "standard market" to use William Skinner's terminology—where most peasant transactions were carried out, independent of the larger social and political hierarchies?[20] Or was the market itself an extension of these hierarchies? If the latter, to what degree were the merchant's opportunities and constraints framed by the larger social property system? In this case, would the best strategy for the merchant have been to exercise monopsonistic controls over the immediate producers, squeezing high interests out of them and strategically buying into gentry status? What impact would this have had on the merchant's incentives for investing in improving production technology?

In Chapter Seven I test some of the hypotheses raised in the earlier chapters by following the divergent histories of sugar manufacturing in late nineteenth-century Guangdong and Taiwan. As the developments of the industrial revolution reached cane-sugar manufacturing, giant refineries and vacuum pans began to make available vast quantities of sugar.[21] In some sugar-producing areas of the world, Cuba for example, industrial technology caused the collapse of small producers, who were replaced by the 1840s with sugar plantations linked to industrial refineries. In South China the demand for cane sugar from modern refineries in Hong Kong led to an increase in the numbers of small-scale sugarcane growers up to about the late 1890s. This chapter investigates what happened to sugar manufacturing on the mainland, which turned to importing sugar by the last decade of the nineteenth century, while neighboring Taiwan, under Japanese colonial rule after 1895, emerged as a major exporter of industrial-grade sugar. Here again, can the concept of social property relations help us understand why Taiwan was able to take advantage of the best technology available to manufacture high-grade sugar for the world market while Guangdong continued along the old lines of small-scale pre-industrial production?

In this book I want to study local historical processes closely without isolating them from global transformations in trade and technology. For while the products of peasant labor were bought and sold on the world market, as William Roseberry reminds us, the village and its institutions shaped the daily lives of the peasants.[22] The demands of the world market could be translated into peasant practice only through these local power structures. In pursuing this dual level of analysis and explanation of the global and the local, I have drawn on the complementary strengths of anthropology and history. The anthropologist's virtue lies in being able to describe the totality of interactions at the local level, for example, among direct producers, and between the producers and the surplus extractors. This is the only way to show how property relations actually operated, how decisions were made in everyday life. Qing historical documents such as land-sale deeds, mortgage deeds, contracts, and legal cases provide little information of this nature. They capture an isolated facet of economic activity, but give few clues about how the community as a whole perceived questions of who was entitled to sell the land and who would be able to move into the settlement as the result of the land sale. In reconstructing the social history of South China in Chapters Four and Six in particular, I have frequently turned to the findings of anthropologists for guidance. For, without their insights, the historian cannot complete an analysis of the innumerable points of social power at the ground level. Yet I am conscious of the century-long divide that often separates the anthropologists' observations and the historical record and the limits of relying on ethnographic accounts for understanding the past. Here the historian's craft of using state archival material, the writings of local literati, genealogical records, legal documents, trade data, agricultural treatises, and contemporary accounts by European visitors has been indispensable in completing the portrait, verifying the links between community and polity in an earlier period.

This book seeks to offer a reinterpretation of the fundamental question of how China, universally acknowledged to be one of the most developed economies up through the mid-eighteenth century, paused in this development process in the nineteenth. Plainly, as I hope to show, the economy of late imperial China was not stagnating nor was the state suppressing trade. The Chinese economy was certainly not awaiting the "historic contribution of the modern West to ease and then break the high-level equilibrium trap."[23] But, just as clearly, the development process did not succeed in transforming the social organization of production or setting in motion sustained economic development. I want to explore the complex linkages between the whole gamut of property and production relations in Guangdong and Taiwan and the role of the state in sustaining these relations, their cumulative impact on the potentialities and limitations of commercial agriculture to take advantage of existing world demand, and their ability to create a local demand for a range of commodities, including sugar. Unlike silk and tea, items that were used primarily by the wealthy in China and were special products available solely from China until the nineteenth century, cane sugar was produced for trade in many parts of the world. This is precisely why I have selected to study the history of Chinese sugar manufacturing, for it allows me to locate China within a framework of global history. In framing this reconceptualization of Chinese history, I propose to integrate the divided worlds of local and global history and show that only by analyzing the confluence of the two can we begin to recast our understanding of Qing history.

ONE

CONSUMPTION AND DEMAND: PARAMETERS OF THE DOMESTIC MARKET

> Air that is fragrant, colors that are muted, and tastes that are sweet are generally desired by all.
>
> —*Tiangong kaiwu*, 1637

SONG YINGXING IN HIS COMPREHENSIVE treatise on industry and agriculture, *Tiangong kaiwu* (The Development of Commodities by Nature and Human Skill), draws our attention to a universal phenomenon: humans like sweet tastes.[1] There has been considerable debate whether this desire for sweet tastes is due to our hominid evolution from fruit-eating primates or whether it is because all milk, including mother's milk, is sweet and is the first taste humans are exposed to.[2] Nutritionists stop just short of calling sugar addictive, but the demand for sweeteners has increased steadily worldwide in recent centuries.

Although there are many types of sugars, sugar from a type of grass that came to be called "sugarcane" was the source of most of the sugar consumed until the mid-nineteenth century. A dark brown cane sugar was already being produced around 800–700 B.C. in northeastern India and the region that was later known as Bengal; this may have been the first area in the world to extract cane juice and evaporate it to a semi-solid.[3] Cane sugar nevertheless played a relatively modest role in the diets of the general populace in most parts of the world for almost two thousand years after it was first developed. Then, from the sixteenth century onwards, the demand for sugar in Europe grew sharply and gained further momentum by the eighteenth century; its cultivation transformed economies from Jamaica to Java. By the early nineteenth century, the quantities of sugar used in some parts of Europe had changed diets permanently. In England, sugar became integral to daily life as an item of food, providing one-sixth of the total calories consumed by 1900. In countries such as France, the increase was not as dramatic in the first half of the nineteenth century, and the rapid increase came slightly later.[4] From towering sculptures of Greek temples made with sugar, lard, and marzipan savored by the elites of the Second Empire to the workaday sweetened tea of Victorian England, the spectacular increase in western European sugar consumption became a barometer of the domestic market and its purchasing power.[5]

In comparison, Chinese demand was slow to emerge. But recent indicators suggest the Chinese like sugar almost as much as everybody else. Per capita Chinese sugar consumption on the mainland increased from two pounds in 1952 to almost eleven pounds in 1984, after which, due to inflation, the increase, though continuing, has slowed. It seems that in China, like elsewhere, when people experience increases in income, the diet changes and consumables like meat, sugar, and soft drinks are purchased in larger quantities.[6] The Household Sample Survey data show that expenditures for sugar went up with income levels in the 1980s. Those who were earning more than 70 Rmb. per capita monthly spent more than three times the amount on sugar than households with incomes of 25 Rmb. or below.[7] In Taiwan, where sugar has been more generally available at low prices since the 1950s, annual per capita consumption had already reached over 40 pounds by the early 1970s and has continued to grow ever since.[8] Among Malaysian Chinese sugar consumption is even higher—by the 1970s school children were getting 25–30 percent of their daily calories from white sugar.[9]

But then, if the Chinese share an almost universal sweet-tooth, why did per capita consumption of sugar in Qing China remain relatively minuscule even though a large amount of sugar was being produced in the country? What were the specific conditions of production and consumption? Sidney Mintz has listed five principal and overlapping uses for sugar in premodern Europe: medicine, spice-condiment, decorative material, sweetener, and preservative.[10] Can parallel uses be found in pre-industrial China? This chapter provides an overview of Chinese demand and consumption patterns from the earliest recorded times up to the end of the Qing. In the conclusion, we return to the questions: What were the parameters of Chinese sugar consumption? And how did this affect the expansion of the domestic market?

The Northern Chinese Discovery of Sugarcane

The first manufactured sweetener available in north China was maltose or malt sugar made from grains. Maltose was certainly generally known by the second century B.C. and perhaps even earlier in several parts of north China.[11] Malt sugar, made from barley and Chinese sorghum (*gaoliang*), continued to be manufactured and is still eaten today as *maiya tang*. But gradually, sugar made from cane emerged as the most common sweetener all over China.[12]

Sugarcane was introduced into southern China either from Southeast Asia or from easternmost India probably no earlier than the third century B.C.[13] The basic term used for sugarcane now is *ganzhe* and this is typically now translated in Chinese-English dictionaries as *Saccharum officinarum*.[14] One of the oldest surviving texts on subtropical and tropical botany, *Nanfang caomu zhuang* (A Prospectus of Plants and Trees of the Southern Regions), written ca. 305, uses the term *zhuzhe*, but adds "it is also called *ganzhe*," as if the latter were a new term.[15] It is possible that the term was a recent transliteration of the Sanskrit *khanda*[16] used for a variety of cane, for, as we see below, Indic influences via Buddhist institutions were beginning to become important in China at around this time, including information about the sugarcane plant. Most Chinese agricultural treatises and pharmacopoeias did not distinguish varieties, but differentiated types of cane according to usage. The main distinction made was between cane cultivated for making sugar versus cane cultivated for chewing fresh as a variety of fruit. There were other varieties cultivated only for medicinal use. The sugarcane species most widely cultivated in China for making sugar prior to the twentieth century were hybrids of the species *Saccharum sinense*.[17] Terms such as *duzhe, baizhe, shuzhe*, and *ganzhe*

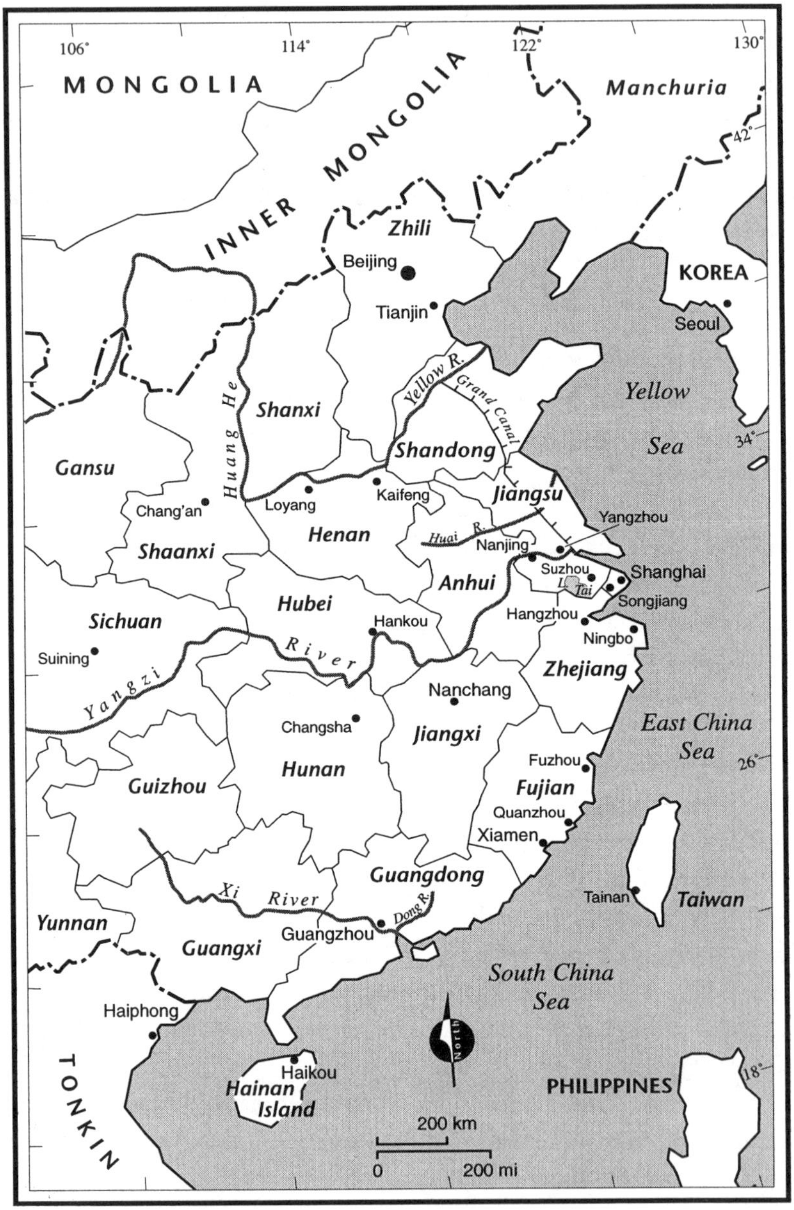

MAP 2. Late-imperial China, inner heartland: river basins and relevant locations

were all used to describe cultivars of this species. A variety of red cane used for chewing and called *kunlunzhe*, indicating its origins in areas to the west and south of the province, was grown in Sichuan during the twelfth century.[18] But in Guangdong, a variety of extremely slender, brittle, and very juicy cane called *xuezhe* and *nanzhe* was considered to be the most suitable for chewing, according to a text from the seventeenth century.[19] Here a dark purplish colored cane also called *kunlunzhe* or *yaozhe* (medicinal cane) was grown for medicinal purposes.[20] These different regional terms and varied descriptions suggest that numerous local hybrids had evolved over time, and a range of varieties could be found in the cane-cultivating provinces.

The first known reference to cane sweeteners is found, not surprisingly, also from the literature from the south. It is from the "Invocation to the Soul" ("Zhao hun") in the collection *Chu ci* (Songs of the South). Composed in the third century B.C. for a sick or dying king in the central Yangzi valley, the poem lays out all the attractions available to entice the soul back to earth and proclaims: "Bitter, salt, sour, hot and sweet: / there are dishes of all flavors / . . . , / Lightly boiled turtle and roast kid with sugar cane sauce / . . . / Fried honey-cakes of rice flour and malt-sugar sweetmeats."[21] Sugarcane may have become quite well known by the second century B.C. in these regions of the south. The tombs of the Marquis of Dai (r. 193–186 B.C.) and his wife (d. 168 B.C.) discovered in Mawangdui (Hunan) contain pottery vessels and hemp bags filled with various types of foods and grains. There are also bamboo slips on which the names of foods and cooking procedures had been written down. On two of the bamboo slips, no. 115 and no. 121, the character for cane sugar is written, suggesting at least the local elite were familiar with it.[22]

Did sugar or sugarcane have any symbolic value? The sources are few and far between. A requiem (*ji wen*) by Xie Huilian (394–430) for two wealthy, but unknown, individuals in Jiangsu laments the disrepair the graves have fallen into and notes: "Sugarcane segments still joined / Melon seeds scattered all around."[23] The preface to the requiem states that the poet found "strangely shaped burial artifacts made of various woods, tiles, copper and lacquer; carved wooden figures" and "in the water at the bottom [of the damaged coffins] sugarcane segments, the kernels of plums and melon seeds all scattered."[24] Sugarcane may have been one of the special local products offered to the departed; it may have also had significance as a burial object for, as in much of south and southeast Asia, it continued to have a special role in the religious rituals of southern China well into the twentieth century.[25]

By the beginning of the Christian era, several regions of China south of the Yangzi river certainly knew and used sugarcane. The standard lexicons of the day, such as the *Shuowen jiezi* (Analytical Dictionary of Characters) compiled ca. 100, provide the characters for sugarcane and cane sugar.[26] Since it did not grow naturally even in the southern regions of China, it can be assumed that it was a cultivated plant. A little bit of juice could certainly be extracted by grinding the cane. But can one infer from these scattered references to cane that the Chinese extracted the juice in sufficient quantities to produce some form of sweetener for commercial purposes?

Yang Fu, who lived in Guangdong during the first century, noted in his *Nanyi yiwu zhi* (Strange Things from the Southern Borders):

> There is sugarcane everywhere. The cane produced in Jiaozhe is the best. There is no difference in the thickness [of the stalk] between the top and the bottom, and the taste is even. The circumference is several *cun* [inches] and it grows to more than a *zhang* [ten feet] in height. You can cut it and eat it, and it is sweet. It is crushed to extract the juice. You can boil it and dry it in the sun. Then it is like malt sugar; it is called *tang* and is even more precious. It becomes both solid and crystalline; it is brittle. When eaten, it dissolves in the mouth. This is what people of the time called *shimi* [lit. "stone honey"].[27]

This process would have made a kind of cane sugar. But was Yang Fu describing sugar made in Guangdong, which was the northernmost part of the commandery of Jiaozhe in Han times or was it made further south in the commandery which included the Tonkin Delta of Vietnam? Sugarcane products, along with Brahmin priests and Indian textiles, were certainly more common further south in kingdoms like Funan that reached into present-day Cambodia.[28] And the Chinese elite taste for cane sugar may have been nurtured through these connections.

An anecdote from a period a bit past the turn of the third century suggests that cane sugar was a tribute item from Vietnam and neighboring regions. The *Sanguo zhi* (History of the Three Kingdoms), compiled by Chen Shou (ca. 233–297), tells of how "Sun Liang [the Prince of Wu] sent his eunuch to the official of the imperial warehouse to get from him the sugarcane syrup (*tang*) sent as a tribute item from Jiaozhou [i.e., Guangdong, Guangxi, and Northern Vietnam]," only to discover that the eunuch in charge had mixed some rat feces into the syrup to settle a score with the custodian.[29] The early fourth-century botanical prospectus, the *Nanfang caomu zhuang*, also furthers the impression that sugarcane products were sent as tribute from Indochina and notes, "Southern people say sugarcane can dissipate the effects of wine." Sima Xiangru says in the *Yao ge*, "A plentiful goblet of wine will diminish morning hangover. This is indeed true. In the sixth year of Tai Kang [286] the country of Funan sent in tribute cane which had three joints to each *zhang* [ten-foot piece]."[30]

References to cane-sugar sweeteners from the sixth century onwards varied from descriptions of syrups to more concentrated products that were somewhat crystallized. The most commonly known product was called *shimi* or "stone honey." This *shimi* would have been a deep brown raw sugar because there is no mention of separating the molasses in any of the texts.[31] Starting also at around this time, a new term and a new product called *shatang* began to be used by the Chinese. Literally *shatang* means "granulated sugar" or "sandy sugar"; the name may have come from the literal and phonetic translations of the Sanskrit term *sarkara* (granulated sugar) as some scholars have suggested,[32] or it may have simply derived from the raw sugar's sandy texture and color. By the end of the sixth century there was also a cane sweetener used in China called *banmi* (lit. "half honey" or a possible transliteration of the Sanskrit *phanita*, used for a concentrated syrup).[33] The *Sui shu* (History of the Sui), compiled ca. 636, mentions *banmi* as an important import from India.[34] The most commonly used term for cane sugar, however, was *tang*. This was written with a character similar to the term for malt sugar, but written with the rice radical instead of the food radical. Even much later texts, however, sometimes left out the rice radical and wrote the word for sugar with the homonym "Tang" denoting the ruling dynasty.[35] This profusion of terms for various types of cane sugar and the use of the same term for maltose and cane sugar suggest that, as yet, there was no standard product made from sugarcane.

Even as late as the sixth century, eight centuries after the plant had been introduced into southernmost China, cane sugar was far from being a part of everyday life for anyone. The *Qimin yaoshu* (Essential Techniques for Common People), written by Jia Sixie between 533 and 544, the best-preserved and most comprehensive of the early agricultural treatises, still places sugarcane under southern exotics in the section entitled "The Five Grains, Fruits, Melons, Vegetables and Roots that Are Not Produced in China."[36] Although based in Shandong, Jia traveled fairly widely in north China and looked through some 160 books before writing; he gives all the known terms for the sugarcane plant and repeats the brief entries on sugarcane from various lexicons; the only detailed extract is from the *Nanyi yiwu zhi* that is given above. Jia's own long discussion of sweeteners focuses on making malt barley sugar, including white barley sugar and soft malt sugar. Making such malt sugars was considered an essential part of the domestic economy, along with various types of fish and meat preserves and condiments (*jiang*) that also used malt sugar, salt, dried ginger, and orange-peel;[37] but Jia's neglect of cane-sugar products in these recipes also underlines the fact that cane sugar was still far from a common item in northern China.

It is also unlikely, then, that by the sixth century very many people in north China would have tasted cane-sugar products, although the educated strata would certainly have known of it. Perhaps only the elites at court in Chang'an, able to partake of tribute items from the south, tasted some type of cane sugar in their lifetime. But this history of slow expansion of cane cultivation and infrequent use of cane-sugar products was to change suddenly in the seventh century under the Tang.

Tang: The Expansion of Sugar Manufacturing

Increased contacts with other parts of Asia, the further absorption of the southern regions into the empire, and improved transportation through the construction of extensive canals, brought new fruits, vegetables, spices, and delicacies into the northern Chinese diet.[38] From fruits like litchees from Sichuan to spices like black pepper imported from Southeast Asia, Tang cuisine discovered a vast range of ingredients with which to embellish the diets of the wealthy. Increased use of cane sugar was one reflection of changes in the diet. But there was also an active interest in increasing cane-sugar production from an unexpected quarter—the Buddhist monasteries.

To begin with, there was a simple coincidence; the holy land of Buddhism was then, as now, the heartland of sugar manufacturing in India. The gratifying properties of the plant had given rise to a variety of myths and legends that are common to Buddhism, Hinduism, and Jainism. Sugarcane had become one of the auspicious items connected with religious ritual in Hinduism, and this was elaborated on in Mahayana Buddhism.[39] The Sākyamuni himself was said to have been descended from the Iksvāku (sugarcane) line.[40] Other stories have him breaking his fast after enlightenment with a taste of sugarcane juice, a motif that was used also in Jain religious paintings from a later date. In the heyday of Buddhism in the early Tang China, the king of the southern kingdom of Nanchao presented a dance called "King of Sugarcane" at the Chinese court. The dance apparently depicted the idea that "the instruction of the people by the Buddha is like the sugarcane in its sweetness and all rejoice in its flavor."[41] Since the Buddha lived and preached in a sugarcane-growing area, sayings and teachings attributed to him are rich in metaphors dealing with sugarcane. For example, the Buddha is supposed to have said that the effects of having women enter the *sangha* were like the red-rot disease which surreptitiously destroys sugarcane; the dead body of someone dying of old age and the funeral pyre are compared by the Buddha to the burning of bagasse after the cane juice has been extracted.[42] These sayings and compilations of tales of the Buddha's former births such as the *Jataka* and the *Lalitavistara*, and sections of the Pāli canon such as the *Sūttapitaka*, translated into Chinese very early in the fourth century, probably provided more than a casual introduction to the plant to the northern Chinese.[43]

We do not know whether these mystical links between the Sākyamuni and the humble sugarcane or the more mundane benefits of sugar gave rise to the Chinese legend that a Buddhist monk taught the Chinese people to make refined sugar:

In the reign period of Da Li [Tang Daizong, r. 763–779] there was a Buddhist monk named Zou. It is not known where he came from. Riding a white donkey, he ascended San Shan [in Sichuan] and built a thatched hut to live in. Whenever he needed salt, rice, firewood, or vegetables, he would write it down on a piece of paper, tie it together with some money, and send the donkey to carry it to the marketplace. People knew it was from Zou. They would take the right payment, hang the goods on the saddle, and let the donkey return home.

One day the donkey ran amuck and trespassed into a field of sugarcane sprouts belonging to Mr. Huang. Huang asked Zou to pay for the damage. Zou responded, "You do not know how to make cane sugar into crystallized sugar. The profit [that you could make] could be ten times greater. I'll teach you in order to repay my debt." . . . From this time on the method spread.[44]

The people apparently discovered in due course that Monk Zou was none other than the Bodhisattva Mānjuśri.[45] Boddhisattva or not, a Buddhist monk in Sichuan may have indeed known how to make refined sugar, for Buddhist monasteries routinely used sugar in three interrelated categories—medicinal, dietary, and ritual.

Although the extent of Buddhist Indian influences in Chinese medicine are yet to be fully studied,[46] there is plenty of evidence that the missionary value of medical treatment was recognized very early by Buddhist monks in both India and China. Some medical texts had already been translated into Chinese by the middle of the fifth century.[47] The *Vinaya Pitaka* (Disciplinary Codes of the Order), taken back to China by Fa Xian in 414,[48] also contained numerous discussions of medical matters because medicine was one of the four resources permitted to a monk. Convents and monasteries in both countries set up dispensaries as part of their charitable activities. A Bodhisattva of Healing, Bhaisajyarājan, emerged early in the Buddhist *sangha*, and excavations have identified an *ārogyavihāra* (infirmary) attached to the Buddhist monastery at Pataliputra.[49] Monks were sent by the first two Tang emperors, Taizong (r. 627–650) and Gaozong (r. 650–683), to collect medicinal herbs in India and send back samples.[50] These connections between material and spiritual well-being were incorporated into ritual worship. Maigre feasts and offerings made to sages and saints at the Buddhist monasteries included offerings of medicines along with food, tea, and incense.[51]

Indian Buddhist universities and monasteries at Taxila and Nālandā were centers of general education as well as medical education. Chinese monks visiting Nālandā during the seventh century studied Indian pharmacopoeia and therapeutic systems. Some, like Tan Jun, a monk with a "profound knowledge of the arts of exorcism and metaphysics," may have come because of their interest in medicine and after arrival specialized in *cikitsā shāstra* (therapeutic treatises and techniques).[52] Well-known Indian medical texts such as the compendia of Charaka, the *Charaka Samhitā*, (ca. first to second century A.D.), and the compendia of Susruta, the *Susruta Samhitā* (ca. fourth century A.D.), studied by the monks, used cane sugar for both medicinal and curative purposes. In the sections on pharmacology, these texts called for the use of granulated sugar, *guda*,[53] sugarcane molasses, and other cane-sugar products to treat a variety of ailments. The *Susruta Samhitā* held that "sugarcane is sweet in taste and digestive; is heavy, cool, demulcent, strength-giving, spermatopoietic, and diuretic."[54] Through these monks and through translations of some texts that are now lost such as the *Bolomen yaofang* (Prescriptions of the Brahmans), some Indian and Buddhist influences entered Chinese medical literature. It is difficult to determine, without a range of extant texts, what the links were between the expanded use of sugar in the Tang materia medica and Indian ideas about the properties of sugar. But there was a shift in the way cane sugar was perceived in Chinese materia medica before and after the seventh century.

Tao Hongjing (452–536), the renowned physician, naturalist, and author of the *Mingyi bielu* (Records of Famous Physicians), a comprehensive account of contemporary pharmaceutical knowledge, had merely noted, "In Guangzhou people plant cane, which grows for several years, is like a large bamboo, and is more than a *zhang* in height. The juice obtained is used to make granulated sugar, which is extremely beneficial to humans."[55] The implied beneficial properties were left to the imagination. On the other hand, the imperially sponsored *Xinxiu bencao* (The New Revised Materia Medica), compiled some hundred and fifty years later in 659 by Su Jing and a team of collaborators, seems to draw conclusions similar to the Indian texts regarding the properties of sugar: "Sugarcane is sweet, non-poisonous. It is stomachic, regulates the center [the abdominal cavity], invigorates the spleen, and is a laxative. *Shimi* is sweet, cold, and non-poisonous. It is soothing, is stomachic, dispels a dry throat, and is cooling by nature. . . . *Shatang* has the same merits as *shimi* and is even more cooling."[56] In any case, either as a result of Indic influences or of the evolution of indigenous ideas regarding the therapeutic properties of cane sugar, sugarcane juice and granulated sugar became firmly ensconced in the subsequent Chinese pharmacopoeia as a cooling agent.[57]

There were three ways in which sugar was used in making up therapeutic prescriptions: to enhance the properties of other herbs and potions, to disguise their unpleasant taste, and for its intrinsic properties of providing quick energy. The first category of use was so general and the quantities of sugar involved so variable that it is difficult to estimate the amounts used. Several prescriptions involving new medical herbs introduced in the Tang such as the bitter and sour myrobalans, for example, used substantial quantities of sugar, as did the prescriptions for these found in contemporary Central Asian and Tibetan texts.[58] The teeth-clenchingly-sour emblic myrobalan, *āmalakī* (*Phyllanthus emblica*, transliterated from the Sanskrit into Chinese as *anmole*), which we now know contains phenomenal amounts of vitamin C and is still a cornerstone of Ayurvedic tonics mixed with sugar and honey, was regarded in the Tang as no less than a magical drug for its rejuvenative properties.[59] The *Qianshou, qianyen Guanshiyin Pusa zhibing he yaojing* (Sutra of the Thousand-Handed, Thousand-Eyed Avalokiteśvara Bodhisattva on the Treatment of Illness and Preparation of Drugs), translated into Chinese between 625 and 650, provides prescriptions in which the cooling and soothing properties of sugar were primary: "For coughing, take one *sheng* of peach pits heated over fire, combined with sugar—all taken as one dose after the victim has recited the spell [*dharani* or protective spell] 108 times."[60] Another prescription reads: "When someone suffers from anal itching, prepare a hot (potion) of finely ground *ts'ao-chien-lo* fruit, add sugar, recite the spell 108 times and rub [the liquid] on the anus three times daily. This relieves the symptoms."[61] These uses of sugar became commonplace, for the "Prince of Pharmacists," as Needham calls Li Shizhen, writing his *Bencao gangmu* (The Great and Complete Pharmacopoeia) around 1590 after a survey of some 800 books, also recommends treating coughs as well as sores and itches with cane sugar.[62] Thus in Tang China, as in medieval Europe, cane sugar may have initially entered the lives of commoners as an item from the apothecary's shelf.

Monasteries used sugar in other ways, blurring the line between medicine and nourishment. Fasting monks and nuns consumed watered-down versions of cane sugar and molasses; these sweet drinks did not violate a fast unlike more concentrated forms of cane sugar. The *Disciplinary Codes* stipulated that while *gulodaka*, a drink made by mixing cane-sugar molasses with water, was permissible on a regular basis, *gula*, the more concentrated form of sugar, was permitted only when monks were sick.[63] Several other sections of the *Disciplinary Codes* like the *Pātimokkha* and the *Bhaisajyavastu* recommend "ghee (clarified butter), oil, *phanita* (concentrated sugar syrup), honey, and *sarkara* (granulated sugar)" to be taken as medicine.[64] These typical combinations of fats and sugars no doubt provided quick energy and a restorative for practitioners of an otherwise ascetic discipline.[65] Sugar was a potent food; this discussion of the uses of sugar as "medicine" rather than "food" was not restricted to Buddhist circles. In the thirteenth century the "medicinal nature" of sugar formed the core of a theological debate in the Christian church—did eating spiced sugars violate a fast? An authority as eminent as Thomas Aquinas found that "though they are nutritious themselves, sugared spices are nonetheless not eaten with the end in mind of nourishment, but rather for ease in digestion; accordingly they do not break the fast anymore than taking of any other medicine."[66]

Sugar was also used in Chinese public rituals such as the "Bathing of the Buddha."[67] The celebrations surrounding the birthday of the Buddha (usually the eighth day of the fourth month) included a procession of all the Buddha images in the city and a ritual bathing of the images and icons. The sugared water in which these images were bathed was then distributed for its blessed properties. The ceremony was based on the belief that when the Buddha was born he was bathed with sweet, scented water that poured from the heavens. This festival was widely celebrated first in Tang China. In the city of Loyang over a thousand Buddha images were carried in formal procession and bathed, and the entire population apparently turned out to participate.[68] The population of Loyang was over a million in the eighth century, so that even if half the people of the city actually received some sugared water, a fair amount of sugar was needed for this particular festival in this one city alone.[69] Although one can only guess how much sugar would have been used at this festival and similar functions in addition to medical and other uses, the number of people beginning to use some cane sugar in the Tang could have been substantial; at the time of the Buddhist persecutions (843–845) we read, for example, that 265,000 monks and nuns were returned to the status of lay people, not counting the novices, who numbered several hundred thousand.[70] Later evidence suggests that monasteries in all other cities also celebrated the festival, so the number of users of cane sugar at least on this one day may have run into a few millions. It was certainly a popular festival, for even after Buddhism was formally proscribed at court, Meng Yuanlao, writing in 1150, describes the festival in Kaifeng, "The ten largest monasteries all have the festival of 'Bathing the Buddha.' Sugared water in which fragrant herbs have been boiled is distributed. It is called *yu Fo shui* [lit. 'bathing the Buddha water']."[71]

This combination of medicinal and ritual uses of sugar by the Buddhists established a regular demand that went beyond the occasional use by the elites in the fourth and fifth centuries. The main producers in China were Guangdong, Yizhou (Yunnan and Sichuan), Jiangdong (Jiangsu, Anhui), and Xirong (Tibet and the lands west of it). But it is not possible to tell how much sugar was produced nor the quality of the product. Much-valued *shimi* and *shatang* were also sent as tribute and gifts to the Tang court from India, Bukhara, Khawarizm, and Persia.[72] When the Tang emperor Taizong became interested in Buddhism, he sent envoys to the Indian kingdom of Magadha in 647 to "learn the art of making sugar." Although mentioned in both Tang dynastic histories,[73] a more detailed account of the episode is given in the Buddhist histories. The *Xu Gaoseng zhuan* (Additional Biographies of Eminent Monks) by Dao Xuan (596–667) records that Wang Xuance, an envoy frequently sent on missions to India, was directed by Tang Taizong to bring over the artisans:

After the envoys returned from the West, again the Emperor ordered Wang Xuance and more than twenty others to go back to Daxia.[74] They were bestowed [by the Emperor] with more than a thousand bolts of brocade and silk. Wang and the monks each received a different quantity of gifts [for the monasteries they were to visit]. Also through the monks of the Mahabodhi monastery [in Bodh Gaya near present day Patna in India] *shimi* artisans were summoned. Thereupon two artisans and eight monks were sent to the east of China. And soon by imperial decree they were sent to Yuezhou [in Zhejiang] to find sugarcane and process it. They were successful.[75]

Sugar manufacturing at Yuezhou seems to have done very well. The *Xin Tang shu* (New History of the Tang) records that the *shimi* manufactured there was sent up to the imperial tables as local tribute.[76] Many other areas, several of them north of the Yangzi, also began to produce cane sugar in this period. There were at least nine prefectures from all over the empire sending up cane or cane-sugar products as tribute to court. These included areas in the western part of the empire such as Luzhou in Shanxi. Some of the producers were noted Buddhist monasteries, like the ones at Yuezhou, Yangzhou, and the Fa Bao Yuan monastery in Sichuan.[77] Cane-sugar manufacturing developed as far to the northwest as Dunhuang, though the sugar produced here may have been used only in the monastery for there is no mention of its being sent up as a tribute item.[78] Monasteries in even more remote places undertook sugarcane cultivation; Fa Xian on his journey to India via Central Asia found sugarcane being cultivated in Skardo, a Buddhist principality to the east of present-day Ladakh.[79] Several types of manufacturing developed in the monasteries in response to particular needs; for example, oilseed processing had developed to meet the need for large quantities of oil for the votive lamps.[80] The development of sugar manufacturing in monasteries can be understood as a similar process.

Outside the monasteries, the cities experienced an increased demand for sugar from the large numbers of Arabs and Persians residing in them by the eighth century. Yangzhou, Chang'an, Loyang, and

Guangzhou all had several thousand Arab and Persian merchants in addition to Indians and Southeast Asians.[81] The cuisine of many of these foreigners, particularly of the Arabs and Persians, favored the use of cane-sugar sweeteners. Sugarcane had been introduced into Arabia via Persia in the seventh century, and both cultivation and manufacture had spread rapidly.[82] Sweet and sour sauces, sweet starchy jellies (today's "Turkish Delight"), sweetened drinks made with scented waters, candied fruits, and scores of confectioneries gave sugar a prominence in Arab cuisine unequaled elsewhere in the contemporary world.[83] These merchant communities continued their customary style of cooking in China. Describing Arab feasts in eighth-century Guangzhou, a Chinese author noted: "The feasts used a lot of sugar, honey, camphor, and musk; the fish though sweet was rancid."[84] Touched by these exotic influences perhaps, Chinese elites too increased their consumption of sweeteners including cane sugar. "Honeyed bamboo shoots" and "honeyed ginger" made with cane sugar and introduced around this time are popular to this day. Preserved meat, shellfish, and fish condiments (*jiang*) made with grain-based yeast starters or wine lees, salt, and maltose had been popular since Han times;[85] these were now made with cane sugar; delicacies such as pickled, sugared, crab *jiang* were apparently much in vogue in the Tang.[86] Another Tang favorite, a heavy cake made by boiling sugar and rice powder in carabao milk,[87] seems to have enjoyed a much shorter-lived fashion, for it is not mentioned in later texts.

From all accounts then, cane sugar was far better known at the end of the Tang than in earlier times. But it was still not a commonplace item. As late as the reign of Daizong (763–779), the emperor saw fit to bestow twenty stalks of sugarcane on a subject as a "rare and wonderful gift."[88] Not until the Song period did cane sugar become a familiar item in urban China.

Song: Urbanization and Sugar Consumption

The early thirteenth-century night market of Hangzhou, described by Wu Zimu in his *Meng liang lu* (The Past Seems a Dream), had so many items made with sugar that it would have satisfied even a present-day sugar addict. One could buy sugar and honey cakes, ten-colored candy, flower-shaped candy, sweet rice porridge, spun sugar, flavored pastes made with sugar, musk-flavored sugar, preserved fruits in sugar, and, of course, plain old sugar syrup. There were seven shops in this night market that specialized in selling only sugar.[89] Colligating descriptions of items on sale in the markets of Hangzhou and Kaifeng, the two major cities of the Song, one finds no less than thirty-seven varieties of cakes, candies, and syrups made from cane sugar. A study of two cookbooks from the mid-thirteenth century shows sweeteners being used in 16.9 percent of the recipes in one text and 25 percent of the recipes in the other.[90] That Lin Hong's *Shanjia qinggong* (The Simple life of a Mountain Dweller) should have used sugars and sweeteners in almost 17 percent of the recipes in "a simple life" is an indication of just how commonplace the use of cane sugar and sweeteners had become. The author of the *Zhongkui lu* (The Cookery Manager's Records) is only known by her last name, Wu. This first-known cookbook by a woman in China shows that a well-stocked larder could be expected to have ordinary sugar, white sugar, brown sugar, refined white sugar, white powdered sugar, and sugared flour.[91]

Some Song confections called for substantial amounts of sugar. The recipe for a molded confection, a kind of marzipan, for example, is: "Finely grind pine nuts or walnuts. Mix well together with equal amounts of sugar until it is like a smooth honey-like paste. [The paste is then to be put into a mold.] When finished, take them out, and they can be eaten right away; they can be molded into square or round shapes. The confection can then be impressed with flower designs, engraved with figures, according to individual wishes."[92] Edible sculptures, consisting of flavored, concentrated sugar pastes in the shape of lions, birds, flowers, and fruits were also very popular. The demand for these sculptures was so great that some vendors cheated customers by weaving bamboo and reed frames in the desired shapes and only coated them with sugar.[93]

While tea and sugar in China were never to be intimately linked as in Britain, both were recent urban amenities in Song China. Tea houses and taverns, which sprang up in the Song cities and in small county towns, served, in addition to tea, wine, pickled vegetables, and salted melon seeds, dozens of sugared and preserved fruits. It is likely that the major increase in cane-sugar consumption in the Song came less from its direct use in candies and cakes and more from its use as a preservative for fruits. The many new varieties of fruits now available from the distant provinces of Sichuan, Guangdong, and even Vietnam were a passion in Kaifeng and Hangzhou, and cane sugar made it possible to taste fruits from thousands of miles away. Sugar itself is durable and keeps well for years if stored away from moisture. When used for preserving fruits, it can disguise tart or overripe flavors, retard microbial activity, and considerably extend the shelf life of perishables. Preserved and candied fruits were so popular that even street vendors hawked small jars of preserved fruits on the streets of Hangzhou and Kaifeng; elaborate porcelain jars filled with preserved fruits became fashionable gifts among Song urban elites.[94] As the painting in Figure 1 shows, sweetmeat vendors had become a common urban sight with stalls at street-corners selling cakes, candied fruits, and various sugars; children then, as now, were among their best customers! All this increased use of cane sugar brought some familiar problems. Zhu Zhenheng (1281–1358) noted in his pharmacopoeia, "Sugar rots teeth and produces worms."[95]

A technical development in sugar manufacturing enabled it to be transported to and consumed in areas distant from where it was grown. As we shall see in Chapter Three, this was the development of processes for crystallizing sugar—the contribution of Monk Zou according to the Buddhist legend. Tang dynasty cane-sugar products such as *shimi* contained a very large proportion of molasses, and therefore rapidly degenerated into a sticky mess in hot and humid or rainy weather. The technique for crystallizing sugar developed in the Song separated the sugar crystals more fully from the dross by boiling the sugarcane juice till it was supersaturated and thick and produced a kind of rock candy. The crystals were called *tangshuang* (sugar frost), the subject of the poet's praise. These chunks of sugar would then be dried further in the sun before being packed in jars. Although this process of manufacture was slow and laborious, with often unpredictable results, the sugar produced was in every way superior to *shimi*.

Sugar was certainly available in the major cities of the Southern Song, but to what extent was this true for the rest of the country? The court received sugar as part of special tax quotas from Fujian, Sichuan, Guangdong, Hunan, and several other areas of the south. At the beginning of the Xuanho reign (1119–1126), Prime Minister Wang Fu created a short-lived bureau to manage the sugar exports from Suining county, Sichuan, one of the major sugar-producing areas in the Song. This one county sent up several thousand piculs of sugar to the court.[96] Other areas noted for sugar manufacturing in Sichuan included Xiaoxi county, Fengtai garrison, and Fengxi county. In Guangdong, as Map 3 indicates, the counties that were to emerge as major producers in the Qing had already started producing sugar in the Song. We read that in 1190, Panyu, Nanhai, and Dongguan counties produced granulated sugar for the capital.[97] In Fujian the counties producing sugar for export to other parts of China included Quanzhou, Xinghua, Fuzhou, and Dingzhou.[98] The cultivation of cane affected cropping patterns in some localities, causing concern among officials such as Fang Dacong (1183–1247), who noted: "The fields of Xianyu county (Fujian) are overrun by sugarcane. Every year, I do not know how many thousands and tens of thousands of jars of sugar are shipped to the provinces of Huainan and Liangzhe. There is no doubt that sugarcane interferes with rice fields."[99] But did this increased production mean that the urban rich were consuming more sugar than the elites in the Tang, or that the use of sugar was spreading downwards into peasant households?

In the counties where sugar was manufactured, peasant families may have used some sugar or, more likely, chewed stalks of sugarcane. But such use was limited. Even in Fujian one finds that in the villages of Wu, sugar was eaten as a special treat only during the New Year's festivities.[100] Shiba Yoshinobu's detailed study of thirty-four village markets in the Lower Yangzi region, the most economically developed region of the country, shows that none of them sold sugar.[101] In the major urban centers sugar was, of course, readily available and the sheer size of some of them, like Hangzhou, with over a million people, set up a regular demand for sugar and other commodities.[102] The markets of most, if not all, of the 1,800-odd townships in Song China probably also sold some sugar.[103]

It is difficult to estimate whether there was any increase in the

FIGURE 1. Sweetmeat vendor and a child, early fourteenth c. Anonymous. Charles B. Hoyt Collection. Reproduced by permission of Museum of Fine Arts, Boston.

consumption of sugar in the monasteries. Under the patronage of the Song emperors, the size of the *sangha* increased so that by 1221 there were 397,615 monks, 61,240 nuns, and 40,000 temples.[104] Several Song literary references to cane sugar are written in monasteries. The poem by Su Shi, with which this book begins, was written on the occasion of a monk's departure from Jin Shan Temple in 1074.[105] A poem by Huang Tingjian (1045–1105) written in 1098 thanked a monk for sending crystallized sugar.[106] Wang Zhuo comments on the high quality of sugar produced at the Fa Bao Temple in 1153. These suggest that sugar manufacturing by the monasteries, started in the Tang, continued in the Song. But even here sugar was probably still not used casually. Lu Yu, a scholar-official, traveling from Zhejiang to Sichuan in 1170, stopped at many a monastery on his way. His diary records the different types of food served at the feasts held in his honor but does not mention cane sugar or other sweeteners served in any quantity.[107]

Popular though sugar may have become, it was also not considered a necessity. Wu Zimu did not list sugar among the daily necessities, which included firewood, rice, oil, salt, soy sauce, vinegar, and tea. Other contemporaries added wine, vegetables, ginger, and pepper but not sugar to Wu's list.[108] Sugar, while not prohibitively expensive, was still quite valuable. We find, for example, that the last prime minister of the Song, Jia Sidao (1213–1275), hoarded away "several hundred jars of sugar and eight hundred piculs of pepper" against a rainy day.[109] And in Sichuan, the local elites extorted and requisitioned refined sugar from the villagers. Wang Zhuo explains that some villages stopped making the large sugar confectioneries like animal sculptures which used a lot of sugar, because "the villagers feared the powerful in the prefectures and counties would demand all [the sugar], and they would have nothing to answer them with."[110] I am therefore inclined to conclude that while cane-sugar consumption increased markedly in the Song, only the wealthy ate it often. For the vast majority it remained a rare treat. Peasants living outside the sugarcane-producing areas probably never even tasted it in their lifetimes.

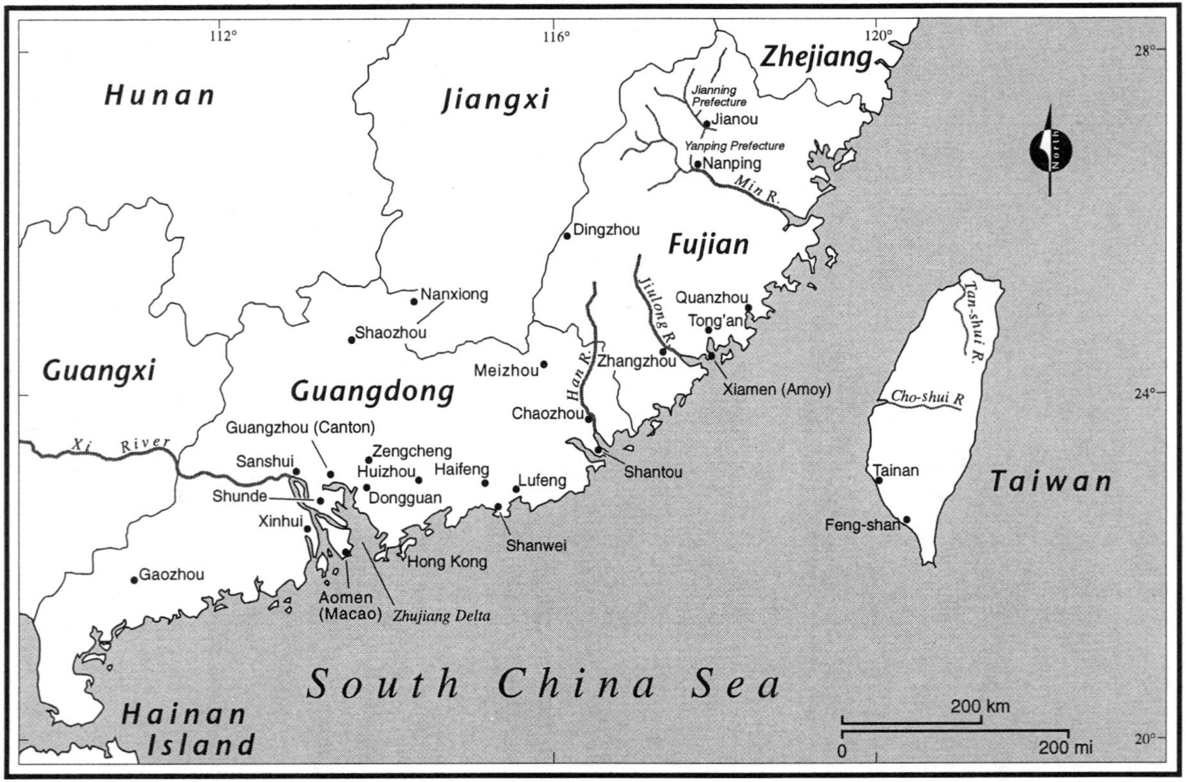

MAP 3. Southern Chinese county towns: relevant historical sites, ca. 1700–1800

Yuan: Imperial Sponsorship of Sugar Manufacturing

By all accounts Mongols and other Central Asians in Yuan China, despite regular contact with the Han Chinese, still ate foods cooked in the manner of steppe people.[111] A Dominican friar, John de Cora, visiting China in 1330, noted: "They eat meat of all kinds of beasts, and when they make a great feast they kill camels, and make fine dishes of the flesh after their own fashion."[112] In this predominantly meat-eating culture, sweeteners had been limited to honey in the twelfth and thirteenth centuries. The Liao (Khitan) used honey and were probably not familiar with cane sugar. The semi-sedentary Jurchen sold only honey and beeswax in the markets of the Liao.[113] Further west, out in Qarakorum, the capital of the Mongols, the four major markets sold many luxury products brought from distant lands of this far-flung empire. Sweetened flavors were popular among the locals, for an elaborate silver fountain at the palace in Qarakorum continuously dispensed *bal*, a mead-like drink made from honey, sweet rice wine and fermented mare's milk (*caracomos*). But again, there is no mention of cane sugar or sugar confectioneries either at the palace or in the markets.[114] It is therefore unclear whether Kubilai Khan's apparent interest in sponsoring cane-sugar manufacturing in China was a result of recently acquired tastes or a desire to emulate the Egyptian and Persian nobility, who were by this time using enormous amounts of cane sugar.[115] In any case, early in Kubilai's reign, according to Marco Polo, who probably visited China between 1276 and 1292, sugar artisans were brought over from Egypt.

And at the end of three days journeys, at fifteen miles, one finds a city which is called Vugen,[116] where a very great quantity of sugar is made. And from this city the great Kaan has all the sugar that he has used in his court, which is indeed so much that it is worth treasure enough, which cannot be told. But you may know that before the great Kaan had conquered them the people in those parts did not know how to do up or make sugar so finely and well as it is made in the parts of Babilonie; for they used not to make it set and cling together into loaves, but making it boil they only skimmed it and then when it was cold it stayed like paste and black. But when it became subject to the great Kaan, people from the regions of Babilonie were found at the court, who going to those parts taught them to refine it with the ashes of certain trees.[117]

Marco Polo was of course an unabashed propagandist for the Mongols, so it is difficult to judge whether all the Chinese cane sugar was indeed of such poor quality. Ibn Battūta, who may have traveled through the same region of Fujian within twenty-five years of Marco Polo's visit, considered the quality of the local sugar very good, "You find in China a great deal of sugar as good as that of Egypt, better in fact."[118]

The wholesale devastation of the economy of Sichuan that accompanied the Mongol invasion had destroyed a major source of cane sugar. Though Guangdong and Fujian were less affected by the turmoil, the overall quantity of cane sugar produced there too may well have declined when compared to the Song. Perhaps for these reasons the Yuan made efforts to increase sugar production by both bringing in the artisans from Egypt and detailing recommendations for cane cultivation and sugar manufacturing in the imperially sponsored agricultural treatise that was distributed all over the country, *Nongsang jiyao* (Fundamentals of Agriculture and Sericulture) of 1286. The other, later agricultural texts from the Yuan, however, such as the *Nongsang yishi cuoyao* (Essentials of Agriculture, Sericulture, Clothing, and Food) by Lu Mingshan (1314) and Wang Zhen's *Nongshu* (Agricultural Treatise) (1313) do not discuss cane sugar.[119]

Their residence in China probably also began to influence Mongol medical and dietary practice, though the prominence of meat in the diet was maintained. The *Yinshan zhengyao* (The True Principles of Eating and Drinking), presented to the Yuan emperor in 1330 by the royal dietician Hu Sihui (Hoshoi?), shows a combination of Chinese and Central Asian influences and contains primarily therapeutic recipes.[120] Dealing with foods for maintaining good health, foods forbidden to pregnant and nursing women and the treatment of diseases through improved nutrition, much of the book is devoted to information on what sorts of meat and cereal combinations to avoid along with some recipes for "rare and precious dishes." We see that cane sugar was no longer a novelty for the Mongols. In addition to numerous recipes for sweet and sour sauces, the section on alcoholic beverages features several prescriptions for dealing with intoxication in which cane sugar features prominently along with *wu wei zi* (*Schisandra Chinensis*).[121]

Among the Han Chinese cane sugar continued to be used much as in the Song; fruits preserved in sugar syrup were still the most common use, "bright dragon-twined jujubes kneaded in sugar" and "ginger threads split fine and dipped in honey sugar" from Zhejiang and Jiangxi were sold in all the markets of northern cities such as Loyang.[122] Several European monks and friars traveling through South China in the Yuan noted the abundance of rice wine and the absence of olives but remarked, "Sugar . . . they have in very great quantities, and therefore it is very cheap there."[123] Continuing the trend noted in the Song, cane sugar was so commonplace in urban China that it could be found in most households. *Jujia biyong shilei quanji* (All that Is Needed for the Home), an encyclopedia compiled in 1301, uses honey in the preparation of several tonics and restoratives for common household use, and suggests using sugar if honey is not available.[124]

At the other end of the economic scale, it is difficult to determine whether the use of sugar had also spread in peasant society. Shinoda Osamu, the preeminent specialist on the history of Chinese food, concludes that the Chinese peasantry subsisted like their Asian and European counterparts on little else but cereals, beans, and vegetables during the Yuan and Ming periods. However, the Chinese diet was richer than the contemporary Japanese diet. Chinese used four to five times as much oils and fats as Japanese, and daily cooking used more flavorings and condiments. Lists of daily necessities from the Yuan include fuel, rice, oil, salt, soy sauce, vinegar, and tea. And, in contrast to the Song, some lists of essential items include sugar and wine.[125] Wealthier families living in the countryside probably consumed all these items, but there is little information on the quantities. There is a great difference between using sugar as a sweetener, as a filling, and for making marzipan and confections versus using a pinch of sugar as a flavor enhancer for a sauce. It is likely that in the Yuan most people who lived in rural areas distant from the sugarcane-cultivating regions at best consumed sugar only in tiny amounts except for special festivals and feasts.

Late-Imperial China: The Expansion of Consumption

Even prior to the sixteenth-century expansion of commercial activity and growth in urban population, the range of fruits, vegetables, and other foods available to the Chinese by the Ming period was more varied than that of other pre-industrial societies.[126] *Yinshi xuzhi* (Essential Knowledge for Eating and Drinking), written by the centenarian Jia Ming and submitted to the Emperor in 1368 as a guide to good health through proper diet, contains a fairly comprehensive list of foods found in the empire. The book is divided into eight chapters and lists 50 kinds of grains; 87 kinds of vegetables; 62 kinds of fruits and nuts; 33 kinds of condiments and seasonings; 65 types of fish and shellfish; 33 kinds of fowl; and 40 kinds of meats, making for a total of 370 ingredients.[127] So, unlike the Tang period when there was an enormous increase in the range of foods and flavorings compared to the Han due to new introductions, the repertoire of Ming or Qing epicures was not dramatically altered by the use of new ingredients and spices. But many of these known ingredients became more widely available and in larger quantities as a result of the commercial expansion of the sixteenth century.

The ingredients used in preparing the daily oblations made at the Temple for Offerings to the Imperial Ancestors (Fengxian Dian) suggest that most of the foods on Jia Ming's list of 370 items were commonly eaten. The offerings made at this temple by the imperial consorts in the 1370s have been used as a convenient indicator of "the tastes and food ideals of the former poor peasant family which now found itself the imperial family, and that the foods offered were also those actually eaten in the imperial household."[128] While this was certainly an upwardly mobile peasant family and mobility could have changed their diet, there was still an emphasis on offering everyday foods to the ancestors. The regulations established by the Minister of Rites stipulated, "Such sacrificial offerings should employ ordinary daily foods and be conducted as private household rites."[129] Different items were presented according to a daily schedule and fresh produce of the season was offered according to a monthly schedule. Steamed mutton rolls, fried pork, chicken and duck eggs as well as various types of poultry and fish were offered in addition to the somewhat special meats such as swans, cormorants, and storks. Sugar was frequently used: "On the second day, finely granulated sugar; . . . on the fourth day, sugared butter cookies; . . . on the eighth day, sugared steamed biscuits; . . . on the tenth day, sugared jujube cakes; . . . on the twelfth day sugar-filled steamed breads; . . . and on the twenty-seventh day, sesame-sugar filled baked breads."[130] The offerings on several other days included cakes which could have been sweetened with either sugar or honey. Sugarcane was offered as a "fresh produce of the season" in the Eleventh Month. At the Imperial Ancestral Temple (Tai Miao), maintained by officials of the state outside the palace precincts, allocations for granulated sugar ranged from 12 to 13 *jin* (16–17 pounds) per month to almost 70 *jin* (over 90 pounds) for certain months that had numerous festivals and rituals.[131] Some dishes clearly required the greater use of sugar in some months, but the specifics are not known.

A clearer picture of the changes in diet of the elites and the wealthy begins to emerge by the mid-sixteenth century. The most noticeable change was the quantity of meat and seafoods eaten. Literatus and minor official He Liangjun (1506–1573) noted,

> When I was a small boy, at parties there were only five plates of fruit and five dishes of food. Only when the most important guests or in-laws [*sic*] came would they add dishes such as shrimp, crab, and clam, and this only happened once or twice a year. Now, even at common parties, there are always, without exception, ten dishes of land and sea delicacies.[132]

Official functions reflected this trend. The menu of a feast held in 1592 in the northern province of Hebei, Wanping county, to honor new provincial graduates (*juren*) was quite extravagant when compared to the modest repasts served to the higher-ranking new metropolitan graduates (*jinshi*) in the fifteenth century. Menus of graduation feasts in the fifteenth century make no specific mention of sugar or preserved fruits. The food seems quite ordinary. Meats were combined with starch and some vegetables; dishes such as lamb fried rice and *mantou* (steamed flour buns) were the main items served in quantity.[133] By the sixteenth century, generous quantities of preserved fruits, sugared cakes, and *bing* (pancakes) were being served up in all categories of formal official feasts. A feast assigned the status of a "lower middle grade" with 211 *xi* (place settings) for the graduates of the provincial level examinations used 20 *jin* (over 26 pounds) of sugar—12 *jin* of brown sugar and 4 *jin* each of white and rock candy—a little over 2 ounces per person.[134] Meat was the main attraction at these feasts. This particular feast used over 900 pounds of meat (420 *jin* of pork, 134 *jin* of beef, 134 *jin* of lamb) in addition to 24 geese, 114 chickens, over a hundred *jin* of tripe, and 280 eggs. Large amounts of fish, refined flour noodles, and various types of fruits and vegetables rounded out the meal. But even as the *juren* were sitting down to enjoy their gargantuan feast in northern China, other changes had already begun in the South which were to affect consumption patterns further.

By 1550 over 68 percent of Chinese households lived south of the Yangzi, and there was a corresponding increase in the number of markets in this densely populated region. If the Song period was notable for the efflorescence of major urban centers like Hangzhou and Kaifeng, the late Ming period was marked by a steady increase in the number of periodic markets and manufacturing centers such as Songjiang and Linqing. From a few thousand markets in the Song, over ten thousand markets had developed by the late Ming.[135] There are few reliable population statistics for late Ming and early Qing cities or information on the number of people engaged in wage-work.[136] But we do know that the population of many of the thirty-three cities important enough to have customs houses established by the Ming government ranged from one hundred thousand to over one million, as in Nanjing. Suzhou apparently grew from one-half million in the sixteenth century to perhaps one million by the beginning of the seventeenth.[137] The sixteenth century also marked the beginning of direct European trade with China. With the arrival of the Portuguese and Spanish in the sixteenth century, and then the Dutch and the English in the seventeenth century, the pace of manufacture for export increased particularly in the coastal regions. Late-Ming observers noted the increase in the volume of commerce: "Day and night goods from Hebei, Shaanxi, Shanxi, Shandong, Henan, and the Huai River are carried by merchants for sale to the South while goods from the Barbarian Southern Seas, Fujian, Guangdong, Anhui, Hubei, and Zhejiang are incessantly carried to the North."[138] Others, like Wang Shimao (1532–1587), commented on the increased regional trade:

> There is no day that the thin silks of Fuzhou, the gauze and pongee silks of Zhangzhou, the indigo of Quanzhou, the ironwares of Fuzhou and Yenping, oranges from Fuzhou and Zhangzhou, litchees from Fuzhou and Xinhua, cane sugar from Quanzhou and Zhangzhou, and paper made in Sunchang are not shipped along the watershed of Pucheng and Xiaoguan down to Jiangsu and Zhejiang like running water. The quantities of these goods shipped by seagoing junks are still harder to calculate.[139]

This sixteenth-century national trade was to further expand along coastal routes in the seventeenth and eighteenth centuries rather than inland river-routes.[140] Both these trade networks affected the sale and volume of sugar on the market. While the distribution of Guangdong and Fujian sugar expanded in northern China via both inland routes and coastal trade, new regions such as Taiwan emerged as major producers of sugar in the seventeenth and eighteenth centuries supplying primarily coastal markets.[141] Changes in sugar-manufacturing technology in the sixteenth and early seventeenth century also increased the varieties of sugar on the market. Refined white sugar, a higher grade and drier sugar than the brown sugar with molasses, became generally available (see Chapter Three). Moreover, numerous confections made with this refined white sugar also became more widely used around this time.

Two Augustine friars visiting Fujian in 1575, Martin de Rada and Miguel López de Legazpi, found that refined sugar was widely used to make edible sculptures.[142] At various banquets the friars were treated to music and "[I]n the meane time of their musicke, there was brought foorth great store of conserues [conserves], marchpanes [marzipan] and thinges made of sugar, and excellent good wine."[143] Throughout their trip the Europeans were given confections made of sugar: "Unto euerie one of their guestes they doo set a table . . . upon the first table (where sitteth he that is inuited) they set the victualles readie dressed, sweete meates, or march-panes, which is the last seruice."[144] At the governor's elaborate banquet in Fuzhou, the friars found a custom that they considered unusual, "On the first Table was set to euery one of the guestes, little baskets wrought with golde and silver wyre, full of sweete meates made of sugar, as marchpanes [marzipan], castels, pitchers, pots, dishes, dogges, bulles, elephants and other things verie curious . . . ."[145] Table settings, rituals, clothing, jewelry had all become more elaborate by the late Ming.[146] Sugar sculptures in baskets of gold and silver wire certainly added to this conspicuous display of wealth.

These "things very curious" were, of course, similar to the confections sold in thirteenth-century Kaifeng. They were also somewhat similar to sugar sculptures fashionable in contemporary sixteenth-century Europe, particularly Italy, France, and England, though the Spanish and Mexican friars may not have seen them. Known as "sotylties" (subtleties), sugar and almond paste sculptures were served to mark the intervals between "courses" or sets of dishes. These confections were also used to decorate the table and were eaten either at the end of the course or given to the guests as presents.[147] These European recipes, influenced by Persian and Arab confections, invariably combined almonds, scented waters, oils, egg white, and vegetable gums. The pliable paste then could be shaped into very elaborate and sometimes towering sculptures. The Chinese sculptures were modest in size, quite delicate, and only in Fujian do they seem to have used marzipan. The *Tiangong kaiwu* provides considerable detail for making pure sugar sculptures:

> To make animal-shaped candy, for every large cauldron put in fifty *jin* [approximately 66 pounds] of sugar. Start a fire and heat on a slow simmer. Heated from a side of the pot, the top of the sugar will come to a rolling boil. If the fire is placed directly under the center of the pot, it will completely boil over and overflow to the ground. For every cauldron, use three egg whites, throwing away the yolks and taking the whites, mixed with 5 *sheng* [approx. 1.5 gal.] of cold water. Add drop by drop to the heated sugar. Then the scum and black dregs will rise to the surface. Skim with a bamboo

ladle. [The clarified sugar syrup is then to be transferred to a copper pot and simmered further till it reaches the required consistency and is poured into molds]. The lion and elephant molds have two halves of pottery that are joined together [to form the whole shape]. Ladle the liquid sugar into the mold [to coat the molds] and pour out [the extra syrup]. Since the mold is cold and the sugar hot, a thin layer of sugar will stick to the mold and congeal. This is called "festive candy" and is used at banquets.[148]

This type of hollow sugar confectionery remained popular in China down to the twentieth century, though the technique changed a little. Peddlers making *tang ren* or "sugar dolls" were popular in towns and villages everywhere. Carrying a charcoal stove, a blow tube, sugar, and an assortment of molds shaped like animals, fish, famous characters from the Chinese opera, and dolls in the shape of little boys and girls, the peddlers made the candy on order. A little bit of sugar would be put into the mold, heated, and liquefied on the stove, the mold would be coated by using the blow tube, and in a few minutes when the mold cooled, an elaborate sugar sculpture was ready to be played with and then eaten.[149]

Besides these confections served at banquets, sugar allocations continued to indicate the rank of the guests in the seventeenth and eighteenth centuries. This can be seen most clearly in the regulations for the Court of Entertainments (Guanglu Si) established during the Qianlong period (1736–1795) to honor Chinese and foreign guests. The quantities of fruits, grains, eggs, and sugar to be used for each type of banquet and each rank were formally stipulated and entered into the "yellow registers" at the end of each month. For the formal banquets, the allotments for the highest level of the six-tiered hierarchy in which the guests were ranked included 18 *jin* of white sugar, 4 *jin* of white honey, 1.25 *jin* of the higher grade of rock candy, and 10 *liang* of a flavored sugar called "eight precious sugar," making for 31 pounds of sugar in all. This amount was to be used for "each sitting" (*meixi*) of ten to fifteen individuals. Even if we assume fifteen people at the feast, they would have been getting over 2 pounds of sugar and sweeteners per person at a single meal. At the second level of this hierarchy, 18 *jin* of white sugar was still included though the amount of white honey was reduced; those in the third tier received only 15 *jin* of white sugar and yellow honey instead of white. The lowest-ranked guests, which included envoys from the Ryukyus and the Europeans, received only 2.8 *jin* of white sugar for each sitting, and all other types of sweeteners were dropped from the menu.[150] Similar sets of regulations for each level of official rank existed for funeral feasts.

The personal tastes of the Qing emperors in food were far from flamboyant.[151] However, perhaps reflecting how widespread the use of sugar had become among the elites, the total allocation of sugar for the Inner Palace came to a hefty 10,635 *jin* or around 14,000 pounds a month by the Qianlong period.[152] The dozens of temples within the Forbidden City with their complex hierarchies were also differentiated by differing levels of sugar allotments. The Temple of Imperial Longevity (Shouhuang Dian) received 45 *jin* of sugar candy and 45 *jin* of "eight precious sugar" or almost 120 pounds of sugar every five days, though the Temple of Eternal Repose (Yongning Si) received a mere 5 *liang* each of sugar candy, white sugar, and brown sugar.[153] And the delicate pastries of the Ming imperial offerings had given way to more heavily sweetened imperial confections such as, "ten *jin* [over 13 pounds] of white sugar simmered over a slow fire with two ladles of water and two ladles of milk."[154]

Despite this increase in the use of sugar, however, sweet dishes were not the focus of a formal meal in China and certainly ritual uses of sugar were nowhere as prominent as they were in England. Though sugar was still very expensive in England, as Gervase Markham's *The English Hus-Wife Contayning, the inward and outward vertues which ought to be in a compleate woman* (1615) makes clear, lower court nobility and "gentlewomen" concerned with the proper ways of giving dinners were using assorted sweets, conserves, cakes, "jumbels, leaches, marmalades, suckets," jellies, and marzipans as necessary "banquetting stuff" to make the right impression.[155] As Sidney Mintz has noted, sugar here was more than a food ingredient. Rituals involving sugar had evolved so that elaborate sweet confections marked either the beginning or the end of the meal.[156] By contrast, in China, dishes using sugar were simply pastries or side dishes complementing the main courses in a formal meal.

The tastes of the opulent Jia household in sweets and desserts in Cao Xueqin's mid-eighteenth-century semi-autobiographical novel, *Hong lou meng* (Dream of the Red Chamber, ca. 1795), for example, ran to delicate "marzipan cakes made of ground lotus root and sugared cassia flower."[157] They did not indulge in sweets and sugars, which were after all so commonly available in China. Instead they affirmed their social position by casually eating pigeon eggs, which cost an ounce of silver each.[158] Status foods in China involved birds' nests, deer tongues, and bears' paws. A "first-class banquet" with the obligatory sixteen dishes usually paid close attention to these foods. Wealthy merchants from Jiangsu and Zhejiang in 1799, routinely served bear paws, deer tails, shark's fins, bird's nests, and sea cucumbers in addition to various types of meat, poultry, fish, and shellfish when entertaining.[159] Sweet dishes made with cane sugar and sometimes honey, while always included in menus, played a minor role. The scarcity value of imported bird's nests and shark fins connoted status and wealth as imported sugar did in England.

In a comfortable but not extraordinarily wealthy household, such as that of Yuan Mei (1716–1798), doyen of literati aesthetes and a gourmet, tastes in desserts and sweet dishes upheld the elite culinary principles of subtle and understated flavorings. As the desserts and pastries named "snow-flower cake" and "white-cloud morsels" suggest, most of these recipes used sugar as a frosting and occasionally as a filling. Yuan Mei's cookbook of 1797 *Suiyuan shidan* (Menus from Suiyuan) has over twenty recipes for cakes, candies, pancakes, wafers, and sweet dumplings, including one for a crêpe au sucre.[160] This was probably a novelty, given the detailed description of the implements used:

Vice-Censor-in-Chief Yang's Western Crêpe (*xiyang bing*): Mix egg whites and flour into a thick paste; put into a bowl with some water in the middle. Beat a pair of copper scissors so that the tips become shaped like a pancake (*bing*), the size of a large saucer. Between the top and the bottom of the two surfaces of the copper [scissors] there should not be even a *fen* [0.1 inch] of space. Stir up the water into the thick paste, pick it up on the scissors and toast it. It will become a crepe, white as snow and translucent like silken paper. Add crystallized sugar and pinenuts.[161]

Among the even less affluent literati, as portrayed in Wu Jingzi's novel *Rulin waishi* (The Scholars, ca. 1750), wine, meats, and fish were the main dishes at feasts. Here the emphasis was not on exotic imported foods, but on the preparation of commonly available foods like sliced pork or ham and duck served in generous amounts. Sugar cakes did not arouse the gluttonous abbot in quite the same way as did the prospect of a large chunk of sliced ham.[162] Sweetmeats such as dumplings filled with sugar and goose fat, sugared cakes, and biscuits made with walnuts and melon seeds coated with sugar were certainly savored but not eaten in large quantities.[163] For those with limited resources, the distinctive varieties of wine and tea excited the gourmet, not sugar candies. Indulging in sweet pastries and desserts may have also stretched the budget. Sugar was still expensive enough to be given as a gift. For example, the brilliant scholar Du Xiaojing, falling on hard times, was overjoyed to receive a gift for the Festival of the Double Fifth (*Duanwu*) from his patron consisting of, "a brace of duck, a hundred sticky dumplings, two catties of white sugar, and four taels."[164] And among those with even more reduced means such as the artist Shen Fu (1763–1809?), sugar remained a flavoring. Often having to make a virtue out of necessity, Shen Fu relished the "wonderful" simplicity of salted beancurd with sesame oil and sugar.[165]

The most common consumption of sugar at the level of the village market may have been in the form of plain boiled sugar candies, spun sugar candies, and peanut brittle. Qu Dajun, writing around 1690 in Guangdong, noted various types of sugar candies in the markets with evocative names like "cocoon candy" (*jian tang*) and "spun-silk nest candy" (*kesi tang*), molded hollow candies called "blown candy" (*chui tang*), sesame sugar candies (*zhima tang*), and a chewy dark-brown candy called "cow-hide candy" (*niupi tang*).[166] The peanut was introduced into China soon after the Portuguese landed in Guangzhou in 1516, and soon peanut brittle and powdered sugar and crushed peanut candies became common confections throughout the country. Sugar and peanuts were often paired in desserts as well. As Eugene Anderson has noted, "Ground or broken peanuts abound in pastries, candies and sweets, and when a new sweet is borrowed from the West, a large dose of peanuts is often a step in making the borrowing into a true Chinese product."[167]

This increased availability and use of refined sugar in the late Ming and Qing did not arouse any sharp medical controversies as it did in contemporary Europe.[168] The line between sugar as medicine and as nutrition had after all been a thin one in China when prescriptions of medicinal tonics typically began including sugar back in the seventh century.[169] Li Shizhen's late sixteenth-century *Bencao gangmu,* the standard reference source on materia medica down into the twentieth century, lists twelve remedies involving cane sugar and cane juice. Warning that eating too much sugar produces cavities among the young, cane juice and sugar are primarily recommended for treating problems of the spleen, bronchial problems and dry coughs, malarial as well as other fevers, nausea, urinary problems, dysentery, and diarrhoea. The use of sugar to treat diarrhoea to prevent exhaustion and a drop in blood pressure while keeping up some easily absorbed caloric intake is now a recognized remedy worldwide. The Chinese text does not analyze why sugar is to be used for diarrhoea but experience may have identified this use. One of Li's more unusual recommendations included using cane juice mixed with golden thread (*Rhizoma coptidis*) as an eye wash for swollen and infected eyes.[170] Presumably the anti-bacterial properties of cane juice would have relieved local infections especially if a camphor-wood (also anti-bacterial) trough had been used as suggested by Li.[171] Sugar was also recommended for fatigue, consumption, and wasting diseases. Huang Gongxiu's *Bencao qiuzhen* (The Ultimate Pharmacopoeia) of 1773 recommends using an infusion of sugar and wine for unconsciousness caused by excessive loss of blood during childbirth as well as for coagulation of blood (*xue yu*).[172] Folk medicine may have used sugar more widely for these energy-giving properties. For women going into labor a tonic called *ding xin tang* or "heart-stabilizing soup" was highly recommended, the "soup" being nothing more than warm, heavily sugared water with a dried shrimp.[173] In the traditionally minded lower-middle-class Beijing household at the turn of the twentieth century described in the *Adventures of Wu,* the young mother was allowed only sugared cakes, various types of eggs, and thick millet porridge sweetened with dark-brown sugar and sprinkled with roasted walnuts for a full thirty days after childbirth.[174] Even poor women in the village of Taitou in Shandong could hope to taste sugar during and after childbirth.[175] Sugar in these cases was food and medicine at once.

Li Shizhen noted sugar was also good for soothing a dry mouth especially if one had a fever.[176] These same properties were put to use in a premodern Chinese version of chewing gum. An essential ingredient in "thousand-mile tea" (*qian li cha*) recommended in a seventeenth-century traveler's manual, the recipe suggested: "Take 4 *liang* [ounces] of white granulated sugar, 3 *liang* of China root, 4 *liang* of *bohe* leaves [*Mentha arvensis*, the common field mint], and 1 *liang* of licorice root. Grind them to a paste. Knead it all together with honey and make them into pills shaped like dates. . . . Even if you have to travel a thousand miles, your throat will not be parched while on the road."[177]

Molasses, the byproduct of crystallized sugar, was commonly made into rum in the Caribbean. But in China, the popularity of rice, sorghum, and other grain-based wines and spirits seemingly limited the market for other types of alcoholic beverages. There are some references in the Tang period to wine called *tangjiu* made from sugarcane juice. Later this type of wine was no longer common; only in Taiwan do visitors in the nineteenth century from the mainland mention a reddish-golden wine made from sugar cane.[178] Elsewhere, molasses was mixed with rice wine and litchee wine to produce a darker and sweeter beverage, but most commonly it was just mixed with water to make a sweetened drink.[179]

In these and dozens of other minor ways, the use of sugar in the Qing had evidently expanded beyond the sugar-producing regions, and its use was no longer confined to the wealthier families. So how much sugar did the Chinese produce and consume?

There was, as we have seen, no dramatic increase in national consumption in the Qing, merely a casual and widespread use of sugar when and where it was available. But in a nation of almost 300 million by 1800, even small per-capita consumption could lead to a significant domestic market by late-eighteenth-century standards.[180] Data on "average levels of consumption" are unsatisfactory because they mask variations according to class and region. Therefore, "per capita" surveys provide at best only a framework for comparison. Bearing this in mind, we can use a Japanese survey from the late 1880s to arrive at an approximate estimate of per capita annual consumption of 2 *jin* (2.6 pounds) of sugar.[181] There is no indication in any of the literature that the use of sugar increased markedly in China after the beginning of the nineteenth century. Therefore, accepting that sugar consumption may have increased only slightly by the 1880s, we can use a rounded-out figure of 1.50 *jin* (a little less than 2 pounds) as the average level of sugar consumed in 1800. (Such an amount was not particularly low by the standards of some parts of the pre-industrial world, including parts of Europe. It is quite comparable to that of France, for example, where in 1788 the annual average consumption is estimated to have been around 1 kilogram [2.2 pounds] per person.)[182] At this rate, in the Chinese population of 300 million, total consumption works out to approximately 561 million pounds (250,446 tons). All of this demand was met through domestic production, and it was by no means insignificant by world market standards. The entire output of sugar reaching the world market, for example, around 1800 has been estimated at about 245,000 tons.[183] This admittedly crude arithmetic suggests that China was certainly one of the largest producers of cane sugar in the pre-industrial world. But then why did Chinese consumption of sugar not increase until well into the twentieth century? And what were the factors which led to the extraordinary increase in sugar consumption elsewhere, such as Britain where per capita annual consumption increased 400 percent between 1700 and 1800?[184] What were the underlying distinctions shaping the purchase of goods on these two domestic markets? Such a comparison, and the contrast, may help us clarify the particularities of the domestic market in China.

Conclusion: The Domestic Market in China and England

Sugar in Britain, as Mintz points out, "came to the fore in connection with three other exotic items—tea, coffee and chocolate."[185] Sugar production in the British West Indies, particularly after the conquest of Jamaica, kept pace with this increased consumption. Sugar moved from its limited roles of medicine and spice-condiment to use as a sweetener for beverages and a myriad of English puddings as the eating of desserts became common in all classes. Sugar prices in Britain had begun declining within decades of the conquest of Jamaica. Mintz writes, "On many sides there is ample evidence of a real push to seize more colonies, establish more plantations, import more slaves to them, build more ships, import more sucrose and other plantation products. And as these substances come within reach of the poor, the possibility of a steadily expanding domestic (national) market, as opposed to an export market, become clearer." Mintz relates increased sugar consumption in Britain not simply to a British preference for sweets, but to the "inside meaning" of sugar in this society, "because the meanings people gave to sugar arose under conditions prescribed or determined not so much by the consumers as by those who made the products available."[186] The suppliers, in other words, had much to do with the shaping of demand. Mintz argues that the complex interrelationships among sugar consumption and production, the symbolic realm of power, and the material base of profit gave sucrose an altogether special dimension in Britain. This, in turn, provided the context for the high level of consumption.

Although Mintz has laid out the parameters of sugar dependency in England eloquently, this framework alone cannot explain the apparent connection between industrialization and sugar consumption as a global pattern. True, sugar consumption escalates first in Britain but then the same pattern can be observed in France and Germany, the United States and Japan, and more recently in Taiwan and Malaysia. Today, for example, the Japanese consume 110 pounds of sugar per capita annually, a level of consumption almost identical to that of the British.[187] Therefore rather than examine how sugar production and consumption molded the domestic demand, I would like to invert the question. What were the circumstances that accounted for the early expansion of both sugar consumption and the domestic market in Britain and conversely limited them in China?

Eric Hobsbawm, discussing the origins of the Industrial Revolution in Britain notes, "The domestic market, large and expanding as it was, could grow in only four important ways. . . . There could be growth of population, which creates more consumers (and, of course, producers); a transfer of people from non-monetary to monetary incomes, which creates more customers; an increase of income per head, which creates better customers; and a substitution of industrially produced goods for older forms or manufacture or imports."[188] "The transfer of people from non-monetary to monetary incomes" refers to the creation of an increasingly urban wage-labor force located within a capitalist system of production and relying on the market for all its needs. For though it is no longer considered odd to speak of the preindustrial consumer and we know rural households are not necessarily self-sufficient, a dependence on wages is crucial to the development of any sort of mass market. In England, starting with the sixteenth century a surprisingly large percentage of the agricultural population had already begun to depend on wages and used them to purchase groceries like sugar, tobacco, tea, and coffee.[189] Rural manufacturing and wage labor had begun to transform the economy long before the end of the eighteenth century; in numerous counties only between 10–25 percent of the population cultivated field crops by the late seventeenth century.[190] But it was the English urban working class which was to become the largest consumer of sugar in the late eighteenth and the nineteenth centuries.

It is now become generally accepted that Britain underwent a markedly slow rate of growth during the last decade of the eighteenth century and the first twenty-five years of the nineteenth.[191] The rise in real wages in aggregate may have come even later, perhaps not until the 1840s.[192] And it was during this period at the end of the eighteenth century, with real wages stagnating and even declining, that more nutritious and expensive foods were replaced by cheaper ones.[193] As milk and the malt used to make beer became too expensive for the working class, sweetened tea emerged as the substitute with which to eat the basic meal of white bread and potatoes. This nexus between the consumption of tea and sugar noted by Mintz, is further explained by John Burnett, a scholar of British nutrition: "White bread and tea were no longer luxuries, but *the irreducible minimum* below which there was only starvation."[194] And as the price of sugar continued to decline relative to that of other foods throughout the nineteenth century owing to the availability of beet sugar and industrial manufacture in Europe, the consumption of sugar among the poorer classes came to *exceed* that of the wealthier classes. Sweetened tea was drunk at every meal. The meal marking the end of the working day was designated "tea" and became a meal where the beverage was accompanied with sweetened condensed-milk, store-bought sweet biscuits, and bread and jam.[195]

This shift in consumption accompanied an epochal shift in where the British population lived and worked. By 1800 only about 35 percent of the total working population was engaged in *any* form of agriculture; by 1851, the percentage had declined to 16 percent and by 1911 less than 8 percent of the British population was engaged in agriculture.[196] The census of Britain in 1801 showed that only 20 percent of the population was urbanized; by the early twentieth century, 77 percent lived in the cities.

In China, by contrast, "in the 1840s, with the regional population [of North China] swollen to approximately 120 million, the combined population of North China's top ten cities came to less than two percent of the total."[197] Even in the Lower Yangzi region, the most economically developed region of China, less than 8 percent of the population lived in urban centers in the 1840s.[198] William Skinner, Mark Elvin, Dwight Perkins, and Kang Chao, though suggesting slightly different total percentages, come to the same conclusion, namely, that a smaller percentage of the Chinese population was urban in the late nineteenth century than in the twelfth and thirteenth centuries. Around 21 percent of the population of China south of the Yangzi was probably urban in 1220,[199] whereas Skinner's figures suggest that by 1893 only 6 percent of the population was urban. Kang Chao revises these figures upwards to 6.9 percent in 1820 and 7.27 in 1893.[200] But since landlords and merchants living on rents and payments in kind constituted a substantial part of this urban population, the percentage of the population actually buying all their needs, particularly food, on the market would have been even smaller. The industrial proletariat in China numbered perhaps no more than 100,000 in 1894 when the total population was estimated at 386,700,000.[201]

A fundamental distinction thus marks the potentialities of the domestic market in late imperial China; as much as 90 percent of the population remained rural. In a pre-industrial economy with a dominant agrarian sector, peasant households are only marginal consumers, buying very little of their needs on the market—one of the "demand-limiting characteristics of the preindustrial economy" as Jan De Vries identifies this phenomenon.[202] Only an urban population, a wage-labor force embedded in capitalist production, and lacking the means to produce their food must buy all its consumption requirements on the market.[203] The ability to buy consumer items on the market is also determined by the price of the particular goods. And here, too, a divergent pattern emerges when the price of such groceries as sugar are compared.

References to sugar prices in China are few and far between, probably a reflection of the fact that it was not considered a necessity by anyone. Most of the data we do have come either from references to purchases made by the imperial larder or from the records of the compradors' contracts for provisions for foreigners trading in Guangzhou from the seventeenth to the nineteenth century. At the beginning of the seventeenth century, cane sugar was cheaper in China than in contemporary Spain, where the influx of silver from the New World had resulted in inflation. Father Diego de Pantoia, one of the Jesuits visiting Beijing in 1602, commented, "All things are very cheape, without comparison cheaper than in our Countrey. A pound of Sugar is worth eight or ten Maravedis and sometimes sixe; and if they buy any quantitie at once, one hundred pounds weight are worth nine or ten Rials of Plate. And here at the Court (where all things are dearest) a pound is worth twenty, or foure and twenty Maravedis."[204] Even at the cheaper rate prevailing outside the court, the price of sugar, based on those estimates, works out to nine or ten ounces (tael) of silver per picul (approx. 133.3 pounds).[205] Sugar in Beijing was considerably more expensive than in Guangzhou, where in 1600 the Portuguese purchased one picul of white sugar for between 1 and 1.5 to 2 taels. Even this lower price was, however, four to five times the price of rice on the same market; and contrary to expectations, foreigners did not always pay the highest prices.[206] Consequently, even though sugar may have been more widely available in seventeenth-century China than in contemporary Europe, and was cheaper than in countries like Spain, it was still quite expensive compared to basic food prices.

As Table 1 shows, sugar prices generally rose in the late eighteenth century. In 1792, the export price of white sugar in Guangzhou was 5 taels per picul, but in Beijing the imperial household paid 10–17 taels per picul.[207] This price was, of course, for the best-quality sugar, and it is hard to tell what the mark-up may have been for the imperial larder. Similar prices were paid by the Macartney mission in 1793, which also paid higher prices for everything.[208] It was probably more difficult to inflate the price of rice for the imperial larder since prices for rice were monitored carefully. On the same price list of the imperial household, rice cost 1 tael and 300 copper cash per *dan* (approx. 185 pounds) or enough rice to feed an adult male for a hundred days.[209] By contrast, one *jin* (1.33 pounds) of white sugar cost 100 copper cash, according to the Macartney price lists, about the same as the daily wages of a Chinese foot-soldier and 20 copper cash higher than the daily wages of the boatmen who were hired by the Macartney mission. Even at Guangzhou prices, sugar was still very expensive. A bean-curd presser in 1791 received 710 copper cash per month plus food, and in 1795 a sugar-press worker in South China received 500–750 cash monthly. A paper press worker between 1774 and 1816 received 750–900 cash per month.[210] Wages in the agricultural sector were even lower: short-term agricultural workers, for example, received only 450–500 cash per month, though wages as low as 200 cash were not unknown.[211] Given this wage-and-price structure, it is unlikely that the laboring classes would have bought any sugar at all. They could at best afford peanut brittle or spun sugar candies, and pieces of candied fruits, which sold for 1 or 2 cash.[212] The regular demand for sugar and such commodities came from the class of landlords and gentry elites, approximately the top 2 percent of the total population, whose per capita income was about sixteen times that of commoners.[213]

The transformation of sugar into a food and a daily necessity during the course of the nineteenth century in Britain could be sustained

TABLE 1
Sugar and Rice Prices at Guangzhou, 1586–1810
(prices in taels per picul of sugar or *dan* of rice)

Year	White sugar	Sugar candy	Rice
1586	4.00–5.00	–	1.30–1.67
1600	1.50–2.00	–	0.35–0.40
1620	1.20–1.60	–	–
1637	2.30–2.90	–	–
1664	4.00–5.00	–	–
1684	1.60	–	–
1705	2.50	4.00	–
1711	1.20–2.30	–	–
1723	3.00	6.00	0.90
1724	3.00	5.80	0.80
1732	2.35	4.45	0.83–1.20
1733	2.80	4.40	1.00–1.50
1751	3.05	5.05	1.32–1.85
1774	4.00	9.40	1.59–1.87
1792	5.00	10.00	1.45–1.57
1810	6.50	10.00	–

NOTE: All prices of sugar converted to taels per picul according to conversion rates of the common contemporary trading currencies (e.g., rials, guilders; see Appendix for weights, measures, and money).
SOURCES: Boxer, *The Great Ship from Amacon*, p. 184; Chen Chunsheng, "Qingdai Qianlong nianjiian Gunagdong de mijia he miliang maoyi," appendix 2.16; Chuan and Kraus, pp. 154–160; Gonzalez de Mendoza, vol. 1. p. 14; Glamman, p. 154; Milburn, p. 491; Miyazaki Ichisada, "Shinsho bōeki ni kansuru ichi shiryō," pp. 440–441; Morrse, *The Chronicles of the East India Company*, vol. 1, pp. 35, 16, 133, 172, 180, 211, 219, 291; vol. 2, p. 203; vol. 5, p. 196.

because there was a dramatic decline in prices. In the sixteenth century, even after Caribbean sources of sugar became available, a pound of sugar in England still cost as much as a laborer's wages for two whole days of work. Over the course of the seventeenth century, the price dropped by half and between 1700 and 1750, and then the price went down again by another third.[214] The most dramatic declines in sugar prices in Britain came between 1840 and 1850 when prices declined by 30 percent and a further 25 percent in the next two decades. This downward trend in prices was a product of sweeping changes in the technology of manufacture developed in Europe in the wake of the Industrial Revolution. Not only did steam-operated crushers, vacuum evaporation pans, and revolutionary changes in transportation bring cheaper cane sugar from the colonies; but by the mid-nineteenth century, new industrial technologies made available ever larger quantities of beet sugar from Eastern Europe and France. While price alone cannot explain the increase in sugar consumption in Britain, there is ample evidence that the demand for sugar fluctuated in direct relation to price.[215] Elsewhere in nineteenth-century Europe, lower prices for sugar were also followed by higher levels of consumption.[216] Then, as real wages continued to rise in Britain, especially after the middle of the nineteenth century, expenditures on food in working-class families began to reflect an improved standard of living. The quantity of cheapest carbohydrates eaten such as bread and potatoes declined, fresh meat (as opposed to bacon) was purchased in addition to tinned foods, raisins, currants, and fruits, and new drinks such as cocoa at supper further increased the total intake of sugar.[217] Cheap beet sugar from the European continent, produced with government subsidies, rather than cane sugar from the colonies, was increasingly used by British industries to manufacture jams, marmalades, confections, and sweet biscuits to cater to the appetites of this class.[218] Contra Mintz, it was not just the fall of sugar from the symbolic to the mundane that propelled consumption in Britain. The eclipse of inefficient colonial slave-labor-based cane-sugar production in the Caribbean for European industrial beet-sugar manufacture was but one indicator of the fundamental changes produced by maturing capitalism that provided both the urban workers and the consumers for commodities like sugar.

In nineteenth-century China, the domestic market for all commodities remained restricted, and sugar is but one example. The continued use of sugar, refined white flour, oils, sesame, dried fruits, tea, and even fresh fruits as status demarcators at formal official banquets[219] underlined the absence of these products in the everyday lives of the majority. The pattern of trade further illustrates the limits of the domestic market. Basic cereals formed the bulk of the goods traded on the national market, followed by cotton cloth. As Wu Chengming points out, however, only 14.3 percent of the total output of cotton cloth was marketed on the eve of the Opium War (1839–1842).[220] The rest was spun and woven for consumption within the peasant household economy. Although Wu excludes the portion of grains, cotton cloth, silk, tea, and salt sold for purposes of tax payments, and their inclusion would revise the totals upwards somewhat, the basic limits of this market are evident. Fan I-chun, tabulating the customs revenues, also sees a plateau in the volume of trade after 1750 and a downward trend after 1777.[221] This, given the increasing size of the population, underlines the limits of the domestic market. As has been amply demonstrated by the vast literature on incipient capitalism (*ziben zhuyi mengya*), the Chinese peasant producers were linked to the market as producers.[222] But it is also apparent that they were not completely dependent on the market as consumers themselves; they did not have to buy all their necessities in order to survive. A brief examination of a commodity that was even more integral to Chinese dietary preferences, such as tea, underlines this point. Tea accounted for only 7.75 percent of the total value of commodities in circulation in 1840.[223] By the nineteenth century therefore, the British worker not only ate more sugar but also drank more tea than the Chinese peasant whose usual drink was the so-called *baicha*, "white tea," that is, hot water. The constraints of the domestic market were such that Jianning, a major tea-producing region by the late Ming, did not develop further and had reached a plateau in its output as early as the sixteenth century.[224]

The consumer market for items such as tea and sugar was probably further affected by the nineteenth-century rise in prices of basic commodities, including rice. Wang Yeh-chien, using data collated from four price series, has roughly divided the history of prices in the Qing period into five phases: (1) From 1644 to 1682, during the years of war and massive dislocations in the economically developed coastal areas, prices fell. (2) From 1682 to 1800 there was mild inflation. (3) From 1800 to 1850 there was a severe deflation, which further reduced the cash income of peasants. (4) From 1850 to 1875, there was a rapid rise in prices, followed by a precipitous fall. (5) From 1875 to 1911, there was a sharp inflation in prices particularly after 1885–1911, during which time prices increased by 150 percent.[225] Throughout the nineteenth century real wages for workers remained stationary at best, with periods of sharp decline.[226] Even teachers, a relatively privileged stratum, experienced no increase in real salaries.[227] Of the four criteria for growth of the domestic market enumerated by Hobsbawm above, the market in China had then grown only through population increase. It was marked by an absence of transfer from non-monetary to monetary incomes, increase in income per head or the substitution of industrially produced goods for goods manufactured within the household.

But were there other possibilities of developing the market for Chinese sugar? The importance of the market has been stressed repeatedly in the literature on economic development. Several theorists, starting with Adam Smith in the eighteenth century, have suggested that the rise of trade between hitherto separate economies leads to specialization as producers seek to buy what was unavailable before and produce what is in demand for sale. Smith expected these exchanges in due course to bring about innovation and accumulation for the anticipated sequence was that individual producers facing competition would respond by cutting costs, generally by adopting the most efficient technology available, thus exerting a *systematic* and continuous pressure on others to do likewise. The process multiplied many times would lead to continuous growth of per capita output. This, as Brenner notes, is the distinguishing feature of modern economic growth.[228] Marx, particularly in volume 1 of *Capital,* also discusses the role of trade and the world market in ushering in this modern epoch: "The circulation of commodities is the starting-point of capital. The production of commodities and its circulation in its developed form, namely trade, form the historic presuppositions under which capital arises. World market and world trade date from the sixteenth century, and from then on the modern history of capital starts to unfold."[229]

Many scholars of both European and Chinese economic history, both Marxist and non-Marxist, have interpreted trade and demand as the crucial solvents in the dissolution of feudalism.[230] Much research on incipient capitalism in China, including that of Wu Chengming cited above, owe their focus on the market to these interpretations of Marx.[231] Other scholars of Chinese economic history are far more explicitly Smithian in their inspiration. David Faure notes: "The commercialization of the Chinese countryside was a continuous process of transport and industrial development that broke down the seclusion of local economies," and concludes: "[A]s it was, rural China was poor not because there was excessive trade, but because there was not enough of it."[232] As this chapter shows, however, there were structural inhibitions to the expansion of the domestic market. A peasantry, who by and large produced their subsistence needs and most of their own food and clothing, did not have to have recourse to the market for consumer goods except for small items such as salt, soy sauce, matches, and a bit of oil.

The market for Chinese sugar was to emerge overseas. For elsewhere, including neighboring Japan, the conditions of economic reproduction of the peasantry were beginning to change. The world market from the sixteenth century onwards presented the Chinese with ample opportunities for expansion. What was the transformative potential of this trade? In the next chapter we turn to a discussion of the world market and China's involvement in this market.

TWO

THE WORLD MARKET: CHANGING PATTERNS OF TRADE

> This China trade once settled, we shall be able to bring home such quantity of sugar as will not only supply England but the rest of Europe; besides which, being brought to a perfection, it will be worth more to his majesty than Brazil was to the Kings of Portugal before the Hollanders disturbed them. It will likewise furnish Achin and India with sugar, in which places it yieldeth reasonable profit.[1]
>
> —Peter Mundy, 1637

PETER MUNDY, WHO HOPED TO BREAK the monopoly of the London merchants in the British East India Company by visiting China on behalf of their rival Courteen's Association, and its backer, King Charles I, was not far off the mark.[2] Chinese sugar came to be sold in Europe at a handsome profit in the seventeenth century and sold extensively in India by the eighteenth century.

China's intra-Asian foreign trade in the sixteenth and seventeenth centuries carried out by Chinese merchants from China and Southeast Asia has received limited attention by scholars writing in English.[3] The nineteenth-century experience, moreover, has colored readings of Chinese overseas trade in the earlier periods.[4] Early-nineteenth-century evaluations of Chinese foreign trade were shaped by comments such as those of Adam Smith: "The home market of China is, perhaps, in extent, not much inferior to the markets of all the different countries of Europe put together. A more extensive foreign trade, however, which to this great home market added the foreign market of all the rest of the world . . . could scarce fail to increase very much the manufactures of China, and to improve very much the productive powers of its manufacturing industries."[5]

Smith, as we have seen, clearly overestimated the extent of China's domestic market. This chapter will show that he had similarly underestimated China's foreign trade. Such inaccuracies, however, are to be expected since Smith wrote in 1776 and relied on limited European sources. What is curious is that Smith's impression of Chinese foreign trade has not been substantially revised some two centuries later. Several scholars, who approach the issue from British sources which discuss the "opening of China" as a prelude to the Opium War (1839–1842), have accepted the view that the Qing government was actually powerful enough to impose its will thousands of miles away, that Canton's trade restrictions on Western traders defined the possibilities of overseas trade, and that this was the sum total of Chinese foreign commerce.[6] China's foreign trade and the consequences of China's increased involvement in international trade in the post–Opium War period have also been the subject of inquiries with models based on Frank's dependency theory and particularly Wallerstein's world-system theory.[7] Despite these innovative approaches their tendency has also been to assume uncritically that China's foreign trade on the eve of the Opium War was limited to the Western trade at Canton and that Chinese traders were entering the nineteenth century as hapless victims of Beijing's disdain and Western predation

These assumptions tell only half the story of Chinese foreign trade. By abstracting the commerce with Western nations from the context of intra-Asian trade in which the Chinese played a dominant role, the expansion and dynamics of Chinese foreign trade as well as the extent of the Chinese market in Asia during the Qing are ignored. Exports to the West and intra-Asian trade appear as unconnected phenomena; the control of Chinese traders over trading networks is equally dismissed. This chapter begins with an overview of the separate trading worlds of Europe and Asia on the eve of European expansion into Asia in the sixteenth century. It then traces the changes that occurred during the course of the seventeenth and eighteenth centuries by following the trail of the sugar trade throughout the world. There are two basic questions which link this overview. Was Chinese trade at a disadvantage compared to European trade in the Pacific arena even *prior* to the Opium War? Or did China's Asian trade have the possibility of generating a surplus which could make capital potentially available for investment in manufacturing—thus initiating a market-led process of development?

The European Sugar Market and the Beginnings of European Trade in Asia

> On 18 October 1513, the king of Portugal offered the Pope a lifesize sugar effigy of himself, surrounded by twelve cardinals, and three hundred candles, one and half meters high.[8]

The display of such elaborate subtleties to underline rank and wealth reached new levels in sixteenth-century Europe among the very rich. But sugar was no longer a prerogative of the aristocratic elite. Culinary preferences of wealthy commoners followed suit; the mid-sixteenth century German saying "Sugar spoils no dish" reflected this general trend.[9]

A major change had taken place in the structure of the European sugar trade by the sixteenth century. Cultivation and refining were now split between producers in the New World and refiners located in various northwestern European centers. Previously, in the fourteenth century and the early part of the fifteenth century—when the sugar trade was based in the Mediterranean and Venice functioned as the primary European entrepôt—famous mercantile houses such as the Cornero and Martini had first discovered the enormous profits to be made from centralized refining and distribution.[10] But although a few refineries had been started in Venice and Bologna, cultivation was still directly linked to the refiners; for example, the great estates of the Venetian mercantile Cornero family on Cyprus produced the raw sugar that was then refined and marketed by the family in Venice. Basic changes in this nexus of cultivation and manufacture began evolving by the end of the fifteenth century when European trade shifted from the Mediterranean firmly toward the Atlantic. Political transformations within the Mediterranean due to the rise of the Ottoman Empire combined with competition from Flemish and Iberian traders and the revival of Greek, Turkish, Jewish, and Armenian merchants accelerated this shift.

Sugar was the first of the long-distance commodities to be revolutionized by "the oceanic challenge" of the Portuguese.[11] With their interest in the sugar trade, the Portuguese had expanded cane cultivation to Madeira in the 1420s as soon as the first settlers arrived. Shortly thereafter cultivation spread to the Canaries, the Azores, and São Tomé.[12] In every case, sugarcane cultivation followed swiftly on the heels of discovery of new lands. The export trade in sugar from the islands, particularly Madeira, was controlled by Flemish, English, Jewish, and Genoese merchants. Among the navigators of the sugar-cargo ships was a Genoese, Christopher Columbus. Probably becoming aware of the possibilities of cane cultivation in the Caribbean from his own experience in the business in Madeira, Columbus is credited with bringing sugarcane to the Americas.[13] On his second voyage in 1493 he was apparently ordered by Ferdinand and Isabella to take "twenty field experts in cultivation and a supply of all sorts of seeds and plants."[14] Cane cultivation and sugar manufacture were thus introduced very early to Hispaniola and shortly afterwards to Puerto Rico, Cuba, and Jamaica. The enterprise on Hispaniola, however, did not succeed as spectacularly as the venture in Brazil, reached by Pedro Alvares Cabral in 1500.

Cabral probably did not have the plant on board his ship. But it must have been introduced soon after, and its cultivation spread extremely rapidly.[15] A charter granted by King Dom Manoel I in 1516 included the recommendation that the people sent to Brazil were to include "a man practised and capable as chief of a sugar factory."[16] By 1526 Brazilian sugar was paying duties in the Lisbon Custom House. The rise of Brazil as the major source of raw sugar and the dominance of Portugal as the main supplier to the European continent was heightened by the eclipse of Venice as an entrepôt and the decline of the Mediterranean trade in sugar.[17]

Concurrent to this expansion in the Americas, Portugal developed sea-trade with Asia. Portuguese monopoly of this trade in Europe was initiated from the moment Vasco da Gama, with the help of local pilots, crossed the Indian Ocean and learned the basic wind systems in 1498; it was sustained through strict secrecy of the "trade winds" navigation charts for over a century.[18] A pattern of Portuguese trade based on territorial control of the trading posts had already been established in western Africa and in America. This pattern was repeated in Asia as colonial outposts were set up in Goa (1510), Malacca (1511), Hormuz (1515), Colombo (1518), and then in Macao by the 1550s. However, the realities of the *Estado da India* (the State of India), the name given to this enterprise by the Portuguese Crown, were far less impressive than the king's title, "Lord of Conquest, Navigation and Commerce of Ethiopia, Arabia, Persia and India" would suggest. Only seven ships per year on average sailed from Portugal for the Indian Ocean during the years 1500–1634; of these 28 percent were lost at sea and fewer than four ships a year made it back from Asia via the Cape.[19]

In spite of its early prominence in the European sugar market, the Iberian peninsula did not inherit Venice's status as the entrepôt of Europe. By the mid-sixteenth century, the commercial and manufacturing center of Europe was located in the Low Countries, with Antwerp emerging as the primary locus of both finance capital and various types of processing including sugar refining. The Portuguese sold the sugar from Madeira and Brazil there. Nineteen sugar refineries (more than any other city) had been established in Antwerp by 1550.[20] But Antwerp's preeminence was soon destroyed by war and the division of the Netherlands between 1572 and 1585. From this war emerged a new independent nation, the United Provinces of the Netherlands, and Amsterdam became the new commercial and financial center of Europe. It was here that enormous warehouses, combined with the development of large banking exchanges, transformed the nature of wholesale trade in Europe.[21] A variety of industries including sugar and cocoa refining, brewing, distilling, and tobacco processing developed to supply the tastes of the new bourgeoisie.[22] Whereas in 1595 there had been only three or four sugar refineries in the Northern Netherlands, there were twenty-nine in 1622; twenty-five of these were located in Amsterdam. By 1640 there were forty refineries and by 1661 the number had increased to over sixty.[23] The only problem, from the Dutch point of view, was that the supply of about 45 million pounds of raw sugar came from Portuguese-controlled Brazil—a trade which alone yielded a minimum profit of 4,800,000 guilders a year by the 1620s.[24] As Dutch-Iberian political and religious conflicts intensified (Portugal had become a province of Spain when Philip II of Spain enforced his claim to the Portuguese crown in 1580), long-distance maritime trade in the Indian and the Atlantic oceans became additional spheres of rivalry and struggle.

The Dutch-Iberian sea war in the Atlantic from the 1580s onwards had begun with the harassment of Portuguese ships returning from Asia. Interested in developing a trade route to Asia, Holland's early attempts had focused on finding a route via the north of Russia and then via northern America. Not surprisingly, only the Cape route and the Indian Ocean emerged as viable alternatives. By 1595, sufficient information had been collected to send a trading voyage to Java. With expanded trading opportunities, the corporate trading associations that had thus far organized Dutch trade in the Mediterranean and West Africa gave way to a more complex enterprise—De Verenigde Oost-Indische Compagnie, United East India Company, chartered in 1602.[25] Acquisition of pepper, nutmeg, mace, and cloves formed the primary motivation for this trade. The profits to be made were impressive; the cargoes of just two captured Portuguese ships auctioned off in Amsterdam fetched six million guilders.[26] Asian sugar, as a profitable ballast stabilizing the hold and filling the cargo of porcelain, was merely a welcome addition.[27] Then suddenly, events in Brazil sparked the interest of the Dutch East India Company in sources of Asian sugar and made it a major commodity of import.

Open hostilities between the Dutch and the Portuguese broke out in Brazil in 1624, and intensified toward the end of the decade in the sugar producing areas of the Nordeste. By 1635, when they occupied Paraíba, the Dutch found that the Portuguese military commanders in Brazil had destroyed much of their cane-processing machinery and property rather than let them fall into the hands of "heretics," that is, Dutch Calvinists.[28] As Braudel points out, "The odd paradox of the Dutch occupation of the sugar-producing Nordeste was that it interrupted the flow of Brazilian sugar to Amsterdam, where it had previously been plentiful; the price went up as well."[29] The 1620s and 1630s coincided with the increased efforts of the Dutch East India Company to expand their trade with China.

East Asian Trade in the Sixteenth Century

Much of the Chinese trade to and from Southeast Asia, both in the form of tribute-related and private trade, had existed since the Tang dynasty. Silk skeins, brocades, and gauzes formed the bulk of the Chinese exports,[30] while sugar was still imported as a tribute item in the seventh century. By the Song it seems a maritime trade in sugar was beginning in Southeast Asia. Zhao Rugua, Inspector of Foreign Trade in Fujian, wrote in his miscellaneous notes on foreign countries and their products in 1225 that sugar was imported into many countries of Southeast Asia and "foreign traders" (*fan shang*) sold sugar in Annam, Palembang (Srivijaya in Sumatra), and on the Malayan Peninsula.[31] Sugar is listed alongside silk, silk brocades, porcelains and iron wares. These goods are most likely to have been exports only from China at this time, although the traders bringing them to the ports may not have been Chinese.[32] The details of Chinese trade to Japan in this early period are even less clear. It is known that merchants from Quanzhou, Fuzhou, and other ports of Fujian traded actively with Japan. Small amounts of sugar along with silk, porcelain, and Southeast Asian products were brought to Japan by these "Sōshōyaku" (Song merchant guests), for Japan did not have the sugarcane plant as yet.[33]

During the Yuan, formal official contact with Southeast and South Asia increased after the conquest of South China in 1278. Trade with Southeast Asia expanded significantly; contacts multiplied with the various military campaigns against Annam and Champa, the spectacular invasion of Java in 1292, and the far more cordial relationships with the kingdoms of Siam and Malabar (southwestern India).[34] The Chinese exported various types of silks, porcelain, copper coins, both white and crystallized sugar, iron pans, lacquerware, and dozens of other products.[35] Though quantitative estimates of this export trade are not available, the total quantities involved were probably substantial; there was enough at least to support various pirate communities who cultivated little and lived off plundering the Chinese traders.[36] As Wang Dayuan's *Daoyi zhilue* (A Record of the Islands and Their Barbarians) of 1350 noted, "Everything the inhabitants of Tumasik (Danmaxi, Old Singapore) possess is a product of their plundering of Chinese junks."[37] The main Chinese import was pepper. The use of pepper and cloves in China, on the increase since the Tang, grew sharply in the thirteenth century. Marco Polo, with some of his usual exaggeration reported: "I assure you that for one shipload of pepper that goes to Alexandria or elsewhere destined for Christendom, there come a hundred such, aye, and more too, to this Haven of Zayton [Quanzhou]."[38] The ships which Marco Polo describes were large junks (from the Malay *adjong*, a large ship) that were loaded with pepper when returning from Southeast Asia: "Each of their great ships requires at least 200 mariners (some of them 300). They are indeed of great size, for one ship shall carry 5,000 or 6,000 baskets of pepper. . . ."[39] Van Leur has estimated that the bulk of the annual production of around 9.3 million pounds of Southeast Asian pepper in the seventeenth century went to China before the Dutch got involved in the trade.[40] Large profits were to be made from this commerce. Pepper sold in China at 750 to 1,000 times the original price. Sappanwood, a dyewood yielding red and purple colors, was also a major import from Southeast Asia and fetched several hundred times the purchase price.[41]

The tension between the Chinese government's attempts to control overseas trade versus the interests of private traders which marks the later history of Chinese foreign trade was muted in the Yuan. Generally supportive of merchants and long-distance trade but eager to increase tax revenues, the Yuan government used a licensing system for Chinese ships going abroad. Administrative regulations and Maritime Trade Offices (Shibo si) were established in Quanzhou, Ningbo, Shanghai, Ganpu, Wenzhou, Hangzhou, and Qingyuan following the Tang-Song model. The registration of foreign ships and payments of duties on foreign goods were regulated by a code introduced in 1294.[42] Then, in 1368, with the advent of the Ming Hongwu emperor the role of the state in controlling private ventures overseas was greatly amplified. The first edict prohibiting Chinese from foreign travel and banning trade was issued in 1371, and the import trade was restricted to goods brought by tribute missions or embassies.[43] The Mingzhou, Quanzhou, and Guangzhou branches of the Maritime Trade Office were closed in 1374.[44] There are two widely variant interpretations of these and other Ming restrictions on foreign trade. To several specialists of China's international trade, including John Wills, the tribute "embassy was the center of a rather tightly integrated system for the management of all foreign relations" designed to insulate the "empire from dangerous contact with foreigners."[45] The other interpretation, Ts'ao Yung-ho's, for example, sees these restrictions as a preemptive bid by the Ming government seeking "to exclude any domestic rivalry, strictly maintaining the policy of prohibiting private trade on one hand, and developing the government monopoly of foreign trade to satisfy the demand for tropical goods on the other."[46] We cannot enter here into a lengthy discussion on the politics of the Ming state which prompted these measures; more pertinently the narrowing of overseas trading opportunities in China through such state prerogatives had two main effects. First, it increased the direct contacts of Northeast Asia with Southeast Asia, and goods from Southeast Asia were brought into China indirectly.[47] Second, the increase in trade and tribute missions from Southeast Asia were accompanied by increased piracy in East Asian seas.

The rise to prominence of the Ryukyu Islands as a major importer and re-exporter of Southeast Asian products to China started immediately after the Ming Hongwu ban in 1371. The first official tribute mission was sent to the Ming court in 1372. This was followed by annual missions, sometimes missions were sent even twice a year. All the tribute missions were rewarded with generous gifts, and the typical gifts the Ryukyuans received from the Ming government were seagoing vessels. In fifty-four years (1385–1439) the Ryukyuans received at least thirty ships,[48] scarcely the actions of a state bent on isolationist policies.[49] And that was not all. In 1392, the king of the Ryukyus requested that the Ming court send crews from Fujian so that they could manage the navigation of these ships for long voyages. The request was honored.[50] The Ryukyuan tribute missions brought large quantities of pepper, sappanwood, and other tropical products to the Ming government.[51] The Ryukyu Islands became, in effect, safe and controllable intermediaries for the flow of Southeast Asian products to the Ming.

The Hongwu ban also sparked a flurry of tribute missions from Southeast Asia to China. Champa, Java, and Samudra-Pasè (on Sumatra) sent numerous missions, but the Siamese outdid them all. Well before the noted voyages of Zheng He (1405–1436), which were obviously designed to raise the prestige of the Chinese state further, no fewer than twenty-two missions were sent to China from Siam in fifteen years.[52] The *Ming shilu* notes that each of the Siamese missions of 1372, 1377, 1386, 1387, 1389, and 1390 brought large amounts of pepper, sappanwood, cloves, and elephant tusks into China; the mission of 1387 brought 10,000 *jin* (over 7,500 pounds) of pepper and 100,000 *jin* (over 75,000 pounds) of sappanwood, which the government then sold.[53] The Siamese initially also sent missions to Korea starting in 1391. As direct Siamese missions to Japan did not seem forthcoming, raiding the missions to Korea became attractive in northeastern Asia. The Siamese mission of 1393 was raided by "Japanese pirates," as were the missions of 1396 and 1406.[54] All of this somewhat dampened the interest of the Siamese in pursuing tribute missions to Korea, although they continued with missions to China. Increased piracy in East Asian waters, which so put off the Siamese, was however, to become the dominant private response to the Ming state's continued attempts to abrogate profits from foreign trade.

Piracy, or illegal trade by another name, had long been part of Southeast Asian and East Asian trade networks as particular states sought to control vital trading channels.[55] The *wokou* or *wako* (literally Japanese bandits), subject of such disapprobation by the Ming government, had first made their appearance off the coast of Korea in 1223.[56] What was different about the illegal trade in the fifteenth and sixteenth centuries was its scale and the extensive involvement of Chinese gentry, high-ranking officials, and merchants in various aspects of this trade; by the 1540s all the leaders of the fourteen *wako* gangs, save one, were Chinese.[57] The rapid expansion of piracy reflected the increased volume and high profitability of East Asian maritime trade, especially the increasing sixteenth-century trade in precious commodities like silver from Manila and Japan.[58] The frequency with which various edicts banning trade had to be issued is a further indication of how vital this overseas trade had become. As Xie Jie, a 1574 graduate from Fujian (who later became Minister of Revenue) astutely noted, "The pirates and the traders were the same people. When trade flourished, the pirates became traders; when trade was banned, the traders became pirates. . . . The more strictly enforced the ban, the fiercer the piracy."[59] Thousands of Chinese managed to continue private maritime trade in defiance of the Ming statutes. The prologue to the expansion of East Asian trade in the sixteenth and seventeenth centuries, in which the Portuguese and then the Dutch were to enter as adjuncts, lies in this history of piracy and evasion of government edicts.

The growth of trading emporia in Southeast Asia also helped to circumvent the Ming restrictions, for they eliminated the necessity of traveling directly to China as long as Chinese goods could be brought over. These trading ports, optimally located in the Straits of Malacca where various kings and sultans found it in their interests to sponsor trade, became the great marketplaces for the exchange of goods from East, West, South, and Southeast Asia and Eastern Africa. Malacca (Melaka), as Ma Huan (ca. 1380–1460) noted on his voyages between 1413 and 1433, was well on the way to becoming the most important of these ports by the fifteenth century, and Chinese trade was already a major component.[60] In 1511, when the Portuguese conquered the port, it had become the central locus for transshipment of Asian trade in spices, textiles, silks, and porcelains. Arriving shortly after the capture of Malacca by the Portuguese, Tomé Pires (the Portuguese apothecary and later ambassador to China) found that Chinese trade accounted for almost 10 percent of all transactions. Trade from Bengal and the Coromandal coast of India accounted for another 10 percent while 4 percent was from Western India and beyond.[61] The bulk was composed of Javanese and intra-archipelago trade. From further to the east, traders, possibly of Chinese origin, brought gold, forest products, and foodstuffs from the

Irogots and Illocos of the Philippines islands.[62] Junks from China to Malacca brought silks in large quantities, sugar, porcelains, copper and iron wares, salt, and goods of high value but small bulk such as camphor, sulfur, alum, saltpeter, pearls, and gold. The quantities involved for any of these products are not specified; Pires only writes, "The land of China produces plenty of good sugar."[63] For their return voyage the Chinese bought sandalwood, cloves, elephant tusks, and pepper. As Pires comments, "Pepper apart, they make little account of all the rest."[64] The various ports of Asia involved in international trade in the sixteenth and seventeenth centuries are indicated on Map 4.

Even in this early period of international trade at Malacca, a division of markets had apparently developed. Except for specialty cotton textiles, such as the type of fine muslin called *beibu*, the common Indian chintz textiles so widely traded in Southeast Asia were not purchased by the Chinese for the return voyage.[65] The sugar market was also similarly divided. Though several areas such as Java, Sumatra, Taiwan, and the Philippines cultivated sugarcane, prior to the seventeenth century, there were only a few producers of sugar in Southeast Asia such as Quangnam (south-central Vietnam) and Siam.[66] The two major sugar-exporting regions of Asia were Guangdong and Fujian in China and Bengal in eastern India. The sugar markets of Japan and the Southeast Asian areas east and south of Malacca seem to have been exclusively supplied by Chinese traders while markets to the west of Malacca, such as Pegu and Arakan, were supplied by Bengali producers, as were the markets of Western India, Persia, and beyond.[67]

Since much of the Chinese, Indian, and Arab trade at Malacca was based on the availability of pepper, Portuguese attempts to break the monopoly of Asian traders affected this trade. As the *Dong-Xi yangkao* (A Study of the Eastern and Western Oceans) by Zhang Xie (1617) was to comment, "Since the Folangji [Franks] conquered Manlajia [Malacca], it has been ruined and there are few goods. The regulations were changed and the Chinese repeatedly treated so unscrupulously that the merchants ships now avoid Manlajia and sail directly to Sumandala [Semudera, on the island of Sumatra]."[68]

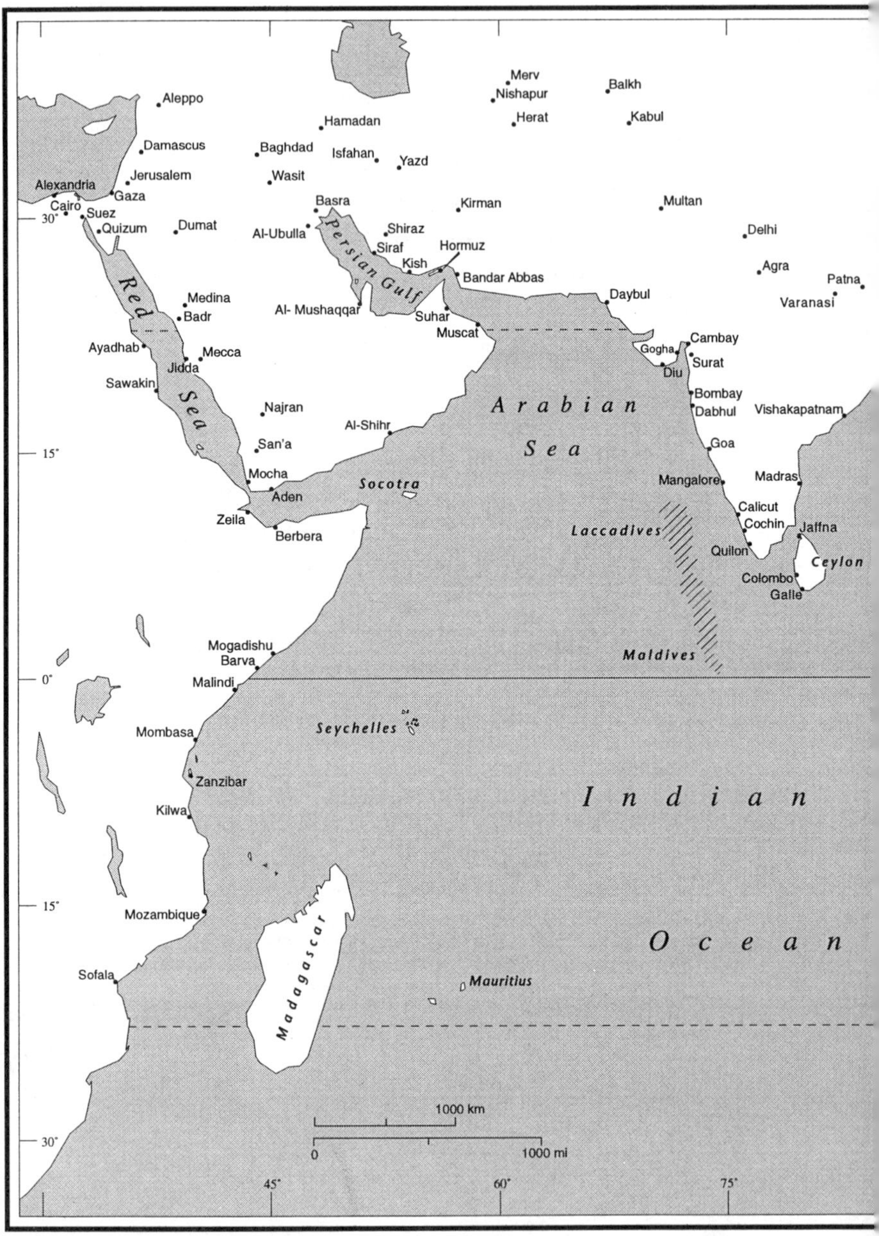

MAP 4. International trading ports, cities, and regions of Asia and East Africa, ca. 800–1850

Beijing
Luoyang
Chang'an
Nanjing
Zhapu
Hangzhou
Dinghai
Ningbo
Wenzhou
Shacheng
Fuzhou
Quanzhou
Anhai
Xiamen
Zhangzhou
Guangzhou
Aomen
(Macao)
Korea
Pusan
Tsushima-han
Japan
Edo
Hirado
Nagasaki
Kii
Satsuma-han
Tanegashima
Naha
Ryukyu Islands
Pacific
Ocean
Tropic of Cancer
Tainan
Taiwan
Calcutta
Satgaon
Tamralipti
Tonkin
Thanh Hoa
Hainan
Island
Annam
Champa
Pegu
Cambodia
Hue
Quangnam
Bay
of
Bengal
Bangkok
Sanf
Sanzhou
Andaman
Islands
Cambodia
Champa
Manila
Philippine
Sea
South China Sea
Ligor
Sulu
Islands
Mindanao
Patani
Kedah
Malaya
Acheh
Pase
Pedir
Kuala Selangor
Malacca
Singapore
Riau
Sumatra
Borneo
Sulawesi
Ternate
Equator — 0°
Molucca
(Maluku)
Islands
Amboina
Bandjarmasin
Srivijaya
Macassar
Bantam
Demak
Tuban
Batavia
Gresik
Tropic of Capricorn
North
90°
105°
120°
135°

Banten, located on the western end of Java and a major collection center for pepper, was one of the ports that picked up the Malaccan trade. Chinese, most of them Fujianese, operated here as middlemen, selling pepper and other products to the Europeans; its sultan and the port were said to owe their prosperity entirely to Chinese trade.[69] Along with Banten, numerous Chinese traders were also active on the east coast of Sumatra, and in Patani and Johore.[70] Sugar, silks, drugs, and copper coins were the primary items brought from China. The demand for sugar was sufficient to permit a substantial markup. John Saris, who lived in Banten from 1605 to 1609 while commanding a voyage of the East Indian Societie, noted in his diary, "Item: in the Moneths of February and March, heere commeth three or foure Junckes from China, very richly laden with Silkes raw and wrought, China Cashes, Purseline, cotton cloath . . . Sugar white the Peecull, three Rials and a halfe, very drie: Sugar Candy very drie, five Rials the Peecull. . . ."[71] Since we have seen in Table 1 that the Portuguese were paying between 1.5 to 2 taels per picul in 1600 at Guangzhou, the markup at Banten was 75–125 percent, not a bad margin for a bulk commodity.

Clearly, with all this trade despite prohibitions, Ming restrictions on private trade were under severe challenge by the mid-sixteenth century. So many bands of pirate-traders existed by this time that the state had to create a special command with control of both military and civil institutions of the coastal provinces of northern Guangdong, Fujian, and Zhejiang. But the money to be made was too lucrative a proposition and some of its own officials turned to overseas trade. A few of these officials-turned-merchants were probably like Lin Xiyuan (1480–1560). A chief judge of the prestigious Court of Judicial Review (Dali Si), he turned merchant and local warlord (*tu hao*) after his falling out with the Ming government over policy issues and his return home to Fujian. There he had a large fleet of ships built for himself, calling them "ferry boats," or *yu huang*, to avoid prosecution. Lin became an extremely wealthy man through trade with Southeast Asia, from the commissions he garnered by acting as a receiver of stolen goods and a "harboring host" (*wo zhu*) for pirates, and by buying and selling goods to the Portuguese.[72] The power of such merchant-pirates was a match for any official of the Ming state. Zhu Wan (1494–1550), a tireless crusader against illegal trade, found local gentry and officials in Fujian in debt to the tune of hundreds and thousands of taels to the merchant-pirates. Despite immense power as vice-censor-in-chief (*fudu yushi*) and governor of Zhejiang and Jiangxi (Nan Gan) with special jurisdiction over coastal Fujian, Zhu ended up humiliated; he was demoted and died in prison when he proved too enthusiastic an enforcer of the trade restrictions.[73] Given the losing battle, finally in 1567 the Ming government was persuaded by Tu Zemin (then governor of Fujian) to liberalize trade restrictions at least to Southeast Asia while Japan was still to remain off-limits. The contrasts between tribute-trade and private trade are only too apparent. Only one to two tribute ships had come in annually to Fujian between 1425 and 1644.[74] In 1567, when official sanction was given for overseas trade to Southeast Asia, close to one hundred Chinese ships left port.[75] That so many ships could be purchased and outfitted indicates the level of private accumulation that had already occurred and the extent to which Chinese traders were poised to challenge and compete with the Europeans entering the trading realm of East Asia.

The Iberian Impact on the Trading World of East Asia

Setting up trade in China had not been easy for the Portuguese. The embassies sent to the Ming court in 1517 under Pires and again in 1521–1522 had come to naught. The death of the Zhengde emperor and the "outrageous and high-handed" behavior of some of the Portuguese commanders had led to their expulsion. Concurrently, edicts had been issued banning trade with them.[76] The anti-*wokou* measures of the Ming had resulted in the closure of both Ningbo and Quanzhou in 1522, leaving only Guangzhou open for limited trading. This further narrowed the options available to the Portuguese. From the beginning Sino-Portuguese trade became an alliance of those Chinese who sought to circumvent Ming restrictions on overseas trade by using the Portuguese as intermediaries, and the Portuguese, who, denied formal permission to trade, had few alternatives but to settle for what they could get via Chinese intermediaries. As Antonio Bocarro, writing in 1635, noted, referring to the Chinese brokers (*jingji*) as "Quevees," they "are most esteemed among them, and there are many of these who entrust great sums of money and goods with the Portuguese, and consequently the Portuguese with them."[77] For the next thirty years, Portuguese trade on the South China coast continued—sometimes despite the opposition of local officials, but more frequently with their connivance.

The beginning of Portuguese trade with Japan in the late 1540s fundamentally altered the structure of Sino-Portuguese trade. Although Marco Polo had written a hearsay account of the fabulous islands of "Zipangu," it was Tomé Pires writing his *Suma Oriental* in Malacca between 1512 and 1515, who provided the first European description of Jambon (Japan).[78] The trade route was finally confirmed in 1542 for the Europeans with the accidental arrival of a few Portuguese in a Chinese junk at Tanegashima.[79]

Trade with Japan had become all the more valuable because of the opening of several new Japanese silver mines at this time. More than fifty gold mines and thirty silver mines were developed in the mid-sixteenth century.[80] Yet this trade could not be routinized by the Portuguese without a permanent base in South China; a base in Macao (Aomen) proved to be the solution. The origins of Portuguese control of Macao are shady. It seems that Wang Bo (jinshi of 1538), then intendant of the Guangzhou Circuit (*Haidao fushi*), was personally involved in foreign trade and permitted the Portuguese to trade in Guangdong on the same terms as Siamese. Furthermore he let them set up in Macao in the early 1550s.[81] Whatever the origins of the Portuguese control of Macao, they were recognized and well established there by 1557 and, given the Ming restrictions, were well-placed to carry on Sino-Japanese trade. As the missionary Luis Frois, writing from Malacca on 1 December 1555, shrewdly noted: "Last year we learnt from the ships that came here from China that there were very great quarrels and disputes between China and Japan. . . . The discord between China and Japan is a great help to the Portuguese who want to go to Japan; for as the Chinese do not go thither to trade with their merchandise, the Portuguese merchants have a great means of negotiating their worldly business."[82] When the Portuguese acquired a base in Nagasaki in 1571, they were indeed in a uniquely powerful position.[83] For the next few decades they were the primary importers of Chinese goods into Japan.

But the Chinese traders, now able to legally trade with Southeast Asia, did not do badly either. Spanish involvement in Asia had opened up trading opportunities for the Chinese via Manila to Acapulco. The new trans-Pacific commercial circuit was established in 1573 when two Manila galleons arrived in Acapulco carrying a load of 712 bolts of Chinese silks, 23,300 pieces of "fine china gilt and porcelain ware," pepper, and cloves.[84] This began the great inflow of silver into China that was to continue for the next two-and-a-half centuries; silks and spices paid for with silver from the mines of Peru and Mexico formed the core of this trans-Pacific circuit.[85] The trade was immensely profitable; the Spanish American merchants could quadruple or quintuple their original investments.[86] It may have been in connection with such trading arrangements that some Chinese merchants traveled to Mexico as early as 1585.[87] Spanish American merchants primarily from Mexico, but also from Peru, Guatemala, and Panama (Tierra Firme), soon began to travel directly to Manila to buy Chinese goods in such large numbers, restricting the market for Spanish goods in the New World, that influential merchants from Seville who handled the trans-Atlantic supply complained the same year to King Philip II, as they saw their profits evaporating.[88] As a result, starting in 1584, restrictions were imposed on the trans-Pacific trade. With various (and oft-repeated) *cedula*, Philip II sought to prohibit direct trade between the Philippines and Peru, Guatemala, and Panama and to limit that trade to 500,000 pesos or a little over twelve tons (28,160 pounds) of silver to be exported annually from Acapulco to Manila. In 1591 the number of galleons allowed to bring back Asian (predominantly Chinese) goods was limited to two per annum, and they were permitted to carry back 250,000 pesos worth of Asian goods.[89] But illegal trade in Chinese goods via Manila continued throughout the colonial period.[90] During the seventeenth and eighteenth centuries large consignments of money were also sent directly to China by the Mexicans and Peruvians. The extent to which the Spanish authorities managed to curtail private trade is unclear; in 1597 alone 12 million silver pesos (675,400 pounds) were supposedly smuggled out from Mexico to the Philippines. And between 1581 and 1800, no less than 44 million pesos (2,470,600 pounds of silver) was sent by the Spanish government to the Philippines.[91] Most of this money was to be used for military, naval, clerical, and administrative stipends. A substantial portion of these stipends went to Chinese merchants to pay for Chinese goods consumed in Manila.

The Chinese did well as the primary suppliers of Manila. As Governor Guido de Lavezaris approvingly noted in 1573, "The Chinese continue to increase their commerce each year, and supply us with many articles, as sugar, wheat and barley flour, nuts, raisins, pears and oranges, silks, choice porcelain and iron, and other small things we lacked in this land before their arrival."[92] Sugar generally had a good market and sold for 6 rials per picul.[93] Beginning with twenty ships in the 1570s, this trade to Manila was to increase to over forty ships from China every year in later centuries.[94] The Spanish trade connections were extensive enough for some of the Chinese merchants trading in Southeast Asia to have learned the language; in 1599, John Davis, an English merchant, ran into one of them in Aceh, and wrote, "I met with a very sensible Merchant of China, that spake Spanish of whom I learned some things, which I hope will give your Lordship good contentment."[95] Manila also provided a convenient cover for Chinese trade with Japan. Japanese traders were beginning to venture to Southeast Asia in increasing numbers under the Tokugawa licensing system of the *shuinjō*. As many as thirty Japanese ships went to Southeast Asia in some years in the first few decades of the seventeenth century, and many bought Chinese goods in the Philippines and Siam.[96] And soon, scores of Chinese traders began venturing directly to Japan.

Sugar and Silk: Emergence of the Japanese Market

Two factors came together in the first decade of the seventeenth century to create a sudden and hitherto unparalleled burst of commercial activity in East Asia. The first was political: the establishment of the *Pax Tokugawa* in Japan and the concurrent collapse of Ming control over parts of South China. The other factor was commercial: a rapid increase in the numbers of private Chinese traders involved in maritime trade as well as the entry of the Dutch and the English into the East Asian trade.

Although the 1522 Ming prohibitions on direct trade with Japan were technically still in effect at the beginning of the seventeenth century, the rescission of the ban to Southeast Asia in 1567 had provided the opportunity for many Chinese traders to resume direct contacts with Japan. By 1597, the number of annual permits issued to Chinese ships going to Southeast Asia had increased to 137,[97] and it was clear even to the Ming officials issuing the permits that once these ships left port the state could not control where they went. So eager were the Tokugawa to encourage the trade with the Chinese that in 1610 Shogun Ieyasu apparently invited a Chinese merchant to his castle at Sumpu (Shizuoka) and promised to protect his trading activities should he run into difficulties with the Ming.[98] Some of these Chinese merchants did very well indeed; one of them, Li Dan (d. 1625), was affluent enough to maintain several houses and warehouses in Nagasaki and Hirado and lend 60,000 taels to the daimyo of Satsuma.[99] The trade was sufficiently lucrative as to be worth risking life and limb: John Saris, now in Japan, noted in 1613: "The twentie three [of June] we had newes of two China Junkes arrived at Langasaque [Nagasaki] laden with sugar. By him we understood that the Emperour of China had then lately put to death about five thousand persons, for trading out of the Countrey, contrary to his Edict, confiscating all their goods; notwithstanding hope of profit enticed these men to put it in hazard."[100]

The vitality of the Asian trade at Nagasaki in these early decades of the seventeenth century is further attested to by the Dutch in 1624:

This year in Nagasaki there were seven small ships (*naveta*) from Macao very richly laden; and another frigate even richer than (the seven ships) went to Manila. There also arrived a Japanese junk, which got her load from the Portuguese, plus one from Cochin China, one from Tonkin, three small ones from Taiwan, two from Cambodia and one from Siam. In addition to that there arrived forty small Chinese junks from the north coast of China, each loaded with 10, 20, 30 piculs of silk, sugar, and porcelain. Altogether they brought a huge treasure so that the price of silk decreased.[101]

Some thirty to sixty Chinese ships were visiting Japan annually at the beginning of the seventeenth century; by the end of the 1630s it was closer to a hundred.[102]

Sugar had been one of the "exotic" items imported from China by Japan. During the Kamakura period (1185–1333), general sugar consumption increased when the eating of sweets like *yōkan* (sweet bean jelly) and *manjū* (rice-flour dumplings with bean jam) became linked with the drinking of green tea.[103] Though cane had been introduced to Japan, there was no organized manufacturing as yet.

Sugar was still regarded as a precious imported item and presented in small quantities as gifts even during the last quarter of the sixteenth century.[104] By the seventeenth century, the emphasis of the Tokugawa *bakufu* on pomp and ceremony and the concurrent rise of a wealthy urban class had led to higher levels of conspicuous consumption of many items, including sugar. New confectioneries were created as the Spanish and the Portuguese introduced caramels, hard candies, cakes, and cookies. Nagasaki was to become famous for a particularly sweet poundcake; *Nagasaki kasutera* (from the Spanish *castella*) remains a specialty of the city to this day. By the end of the century Miyazaki Antei (1623–1697), author of an agricultural treatise, *Nōgyō zensho* (The Complete Book of Farming), was one of many who expressed concern that the consumption of sugar was so commonplace among all classes of people that paying for this imported item was a drain on the national treasury.[105]

A fairly comprehensive run of data on the volume of Chinese shipments from 1637 to 1833 is available from the archives at Nagasaki. The data show that in most years sugar shipments ranged from close to 1 million *jin* to 2 million *jin* (approx. 1,330,000 to 2,660,000 pounds) of sugar. This included all varieties of white, brown, and refined sugar and sugar confectioneries. Occasionally almost three thousand tons of sugar were brought in, as in 1641 when over 5 million *jin* (6,650,000 pounds) were imported on Chinese ships into Japan. The Chinese were not the only ones who brought in sugar. In the early 1600s, the

Portuguese bought it in China to sell to Japan. The Japanese traders in Southeast Asia frequently bought sugar in central Vietnam till Japanese overseas voyages were banned by the shogun in 1635. The Vietnamese and the Siamese brought sugar during the course of their regular trade with Japan. The Dutch bought it where ever they could in Asia, then produced sugar in Taiwan and Batavia (mod. Jakarta) and finally brought it all the way from Bengal by the 1670s.[106] This high level of sugar imports, while not quite comparable to the burgeoning consumption of sugar in contemporary Britain, reflects the general economic transformation and urbanization already under way in Japan.[107] As in Europe, the link between urbanization and the increased consumption of certain foods such as sugar was to become evident in Japan. The per capita annual consumption of sugar rose from five pounds in 1888 to ten pounds in 1897 and to twelve pounds by 1903.[108] At that time, the development of the sugar industry in the newly acquired colonial possession of Taiwan was to become a matter of national priority. In the seventeenth century, however, there were as yet few alternatives to importing sugar.

From the point of view of the Chinese and other merchants, large cargoes of sugar may have also functioned as insurance in these years. While silk was by far the more profitable item for sale in Japan, the market could be uncertain. For example, in 1642 the shogunate moved to curb the use of luxuries by commoners and prohibited them from wearing silk. The price of silk dropped precipitously, causing several bankruptcies.[109] Sugar was exempt from such restrictions and assured good profits. The profits to be made were substantial, as the few years for which we have comparable data from both China and Japan indicate (see Table 2).

Because brown sugar was initially favored, its sale price at the beginning of the seventeenth century was marked up 1,000 percent. The difference between purchase price in China and sale price in Japan ranged from 100 to 250 percent on average. In 1635, for example, the only year for which we have data on purchase and sale prices in all three categories, 3.4 taels in profit could be made on a picul of sugar candy, 4 taels on white sugar, and 3.6 taels on brown sugar. As Iwao Seiichi has pointed out, there was a sharp increase in commodity

TABLE 2
Seventeenth-Century Sugar Prices in China and Japan
(prices in taels per picul)

Year	Sugar candy: Purchase price in China	Sugar candy: Sale price in Japan	White sugar: Purchase price in China	White sugar: Sale price in Japan	Brown sugar: Purchase price in China	Brown sugar: Sale price in Japan
1600	–	–	0.5	3.0–4.5	0.4–0.5	5.0–6.0
1635	3.6	7.0	2.0	6.0	1.4	5.0
1636	–	7.8	–	5.6–6.8	–	–
1637	2.3–3.9	–	–	–	–	–
1640	–	–	–	4.9–6.0	–	–
1654	–	9.0	–	8.0	–	6.0
1658	–	–	–	6.3–6.9	–	–
1664	4.0–5.0	–	–	–	–	–
1680	–	14	–	7.0	–	–
1684	–	–	1.6	–	–	–
1692	–	23	–	14.0	–	–

NOTE: All prices of sugar converted to taels per picul according to conversion rates of the common contemporary trading currencies (e.g., rials, guilders; see Appendix for weights, measures, and money).
SOURCES: Boxer, *The Great Ship from Amacon*, p.184; Glamann, p. 154; Iwao, "Edo jidai," p. 12; Nagazumi, *Tōsen yushutsu*; Morse, *The Chronicles of the East India Company*, vol. 1, p. 35.

prices in Japan toward the end of the seventeenth century. The price of 23 taels per picul of sugar candy in 1692 was a reflection of this general increase but also an indicator of the high demand for sugar.[110]

The sugar-importing ships were all recorded in Nagasaki as "Chinese ships" (*Tōsen*). The ships so designated originated either in China proper, or the captain and the crew were Chinese even if the port of origin was not. Sugar and silk were the major imports, though the cargoes included other high-value, low-bulk goods such as ginseng and medicinal herbs. The Chinese trade was also a conduit for Southeast Asian and Taiwanese products since deer and cattle skins, tropical woods, and buffalo horns were part of the lading. Ships from Anhai were the most numerous with others coming from Fuzhou,

Quanzhou, Xiamen, Changzhou, Guangzhou, Taiwan, Ningbo, and Nanjing in China and Tonkin, Quangnam, Cochin China, Siam, and Patani in Southeast Asia. In some cases (such as Ningbo and Nanjing), sugar was evidently transshipped from southern China, perhaps as part of domestic consignments. This extensive trade reflects the range of Chinese trading networks throughout the Pacific region and the dominance of Chinese traders in the lucrative Japanese market.

The importance of the Portuguese in the China-Japan trade diminished as more Chinese entered into direct trade with Japan. Whereas in 1600 the Portuguese had been the only regular suppliers of Chinese silk and sugar, considering sugar "a very profitable commodity," competition from Fukienese traders by the 1630s eliminated them from this section of the sugar trade.[111] Silk from China in return for silver from Nagasaki (which formed the core of the Portuguese trade from Macao) was threatened by competition from the Dutch. The latter were beginning to buy silk in Tonkin and also enticing Chinese merchants to come to Taiwan by offering them higher prices than at Canton. While many Chinese traders continued to invest in the Portuguese cargoes to and from Japan, by the 1630s there was also mounting concern in Nagasaki over Portuguese bankruptcies.[112] The Portuguese owed 1.25 million taels to various people at Nagasaki and owed the Chinese traders from Fujian and Nanjing well over 700,000 taels when the Portuguese Macao-Nagasaki trade collapsed.[113] This came in 1639 when the shogun declared the exclusion of the Portuguese. Efforts to reopen the Macao-Nagasaki connection ended with the execution of the Portuguese ambassador and his entourage and the burning of the ship in 1640. Finally, though the Portuguese were able to survive in Asia through an expansion of the trade between Macao, Batavia, and India after the 1660s, this trade brought neither the financial gain nor the honor the crown had hoped for.[114]

The Dutch Presence in Asia

The imminent decline of the Portuguese was, however, far from obvious in 1639. When news of the Portuguese expulsion from Japan reached Batavia, the Dutch were said to have held a thanksgiving service.[115] Since their arrival in Asia, the Dutch had been involved in several contests with their Iberian rivals for the control of particular routes and markets. While in Southeast Asia they managed to chase the Portuguese out of the Molucca (Maluku) Islands, as well as Malacca by 1641, successes in East Asia had not been as easy. Attempts to open direct trade with China in 1604 and then again in 1607 had been thwarted by Portuguese interference. Although a factory had been set up in Hirado in southwestern Japan in 1609 and a base established in Batavia in 1619, direct trade with China remained elusive.[116] Finally, after an abortive attack on Macao in 1622, the Dutch resigned themselves in 1624 to setting up a base at what is now An-p'ing (Tainan), in Taiwan.[117] The Spanish, based in northern Taiwan, mounted a half-hearted opposition but were successfully driven out in 1642. Although it is not certain that the Ming court ever gave formal permission for trade with the Dutch in Taiwan, an informal agreement seems to have been worked out allowing Chinese traders to bring merchandise to them.[118] The development of a Dutch base in Taiwan was far from detrimental to the expansion of Chinese trading networks. The Dutch were so eager for trade that they were willing to pay high prices and more than willing to help their suppliers circumvent the Ming authorities.

Sugar featured in Dutch trade as a commodity for sale in European as well as in intra-Asian markets from the earliest days of their presence in Asia. The possibility of transporting sugar from China to Amsterdam may have been first noted at Banten, on the island of Java. Cornelis Matelieff, a Dutch admiral who had arrived in Asia in 1605 and was trying to break the Portuguese monopoly of the Chinese and Japanese trade, left for Holland in 1607 from Banten with "twelve thousand sackes of Pepper, foure hundred sackes of Nutmegs, Sugar, Ebony wood, and some raw Silke."[119] Other Dutch ships carried similar cargoes. John Saris noted, "The fourth of October, 1606 the China quarter was all burnt downe, yet it pleased God to preserve Ours. The same night, the Carracke of the Flemmings set saile for Holland, her lading was fifteene thousand sackes of Pepper, some rawe Silke, and great store of China Sugar."[120]

The directors of the Dutch East India Company, recommended

regular trade in sugar, both as ballast and as a profitable commodity from Asia as early as 1616.[121] In 1622 the first Dutch cargo of approximately 106,000 pounds of powdered Chinese sugar arrived in Amsterdam, nearly half of the 242,000 pounds total for the year.[122] As the Dutch-Portuguese conflict in Brazil intensified and drove up the prices of West Indian and Brazilian sugar in Amsterdam, interest in Chinese sugar rose correspondingly. In 1631, the directors sent an order to Batavia for 440,000 pounds of sugar. By 1633 this was increased to over 650,000 pounds, in 1636 to 1.1 million pounds. In 1637 the directors asked for an "unlimited quantity," and received 4,125,000 pounds.[123] The Dutch possibly had difficulty rounding up these large quantities at short notice, since the demand for Chinese sugar on the Japanese market had also increased. Shipments of Chinese sugar made up the bulk of the sugar sent to Europe, and these steadily increased to over 4 million pounds in 1637.[124] Bengali and Siamese sugar were also sent in the sugar consignments from Asia; but the directors repeatedly requested that Chinese white, candied, and powdered sugar be sent, for only these were of suitable quality for use in the Amsterdam refineries.[125] In 1642, the Dutch must have bought the bulk of the Chinese output, for there was a small shipment to Japan while over 2 million pounds of powdered sugar from China were imported into Amsterdam.[126] Throughout the decade of the 1640s approximately 440,000 pounds of powdered sugar and 220,000 pounds of sugar candy (*bingtang*) continued to be ordered from China.[127] There was another peak period in 1649 when 2.5–3.0 million pounds of sugar was requested.

Dutch profits from Chinese sugar imports were not negligible, though clear runs of data do not exist. The directors of the Dutch East India Company considered dispatching a small ship solely for the purpose of getting sugar from Asia in 1636. According to their estimates, at a very conservative level there would be a net profit of 75 percent per investment or 52 percent per annum if sugar was imported directly from Asia.[128]

The apparent profits to be made encouraged the Dutch to sponsor sugar cultivation and manufacture in both Taiwan and Batavia. In 1636, Taiwan was able to export some sugar to Europe in addition to

12,042 *jin* (16,015 pounds) of white sugar and 110,461 *jin* (146,913 pounds) of brown sugar to Japan.[129] By 1645, production in Taiwan had increased to permit an export of 1,500,000 *jin* (1,995,000 pounds) and by 1660 that increased to 2,000,000 *jin* (2,660,000 pounds). In Batavia, with the demand for pepper on the decline in Europe after 1650, sugar was seen as an alternative. One letter from Batavia to the company's directors, commenting on the sugar trade, hoped: "In sum, God be praised, we will live to see a prosperous century in Batavia."[130]

But the European sugar market did not prove to be Batavia's salvation. Demand for Asian sugar remained fairly high in the Netherlands only until 1655. Then the price began to fall owing to the recovery of the Brazilian sugar industry and the development of several new areas of supply in the West Indies.[131] By the end of the decade, Chinese sugar was dropped from consignments to Europe. Much to the chagrin of the Batavian officials of the Dutch East India Company, the directors in Amsterdam also did not want large quantities of Javanese sugar on a regular basis because of its loss through leakage on the longer voyage from Asia and the low price of Asian sugars on the Amsterdam market.[132]

Yet not all was lost. The two terminal points of the intra-Asian trade, Japan and Persia, were among the largest markets for sugar in Asia. The Dutch entered both these markets with sugar produced in areas under their colonial domination. For example, Taiwanese sugar produced for export totaled 2,249,000 pounds in 1658. Of this 780,000 pounds was sold by the Dutch to Japan, and the rest to Persia.[133] This trade between East Asia and West Asia elaborated on patterns of trade set up by the Portuguese galleons or "great ships" that connected the colonial possessions of Goa and Macao. The Dutch developed it further with their trade between Bengal and Nagasaki.

As early as 1614, Jan Pieterszoon Coen (later the governor-general of the Dutch East India Company in Batavia) had argued that the company must develop a policy for trade within Asia distinct from its original business of carrying goods to Europe.[134] Coen's recommendation reflected a shrewd assessment of contemporary intra-Asian trade, noted the possibilities of its expansion and profitability when crucial points of transshipment were controlled, and proposed that the Company's entire Euro-Asian trade could be financed through the profits of the intra-Asian trade.[135] As a policy, it was not easy to implement. Competition in East Asian and Southeast Asian waters was keen in the 1620s because of the large numbers of Chinese and Japanese ships already involved in the expanding trade. Unless the Dutch had silk to sell, they were in effect cut out of the most profitable nexus in the trade circuit, the silk-for-silver trade at Nagasaki. Plaintive reports dispatched to Amsterdam from Taiwan illustrate their dilemma:

> 13 Dec., 1626: Our people in Taiwan are complaining over the manner of silk trading . . . because we are not masters of her trade. The Chinese merchant Simsou [Xu Xinsu] (with whom we got in touch for the matter of trade as a middleman) is the only one who carries out the negotiations with China, and it seems no one else has the license [to trade]. He conveniently owns the merchandise in the form of leases, [which is a problem because] he is very slow in ordering the stuff. Sometimes instead of a month or six weeks as agreed upon, he is three months behind.
>
> Our people cannot meet the bills because our money is outstanding and this has already caused so many arrears that fewer than 200–300 piculs of silk have been sent to Japan. It seems that Simsou plays around with the money in China and uses it in other quarters before it is finally used for the Company. . . . [The Dutch then tried raising the price of silk in Taiwan hoping to get independent traders to come without going through Simsou, but only got 150 piculs which was not enough]. . . .
>
> So for the time being we have to bow our heads and put up with this monopoly. That is more important than the standstill of this trade with China. We also wanted to buy green ginger and sugar which you recommended we buy in Taiwan but up to now we have not made any progress. . . .[136]

Dutch access to Chinese goods became ever more problematical in the 1660s when the Dutch were expelled from Taiwan by the Zheng forces, a Fujian-based mercantile family of maritime adventurers. These problems multiplied when the Manchu Qing government evacuated China's coastal regions in an effort to starve out the Zhengs. Consequently, the Dutch turned their attentions more closely to Southeast Asian and Indian sources.

Silk from other sources seemed to be the answer; and in cargoes bound for Japan, Bengali silk and sugar were soon substituted for Chinese commodities. Whereas Bengal had been previously seen as a source of staples such as sugar, rice, cotton textiles, and saltpeter, in 1631, the Dutch governor-general and his council at Batavia pointed out to the directors back in Amsterdam that a considerable amount of raw silk could also be obtained in the province.[137] It became possible to take full advantage of this potential when regular Dutch East India Company trade was resumed after Mughal forces drove the Portuguese out of Bengal in 1632. The blueprint of trade as envisioned by Governor-General Coen became a reality with some modifications. Silver and copper from Japan and gold from Taiwan were sold in Bengal, Surat, and the Coromandal coast around Madras. Silk from Bengal was taken back to Japan. This became a well-defined and profitable circuit of trade.[138] Goods from Bengal enabled the Dutch East India Company to turn a gross profit of around 100 percent from Bengal silk in its trade with Japan during 1656–1672.[139]

Ultimately, however, the Dutch were not able to supplant the Chinese traders as the primary suppliers for either sugar or silk to Japan. This was particularly the case when Chinese trade began its recovery from the coastal evacuation in the 1680s.[140] Since Batavia still had plenty of sugar to sell, Dutch East India Company interests turned to competing with Bengali sugar on the Indian and Persian Gulf markets.

The markets for sugar in western India and the Persian Gulf were linked to the role of ports such as Surat and Bandar Abbas, which were entrepôts for spices from Southeast Asia. After the defeat of Banten in 1682 by the Dutch, the much sought-after cloves, pepper, mace, and nutmeg were all from areas now under Dutch control.[141] The Dutch began bringing Batavian sugar, Japanese copper, Malayan tin, Indonesian spices, and Chinese silks and porcelains to Surat in exchange for textiles and indigo. They then took the Mughal silver rupees from Gujarat and used them in Bengal for making the Dutch East India Company purchases to Europe.[142] To the east, they started exporting larger quantities of opium from Bengal to Batavia where Chinese, Indonesian, and Malayan traders bought opium in exchange for Chinese raw silks and porcelains.[143] We cannot enter into the various factors specific to Indian history that made the Dutch impact on South Asia more profound than their impact on China and Chinese trading networks;[144] but since the decline of Bengal trade in sugar was to provide the rationale for the later Indian imports of Chinese sugar, the background can be sketched out here briefly.

Initially, Bengali sugar was cheaper than Javanese sugar when the Dutch began this trade. By the last decade of the seventeenth century, the pricing policies of the Batavian government on the one hand and the increase in agricultural prices in India on the other[145] gave Javanese sugar a price advantage.[146] Consequently, the Surat market grew to be the largest purchaser of Batavian sugar. This Dutch control of the South Asian sugar trade is directly attributable to the rapid development of the Javanese sugar industry under the Dutch East India Company. In 1652, only 1.65 million pounds had been produced in Dutch-controlled Java, but by 1710–1711 there were 131 mills already producing over 8.8 million pounds with a production capability of over 14 million pounds. These 131 mills belonged to 84 entrepreneurs, 79 of whom were Chinese, 4 Dutch, and 1 Javanese. All the employees, including those of the Chinese-owned mills, were under the direct supervision of the Dutch sheriff and his men. The Dutch East India Company controlled the prices and the quantities to be purchased, thus forcing reductions in the purchase price to suit the Dutch East India Company's interests.[147] Though these policies were to lead to bankruptcies among the Chinese and contribute to the social unrest which erupted in the massacre of the Chinese in 1740, these mechanisms enabled Batavia to become a major producer of sugar in the seventeenth century.

By linking the trade with Japan at one end with Persia at the other, the Dutch had established an international trade which, in terms of distances covered, was "of almost the same magnitude as the sea route from the North Sea to Ceylon and Batavia."[148] Trade exchanges in Japan became joined to a chain of trading links, the other end of which lay in the markets in Persia. The older, centuries-long pattern of intra-Asian trade, when traders from India, the Persian Gulf, China, the Indonesian Archipelago, Philippines, and Siam all congregated in one location, first at Malacca and then at the other Southeast Asian ports, was transformed in the process. Yet even as Dutch control of segments of the intra-Asian trade reached new levels in South and West Asia, maritime trading circuits in East Asia were shifting and regrouping, not least due to the activities of Zheng Chenggong (1624–1662), the scion of the family of maritime adventurers and a Ming loyalist.

The Zheng Challenge to Dutch Expansion in East Asian Trade

Chinese trade in the decades following the collapse of the Ming had expanded primarily under the aegis of Zheng Chenggong (or Koxinga as the Dutch called him) and his affiliates. In direct competition with the Dutch, the Zheng, too, had developed a vast trading network that linked suppliers from Southeast Asia and China to the market in Japan. As Batavia reported to Amsterdam regarding the status of trade at Nagasaki in 1658:

> Last year 47 Chinese junks reached Nagasaki, 28 from Anhay [Anhai, Fujian, a Zheng family stronghold] 11 from Cambodia, 3 from Siam, 2 from Quinam (Quangnam or Cachan in Vietnam), 2 from Patany (Patani) and 1 from Toncquin (Tonkin). As far as we were told, they all belonged to the great trading merchant Cocksinja and his adherents. Not a junk came from the maritime regions near Nanjing, where the Manchus have a good hold. The main cargo of these junks was 112,000 catties [*jin*] of assorted raw silks, 636,000 catties of white and brown sugar, various silk manufactures, skin merchandise, medicaments, fancy goods, etc.[149]

Because the Dutch kept records at Nagasaki based on the Gregorian calendar, they did not note the three ships from Nanjing which had come in earlier that year according to the lunar calendar which the Japanese used for their records.[150] However, the assessment that these ships belonged to the Zheng family was accurate. The sugar on these ships had been loaded at various ports; most of it came from Anhai and Quangnam.

It is difficult to arrive at a quantitative assessment of the Zheng maritime fleet. Though the "over one thousand vessels" that the fleet supposedly contained cannot be taken literally, the Zheng represented the largest commercial network of Chinese merchants involved in overseas trade.[151] There were at least ten mercantile groups, or *hang*, under the control of the Zheng, five of whom were located in Hangzhou. These *hang* had the responsibility of collecting silk fabrics and cotton textiles from Hangzhou and Suzhou and getting them down to Xiamen (Amoy). The other five *hang* were located in Xiamen and controlled the export of these goods and other products from Fujian to Taiwan and overseas including Japan. The Zheng-controlled *hang* were at the fulcrum of a three-way trade linking Southeast Asia, China, and Japan. Ships from Siam, Ligor (Nakhon Sithammarat), and Patani brought tin, sappanwood, ivory, bird's nest, pepper, and so forth to Xiamen or Tainan for the Chinese market. They were exchanged for Chinese silks, teas, and sugar to be carried on to Japan. Sailing back from Japan, the ships brought Japanese silver and copper to China, where they were exchanged for Chinese goods bound for Southeast Asia.[152] Others, including members of the Siamese royal family and rich Chinese immigrant merchants, participated in this trade with their own ships; but considerable evidence suggests that the Zheng trade network was tightly controlled by members of the Zheng family. The trade at Nagasaki was headed by an uncle, Zheng Tai, and extortions from merchants within the ambit of the Zheng empire were common.[153]

There was also some attempt by the Zheng to establish monopolies in the more profitable commodities. Captain Limbrey of the English East India Company ship, the *Return*, which was sent to Taiwan in 1671 to set up a factory there before proceeding to Japan, found,

> [t]he Company had rec[ieve]d: strange information of this place, as if all the Sugar and Skinns which the Island affords considerable quantities of, would bee at their devotion, but wee found otherwise of it, and doe admire with what reason any man could dreame of such a thing, for the King of Tywan ingrose all those commodities to his pticular use, with which he drives an advantagious trade to Japan, sending yearly 14 or 15 juncks; whereas wee could not procure soe much Sugar as for the necessary provision of the ship. . . .[154]

The "King of Tywan" was Zheng Jing (d. 1681), the son of Zheng Chenggong, who ruled Taiwan after his father's death in 1662. Zheng Jing had apparently declared the trade in sugar and deer skins for Japan as his official monopoly and sold 5,000,000 *jin* (6,650,000 pounds) of sugar and 200,000 deer skins annually. The sugar, which cost 2 rials per *jin*, was sold in Nagasaki at four times the original price, while the deer skins fetched three-and-a-half times the original price.[155]

Overall, the period 1644–1684 saw temporarily reduced Chinese trade owing to the oft-cited Qing edict of 1656 "forbidding even a plank to drift to sea,"[156] which was one of the measures taken by the government in its war against the Zheng forces. As the coastal evacuation ordered by the Qing government took effect during heightened efforts to subjugate Zheng Chenggong, mainland Chinese trade to Japan was probably affected the most. A few ships, primarily from Guangdong and Fujian, still made it to Japan; but, until the ban was lifted in 1684, the bulk of the shipping designated "Chinese ships" (*Tōsen*) by the Japanese actually originated in Southeast Asia.[157] As Table 3 indicates, the disruption of sugar and silk supplies led to fluctuations in the level of imports into Japan.[158] The volume of the sugar trade, compensated no doubt with supplies from Taiwan and Siam, did not decline as much as the silk trade, which depended on mainland suppliers.

But it would be inaccurate to assume that all Chinese trade came to a standstill because of the Qing edict. Chinese trade with Batavia, Nagasaki, and Manila had continued even during the 1660s and 1670s when the coastal regions of Guangdong and Fujian had been evacuated. As Table 4 shows, trade with Batavia, resumed tentatively in the 1660s, had picked up quite rapidly in the 1670s. Given Zheng's hostile relationship with the Dutch, these Chinese ships were clearly not part of his entourage but were part of other trading networks. The number of Chinese ships calling at Batavia numbered twenty-eight, compared to the fifteen "Macao Junks" as the Portuguese ships were called. Chinese ships from Southeast Asia calling at Nagasaki, as indicated in Table 5, numbered 300 compared to the fifty-one Dutch ships at Nagasaki during the 1670s. When we look at the trade at Manila

TABLE 3

Sugar and Silk Yarn Imported into Japan on Chinese Ships during the Period of Coastal Evacuation, 1663–1683
(weights in *jin*)

Year	Sugar	Silk yarn
1663	1,946,942	47,614
1664	2,391,514	119,208
1665	2,577,121	163,042
1666	43,250	–
1671	–	50,000
1674	–	220,000
1676	–	133,282
1680	2,418,134	190,853
1682	2,600,165	73,323
1683	2,130,644	11,291

SOURCES: Iwao, "Kindia Nisshi bōeki ni kansuru sūryōteki kōsatsu," pp. 28, 31; Iwao, "Edo jidai no satō bōeki ni tsuite," pp. 4–5; Nagazumi, *Tōsen yushutsu.*

TABLE 4

Chinese and Portuguese Ships at Batavia during the Qing Ban on Trading, 1665–1683

Year	Macao junks	Chinese junks
1665–1669	1	0
1670–1674	13	5
1675–1679	15	28
1680–1683	6	10

SOURCES: Blussé, p. 120; Chaunu, pp. 164–169; Innes, pp. 636–640; Iwao, "Kindai Nisshi bōeki," p. 12–13.

TABLE 5

Chinese and Dutch Ships at Nagasaki during the Qing Ban on Trading, 1665–1684

Year	Dutch ships	Chinese junks
1665–1669	41	185
1670–1674	32	159
1675–1679	19	141
1680–1684	20	115

SOURCES: Blussé, p. 120; Chaunu, pp. 164–169; Innes, pp. 636–640; Iwao, "Kindai Nisshi bōeki," pp. 12–13.

TABLE 6

Chinese and Portuguese Ships at Manila during the Qing Ban on Trading, 1665–1684

Year	Macao junks	Mainland Chinese junks	Taiwan junks
1665–1669	0	12	15
1670–1674	1	2	16
1675–1679	0	27	5
1680–1684	5	6	6

SOURCES: Blussé, p. 120; Chaunu, pp. 164–169; Innes, pp. 636–640; Iwao, "Kindai Nisshi bōeki," pp. 12–13.

during this decade, as in Table 6, a similar picture emerges. Between 1675 and 1679, not one Portuguese ship made it to Manila, while there were twenty-seven Chinese ships from the mainland and five from Taiwan. So, even when compared to that of the Portuguese and the Dutch trade during the years when overseas contact was the most restricted, Chinese trade in the Pacific was not insignificant. The data on the tonnage of ships also supports the conclusion that Chinese trade in the Pacific was far more substantial than either that of the Dutch or the Portuguese. The ships from Guangdong and Fujian going to Batavia and adjacent areas during this period later ranged from 400 to 1,000 tons while those going to Manila and Taiwan were smaller vessels of 40 to 100 tons.[159] Collating various sources of information on the tonnage of vessels used, Ts'ao Yung-ho has suggested that the total tonnage of Chinese junks in Asian seas in the 1630s may have been around 40,000 tons compared to only 12,000–14,000 tons in total for the Dutch.[160]

The Pax Manchurica and Chinese Trade

After the conquest of Taiwan in 1683 and the rescission of the ban on overseas trading in 1685, there was an unprecedented increase in overseas trade from China.[161] Elimination of the Zheng family monopolies may have permitted a number of newcomers to enter the overseas trade networks. In Xiamen the rush to enter this trade brought so many small shipowners to the fore that Shi Lang (1621–1696), the Ming-Qing admiral credited with the Manchu conquest of Taiwan, recommended that overseas trading permits only be granted to larger ships.[162] Since seagoing junks cost around 4,000–5,000 taels to build, according to contemporary Lan Dingyuan's calculation, the availability of capital among Chinese traders is obvious.[163] Cities like Xiamen were visibly so prosperous by the beginning of the eighteenth century that local officials approvingly noted the beneficial aspects of overseas trade.[164]

Trade could also expand because none of the first three Qing emperors was fundamentally opposed to overseas trade per se.[165] Given the financial interests of the Imperial Household in the ginseng and copper trade and its close alliance with favored mercantile families such as the Fan lineage, this was not surprising.[166] Consequently, unlike those of the Ming, the Qing policies were designed to permit a degree of private trade—as long as the imperial treasury and its favored officials could benefit from it. Accordingly, the Kangxi emperor removed all restrictions in 1685 with the edict, "opening the seas to trade, we want to allow the people to earn their living."[167] This benevolence regarding the common people and their participation in overseas trade may also have been furthered by the reluctance of the

Tokugawa at this time to have anything to do with the Manchu government,[168] and Japan was a necessary source of the copper used for Chinese coins.

The Kangxi emperor was quite explicit in his support of private traders. In 1686, officials from Fujian attempted to monopolize the Taiwanese sugar and deer-skin trade to Japan as a means of raising revenues. The Kangxi emperor agreed with the recommendation of some officials who criticized this. Shi Lang and other bureaucrats in Fujian were ordered not to send official trading missions to Japan: "The government should not send trading ships with Taiwanese sugar and deerskins; this should be left to merchants from among the people."[169] In order to encourage trade, tariffs on foreign ships coming into Guangdong, Fujian, Zhejiang, and Jiangsu were lowered to 20 percent of the total amount in 1686.[170] Later, in 1698 another edict expressed concern that local officials (such as those in Guangdong) were imposing duties on "insignificant articles," which was "unbecoming to our dignity." It was ordered that the duties be reduced.[171] There was a remarkable increase in the number of Chinese ships trading with both Japan and Southeast Asia during those years of the Kangxi reign when there were no restrictions on overseas trade. As Table 7 indicates, the total number of Chinese ships going to Batavia were two to three times the number of Portuguese ships. The disparity between the volume of trade conducted by European traders and the Chinese is most evident from the data at Nagasaki. As Table 8 shows, as many as 540 ships from China rushed to Nagasaki as soon as the Qing government restrictions were lifted in 1684. Only 128 of these ships, however, were given permission to land by the Japanese authorities. For the next twenty years, every year well over 100 ships came to Nagasaki from China while the Japanese government, seeking to control this trade, routinely turned away dozens of them. The number of Dutch ships at the port of Nagasaki during 1688–1708, on the other hand, never exceeded a total of 26 ships for any given five-year period and typically numbered only four to five ships per year. The contrast between European trade and Chinese trade was just as striking at the port of Manila. As indicated in Table 9, while the Chinese traders

TABLE 7

Chinese and Portuguese Ships at Batavia, 1684–1718

Year	Chinese junks	Macao junks
1684–1688	51	17
1689–1693	38	8
1694–1698	45	5
1699–1703	82	17
1704–1708	59	28
1709–1713	63	36
1714–1718	65	33

SOURCES: Chaunu, pp. 168–180; Innes, pp. 636–640; Nagazumi, *Tōsen yushutsu*; Souza, pp. 134–137.

TABLE 8

Chinese and Dutch Ships at Nagasaki, 1684–1718, prior to Japanese Restrictions

Year	Chinese junks[a]	Dutch ships
1684–1688	128 (412)	19
1689–1693	350 (63)	18
1694–1698	338 (51)	26
1699–1703	338 (24)	22
1704–1708	379 (73)	20
1709–1713	261 (18)	19
1714–1718	150 (13)	6[b]

[a]The figures in parentheses indicate the number of ships denied permission to land.
[b] Includes only the years 1714 and 1715.
SOURCES: Chaunu, pp. 168–180; Innes, pp. 636–640; Nagazumi, *Tōsen yushutsu*; Souza, pp. 134–137.

TABLE 9
Chinese and Portuguese Macao Ships at Manila, 1684–1718

Year	Chinese junks	Macao junks
1684–1688	63	3
1689–1693	59	0
1694–1698	85	4
1699–1703	76	7
1704–1708	89	2
1709–1713	94	1
1714–1718	51	0

NOTE: In each of the years 1684, 1711, 1713, and 1716, there was also one ship from Taiwan.
SOURCES: Chaunu, pp. 168–180; Innes, pp. 636–640; Nagazumi, *Tōsen yushutsu*; Souza, pp. 134–137.

annually sent anywhere from eleven to eighteen ships per year, often not a single Portuguese ship called at Manila.

The boom years of the trade to Japan, however, could last only a few decades. Even before the Chinese liberalization of trade restrictions, Edo had reissued an edict in 1685 proscribing the export of monetizable metals, silver and copper, which were needed in the expanding commercial economy of Japan. These two metals were the main Chinese imports from Japan. Japanese copper coins were also in demand throughout Southeast Asia. Consequently, when the Kangxi edict permitting trade was issued and there was a rush of 102 Chinese ships to Nagasaki followed by 194 ships in 1688, Edo authorities decided to limit the number of Chinese ships permitted entry at Nagasaki to 70 per year; and the value of the trade was limited to 6,000 *kan* (approx. 600,000 taels).[172] As seen above, ships in excess of the permitted quota were refused entry at Nagasaki. For a time, these trade restrictions were circumvented by an increase in the Chinese trade carried out indirectly via Korea with the far western Japanese fiefdom of Tsushima-han; but this, too, came to an end in the early eighteenth century.[173]

The debates on permitting export of monetizable metals gained a new momentum with Arai Hakuseki (1657–1725), the principal advisor to the sixth and seventh shoguns. Proponent of a philosophy somewhat akin to European bullionists seeking to curtail the export of precious metals, Arai implemented a policy designed to reduce foreign trade in 1715.[174] The number of Chinese ships permitted entry was reduced to thirty. Known as the *Shōtoku shinrei* (The New Shōtoku Act), these Japanese regulations "signalled the transition to an era of reduced foreign trade and import substitution."[175]

But the Chinese government continued to sponsor private trade to Japan to meet the demands of the Board of Revenue for copper. Japanese copper had been a major import into China since the seventeenth century and starting in the 1740s, private traders in copper acquired the status of "state merchants" and began to receive large loans from the Qing government for the Nagasaki copper trade. "State" merchants (*guan shang*) received loans of up to 650,000 taels a year from the Imperial Household Department and then pooled their capital with twelve "quota" merchants (*ou shang*) from the Yangtze basin who used their own private capital to buy the 1 million to 2 million *jin* of copper imported every year from Japan.[176] This was a trade which continued throughout the eighteenth century and well into the nineteenth.

In terms of imports into Japan, though the Shōtoku Regulations curtailed trade, the initial impact on sugar imports was not quite as dramatic. The regulations set a total import quota of 4,500,000 *jin* (approx. 6,000,000 pounds) for sugar of which approximately 3,500,000 *jin* (approx. 4,665,500 pounds) were imported by the Chinese and the Dutch.[177] This was fairly close to the general volume of sugar imports prior to the regulations. The actual reduction in imports came in the latter part of the eighteenth century as the efforts to produce sugar domestically began to yield results. As a result, the quantities of sugar imported on Chinese ships show a steady decline up to the beginning of the nineteenth century. As far as the market for Chinese sugar was concerned, however, reductions in the size of the Japanese market for Chinese sugar were more than compensated for by the development of the export trade to India through the British.

Canton Sugar for Bombay Cotton: The Expansion of British Trade with China

The English East India Company received its first charter granting permission to trade on 31 December 1600. Although by 1615 the Company had seven factories in India, eleven in Southeast Asia, and one in Japan, as yet there was only indirect trade with China through Chinese merchants at Hirado.[178] The English were frustrated in their attempts to establish direct trade with China by their Portuguese and Dutch rivals until 1637. A well-equipped squadron of four ships from Courteen's Association, carrying Peter Mundy among others, strong-armed its way into Guangzhou that year. One of the four ships, the *Catherine*, carried 1,208,600 *jin* (1,607,438 pounds) of sugar and 50,000 *jin* (66,500 pounds) of sugar rock-candy back to England in this first cargo.[179] Six English ships carried back a total of 750 tons of Chinese sugar in 1637.[180]

Company trade with Guangzhou remained sporadic for the next few decades. Civil war in England (1642–1648) and wars with Holland (1652–1654 and 1665–1667) retarded the growth of the Company at home while private traders and Company ships attempted unsuccessfully to trade at Macao during the years of the Qing evacuation of the coastal regions. By the beginning of the eighteenth century, "the English had thrust their feet over the threshold of the China trade but had not yet obtained a seat at the table."[181]

The "table" was richly laden by all accounts. Jacques Savary des Bruslon, appointed to the position of inspector-general of the customs house in Paris in 1686, dedicated the next thirty years of his life to collecting all available information on trade, and particularly what was known about Asian trade. Published as an encyclopedia, the entry under China reported,

> They [the Chinese monarchy] now not only suffer, but encourage, both near and distant nations, particularly Europeans, to come and trade with them, and bring them their most valuable commodities; and at the same time, allow their own people to disperse themselves into a great number of foreign parts, wither they carry their silks, porcela[i]n, japan, and other curious

manufactures and knicknacks, as well as their tea, medicinal roots, drugs, sugar, and other produce. They trade into most parts of India; they go to Batavia, Malacca, Achem, Siam, &c. especially to the islands of Japan and Manillas, which are but a small distance from them, and from which they bring, among other things, great quantities of silver and gold; and that which comes from Mexico to the Philippine Islands, is carried to Canton, and then dispersed through the whole empire.[182]

Ultimately, it was British success in this intra-Asian trade[183] that determined the long-term outcome for the trading-world of China. "Country trade," as the South Asian intra-Asian trade was called, expanded with British involvement and was conducted by individual traders and by trading firms who operated under license from the East India Company. Country trade became the mainstay of private business—the realm where "East India fortunes" were to be made. After 1700, the stronger political position of the English in South and Southeast Asia aided the expansion of this private trade.[184] By the early decades of the eighteenth century several ports in India regularly imported Chinese goods via Portuguese and British companies as well as via private traders of European, South Asian, and Armenian origin. One of the most lucrative connections was the trade between Madras, Manila, and Canton in silver and gold bullion.[185] Silver from India, along with iron goods and textiles, was taken to Manila. There additional silver was picked up and traded to China. Chinese gold was imported back into India, for the price of gold in China was considerably lower than in India and demand was high; as a letter dated 1702 to Thomas Pitt, governor of Madras, noted, "Our silver is generally carry'd for China, and a great deale of that gold which returns is Carry'd up into the Countrey for the making of Jewells and coining it in their own Mints. . . ."[186] But because the precious metals provided little ballast, other goods were carried, sugar being one of the "China goods" brought back to India. Sugar was, for instance, listed on the 1716 manifest of the *Marlborough* along with copper, tutenag (an alloy of copper, zinc, and nickel used for casting vessels in India), quicksilver, and alum.[187]

Both Madras and Bombay became regular importers of Chinese sugar through the 1720s. The trend increased in the following decades with anywhere from 3,000 to 6,000 piculs (400,000–800,000 pounds) of sugar candy exported on each ship carrying cargo to India.[188] The English were not the only group interested in importing Chinese sugar to western and southern India. The Dutch, who had been selling Javanese sugar on the West Coast and had successfully displaced Bengali sugar, faced a crisis in supplies with the revolt and massacre of the Chinese in Java in 1740. This undermined their ability to provide sugar at cheap prices, and they had to turn to Chinese sources. Already struggling to keep their markets in Japanese copper, spices, and sugar in western India, the Dutch found their old nemesis, the Portuguese, also bringing Chinese sugar from Macao and Guangzhou to sell and undercutting them.[189] These problems of the Batavian Dutch in securing supplies in the mid-eighteenth century reflected not only the decline of their dominance in intra-Asian trade but also the many ways in which the trading and political world of Asia had been changing with increased momentum since the 1740s.[190] These changes came together in one crucial decade of 1756–1766.

During the first half of the eighteenth century, the decay of the dominant political formations of the Mughals in India and the Safavids in Persia, combined with the civil wars in the Persian Gulf such as Ottoman-controlled Basra, had eroded the West Asian markets and weakened traders who relied on these markets, including the Batavian Dutch, the Indian Gujarati, and the English country traders. The English, however, were able to recoup very rapidly. The victory of the British in 1757 at the Battle of Plassey against the nawab of Bengal gave them control of a major Indian region, where, by initiating direct colonial rule, they began to change the equation of power that had existed up to that point in South Asia. Simultaneously, the British gained considerable economic clout on the west coast. In 1759, Surat Castle was captured by English forces; Bombay had already been acquired in 1662 as part of the dowry of Charles II's Portuguese queen. The political and economic power gained by the control of these two major ports on the west coast of India was further consolidated when the Marathas, the major challengers to British hegemony in western and northern India, were severely defeated by an Afghani expedition in 1761.

With increased power in India and a major economic base, the British were also successful in challenging Batavian Dutch hegemony in Southeast Asia. The position of the Batavian government was undermined by a combination of disaffection in their own ranks and policy differences between Amsterdam and Batavia. The insistence of the Batavian government and the Dutch East India Company on preserving trade monopolies alienated many of its officials, who started linking up with the British and Armenian traders to further their own private interests at the expense of the Dutch East India Company.[191] At the same time, there had been growing disagreements between the Batavian government and the Dutch East India Company's directors about whether the dispatch of Dutch ships directly from Amsterdam to China was more profitable than having the Chinese junks come to Batavia. The former enriched the Dutch East India Company; the latter added to coffers of the Batavian government since they collected fees from the Chinese traders.[192] The Dutch East India Company directors had started sending ships directly from Amsterdam to Guangzhou in the late 1720s. Finally, there was an open break in 1756 when the directors decided to deal with the China trade directly and leave Batavia entirely out of the picture.[193]

The Batavian Dutch were further distracted by the Bugis, traders and maritime adventurers from Macassar. After the destruction of the Macassar spice trade through Dutch monopolies, starting in the 1720s the Bugis had moved to control ports on the Malayan peninsula. Open confrontation reemerged with the Bugi attack on Dutch-controlled Malacca in 1756. Although the Bugis were subdued by 1758 and the Dutch gained some concessions, the fluidity of political alliances on the Malayan peninsula and northern Sumatra enabled the British to establish trading bases in short order at Aceh, Kedah, Kuala Selangor, and Riau.[194] These connections in Malaya and Sumatra were necessary to the growth of the British India-China trade, for both tin and pepper were important commodities in the trade at Guangzhou. By 1757, the volume of foreign trade was five times greater at Guangzhou than it had been at the beginning of the century.[195] The British had emerged as the dominant trading partner of the Chinese. The same year, the Qing government moved to keep a tighter rein on the western trade by confining most European traders, with the exception of the Spanish, Portuguese, and Russians, to Guangzhou.[196]

As the English East India Company and private British-Indian trade with China increased after the 1760s, the demand for goods that provided ballast became important. A trade in Bombay cotton for Canton sugar had already developed in the early eighteenth century, both ideal commodities for use as ballast. For example, in 1704, the *Catherine* carried 1,116 piculs (148,428 pounds) of raw cotton, which had been picked up on a "trial basis" in Surat, apparently the first shipment of western Indian cotton sold by the British in China. It was taken to Xiamen, where it bought 5.50 taels per picul. Sugar in Xiamen, however, could be purchased for 2.50 taels per picul, almost paying for a return cargo close to twice the weight of the cotton shipment. The *Catherine* carried back 2,500 piculs (332,500 pounds) of granulated white sugar and another 800 piculs (106,664 pounds) of sugar candy at 4.00 taels per picul.[197] Then, as changes in the domestic trade networks of both India and China created additional demands, trade in both these commodities increased significantly by the end of the eighteenth century.

In the early eighteenth century, we have seen, cheaper Batavian sugar started gaining ground on the west coast of India in competition with Bengali sugar. These trends increased in the second half of the eighteenth century. Output of Bengali sugar had also declined. Cane lands in Bengal were turned into indigo fields, and sericulture expanded as the export of raw silk increased.[198] With reduced availability and local wars, the price of Bengali sugar went up further; by the 1770s the price of Bengal sugar had increased 50 percent over pre-1756 prices. By the early nineteenth century even the limited production was further reduced when jute replaced sugar-cane fields.[199] Bengal ceased to export sugar altogether.

There had been a simultaneous shift in the trade circuits of western India. In earlier centuries, when Surat imported large quantities of Bengali sugar, it exported cotton to Bengal, which had extensive textile manufacturing but inadequate supplies of cotton. By the end of the eighteenth and early nineteenth centuries, however, cheaper cotton became available in Bengal as cotton cultivation expanded in western Bengal and in the United Provinces. The consequent dislocation of the sugar-cotton nexus between eastern and western India left west coast cotton available for export.

In China, by contrast, increased textile exports had left a shortage of cotton in the south at about the same time. Earlier, during the seventeenth and early eighteenth centuries, sugar from Guangdong and Fujian was sold up north in Zhejiang, Hubei, and Jiangsu for ginned cotton.[200] Chu Hua, author of the late eighteenth century *Mu mian pu* (A Treatise on Cotton) was one of several observers who commented: "In the Second and the Third Month people from Min (Fujian) and Yue (Guangdong) come carrying crystallized sugar for sale. In the autumn they don't buy cloth, but only ginned cotton and return to the south. Hundreds and thousands of ships all load up, pile upon pile of bags, because there [in Min and Yue], among themselves they can spin and weave it."[201]

Beginning with the increased European trade in Chinese textiles, the Jiangsu-Zhejiang export trade in cotton to Guangdong began to change in the 1780s. A rapid increase in the export of "nankeens" (a type of cotton cloth from the Songjiang area of Jiangsu) used up a far greater proportion of the Jiangnan raw cotton surplus, thus creating a shortage of cotton for sale to Guangdong. While it seems that some cotton continued to be exported to Guangdong, the volume was no longer adequate to the demand. Indian raw cotton, exported through Bombay and Surat, was at this point slightly inferior to that of the Jiangnan region, but adequate for hand spinning and for producing the low count yarn manufactured in Guangdong.[202] As the demand for Bombay cotton in Bengal declined, Bombay was in a position to benefit from the rising cotton prices in China by exporting cotton.[203] Figures from a slightly later period show that the price differential may have favored Indian cotton over Jiangnan cotton by as much as 1 tael per picul.[204]

Until 1823, raw cotton was the most important Indian export to China—more valuable than opium.[205] Between 1785 and 1833 approximately 27 million *jin* (almost 36 million pounds) of cotton were imported annually, on average, from India to Guangdong. The volume of the cotton trade rose to 43,800,000 *jin* (58,254,000 pounds) by 1831–1833.[206] Most of this cotton came from western India. After 1800, when the Gangetic Doab was brought under cotton cultivation, some cotton to China was also exported through Calcutta.[207] On the return voyages the ships carried Chinese sugar.

Sugar and sugar candy became the chief commodities of the China trade for the Indian market, constituting approximately one-quarter of the total volume of the trade till 1833.[208] As one of the "bulk" items in the country trade, annual export figures for sugar are difficult to locate in a series, but the contours of this trade can be readily gauged by comparing figures for 1792 and 1820–1833. In 1792, for example, as Table 10 indicates, twenty "country ships" carried out a total of 2,609,800 *jin* (3,471,034 pounds) of white sugar and 1,074,900 *jin* (1,429,617 pounds) of sugar candy. Since Dutch, American, and other traders also purchased sugar and since it was also exported to Japan, the Indian market did not account for the entire volume of the Chinese sugar trade in 1792. Nevertheless, it was by far the largest segment. Sugar carried by the country ships alone was valued at 237,980 taels out of total exports valued at 394,645 taels.

As Table 11 indicates, the export-volume of sugar fluctuated abruptly in certain years. The contrast, however, appears greater than it probably was; for the only data available for some years are for sugar exports on private account and do not show Company account. The overall increase in the volume of sugar exports since the 1790s is clearly indicated. The linking of the Indian cotton trade to China with the export of sugar was the logical extension of the pre-colonial sugar-cotton trade circuits that had existed both in India and China.

Other buyers of Chinese sugar also emerged during this period as China's direct trade to America increased. While silk and tea formed the primary items of export, sugar was commonly exported by American ships for Europe, South America, and the United States.[209] American trade in the first two decades of the nineteenth century was based on collecting products from India, China, the Pacific Ocean, and South America, and exporting to Europe via transshipment at the United States' Atlantic ports.[210] There was considerable interest among the Americans in exporting sugar. The instructions given by

TABLE 10
Amount and Value of Sugar Exported from Canton in Foreign Ships in 1792
(weight in piculs; value in taels)

Type	Number of ships	Sugar	Sugar candy	Value
British East India Company	20	593	47	3,435
Country	20	26,098	10,749	237,980
French	2	1,969	1,006	19,905
Swedish	1	4	–	20
Danish	1	3,985	598	25,905
Dutch	4	4,814	–	24,070
American	4	4,576	–	22,880
Genoese (English)	1	3,930	115	20,800
Tuscan (English)	1	3,930	2,000	39,650
TOTAL		49,899	14,515	394,645

SOURCE: Morse, *The Chronicles of the East India Company*, vol. 2, pp. 203–204.

Joseph Peabody and William Ropes of Salem to Mr. Benjamin Shreve, supercargo of their ship *Canton*, were not atypical:

8 May, 1816. We think to stow the Brig to advantage, you will be able to fill the lower hold with sugar, in cases or Bags as you shall judge best, and perhaps more, as far up as a foot above the Beams and on top of the sugar stow Nankins and on top of them the Cassia, enough to make her completely full. The few chests Tea, say 50 Hyson, 50 Soucheng and a few Gunpowder to where it will stow to most advantage. You will take as much pulverized candy as you may think best. . . .[211]

A peak in the sugar exports to America was reached in 1819–1820 when almost 5 million *jin* (approx. 6 million pounds) were exported. Exports of around a quarter of a million *jin* continued into the 1830s.[212] Then, as more sugar was produced in the plantations of South Carolina and Louisiana and manufacturing was started up in

TABLE II

Shipments of Chinese Sugar in British Ships, 1820–1833

(weight in piculs; value in taels)

Year	Weight	Value
1820	92,733	515,878
1821	100,259	537,285
1822	–	–
1823	–	–
1824	79,848	569,775
1825	89,000	488,800
1826	153,255	791,608
1827–1828	43,559*	188,700*
1829	4,925*	23,935*
1830	952,520	1,034,802*
1831	560,349	714,358*
1832	221,885	420,261*
1833	264,140	–
1834	28,439*	198,105*

*Data from Phipps. Phipps gives weight, value, or both for private account only. Values given in dollars by Phipps have been converted to taels (see Appendix for weights, measures, and money).

SOURCES: Morse, *The Chronicles of the East India Company*, vols. 3 and 4 (appendixes); Phipps, pp. 175–189.

Hawaii with the help of Chinese artisans, interest in sugar exports from China dwindled.[213]

The market for sugar and cotton in Asia also changed in the 1830s. The China-India country trade in sugar and cotton began to diminish in volume in the 1840s. Increased imports of Manchester-made yarn rendered Indian raw cotton imports obsolete in Guangdong.[214] Demands for Chinese sugar in India declined as a modern Indian sugar industry developed under the impetus of British capitalists relocating to India after the emancipation of slaves in the Caribbean in 1834–1838. Some West Indian planters, unable to survive competition in the Caribbean, decided to begin over again in India.[215] The China-India trade in sugar did, however, leave a linguistic legacy. In most Indian vernacular languages the word *chini* (i.e., Chinese) became the term for granulated white sugar.[216]

The concept of a monopoly organization such as the East India Company itself had become anachronistic in the changed commercial environment of the 1820s and 1830s. Under its regulations, it had been illegal for private British subjects to trade in goods directly from China to England. Prior to the development of Singapore, private traders at Guangzhou could transfer funds to Britain only via the East India Company's bills of exchange on London. The establishment of Singapore as a free port in 1819 deprived the East India Company of the power to control the shipping of Chinese goods to England. As Singapore became available as a base of transshipment, and Chinese traders and others bringing in goods multiplied, private English traders could easily circumvent the Company's monopoly of the Anglo-Chinese trade.[217] The increase in the numbers of American traders at Guangzhou also made it possible for the free traders to use American bills and American drafts on London as an alternative to dependence on the East India Company. The lucrative European tea market was increasingly supplied by American traders bringing Chinese tea directly to Hamburg, Le Havre, and Mediterranean ports; the British Parliament set up dozens of hearings to deal with "American interference."[218] The compromises between the private merchants and free traders on the one hand and the East India Company on the other were no longer adequate; over half the British trade with China was already in the hands of private traders.[219] The campaign against the Company by the free traders began in earnest in 1829, and the abolition of the charter of the English East India Company in April 1834 registered the end of a trading era.

Conclusion: China's Intra-Asian Trade on the Eve of the Opium War

Chinese traders had survived and indeed managed to hold their own on several fronts through all these changes of the eighteenth and early nineteenth century. Chinese intra-Asian maritime trade networks had been restructured during the late eighteenth century. The junk trade in Southeast Asia, previously focused on Batavia, had begun to shift in the 1740s in the aftermath of the Chinese massacre. As the Dutch East India Company started sending ships directly from Holland to Canton, the locus of the profitable tea trade shifted from Batavia to Canton and made Batavia a less relevant port of call for Chinese traders.[220] Chinese traders turned toward the Malayan ports such as Riau where Bugi, and then British private traders, had an increasingly active trade in opium, Spanish dollars, and textiles in exchange for tea, silk, and sugar.[221]

A trade in bulk commodities, particularly rice, also shifted intra-Asian Chinese trade to other ports of Southeast Asia. Tax exemptions had been given to Siamese traders who brought in rice from Southeast Asia by the Chinese government in the early eighteenth century. In the 1720s this privilege was extended to Chinese merchants, who began bringing in rice along with the higher-value goods such as sea cucumbers and swallows nests.[222] Then, in the latter half of the eighteenth century, the Qianlong emperor's interest in promoting specifically a rice trade encouraged an enormous expansion. As early as the 1750s local merchants from Fujian and Guangdong were rewarded with titles and honorary ranks according to the volume of rice imported.[223] Rice imports from the Philippines increased in the late 1780s as Chinese and even English merchants were encouraged by the Qing government to bring in rice.[224] Since many of the Chinese merchants from Fujian involved in the intra-Asian trade were already having their ships built in Siam, where teak was much cheaper than in China, and were using these ships for importing silver from Manila, they readily expanded their trade to Manila and Siam, where rice, too, was cheaper than anywhere else in Southeast Asia.[225] It was this ability of the Chinese trading networks to realign their trade at short notice, and maneuver around vicissitudes such as regional piracy, that accounted for the vitality and continued growth of the junk trade in the eighteenth and nineteenth centuries.[226]

The 1757 decree of the Qianlong emperor confining most European and American traders to Guangzhou, the subject of such comment and criticism by Western traders in the nineteenth century, was not, it would seem, particularly inconvenient for the Chinese traders.[227]

To begin with, the edict did not affect the trade from Southeast Asia. The ports of Xiamen, Zhangzhou, Shanghai, Ningbo, and Zhenhai continued to trade and receive ships from Luzon, Java, Sulu, and Siam. And even some European trade continued at the other ports. The Portuguese could trade at Guangzhou and at Macao; the Spanish had permission to trade at Xiamen. By flying the Portuguese flag, ships could call at ports closed to British European ships.[228] British private traders, with the cooperation of Chinese merchants from Guangzhou, carried out business at Xiamen under Spanish colors. For example, James Matheson, as a junior partner of a Spanish firm, traded between Xiamen and Manila in the early decades of the nineteenth century on a regular basis. So did Beale and Magniac, the forerunners of Jardine Matheson and Company.[229]

During the approximately seventy-year period from the beginning of British control of Bengal in 1757 to the end of the East India Company charter in 1834, intra-Asian trading had coalesced around two primary networks: Pacific and Southeast Asian trade and British trade from India to China via Southeast Asia. Chinese traders still exercised considerable dominance in both the Pacific and in Southeast Asia. As a Captain Oliver, questioned by a committee of the British Parliament about Chinese trade with Southeast Asian islands, noted in 1820, "To an immense extent the junks are passing as freely in the China seas to all those islands as British ships pass across the Atlantic."[230] As Table 12 indicates, some idea of the extent of Chinese shipping can be arrived at by tabulating the reports of John Crawfurd and John Phipps submitted to the British Parliament in 1830. These reports indicate that the number of junks from Guangdong, Fujian, Zhejiang, and Jiangsu trading in Southeast Asia numbered 214.[231] There were also dozens of smaller junks mentioned in these reports that are not tabulated here. Many of the small junks were from Hainan Island (presumably of Cantonese ownership), and we are told that there were as many as 50 of these smaller junks trading with Siam while another 43 traded with Cochin China.

Several of these junks were of considerable size. Crawfurd, the British envoy to the Thai court, noted that among the junks from Zhejiang and Jiangsu coming to Southeast Asia, "the average burden

TABLE 12
Chinese Shipping in Southeast Asia, 1830

Destination	Number of ships
Japan*	20
Philippine islands	13
Sulu islands	4
Celebes	2
Borneo	13
Java	7
Sumatra	10
Riau	1
East coast of Malay Peninsula	6
Siam	89
Cochin China	20
Cambodia	9
Tongking	20

*10 junks, two voyages annually
SOURCES: Crawfurd, pp. 109–110; Phipps, pp. 202–203.

does not fall short of 17,000 tons." He estimated that the total tonnage of the Chinese intra-Asian trade was around 80,000 tons.[232] This was clearly not the total tonnage because there were also Chinese residents in Southeast Asia, including Siam, who owned ships. There, apart from the twenty-odd junks owned by the Siamese king and members of the nobility, resident Chinese (mostly from Chaozhou, Guangdong) owned a fleet of 136 junks. Thirty-two of these junks traded with China, and 54 with other parts of Southeast Asia.[233] It is possible that these traders in Siam were linked with trading networks from China, but they may have also operated as competitors.[234] For example, the Chinese immigrants from Chaozhou developed sugar plantations in Siam and began exporting to Singapore, a market on which Chinese from Guangdong and Fujian were also selling sugar in the 1820s.[235]

Quantitative data indicating the volume of exports unfortunately do not seem to exist for this trade. Tian Rugang, extrapolating from

TABLE 13
Foreign Shipping at Canton, 1833

Origin	Number	Tons
East India Company	25	28,167
Country	82	36,326
American	59	24,000
Dutch	8	3,200
French	7	2,800
Danish	4	1,600
Belgian	1	400
Prussian	1	400
Hamburg	1	400
Mexican	1	400
TOTAL	189	97,693

SOURCE: Morse, *The Chronicles of the East India Company*, vol. 4, p. 343.

the tonnage of shipping, has estimated that Chinese shipping in the Pacific and Indian Ocean was around 85,000 tons annually at this time.[236] The total tonnage of the British East India Company at Canton, on the other hand, never exceeded 30,000 tons annually. This extrapolation is corroborated by data available from H. B. Morse and the East India Company records.[237] The extent of Chinese trade in the Pacific and in Southeast Asia can also be gauged by the evidence that *all foreign shipping* in 1833, including British shipping up through 31 March 1834 and others up to 31 January 1834, at Guangzhou totaled only 97,693 tons (see Table 13).

The importance of Southeast Asia as an integral part of the trade networks of Guangdong and Fujian suggests that the land-based structure of trade used by G. William Skinner in developing the macroregional framework separating the two provinces may need not only a maritime extension but also a reintegration.[238] The coastal regions of Guangdong and Fujian were linked with each other—rather than isolated—in terms of international trade at the beginning of the nineteenth century. And together they represented a more substantial challenge to British and American traders seeking to expand trade in

Southeast Asia and East Asia than is apparent when the focus is only on Guangzhou.

More important, the data show that Chinese merchants involved in private trade with Southeast Asia and Japan were not entering this new era of the nineteenth century entirely without power. An 1833 discussion at the East India House in London noted that while the trade between India and China was worth $32 million, and the trade between China and Britain $11 million per annum, the Chinese junk trade to Southeast Asia and Japan was estimated to be worth an impressive $70–80 million per annum in contemporary values.[239] Phipps, another contemporary, placed the British trade, including Company trade, at $44,450,063 and the India-China trade at $27,439,370 and suggested that the Chinese junk trade was at least the value of the total British trade, a figure that is close to the estimate given in the other report.[240] Besides this advantage in shipping tonnage and value of the trade, cultural and linguistic connections helped the Chinese in Southeast Asia. In some ports, such as those in Siam and at Singapore, the Chinese fared better than English and American traders even when they arrived later than the Westerners, and were often able to dispose of their goods faster and at better prices.[241] As a result, in Singapore in 1833–1834, for example, the value of Chinese trade was greater than that of either England or British India, and the competition provided by the Chinese was keenly felt.[242] Thus, not only were many Chinese merchants vigorously involved in world-market trade for some two-hundred-and-fifty years prior to the Opium War, but the fact that commodities were still carried on Chinese ships in the 1830s suggests the profits from trade accrued to Chinese merchants during later years as well. There was no simple equation between India's being "incorporated" into the world capitalist economy in the period 1750–1850 and China's becoming part of the external arena awaiting incorporation, as has been suggested by Wallerstein.[243] Nor was the triangular India-China-Britain trade in opium, tea, and cotton set up in this period unique.[244] While it is true that the quantities involved in both exports and imports from China increased dramatically as American and British traders arrived in larger numbers in the nineteenth century, Chinese purchase of opium via Dutch and Chinese traders in Southeast Asia and the sale of Chinese silk and tea had long existed in intra-Asian trade. The arrival of the English, American, and other traders in larger numbers in the early nineteenth century also did not precipitate the collapse of Chinese merchants. A few examples suffice to point to the availability of private Chinese capital and increased Chinese mercantile involvement on the world market.

Pan Zhencheng (1714–1798), or Puankequa[245] as the Westerners called him, one of the major officially licensed (*hong*) merchants permitted to trade with Westerners at Guangzhou, traveled to Manila quite a few times and had a working knowledge of both Spanish and English. He also traded with other Southeast Asian ports and had his own ocean-going trading company (*yanghang*) called the Tongwen hang.[246] Already trading with the East India Company as early as 1753, Pan Zhencheng began investing in the Swedish East India Company trade in the 1770s.[247] In this international trade nexus, Swedish copper, iron, and timber products were sold for Spanish silver in Cadiz, which was then imported into Guangzhou. He had a close working arrangement with the Spanish as well. His son inherited a fortune of some 20 million Spanish dollars. The Pan lineage and its numerous branches continued as a major business family well into the 1850s.[248] Another hong merchant, Liang Jingguo (1761–1837), called Kingguan or Kingqua by the Europeans, had accumulated personal assets of 608,865 taels by 1794. He was widely respected for his business acumen.[249] His son, Liang Lunshu (1790–1877), also called Kingqua by the Westerners, contributed 95,000 taels to the government for a public works project in 1828 and another 20,000 taels in 1822 for a coastal defense fund.[250]

Wu Bingjian (1769–1843), called Houqua or Howqua like his father, Wu Guoying (1731–1800), also a hong merchant, started shipping tea to Europe on American ships by 1810. The insurance claim forms for two American ships captured by Danish privateers in 1810 show that one ship destined for Gothenburg carried over $38,000 worth of tea belonging to Chinese merchants at Guangzhou in addition to goods for American merchants. The other ship carried no goods for American merchants but had $58,000 in tea belonging to

Wu Bingjian and $32,000 belonging to a hong merchant called Consequa (Pan Kun, 1759–1823).[251] John P. Cushing, another partner in Russell and Company, worked with Wu Bingjian as an agent in 1833 when Wu Bingjian shipped tea to Hamburg and hired the entire 200-ton Prussian vessel for his merchandise.[252]

The American traders clearly considered Wu Bingjian an important business partner, and so did he. With the start of the Opium War in 1839, Wu Bingjian became one of the few sources of Chinese information to the Western community. As M. S. Hooper, a small-time American businessman in Canton, noted in his journal in April of 1840, "[Howqua] the senior Hong merchant was passing on to the Americans news of government decisions that he had been able to pick up."[253] During the course of the war, when the position of the hong merchants also became rather tenuous, Russell and Company suggested to Wu Bingjian that he might wish to visit the United States or the West Indies until matters settled down.[254] Wu Bingjian did not accept the invitation but decided to invest in the United States with the stipulation that Russell and Company could retain use of the capital as long as they made annual interest payments to his descendants. Wu Bingjian invested in American railroads such as the Michigan Central Railroad, the Burlington, and the Missouri River Railroad through both John Murray Forbes and Robert Forbes, who were partners in Russell and Company. Wu Bingjian's funds were further used by John Murray Forbes in setting up the American Stock Investment Company and included investments such as the Albany and Boston Mining Company.[255]

By the early 1830s Wu Bingjian had also set up independent trade networks in India with Parsee merchants, such as Jamsetjee Jeejeebhoy at Bombay, selling Chinese silk and cassia on commission from him. He had his proceeds from silk sales in London returned in East India Company bills on Calcutta.[256] As his correspondence with John Cushing and John Forbes shows, Wu Bingjian was fully involved in the dynamics of the changing international market, a far cry from the prevalent image of the pidgin-speaking Chinese trader unaware of the world beyond. A letter to Cushing, for example, dated 1 June 1840 reads,

. . . I write now chiefly to say that I have made a shipment of teas on board the "Akbar" to amount of about $50,000, which goes on her to Singapore & thence per British vessel to London to Forbes Forbes &Co in case it cannot be sold at Singapore at 40% profit, and I intend to give all the profit on this adventure to Mr. J. P. Sturgis after charging interest at 8 percent per annum, and in case of loss I shall bear it myself. I am in hope Mr. Sturgis will make some forty or fifty thousand dollars this year, & besides I relinquish to him about thirty thousand dollars which he owes for me interest on old account.[257]

Wu Bingjian notes in a letter to John Forbes on 28 June 1840, "I have a large amount of funds in America and Europe of which you must take the best care you can and place them in safety and where they will be productive of interest; after the English business is settled send all my funds back to China to my friends Russell & Co. in Hard Dollars or Bills on Bengal whichever you think may be best for me."[258] Wu Bingjian's fortune of some 26 million silver dollars (approx. US$56 million) in 1834 was thought to be the largest mercantile fortune in the world.[259]

Wu Bingjian's grandson Wu Chongyue (1810–1863) inherited the trading company and continued to invest extensively with Russell and Company. He received regular dividends from the investments of his grandfather in American railroads and other activities through the Baring Brothers Bank. During 1858–1879 the Wu family seems to have received over U.S.$1,250,000 in dividends.[260] When Russell and Company declared bankruptcy in 1891 and John Murray Forbes became the trustee for the Wu family, the records showed Russell had over U.S.$1,000,000 in a trust fund belonging to the Wu family and that the family representative had received between U.S.$39,000–45,000 a year in income during the years 1878–1891. [261]

The Wu family, though probably the richest mercantile family in China at the time, were not unique in their American connections. The Boston firm of Perkins and Company also had a very close partnership with several other Chinese merchants; their extensive silk trade was carried out through a private Chinese trader named Yeshing, who amassed substantial wealth through this.[262] Both Chinese and foreign traders suffered from problems of liquidity in this system of forward dealing. Many American traders borrowed heavily from Chinese merchants for their operations. Pan Kun (Consequa) wrote to President Madison in 1815 complaining that American traders owed him $1,000,000 and had not paid up.[263] Some twenty-one merchants in Philadelphia together apparently owed Consequa half a million U.S. dollars, a fortune in those times.[264] Various American companies were hired to help the Chinese merchants press their claims even during the Opium War. As Edward Delano, then working as a clerk with Russell and Company in 1841, noted, "[b]usy all day and evening making out powers of attorney for various Hong merchants to the end that they may recover back monies for teas &c. sold by them to a man calling himself an American under the cognomen of T. Woodhouse Stevens—he has absconded to Bombay on his way to England and France."[265]

American traders also brought specie to China; it has been estimated that some U.S.$150–180 million in silver was shipped to China between 1784 and the Treaty of Wangxia in 1844.[266] Anecdotal evidence suggests that some merchants connected with the American trade were so affluent that they could be casually generous. Wu Bingjian apparently once tore up an I.O.U. of $72,000 from an American to enable the trader to go back home to the United States.[267] Clearly there was no absolute shortage of capital among several of the major traders.[268]

If, then, investable surplus (capital) was available, and just as clearly China was involved in the world market producing and exporting commodities made with Chinese labor and Chinese technology well before the Opium War, it follows that China did not have to wait till the post–Opium War period to be "opened up" by Westerners to avail itself of the opportunities provided by international trade. There already existed ample opportunities to raise profits through investments and to unleash the transformative potential of trade. Such investments would have maximized the cost-output ratio by minimizing the unit cost of production and adopting the most efficient technology available. With the burgeoning world market demand in silk, tea, and sugar, if market demands alone had been adequate stimuli to transform the economy and set in motion a process of continued development and technological innovation, suitable preconditions existed *prior* to the intrusion of imperialism. But then what happened in China? Was the technology to raise productivity not available? Was there a technological standstill, "less technological progress during this time [the last three centuries of pre–Opium War Chinese history] than at almost any other moment in two-thousand years of Chinese history"?[269] To answer these questions, we next turn to the technology of sugar manufacture prior to the Opium War.

THREE

FROM CANE INTO SUGAR: THE TECHNOLOGY OF SUGAR MANUFACTURE

> Sagacious men invent things, the skillful inherit and preserve them. This act is generally called manufacture. Therefore we owe the hundred kinds of artifacts to the sages.[1]
>
> —*Kaogong ji*, 140 B.C.

THE *KAOGONG JI* (THE ARTIFICER'S RECORD), one of the earliest sources of commentary on technical matters in the world, already reflects the seemingly universal predilection to distinguish between those who invent and those who merely reproduce and pass on the technique. Names of famous inventors and the origins of inventions occupy the front pages of books on the history of science and technology, including those on China;[2] the relatively recent history of scientific breakthroughs has produced an anachronistic and mythical popular literature on technology reinforcing notions of a parallelism between dramatic invention and its transformative applications.[3] As George Basalla points out, "The prevalence of artifactual continuity has been obscured by the myth of the heroic inventive genius, by nationalistic pride, by the patent system, and by the tendency to equate technological change with social, scientific and economic revolutions. However, once we actively search for continuity, it becomes apparent that every novel artifact has an antecedent."[4] The long history of sugar-manufacturing technology traced below, like the technological history of many other sectors of manufacturing prior to the eighteenth century and the Industrial Revolution, is a story of incremental change and continuities rather than one of heroic innovators. But, unlike some other types of manufacturing in which the technological changes came only in the nineteenth century, the intimate link between increased sugar consumption and the European discovery of the Americas added a specific dimension to the technical history of sugar manufacture even in the pre-industrial period.

In the early seventeenth century the pace of technological change worldwide in cane-sugar manufacturing underwent fundamental transformations. At one level this was a reflection of a basic shift in the social organization of production in the Americas, the type of labor used there for production, and the connection between sugar plantations and capitalism in western Europe.[5] That nexus changed the basic logic of production. Extracting the maximum amount of sugar in the shortest possible time and at the cheapest possible rate became the organizing principle of plantation enterprises.

Sugar-manufacturing techniques in China had continued to evolve over a thousand-year period. Were Chinese technologies also transformed in the seventeenth century, and did the quality of sugar produced equal the standards of the world market? The questions that arise are many. What was the technological baseline of Chinese manufacture and the extent of Chinese inventions? Or was there a "technological standstill" from the late sixteenth century on, even though, as we have seen, the merchants trading in sugar and other commodities on the world market had no absolute shortage of capital? How did the social organization of production shape the technology of manufacture? And was the technology of sugar manufacturing a particular and unique case or did the social organization of production in rural China shape the selection of other technologies as well? This chapter looks at these questions in comparative perspective and focuses on the processes of technological selection that were at work. I begin with an overview of the general problems confronting pre-industrial manufacturers of sugar, for such a producer faced many obstacles that are not readily apparent since these problems have been largely alleviated by the availability of industrial technology.

The Logistics of Manufacturing Sugar

The first obstacle the producer faced was the mechanics of crushing. Cane rind is hard and brittle, and steady pressure is necessary to extract the juice. The amount of cane juice extracted from a given acre of cane depends not only on the variety of cane, but also on the efficiency with which the machinery manages to extract it. Methods of crushing that grind the cane down completely are not the most suitable because bits of cane bagasse in the juice impede crystallization. Furthermore, organic substances present in the cane juice, such as albumin, ferment when the juice is exposed to air.[6] Although harvested cane can be kept in storage for some time if totally undamaged and the rind unbroken, it cracks easily when harvested by hand and stored under common pre-industrial agricultural conditions. Such damage lets air into the cane cells and fermentation sets in. Once fermentation has begun, the juice cannot be used for making crystallized sugar. Prior to the development of cold storage and rail transportation in the nineteenth century, cane was processed within forty-eight hours of harvesting in or near the area it was cultivated.

Producing crystallized sugar after extracting the juice is a complicated process. Fermentation proceeds rapidly because the juice is in full contact with air, so the producer has to start boiling the juice soon after extraction. The cane juice at this point, however, is a slimy liquid with gummy albuminoids from the cane cells and other undesirable matter floating in it, all of which have to be removed by careful tempering with additives like slaked lime (calcium hydroxide) and other substances. These additives cause the impurities either to float to the top of the boiling juice, where they can be skimmed off, or sink to the bottom, where they can be removed by decanting.

Next the juice needs to be boiled down to evaporate the water and produce a supersaturated solution. The temperature while boiling has to be carefully controlled, for heat changes the structure of the sucrose molecules. First the sucrose melts. But then as heating continues, the sucrose molecules part with successive molecules of hydrogen and oxygen. These molecules become converted into non-crystallizable forms of sugar, such as glucose, which, due to the caramelization of the molecules affected by heat, are lost as molasses.[7] Using too high a temperature to concentrate the cane juice results in the whole batch turning into burnt, non-crystallizable syrup.[8] Judging the exact moment when the sugar syrup was "done" required considerable expertise before the advent of industrial technology and temperature-controlled vacuum-pans for boiling. After boiling, separating the sugar crystals from the molasses and drying the sugar presented another set of formidable problems.

Different techniques evolved to resolve these problems of production in the sugar-producing regions of the world. Chinese techniques, presented here in chronological sequence, show a combination of adoption, adaptation, and energetic innovation.

The Mechanics of Crushing Cane in Tang-Song China

Of all the texts describing the Chinese sugar industry, the earliest extant illustration of a sugarcane crusher in China is from the seventeenth-century *Tiangong kaiwu*.[9] As seen in Figure 2, it was a vertical two-roller cane crusher of a design used, with minor modifications, both in China and India well into the twentieth century. The prevalence of this type of vertical two-roller crusher since the seventeenth century, however, has led to an assumption that it was the one and only type of cane crusher used in China.[10] This was not the case.

The first detailed description of the machinery used for crushing cane in China is the ninth-century fragment on sugar manufacturing discovered in Dunhuang. It reads: "When making it [sugar] first take the sugarcane stalks, strip away the leaves, cut the stalks into five *cun* [inch] pieces and place in a large wooden mortar (*jiu*), harness an ox and crush to extract the juice which will collect in the earthenware jar. Then boil it in fifteen *cheng* (tripod vessels used for heating wine)."[11]

Although the small, hand-held mortar and pestle was widely used in China, this type of wooden, ox-driven mill with a "large wooden mortar" was altogether atypical.[12] The description of this Chinese mill, however, closely fits that of the Indian annular mortar-and-pestle mill, or the *kolhu*.[13] The *kolhu*, usually made out of a hollowed out tree trunk, is the earliest form of the cane crusher found in India; the mill

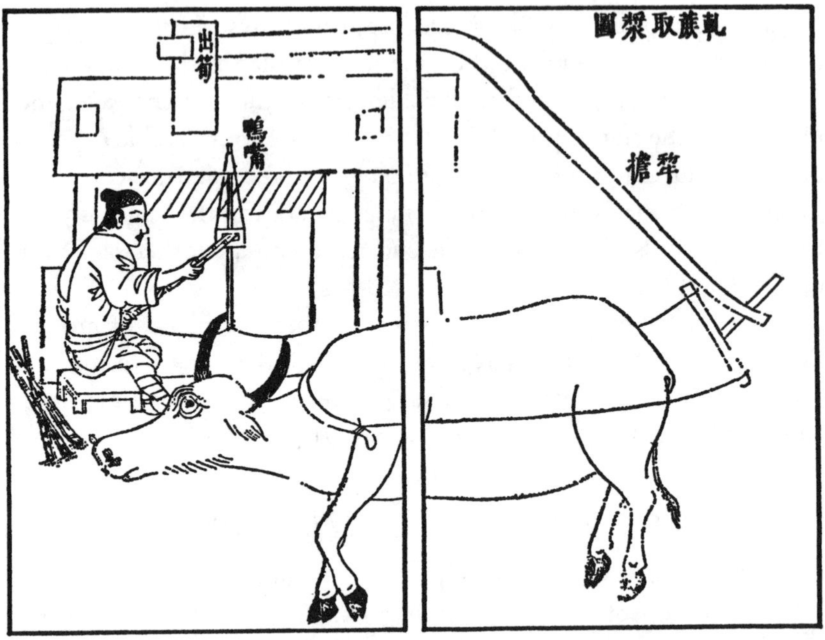

FIGURE 2. Vertical two-roller sugarcane crusher (*Tiangong kaiwu* [1637]). This is the first available illustration and mention of the device in China.

continued to be used well into the twentieth century. As Figure 3, an East India Company illustration from 1822, shows, a canal cut obliquely into one side of the mortar let the juice squeezed from the cane run into a vessel located in a hole under the spout of the canal.[14] The operation of this mill has been described by many: John Gerard's description of an Indian sugarcane crusher written in 1597 points to the similarity of the process as described in the Dunhuang fragment:

Notwithstanding I think it not amisse to shew unto you the ordering of these reeds when they be new gathered, as I received it from the mouth of an Indian my servant, he saith: They do cut them in small peeces, and put them in a trough made of one whole tree, wherein they put a great stone in maner of a milstone, whereunto they tie a horse, bufle, or some other beast which draweth it rounde: in which trough, they put those peeces of canes, and so crush and grinde them, as we do the barkes of trees for Tanners, or apples for Cyder.[15]

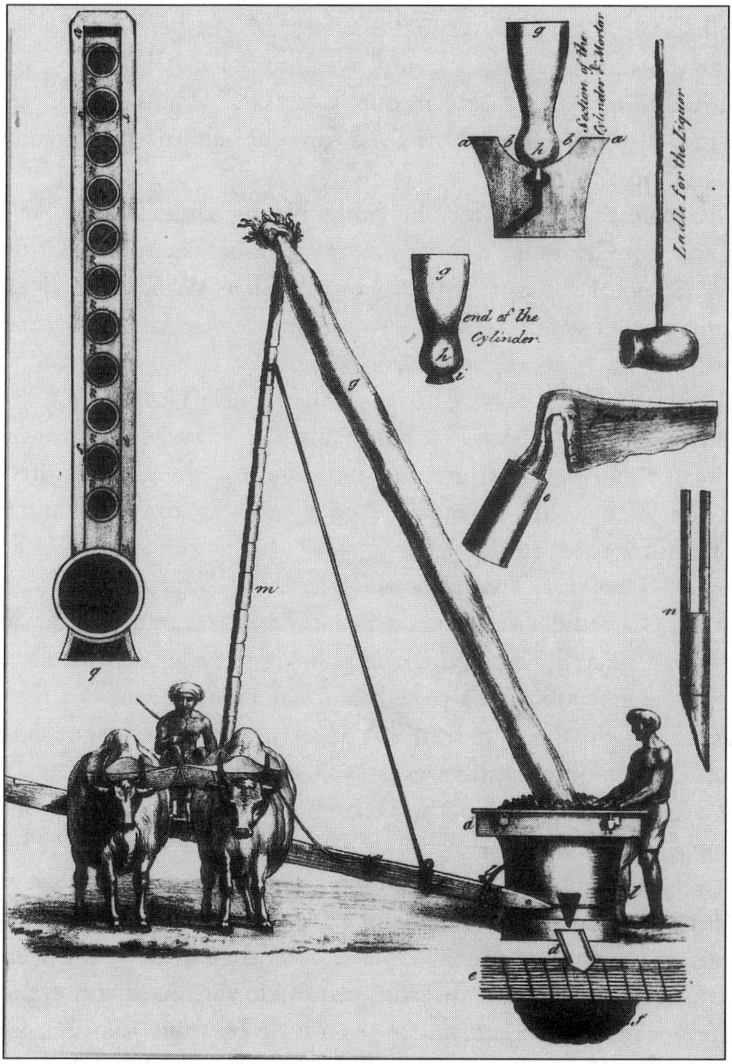

FIGURE 3. Indian annular mortar-and-pestle mill (*kolhu*) and multi-aperture boiling stove (East India Sugar Papers [1822], p. 24)

The Indian annular mill may have been taken to Dunhuang by the Indian artisans who came in the Tang to teach "the art of sugar-making" in the monasteries. The mill required a very labor-intensive process; as the Dunhuang fragment and Gerard both point out, the cane had to be cut into very small slices. Maybe because of this, the use of the mortar-and-pestle mill was limited in China, and only a brief mention of it is found in one later text.[16] The adoption of this mill may also have been short-lived for other alternatives already existed in China.

Our primary source for the Song, Wang Zhuo's *Tangshuang pu* (Treatise on Crystallized Sugar, 1142), describes the mill used for initial crushing of the cane in Sichuan as a *nian*; Wang's text does not contain any illustrations.[17] *Nian* was a generic word used for all mills; in other texts from the same period and later, *nian* was commonly used to describe all sorts of edge-runner mills. The typical Chinese edge-runner mill, used for grinding and decorticating grain, was the *niu nian* or *shi nian*. Illustrated here in Figure 4, the nian was first depicted in Wang Zhen's *Nongshu* (Agricultural Treatise, 1313) and then, among other texts, in the *Tiangong kaiwu* (1637) and in the *Nongzheng quanshu* (Complete Treatise on Agricultural Systems, 1639).[18] The *Nongshu*, written between 1300 and 1304 and reflecting conditions in southern China, describes the *nian* as having a roller which was about two feet in height, with a trough and the circumference of the base measuring "several tens of feet."[19] The circumference of the base of the common edge-runner mills was 25–30 feet.

Wang Zhuo's mill, on the other hand, is described not only as having a much smaller trough, but also a much larger roller, "There is the cane mill (*zhe nian*) to which oxen are harnessed [in order to] to crush the pared cane. It is made of a big piece of hard stone, is five to six feet in height, and more than a thousand *jin* in weight. Beneath it there is a receptacle base [mortarium] made with hard stone; the circumference of the receptacle base is a little bit more than ten feet."[20] The ten-foot mortarium or base of the mill described by Wang Zhuo would have been much smaller than that of the usual edge-runner mill, while the height and weight of the grindstone, in contrast, was far larger and heavier than that of the wheel or roller of the edge-runner mill. In describing the grind stone as weighing a "thousand *jin*," Wang was pretty close to the mark, for a five-foot high stone cylinder with a specific gravity of 3.5 (not very dense), and 1 foot thick in

FIGURE 4. Rotary double edge-runner mill (*shi nian; Tiangong kaiwu* [1637]), similar in design to that shown in the *Nongshu* (1313). The use of the trailer for sweeping the grain back into the trough is a later addition from the *Gujin tushu jicheng* (1725).

FIGURE 5. Oil mill with single stone roller (Hommel, p. 88). The trough scraper is not visible in the photograph. Reproduced by permission of M.I.T. Press.

diameter would weigh 1,095 pounds at 219 pounds per foot.[21] The mill described by Wang Zhuo clearly was not the type of edge-runner mill used for crushing grain. But interpreted as being similar to mills used for crushing oil-seeds in China in the Song as well as later,[22] the mill described by Wang bears a striking resemblance to an oil mill as seen in an early-twentieth-century photograph from Zhejiang province by Rudolph Hommel, reproduced here in Figure 5.[23] Needham noted that oil mills with only one running stone and a small travel circle were more common in Sichuan province than in other parts of China.[24] I am interpreting Wang Zhuo's mill as similar to the *mola olearia,* which as Needham points out, was an analogue to the Indian annular mortar-and-pestle mill.[25] The Greek and Roman olive-oil mill, or *mola olearia,* had one or two rather narrow rollers or edge-runners with a small travel circle in the trough. There was a tendency in all of the early cane-sugar-producing regions of the world to adapt the technology used for seed-oil extraction to that of cane juice extraction. In India, the *kolhu* was used for both; even the occupational categories of oil extractors and sugarcane crushers were subjected to the same types of taxes as early as ca. 300 B.C.[26] In most of western Asia and the Mediterranean, the edge-runner mill, whose origins have also been traced to the oil presses of the Hellenistic world, was used as the primary type of cane crusher during the course of the thirteenth century.[27] In some of these areas, an olive-oil press was used to extract the juice after boiling or soaking the macerated cane.[28] After crushing in the edge-runner mill, the cane was pressed in a stationary press like a wedge press to extract the juice.[29] Clearly the Chinese were using a similar technique. This interpretation of Wang Zhuo's text allows us to reconstruct the sequence of cane-sugar manufacture in the Song; it may also help explain why the Dunhuang annular mill that was used in India for both crushing cane and oil-seeds did not become more widely used in China, where a very different type of oil mill was in use.

The Chinese method of preparing the cane for crushing was far more labor intensive than either the Indic method using the annular mortar-and-pestle mill or the edge-runner mill used in the Mediterranean. Although the cane had to be sliced into small pieces in all these mills, the extant Indic and Mediterranean descriptions of crushing sugarcane do not mention peeling or paring the outer surface of the cane. Wang Zhuo's description of the Chinese process, on the other hand, makes it quite clear that the cane was to be stripped of its outer rind before crushing: "Then there is a cane bench, which looks like a small stool; in one corner a hole is chiseled, to stand a wooden fork. Bunches of cane, three or five (at a time) are placed on the fork to straighten them out and one straddles the bench at an angle to pare them."[30] After the cane was peeled, it was chopped into little pieces, "the size of coins," and put into the edge-runner mill and crushed.

Next, the peeled and mashed cane pieces were placed in a woven or plaited bamboo basket and steamed. This step, too, is reminiscent of oil-seed processing in China. But the final stage of extraction was not done in the wooden wedge-press commonly used for oil extraction in China. After steaming, the macerated pulp was put into a "pressing bowl" (*ca dou*), also called a "bamboo basket" because it was woven out of tender bamboo slats and the whole basket was placed in the press. Wang Zhuo gives only a sketchy description of this press: "There is the pressing bed to hold the basin. On top of the press-bed there is a frame with a large beam; below there is a rotating axle, which draws [down] a rope to press [the prepared cane bits]."[31] The references to a rotating axle and rope suggest that Wang could be describing some version of either the wine-press or a rope-clutch press illustrated here in Figures 6 and 7.[32] These are the only two Chinese presses I could identify that operate with a rotating axle and could have been used for extracting liquids.

A significant amount of sucrose was lost in the juice processed in

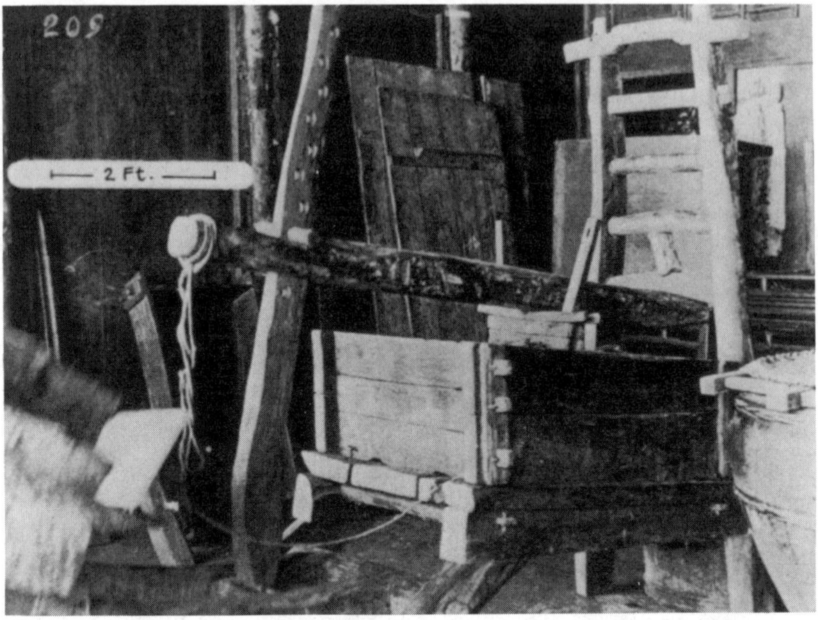

FIGURE 6. Chinese wine press with horizontal lever beam and stone weight (Hommel, p. 108). Similar in construction to the beancurd press. Reproduced by permission of M.I.T. Press.

the annular mills of India because of the waste and albumin from the rinds incorporated in the massecuite.[33] The Chinese method of peeling the cane before crushing, then steaming it and expressing the juice, would have produced a cleaner juice. A greater proportion of the juice would also have been extracted because the cane would have been squeezed more thoroughly. But the Chinese method would also have required more labor for the various steps as well as more fuel to boil down the cane juice (because of the water absorbed from the steaming) than the one-step crushing in the annular mill.

The boiling of the juice, according to Wang Zhuo, was likewise done in two stages:

[After] boiling the juice and steaming [the macerated pulp in order to squeeze out more juice] in sequence, wait for three days after it is done. If [you] wait more than three days, then it will turn sour. Take the syrup which is left [after initial evaporation] and boil again till it is nine-tenths

FIGURE 7. Chinese wooden rope-clutch press (Hommel, p. 109). The horizontal press-beam is pulled down with a rope and windlass. Reproduced by permission of M.I.T. Press.

done and thick like malt sugar. If you boil till it is a hundred percent thick, then it will turn into "sandy foot." Insert bamboo sticks [pieces] throughout the jar, and only then should the massecuite be poured into the jar. Cover with a winnowing fan. And this is the way to make crystallized sugar.[34]

From a technical point of view, Wang Zhuo shows an awareness that underboiling the cane juice would lead to fermentation of the sucrose molecules and the souring of the juice and that overboiling would concentrate the juice too much. The latter would lead to the formation of what is known as "false grain" or "sandy foot" as Wang Zhuo calls it. This is the formation of minute crystals that cannot grow larger because the massecuite is too thick and the uncrystallizable residue cannot be separated during evaporation.[35]

The process of crystallization recommended in the Tang was in many ways more labor intensive than the process used in the Song. The Dunhuang fragment recommended that the supersaturated boiled sugar be whipped (beaten) for an hour until small granules (sandy sugar) formed.[36] Beating a supersaturated syrup in a rapid motion separates the solid from the liquid, and although very labor intensive, this method can produce sugar granules within a very short time. The other method, less labor intensive, was to pour the supersaturated sugar syrup in a bucket that had a hole or slot in the bottom; the molasses drained out into a pottery jar placed below to catch the "water," which was then made into wine.[37] Both these methods, beating the sugar and pouring the syrup into a bucket, continued to be used in the Song. But the slotted bucket was not used any more, and the sugar was allowed to crystallize through simple evaporation. Wang Zhuo's recommendation to "[i]nsert bamboo sticks into the jar, and only then pour the massecuite into the jar" at this stage was innovative.[38] Crystals deposit more rapidly if twine or bamboo sticks are inserted into a super-saturated sugar syrup.[39] Other than inserting these bamboo sticks, however, Wang Zhuo does not suggest that the jars used for crystallization were specially designed to allow the molasses to trickle out. After the sticks were inserted, there was a long waiting period to find out if the sugar actually crystallized or if the whole lot was the inferior "sandy foot." As Wang Zhuo writes:

> After the syrup has been in the jar for two days, there will be gruel-like streaks on top in the jar. When you dip your fingers [lit. "color the fingers"] to look at it, you will find that it is like fine sand. After the fifteenth of the first lunar month, it will crystallize into little lumps, or there will be granules like the ears of grain on the tips of the sticks [of bamboo]. Slowly they will become larger like beans, and then like the joints of fingers. Eventually they may even go as far as becoming like stalactites and artificial mountains [lit. rocks in a garden]. This is commonly referred to as the fruiting of the fruit. By the fifth month, when the growing energy of spring and summer have already been spent, the crystals are fully formed [they will not grow any larger]. Then strain out [the molasses from] the jar.[40]

The text then goes on to discuss how the crystals should be taken out of the jar and further dried in the sun, adding no doubt to the five-month processing period mentioned above. This process of crystallizing through evaporation and sun-bleaching for sugar was very similar to the process of making table salt in China; the making of salt has been described in detail by Jia Sixie in his sixth-century work, the *Qimin yaoshu*.[41]

Although Wang Zhuo provides enough detail for anyone contemplating making cane sugar, a survey of all the equipment necessary for processing and crushing the cane shows that it was not a simple matter to undertake manufacture.[42] No less than eleven items plus at least one ox would be needed. These included a paring knife, the cane sickle, the bench on which the cane would be positioned for peeling and chopping, the mill, the basket in which the macerated pulp would be placed, the pestle for driving the cane into the crusher, and the press—all used for the mechanical process of juice extraction. In addition, various types of vessels were needed: iron or copper cauldrons for steaming the pulp, vats for holding the juice as it was expressed, metal pots for boiling the juice, and the jars in which the final crystallization would take place. Only a portion of this equipment was standard farm equipment. The mill and the press were two of the more expensive items, and although the mill was similar in design to those used for oil-pressing, oily residues would make it impractical to use a single mill for both purposes. Much labor was also required. According to Wang Zhuo, between ten to twenty people were needed to ensure that all the steps were carried out rapidly enough to prevent spoilage.

This rather complicated list of the equipment and labor inputs, as well as the five-month waiting period necessary before the sugar could be marketed, suggests that sugar production (at least as described by Wang Zhuo) could not have been casually undertaken. The specific expenses as well as the high labor requirements would have made individual small-scale peasant household production difficult. In the Tang and Song periods, sugar manufacturing of this type may have been done primarily on manors or estates and monasteries where labor and resources were readily available. While there is ample evidence that sugar did become a commercial product in the Song and was sold in the markets of major cities like Kaifeng, output and the total number of large producers were probably limited by the costs of labor and equipment. Elsewhere in the Song, as in the Yuan and early Ming, small peasant producers may have used the pedal-tilt hammer and far less efficient methods of manufacture such as those described below.

Cane-Processing Techniques in Yuan and Early-Ming China

The only text with discussions of sugar manufacturing in the Yuan is the late-thirteenth-century *Nongsang jiyao* (Fundamentals of Agriculture and Sericulture) compiled under Yuan imperial sponsorship. As we have seen, neither of the two other major contemporary works on agriculture, Wang Zhen's *Nongshu* and Lu Mingshan's *Nongsang yishi cuoyao*, discuss sugarcane or sugar manufacturing, attesting perhaps to the northern orientation of these authors.[43]

The discussion of the actual machinery of crushing cane in the *Nongsang jiyao* is extremely brief, and more attention is devoted to the procedures for cultivation than to manufacture. But instead of the elaborate processing using an edge-runner mill and rope-clutch press described by Wang, the *Nongsang jiyao* suggests that the common domestic tool used for decorticating grain, the pedal tilt-hammer or hammer mill, was used for crushing cane: "If after harvesting [the cane] you leave it for more than ten days, then it will not be suitable for boiling. Take the freshly cut stalks and strip the leaves. Dice into pieces two inches long. Pound in a *dui* [pedal tilt-hammer mill] to crush. Using a fine textured basket or a cloth bag filled [with the pulp] make ready to press, and squeeze to take out the juice."[44] The text then goes on to discuss the boiling of the juice. Pedal tilt-hammer mills are considered to be indigenous to China and were in use at least since the fifth century B.C. for hulling and polishing cereals.[45] As seen in Figure 8, in a second-century Han dynasty tomb pottery, it was as common a kitchen item as the quern sitting next to it. It is difficult, however, to judge the efficiency of the *dui* for purposes of crushing sugarcane. All available replicas and later illustrations of the *dui*, such as from the *Nongshu* (1313) and the *Nongzheng quanshu* (1639), show that the stone mortar was set into a depression dug into the ground to stabilize it when the grains were pounded. Similar tilt-hammer mills

FIGURE 8. Model of a pedal tilt-hammer mill. Anonymous, Chinese, ca. 1st c., red earthenware with green lead glaze. Reproduced by permission of University of Michigan Museum of Art, Gift of Domino's Pizza Inc., 1963/1.61.

were also used for pounding ores and powdering clay for making porcelains.[46] In China and elsewhere, in the dozens of uses listed for the tilt-hammer mill, it seems to have been used for decorticating grains and for pounding and pulverizing solids.[47] The known design, and none of the hundreds of surviving samples of the mortar of the tilt-hammer mill, show neither a bowl-shape nor a channel for drawing away liquids. Its use for crushing cane, as discussed in the *Nongsang jiyao*, is therefore quite unusual. Although the pedal tilt-hammer had the advantage of being a common household tool, it would certainly have spattered and wasted much of the cane juice in the process of pounding cane. There is no way of knowing whether the sugar-producing regions of China in the early fourteenth century were actually using the *dui*, or whether other types of larger mills like those described by Wang Zhuo were still in use. The use of the *dui*, instead of the edge-runner mill, makes sense only if we assume either that the amount of cane crushed was very little or, as I suspect, the author recommended its use in an effort to promote cane processing in more households; as noted earlier, the *Nongsang jiyao* was part of the Yuan imperial effort to aid and improve Chinese agriculture affected by the Mongol invasion.

Had Chinese techniques of sugar manufacturing deteriorated since the Song? As we saw earlier, Marco Polo found the sugar in Fujian "like paste and black," a far cry from the Song poet's vision of "amber crystals" and Wang Zhuo's "sugar frost." Marco Polo suggests that Chinese sugar was black because the Chinese did not know how to clarify the cane juice and artisans from Egypt had to be brought over to teach them the technique of clarifying with wood ashes.[48] Clarifying rid the juice of the fine bits of cane stalk and bagasse, wax and gums from the rinds, and sand and clay from the roots of the cane as well as albumin from the green parts of the cane. Adding any one of a range of ingredients, such as milk, blood, charcoal, egg whites, wood ashes, slaked lime, and sulfuric acid, to the juice during heating causes the gummy matter and albumin to coagulate and tangle with the other undesirable particles, which can then be skimmed off when the scum rises to the top of the boiling juice. Milk was widely used in India and Persia for purposes of clarifying cane juice at least since the seventh century.[49] In the Tang, when various types of sugar products were imported from India and Persia, it was known in China that boiling with milk produced a whiter sugar.[50] But, probably due to dietary preferences established by the Song, the use of milk did not become part of sugar manufacturing. Neither the Song nor the Yuan texts say anything about adding clarifying ingredients to the cane juice. We then have to assume that using clarifying substances was not commonly known in China as of the fourteenth century and efforts were made to clean the juice mechanically.[51] Wang Zhuo's complicated method of crushing the cane in the plaited bamboo basket was perhaps one such effort to strain the juice as best as possible and rid it of the larger bits of pulp.

In the Yuan, as the *Nongsang jiyao* suggests, the crushed cane was put into a fine textured basket or cloth bag and the juice squeezed out, a process that was certainly necessary as cane crushed in the hammermill would have left plenty of cane fragments.[52] However, straining the juice at best gets out only the larger bits of the fiber and stalk but cannot remove the albumin and gums that can burn as the juice is boiled down. The use of wood ashes for clarifying as taught by the artisans from Egypt in the fourteenth century may have had a local impact in Fujian, but only in the late-Ming *Tiangong kaiwu* do we see any systematic discussion of clarifying cane juice. The commonly used ingredient at that time was slaked lime.[53] But there was some advance over the Song methods in the Yuan; there was a greater awareness of temperature control, and slotted vessels were used for straining out the uncrystallizable molasses after boiling the juice. The compilers of *Nongsang jiyao* note:

Using a copper pot, boil the [extracted] juice with a slow or quick fire, taking into consideration the amount [of juice]. Place this pot and arrange the fire outside the partition wall.[54] Do not let any smoke get into the pot; have a person solely watching over this. Boil till thick and sticky like the color of *heizao* [*Diaspyros lotus*, or wild persimmon, a light golden color].

Use a pair of earthenware vessels. At the bottom of the upper one, drill a hole the size of the head of a chopstick. Place a jar below the vessel [with the hole] to catch the molasses. Take the boiled juice and using a ladle, pour it into the vessel. The best stuff becomes clarified [lit. "becomes pure"] and stays in the vessel; the stuff that flows into the jar can only be mixed with water and used as a drink. Take out the good stuff and then, using the eye to judge [the degree of drainage], store the vessel holding it. Or it can also be poured into an earthenware jar and covered. Eat it as you wish, but be careful not to place it on a hot *kang* [brick bed]—otherwise the heat will change it.[55]

Draining out the molasses was clearly recognized as necessary, and the text recommends using specially designed pots with a hole. The shape of the vessel is not given although in other parts of the world by this time conical vessels were commonly being used for curing sugar.[56] The Yuan process of evaporation and crystallization, while far faster than in the Song because the molasses could now drain out, was still slow and depended on the vagaries of the weather. When the upper layers of sugar crystals formed in the pot, the molasses would trickle to the bottom of the jar and into the pot below. The higher-grade product, the upper layers, would have been a light golden or a light brown in color and the quality would have been similar to the cane sugar produced in contemporary sugar-manufacturing centers in various parts of the world that was known by the Portuguese term *muscavado*.[57] The layers of sugar at the bottom of the draining vessel, produced according to the Yuan method, would still retain a large proportion of molasses and be quite dark and sticky. I think it is likely that Marco Polo saw this inferior grade of sugar and, given to generalizations, formed his poor opinion of all Chinese sugar. And soon, Marco Polo's evaluations notwithstanding, an even higher grade of white sugar was to be produced in China through the technique of claying as discussed below. Overall, reviewing the techniques of manufacture from the seventh to the fourteenth century, we see that there had been more developments in the refining of sugar than in the crushing of cane. Cane was still crushed with a range of different and perhaps not very efficient equipment. This, too, changed shortly.

China and the Americas: Innovations and Adaptations

In both China and the Americas the sugarcane industry was transformed during the course of the late sixteenth and early seventeenth centuries. Monoculture, the development of vast plantations extending across hundreds of acres, and dependence on slave labor became the norm in the sugar colonies of Brazil, Peru, and the Caribbean. The technological parameters of production were transformed under the imperatives of producing as much sugar as possible for the markets in Europe. In China, sugarcane cultivation also expanded dramatically as exports rose in the seventeenth century. Here, too, there was a social transformation undergirding the technology of production, the reinvigoration of small-scale peasant agriculture that is explored in the next chapter. In both these worlds, at about the same time, specialized vertical-roller mills designed to crush sugarcane became available. Powered by animal, water, and wind, these new vertical-roller mills sharply reduced labor needs while raising productivity. The cane did not have to be chopped into pieces before crushing as with edge-runner mills, and crushing the entire stalk without pulverizing it produced a relatively clean juice that did not have to be strained. The dried, crushed stalks of cane (bagasse) provided ready fuel for boiling the syrup. Simultaneously a range of techniques also evolved to hasten the processes of crystallization and refining.

Vertical-roller sugar mills appear suddenly worldwide. The earliest clearly documented records are contained in a manuscript from Peru dated 1613 with an illustration of a three-roller crusher that is reproduced here in Figure 9,[58] and a description of a two-roller mill from the Philippines in a Spanish-Tagalog dictionary that is also dated 1613,[59] and an illustration and discussion of a two-roller mill in the *Tiangong kaiwu,* dated 1637 and given above in Figure 2. This is the earliest description and illustration of the device in China. The question of where the technology of vertical-roller cane crushers first developed is, however, not easily resolved.[60]

The two best-known late-Ming works on Chinese agriculture are the *Nongzheng quanshu* (composed 1625–1628, printed 1639) and the *Tiangong kaiwu* (composed 1634–1636, printed 1637). The only other text slightly predating these two with some information on agriculture is the pharmacopoeia of Li Shizhen, *Bencao gangmu* (printed in 1596); it has a discussion on cane, but the focus of the work is on the varieties cultivated and the various types of sugar produced rather than on the techniques of extraction; the text simply declares "the juice is extracted."[61] The *Nongzheng quanshu* and *Tiangong kaiwu,* although compiled within a decade of each other, show very different stages of development in the history of Chinese sugar manufacturing. Xu Guangqi (1561–1633), the author of the *Nongzheng quanshu,* was one of the highest officials in the realm and one of several late-Ming literati who were becoming interested in European geography and technology. Having spent his early working-life in Guangdong, where he came into contact with European missionaries, Xu was particularly attuned to new agricultural and technological developments; he wrote books on the then recently introduced sweet potato, collaborated with Jesuits in translating works on geometry and irrigation, and was an activist-bureaucrat who carried out agricultural experiments on his own farms. Xu was by all accounts acutely interested in contemporary technical developments. In his *Nongzheng quanshu,* however, Xu repeats the information from the three-hundred-and-fifty-year-old

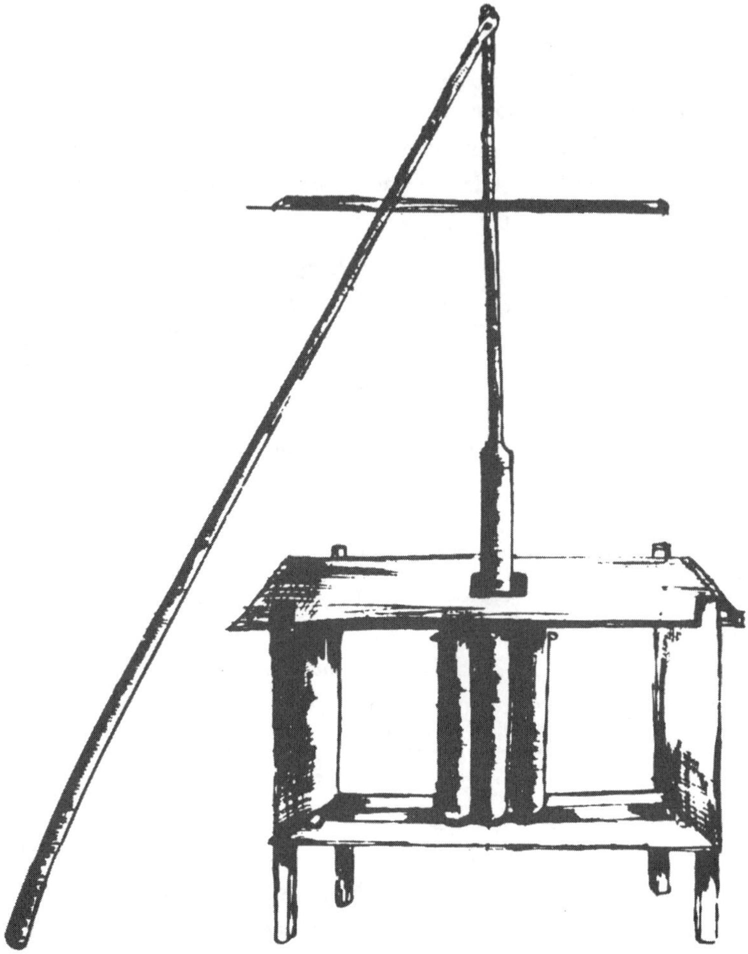

FIGURE 9. Sketch of three-roller vertical mill, Peru, manuscript dated 1613, Ajuda Palace, adapted from Mauro, pl. III, opp. p. 203.

Nongsang jiyao and briefly discusses the pedal tilt-hammer for crushing cane. There are no commentaries inserted to suggest that the method described was other than a contemporary procedure. The *Tiangong kaiwu*, on the other hand, describes a completely different process for both cane crushing and refining; the vertical two-roller cane crusher (*tang che*) is described in some detail:

Apparatus for making sugar: Use two wooden boards, five feet in height, five inches thick, and two feet wide. Drill holes at the two ends of the boards to accommodate the supporting posts. The upper ends of the posts should protrude a little, while the lower ends of the post extend two or three feet below and are buried in tamped earth in order to make them stable.

Two holes are made in the middle of the upper board in which two large rollers (made of hard and heavy wood) are aligned next to each other. It is best if the rollers measure seven feet in circumference. Of the two rollers, one is three feet, and the other four feet and five inches. On the protruding end of the longer one a fifteen-foot-long curved wooden plough pole is attached in order to harness to an ox walking round and round [and thereby turning the rollers]. On both the rollers teeth [cogs] are chiseled which fit into each other like female and male; they must be directly placed so as to fit together and mesh when turned. The sugarcane placed between [the rollers] will be crushed as it passes through. The principle is the same as that of the cotton gin. As the cane passes through, the juice flows out. The residue [bagasse] is entered through the "duck mouth" [opening] on the rollers and pressed again. After three pressings the juice [in the cane] is exhausted. The bagasse is used for fuel.

On the lower board, niches one-and-a-half-inches deep are chiseled out to accommodate the bottom end of the rollers. The board is not drilled through so as to collect the juice. At the end of the rollers, iron bearings are fixed in the center in order to facilitate the rotation. There is a trough on the board through which the cane juice flows into a vat.[62]

As we see in the Ming illustration of the cane crusher (Figure 2), the gear teeth at the top of the wooden rollers are oblique cogs.[63] It also shows the "duck bill" (*yazui*) quite prominently. This duck bill operated as a pressure feeder and compressor for the cane and was particular to the Chinese design. The feeder, by locating the entry-point for the cane to be crushed within an enclosed frame, may have prevented the kind of accidents described below in Brazil where the crushers did not have this feature. The two-roller Ming design was to become the standard in China; the three-roller cane crusher that became so common in the Americas was never used in China. There is no documentary or other evidence to suggest that a vertical three-roller crusher was ever known in China.

In other parts of Asia besides the Philippines and China, the first written references to the use of any sort of vertical crushers come rather late.[64] In India, in 1695, the Italian traveler Giovanni Careri noted seeing near Bombay, "Sugarcanes Press'd between two great wooden Roulers, turn'd about by Oxen, whence they come out thoroughly squeez'd."[65] The three-roller cane crusher was never common in India, but in contrast to China, it was observed in use in some areas, including areas far from the coast. In the nineteenth century, for example, it was noted as being used in central India in the Chattisgarh area, a rather isolated region in central India, and in another location near Meerut.[66] In the major sugar-manufacturing areas in the plains of eastern and western India, however, the *kolhu,* or the mortar-and-pestle mill, continued to be the most commonly used cane crusher well into the twentieth century.[67] In northeastern Asia, a vertical two-roller cane crusher was used at first, but horizontal two-roller crushers and vertical three-roller crushers were in use by the late seventeenth century in the Ryukyus and by the mid-eighteenth century in Japan.[68] In southeast Asia, such as Vietnam, Thailand, and Java, the vertical two-roller crusher seemed to have become standard equipment; but since cane-sugar manufacturing was developed in these areas by Chinese immigrants, it stands to reason that the mill was introduced by them in seventeenth century.[69] Other than the Philippines, therefore, all references to the vertical-roller cane crushers in Asia, including China, are dated to the period after the 1630s. Was this vertical-roller cane crusher, far more efficient than any of the prevailing techniques for crushing cane, a Chinese invention as has been argued,[70] or was it an example of diffusion and adaptation of a design which was introduced into Asia from other parts of the world?

There were still several types of mills in use in the cane-sugar-producing regions of the Mediterranean, Brazil, Peru, and the Caribbean in the mid-decades of the sixteenth century. Water-driven and animal-driven edge-runner mills were by far the most common.[71] The shortage of animal-power in some regions of the Americas may have promoted an early and greater use of water power here than in other parts of the sugar-producing world. Many estates had more than one mill and used various types of power; there are several examples from the Americas similar to a letter from the bishop of Puerto Rico written in 1548 noting, "G. de Santaolla, an old established resident, has with great difficulty and expense, established a powerful water-driven sugar mill in the immediate vicinity of San Juan city. . . . He has two other horse-mills."[72] Numerous engravings of such mills were printed. One of the earliest illustration of cane crushing from the Americas is an engraving by Theodor de Bry dated 1590, given here in Figure 10. When there were shortages of animal-power, the grindstone was apparently moved by whatever means available, including human labor. Such engravings, called *compilatiewerk* by the Dutch, depicted a scene often compiled from several different sources rather than an actual scene from one plantation. In the de Bry illustration we see, for example, an overshot waterwheel in the right-hand corner of the illustration; it is therefore not clear why water-power was not used to turn the edge-runner mill in the scene, unless the artist was further emphasizing the title of the illustration, "The Negroes, having exhausted the metallic veins, had to be given work making sugar."[73] Although edge-runner mills like this one continued to be set up in some sugar producing estates in the Americas even in the 1630s,[74] in most areas the machinery used for crushing was rapidly transformed. The three-roller crusher became widely used in the Americas from the seventeenth century onward. But a two-roller version also existed in some parts of the Americas including Brazil. Richard Flecknoe's vivid account, written in 1648 as a letter to his patrons in Europe, noted the method of crushing and manufacture; it also shows the intensity of the process on a Brazilian plantation. Flecknoe's reference to the use of iron to plate the rollers is also interesting and relevant to our discussion below:

Their Sugar canes are prun'd to the height of standing corn: nor need they other culture, but every second year to cut them close by the roots as we do Osier [*Salix viminalis*, a species of willow] when against the next year they never fail to spring up again, the flaggs of which Canes are a pleasant green, and shew a far off just like a Field of Corn, which being ripe about the month of June, they joint them in pieces some foot long, and carry them to the Mill, turn'd by Oxen, or Water, consisting of two round Cylinders, about the bigness of Mil-posts, plated with Iron, which turning inwards, and joining all close together as they can meet, so squeeze the canes passing

FIGURE 10. *Negritae exhaustis venis metallicis,* Theodor de Bry [America], Frankfurt, 1590, Part v, pl. 11, (*KB 1590). Reproduced by permission of Rare Books Division, The New York Public Library, Astor, Lenox and Tilden Foundations.

through them, as they come out on th'other side all bruzed [*sic*] . . . which Liquer is conveyed by Troughs to certain Cauldrons, whe'tis boyl'd, still retaining its amber colour, till powr'd out at last in to their forms or coolers, with a certain Lees 'its rendered white; And while these Mills (during the Season of making Sugar) they work both day and night, the work of immediately applying the canes into the Mill being so perillous as through drousinesse or heedlessnesse a fingers end be but engag'd bewixt the Posts, their whole body inevitably follows, to prevent which, the next Negro has alwayes a Hatchet readie to chop off his Arms, if any such Misfortune should arrive.[75]

Extant illustrations of the two-roller mill in the Americas are not known. A large number of engravings and illustrations of the vertical three-roller mills in the Americas are available, for these were by far more common. Several of the illustrations are from Brazil from the 1630s and 1640s where this type of mill is thought to have been introduced by a Spanish priest sometime after 1600[76] and had become prevalent by 1618.[77] Many illustrations show two or more sets of vertical three-roller mills located side-by-side being worked by teams of oxen as well as waterwheels.[78] Barlaeus (Kaspar van Baerle), an engraver in the entourage of the Dutch governor of Brazil Johan Maurits in the 1640s, produced numerous *compilatiewerk* depicting scenes from the Americas, including that of sugarcane plantation.[79] The segment of his engraving reproduced here in Figure 11 shows a massive waterwheel turning a three-roller mill. Similar engravings by other artists, such as in Pierre Pomet's *Histoire générale des drogues* given in Figure 12, added tobacco plants in the foreground of the sugar mill for good measure;[80] the two major products of the Americas were linked items of consumption for many Europeans. All these seventeenth-century illustrations of sugar mills have two features in common: the vertical three-roller mills shown are powered either by waterwheel, windmill, or by large teams of oxen, and the process of evaporation is shown, discussed below, as being carried out on multiple-aperture stoves.

By the 1630s use of the three-roller crusher extended beyond Brazil to other sugar colonies in the Atlantic when, with expansion of the sugar industry into Barbados under combined English and Dutch auspices, it was introduced into the Caribbean islands.[81] In the west, vertical crushers were certainly being used also on the Jesuit estates in Peru by the middle of the 1630s.[82] This is not surprising given that the manuscript illustration showing a vertical three-roller crusher in Peru is dated 1613; indeed there is even some suggestion that a vertical-roller mill was in use there as early as 1581.[83]

The independent development of the vertical cane crusher at two ends of the globe within a short period of two to three decades, with such marked visual and functional similarities[84] when those two areas were in well-established contact with each other, seems altogether unlikely. The evidence of the vertical two-roller mill in the Philippines in 1613 at a time when two-roller mills were also known and used in the Americas and its mention in China only after the mid-1630s leads one to query an interpretation positing a Chinese origin for this machinery.[85] To mechanically attribute all inventions to China is problematic; Lynn White's caution is perhaps relevant here, "But while no one

FIGURE 11. Waterwheel-driven three-roller vertical cane crusher, Brazil, ca. 1640, attributed to Barlaeus, detail enlarged and adapted (Reesse, pl. 12).

FIGURE 12. Vertical three-roller cane crusher and sugar boiling house (Pierre Pomet, *Histoire générale des drogues* [1694], p. 94). A channel led the juice directly from the crusher to a vat near the stoves. Reproduced by permission of Special Collections Library, Duke University.

can fail to be filled with admiration for Chinese inventiveness, is it conceivable that our history of technology, in estimating Asia, may still be in bondage to the Jesuit enthusiasms?"[86] The hypothesis explored below is that the vertical-roller cane crusher was an American invention, driven by the logic of sugar production on a massive scale and that its widespread adoption in China in the seventeenth century is a remarkable example of technological adaptation and receptivity to technological change in the agrarian sector.

The likelihood of the vertical-roller cane crushers evolving outside Asia can be better explored by tracing the antecedents of this technical development. Joseph Needham has proposed that the cotton gin and the sugarcane roller mills are based on the same principle of two rollers turning in opposite directions and asserts that the operational principle of these two devices make them "the ancestors of all steel-rolling mills, mangles and paper or textile machinery."[87] Given the tendency for "every new artifact to be based to some degree upon a related existing artifact"[88] and histories of technological continuities that abound in every sector of manufacturing, identifying the connection between the cotton gin and sugar roller mill is relevant here. This nexus is most readily evident in the horizontal-roller mill cane crushers that were in use in some areas prior to the development and widespread use of the vertical-roller sugar mills. These cane crushers commonly operated with two horizontal rollers[89] and were strikingly similar in design to the cotton gin but with an attached trough to direct the cane juice into a bucket. Accepting Needham's insight that the cotton gin was the antecedent to all other roller mills, it stands to reason that such a development would have taken place in an area where there was both cotton manufacture and cane-sugar manufacture. There is a temporal disjuncture, however, when we try to locate the sequence of this development in Asia; the horizontal cane crusher is found rather late in parts of Asia and not at all in China.

Cotton cultivation and cotton technology are of course very ancient in India, and the cotton gin seems to have evolved there around the mid-sixth century A.D.[90] The typical design of the cotton gin from the Indian-culture area consists of two oppositely rotating horizontal rollers engaged by elongated worms placed side by side. But cane crushers with horizontal rollers were noted in India only in a limited area in the northwest and at a much later date than even the seventeenth century when the vertical-roller mills came into use.[91] Elsewhere in Asia, horizontal-roller cane crushers were noted also at a much later date.[92] In Japan, for example, horizontal-roller crushers were noted in use only in the late eighteenth century.[93] Areas in Southeast Asia such as Cambodia had the Indian cotton gin by A.D. 1000.[94] But here, as in the rest of Southeast Asia, besides the mortar and pestle, the only type of sugar mill used seems to have been the vertical two-roller mill.[95]

In China the cotton gin, along with the increase in cotton cultivation, became known during the course of the thirteenth century. The earliest illustration of this gin is found in Wang Zhen's *Nongshu* of 1313[96] (see Figure 13). As we see, the Chinese gin did not have gearing like the Indian version, but instead had a crank handle for each roller. But there is no evidence of a horizontal cane crusher evolving from this gin in China, and efforts to suggest such a development remain conjectural.[97] In fact, given the general preference of Chinese artisans for using a horizontal axis for machinery,[98] the adaptation of the horizontal-roller cotton gin to a vertical-axis cane crusher seems an unlikely modification. The only connection between the cotton gin and the cane crusher in China comes from a source other than its technical genealogy, namely, the generic similarity of the rollers of the vertical sugarcane mill to the cotton gin alluded to in the *Tiangong kaiwu* passage given above. The *Tiangong kaiwu* reflects techniques of manufacture and agriculture in Song Yingxing's own locality of southern China.[99] Given that this was a cotton-growing area, Song's reference to the cotton gin can be read as his way of introducing an unfamiliar piece of equipment by referring to a familiar device. I think this is the most probable explanation for the reference, for there were no other devices in China that operated with similar types of rollers. Unlike Asia, however, elsewhere various types of roller mills including one for crushing cane that resembled the cotton gin had come into use by the sixteenth century.[100]

Cotton was introduced into Spain by the Arabs in the eighth cen-

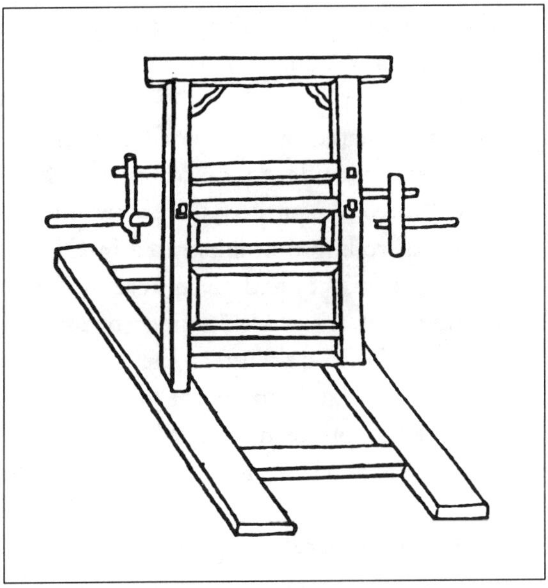

FIGURE 13. Two-roller, crank-handled cotton gin (*Nong-shu* [1313]). The gin was fixed on a ground frame.

tury and spread to France, Flanders, and Germany during the course of the twelfth to fourteenth centuries, where it was used to manufacture fustian, a cloth made with a warp of flax and a woof of cotton.[101] A type of cotton gin consisting of "two wooden rollers fluted with grooves which revolved against each other in opposite directions when turned with a crank" is recorded in use as early as the twelfth century in Italy.[102] In several of these same areas of the Mediterranean, horizontal two-roller cane crushers were used widely *prior* to the development of the vertical-roller mills. All these areas also had extensive textile manufacturing, sometimes with very close connections between the two. The Cornero cartel of Venice, for example, controlled the trade in both sugar and cotton from Cyprus.[103] Along with cane-sugar manufacturing, the horizontal-roller mill first spread to the Canary Islands, and then to Hispaniola and other parts of the Americas in the early sixteenth century. In Mexico it was in use perhaps as early as 1534.[104] It was also used in Brazil and Peru in the early sixteenth century.[105] The absence of any sort of two-roller horizontal mill for crushing cane in China and its limited and late use in Japan and India leads me to suggest that the adaptation of the cotton gin for crushing cane took place outside Asia.

This possibility is furthered by the evidence of the concurrent development of other devices similar to the cotton gin in which the basic design was modified for other purposes, for example, as in the horizontal two-roller metal rolling mill illustrated in Giovanni Agostino Pantheo's *Voarchadumia* of 1530, and given here in Figure 14. George Basalla has suggested that there are "periods of rapid technological change and periods of relative stability" in the history of technological development.[106] The mid-sixteenth to the mid-seventeenth century was certainly a period of rapid technological change in global history, and particularly in Europe. Many new types of technologies evolved during this period including numerous innovations in grinding, pressing, and rolling machinery.[107] Agostino Ramelli (1531–1608), a French military engineer, illustrated and discussed no fewer than 20 designs for grain mills along with 110 water pumps, 14 screwjacks, and 10 cranes among other types of practical devices in his *Le diverse et artificiose machine* (The Various and Ingenious Machines). Published in 1588, the work has been called a "celebration of technological possibility"; designs of Ramelli's mills were copied and elaborated upon by others, including Fausto Veranzio, who devised a portable roller mill for grinding grain.[108] Both Pantheo's rolling mill and Ramelli's iron flour-mills operated on the principle of having the rollers turn in the same direction rather than opposite directions as in the cotton gin and later the vertical three-roller sugar mill. The identifying principle of all these devices, however, was the same; geared rollers encased in a free-standing structure that could be hooked up to a range of sources of motive power. And, as in the Flecknoe account of the two-roller cane crusher in Brazil, many of these new mills in Europe and in the Americas tended to incorporate iron plate into their basic design.

Innovations in the designs of machinery developed in Europe could be swiftly adopted across the Atlantic, for there were hundreds of European artisans in the new colonies. As we see in the illustration of the three-roller cane crusher from Peru (Figure 9), the roughness of

FIGURE 14. Two-roller horizontal metal rolling mill (A. Pantheo, *Voarchadumia contra Alchemiam* [1530]). Reproduced by permission of Special Collections, Lehigh University Information Resources.

the ink sketch of some basic technical details suggests the hand of an artisan rather than that of an artist making a finished drawing for publication. Few areas in the world had a higher concentration of artisans and technicians than Peru in the sixteenth century, where it has been calculated that out of a Spanish population of around 10,000 in 1560, as many as 2,500 were probably artisans.[109] There were also other Europeans—Genoese, Venetians, and Dutch—in Peru; some like the Genoese Rostrán Tujia, a well-known carpenter, made their reputations with the construction of large sugar mills.[110] I suggest that it is perhaps these artisanal connections in Europe and in the Americas and the technical milieu of the sixteenth century in these areas that we must look to for the development of the vertical two-roller and three-roller mills and consider the possibilities of its diffusion to Asia via the Americas.[111]

The possible agents of rapid technological transfer connecting China and the New World in the late sixteenth and early seventeenth century were many, for, along with commodities, people also traveled. The ready availability of Jesuit texts and their own detailed accounts promoting Christian contributions has perhaps led to a disproportionate level of attention being given to the Jesuits as conduits of technological transfer between Europe, Asia, and the Americas.[112] Consequently not only is the eastward route to China from Europe via India better studied than the trans-Pacific connection, the contributions of artisans and merchants in technological transfers is obscured, for there are no written records for them comparable to the Jesuit archives. More relevantly, since the realm of Asian artisans and merchants intersected only infrequently with those involved with the transfer of more formal systems of knowledge such as science and astronomy, mundane technological transfers have seldom been recorded. At another level, however, these two worlds were not quite separate. Commodities like sugar were the *raisons d'être* of so many in the New World that it was inevitable that interests as diverse as Portuguese Jews in Brazil, Jesuits in Peru, and Spanish bishops in the Caribbean were all involved in the development of haciendas, sugar mills, and trade.[113] Technical information could have been transferred via Portuguese and Spanish travelers and missionaries who came to Asia from the Americas after visiting various sugar estates. Several friars from Spain, Portugal, and Italy often took the route used by the Franciscan Friar Martin Ignatius, who traveled due west, from the sugar estates in the Canaries to the sugarcane plantations of Hispaniola, then on to the American mainland, and arrived via the Pacific to the Philippines to reach Fujian and Guangdong in 1584.[114] The Spanish from the Philippines also had a colonial outpost in northern

Taiwan (1626–1642), where the Spanish population, estimated to have been around five hundred, consisted mostly of people who came from the Spanish colonies in the Americas.[115]

Similarly, there were many Chinese traders and artisans who were in regular contact with travelers from the Americas at Macao, Nagasaki, and Manila. Already by 1586 there were more than ten thousand Chinese residing in Manila, and among them were scores of artisans. Martin Ignatius found "many handicrafts men as shoemakers, taylors, goldsmiths, blacksmith and other officers and some merchants."[116] Friar Domingo, bishop of the Philippines, noted in 1590 in a long report to the Spanish king that not only did the Chinese in Manila make "much prettier articles than are made in España, and sometimes so cheap that I am ashamed to mention it" but that "they are so skilful and clever that, as soon as they see any object made by a Spanish workman, they reproduce it with exactness." He went on to note, "They make chairs, bridles, and stirrups of so good a quality and so cheaply that some merchants wish to load a cargo of these articles for Mexico."[117] There was also some traffic the other way; we have already noted that a few Chinese merchants traveled to Acapulco in 1585. There were also at least seven Filipino "ship boys" on board with Captain Sebastian Rodriguez Cermeno in 1595 when the *San Augustin* sailed east across the Pacific and explored San Francisco Bay.[118] "Oriental slaves" were sent to work in the industries and manufacturing crafts in New Spain.[119] And there were more than a few Spanish American merchants from Peru traveling to Manila during the last decades of the sixteenth century and the early decades of the seventeenth.[120] Along with them, new crops were introduced and Aztec words entered the languages of the Philippines. For example, the sweet potato, introduced in the 1570s into Asia, is known by its Aztec name *camotl* in all the languages of the Philippines.[121] Besides the direct Spanish connections, the increase in intra-Asian trade also resulted in many Chinese traveling between the various ports, and some of these traders were also of artisanal backgrounds. For example, a carpenter called Jan Con by the Dutch (probably based on his Cantonese nickname Sumkon) was one of the first Chinese to arrive in Batavia. Working as an intermediary in the Dutch trade with China and on various ventures including sugar manufacturing in Batavia, he traveled several times to and from Batavia to Taiwan and Fujian and back to Southeast Asia in the 1620s and early 1630s.[122] In this environment of trans-Pacific contact, technology, illustrations of machines, and designs of various kinds could be transferred from one shore to the other fairly rapidly, for copying designs was a common enough endeavor in China.

The illustration of the revolving bookcase is a typical example of one such an effort. In 1588, Ramelli had published the design of a revolving bookcase that allowed a scholar to consult several books without getting up from his seat. This was copied in detail in the Chinese illustration down to the books bound in European style in the 1627 Jesuit-sponsored work, the *Qiqi tushou* (Diagrams and Explanations of Wonderful Machines)[123] (see Figures 15 and 16). As we see, the Chinese draftsman valiantly tried to copy even the unfamiliar gear-wheel system in an effort to remain as close as possible to the original design. In the silk and porcelain trades there are other, more successful, examples of Chinese copying manufacturing designs, this time brought from the Americas. In addition to the raw silk from China that had already become the mainstay of the Mexican silk industry by the late sixteenth century, various types of finished silk goods were made in China for the Mexican and Peruvian markets. Ships from Mexico, Peru, Guatemala, and Panama came to Asia loaded with silver to buy large quantities of *ropas de China* in Manila.[124] Chinese manufacturers learned new designs of Western-style clothing expeditiously. They turned out silk stockings (more than 50,000 pairs were carried on one galleon alone!), velvet bodices, and skirts for the wealthy in Lima and Acapulco. They also made vestments and tapestries for the service of hundreds of churches and convents extending from Mexico to Chile.[125] Chinese wood carvings and ivory and lacquer work had notable influence on the art of Spanish America.[126] And, as the Andalusian silk merchants in Spain, fearing the ruin of their business, frequently complained to the king, Mexican and Peruvian traders were taking specimens of Spanish designs of brocades to serve as samples for the Chinese weavers in the 1590s.[127] These complaints obviously did not stop the trade, for by the late seventeenth century, citizens of Mexico were regularly sending as much as 400,000 pesos directly to China for investment.[128] Chinese artisans also efficiently copied wooden samples and sketches given by the traders for manufacturing porcelains for the European market. Salt and pepper cellars, covered mustard pots and butter dishes, brandy cups and wine jugs, were turned out in the hundreds of thousands based on designs provided by the European, mainly Dutch, traders.[129] In 1642, for example, design specifications were included in an order of 192,000 pieces given by the Dutch in Taiwan to a mainland Chinese merchant called "Jousit." The order was delivered promptly five months later and included European-style items which Chinese artisans would have had to learn to make, such as 3,000 covered butter dishes and 2,000 pear-shaped wine jugs.[130] Did somebody like Jan Con adapt the design of a vertical sugarcane crusher based on a Portuguese, Spanish, or Dutch sketch seen in the Philippines?

Some scholars have argued that the new design of the vertical-roller cane crushers was a Chinese innovation by way of inspiration from the Indian cotton gin that was then adapted to use in the Americas, and that its first mention in the Philippines rather than in China is mere coincidence.[131] But the evidence for such an interpretation is missing. A Sinocentric worldview can creep into various reconstructions of history; it cannot be assumed *a priori* that all that was invented or introduced in the Pacific region had its origins in China. The 1613 Spanish-Tagalog dictionary reference from the Philippines reads: "Sugarcane Press; there are two poles (*palo*), the one is fixed and the other goes up and down, and they press the canes there between them; there is another of the same name, which from the Sangleys [Chinese], which the Indios now use, which works like a *noria* [lit. "chain-pump, draw-well"]; it is two logs (*palo*) both toothed together so that one fits solidly into the other."[132] Another entry in the dictionary under the term *palos* indicates that two logs that rotated in opposite directions were used for crushing.[133] In the translated excerpt, we see that the Chinese (Sangleys) and the Filipinos (Indios) were both noted as using the cane crusher. But the Chinese could have been local Chinese, rather

FIGURE 15. Revolving bookcase (Agostino Ramelli, *The Various and Ingenious Machines* [1588], pl. 188). The epicyclic gear train kept the books at the same angle when the book-wheel was rotated. Reproduced by permission of Johns Hopkins University Press.

than Chinese from China. There is no reason to assume otherwise. After all, Filipino-Chinese had been resident in the islands for centuries and were actively involved in various commercial endeavors.[134] Attributing the crusher to the "Sangleys" does not mean that the machinery originated in China, as has been suggested by Daniels.[135]

A Chinese-Filipino artisan could have copied the design of the vertical-roller cane crushers from a Spanish-Peruvian model just as easily as he copied designs of bridles and stirrups. The role of the Philippines in the transfer of silver from the Americas to China has been

FIGURE 16. Revolving bookcase (*Qiqi tushuo* [1627]). The Chinese drawing was copied from the illustration by Ramelli (see Figure 15).

well noted; its role as a transmitter of technologies is as yet understudied. I suggest that given the far broader spectrum of mechanical innovations in milling and grinding devices occurring in the region stretching from Italy to the Netherlands, and the fundamental logic of maximizing both output and labor productivity that governed the sugar plantations in the Americas, these areas were a more likely site for the development of efficient cane crushers than China or India, where no such imperatives existed. Food crops, such as the sweet potato and maize, and commercial crops such as tobacco introduced from the Americas at around the same time were also rapidly adopted in China.[136] This embrace of new methods of manufacture and new crops in the agrarian sector highlights the general climate for technological adaptation and innovation in the seventeenth century. For ultimately, looking beyond the question of the origins of an invention, it is the alacrity with which this new technology of the vertical-roller sugar mill caught on in China that is interesting in historical perspective.

The vertical two-roller cane crusher required less labor than Song and Yuan mills and less fuel since its bagasse could be burned to boil juice. As discussed below, moreover, it could be adapted to use more than one source of motive-power. For all these reasons, it became the preferred type of cane-milling equipment.[137] Although there is one reference from the late eighteenth century that suggests that a horizontal single-roller mill (*gun nian*), an angulated roller of hard wood drawn over layers of cane laid over planks, was used to crush cane,[138] none of the Chinese texts discussing sugar manufacture written after the seventeenth century mention any type of crushing equipment other than the vertical two-roller mill.[139]

In later centuries, there were some modifications in basic design of the vertical two-roller cane crusher in China. Late-eighteenth century travelers found that the rollers were more commonly made of stone rather than hard wood.[140] By the nineteenth century, all the vertical, two-roller sugar mills seemed to have rollers made of granite or other hard stone; Figure 17 illustrates a typical stone-roller cane-crusher. Other parts of the crusher, such as the binding-beam for securing the rollers, continued to be made of wood. Although the crusher was far from a precision instrument and the dimensions of the equipment did not change much over the centuries in China, the stone rollers were always bigger in circumference and heavier than wooden rollers used elsewhere.[141] The iron ingots which served as bearings for the wooden rollers in the Ming design gave way to wooden spindles inserted into the center of each stone roller at the top and bottom. The bed-plate, although sometimes made of wood, was also now made of granite. The gear design was modified on the stone rollers from the oblique cog structure of the late Ming to a simple lug-tooth construction with approximately sixteen teeth to each roller.[142] Wooden cogs were in-

FIGURE 17. Chinese two-roller vertical sugarcane mill, with stone rollers, stone and wooden cogs, and wooden framework (Hommel, p. 113). Reproduced by permission of M.I.T. Press.

serted into holes made in the stone to function as gears for the rollers. This would have made the replacement of worn-down gears far less expensive than if the entire apparatus of the rollers had to be replaced. While there were technological limits in the widespread use of the stone rollers, they nonetheless had some definite advantages over wooden rollers. Stone was far more readily available throughout the southeast than the very hard wood recommended by Song Yingxing. Wooden rollers were susceptible to rot; stone mills could be left exposed to the elements in the off-season and could withstand much more wear and tear. Well-aligned stone rollers, being heavier with greater surface rigidity than wood, would have also served to increase the pressure on the canes crushed. The heavier stone rollers, however, required greater traction power. They required a draft of about three hundred pounds for an average load. To operate these mills, for the twelve-hour workday common during the cane-crushing season in China, teams of four oxen working in shifts were considered optimal although fewer sufficed. The widespread adoption of the vertical two-roller cane crusher, increasing both productivity and speed while reducing wastage of the juice, enabled adequate output for Chinese sugar to become a major item of export in the expanding world market in the seventeenth century. New techniques of refining that had been developing since the fifteenth century added to the quality of the Chinese product.

Ming-Qing Developments in Techniques of Refining

One of the common problems faced by pre-industrial sugar manufacturers everywhere was the large amount of fuel required to boil the cane juice to the necessary consistency for crystallization. In those sugar-producing regions where one furnace was used to boil one cauldron of juice, as in eighteenth-century Cuba, land was often abandoned because deforestation so lengthened the distance between firewood supply and the cane mill that it added significantly to production costs.[143] Chinese methods were far more fuel efficient.[144] The *Tiangong kaiwu* suggests in its section on refining: "The Making of Sugar by Boiling the Juice: Set out three pots in the shape of the character *pin* 品 [i.e., in a triangle]. The syrup that has been [already] thickened is put into one pot, then thin [raw] juice is added to the other two pots."[145] In mid-nineteenth-century Guangdong, a description of the triple boiler—"each of the pans spreading from the center like a clover leaf"—shows Song Yingxing's stove in the shape of *pin* was still being used.[146] The opening for fuel for these stoves was located outside the boiling house.

These multiple-aperture stoves operated on the principle that the cold, raw juice required a higher temperature to come to a boil than the already boiling juice which could be left to simmer on the back of the stove. The first pan, nearest the furnace, would get the juice directly from the tub at the press.[147] The design of this fuel-efficient system for evaporating the cane juice, similar in concept to the traditional Chinese kitchen stove, was a major innovation in sugar manufacturing. Its use, like the vertical-roller mills, seems to have spread

FIGURE 18. Sugar boiling house with multi-aperture stoves and drying room, Brazil, ca. 1640, attributed to Barlaeus, detail enlarged and adapted (Reesse, pl. 12).

world-wide around the same time. As noted above, the mid-seventeenth-century engravings from Brazil and the French Caribbean all show this type of stove. These stoves came to be known as "Dutch ovens."[148] As seen in a segment from the engraving by Barlaeus in Figure 18, stoves with multiple apertures held enormous pans that were boiled simultaneously and the massecuite was then put into conical vessels in an adjacent drying area. The appearance of this stove in cane-sugar manufacturing elsewhere outside China cannot be dated to a period earlier than 1641.[149] The date suggests that it is likely that the multiple-aperture stove was a Dutch introduction into Brazil (hence the nomenclature) from their copying the Chinese stoves used in Java and Taiwan. Later American developments, such as the Jamaican train, where a series of pans, sometimes as many as ten or fifteen set in a straight line, were similarly common to both China and India in sugar manufacturing, and this design too may have been an introduction to the Americas from Asia.[150]

The other hurdle faced by sugar producers worldwide was to make the sugar as white as possible. A preference for white sugar as the purest and most desirable product had developed quite early among most consumers, for, as the purer product, it was also the most durable. Prior to the late sixteenth century, white sugar had been derived literally by "*re*fining." After the sucrose crystals first formed, they were remelted in water, then boiled, reclarified, and recrystallized. As in the case of salt manufacturing, in which a similar technique was used, repeated dissolving, reboiling, and recrystallizing produced a higher-grade and whiter product. The Chinese producers used the standard method but with some additions; the 1503 gazetteer of Xinghua county in Fujian recorded:

> White Sugar: Take well-dried granulated sugar and place in a large cauldron and boil. Putting in ducks eggs, with the white and yolk beaten together, will cause the scum to float to the top of the liquid. With a wire skimmer remove [the scum] and clean out [the syrup]. Watch that the fire is adequate. Use two vessels, an upper and a lower, one on top of the other. The upper one is called "the chamber" the lower one the "pot."[151] The bottom of the "chamber" tapers and has a hole. The "pot" is empty and on the ground. Using straw cork up the hole [in the upper chamber]. Take the boiled sugar syrup and place it in the chamber and stir it while it is still warm. Then let cool. The sugar will crystallize. The molasses (*tang you*) will fall into the pot.[152]

Although the Chinese methods were similar to those used by contemporary Europeans, this technique was certainly arrived at independently, for this reference predates the arrival of the Portuguese in East Asia by over a decade. The specific procedures followed to make refined sugar by the great sugar houses of Venice and Bologna in the fifteenth century were considered "trade secrets" and so were not written down.[153] But it is known that as in China, they were also produced by this process of repeated boilings.[154] Refining was commonly used also to grade the sugar. As Wang Shimao, describing sugar manufacturing in Fujian in his *Min bu shu* (Annals of Fujian) in 1580 writes, "red sugar" reboiled once was known as "white sugar" (*baitang*); when this white sugar was reboiled and refined again, it was known as "crystal sugar" or sugar candy (*bingtang*).[155] This method of repeated refining, however, was both time-consuming and extremely labor-intensive; only relatively small batches could be reprocessed. The technique of "claying" or "bleaching" sugar on the other hand, introduced in the sixteenth century, could produce white sugar in far larger quantities.

The various procedures for whitening sugar by claying and washing that developed were all based on the fact that impurities such as the molasses coating the crystals and giving the sugar a brown or black tinge are far more readily soluble in water than the harder core of sugar crystals. But too much water would dissolve the sugar crystals before they had fully formed; so it was necessary to have minuscule amounts of water trickle through, slowly dissolving only the surface material on the crystals; the process came to be called "washing." One of the common ways in which small amounts of water can be made to percolate slowly through the crystals is to cover the top of the drying massecuite in a drainage vessel with a moist layer that will slowly release water. Aquatic weeds and wet rags were used in many areas for this purpose. The sugar crystals immediately below the layer of weeds or rag would be "washed," and the molasses would trickle down with the water. Then, the topmost layer of crystals would be removed and set out to dry in the sun. The moistened weeds or rags would then be reapplied to the next layer of crystals in the drainage vessel. This was a widespread process in many parts of Asia even in the nineteenth century,[156] but it was also extremely slow and laborious and produced only a very small quantity of washed sugar crystals each time. In contrast, starting with fifteenth century, the Chinese began using a fine paste of clay that not only "washed" the crystals, but utilized the absorbent properties of clay.[157]

The first readily available Chinese depiction of claying dates from the early decades of the sixteenth century; a detailed description is given in the *Guangyang zaji* (Miscellaneous Notes from Far and Wide), a collection of essays and jottings of Liu Xianting (1648–1695), who cites this report as the work of a scholar from the sixteenth century:[158]

Before the Jiajing period [1522–1566] there was no white sugar in the world. All that was boiled [made] by the people of Fujian was black sugar. [This is literary license for, as noted, refined sugar was produced in Fujian at this time.] During the Jiajing period, a roofing tile accidentally fell into the draining jar of a sugar-making household. It was seen that, unlike the usual, the color of the sugar on top was white as snow and the taste sweet and good. The middle [section] had yellow sugar and the bottom, black sugar. It was extraordinary. From then on, clay has been pressed onto sugar hundreds of times without failure. White sugar has been seen in the world since then.[159]

Accidents aside, how this method of claying was discovered is unclear. Like this Chinese report, other references to the discovery of claying are also anecdotal. European sources from this period on the invention of claying are equally fanciful. The earliest such story is from the natural history of Mexico by Francisco Hernandez de Toledo, written in 1577, and tells of a hen with damp earth on its feet walking over mounds of drying sugar and behold, the sugar turned white; people were thus alerted to the potential of claying sugar![160] By the seventeenth century the process had been standardized. Song Yingxing suggests using "yellow mud water" (*huang ni shui*) for claying, although presumably any type of fine clay might have sufficed, for later observers noted clay from the bottom of ponds and canals that had a high proportion of calcium (from the shells of snails in these canals) being used for the same purpose.[161] The massecuite was first poured into barrels. After it reached a semi-crystallized stage and dark granules had formed, the sugar was placed in specially designed drainage vessels, as we see in the Ming drawing in Figure 19:

Then place over a large vat an earthenware drainer (potters can be instructed to make them) which is wide at the top and tapering at the bottom [i.e., a funnel shape]. At the bottom [of the conical drainer], there is a small hole plugged with straw. The dark granules are poured into it. When the dark granules have crystallized and settled, the straw plug is then removed from the hole and yellow-mud water is applied and allowed to drip through it. The black dregs [i.e., the impurities] run off into the vat and only white crystallized sugar is left in the drainer. The topmost layer is about five inches thick, is extremely pure and white and is often called "foreign sugar" (because sugar from the Western Oceans is so absolutely white and excellent). The color of the layer below this is somewhat yellowish brown.[162]

FIGURE 19. Refining crystallized sugar with yellow-mud water (*Tiangong kaiwu* [1637]). The conical shape of the vats is exaggerated in the drawing; if the top had indeed been so much broader than the bottom, the vats would have been unstable when full.

Song Yingxing does not clearly indicate the proportion of clay and water used nor the size of the jars.[163] Later, a fairly standard measure used throughout China was based on variations of the picul, and each jar contained between 133 and 200 pounds avoirdupois of massecuite.[164] After claying, the top 5 percent of sugar was labeled the highest grade of white sugar; the second layer, consisting of approximately 15 percent of the sugar, fell into the next grade and so on, down to the very dark sugar at the bottom; about 30 percent of the massecuite drained out as molasses. The more efficient techniques of draining also abbreviated the time spent for crystallization. Although Song Yingxing does not specify the time needed for the entire process of crystallization, it probably took 30–40 days as noted in later studies,[165] a substantial reduction from the five-odd months spent waiting for the sugar to crystallize in the Song.

Higher-quality white sugar was produced primarily for the export market and the more exclusive domestic market such as the imperial larder. Had Song Yingxing seen "Western sugar" as his comment suggests and used it to establish the standard? It is difficult to tell; writers following Song Yingxing began to use the term "foreign sugar" (*yangtang*) to indicate sugar intended for export to the West. Qu Dajun was to write at the end of the seventeenth century, "The whitest sugar is that which is dried in the sun, it is as fine as powdered snow. It is sent both to the Eastern Oceans and the Western Oceans. It is called foreign sugar (*yangtang*)."[166]

These processes of claying and refining developed in the seventeenth century generally continued in use into the twentieth to produce white crystallized sugar. But a soft sugar was also popular for domestic consumption. A method reminiscent of the technique used in ninth-century Dunhuang was still in use in Shantou, southeastern Guangdong, where the Reverend John Scarth noticed in the 1870s:

> Now comes the Herculean work of our strong friend. . . . He seizes a spade-like implement, and bending over the hot mass of syrup, begins to spread it about and mix it in all directions. As it cools it thickens; his work gets harder and harder; over the side, up the middle and down again, backwards and forwards he works the stiffening sugar until it loses its liquid state. Then he takes up a short piece of wood with two upright handles; holding these he commences to rub over the sugar hard, very hard. You see the labor by the working of his muscles. Gradually the stiff mass assumes a sand-like appearance, its colour gets lighter and lighter; and within an hour of its being merely sap in the cane, the juice is expressed, boiled, cooled and made into sugar,—real Muscovado.[167]

The soft muscovado sugar was then refined and dried and bleached in the sun to produce "white sugar." A similar method of producing soft, light-colored sugar was also used in India and in other parts of Asia.

In practical terms, the vertical two-roller cane crusher represented a substantial saving of labor power and time over the Song technology while still enabling large amounts of sugar to be processed. The cane was now crushed directly and did not have to be peeled, chopped, steamed, and so forth. The late-Ming and Qing techniques were more fuel-efficient; the strips of cane bagasse provided the main fuel. Two people could operate the crusher and extract the juice, compared with the ten or twenty people needed in the Song to carry out crushing. Overall, only one large piece of machinery was now needed instead of the several types of wooden presses, crushers, benches, and knives. Qing developments, such as the use of stone for the rollers, meant that the machinery probably lasted a lot longer than the wooden version.[168] Did the Qing techniques of crushing cane and processing sugar then represent the limits of premodern technology?

Social Parameters and Technological Development

In broad outline the history of Chinese cane-sugar manufacturing can be summed up as:

1. The gradual introduction of the plant and its products, culminating in an era of Indic influences in techniques of cane crushing during the eighth and ninth centuries, as evidenced by the Dunhuang manuscript fragment.

2. An increased interest in sugar manufacture, reflecting urban demands, and elaboration of methods of extraction similar to those used for oil extraction in major sugar-producing regions by the twelfth century. Major new developments in techniques of crystallizing and refining leading to the manufacture of crystallized sugar.

3. Further developments in crushing and particularly the refining of sugar from the thirteenth to sixteenth centuries. The pedal-tilt hammer was also used for crushing cane, although this type of crushing probably coexisted with the use of the more elaborate machinery used in the eleventh and twelfth centuries. Developments in the process of crystallization included the use of specially designed drainage vessels by the fourteenth century and the manufacture of refined sugar and clayed sugar by the fifteenth century.

4. A period of major developments in Chinese sugar manufacturing both in the machinery used for crushing and in the techniques of processing occurring in the late-sixteenth and early-seventeenth centuries. Primary among these developments were the use of the vertical

two-roller cane crusher and the widespread adoption of techniques of clarifying and claying sugar.

Within the limits of pre-industrial technology, there were three aspects of manufacture that could have been improved: more efficient grinding devices that extracted a higher percentage of the juice from the cane, the speeding up of the processes of crystallizing and drying the sugar, and the use of motive power that could be maintained at a lower cost than teams of oxen, permitting the mills to operate longer hours while turning the rollers faster.

Neither type of crusher, the three-roller versions used in the Americas nor the two-roller models used in China, extracted cane juice very efficiently. In both types of mills, the pressure and resistance of the canes pushed the rollers out of alignment and affected the mill's productive output. But the wooden three-roller crusher found throughout the Caribbean and in Brazil, Peru, and Mexico still had some advantages over China's two-roller stone devices. At first pressing, the former could recover 30–35 percent of the weight of the cane in the form of juice, as opposed to the Chinese average of 20–30 percent. In contrast to stone, moreover, wood allowed for the insertion of wedges and adjustment of the distance between rollers so that a second pressing was more effective in obtaining additional juice.[169] In China, only extra labor could improve results; but even when the cane was passed through the rollers two or three times, no less than 25–40 percent of the juice in the canes was still lost.[170] Moreover, the three-roller crusher was faster. The cane could be passed between rollers one and two and returned immediately between rollers two and three by having two workers stand on either side of the mill. In some areas of the Americas, a *doubleuse* or "dumb-returner" was later attached to the vertical three-roller crusher. This was a curved metal plate positioned along one side of the rollers that automatically pushed the cane back in for a second crushing. This gadget freed up the labor of one or two slaves, and in addition a faster pace was achieved by processing mechanically rather than manually.[171]

The common use of stone rollers for the vertical mill in China also created several problems. Although iron was widely used in the agricultural sector in China, the shift to stone rollers eliminated the possibility of using iron bearings, as was evidently done in the Ming. Hard granite rollers were more durable, but the combination of wood and stone also caused the wooden parts, such as the binding beam and the spindles at the base of the rollers, to wear out rapidly with the friction between stone and wood.[172] This meant that the distance between the rollers and the pressure exerted on the cane varied and had to be corrected constantly for efficient crushing. Awkward and heavy, the stone rollers were difficult to align, as is visible in the photograph given in Figure 17 above.[173]

Another limitation of pre-industrial technology was the time it took for the sugar to crystallize naturally. Squeezing out the molasses by placing the massecuite in bags of coarse sack cloth with weights on top (common in India) and stirring the sugar with large paddles (as in China) were efforts to speed up the process of separation.[174] Only small batches in particular areas, however, could be processed in this manner. The bulk of the sugar produced was simply set out to drain in the conical jars typically for 30–40 days in the cool but damp winter months following the harvest in south China. The whole process of draining and drying was repeated to refine and produce clayed white sugar and all manufacture including claying and refining was carried out where the sugarcane was crushed. Even within the same village different grades of sugar of uneven quality were produced.[175] As early as the fifteenth century, by contrast, European manufacturers speeded up processing and ensured quality control by centralizing the process of refining.

The great merchant houses of Venice—the Cornaro and Martini—were among the earliest to develop centralized refineries. Raw sugar (muscavado) produced on a number of estates was brought to a single location for the express purpose of manufacturing white sugar, the volume of raw sugar brought in making it economical to refine large amounts simultaneously. In 1449, Pietro Casola, an Italian clergyman traveling to Jerusalem, noted on the Cornaro and the Martini estates in Cyprus:

> I can only speak of a great farm not far from Limasol, which belongs to a certain Don Federico Cornaro, a patrician of Venice, and is called Episcopia where they make so much sugar, that, in my judgement, it should suffice for

all the world. Indeed it is said to be the best which goes to Venice, and the quantity sold is always increasing. It seems to me that no one ought ever to die there [from starvation]. It was very interesting to see how they make sugar both the fine and the coarse and so many people at work. There were not less than four hundred persons there, all employed some in one way, some in another. It was interesting too, to see such a number of utensils; it was like another world to me. There were cauldrons of such a size that if I described them no one would believe me. One of the factors of the aforesaid Don Federico told me that every man was paid every Saturday.[176]

Cornaro and Martini muscavado was also sent to Venice for refining and marketing. Bologna also had similar refineries in the fifteenth century. These Venetian and Bolognese sugar refineries were the predecessors of the Belgian and Dutch refineries at Antwerp and Amsterdam, when the sugar trade moved from the Mediterranean to the Atlantic seaboard.[177] The Dutch further hastened the refining process by constructing "drying rooms." Loaves of crystallized sugar (formed in cones) were taken out after only eight to ten days of drying, put on trays, and dried in multistoried structures. A coal fire was built to heat all the various levels of the buildings simultaneously to a temperature of 114°F. The sugar would be fully dried in just five to seven days.[178] The genesis of these refineries lay not just in the cooler climate of Europe, which necessitated the use of additional heat to evaporate the sugar, but in the quantity of sugar processed and the centralization of manufacture. The Dutch refineries were a product of the economies of scale and a reflection of the underlying differences in the imperatives of manufacture between China and the Netherlands.

Quality control was more feasible in centralized operations. Since the "sugar master" (a specialist who determined that the sugar had been boiled to the correct consistency) kept records of how much refined sugar was manufactured from a particular batch of raw sugar purchased by the refinery, and the consistency at which the sugar was to be removed from the fire, procedures for both stages of manufacture became standardized. The employment of managerial staff to oversee production made it possible for the Cornaros to control both quality and quantity, to make sure each estate delivered the cane on time, and schedule sales on the market. The same logic applied in the

American plantations, where even in not particularly efficient centers of production such as Martinique, drying ovens were constructed to hasten the process.[179] Sugar was an annual crop harvested in December in south China, when freezing temperatures are common, and the weather is cool and rainy through much of January, February, and March; so any type of slow heating would have aided the evaporation here as well. But the structure of Chinese manufacturing remained decentralized and the imperatives of standardization of product, economies of scale, and speed of manufacture driving sugar manufacture elsewhere did not apply.

This divergence is most clearly visible when we look at the sources of power used to drive the sugar mills, for in many ways the most fundamental limitation of all pre-industrial technology was motive power. The source of power used for turning the cane crushers was the final determinant of the production capabilities of a particular mill. Animate power—human or animal—is ultimately limited and renewable only at considerable costs of feeding and resting. Both volume of production and work intensity are determined by the amount of motive power available.

In the Americas the largest portion in the initial expenses of setting up a sugar hacienda was the cost of slaves. But close to that was the cost of teams of oxen. In one Jesuit estate in Peru set up in 1632–1634, for example, initial expenses included 97 slaves and 60 pairs of oxen to operate a sugar hacienda with six edge-runner mills.[180] Enormous teams of oxen were used in many places such as Cuba (where cattle ranchers were involved in expanding the sugar industry in the late eighteenth century), and as many as fifty and eighty yokes of oxen were used. In Brazil, twenty percent of the mills used water-power with animal-pack backups, and water-driven mills and windmills played an increasingly important role in the eighteenth and early nineteenth centuries.[181] In China, one ox, or at most small teams of two to four oxen, formed the sole means of power. The Ming illustration in the *Tiangong kaiwu* (see Figure 2) shows only one ox. Qu Dajun, writing in the late seventeenth century, describes teams of three oxen being used for operating cane crushers.[182] A description of cane crushing in 1724 from Taiwan notes the use of four oxen,[183] although another contemporary illustration from Taiwan (see Figure 28 in Chapter 5) shows a team of only two oxen. In the non-pastoral economy of south China, using sizable teams of oxen or buffaloes was not a feasible option.[184] But water power was.[185]

The difference between a water-powered mill and one powered by animals is significant. In Hispaniola where Spanish American entrepreneurs experimented with a horizontal two-roller cane crusher in 1515, engineers calculated that the mill could produce 125 tons of sugar if water-powered and perhaps a third of that tonnage if powered by animals.[186] Others have calculated an even greater difference in output and suggested that three-roller vertical crushers hooked up to a water mill could crush twice the amount of cane in the same period of time as an ox-driven mill of identical design. In Brazil, the sugarcane plantation owners who leased land based their calculations of how much cane a mill could grind in a twenty-four-hour period—the standard calculation was 20–35 cartloads of cane for a mill driven by oxen, and 40–50 cartloads for one driven by water-power.[187] However, no known attempts were made in China to use water power to crush cane in the major sugarcane growing regions of Guangdong, Taiwan, or Fujian. Yet it was used for just this purpose in neighboring Ryukyus and then in Japan.

Owing to extensive contact with Fujian in the Song and the Ming, sugarcane cultivation had been introduced to the Ryukyus perhaps as early as the fifteenth century.[188] In 1534 a Chinese official noted it was grown on Okinawa, the principal island of the Ryukyus; sugar manufacturing and refining had started there by 1623.[189] The cane crusher used at this time was a vertical two-roller model, similar to the Chinese version, and is thought to have been introduced from Fujian.[190] As we have seen, however, the vertical two-roller model does not seem to have been common in China as yet; so it could have been an introduction directly from the Philippines given Ryukyuan trade links with southeast Asia. And unlike China, economic and sociopolitical changes of the seventeenth century were to give sugar such a unique importance in the Ryukyus that they were to foster yet other changes in the technology of manufacture.

The Ryukyuan economy had become closely linked to the Japanese economy via Satsuma *han*. The five northern islands of the Amami chain adjacent to the Ryukyus had long had a vassalage relationship with the Ryukyuan kingdom; they were occupied by Satsuma in 1609 ostensibly to punish the Ryukyuan king for disrespect to the Tokugawa shogunate.[191] The Ryukyuan kingdom was allowed to retain a fictitious independence so that the Satsuma's immensely profitable trade with China could be continued under the guise of Ryukyuan missions bypassing Bakufu restrictions.[192] The status of the Ryukyus itself became that of a vassal state with an annual tribute to be paid to the Shimazu lords of Satsuma. Sugar was regularly sent by the Ryukyus to Satsuma and was substituted for one-third of the 20,000-*koku* rice tribute.[193] The demand for Ryukyuan sugar in Japan was significant enough for the Bakufu to permit Satsuma in 1655 to buy additional sugar from the Ryukyus with its locally minted copper coins called "Ryukyu *tsūhō*."[194] On an average, Satsuma began importing between 700,000 and 800,000 *jin* (around a million pounds) of Ryukyuan brown sugar each year throughout the seventeenth century.[195]

The Ryukyuan government found sugar to be a highly profitable source for raising revenues in the new economic arrangements that followed the conquest by Satsuma. The kingdom had run up tremendous debts to Satsuma in the course of fitting out ships for the trade-and-tribute missions to Ming, and then Qing, China. Centralized control of sugar prices was used by the kingdom to repay the thousands of *kan* that it owed.[196] Sugar had become much too valuable a commodity to be left in private hands; in 1646 it was made a government monopoly. In 1662 all production was put under the agency of the *satō-za* (sugar guild).[197] The government began providing the producers with iron tools, refining pans, and other necessary equipment to increase output. These arrangements between the Ryukyus and Satsuma became yet more important when the Ryukyus were exempted from the trade restrictions imposed by the Bakufu in 1717, which specified the quantities of sugar that could be imported by the Chinese, Siamese, and Dutch in Nagasaki. Throughout the eighteenth century, and for most of the nineteenth, Satsuma's control over the Ryukyuan sugar manufacturing intensified; the increased productivity of the Ryukyuan industry is also evident; the Ryukyus provided 5 to 6 million *jin* (about 6.5–7.9 million pounds) to Japan by the Tempō period (1830–1844).[198]

The overwhelming importance of sugar in the Ryukyuan economy led to a series of technological innovations. Although the two-roller cane crusher was already in use, Makiya Sanekiyo (dates unknown) of Shuri apparently developed a vertical three-roller crusher in 1671; earlier we have noted the difference in output between the two types of crushers.[199] Experiments with sugarcane cultivation and processing were, however, not unique and occurred alongside other technical developments encouraged by the Ryukyuan authorities. Sai On (1682–1763), an eminent scholar-statesman and advisor to the Ryukyuan king, for example, not only was interested in cane culture but also ordered Ryukyuan scholars to construct a telescope and an observatory and was interested in promoting Rangaku (Dutch studies) then developing in contemporary Japan.[200] During this period, new irrigation and land reclamation projects were undertaken in the Ryukyus, and agricultural inspectors assigned to each district office to encourage the cultivation of cane, sweet potatoes, tea, and abaca (*musa textilis*), a fiber-producing plant.

Sugarcane cultivation did not become part of an exclusive slave-labor-based plantation culture in either the Ryukyus or in Amami, as it had in the Americas. But intensified cultivation and manufacture nonetheless were subjected to similar demands of a colonial power, particularly in the Amami islands. Sugarcane cultivation had been introduced here from the Ryukyus in the seventeenth century, and a sugarcane inspector (*kibi kenja*) was appointed by Satsuma in 1695 on the two main islands followed by various other systems of oversight in the eighteenth century that further strengthened Satsuma's control over sugar production in the Amami islands.[201] Taxes payable in grain or beans were commuted to sugar in 1745.[202] The pressure to grind more cane may have led to the innovation of 1717 when an official from the Ryukyus, Tabata Sabuni (1678–1764), successfully connected the three-roller crusher to a waterwheel.[203] By the 1830s the island of Oshima was providing 6 to 7 million *jin* (about 8–9 million pounds) of sugar to Japan.[204] The Ryukyuan and Amami responses to the accelerating demand for sugar, although forced upon them, transformed the local organization of sugar production. Furthermore, the importance of sugar in the economy encouraged innovation and adoption of more efficient production technologies. Most relevantly, as we see below, the water-mill-operated three-roller cane crusher was an innovation that adapted existing technology long used for driving water mills in both China and Japan.[205]

There was also considerable interest in official circles in sugar manufacturing in Japan, for the drain of silver to pay for the imports was a concern of the shogunate. In the 1720s, Shogun Tokugawa Yoshimune (r. 1716–1745, d. 1751) ordered cane seedlings from the Ryukyus and distributed them in various parts of southwest Japan such as the Bōsō Peninsula in the Kantō and Kyushu as well as in the Tokugawa lands. Like Tokugawa Mitsukuni (1628–1700) before him and his contemporary Sai On in the Ryukyus, Yoshimune's sponsorship of sugar manufacturing was part of a range of elite interests in technical matters, including the collection of plant samples, books and information on agriculture, technology, medicine, military strategy, and so on.[206] Magistrates at Nagasaki were directed to order Chinese traders to bring in agricultural treatises and seedlings of various plants and crops and find people who had information about their cultivation and manufacture. Yoshimune personally experimented with manufacturing of brown sugar on his estate near Edo Castle; his enthusiasm for expanding sugarcane cultivation led to detailed discussions in 1727 with a knowledgeable Fujianese captain of a junk from Xiamen, who apparently gave information on the mechanics of sugar manufacturing.[207] The project was so successful that within a couple of decades of the introduction of cane into the Tokugawa fiefdom of Owari, sweetmeat shops using local sugar could be found in Nagoya.[208] Yoshimune took such an active interest in sugar manufacturing that it received special mention in his official biography.

The earliest types of cane crushers used in Japan were two-roller models similar to the Chinese design. Hiraga Gennai (1728–1779), the Japanese botanist, wrote the first history of sugar-making in Japan as a supplement to his *Butsurui hinshitsu* (The Identification and Classification of All Matter) in 1763. He drew his information from the *Tangshuang pu* and the *Tiangong kaiwu* and suggested these as models.[209] There were several other individuals such as Ikegami Tarōzaemon (1718–1798) and Tamura Genyū (1718–1776) who were also experimenting with cultivating cane and making sugar candy.[210] As cane cultivation and manufacture spread in Japan, different types of cane crushers were used, depending most probably upon the amount of cane to be crushed, and these ranged from using the edge-runner mill to the vertical two-roller mills.[211] During the second half of the eighteenth century a three-roller mill was also introduced here. Illustrated in a 1797 text on sugar manufacturing, *Satō seikakuki* (Notes on Sugarmaking) by Kimura Yoshiyuki, it is reproduced in Figure 20.[212] As we see in Figure 20, this mill was operated by water power, although other illustrations in the same text show the three-roller crusher being turned by human labor.[213] There is no reference to a vertical two-roller mill in this text, which sought to be comprehensive and included various mills including the first illustration of a horizontal two-roller crusher in Japan.[214] This suggests that in the thirty-odd years that had passed between the writing of the *Butsurui hinshitsu* and the *Satō seikakuki*, the three-roller model had already replaced the vertical two-roller crushers as the standard design. The source of the vertical three-roller model in Japan could have been the Ryukyus; this has been the accepted interpretation.[215] But there is also a possibility that the design of the three-roller cane crusher marked an independent introduction into Asia from the Americas in both places, but this time by either the Dutch or the English rather than the Spanish.

This hypothesis is prompted by the design of the crushers, the existence of possible avenues of introduction, and the comments of contemporaries. The *Kansha ki* (An Account of Sugarcane, 1764), a manuscript by Gotō Rishun (1696–1771) with a preface written by the physician to the shogun attesting to the high standing of the author, describes the Japanese three-roller crusher in detail.[216] Gotō notes that the three rollers of the crusher are set in a line, and are 23.8 inches high with a diameter of 17.9 inches. These rollers were distinctively more slender than the average Chinese versions; the *Tiangong kaiwu*

FIGURE 20. Waterwheel-driven twin vertical three-roller cane crushers from Japan (*Satō seikakuki* [1797]). The drawing suggests the rollers were made of stone to which wooden collars with cogs were attached. Courtesy Library, University of California, Berkeley.

described the circumference of the rollers as being 27 inches, and the later stone models were larger still.[217] On the other hand, very slender rollers were commonly used in the Americas. Besides the illustration from Peru (see Figure 9), rollers as slender as 15–18 inches were, for example, noted on sugar mills in Martinique in 1696.[218] The design of the vertical three-roller crusher, with the rollers turning in a counter-clockwise direction,[219] also suggests an American connection, where this was the typical design.

The enthusiasm for Dutch learning at the Ryukyuan court could have provided a channel for the introduction of various mundane technologies. The Ryukyuan tribute missions to the Chinese included elites who were interested in learning about various types of technology and manufacture; several of them are credited with numerous introductions.[220] During these missions the Ryukyuans came into contact with many others besides the Chinese, including the Dutch and the English from whom they bought goods. In 1683, for example,

Satsuma was reprimanded by the Tokugawa bakufu for selling in Osaka and Kyoto certain commodities acquired in the Ryukyus; the articles in question were plaids, tartans, and other woolen goods that were being labeled "Ryukyuan items."[221] These contacts could have been the source of technical information. Finally, contemporaries in Japan also thought that the three-roller crusher was a Dutch introduction. In his preface to the *Satō seikakuki*, Kimura Yoshiyuki, for example, attributed the introduction of the new three-roller mill to Yasuda Tai (dates unknown) and credited him with learning this from the Dutch at Nagasaki and bringing it back to Kii (Wakayama).[222] Although Higuchi Hiroshi's caution that there was a tendency to label all new technology from Nagasaki as "Dutch" is perhaps well-taken,[223] given that all other models of cane crushers used at this time in China, India, and Southeast Asia were similar to the Filipino-Chinese model of two rollers, it is likely the three-roller cane crusher marked a distinct phase of technical introduction from the Americas by the Dutch to the northeastern Asia. And in Japan, as in Oshima-Amami, the concept of using water-power to drive the mills followed closely on the heels of the introduction of the three-roller crusher.

As Figure 20 shows, two sets of three-roller cane crushers with right-angle gearing were hooked up to a waterwheel and operated simultaneously. Given the higher output of water-driven mills, the three-roller mills in Oshima-Amami or Japan had the capacity to extract, on an average, 10–15 percent more juice per cane crusher operated than existing Chinese models and extract twice the amount of juice in a given span of time.[224] Why, despite demands of a dynamic international market to which China was linked, did the Chinese apparently make little attempt to utilize readily available technology and water-power, which would have further promoted the output of cane crushers? The radical improvements in the design of cane crushers and refining techniques in seventeenth-century China went only so far and no further.

The potential improvements certainly did not represent a technological barrier requiring invention, for none of the technology used to operate hydraulic sugar mills in Japan and Amami, for instance, was

FIGURE 21. Square-pallet chain pump (*Tiangong kaiwu* [1637]), with horizontal waterwheel and right-angle gearing. Also illustrated in the *Nongshu* (1313).

alien to China. The use of water-mills had, in fact, initially spread to these areas from China in the seventh century.[225] Using water-power to drive a variety of machinery from hydraulic trip-hammers to water-driven quern mills was common in China from the Han period on.[226] The right-angle gearing used to operate the Japanese crusher was conceptually quite similar to the Chinese use of gearing in chain pumps worked by horizontal waterwheels.[227] The square-pallet chain pump given in Figure 21, and illustrated in both Wang Zhen's *Nongshu* of 1313 and Song Yingxing's *Tiangong kaiwu*, shows that right-angle gearing technology was very well developed. Similarly, the *lianmo* or geared, animal-driven milling plant as illustrated in Figure 22 shows

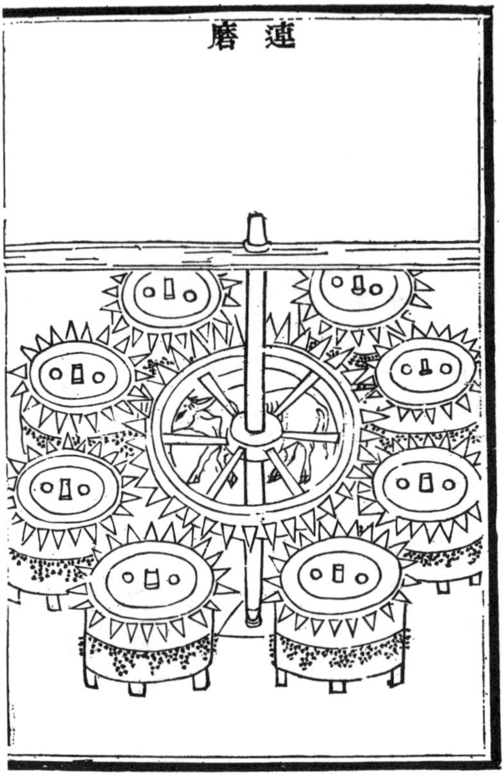

FIGURE 22. Geared, animal-driven multiple mill (*Nongshu* [1313]). A central whim wheel operated the eight grinders.

that the concept of a right-angle gear-drive to operate multiple grinders was also known in China. The use of water-powered mills for grinding and pounding was quite common in the late Ming. According to Song Yingxing, water-powered tilt-hammer mills (*shui dui*) were used extensively in the mountainous regions of Jiangxi for pounding rice. There were even multipurpose water mills that could simultaneously work a flour mill, operate a mill for polishing rice, and draw water (like a noria) to irrigate rice fields.[228] In mountainous regions where limited grazing lands produced few draft animals, water power was used for all sorts of grinding;[229] water-powered mills were also used in many areas besides the mountains and highlands in China. Wang Shimou commented that water-powered trip-hammers were most common in Fujian and noted that those manufacturing paper often used trip-hammer mills mounted on boats (ship-mills) that were moored midstream and were driven by the flowing currents of rivers and streams.[230] Known as *huofa mo* (movable-method mills, lit. "live mills") and *wei chuan* (mill ships), these portable devices did not need permanent structures or any special structural modifications for their operation on land.[231] In the same areas as sugar manufacturing, porcelain factories in Guangdong used water-driven trip-hammer mills to pulverize clay.[232] Additionally, Hommel recorded several examples of water mills used for polishing rice and grinding grain in twentieth-century Zhejiang.[233]

There is one common characteristic found in all these examples from China; the water-powered mills were used in enterprises that were either separated from peasant production (for example, paper and porcelain manufacturing) or linked to perennial endeavors such as rice polishing and flour mills. Did the decentralized, seasonal aspect of sugar manufacturing in south China, which was located within peasant households, set limits to technological developments and adaptations? Perhaps a brief investigation of other sectors of manufacturing that were considered supplementary sources of income in the agricultural sector such as spinning and weaving can help us ascertain whether this selection of particular technologies was unique to sugar manufacturing or whether the logic of selection represented a general pattern evident in other sectors of rural China.

Conclusion: Technological Selection in a Small-Producer Economy

Cotton, ramie, and silk textiles were among the primary commodities of the great commercial development that began in the late Ming and accelerated with the expansion of the world market. Silk manufacturing, with its close links to meeting the demands of the state, imperial household, and the urban elite, was an atypical handicraft manufacturing sector. Since the Song period silk manufacturing had become separated into two fairly distinct spheres. Sericulture and reeling remained located in peasant households, while weaving the finer, multi-colored, and textured textiles was a specialized and centralized enterprise frequently located in imperial workshops in urban centers.[234] Consequently, many aspects of silk manufacturing were distinct from the technological parameters of rural manufacturing. By contrast, cotton and ramie cloth were produced entirely within peasant households. Here we can further examine the potential constraints of small-scale manufacture.[235]

Although cotton (*Gossypium herbaceum*) has a long history of cultivation in China dating back to the second century,[236] there was a rapid expansion of cultivation in China during the twelfth and thirteenth centuries. Initially a hand-operated cotton gin was used to separate the fiber from the seeds; the balls of cotton were rolled under a single, small iron or wooden roller. Slow and laborious, the process was only marginally more efficient than picking the seeds out by hand.[237] Sometime between 1295 and 1313, the ginning frame (*jiaoche*), illustrated in Figure 13 above, was developed.[238] This was the cotton gin that is thought to have led to the design of the two-roller cane crusher. While far more efficient, it was comparatively labor-intensive for a basic device. Three people were required to operate it. One person had to feed in unginned cotton while the two others turned the two crank-handles. By 1628, however, when the *Nongzheng quanshu* was composed by Xu, in addition to the three-person-operated *jiaoche*, a small foot-treadle-operated gin (*yache*) that could be operated by one person had come into use. It is supposed to have been developed in Jiangsu and became quite common in all the provinces.[239] As we see in Figure 23, the person operating the gin would have turned one roller with the right hand, used a treadle to move the other roller, and fed the unginned cotton in with the left hand. The lower roller was turned by a hand-crank, while the upper roller was worked by the treadle attached to a radial bob flywheel, although the latter detail is missing in this illustration. This small gin was inefficient when measured by output per operator. A highly skillful operator could gin only 2 *jin* (2.2 pounds) of cotton in ten hours.[240] But unlike the *jiaoche* operated by three people, it could be readily accommodated within the small-scale peasant household manufacture. Since it required the labor of only one person instead of three, it certainly permitted a more

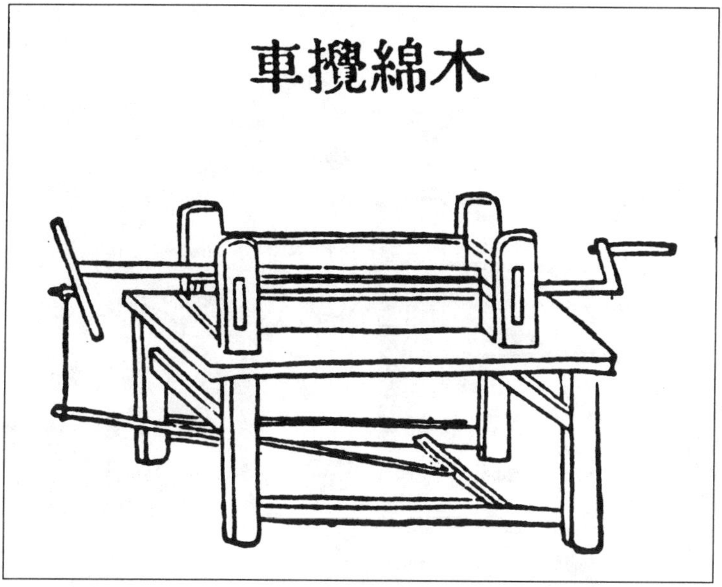

FIGURE 23. Foot-treadle-operated cotton gin (*Nongzheng quanshu* [1639]). The small upper roller, often made of iron, was worked by a treadle with the momentum controlled by the radial bob flywheel; the lower and slightly larger wooden roller was worked by a hand-crank.

flexible work schedule. Ginning typically became the work of women.[241] Although several methods of ginning continued to be used, this single-worker-operated gin became the standard equipment used in rural households, and its use continued well into the twentieth century.

In the spinning of cotton, as Kang Chao has shown, up to the 1740s and the beginning of the Industrial Revolution, the level of technology used in spinning cotton in China was unparalleled anywhere in the world.[242] As early as the fourteenth century, a big multispindle spinning wheel (*da fangche*) used for ramie had been developed. Described and illustrated in detail in the *Nongshu*, the frame of this "big spinning wheel" was twenty feet long, five feet wide and five feet high, with thirty-two spindles. It could be turned by draft animals or if necessary human labor. The *Nongshu* also shows a similar multispindle spinning frame used for ramie that was entirely water-

FIGURE 24. Multi-spindle, water-powered ramie spinning wheel (*Nongshu* [1313]). The design used iron for several parts, such as the spindle shafts. The drawing is somewhat misleading in giving a tooth-like shape to the cylindrical boxes that contained the yarn.

powered (*shui zhuan da fangche*), which is reproduced here in Figure 24. As has been suggested, this spinning-frame contained several of the essential features of the "spinning jenny," and with some modifications this multi-spindle spinning wheel could have been adopted for cotton spinning.[243] Indeed, the modifications necessary to convert it were made in the twentieth century when during World War II interior regions of China like Sichuan were cut off from both foreign imports of cotton yarn and from yarn produced in the Japanese-controlled coastal factories.[244] During much of late imperial China, however, the trend was not in the direction of developing the large spinning frame and speeding up the production of cotton or ramie. Instead, there was a wider use of the two-spindle and three-spindle spinning wheel throughout China.

As seen in Figure 25, in a Qing illustration of the treadle-operated

FIGURE 25. Treadle-operated two-spindle spinning wheel for cotton (*Tiangong kaiwu*, later addition from *Gujin tushu jicheng* [1725]). This device was similar to the multi-spindle spinning wheel with a square yarn frame used for doubling cotton yarn discussed in the *Nongshu* (1313).

two-spindle spinning wheel, this device, and the comparable three-spindle spinning wheel, allowed more than one strand of yarn to be spun in parallel. These two- and three-spindle spinning wheels were developed sometime in the thirteenth or early fourteenth century and were most likely based on the existing technology for spinning ramie. The three-spindle spinning wheel was a relatively efficient device, for elsewhere, until the development of James Hargreaves's multi-spindle "spinning jenny," spinning wheels tended to have only one spindle. Working with a three-spindle treadle-operated wheel, an efficient worker could triple the amount if spinning medium- to low-grade yarn.[245] The three-spindle treadle-operated spinning wheel was both time- and labor-saving; and most important, unlike the large multi-spindle frame, it was easily located within the space and rhythm of household production. There was also a simpler version, a hand-operated as well as a treadle-operated single-spindle spinning wheel.[246] Using this, a woman could spin only 4–6 *liang* (5.25–7.9 ounces) in a 10–13 hour period of work.[247] By the twentieth century the treadle-operated single-spindle spinning wheel was to become the most commonly used spinning wheel in China.[248]

The small scale of manufacture and the apparent tendency toward selecting technology that needed only one operator also apparently determined the long-term use of the drawloom in China. The drawloom or figure loom (*huaji*), used for weaving patterned cloth, is illustrated in the *Tiangong kaiwu* (1637). At a total length of sixteen feet, it was large and required at least two workers to operate. In addition to the weaver who sat in front of the loom, the complex designs woven on this loom required another person who controlled the numerous harnesses and drew up the proper combinations for the design being woven.[249] But gradually, during the course of the Qing, cotton cloth woven with intricate patterns became less common as the treadle-loom and the back-strap loom (*yaoji*) operated by only one weaver became the typical looms found in peasant households.[250] Fairly good cloth for sale could be produced on either of these looms. Although weaving was primarily considered to be women's work, given the importance of weaving as a secondary source of income, labor on these looms was not strictly gender differentiated. There were, however, other looms where the work was done entirely by women. These produced coarse cloth for common wear called "woman's loom cloth," and there were even simpler looms for weaving ribbons and the strong tape used for binding feet.[251]

Bast fibers such as ramie, hemp, and kudzu continued to be important crops even after the expansion of cotton cultivation in the Ming. In the south, ramie was cultivated more extensively for making fabrics, while hemp was used only for manufacturing rope. In Guangdong, Fujian, and Taiwan a particular variety of ramie called "green ramie" (*qingma*) and abaca were common.[252] Ramie was by far the most important commercial crop. It was used for manufacturing summer garments, underwear, curtains, and mosquito nets. Sold in rolls of ten *zhang* (almost 35 yards), a coarse weave sold for one ounce of silver. Finer-quality cloth could sell for as much as four to ten ounces of silver per roll.[253]

The water-driven, multi-spindle frame, discussed above, was widely used for spinning ramie in the Yuan. It was said to have a spinning capacity of about 100 *jin* (132 pounds in the Yuan) of yarn in twenty-four hours. Although efficient, for it saved time, it did require several individuals to oversee the operations. The yarn boxes, where the material to be spun was placed in layers, had to be kept constantly filled. The speedier water-driven spinning frame required a large supply of carded fibers; this meant that several individuals could do nothing else but work on separating the ramie fibers and preparing the rove for spinning. This was a slow and laborious task without any mechanical shortcuts.[254] The stem of the ramie plant consists of three layers, the outer skin, the layer of fibers, and the inner body of the plant (which is hard and woody). The fibers are coated with pectins and gums which have to be removed immediately after harvesting before they have dried. The *Nongzheng quanshu* and *Tiangong kaiwu* further describe the process. First the fibers were soaked to complete the process of degumming. They were then boiled or soaked again in an aqueous solution of ash of rice or millet stalks or mulberry brushwood and lime to bleach the fibers. Next, after repeated rinses in running water to rid it of the chemicals, it was dried in the sun before each strand was spliced by hand.[255] The output of an entire day's work was only 3–5 ounces of fiber.[256] This may have been the reason why, writing in the early fourteenth century, Wang Zhen suggests that several households came together to spin yarn in the water-powered multi-spindled frame.[257] Regular supervision and coordination was also necessary to make sure that the spun yarn was removed at appropriate intervals. Hence, although the multi-spindle frame was undoubtedly more efficient, it remained labor-intensive and could not be accommodated conveniently into the schedule of peasant household manufacture, where spinning was a secondary occupation carried out between other tasks. By the late Ming, the large multi-spindle frame, although still known, was no longer common. The large spinning frame further faded in importance in the Qing as small-scale, individual-household manufacture of ramie cloth increased. The single-operator treadle-powered spinning wheel became the commonly used equipment for spinning ramie.[258] As in the case of cotton spinning, this spinning wheel was efficient enough for the needs of a secondary occupation.

The logic and chronology of this technological preference has been given a demographic explanation. According to Kang Chao,

> The other profound impact of overpopulation was on the technological preference of producers. Again, the twelfth century may serve as the approximate line dividing two patterns of technological orientation in the agricultural history of China. Up to that time there had been a flow of inventions of new farm implements, including the improved plow that required less draft power, the shareplow that could turn over sod to form a furrow, and the deep-tooth harrow. All of these devices were labor saving by nature. This stream of inventions had run its course by the end of the twelfth century.[259]

This linear equation between the increase in population in the late imperial period and technological preference toward labor-intensive usage is problematic. Indeed there are several instances given above—such as in the selection of the loom, spinning frames, and the cotton gin, as well as cane crushers—where the preferred innovation obviously required fewer people to operate. Other aspects of agricultural practice replicated this tendency, for example, in irrigation. The square-pallet chain pump, a scoop wheel pump essential for lifting water two to three feet for irrigation, was one of the most common sights in the Chinese countryside. Although the device could be driven more efficiently by either right-angle gearing from the axle of a horizontal waterwheel or by an ox (as given in Figure 21 above), the most common version was one treadled by two people as seen in Figure 26. Moreover, since field irrigation was carried out on a household basis during the Qing, the version that required the labor of two adults was more common than one modified with turn-sticks to allow for operation by a single man.[260]

The idea that an excess of labor and a Malthusian logic governed

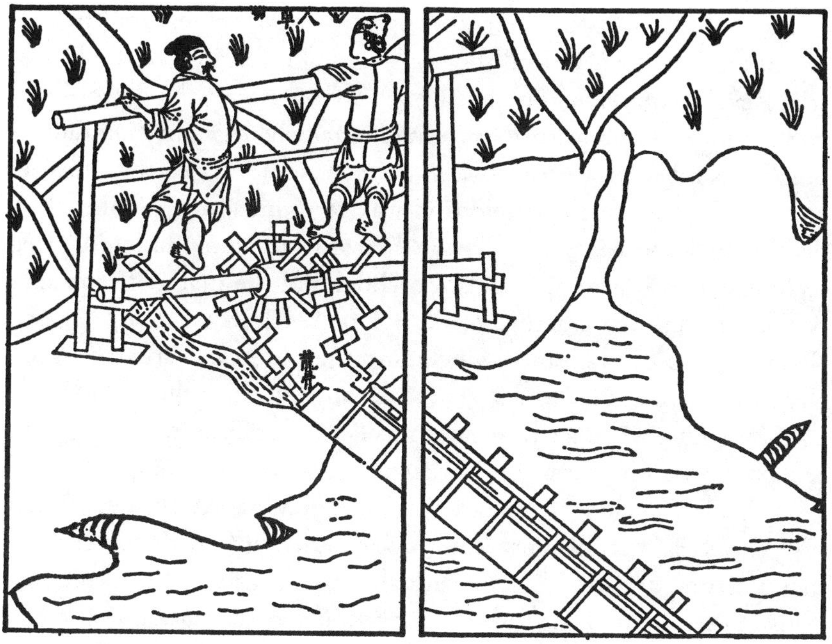

FIGURE 26. Square-pallet treadle chain pump (*Tiangong kaiwu* [1637]). Also known as the endless chain pump. The beam rotates as each worker steps from one spoked foot-lever to the next.

all aspects of the Chinese economy—including technological selection—cannot be assumed. Such an assumption presupposes that Chinese peasants were irrational or had no means of controlling fertility. Instead, I suggest that the tendency toward labor-intensive practices in cultivation were simultaneously counterbalanced by the selection of technologies of manufacture and technologies of agriculture, as discussed below in Chapter Five, that required a minimum number of operators. Production was expanded by multiplying the number of units of manufacture, rather than by centralizing production and using technologies that increased production by speeding up the process. I think the technologies selected reflected the social organization of production, rather than an assumed disjuncture between technology and the institutions of production[261] or a conscious "management solution" being given priority over "technical solutions."[262]

As Hobsbawm points out, surveying the developments of the cotton industry in England, all the fundamental inventions of the Industrial Revolution, the spinning jenny, the water-frame, the power-loom and so on, had one feature in common, namely, that they simultaneously expanded production while cutting costs.[263] The trajectory of technological change and selection was very different in China. Evidently, in some cases the tension between accommodating a given technology within the peasant household and the material requisites of commercial manufacture could not be resolved with any finality. Several types of equipment, including the sugarcane crusher as we shall see, remained far too expensive for any but the richer peasants to own individually. In such instances, collective associations of eight to ten poor peasants came into existence to share the equipment and space.[264] In the long run, however, the dominance of the peasant household as the primary unit of manufacture made centralized manufacture, and the technologies that went with it, the exception. This in turn limited the type of innovation and adaptation that could be undertaken. Even when a degree of centralization of manufacturing was carried out, such as in the cotton calendering and dyeing businesses in Suzhou, and several thousand artisans worked under one roof, these large enterprises functioned like a putting-out system, and the artisans rented the equipment individually.[265] There were no attempts to centralize related aspects of manufacture, such as ginning, spinning, and weaving of the cotton cloth, which remained decentralized and located within the peasant households.

The process of technological selection in sugar manufacturing was evidently similar to a pattern observed in other sectors, a tendency toward labor-saving technologies. As we have seen, there was no "technological standstill" as posited by Mark Elvin among others. The technology used for crushing and refining cane in China clearly kept pace with changes occurring in the Americas and elsewhere, and may have initiated some of them. The surge in demand for Chinese sugar in the seventeenth century coincided with the period during which the most rapid changes in technology took place in this sector. But the social organization of production into which demand was translated proved crucial in shaping the ongoing technological responses to demand. The pace of change in the technology of sugar manufacture in China did not lead to innovations in related sectors of manufacturing such as refining. No centralized drying houses were constructed as in Amsterdam. A systemic and continuous pressure to improve production capabilities through new inventions and innovations, to produce more sugar more cheaply in the shortest possible time through more efficient motive power, also did not prevail in China as it did in Brazil or the Caribbean or indeed even in Oshima-Amami. Instead, beyond the dramatic shift to the two-roller cane crusher, there was a consistent thrust toward modification of the technology which ultimately made it possible to accommodate sugar manufacturing within the organization of labor imposed by the small-scale peasant economy of the Qing. Increased demand and the increased output for exports were met by operating many more less efficient cane crushers and by involving larger numbers of small-scale producers in cultivating and manufacturing. This outcome, and the social formation of a small-property-owning peasantry that was to be so characteristic of Qing China, was, however, by no means a given reality at the beginning of the seventeenth century. In the next chapter, we turn to a closer investigation of the social formation of the sugar-producing regions and examine the historical processes through which the small producer came to dominate organization at the point of production. Then, in the following chapters, we will explore the particularities of smallholder agriculture in China which made it possible for small-scale family farms to produce sugar, among other commodities, for the national and international market.

FOUR

THE SOCIAL FORMATION OF LATE-IMPERIAL CHINA

> We had come to learn how the old-world farmers had been able to provide materials for food and clothing on such small areas for so many millions, at so low a price, during so many centuries, and were anxious to see them at the soil and among the crops.
>
> . . . [L]ooking down upon its terraced gardens and tiny fields, we saw men and women busy fitting the soil for new crops, gathering vegetables for market, feeding plants with liquid manure and even irrigating certain crops notwithstanding the damp, foggy, showery weather.[1]
>
> —F. H. King, 1911

THE IMAGE OF MILLIONS of small peasants toiling in carefully cultivated minuscule fields is so integral to any representation of Guangdong that this pattern seems to have existed from time immemorial. Was this indeed the case? What propelled the development of this particular social formation and sustained it even as the burgeoning world market drew this region into an ever more intimate nexus? Scholars of Chinese agricultural and economic history have suggested that larger farms, at least to a certain point in size, usually led to growth in productivity.[2] Since some parts of South China already had close links with the world market, could entrepreneurial landowners have amalgamated small holdings into larger estates which they then operated with wage labor? Or, given that several forms of bonded labor existed in South China, could there have been sugar plantations along the lines of those found in the Americas? More important, would it have made sense in the local context for landowners to do so? This chapter explores the dynamics of social property relations in Guangdong and Taiwan—two of the major sugar-producing regions in the Qing—and the implications of this social formation for sustaining long-term economic growth.

Servile Tenants and Elite Landlords: Pre-Qing Guangdong

The contours of the society and economy of South China prior to the late sixteenth century need only be sketched here in broad outline. First conquered by northern Chinese during the third century B.C., Guangdong, then part of the kingdom of Nan Yue, was brought under firmer centralized imperial rule in 112 B.C. after numerous armed confrontations between the imperial Han government and the local rulers. Land was settled by military colonization from the north, a process that was to gain momentum in the sixth and seventh centuries. Northern Chinese moved into the area—"aggregations of hopeful humanity, supported by troops who killed those natives bold enough to resist, leaving the survivors to be indoctrinated, exploited or enslaved by Chinese agents and their aboriginal collaborators."[3] Swidden agriculture and fishing still formed the basis of the economy, but salt and pearls from the Guangdong delta were sent up to the Han emperors as tribute. There was also an active slave trade in non-Han aborigine peoples sold in the north by slave merchants.[4]

The city that came to be known as Guangzhou was the capital of the Yue people. Its prime location on the Pearl River Delta ensured that it would remain a focal point of economic activity in the following centuries. By the eighth century Guangzhou had become a major port and trading center, but it was still a frontier town, rife with murders, pirate raids, and the depredations of corrupt officials.[5] Its population of some two hundred thousand people was mostly of non-Han origin and consisted of Arabs, Southeast Asians, and Indians attracted there by trade. The profits of this foreign trade also drew the attention of the central government. The Tang imperial government appointed a maritime trade commissioner (*shibo shi*) to collect customs revenues. Primarily a site for luxury trade in pearls, aromatics, gems, and spices from Southeast Asia, India, and Arabia, Guangdong exported pottery, silk, gold, and Chinese coins from all over China.[6]

The economy of Guangdong in the Song was backward compared with that of the Yangzi Delta. Although sugar was produced in Guangdong from at least the sixth century on, and was sent up to the court as a tribute item in the Tang, we do not know how much was produced for sale.[7] Fruits like litchees, longyan, and oranges were also grown for sale up north in the Song, and these, as we have seen, were often packed in jars of sugar syrup for the long journey. The major item of agricultural produce was rice. "Long waist," "jade kernel" and other varieties of rice were exported to Fujian, Zhejiang, and even abroad to Southeast Asia.[8]

The great migration southward during the Song, as the regions north of the Yangzi came under the control of the Liao-Khitan and Jurchen-Chin, brought substantial numbers of ethnic Han immigrants to Guangdong. Genealogies from most areas of the Pearl River Delta refer to the troubled times preceding the fall of the Song as the cause of the southward migration. The first ethnic Han ancestors to the region are said to have settled in Nanxiong, a military garrison in northern Guangdong through which all the overland trade to North China passed (see Map 3). The genealogies of over 60 percent of the population of Xinhui county hold that their ancestors migrated from Nanxiong in the late thirteenth century, and contain colorful stories of heroic escapades.[9] Others claim to have migrated somewhat earlier, like the founders of the famous Deng lineage of Xin'an county.[10] Yet other genealogies from Xiangshan county, on the other side of the Delta, tell of lineage ancestors accompanying the last Song monarch as he fled from the Mongols. Although all these lineage genealogies claim that the ancestors settled the region in the late Song, since the vast majority of the texts are late-Ming compilations,[11] myth and reality have clearly been combined to present a far more coherent sequence of settlement than could have been possible in this frontier province.[12]

Significant economic growth began in Guangdong in the thirteenth and fourteenth centuries, even though it was still quite modest compared to regions of the Yangzi Delta. During this period major dikes were constructed in the Pearl River Delta, often under government sponsorship, and this created rich new agricultural lands.[13] Yuan sources also mention dredging of swamp and reed lands by private landholders. Numerous military agricultural settlements, garrisons, and colonies were established as far south as Hainan island.[14] Transportation was improved, and navigation of the main rivers in the Delta expanded considerably.[15] In the comprehensive land-and-population survey carried out by the Ming government in 1393, the population of Guangdong was recorded at 3,007,932 *kou* (mouths or people) and 675,559 *hu* (households). This official count did not include the substantial non-Han and aboriginal populations of Guangdong.[16] The population of Guangdong was relatively small compared with that of contemporary Zhejiang, which already had over 10 million people, or Jiangxi with almost 9 million.[17]

The data prior to the fourteenth century are too fragmented to give a detailed picture of the patterns of landholding and the social structure of the Delta. Some lineages that became prominent in the Qing may have started on their climb by receiving land grants. The Deng of Xin'an county, for example, apparently received extensive imperial land grants when an ancestor married an imperial princess in the twelfth century.[18] The spate of ancestral estate endowments in some counties in the twelfth and thirteenth centuries, such as Nanhai county, where twenty-three ancestral halls were set up, and Shunde county, where seventeen halls were established, suggests an affluent elite already well able to provide land for corporate lineage estates.[19] The percentage of direct producers who were smallholders, with independent rights to property and land, is also not clear. Several scholars have suggested that, in a process that became far more common by the end of the sixteenth century, smallholders who initially had rights to land were driven by heavy taxation in the twelfth and thirteenth centuries into bondage, pledging their lands and labor to large powerful landowners who, as officials or as relatives of officials, were exempt from both taxation and corvée.[20] Cases like this were seemingly common; even one of the ancestors of the famous Deng lineage lost his title to the land in this manner.[21]

A somewhat clearer picture of the social structure begins to emerge in the fourteenth century. There seem to have been some very wealthy landowners in Guangdong at one end of the scale, as well as a large number of cultivators who either were bonded laborers or had other forms of servile status. The sources of rights in land were varied. Imperial land grants were one source. He Zhen (1322–1388), the Yuan commander of Guangdong who handed over the province to the Ming, for example, received a land grant along with the title of earl (*bo*). The He ancestral estate founded in 1372 had 10,000 *mu* (almost 1,700 acres).[22] Other families acquired land by outright appropriation; a number of "violent seizures" by landlords are mentioned throughout the Yuan and later.[23] Lands may have been also taken over by agnatic-kin groups with numerous able-bodied males through a collective use and show of strength. In the mid-fifteenth century, one such case notes that the Chen of Tianma (Xinhui county) murdered a member of the Feng lineage in a scuffle over land rights; when thirty-five Chen males turned up as "joint culprits" at court, the magistrate let them have the land "in the interests of peace."[24] Yet others, like the Zhao lineage in Xinhui, were able to extend their landholdings and collective social power by granting the right of reclamation only to groups to whom they were related by marriage.[25]

The development of lands through polders and reclamation in the Delta made many initially modest landholdings immense. He Taixiang (*jinshi* of 1592) from Xinhui, who served as a minister of the Ming, accumulated 32,000 *mu* (over 5,300 acres) during his lifetime. A small strip of marshland, casually allotted to his ninth son, who died when a month old, eventually expanded to 6,000 *mu* (1,000 acres). Now a fertile polder, it is still known as Jiuzisha (Ninth Son Sands).[26] The Liu Geng Hall of Panyu county started out with an endowment of just 14 *mu* in 1587, but in about fifty years the same plot had increased to 2,144 *mu*.[27] A member of the Deng lineage, reputedly the richest man in Xin'an county, owned over 10,000 *mu* in the Hong Kong area in 1587.[28] But the true size of these holdings was never clear. As Ming officials such as Huo Tao (1480–1540) frequently complained, much of the property belonging to gentry-landlords[29] effectively evaded assessment and paid no taxes as a result of corruption aided by the delta ecology.[30] Official land registration records for Guangdong in the Ming show a sudden and inexplicable drop in registration in the early sixteenth century; this too suggests gross tax evasion on the local rolls:[31]

1393: 23,734,056 *mu*
1502: 7,232,446 *mu*
1578: 25,686,514 *mu*

By the late sixteenth century not only did no one know exactly how much land the Guangdong gentry held, but no one knew the real size of the population either. As the 1585 edition of the Shunde county gazetteer declared, "the omission of children in the official registers has been an old practice" and elaborated that "the rich and powerful households ally themselves with the local government personnel, so that sometimes only one out of several tens of actual *ding* [unit of male labor service] is entered into the register."[32] These practices were not limited to Shunde county. The population data from 1578, showing 2,040,655 people and 530,712 households in Guangdong, represented a *decrease* of over a million individuals since the beginning of the Ming. Since Guangdong had escaped many of the epidemics that ravaged north China during the 1570s and 1580s, the noted decrease in population was probably an undercount and an approximate estimate at best.[33]

There were some notable large-estate owners in Guangdong similar to the "scholar-official turned entrepreneur-estate manager" found in the Jiangnan region during the late Ming.[34] One such individual, Pang Shangpeng (1524–1581), best known as the Ming administrator responsible for changing and consolidating the imperial taxation system, had a vast estate in Nanhai county.[35] His didactic *Pang shi jiaxun* (Family Instructions) exhorted his heirs to go out into the fields, know which fields were used for paddy or vegetable gardens, supervise planting, and manage the rice harvest. It is clear that the workers in the Pang family fields were not free wage earners or rent-paying tenants but serfs and bonded laborers:

> . . . Thoroughly investigate the number of male and female serfs (*pu*), how many are fit for farming and how many are capable of carrying out trade.

[Find out] how much food and clothing are needed each year. Check the abilities [of the serfs] and their work, whether or not they are in accordance [with orders]. If trading does not yield high profits and there are reckless tendencies, this must be stopped before capital is lost. . . .

Every evening, all the serfs (*tongpu*) must be assigned the tasks for the next day and told the day by which the tasks must be completed. Every evening each must return and make a report. Check for diligence and sloth. If indolent habits are not stopped right away, my family's business will be done in by them.[36]

Ming statutes exempting degree-holders from taxes and the concurrent shifting of the tax burden to the peasants increasingly resulted in many of the impoverished turning over their property rights to gentry-landlords. Servile status in Ming-dynasty Guangdong had many gradations, ranging from hereditary servitude to voluntary indenture for a limited period. The status of *shipu*, whose servile status began when parents sold them as minor children, could vary from that of domestic slaves to that of fictive adopted "sons" with the status of bondsmen in a wealthy family. Although the *shipu* could be involved in farmwork and sometimes rose to the position of trusted overseers, they were typically used for housework and onerous tasks such as carrying sedan chairs, hauling water, and gathering cooking fuel.[37] Another system, known as *touxian*, implied only the surrender of property. *Maishen* (lit. "selling the self"), in contrast, involved pledging one's labor in exchange for food and shelter.[38] Peter Mundy, visiting Guangdong in 1637, noted: "[t]he poorer sort of Chineses selling their children to pay their Debtts or Maynetaine themselves (which itt seems is somewhat tollerated here) butt with this condition, as letting them to hire or binding them servauntts for 30, 40, 50 yeare and after that to bee Freed. Some sell them outrightt withoutt any Condition att all."[39]

The *nupu*, translated as "bondservants" by some scholars and as "serf" by others, were more clearly involved in farming, as were the *dianpu* or bonded tenants.[40] There was another category of bonded laborers who worked in agriculture, *gu gongren*. The legal status of these hired hands was between that of serfs and that of commoners (*liangmin*) and was clearly differentiated in the criminal code of 1588. This category included all laborers who entered into contracts lasting for periods of over a year. Technically, after the termination of the contract, bonded laborers could return to commoner status but it is not clear whether they ever lost the stigma of their bonded status. The Ming legal code upheld the unequal status of master and servant; it stipulated that a landowner who killed his hired hand could receive a maximum sentence of three years of hard labor but not the death penalty. By contrast, the *nupu* were considered to be of such low legal status that they received twice the degree of punishment that a commoner would receive. For example, in a fight involving a commoner and a *nupu*, if they both emerged with "swollen bruises," the commoner would receive 40 lashes, while the *nupu* would receive 80.[41] And when it came to the relationship between master and *nupu*, the legal code provided no penalties for the master for rape or seduction of a *nupu* or her relatives or for killing a *nupu* through negligence or accident. A premeditated killing of a *nupu* by the master would lead to 60–100 lashes and a year's banishment. But the *nupu* would be sentenced to the painful punishment of death by quartering if he or she killed a master. The *nupu* could be hanged for simply rebuking their master or defaming him.[42] By the late Ming, many of the gentry-landlords in several of the southern provinces had anywhere from several hundred to three or four thousand *nupu* on their estates.[43]

The proportion of the servile population by the end of the Ming varied enormously by province. In the Jiangnan region it is estimated that 20–30 percent of the peasants had become attached to wealthy gentry-landlord families through *maishen* or *touxian*. Bonded tenants or *dianpu* may have numbered one-fifth of the rural population.[44] But in some other districts of the Jiangnan by the end of the Ming there were apparently no freeholders left among the commoners.[45] For Guangdong we only have the word of Lin Xiyuan (1480–1560), the colorful official-turned-trader from Fujian, who served in various posts in southern Guangdong. He noted: "At present 50 or 60 percent of the land here is in the hands of the rich houses, and almost none of the people cultivate private land."[46] Bonded labor of various types, it is argued, was more common in areas with small populations both in parts of Europe and China,[47] and this may also have been true of

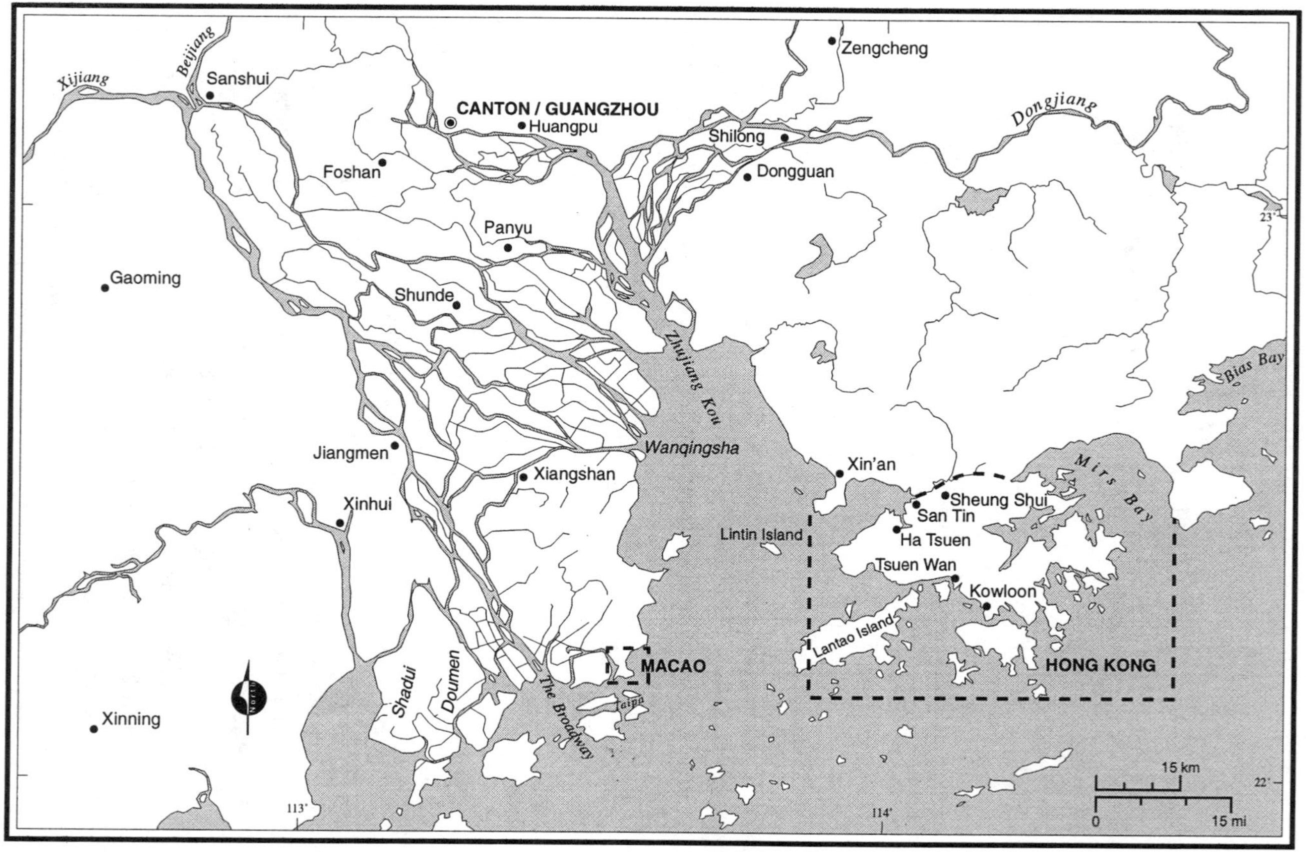

MAP 5. Major waterways, polders, and villages, Guangdong Delta, ca. 1900

Guangdong in the Ming. In addition, a large percentage of the direct producers were in the category of tenants (*diannong*). Such tenants, besides paying rent to the landlord, may not have had other obligations,[48] but their social status nonetheless made them subject to the landlord's power of using larger measures when collecting rent-grain as well as having to pay a range of fees. The standard share-rent of 50 percent of the harvest could easily be transformed into a collection of 70 percent of the harvest.[49] Although some commoners may have continued as freeholders, the intensity and frequency of *nupu, dianpu,* and *diannong* uprisings in Guangdong in the seventeenth century (more frequent than any other province in the empire)[50] suggests the existence of a large servile population as well as a number of tenants.

The Crisis of the Seventeenth Century: The Ming-Qing Transition in Guangdong

The "general crisis" of the seventeenth century, which seemingly encompassed the globe, has received considerable attention.[51] But despite the similarities in the political confrontations that inspired Voltaire in his *Essai sur les moeurs et l'esprit des nations* to list contemporaries such as Charles I of England, Philip IV of Spain, Muley-Ismail in Morocco, Aurangzeb in India, and Li Zicheng in China as examples of a "period of usurpations almost from one end of the world to the other,"[52] the crisis in each case had widely divergent outcomes. The demise of the Ming state and the peasant rebellions accompanying its collapse were to restructure the property rights of the vast majority of direct producers.[53]

The tensions between warring factions of the northern and southern gentry, the struggles for power between professional militarists and the civil bureaucracy, and the corruption of eunuchs were all part of the Ming government's disintegration.[54] By the last decade of the dynasty (1634–1644), military spending was twenty times that of nonmilitary spending and five times that of the level of government expenditures in 1590.[55] One example suffices to underline the fiscal crisis of the state: in 1644 the imperial treasury contained only 4,200 ounces of gold and silver, at a time when military provisions for the troops on the frontier alone took 400,000 taels (ounces of silver) a month.[56] Massive peasant rebellions accompanied this disintegration of the administration at the central and local levels.

Peasant revolts in China were of course nothing new; they had been a common phenomenon since the founding of the imperial state system in 221 B.C. Famine, war, the collapse of state welfare policies, and so on, added to the usual grievances of rent-gouging and the avarice of landlords, certainly contributed to the general number of uprisings in the late sixteenth and early seventeenth centuries. But the revolts at the end of the Ming were distinguished by the particularly clear efforts of the organized peasant struggles to curtail bonded labor and other forms of bonded existence.[57] Whereas during earlier dynastic transitions gentry had sought to use peasant discontent for their own purposes, few of them joined[58] Li Zicheng (1605?-1645) and Zhang Xianzhong (1605–1647), the leaders of the two major peasant rebellions that spread across most of northern and central China from 1627 onward. At times both these rebellions attempted to build a broad popular base by focusing on class issues, the demand being "to equalize the land between the rich and the poor." The broadsheets posted by Li Zicheng declared, "The gentry has no sense of decency. Taxes grow heavier each day."[59] The rebellion of Zhang Xianzhong, which started out in Shensi in 1630 and lasted until 1664 in Sichuan, also targeted the gentry-landlords in the several provinces it swept through. In many places it virtually wiped them out. Several other rebellions that remained localized also shared these sentiments. In Huguang, when the troops of Zhang Xianzhong arrived, *nupu* turned their masters over to rebels and led the movement to kill local degree-holders. One banner declared, "Follow the right Way on behalf of Heaven in killing the wealthy and aiding the poor."[60] Another eyewitness account from Jiangsu in 1645 noted, "Among the bondservants, some are cunning, and they are stirring up a movement for their annulment of their bonds of servitude, saying that the dynasty is changing so how can the regulations for bondservants be as they used to be."[61]

In the south, numerous peasant uprisings against landlords began in the last decade of the sixteenth century and continued into the second half of the seventeenth century.[62] Tanaka Masatoshi's survey of popular uprisings during the Ming-Qing transition throughout the country concludes that, beginning with the turn of the century, there were numerous rent-resistance struggles, led by the still independent tenants (*diannong*). By the 1640s hereditary bondservants (*nupu*) were the major participants, along with bonded tenants (*dianpu*) and bonded laborers,[63] who were joined by hired laborers, small peasant freeholders, and handicraft workers who had been driven by debt into non-hereditary servitude. This tabulation of the participants also reflects the composition of the rebels in South China.

Prominent Guangdong families and lineages who had numerous *nupu* experienced serious attacks. Many members of the Pan lineage, one of the largest landlords in Shunde county, were killed; there the "*nupu* murdered their masters . . . the county capital was attacked by them and the treasury looted."[64] In neighboring Xinhui county, "peasants all went over to kill their former masters"; in Gaoyao county peasants "angrily killed their masters and rebelled," while in Qingyuan county the bonded tenants (*dianpu*) "killed their masters and squatted on the fields."[65] Gu Yanwu (1613–1682), writing at about this time, tells of "bandits and unlawful elements" in the thousands taking over silver mines in Conghua county.[66] Others inducted for labor services in various areas of the Pearl River Delta refused to work. In some areas, serfs organized and formed armies. To quote a report of 1646: "There was an uprising of the Association of Bandits (*she zei*). The organization leading the uprising was also known as the Association of Serf Bandits (*pu zei*). For several years now, serfs have killed or chased away their masters, seizing their lands and houses. The worst of them have taken the wives and children as prisoners and defiled ancestral graves."[67] Famine had brought other supporters to the "bandits." In Guangdong's Xinxing county, "a thousand hungry civilians in Magang and other places joined the bandits en masse and brought their wives and children with them."[68]

The rebels made a range of demands. They wanted the landlords' granaries opened, their wealth redistributed; they wanted lower rents and standard measures for the collection of rent grain; they wanted large estates divided into individual farms, so that peasants would have land of their own. Perhaps the most fundamental challenge to the existing class structure came from the *wan dian kangzu* ("obstinate tenants resisting landlords") movement, a struggle against land rent by the peasants.[69] Such tenant-led struggles occurred on a particularly large scale in Fujian.[70] But Guangdong was not far behind. County gazetteers enumerate as many as 284 "violent events" in Guangdong in the seventeenth century.[71] The Manchu government entering Beijing in 1644, therefore, could not hope to establish stability and collect revenues without considering the issues raised by these numerous rebellions. The process of establishing Qing hegemony in the south was further complicated by civil wars in Guangdong and Taiwan.

Several Ming loyalist groups had fled to Guangdong and Guangxi when north China came under Qing control. Factions of the Ming claimants of the Yongle and Shaowu courts battled around Guangzhou several times, and even after the entry of the Qing forces into Guangzhou in 1647, pro-Yongle resistance continued till 1653. Later, the anti-Manchu Revolt of the Three Feudatories (San Fan, 1673–1681) also affected the region around the Pearl River Delta; Shang Zhixin (d. 1680), one of the leaders of the rebellion, had been based in Guangdong. The villages of Shunde county are said to have burned for twenty-four days as the troops initiated a scorched-earth policy. Judging from the number of prominent Guangdong literati who were disgraced for their Ming loyalist sympathies and support of the rebellion, several prominent gentry-landlord families were also undoubtedly affected.[72] The population of Guangzhou prefecture apparently declined from 399,099 people in the 1640s to 232,541 by 1662.[73]

A more fundamental dislocation of the established social and economic structure occurred when the Manchu government evacuated the coastal regions of Guangdong, Fujian, Zhejiang, Jiangsu, and Shandong in 1662 in order to starve out the Taiwan-based Zheng Chenggong, the most serious remaining military threat to Qing suzerainty. The population of the villages of the core counties of the Pearl River Delta—Shunde, Panyu, Dongguan, Xin'an, Xinhui and Xiangshan—were forced to move approximately fifty miles inland.[74] The evacuation order stayed in effect until 1669, and Qu Dajun has graphically depicted the extent of the dislocation: "People continued to drift around, unable to figure out how to survive. Fathers and sons, husbands and wives, abandoned each other; with anguished cries they parted ways. A son for a peck of grain, a daughter for a hundred cash for purchase by the powerful."[75] Others recorded, "The ground was covered with bones, in the daytime nothing could be heard but the hum of flies, and at night the sound of weeping."[76] Local fishermen, most of whom were ethnic Danmin (Tanka) origin, having lost their means of livelihood during the evacuation, joined the Ming-loyalist forces or bands of pirates. Land, perforce lying fallow, returned to wilderness in this tropical area. The gazetteer of Conghua county noted, "The town is devastated, the people impoverished, the wilderness is filled with the laments [of the impoverished], and everywhere there are barren fields."[77] Xin'an county reckoned that its population had declined from 17,871 in 1642 to 3,972 by 1671 while in Shunde county 368,000 *mu* of land were laid waste as a result of the evacuation.[78]

The Ming-Qing Transition on Taiwan

Conditions on Taiwan at the beginning of the Qing period were different from those in Guangdong but also on the brink of rapid change. On the eve of his Taiwan campaign in 1661 Zheng Chenggong reportedly told his generals: "The year before last He Tingbin portrayed Taiwan as having ten thousand hectares of fields and gardens, a thousand *li* of undeveloped fertile land, and revenues of several hundred thousand [taels per year]. Ship-building and arms manufacture could be done well if our skilled people were concentrated there."[79] Nor was Zheng alone in attempting to seize the opportunities offered by the island.

Its location on the direct seafaring route between Japan and the Philippines (close enough to the mainland to be a practical stopover, far enough from Beijing and the two provincial governments of Guangdong and Fujian to escape strict supervision) had long given Taiwan a strategic importance. Several bands of pirates had used its harbors as safe havens since the promulgation of the Ming edicts against private overseas trade in the late fourteenth century. By the late sixteenth century, there was regular trade with the mainland; and by 1589, between four to eight trading licenses were issued annually by the Ming government to traders going to Taiwan.[80] The Chinese bartered porcelain, cloth, salt, and brass and iron goods in exchange for deer skins, meat, and horns with the aborigines of southwest Taiwan.[81] Never directly claimed by the Ming government, Taiwan was first colonized by the Dutch and the Spanish, who, in their quest for East Asian trade and colonies, arrived on different parts of the island of Taiwan in 1624 and 1626, respectively. When in early 1625 the Dutch East India Company's governor, Martinus Sonck, gave fifteen pieces of trade cloth (*cangans*) to the Sinkan aborigines for a tract of land and proceeded to build the town of Sakam (Tainan) in the hinterland of the islet-fort Zeelandia (Tayouan), the Dutch entered into a new phase of colonization and trading-post settlement in East Asia.[82]

The Dutch attempted to involve the southwestern tribes in trade, sent missionaries to work with them, and began to regulate tribal use of land by imposing head taxes, hunting and fishing taxes, and so on. But developing a viable colony proved difficult; the aborigines were not inclined to produce more grain than they themselves required, nor were they involved in intensive agriculture. Although there were around 1,000–1,500 Chinese immigrants and traders living in the aborigine villages, many more skilled and settled agriculturists were clearly needed to boost local production of provisions and to produce the rice and sugar the Dutch wanted to export. To this end, the Dutch actively encouraged migration from China, a pattern reminiscent of Dutch initiatives in developing sugar manufacturing in Batavia. Su Minggang (also known as Bencon, d. 1644), a wealthy and influential person from Fujian and "captain" of the Chinese in Batavia, who had worked closely with the Dutch in Batavia, went to Taiwan to aid in sponsoring immigration.[83] Su was interested in developing rice and sugarcane plantations on land near Sakam that he and his partners had reclaimed. With the support of the Dutch he brought over laborers from Fujian. Zheng Zhilung (1604–1661), whose son Zheng

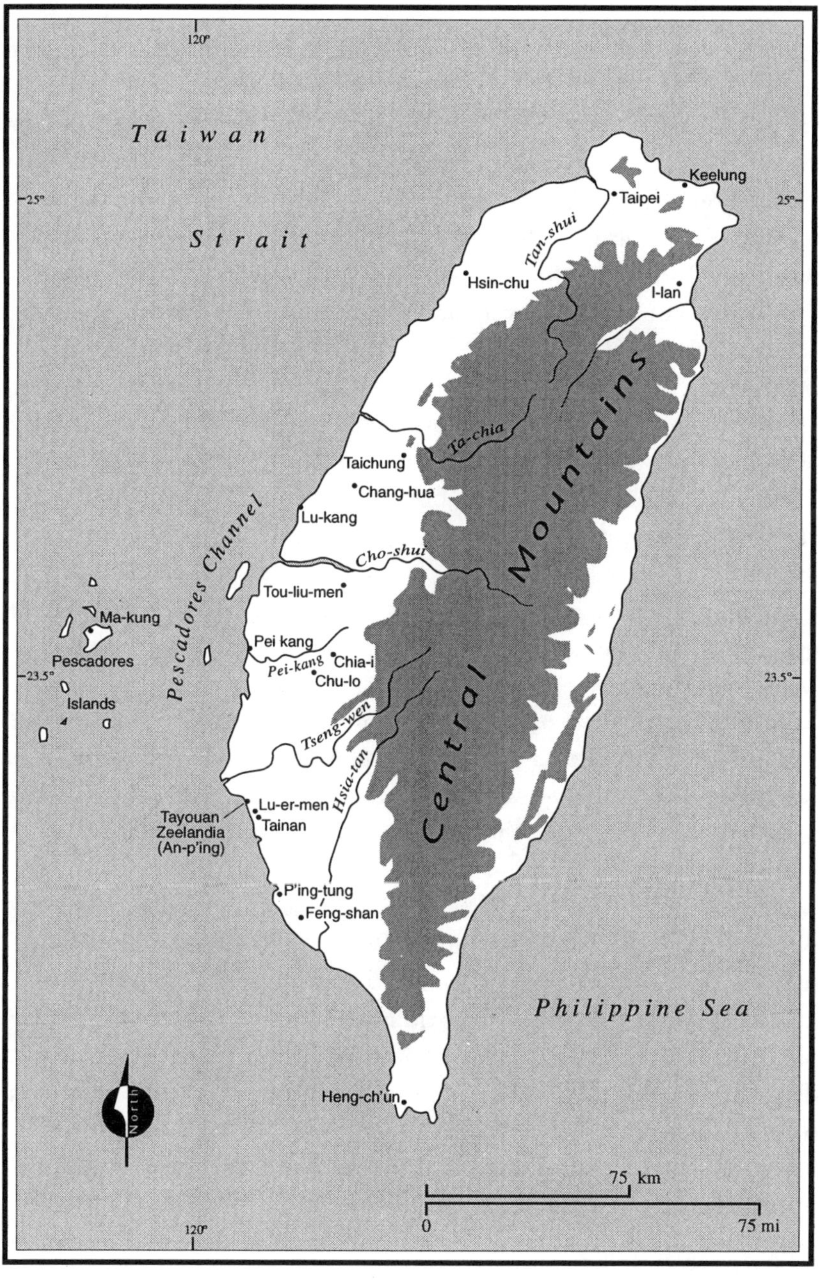

MAP 6. Late-imperial Taiwan, major Dutch and Han settlements

Chenggong was to become the nemesis of the Dutch, was also one of these early recruiters. He apparently shipped "several tens of thousands of people" from drought-stricken Fujian between 1628 and 1631 and gave each settler three taels of silver and each group of three settlers an ox.[84] This was in keeping with Dutch schemes for the promotion of agriculture, which included importing draft animals all the way from India and Batavia and giving those who reclaimed land a five- to ten-year tax holiday and a tax waiver on land devoted to sugarcane cultivation.[85] After the Dutch ousted the Spanish from the northwest of Taiwan in 1642, they once again turned to Chinese labor recruiters and worked out arrangements to settle the lands around Tan-shui and Keelung. In 1638, the Dutch authorities could report: "There are about 10,000 to 11,000 Chinese in Tayouan under the authority and within the territory of the Company, earning their living by deer hunting, rice and sugar cultivation as well as fishing. The number of Chinese is increasing daily. It is time to levy a poll tax in order to reduce the expenses of the garrison."[86] The various tribal aborigines continued their hunting, fishing, gathering and barter economies, although by the mid-seventeenth century an increasingly larger number of those located in the vicinity of the harbor and the southwest-core settlements were also involved in the Dutch-introduced plow agriculture. In 1650 the total number of aborigines was reported to be 68,567.[87]

The success of Dutch policies was evident. In addition to the export of Taiwanese sugar to Japan, Persia, and Amsterdam that we have already discussed in Chapter Two, Taiwan had become much more than a simple colony providing a footing close to China. By 1660, over 30,270 acres[88] of land had been brought under cultivation. The Chinese population had increased to around 35,000 individuals by 1661; since one-third of them were women and children, the population could be expected to grow.[89] In less than fifty years Taiwan was transformed from a lair of pirates into a revenue-generating commercial colony. By the mid-seventeenth century, these developments were attracting the close attention of Zheng Chenggong, a staunch Ming loyalist who, after twelve years of fighting the Manchu forces along the eastern seaboard and a major defeat, was looking for a base from which to continue his trading empire and rebuild his military forces.

In 1661, Zheng Chenggong retreated to Taiwan with some 200 vessels and 25,000 men and laid siege to Fort Zeelandia. The Dutch surrendered the fort nine months later; complete withdrawal from the island came in 1668. Like the Dutch, the Zhengs also sought to increase the agricultural tax base on Taiwan and tried to get officers and soldiers to bring over their families from the mainland. Although not all of them complied, large numbers of refugees, dislocated by the Qing policies of coastal evacuation, came to Taiwan and boosted the population and tax base of the Zhengs. The English factor at Taiwan estimated in 1670 that there were about 70,000 Chinese on the island.[90] In 1683, on the eve of the Manchu conquest of Taiwan, the Han Chinese population of Taiwan is estimated to have been around 100,000. Ninety percent of these Chinese settlements were in the central part of the island around Tainan and in the southern part around present-day Kaohsiung.[91] Continuing the regional pattern of emigration that had started when Su Minggang had recruited immigrants from Fujian, the vast majority of the immigrants continued to come from Fujian province, especially from the prefectures of Quanzhou and Zhangzhou.[92] These early immigrants from Fujian created a powerful ethnic "Fulao" Hokkien identity, which was to bring them into sharp conflict with immigrants from eastern Guangdong who were to arrive somewhat later.

In 1683, Zheng resistance to the Manchu forces collapsed. Taiwan was formally integrated into the empire in 1684 and made into a prefecture of Fujian province and divided into three counties, Fengshan, Taiwan (which corresponded to the settlements around Tainan), and Chu-lo (later called Chia-i). The peopling of Taiwan, however, proceeded very slowly from this time to roughly the middle of the eighteenth century; indeed the population may have decreased for a while when soldiers and civilians were repatriated back to the mainland by the Qing government. John Shepherd estimates that there may have been fewer than 80,000 ethnic Han Chinese on the island in the first decades of Qing rule.[93] Although the surrender of the Zheng forces had been accomplished, Taiwan was nevertheless still a highly militarized frontier society. The Kangxi emperor was concerned that Taiwan harbored Ming loyalists and pirates who might support antigovernment forces. These concerns spawned a variety of Qing restrictions on migration. Even though some of his officials disagreed and thought encouraging Chinese immigration would bring greater stability, and local administration of the restrictions was often lax, Qing imperial policies during the Kangxi period slowed immigration considerably. This ambivalence regarding the settlement of Taiwan was to continue under the following emperors. Immigration policy fluctuated between efforts at total restriction to occasional support for settlement during the next hundred years. Only after 1790 did Beijing finally abandon efforts to control the settlement of Taiwan.

Migration from the mainland was controlled primarily by preventing the immigration of families. In contrast to earlier Dutch practices, until 1732 there were official Qing restrictions on bringing women to Taiwan. Since many of the early settlers were adult males from the ranks of the Zheng troops on Taiwan, the development of households was slow and uneven. The *Chu-lo xianzhi* (Chu-lo Gazetteer) commented in 1717 that it was very difficult for the male migrants to marry because women were so scarce.[94] Lan Dingyuan noted in the 1720s after visiting a village that of the 257 men there only one had a wife.[95] This skewed gender composition had the effect of making women, including aborigine women, highly valued, as Chinese men began to outbid each other and aborigine men for wives. And in contrast to Guangdong, outright slavery of men and women (*nu* and *bi*) was not common, and children could not easily be bought.[96] Government surveillance and restrictions on immigration also made it difficult for large agnate and kinship groups to migrate simultaneously. As a result, as seen below, the lineage and kinship organizations that developed in Taiwan in the eighteenth and nineteenth centuries had somewhat different forms from the corporate organizations commonly encountered in Guangdong.[97] Government intervention in settlement policies also shaped the particular social arrangements under which land reclamation took place and this, in turn, shaped Taiwan's social formation and the pattern of development of private property.[98]

The Qing Restructuring in South China: Strengthening the Smallholder

A new dynasty seeking to establish control over the polity typically reiterated support for the peasantry; after all, agrarian China was the revenue base of imperial China. In the case of the Qing, the widespread rebellions by peasants and others and the long drawn-out civil wars had added urgency to this policy. While the Manchu were anxious not to alienate local elite opinion unnecessarily, the Qing state also moved to ensure that the taxes would actually be collected, and the survival of the regime was ensured as the wealthier Yangzi Delta and then other regions of the south came under control.

The Qing inherited its tax structure from the Ming.[99] The early-Ming taxation system had been based on two interrelated principles with separate levies of land and labor. By the end of the dynasty, however, the land tax and labor services had been commuted into one tax payable in silver. This was the so-called single-whip method (*yitiao bianfa*). Rather than requisitioning labor services from individual households, the state now demanded silver from the adult male head of household and the silver was used to pay persons hired by the state to perform various tasks. The process of commutation was facilitated by the influx of silver from Spanish American, Japanese, and other sources. The Qing taxation system proceeded formally to combine the land tax and the labor service (*di ding*) into one. The poll tax became auxiliary to the land tax; those without land were now exempt from the primary tax dues. The land tax was by far the single most important source of government revenue, representing 73.5 percent of the total down through the eighteenth century.[100] The government therefore had a considerable interest in preserving its tax base; a 1684 memorial from the governor of Anhui makes the logic clear: "Tenants are by nature poor people who till the land and pay rent. . . . If tenants have spare energy, they should be allowed to open up more land in order to increase the amount of taxes to the state. If all the tenants who engage in cultivation become bondservants of official families, then even the profits of the hard labor of small peasants will fall into the hands of wealthy households and will certainly create a waste of taxable land."[101]

In the immediate years after the Manchu conquest, generous tax remissions were provided in much of the country to encourage peasants to return to their fields. In the south, lands abandoned during the rebellions and the evacuation of the coastal provinces were resettled in the 1670s and 1680s. The nationally registered acreage rose from approximately 290 million *mu* in 1651 to over 590 million *mu* by 1691.[102] The destitute were settled on new lands. In Guangdong, for example, 2,819,200 *mu* (almost 47,000 acres) of land were reapportioned to 31,300 people in 1684.[103] Securing rights to land was also used as an inducement to bring people to the police registers; at least one magistrate in Guangdong declared that voluntary compliance with the *baojia* (security groups and tithings, including the community self-defense system) registration would be rewarded with "an officially sealed certificate guaranteeing permanent rights to land."[104]

The Yongzheng emperor actively encouraged reclamation and settler projects both on the mainland and on Taiwan. In 1729, an imperial edict declared that government loans be provided everywhere to help poorer peasants open up new lands on which taxes would be waived for three to ten years. These reclamation policies added significantly to the smallholder's access to land since local officials, whose promotions depended on preventing local unrest and successful collection of land revenues, also supported the measures. Officials in Guangdong, for example, repeatedly urged the Yongzheng emperor in the 1720s and 1730s to provide peasants with security of tenure as a way of attracting immigrants from eastern Guangdong to the sparsely populated western regions of the province.[105] The late 1720s and 1730s were also a period of official support for immigration to Taiwan as part of the larger efforts at land reclamation made during the Yongzheng era. Several officials shared the observations of one memorial to the emperor, "In the newly formed county of Changhua, there is plentiful unopened land that is suitable for settlers."[106] Arrangements were proposed to allow access to aborigine lands by cultivators. The Yongzheng emperor recommended that, "Local officials should be told to investigate all the deer fields belonging to the aborigines that can be reclaimed. The tribes are allowed to rent these to settlers for cultivation and the lands must be registered on the tax registers."[107] Several tens of thousands of people emigrated to Taiwan in this period. As an added inducement, Taiwan's overall land-tax rate was lowered in 1731, while the usual tax write-offs for land reclamation were maintained.[108]

Requests from governors to settle poor people on lands continued in the following decades. In 1742, the governor of Guangdong requested that small plots of land on hillsides and sandy soil be given tax exemptions so that "poor people" could grow sweet potatoes, tobacco, sugarcane, and other cash crops, and this request too was granted.[109] As late as 1745, the request of the governor of Guangdong that one hundred *mu* of hilly land be given to landless poor peasants with a tax waiver for ten years was also approved.[110]

The proportion of direct producers affected by these changes was further increased by state intervention on behalf of some minority groups like the Hakka (*kejia*), the immigrants who had moved from the north to the south in centuries past, as well as the local Danmin.[111] The state sought to accommodate the latter on land. An edict issued by the Yongzheng emperor in 1729 exhorted, "Powerful families and local strongmen must not mistreat them. . . . Officials should encourage the Danmin to open up waste land and take up cultivation as commoners (*liangmin*)."[112] But though the Danmin were legally emancipated, the state was not able to reverse some of these local customary relationships; a few managed to transform themselves into smallholders, but the majority of them continued to live on boats. The Danmin were often hired by the dominant lineages to develop and settle polders only in the initial stages of land reclamation and continued to provide the labor for menial jobs.[113] The state was more successful in placing the Hakka. Starting with the 1720s, the government took the initiative of encouraging Hakka migration from the mountainous regions of northern Guangdong to the Pearl River Delta. Hakka migration from eastern Guangdong to Taiwan also began during this period.[114] Although these new immigrants seldom got the best lands, and their increased migration in the eighteenth and nineteenth century was to be the source of ethnic strife in both Guangdong and Taiwan, they did become part of the peasant communities of South China with full rights to landownership.

The ranks of direct producers were additionally increased by tenants who had been successful in rent-resistance struggles, not only of the seventeenth century but also in the early decades of the eighteenth. In Guangdong's Xiangshan county, for example, tenants in 1736 rebelled against a landlord who demanded "outrageous" rents on his 1,765-*mu* estate. The state intervened and permitted these tenants to open up uncultivated land with ownership rights.[115] This was not an isolated incident, for the governor of Guangdong complained of numerous lawsuits resulting from "evil tenants" laying claims to land and managing to resist both eviction and rent payments on the grounds that they had improved the land and therefore now owned it.[116] Peasant proprietorship, and thus direct access to the means of production, was also sustained because permanent tenancy rights were inheritable and technically salable; as discussed below, there are several examples of tenants who managed to resist being thrown off the land by exercising these rights.[117]

This type of reapportionment did not automatically mean that the neediest all gained access to land or that the wealthy did not take advantage of the land reclamation policies of the state. But this was the best the Qing could hope to do to bolster their revenue base, when in the 1650s and 1660s, in the face of opposition from powerful gentry interests, the state found itself unable to push through a new land survey. It therefore settled for a registered acreage that matched the 1588 Ming survey and some legal controls to ensure that a large percentage of the population would stay on the tax rolls by remaining owners of land.[118] To further sustain the viability of the tax base, the state also took several steps to limit gentry power over tenants and poorer peasants.

To begin with, it restricted gentry access to particular privileges that came with political office. For example, in 1657 the state terminated the officials' and degree-holders' exemptions from payment of the labor tax, and granted only a personal tax-exemption privilege to those who had passed the examinations. The privilege was no longer extendable to family members.[119] Then, perhaps as a demonstration project, the state conducted the infamous Jiangnan Tax Clearance Case (or Tax-Default Case) of 1661 when 13,517 degree-holders and 240 employees of the yamen were investigated and punished by dismissal, confiscation of property, imprisonment, public flogging, and deprivation of degrees and titles.[120] Although the long-term impact of this particular case as a deterrent to gentry manipulations of the tax rolls may not have been what the Manchu government desired, this tax-default case was followed by other similar initiatives.

The other approach used by the state in its attempts to consolidate central imperial authority was to seek to curb the legal privileges of the local gentry. While it is doubtful that the Qing initially envisioned the complete abolition of serfdom in China,[121] the exigencies of restraining local elite power made the emperors wary of relinquishing the power of the central state over a large number of its subjects. The power of the gentry over tenants therefore continued to be a subject of imperial concern; a 1679 edict noted, "Lawless gentry and scholars who privately prepare flogging boards and sticks, and [with them] punish their tenants without authorization; and those who appropriate women of tenant families, making them their female slaves or concubines, shall be deprived of their ranks or titles and punished for their offences."[122] The 1679 edict does not seem to have accomplished the desired goals; for in 1681, the Kangxi emperor again ordered, "From now on if there are gentry and elite households which turn tenant households, convicts, and poor people into slaves (*nu*) and similar conditions, the governor or the governor-general of that province shall impeach them."[123] Of course, here, too, as in the case of the gentry tax-defaulters, the government was not entirely successful in implementing these measures, and in many provinces, including Guangdong, forms of servile labor continued where some peasant communities ended up in relationships of subservience to other more powerful villages and lineages.[124] All status privileges also could not be terminated, for senior officials repeatedly sent up memorials to the Kangxi emperor complaining that families with local official connections were opportunistically using these connections for personal gain.[125] But there was one major success. The widespread enserfment of direct producers, as in the late Ming, was curtailed. The legal status distinctions between landlord and serf, prevalent since the Song through the principle of *zhu pu zhi fen* (distinction between master and servant), were also abolished. If a landlord killed a serf, who now had the status of a commoner, he was to be punished for committing a crime against a commoner, not a servant.[126] Although the state continued to uphold the rights of the landlord to collect rent, the legal right of punishing recalcitrant tenants was taken out of the hands of individual landlords. Some efforts were also made to limit landlord usury.[127]

Many of these policies became codified as state and imperial ideology through the pronouncements of the various emperors. The Kangxi emperor stated, "I reminded the provincial officials that I really was concerned about the people's livelihood, and warned them to permit no fraud or concealment which might prevent my favors from reaching the common people, and not to use these changes to exact new payments."[128] Both the Yongzheng emperor and the Qianlong emperor made similar pronouncements and stressed that landlords should be benevolent and show concern toward the poor tenants. They also warned the rich against hoarding grain and other foodstuffs.[129] These edicts were incorporated into the texts for the didactic village lectures (*xiangyue*) that the state sponsored twice a month.

The ultimate example of such imperial benevolence was the enactment of the *yongbu jiafu* (never raise taxes) decree of 1713. The tax liability of households was fixed at the level of the *ding* tax in 1711. This ensured that there would be no tax liability on additional adult males in the household. As interpreted in practice, this became applicable to the land tax as well.[130] Shigeta Atsushi has pointed out that this decree encouraged the physical mobility of peasants, for the state now no longer kept tabs on the landless for tax purposes.[131] The landless of one province could move to another to take advantage of reclamation projects with state support for settlers to establish land rights. The mobility of labor also made it possible for those without access to land in one region to work elsewhere and use their earnings to buy land in their home districts. For example, in the 1720s agricultural workers from Huizhou and Chaozhou districts of Guangdong went to Taiwan annually in the spring and returned after the autumn harvest and used their income to buy property and support their families.[132]

I think the argument can be taken a step further. One unintended consequence of remitting increases in the head tax also meant that the direct producers now had no constraints on trying to multiply their labor force, for the household could control the additional labor without penalty in the form of tax increases. Increasing the number of workers in a household created at least short-term possibilities for increased income. Qing restructuring of the agrarian relations of production was not designed to herald any dramatic break with the past but to restrain and modify its most oppressive features which, by enabling an increase in servile and bonded labor in the Ming, eroded both the revenue base of the state and the property rights of the peasantry and resulted in fiscal and political instability. The outcome of this convergence of tenant and poor peasant demands for land, on the one hand, and the Qing state's interests in land revenue, on the other, was to strengthen the rights of tenants and smallholders to land. The Qing state undertook a massive effort at reclamation in order to settle as many tax-paying producers as possible. Additional labor could provide a family with some advantages, especially as secondary sources of income through household manufacturing became possible. By the same token, however, the absence of primogeniture among the peasant producers also multiplied the units of production along already existing lines and set in motion a regime of population growth.

Private Property Rights: Lineage, Family, and Community

How did the newly enfranchised peasant communities seek to safeguard their rights to land? Could outsiders, say merchants from Zhejiang and Fujian, involved in the sugar and silk trade with Japan, use their profits to buy land in the Pearl River Delta? In this section, I turn to the primary institutions that shaped and formed the parameters of peasant life in South China—namely the lineage or the corporate-group formation, the family, and the village community—and investigate their combined impact on property relations. These three institutions could overlap in their material interests and spatial locations, and often did. But simultaneously, as part of the configuration of daily life, they also remained distinct loci of social, cultural, and economic relations, mediating rights, responsibilities, and opportunities of their members at each level.

Any discussion of social property relations in South China of necessity involves at least a schematic consideration of the lineage and related corporate-group formations.[133] We begin our discussion with this institution, without being unduly influenced, hopefully, by the "received wisdom of Sinological anthropology."[134] Of course, not all lineages had equal social or economic power, and the efficacy of membership in the corporate structure varied accordingly. Nor did everybody live in a single-lineage, single-surname village.[135] Some lineages clearly became more powerful in the course of the Qing period and, as discussed below, managed to control their neighbors more aggressively through their control of resources, ranging from agricultural lands to markets and systems of transportation.

For our purposes, the term "lineage" is perhaps best understood as "a *corporate group* which celebrates *ritual unity* based on *demonstrated descent* from a common ancestor."[136] Although I am inclined to accept David Faure's modification of the term "demonstrated" descent to simply "acknowledged" descent, for many a lineage invented ancestors when lineage formation was still in considerable flux in the Pearl River Delta in the late-Ming and early-Qing periods,[137] it would seem that there was an acute impetus to develop some form of collective with corporate bases in shared assets. In the absence of agnatic kin, lineage-like associations such as "clans" developed, which "recruit[ed] members on the basis of *fictionalized* descent rather than demonstrated descent from known ancestors."[138] In Taiwan, while there were some large lineages with demonstrated agnatic descent, the particularities of emigration and the greater importance of other forms of kinship in certain localities led to the development of corporate formations such as "same-surname associations" (*zongqinhui* or *tongxinghui*) and "same-district associations" (*tongxianghui*).[139] All of these social organizations, in varying degrees, reconstructed and emulated the agnatic kinship and organizational structures of the lineage and provided their members with benefits derived from jointly owned property. While there is a vast anthropological literature on the distinctions among these organizations,[140] for our purposes there are two features of lineages and related organizations that are of interest: the social outcome of cross-class alliances effected by these group institutions and the impact on the land market through corporate property augmentation.

Although lineage and simulated-kinship organizations had existed prior to the Qing, there is general consensus that they proliferated in the aftermath of the seventeenth-century crisis. It has been argued that the attack on gentry and elite privileges by peasant uprisings, the acquisition of property rights by the majority of direct producers, and the efforts of the state to preserve its tax base were countered by the building up of corporate wealth and authority via a revitalization of the institution of the lineage in south and central China.[141] This was neither a "natural" nor "inevitable" process, as Rubie Watson puts it; numerous case studies have shown that well-organized patrilineal kinship groups were able to take advantage of every opportunity that arose in the tumult of dynastic transition and the coastal evacuation in Guangdong.[142] Initially, the Qing state also saw the lineage as an institutional avenue for restoring order and social control. Other voluntary social associations drawing on members from the poorer classes, such as sworn-brotherhoods and secret societies, did exist in rural society but were suspect because they frequently adhered to proscribed religions or causes. The lineage, by contrast, was seen as benevolent. The Kangxi and Yongzheng emperors, in particular, believed that the lineage could aid in fostering Confucian ideology and organizing social welfare. People were asked to establish ancestral shrines (*jia miao*) and lineage schools (*jia shu*), institute charitable fields (*yitian*), and revise genealogies (*zupu*) "so that distant relatives may be bound together."[143] Lineage ancestral halls proliferated in Guangdong; ancestral halls, built in the official style, "promoted status by association" for all the kin.[144] As Qu Dajun noted at the end of the seventeenth century, "A lineage with a thousand people has several tens of ancestral halls; small surname [groups] and plain families, with lineages which do not even have a full hundred people, still have several ancestral halls. Those called the great ancestral halls are the halls of the first ancestor."[145] In other words, state and gentry-landlord ideological interests converged and permitted the lineage to emerge as a powerful social and economic institution. But why did the militant peasantry of the seventeenth century succumb seemingly so readily to cross-class alliances represented by the lineage and other kin groups? I suggest that cross-class alliances were necessary for the protection of private property and that the need to organize collective defense of the hard-won rights to property was at the core of this alliance.

The roots of the revitalization of the lineage in the Qing lay in the local conditions during the late Ming, and, as I show below, the lineage organization continued to provide crucial security to property owners in the Qing.[146] The ability of the state to provide physical protection and security to the peasant communities in the south had more or less evaporated by the seventeenth century. Taiwan was a military colony with ethnic Han soldier-farmers continuously encroaching on aborigine rights and lands; there were numerous raids, killings, burning of villages, and looting by both sides.[147] In the Pearl River Delta, Chinese and Japanese pirates in the thousands had taken over entire villages and collected fees on junks and boats passing their territories.[148] As foreign trade and the inflow of silver increased, the inducements were many; local strongmen and corrupt officials who were involved in illegal trade provided protection to the gangs of pirates, smugglers, and robbers who lived off the peasants. Even after the establishment of formal peace by the end of the 1680s, the power of local strongmen and bullies (*hao ren*) continued unabated. At the turn of the century Qu Dajun repeatedly writes of crops being robbed at harvest time, of fields being occupied by force (*zhansha*), of brigands holding the harvest to ransom, of local pirate bosses gathering shiploads of followers and descending on the hapless peasants, "brandishing swords and pennants and leaving many injured and dead."[149] Fortified villages and local militia under the lineage banner were natural outcomes of these continuous struggles; villages began to resemble fortresses. The Hakka of Taiwan's P'ing-tung plain surrounded all their villages with protective walls when they built them in the seventeenth century; across the straits, the residents (*bendi*) of Huizhou county, Guangdong, built a twenty-foot-high wall with sixteen parapets in 1737, and surrounded the wall with a ten- to twenty-foot deep moat for good measure.[150]

Endemic violence was also part of an ongoing process of accumulation. Essentially collective struggles to take over land and property, and to gain control over resources such as water and markets by driving out weaker rivals, such armed feuds could go on for three, five, or even ten years.[151] Increasingly violent and well organized by the eighteenth century, the warring factions could call up thousands of men in aid of their well-armed core militia. There is little evidence that peasants in either Guangdong or Taiwan had long stretches of peaceful coexistence. Officials started sending memorials up to the emperor as early as 1728 noting how, "with the ceremonial beating of gongs and displays of weapons," lineages prepared for feuds with sharpened agricultural tools, spears, knives, spears and muskets.[152] By 1766, the Qianlong emperor was expressing serious concern over lineage feuding in Guangdong:

> According to Wang Chien's memorial, the ritual land attached to the ancestral halls in the eastern part of Guangdong frequently caused armed feuds. . . . It is petitioned that the land be divided up in order to put this wicked custom to a stop. . . . We fear, however, that clerks and underlings may use it as a pretext and stir up troubles. . . . Moreover ancestral halls are built and ritual land instituted normally for the purpose of financing the sacrificial rites and supplying the needs of the clansmen. If the land is used lawfully to consolidate and harmonize [kinship relationships] . . . it is not a bad practice at all. But if [it induces people] to rely on the numerical strength or financial power of their clans, to oppress their fellow villagers, or even worse, to assemble mobs and fight with weapons, . . . [such a practice] surely should not be allowed to spread. This wicked custom is especially prevalent in Fukien and Kwangtung provinces.[153]

Known as *xiedou*, these notorious armed feuds of Guangdong, Fujian, and Taiwan were a constant source of peasant vulnerability.[154] On Taiwan, the increased immigration of Hakka and intensifying competition for control of resources led to a phase of severe intra-Han Chinese strife that lasted from 1782 till 1862.[155] The powerful Hakka lineages of the P'ing-tung plain, immigrants from Guangdong, organized paramilitary forces called *Liudui* (Six Units) to perpetuate Hakka alliances in the face of Hakka-Hokkien ethnic violence.[156] There were also feuds between Zhangzhou and Quanzhou immigrants, intra-lineage feuds, feuds between same-surname groups, and feuds between rural and urban residents. In Guangdong too, as one observer noted, "Sometimes the feud would be between village and village, irrespective of clans; sometimes it would be between two clans in the same village; and sometimes it would be between two branches of the same clan."[157] Even before the Opium War (1839–1842), after which arguably the situation further deteriorated in the Guangdong delta, reports such as the following were common:

> The magistrate of Nanhae [Nanhai] district issued a proclamation in 1829 against banditti who cut down the growing crop of farmers; and the farmers themselves, who quarrel about the bounds of their respective lands, collect a multitude and cut down each other's crops. In the vicinity of Canton, Whampoa and Macao, in the districts of Shuntih [Shunde], Tungkwan [Dongguan] and Sinhwuy [Xinhui], the people who cultivate land on the banks of the rivers, are particularly distressed by these practices. The banditti require them to pay for a ticket of security, and plunder those who do not comply.[158]

Opportunities for young men to earn money through wage-work in Southeast Asia may have also unexpectedly aided lineage feuds. Although the comments of the inveterate memorialist Huang Juezi (1793–1853) were probably colored by his concerns about the collapse of the social and moral order brought about by the influx of opium and foreign traders, he suggests that in addition to fighting, "adopted sons" were being sent off overseas to earn money for the lineage and then these funds were deployed for feuds.[159] Those without strong lineage and other collective organizations were all too easily victimized. As Adele Fielde from the American Baptist Mission near Shantou (Guangdong) perceived in the 1880's: "The Stones [Shi lineage] planted and watered their crops, and the Plums [Mei lineage] reaped the harvest. There were perpetual raids on the property of the Stones and they, having no redress for their wrongs, were in danger of utter extinction."[160] Membership in some form of collective was imperative under these circumstances. In South China, only groups without access to landed property rights, and therefore outside the process of accumulation and defense of such resources, such as the Danmin still living on boats or the desperately poor residents of Ploughshare Village in Taiwan, did not generate lineage-type organizations.[161]

For the vast majority of peasant producers, the lineage and village organizations thus became the most readily available safeguards against invasion and appropriation. The lineage elite, with their access to gentry status and officialdom, could call in the government troops as a last resort.[162] As a form of social security, the lineage council could take care of its own and provide recompense to those who died in its cause—even provide cash benefits for the injured, along with the chronically ill, the indigent, and the widowed.[163] In one case, as much as 300 taels was given as compensation to the families of those killed in a *xiedou*. The funds were raised by a special tax levied on the whole village by the lineage council.[164] In other cases "adopted sons" were purchased from the poor, or from poorer lineages or villages that had a subservient position to a dominant lineage. The young men were then sent off to fight. In return for security and protection, lineage members were *compelled* to participate in aggressive forays and defensive action, or pay for "substitutes." According to some lineage regulations, the lineage council asked all men between the ages of sixteen and sixty to show up when called, and those who did not do so had their names struck from the lineage records and lost their rights to settlement as community members.[165] The community defense of the direct producers' property rights thus muted class differences. In the long term this enabled the gentry-landlords to recoup, although in different forms, many of those very prerogatives that had been under challenge in the late-Ming early-Qing peasant uprisings and initiatives of the state.

The other aspect of the institution of the lineage relevant here was the formation of corporate estates, essentially various forms of land and property put into indivisible estate trusts. Descendants inherited "shares" in the income from corporate estates but not the right to dispose of the estate. The "trustees" could range from a handful of family elders in one village for a small estate to lineage council representatives spread over several villages where the lands were dedicated to the maintenance of ancestral temples and lineage rites, not to mention the maintenance of militia. Lineage lands were seldom sold, and there were severe penalties for those who attempted to do so without explicit written permission of all the representatives of the lineage branches (*fang*) that served as public evidence. These restrictions on sales of lineage and ancestral temple lands were enforced by the Qing law codes. A sub-statute added to the code in 1756 clarified that even sons and grandsons could not touch this property. Anyone found selling communal property of up to 50 *mu* (8.3 acres) illegally, "left by his ancestors to support their worship, shall be sentenced to military exile at the distant frontier."[166] Sales of larger plots were obviously out of the question. Lineage regulations also restricted land sales to non-lineage members.[167] Since lineage lands were used to support temples and provided the resources for ideological functions supported by the state as well as help in tax collection, the Qing government helped enforce lineage restrictions on sale.[168]

For all these "property-owning corporations," to borrow James Watson's term, whether lineage or clan or association, the corporate estate and its replenishment and augmentation was vital to continued growth and power.[169] The endowments of course did not occur simultaneously; and the value of the endowments increased over the centuries through continued contributions. In fact, the possibilities for land reclamation through the development of polders in the delta helped make some lineages and gentry-merchant organizations even more powerful and wealthy by the end of the Qing than they had been at the beginning of the period.[170] Consequently, by the twentieth century, the vast proportion of delta polder lands, in many cases the most fertile agricultural lands in the region, were owned by lineages and gentry-merchant landlord associations.[171] In many cases, such as that of the famous Minglun Tang of Dongguan, which owned some 76,000 *mu* (almost 13,000 acres), of which 45,000 *mu* were polder lands, the estate created vast new properties through aggressive land reclamation ventures.[172] Besides polders, lineage trusts included other agricultural lands, commercial properties, markets, pawnshops, transportation facilities, water supplies, irrigation canals, and salt beds for making salt by evaporating seawater. The Chen, Xian, Huo, and Li, the four powerful lineages who ran Foshan township by the eighteenth century, owned and operated wharves, ferries, warehouses, kilns, foundries, and pawnshops under lineage ownership.[173] As James Watson points out, the distinguishing feature of the most powerful and influential lineages in South China was that their corporate property had endured for upward of twenty generations.[174]

The impact of these corporate estates on the land market was significant. Although we do not have data for periods earlier than the twentieth century to trace out the shifts in detail, it appears that in addition to lineages, clans, and temple endowments, other corporate entities, such as gentry academic institutions and local militia, also managed to acquire and lock up a substantial portion of prime agricultural land in both Guangdong and Taiwan; in the one small town of Huicheng, two academies, the Palm Fan guild, and the local militia owned 4,079 *mu*.[175] Together, as a result of these endowments and trusts, much farmland ceased to be individually owned private property available for private sales. In the long-settled areas of the Pearl River Delta, where lineage corporate-property endowments had started out in the thirteenth century, as much as 50–75 percent of the land in a given village was under corporate control by the 1920s.[176] In Taiwan in general, the level of corporate property in villages typically varied from 25 to 50 percent of the paddy fields. But in some areas, such as in the Hakka-speaking region of southern Taiwan, between 50 and 70 percent of farmland was held by corporate associations by the end of the Qing.[177] We can then conclude that lineages and corporate structures affected the land market in two primary ways: by reducing the total amount of land and property that could be on the market at any given time, and by restricting sales of land to individual outsiders by laying down conditions for sale.

The lineage and collective organizations marked one end of the spectrum of social relationships; at the other end was the family or the household as the basic unit of consumption, production, and political authority.[178] The right to divide all property in land, house, movable property such as furniture, clothing, livestock and so on, was legally recognized. Contracts dividing family property were common. All sons, recognized as such by the father, had rights in the patrimonial estate regardless of whether they were the offspring of the primary legal wife, concubines, or female domestic slaves (*bi*). The common practice was to divide property on a ratio of six-tenths to the son or sons of the primary wife, four-tenths to the sons of others.[179] According to the Qing codes, which emphasized the inheritance rights of sons compared with earlier legal codes, even a son born of a proscribed sexual relationship (*jianshengzi*) would receive half the share of a legitimate son.[180] Although property could occasionally be set aside for very young sons, the usual practice was to divide the property after marriage. It was possible for adult brothers to divide the property while the father was still alive. Gazetteers going back to the sixteenth century refer to this; however, there is some evidence that earlier than that it was against the law.[181] The father could not, under any circumstance, legally disinherit a son.[182]

Subject to the payment of the land tax, the right to alienate private property was recognized by the Qing law codes. There was, in fact, a proliferation of complicated deeds of sale during the Qing, and thousands of "unofficial" (*baiqi*) versions of such deeds kept by families have now been collected. Various levels of sale were recognized, including conditional sales that could restrict sales in the future and redemption sales where the seller reserved the right to buy back the property at the original sale price. To be legally binding, a deed of sale had to have numerous witnesses: agnatic kin or a lineage relative, a maternal uncle or maternal cousin, neighbors, and most importantly a middleman-guarantor (*baoren* or *zhong baoren*).[183] The middleman's name had to appear on all transactions, for he had a legal responsibility; if the transaction turned out to be illegal, for the various reasons given below, the middleman was liable to punishment only one degree less severe than that meted out to the contractors.[184] The massive proliferation of land deeds of various types in the Qing, however, rather than suggesting an active market in land, may point to the fact that property rights were unclear and contested.[185] And did these rights of private property permit free alienation of land and free entry of capital? To what extent could the household, the agnatic kin group, and the community restrict the sale of property to non-kin and outsiders?

Much of the scholarship on the question of land sales, based on the prima facie evidence of contracts, has failed to consider specific barriers to purchase and sale and to the entry of capital. Evelyn Rawski argues that "there were no institutional barriers to profit-maximizing responses by the peasants." Shūzō Shiga, writing on family property, states, "Land did, to be sure, most commonly constitute the bulk of household property, but that very land could, depending the household income and expenditures, be bought and sold with comparative nonchalance."[186] Chinese scholars focusing on incipient capitalism (*ziben zhuyi mengya*) have also assumed that land could be freely bought and sold to anyone able to put up the money. I think it is necessary to show, rather than assume, that transactions in land were unfettered.

There were three groups with preemptive rights in any sale of property: immediate agnatic relatives, neighbors, and mortgage holders. In order to make a sale valid, it had to be clear that the first two had no objection and that the third was not involved.[187] I have examined over two hundred land sale deeds from both Guangdong and Taiwan, dating from the mid-eighteenth century to the end of the nineteenth century. All contain the phrase "first informed the relatives of the *fang* [agnatic kin]" (*xian zhao fangqinren deng*).[188] While by the end of the nineteenth century this may have become no more than an empty standard phrase and implied only the right of first refusal, it had earlier clearly indicated a serious restriction on sale.[189] When discussing the difficulties involved in land transactions, George Jamieson, conducting the earliest known statistical survey of Chinese agriculture, in 1888 comments, "On the occasion of a sale a score or more of brothers and cousins may turn up, all of whom are equally interested in the land, and the consent of all of whom is required to give a valid title."[190] Legally it was possible to redeem rights to land sold even two generations past if the deed of sale contained a clause indicating that it was a redeemable sale. Such claims could lead to a new sale being blocked. The proliferation of law cases, and indeed homicides pertaining to land sales, resulted in a revision of the Law Code in 1753, when the Qing government set a time limit of thirty years within which a redeemable sale had to be redeemed or else the sale would be considered final.[191] But thirty years is a long time to wait if the buyer was a potential investor hoping to realize profits through development and land accumulation. In considering land transactions, in addition to the portion of arable land removed from the market through lineage trusts and their restrictions on sale, it becomes necessary to consider the restrictions on free transfer that may have been posed at the level of the household and agnatic kin.

The village and the community can be considered next. This was the arena in which the peasants, the community elites, and the gentry-landlords came together. Many, though not all, villages in Guangdong had large populations by the nineteenth century; as S. W. Williams noted in the 1880s: "In the district of Nanhai, which forms the western part of the city of Canton, and the surrounding country for more than a hundred square miles, there are more than one hundred and eighty *hiang* [*xiang*] or villages; the population of each *hiang* varies from two hundred and upwards to one hundred thousand, but ordinarily ranges from three hundred to thirty-five hundred."[192]

In some instances the village was identical to the lineage, though many lived in communities that were not dominated by a single lineage.[193] The community, too, was not necessarily defined by the spatial and territorial limits of one particular settlement, but could be a multi-village cluster. But regardless of size and the degree of power of the local lineage, members of the villages and communities traced their descent through groups of patrilineal kinsmen who settled in the area. The community determined a common adherence to customary usage regarding marriage, residence, burial, property, and inheritance rights.[194]

Settlement rights were typically inherited. Membership in the community ensured access to the village commons, the right to collect firewood from waste and hilly grounds around the village, the right to build houses within or near the village, and, most important, the right to bury the dead, for this involved the use of land in perpetuity. The unity and identity of the community residents were fostered by participating in the village temple festivities, receiving shares of ritual pork and duck distributed at these ceremonies, reading out the names of all shareholders in the community, and performing rituals pertaining to the village earth god and community exorcism ceremonies.[195] Individual outsiders became members usually through marriage or adoption. In some communities it was possible for outsiders to become members with settlement rights by performing particular rituals, for example, one in which the incoming outsider provided a ceremonial feast for the villagers and literally "entered the register" (*ruji*).[196] However, communities could be completely closed to outsiders. In the Guan villages of Kaiping county, a lineage spread over forty villages and dating back to at least the thirteenth century, there was no non-Guan living within the village boundaries, let alone owning land, even in the twentieth century.[197] The Man (Wen) lineage of San Tin, a cluster of eight settlements and the home of one of the most important lineages of the Hong Kong area since the sixteenth century, did not allow any non-Man, even itinerant hawkers who wished to conduct business in the community, to stay inside the nucleus of subvillages after dark in the 1950s.[198] Similarly there was no question of an individual Hokkien or Hoklo settling in a Hakka village in Taiwan in the eighteenth century, given their long history of subethnic feuding. In both Guangdong and Taiwan, settlement rights in lands that had already been claimed (and hence had a nucleus of settlements) were won, not on an individual basis, but through the collective; an entire group or lineage won rights of settlement by driving out the previous occupants by force.[199] The community then, while not always closed to individual outsiders, could exercise considerable control regarding admission.

Not surprisingly the community also had a say in the alienation of property. As noted above, for a sale to be valid neighbors had to be informed about it. The consequences of disregarding such restrictions could be serious: "A Kuan (Guan) had secretly sold a piece of land to a Fang. His villagers did not like the thought of the Fang intruding into their territories, so there was a feud between the two lineages that lasted several weeks. It was finally settled when the garrison soldiers moved in to restore order."[200] Throughout the Qing such feuds between villages and lineages, involving rights of control over crucial economic resources such as land, water, and markets, were common.

A tenancy deed of 1734 from Xin'an county reflects the caution with which "outsiders" were treated. Although it granted rights of permanent tenancy, the deed stipulated, "Chung Yuk Hing is the tenant specified in this deed to farm the hill land, and *may not privately sublet it to people who live far away* [emphasis added]."[201] One rather unique set of thirty-one mortgage deeds (*dianqi*) of the Du family, obtained by David Faure from Bao'an county, just north of Hong Kong, and dating from 1829, shows that all the sales were to people living in the same village or the neighboring village.[202] These practices continued. In the twentieth century, in the hinterland of Hong Kong, the Man lineage allowed the Poon lineage tenure; but they, too, "would not allow the sale of surface land [rights] to strangers."[203] These practices raise questions about how feasible it may have been for an outsider, say, a merchant from Fujian or further north, to exercise entrepreneurial control over agricultural land in Guangdong in the Qing.

The cumulative impact of these restrictions on land sale to outsiders by the family, community, and lineage arguably presented barriers to the ready entry of outside capital seeking to invest in land. The fact that there was very little change in land prices in some areas in spite of population growth, such as in Bao'an county from 1829 to almost 1890, suggests that such restrictions may have indeed dampened the land market.[204] Wong Wing-ho, analyzing some of the land deeds from Dongguan county from the three-hundred land deeds collected by James Hayes, has also noted the unexpected stability in land prices during this same period.[205] What were the ways in which these kin- and community-based limitations acted to reinforce the existing social property relations? And how much land could an outsider capitalist or an entrepreneurial direct producer hope to buy? We turn next to issues of land tenure and land rights.

Land Rights and the Social Consequences of Small-Peasant Proprietorship

Numerous restrictions on the sale of land, the limited amount of land held in individual parcels as opposed to corporate land, and the general reluctance of smallholders to part with their primary means of subsistence meant that property came on the market in extremely small parcels, providing yet another barrier to outside capital seeking investment outlets. Although there are thousands of land deeds surviving from the Qing period, most land sale and mortgage deeds do not state the size of the property. Typically the official tax due on it is indicated and the plot identified only by trees, ponds, buildings, and levees indicating the boundaries. But a representative sample drawn from the land deeds that do indicate the size of the property illustrate the general point regarding the limited size of the properties that came on the market.[206] As we see from Table 14, the largest plot of land to come on the market was nineteen *mu*, a mere three acres, and that too in the year 1851, when in the aftermath of the Opium War and the first year of the Taiping Rebellion, property in the Pearl River Delta could scarcely have been a secure investment.

Homicide cases from the eighteenth century involving disputes over land sales show that even these small plots of land were deeply coveted. Neighbors fought and sometimes killed each other for properties less than half an acre in size.[207] The use of boundary markers such as trees and so on, in the contracts for land transactions, instead of noting the actual size of the plot on the deed, perhaps reiterated the importance of the local participants who knew the particulars of the boundaries of plots. But this also left the way open for innumerable legal disputes which complicated processes of sale and possession.[208]

The complexity of both land rights and tenancy rights in South China further inhibited casual transactions. Land rights were divided into subsoil rights and surface rights—"the bone" (*tian gu* or *di gu*) and "the skin" (*tian pi* or *di pi*). Consequently each plot of land could have multiple owners; the most common arrangement was the "one field two owners" (*yi tian liang zhu*). But sometimes there were even more with "one field three owners" (*yi tian san zhu*). This system of divided property rights did not begin with the Qing. It was certainly prevalent in some areas by the mid-Ming period, and some versions of limited transfers of land rights and multiple ownerships go back to the thirteenth century.[209] During the Qing, however, it became far more

TABLE 14
Size of Property Sold in Dongguan County, 1748–1901
(in *mu*)

Seller's name	Year	Size
Yuan	1748	8.9
Tao	1823	11.79
Lin	1823	2.7
Xi	1839	10.3
Chen	1840	5.0
Zhang	1851	19.0
Huang	1855	1.4
Xi	1857	1.2
Li	1868	4.0
Huang	1866	5.4
Ye	1876	6.0
Mai	1874	6.0
Li	1875	3.0
Qi	1885	1.2
Liao	1892	3.2
Li	1891	1.5
Chen	1893	3.0
Mai	1893	4.0
Zhang	1894	8.0
Zheng	1901	2.0

SOURCE: Manuscripts in the collection of the Guangdong sheng shehui kexue yuan, Ming-Qing lishi yanjiusuo.

widespread and was by and large the prevalent form of tenure in all the provinces of south China, as well as Jiangxi, Zhejiang, Jiangsu, Anhui, Hunan, Hubei, and Shandong. The diversity of these arrangements and the different types of tenancy make the categories of "landlord" and "tenant" based on the sole criteria of landownership meaningless, for many "tenants" were in practice wealthy landlords who rented large tracts of land and then rented out small parcels with usufruct rights to others.[210]

The complexities of the land tenure system were further compounded by the variety of arrangements under which sale of land could take place. For example, although the Qing legal system provided for "irrevocable sale," in which the vendor surrendered all rights to the land, there was also a legally recognized category of "revocable sale," in which the vendor reserved the right to buy back the property. The latter was very similar in practice to "pledging," which was, however, different from "mortgage." When "pledging" property, the use and income from the property were surrendered, until by repaying the money the property was redeemed. In a mortgage, the debtor did not deliver possession of the property, but paid interest to the creditor, who could secure the property only if the debt was not repaid. As noted earlier, prior to 1753, there was no time limit during which the mortgage needed to be redeemed; after that the limit was set at thirty years.[211] Sometimes the "bones" were mortgaged, while the "skin" was retained, essentially keeping the usufruct rights while selling only the legal ownership. So durable were the original owner's rights to property, that even in the case of "irrevocable" sale, customary law provided for additional payments (*zhaotie* or *zhaoshu*) to the original owner. Demands for such payments were made and honored repeatedly over several generations.[212] In many of the land deeds from Guangdong and Taiwan, other clauses were often added to the irrevocable sale, such as stipulations that tenants who had permanent rights would remain forevermore on the property.[213]

The possibility of splitting property rights into so many different levels of ownership made the direct producer's access to the means of subsistence extremely tenacious. Even those who could not hope to pay for full ownership, or could not retain full ownership for one reason or another, could prevent their complete proletarianization by alienating only a part of their rights. It was possible to buy and sell usufruct rights without establishing full ownership rights. The complex tenancy rights also enabled many to retain access to their means of subsistence through a combination of landholding and rental. In practice, these arrangements curtailed unambiguous access to purchased property. Capital could claim revenue as rent and interest under these circumstances, but could not get full ownership rights or production rights. While the demographic upsurge in the eighteenth century in Guangdong, within the existing framework of multifaceted land-tenure rights, further accentuated certain tendencies that are explored below, these were systemic tendencies embedded in the social formation. This is illustrated by a comparison of landholding patterns in Taiwan and the Guangdong delta. The demographic patterns of the two regions were quite different from each other, but like Guangdong, a rentier class, widespread tenancy, and smallholder-dominated agriculture also evolved on Taiwan.[214]

In the mid-seventeenth century, Taiwan was still a settler colony with a small population base. During two centuries of Qing rule approximately 450,000 hectares (1,111,950 acres) were brought under cultivation. The population of Taiwan grew largely by immigration from 2 million in 1811 to 3 million in 1895. The land-to-population ratio did not begin to decline until the 1920s.[215] Throughout the Qing, there was new land to be opened for cultivation, albeit at the cost of dislocating tribal hunting rights. Demographic growth on Taiwan resulted in further Han expansion into aboriginal areas and increased settlements in new areas such as the I-lan Plain on the eastern side of the island. The very dynamics of settlement, however, also led to the development of multiple tiers of tenancy.

Given Taiwan's history of military colonization, there were army officials as well as civil officials who had laid claim to vast estates in the Zheng-to-Qing transition.[216] Some others, like Shi Lang, who led the Qing naval forces during the campaigns on Taiwan, were rewarded with titles and estates by the government. All these official estates (*guan zhuang*) were settled by bringing in tenants from the mainland. Then, under the Qing policies of reclamation with its attendant benefits of tax waivers, land was settled by entrepreneurs, the *kenshou* or "reclaimer chief." These individuals, and sometimes groups of individuals, either by formal petition to the government or by private arrangement and payment of a fee to the aborigine chiefs, received permission to settle new lands. The *kenshou* were, by and large, wealthy individuals who undertook the reclamation of enormous tracts of several thousand *mu* of land. Known as the "big rent household" (*dazu hu*), these legal owners were responsible for paying the land tax and the meltage fees (*huohao*)[217] to the government. The rights to the "big rent" could be owned by one or more parties. These big-rent households sublet the land to lessees who operated as contractors. These arrangements were usually permanent. The lessee, called the "small-rent household" (*xiaozu hu*), could rent out lands, in turn, to numerous tenants who were the actual cultivators (*xian geng dianren*) for between three and ten years.[218] The lessee in effect was the de facto owner of large tracts of land rented from the de jure owner for a certain fixed amount of rent. His tenants owed him rent and often had no direct relationship with the de jure owner. A contract dated 1781, for example, between a *kenshou* named Liu and an aboriginal group for renting of 191 *jia* (420 acres) of land, agrees on a fixed rent and then lists the names of 61 tenants who were going to be on the land. Among these tenants, in turn, some were clearly going to sublet to yet others, for they were renting plots of over 17 *jia* (almost 39 acres), an area far larger than could be cultivated using family labor alone.[219] The increased participation by aborigine tribes in the land-settlement programs in the eighteenth century did not alter the arrangements between multi-level strata of rentiers and tenants. Making a rapid transition from deer hunters to landlords, several tribes joined the ranks of the *dazu hu*.[220] Some emerged as active partners in land-development enterprises via their Han interpreters working out complicated arrangements for access not only to land but also to water.[221] Elaborate contracts were drawn up enabling two-tiered and even three- and four-tiered rentier arrangements.

In Guangdong, by contrast, the ratio of land to population had begun to decline perhaps as early as the eighteenth century. Data from the eighteenth century do not make it possible to determine what percentage of the direct producers belonged to the category of landowning cultivators and how many were usufruct tenants. One eighteenth-century commentator in Guangdong observed, "All are households of freeholders (*zigeng nong*), and no land is leased."[222] The observer was not quite correct, for, as noted, there was widespread tenancy of various types. Overall a higher percentage of the direct producers may have been owner-operators in the eighteenth than in the late nineteenth and early twentieth centuries. The mid-Qing population figures for the mainland are based on data from 1776–1850.[223] They show that the population of Guangdong was over 16 million in 1787. By

1820, it had increased to well over 21 million, resulting in Guangdong being the ninth most densely populated region in the country.[224] The land-person ratio declined from 7.90 *mu* per person in 1393 to 5.4 *mu* per person in 1685. By 1887, it was 1.1 *mu* per person.[225] Peasant possession of land, with partible inheritance, had resulted in an enormous group of peasants willing to work themselves and household labor as intensively as possible and rent land when their own plots became inadequate.

Qu Dajun noted differentiation within the peasantry based on access to resources. Discussing sugar manufacturing in Guangdong around 1700, he uses the categories of "rich or upper peasant" (*shang nong*), "middle peasant" (*zhong nong*), and "poor peasant" (*xia nong*). Rich peasants were those able to afford their own cane crusher, whereas around five middle-peasant families and eight to ten poor-peasant families would have to pool resources to purchase one. As for draft animals, some households could afford their own, while others cooperatively owned a buffalo. Cooperative arrangements no doubt made it possible for many more families in the *xia nong* category to continue operating small landholdings, for without such arrangements, many more would have had to join the ranks of agricultural laborers. But Qu does not say how much land peasants in these various categories owned, though it is clear he is not discussing tenants. Zhang Jiancun, a late-eighteenth-century *jinshi* and author of *Jiuhuang zhengce* (Strategies for Famine Relief), uses exactly the same terminology as Qu Dajun for describing tenant operations. He classifies those with more than 20 *mu* as rich or upper households (*shang hu*), those with 12–13 *mu* as middle households (*zhong hu*), and those with 4–5 *mu* as poor or lower households (*xia hu*).[226] In the absence of better data, we can only infer that the "middle peasants" described by Qu Dajun probably owned around 10–15 *mu*, enough to meet subsistence needs. These intense pressures on land-to-population ratios, however, while leading to differentiation within the ranks of direct producers, did not lead to complete proletarianization. The proportion of the population without any access to land remained surprisingly small.

There has been considerable research on the rise of "commoner landlords" or "managerial landlords," on the one hand, and agricultural wage-workers on the other in the Qing. Lenin's *Development of Capitalism in Russia*, suggesting that the employment of hired labor was the principal manifestation of agrarian capitalism, has provided the model for the close research on wage-labor and Chinese incipient capitalism. The emphasis on managerial landlords in this research also borrows from the English model of agrarian capitalism.[227] Careful scrutiny of hundreds of homicide cases involving agricultural workers has established that a substantial number of people worked for wages and evidently such wage-workers increased during the eighteenth century. These cases show that there was also differentiation within the labor force in the terms of wages and employment—short-term (*duangong*) versus long-term (*changgong*).[228] But were these Qing agricultural laborers completely landless, and also without access to land as tenants?

Twentieth-century data suggest that the size of this landless proletariat in the Qing must have been very small. C. K. Yang's research on the Pearl River Delta in the 1940s showed that in the vicinity of Canton, only 20 out of 230 families, or 8 percent, were completely landless and worked for wages as their sole means of income. Chen Han-seng found 6.9 percent were landless agricultural laborers in 1933 in the ten villages he surveyed in Panyu, Guangdong. Philip Huang has established that in the 1930s in the Hebei–northwest Shandong area long-term agricultural worker households accounted for 12.5 percent of all village households, while in the Yangzi Delta the incidence of long-term agricultural wage-labor households remained below 5 percent.[229] Even if we accept the higher figures as the norm, the very limited degree of proletarianization in China is apparent when we note that already by 1688 in England, a majority (56 percent) of English rural laborers were proletarians and forced to work for wages. There was a 360 to 420 percent increase in the number of landless peasants between the 1560s and the early 1600s in England.[230] In China, the success of the peasant rebellions of the seventeenth century and the revenue-collection interests of the Manchu state ensured that peasant producers with varying degrees of ownership in land relying primarily on household labor for all aspects of production continued to dominate the economic landscape. The possibility of working as wage laborers indeed enabled some to retain and renew their status as smallholders, as seen above in the case of migrants to Taiwan in the eighteenth century. Additionally, the long-term outcome of the various types of communal restrictions on land sale, the complicated mortgage and sale procedures permitting split ownership rights, and the widespread application of permanent tenancy rights, altogether strengthened the direct access of the vast majority of peasants to the means of reproduction.

By the same token, all of these restrictions also limited the power of landlords to expropriate the peasantry completely. Tenant militancy had certainly not abated in the eighteenth century. A review of a sample of sixty-five documents of the Board of Punishment dealing with major tenant uprisings culled from the sixty years of the Qianlong reign (1736–1795) shows that eight of these sixty-five large-scale rent-resistance movements were in Guangdong. The governor of Guangdong complained in 1735 that there were "evil tenants who cursed their landlords and threatened violence."[231] By the nineteenth century, some tenants, by appealing to the community, were able to form "'rings,' agreeing among themselves that no other person would be allowed to take over cultivation from the peasant in occupation."[232] Similar conditions prevailed in Taiwan where the *Chu-lo xianzhi* of 1717 was already stating, "When the tenant who has occupied the land for a long time does not pay the rent, the taxes are also not paid. The landowner then wants to find other tenants. However, the people cry out and there are uprisings, and the tenant becomes the owner in this corrupt practice."[233] Peasant militancy thus further limited the extent to which landlords could use economic discipline against peasants by evicting recalcitrant tenants en masse. Additionally, as noted, peasant property rights were defended by the Qing state. Ultimately, therefore, the landlords' economic interests were better served by strengthening institutions like the lineage that extended the social power of the elites.

The authority of the lineage council strengthened the landlord's hand when dealing with tenants from within the lineage. Those who failed to pay their rent on time, for example, were punished by *ting zou* or the suspension of the privilege of receiving sacrificial pork, an important ceremony that annually reaffirmed a man's ties to the lineage and the ancestors. Because ouster from the lineage terminated all privileges of access to the commons, water resources, and burial grounds, this was not a casual matter; it was to be "shut out from the community of the living and of the dead members of the *zu*."[234] The lineage and its council also dispensed justice and punished breaches of justice by imposing fines and physical punishments.[235] The lineage exercised control over the labor of all adult males to be used for purposes such as building and repairing dikes, and constructing canals and dams for irrigation. Liang Qichao (1873–1929) recalled that all members of the Liang lineage between the ages of eighteen and fifty had to provide labor to dredge the canal in front of the village as well as to build dikes. Those who did not contribute labor had to pay an "avoidance fee"; those who did neither were punished by the lineage council.[236] The improved fertility of the fields allowed the gentry to levy higher rents. At the same time the increased wealth of the lineage enhanced its dominance over rivals in the area.[237]

The economic relations between landlord and tenant were thus mediated through myriad webs of mutual dependency.[238] Both groups were forced to defend their private property from competing lineages, pirate gangs, and others in the face of incessant strife and armed forays. The lineage elites and their village counterparts acquired social power from the organization of crucial services: the defense of all property, from the household, its goods, and its children,[239] to land, crops, ponds, trees, in addition to ensuring access to water, fodder on hillsides, burial lands, irrigation networks, markets, and so on. But in turn, this social power also allowed the elites to stake a claim to increasingly larger shares of the peasant-produced surpluses when peasants sought to rent land or, as we shall see, when they had to go to the market to buy and sell. Whatever limits to appropriation the peasant victories of the early Qing may have imposed on the gentry were minimized by population growth from the eighteenth century onward. Partible inheritance and the absence of primogeniture opened a clear path to greater income for the rentiers without their having to undertake any fundamental changes in the structures of production. Gentry-landlord and corporate investment went into creating more land through the tax-deferred development of polders, which were then rented out to small producers desperately seeking land and willing to pay rent deposits in addition to rent.[240]

The State, Landlords, Gentry, and Merchants: Taxes and Rents

The basis of the symbiotic relationship between the state and the local landlords' interests was simple: "tax is paid out of rent" (*liang cong zu chu*).[241] Therefore while the state sought to preserve its tax base by supporting the small peasant producer, it had to uphold the right of landlords to collect rent, for otherwise it could not be assured of its own revenues. The state's support for the landlord in matters of rent collection was underlined by its participation in punishing recalcitrant tenants. Furthermore, rent arrears were handled by the revenue office (*hufang*) within the county magistrate's office (yamen).[242]

In Guangdong tax collection began in the seventh month and continued till the end of the eleventh month. The magistrate's promotion depended on his tax-collection record. Failure to collect the proper quota meant a punishment, which could be (depending on the percentage uncollected) a demotion of one to four grades in rank or even dismissal.[243] The magistrate consequently had every interest in collecting the taxes, a process that needed gentry cooperation. As Rev. Krone noted in 1859 in Xin'an county, "When the Mandarins intend to levy the taxes, they announce their intention to the gentry of the villages, one or two weeks, or sometimes a month, before their arrival. They make a progress through the district, accompanied by a sufficient force to protect themselves against large bands of robbers, which sometimes have the audacity to attack the tax-collectors if the escort be not strong."[244]

But notifying the gentry was scarcely enough. The tax was due in cash; most peasant-producer transactions were in kind; and there was no certainty that taxes from individual households could be collected on schedule.[245] Tax farming (*baoshou* or *baozheng*) was a natural outcome. The power of the lineage over the individual in the Pearl River Delta was strengthened by the role of the lineage-head households as tax collectors of the state.[246] In powerful and wealthy lineage estates it was common for the manager to pay the tax out of the estate funds first and then collect taxes from each of the segments.[247] The clout of the lineage, and the social sanctions it could impose, ensured payment in ways that the state could not. In Nanhai county, for example, a lineage had all its members pay taxes at the lineage ancestral hall within three days of notification. If anybody was late, he had to pay a surcharge to the ancestral hall. Not a single person had failed to pay their taxes on time for three-hundred years.[248]

Individual profit via tax farming was also common. A contract for tax collection, sold to the highest bidder by auction, was an arrangement between the magistrate and an authorized tax farmer whereby taxes were to be collected at a certain rate from a specified area and turned over to the magistrate by a certain date. The related institution of *baolan*, a contract for payment made between the tax farmers and the taxpayers, was technically illegal but widespread. Most tax farmers were from the ranks of the clerks and runners of the district yamen and the local gentry. In Guangdong, the elite of the dominant lineages were usually the tax farmers. The *Dongguan xianzhi* (Dongguan Gazetteer) described how the process worked: "This county has one hundred and twenty-seven *tu* [wards]. A copyist accountant [*shusuan*, an unranked sub-official] is assigned to each *tu*, and they keep the local tax records in their home. When the households make their tax payments, the accountants demand a bribe at a certain rate per *mu*. Only after the bribes are paid are the tax payments certified as completed."[249] The position of the accountant was so lucrative that it was "customary to make a gift" of 1,000 taels to the magistrate's office after as little as five years in this job!

As long as the state had to depend on the gentry-landlords for tax collection, the latter could find new ways of extracting a surplus, sometimes with the tacit support of the state or at least its lower-echelon officials. It was widely acknowledged that landlords rigged the scales when measuring the rent crop; but because this was justified as the surcharge for delivering the tax, the state was unwilling to intercede. Tenants in Guangdong, taking advantage of an order by the Yongzheng emperor to unify weights and measures, accused landlords of using larger measures for weighing rent grain and took them to court. But in several instances, in 1732, 1733, and again in 1777, Guangdong provincial and local authorities ruled that rent in kind could justifiably be measured with weights larger than the imperial measures or the ones normally used in the market.[250] The 1777 decision, engraved on a stone tablet for all to see and probably to discourage further acrimony, allowed a measurement as much as 30 percent larger than the standard market size.[251] In Xin'an county it was accepted that the holders of subsoil rights, that is the person who paid the tax, determined the size of the grain measure to be used for weighing the rent; measures 10 percent larger were common, and even a 50 percent larger measure was not unheard of.

A survey of 122 documents pertaining to rents in Guangdong from the Qianlong archival records, extracted from a nationwide list, shows that in 116 out of 122 examples, the rents were a fixed measure of grain weighed by the landlord. The remaining six in this sample were share rent agreements, determined as a percentage of the crop in the field. Data on rent collected for 1796–1820 suggest that actual rents may have varied between 40 and 60 percent of the crop and 50 percent may have been a common arrangement.[252] This is borne out by the comments of various observers from the nineteenth century. Liang Qichao recalled that ritual land of 700–800 *mu* in Chakeng provided the main income for the ancestral hall and that the lineage rented out estate land to tenants on the basis of a 40 percent share of the crop.[253] In Taiwan, where the landlords, both the subsoil owner and the topsoil owner, often lived away from the actual cultivators, it was common to add a charge of 6.25 percent to the rent as a freight charge for moving the rice received as rent. Even when the tenants had to deliver the rent, the charge remained.[254] A landlord in Taiwan (the *dazu hu*, the subsoil owner) renting out a "first-class paddy field" of one *jia* (16 standard *mu* or 2.2 acres) could get over 5 *dan* (925 pounds) of rice as net rent, that is, after paying the government tax. The direct landlord-tenant or topsoil owner on a permanent lease (*xiaozu hu*), renting out one *jia* to other lessees in the 1830s, received as much as 40 *dan* (7,400 pounds) of rice for high grade land while paying only 8 *dan* (1,480 pounds) as rent to the subsoil owner.[255]

Landlords collecting rent in person could squeeze more out of the tenants than just the rent. If the rented lands were at some distance from the residence of the landlord, the tenants had to pay a certain amount of "polished rice and a certain number of ducks to be used for food [of the rent collection party]."[256] Absentee landlords with no contacts with the village were less common in Guangdong than in some other parts of the country well into the twentieth century.[257] Although here too gentry from different surnames and lineages came together in the county capitals or the provincial capital and founded academies (*shuyuan*) and developed metropolitan links, the need to maintain all the embellishments of lineage power and direct involvement in tax collection through the *tujia* system meant that at least one member of the main family often continued to live in the ancestral village home. Ancestral temples and ancestral rites and rituals also helped maintain connections with the village; as Qu Dajun noted, "If there is a temple, the descendants return, for the sake of family roots."[258] These arrangements involving direct contact no doubt helped limit delinquency on rent payments.[259]

It has been suggested that a greater frequency of fixed rents and permanent or long-term leases usually indicates certain incentives to tenants to increase productivity.[260] But although there were permanent tenancy rights, not all leases were long-term leases. In both Taiwan and Guangdong permanent leases were less common for second-tier tenants and those below and became increasingly less so by the late nineteenth and twentieth centuries.[261] And where longer-term leases and labor and material inputs succeeded in raising the productivity of land, there is some evidence that the gains were short-lived for the tenants. For example, in 1776, in Lufeng county, Guangdong, a landlord realizing that tenants were making good "profits" through growing oranges, increased the rent by 50 percent. In Dongguan county in the late eighteenth century, a tenant named Hu rented seventy-five *mu* of land, five *mu* of which was swamp, at a cash rent of 70 taels per year. A few years later, when the landlord found out that Hu had drained the swamp and was also cultivating it, he immediately raised the rent by 10 taels. In a similar case recorded from contemporary Zhaoyang county, the landlord also increased the rent when he noticed the tenants' abundant harvest.[262] By the late eighteenth century, landlords were generally raising rents and typically converting a portion of the rent into a cash demand as well. As demographic pressures intensified competition for land, landlords were able to take advantage of the peasants' need for land and increase the rent, demand prepayment of a portion of the rent, and require substantial rent deposits.

On the other hand, there were few incentives for landlords to undertake cultivation themselves. Working the land oneself with the help of hired labor could actually reduce potential income. In the 1880s, in some areas of Guangdong, for example, agricultural wages were 8–14 dollars (*yuan*) a year plus meals, tobacco, and barber's fees for shaving.[263] Using this and other similar wage data from missionary surveys, Li Wenzhi has calculated that a plot of land which would earn 30 taels net in rent would, if cultivated with hired workers (and without tabulating the costs of one's own labor), bring in only 19.23 taels. In four other provinces, Jiangsu, Zhejiang, Hebei, and Shandong, the same equation held.[264] In every instance it was more profitable to rent out land than to cultivate it. As the saying went, "whoever has land has rent."[265] Ultimately, as seen below, there can be no simple comparison made between income from rent and earnings from managerial farming because the landlord could, and did, add to his income through sales of the rent crop, rent deposits, and usury.

Already by the end of the eighteenth century it had became common for some landlords to demand a portion of the rent in cash, and often at the time of the signing of the lease.[266] This evolved into the institution of rent deposits, which by the nineteenth century were generally 30–50 percent of the rent. Rent deposits could range from 10 percent of annual rent to three years' rent. In the He Shide estate of Xinhui, between 1818 and 1892, rent per *mu* varied between 27.8 *jin* and 38.7 *jin*. Except for the crisis year of the Opium War, rent deposits averaged 60 *jin* per *mu* or almost twice that of the rent.[267] Although lineage rules varied, members of a lineage were not exempt from paying rent deposits; the Guan of Kaiping paid as high a rent deposit as the non-Guan.[268]

Cash generated from rents and other sources was used for lending money, a lucrative source of income. Lineage estates and individuals had moneylending operations. The interest rates varied from 8–10 percent per month in Panyu, to 12–20 percent annually for individuals in small villages in Shantou, to "the customary high rates of interest" of 50 percent per annum in Xin'an county.[269] If the borrower of the lineage funds was unable to pay back the money, and if he owned land, the lineage had the power to foreclose on the land.[270]

How about the merchants? Could they have become entrepreneurial landlords, who, because of their involvement on the world market, should have been interested in raising output? Were there barriers to their reproduction and processes of accumulation? On the contrary, it seems that the sharp distinction between merchant and gentry had been blurred in the south from as early as the Song on,[271] and there were few impediments to their cultural and social reproduction as a class. Landlord families in both Guangdong and Taiwan, in the manner of the elites in south China, included both merchants and gentry members; the term *shenshang* (gentry-merchant) is perhaps the most appropriate for describing this class, rather than attempting to draw distinctions between "gentry landlords" and "commoner landlords."[272] Wealthy merchants could be full participants in gentry culture with all its embellishments, for the route to assimilation was open. Wu Chongyue (Howqua III), for example, not only built a famous garden and became well known as a collector of rare manuscripts and paintings, he also sponsored several major literary projects and became the patron of well-known gentry scholars.[273] Although every now and then a Confucian-minded bureaucrat from another province would send up memorials to the emperor deploring the behavior of Guangdong officials—"behaving like mercantile men and not caring for official warnings"—the fact that several of the prominent gentry academies had headmasters who were of mercantile origin, shows how irrelevant such distinctions were at the local level.[274]

The Qing state recognized a mutuality of interests also at the national level. As long as financial support and gifts were given by merchants, the state was willing to enhance their gentrification. Perry Anderson's comment, made in reference to western Europe, is perhaps equally apt here: "He who privately purchased a position in the public apparatus of the State could then recoup himself by licensed privileges and corruption (fee-system) in a kind of monetarized caricature of investiture in a fief."[275] Since the 1670s, the imperial authorities had created special examination quotas for merchants in Guangdong, Zhili, Zhejiang, Shandong, and Shanxi. In these examinations the chances of success were set by quota at one out of ten in the *shengyuan* examinations and one out fifty in the *juren* examinations, as compared to the success rate of only 1–2 percent in the generally administered examinations.[276] Taiwan, too, received special quotas for the civil examination. Several dozens of military degrees, which required only minimal literacy, were frequently awarded.[277] Those who made money as merchants either rapidly purchased degrees or managed to enter at least the ranks of lower-gentry by taking advantage of these examinations. This trend is most readily discernable in Guangdong where a very large percentage of the "commoner" landlords purchased official degrees and thereby acquired gentry status; Guangdong had the second largest number of *jiansheng* degrees purchased of any province, 38,264 between 1800 and 1830 alone at 108 taels apiece.[278] Such accommodation of the merchants by the state and its bureaucracy, "both registered the rise of mercantile capital and arrested it" in China and elsewhere.[279]

Social mobility also made it more logical for these newly arrived gentry-merchant landlords to rent out their lands instead of working them directly. Even in Taiwan, where with its frontier culture one might have expected a somewhat different outcome, merchant-reclaimers turned to renting and joined the ranks of rentiers. For example, Shi Changling (1672–1742), an entrepreneur who developed an enormous irrigation system that watered a total of 19,000 *jia* (41,800 acres) in Chang-hua county in 1719, nevertheless rented out the land piecemeal to tenants.[280] Similarly, three landowner-traders, who had been among the major reclaimers in Taiwan, undertook a project to irrigate six villages in the I-lan Plain in 1807. The construction took four years to complete and irrigated 247 *jia* (almost 600 acres) at a total cost of 4,868 Mexican dollars. But once constructed, the annual rent income accruing to the landowners from the irrigation system was 700 *dan* of rice, with a cash value of some 500 Mexican dollars.[281] This rental income, unlike the risks on the market, was a secure and highly lucrative return. In Guangdong, too, there are some seventeenth- and eighteenth-century descriptions of cane cultivation covering "thousands of *mu*" of land. Qu Dajun refers to extensive orchards, tea gardens (*cha yuan*) and thousands of *mu* of *chaozhe*, a variety of cane suitable for cultivation on tide land, all owned by a *hui* (merchant association) from Shilong, Dongguan.[282] The Wanqing sha, or Ten-thousand-acre Polder, owned by the Minglun Tang, the gentry-merchant association from Dongguan, was also immense in size. But as in Taiwan, the vast holdings were all rented out in multilayered tenancy arrangements, with as many as four levels of rentiers above the direct producer in some cases.[283]

The point here is not that commoner or managerial landlords did not exist in Guangdong or Taiwan. Indeed with painstaking research Li Wenzhi and Liu Yongzheng and others have culled examples from the archives of the Board of Punishment showing that such individuals operated farms in both provinces.[284] But they are isolated examples, and the data do not suggest that there was a systemic transformation under way. There is also no way of knowing whether ten years down the road, these entrepreneurial commoner families did not purchase degrees and become gentry-landlords. The biographies that exist in fact suggest that this was indeed the case.[285] To sum up then, members of the landlord class—gentry, commoner, and merchant—could receive rent, rent deposits, interest payments, *baolan*, and other fees and dues collected in cash and kind. The gentry-landlords also received income indirectly via the surplus appropriated as tax by the state. Given this range of possible sources of income, undertaking managerial agriculture and submitting directly to the risks of the market made no sense for those who had land to rent.

Conclusion: Peasant Property and the Limits of Change

It was rational, under the circumstances described above, for the gentry-merchant landlords to invest in the acquisition of office via the examination system or purchase and generate more opportunities for rental income via the reclamation of new lands.[286] Throughout the Qing, gentry-merchant landlords were able to increase their possible sources of income through rent deposits and so on at one level and the use of lineage feuds and paramilitary activities at another. They did not face a crisis of economic reproduction until the Qing state itself collapsed.

Increased opportunities in trade and land reclamation undoubtedly brought many new men into the ranks of landlords in the early Qing. But there were no barriers to their gentrification, and thus they could pursue strategies of reproduction similar to those of the existing gentry elites. Merchants having gained official position even changed their name or operated under two names. For example, the first Howqua, Wu Guoying, was better known as Wu Haoguan; his grandson, Wu Chongyue, conducted business under the name of Wu Shaorong.[287] Elite merchants became part of the imperial state; a quick look at the financial contributions of some of the Hong merchant-landlords to the government underlines the symbiotic relationship. Between 1773 and 1832 such contributions exceeded 40 million taels; the Wu family alone gave more than 10 million. Wu Bingjian (also known as Houqua II) contributed 33,000 taels for public works in his son's name and was one of the few to receive a *juren* degree without going through the examinations. Wu Chongyue, who contributed 40,000 taels to a public granary, was a negotiator for the 1857–1858 war with western countries, and was honored with the rank of financial commissioner and the Red Coral Button of the second class, the highest button granted to those who were not formal officials of the state. In Taiwan, the Lins of Wufeng, who started out as local strongmen, owned so much land in the nineteenth century that their rents alone furnished as much as one-tenth of the rice exports from mid-Taiwan. The personal assets of one of them in 1894 was 200,000 taels and the branch of the family at Pan-chiao sent large shipments of rice as donations to north China during the nineteenth-century famines.[288] Such merchants, the gentry members of their families, and their corporate interests, together controlled vast estates. We have already mentioned the estates of the Minglun Tang, which was formed by several gentry-mercantile interests coming together for a corporate endeavor. One can multiply these examples. As long as the gentry-landlords, merchant-landlords, and related elites had a variety of sources of income via their landed properties and their nexus with the state, it was neither necessary nor rational for them to want to undertake the risks of direct production or invest in improving production on properties they already owned.

The direct producers, having won rights to land through generations of struggle and thereby ensured their means of subsistence, were intent on protecting their land. This took the form of community institutions and membership in social organizations that limited the entry of outside capital. While land was the property of persons, the right to alienate it was not. This, in turn, limited the extension of the market in land. Merchants and landlords could develop new lands, but it was far more logical to let the land to middlemen on conditions of permanent tenancy or rent it out through their own corporate structures and live off the rent.

For the direct producers, it was also rational to have many sons, both in order to ensure security in their old age and to maximize family labor on the farm and in household manufacturing. There were no restrictions imposed either by the community or the state on early and universal marriage; some benevolent lineages even set aside funds for the indigent to marry if they had not managed to save the funds for bride-price by age forty.[289] But, inevitably, given the rules of inheritance, this led to fragmentation of landholdings. The overall tendency was to limit the potential for those types of economic activities that depended on economies of scale and required major investments or even large numbers of operators.

Finally, because the direct producers sold their labor power only after working on their own fields, the labor market, too, was limited. For the vast majority, the need for labor led to an urgency to develop cooperative arrangements within the community, ensuring access to labor during harvests and other critical moments in the agricultural calendar. These arrangements, "informal but as binding as a contract," specified the number of people, including the wife and children, the dates and hours of work, and so on. The premise of these arrangements was *gan qing* (sentiment) and a person who contravened them by not performing the promised share of work became known as one "who did not want face" and ran the risk of not receiving help even in a real crisis.[290] On the one hand, these arrangements strengthened the control of the community over the individual producer; on the other, they enabled poor and middle peasants to establish a tenacious hold on the means of production and prevented their complete proletarianization by giving them mechanisms to share a plow, a buffalo, a sugarcane crusher, and other agricultural implements.

These arrangements further enabled a vast number of direct producers to undertake certain types of commodity production, including the production of sugar for the world market. In the next chapter, we will examine the factors that led the direct producers to undertake the cultivation of cash crops, and show how subsistence needs and commodity production were simultaneously accommodated in practice in the peasant producer–dominated economy of south China.

FIVE

COMMERCIALIZATION IN A SMALLHOLDER ECONOMY

> There are three harvests from a field in a year; the winter planting ripens in the spring, the spring planting in summer, and the autumn plantings in winter. . . . There are two harvests from the early rice fields; then in addition to cabbage [*brassica* var. *oleifera*], indigo is planted for dyes, as are yellow ginger [*curcuma* or turmeric, also used for dyes], barley or rape, and sweet potatoes. After the rice fields have been harvested, the stalks are soaked in sea water and then burned to make salt. On the flat hills and ridges there are *di* [*Miscanthus sacchariflorus*, used for making paper], sugarcane, cotton, hemp, various herbs for incense, fruits, and melons. The people are all very hardworking and so diligently devoted to their business [of farming] that it can be said that there is not a patch of uncultivated land nor an idle hand.[1]
>
> —*Guangdong xinyu* (1700)

THE INTENSIVE PATTERN OF AGRICULTURE noted in twentieth-century Guangdong already seemed to be in place in the late 1690s when Qu Dajun in his *New Descriptions of Guangdong* described the agriculture of Nanhai and Panyu counties of the Guangdong delta. Crops like sugar had been produced for sale, as we have seen, in parts of the province since Song times. Was the commercialization of agriculture in the Qing different in any substantial manner from that of the Song or even the Ming period, or was it a matter of greater volume and quantity, meriting the explanation of "involution"?

Several scholars have argued that the latter was indeed the case.[2] But, as this chapter will show, the seventeenth- and eighteenth-century expansion of commercial agriculture was quite distinct from the market-oriented production of the Song and early-Ming periods in two fundamental ways. First, even major commercial crops like sugar and silk intended for the sizable export markets were raised in the Qing entirely by smallholders, who now owned most of the means of production and moreover had direct access to their means of subsistence. Second, agriculture in the south fundamentally incorporated American crops, particularly the sweet potato, into the daily diet; the ready availability of these crops was crucial to sustaining the social formation of the smallholder agriculture that emerged in the Qing.[3]

The phrase "commercialization of agriculture" is at best an imprecise term. It tells us little about the organization and structure of the society in which this production takes place. Several scholars of Chinese socioeconomic history, drawing on neoclassical interpretations of economic behavior, have assumed that peasants were "rational, profit-oriented petty entrepreneurs" taking advantage of expanded markets and population growth.[4] Was this the case? As a general pattern, proximity to urban markets and population density have been important influences on the intensity and degree of specialization in the agricultural sector. But the processes by which these market demands work their way into the rural production structures remain unexplored if we accept a priori that "increased contact with the market" was sufficient to turn the Chinese peasantry into a class of independent entrepreneurs.[5]

Other scholars participating in the debates on the development of incipient capitalism in China have approached the question of commercialized agriculture from an entirely different angle. Innumerable examples of "commoditized agriculture" *(nongyede shangpinhua)* in the Ming and Qing have been presented as evidence of capitalist or proto-capitalist relations in the countryside.[6] This conceptual framework is modeled on Lenin's *Development of Capitalism in Russia,* the basic premises being:

> The growth of commercial agriculture creates a home market for capitalism. Firstly the specialization of agriculture gives rise to exchange between the various agricultural areas, between various agricultural undertakings and between various agricultural products. Secondly, the further agriculture is drawn into the sphere of commodity circulation the more rapid is the growth of the demand made by the rural population for those products of manufacturing that serve for personal consumption; and thirdly, the more rapid is the growth of demand for means of production since neither the small nor the big rural entrepreneur is able, with old fashioned "peasant" implements, buildings etc., etc., to engage in commercial agriculture. Fourthly and lastly, a demand is created for labor-power, since the formation of a small rural bourgeoisie and the change-over by landowners to capitalist farming presuppose the formation of a body of regular agricultural laborers and day laborers.[7]

Lenin and others expected the outcome of this commercial agriculture to be a tendency toward consolidation of landholdings and a concomitant specialization of production. Specialization, in turn, would ultimately lead to universal dependence on the market *even for subsistence needs* (growers of sugarcane would become purchasers of rice), leading finally to capitalism. But was there such an inexorable pressure toward specialization in Chinese agriculture? How did the existing social property relations affect the commercialization of agriculture?

This chapter begins with the empirical evidence on agricultural developments in the Qing. These can be conveniently approached under two rubrics: first, the impact of American crops, and second, the intensification of pre-Qing patterns of agriculture. Then, I turn to three basic questions: What was the direction of change in Qing agricultural practice? How and why did the direct producers enter into commercial agriculture? And, is there any reason to believe that the developmental sequence posited by Lenin was being fulfilled in south China?

New World Crops in South China

One of the distinguishing features of Qing agriculture, setting it apart from earlier periods, was the widespread use of American crops for both commercial and subsistence agriculture. The routes by which new crops and plants were introduced into China varied, as did the routes of diffusion within Asia and large countries like China. The Spanish and the Portuguese were major sources of these introductions; the Spanish were a particularly important source for the southeastern coast of China because in the Philippines they had undertaken a conscious project of crop introductions. One of the first acts of Miguel Legaspi after setting up the Spanish settlement at Cebu in the Philippines was to plant "Castilian seeds," which included many American crops.[8] A rapid diffusion of New World plants and crops followed in the sixteenth century as peanuts, cashews, sweet potatoes, potatoes, cassava (*Manihot utilissima*), maize, tobacco, peppers (genus *Capsicum*), tomatoes, custard apples, guavas, papayas, pineapples, avocado, squashes, and jicama were introduced in rapid succession.[9] Along with crops, the Spanish and the Dutch also experimented with animal husbandry. The Dutch, as we have seen, introduced cattle from India into Taiwan; the Spanish introduced the horse (typically Arabian or mixed with Arabian) into the Philippines and bred these with the Chinese (Mongolian) ponies found there.

These efforts at introducing new types of farm animals did not amount to much, and several of the American fruits and vegetables simply provided minor additional items of consumption in a region like that of southeastern China that was already well endowed with many varieties of both. Other introductions acquired very specific local importance. The use of cassava in China as a staple, for example, was limited to Hainan island. Elsewhere it remained a casual food, as in Guangdong and Taiwan, where it was made into a dessert with coconut milk, sugar, and bits of boiled corn. Similarly, the "white potato" (*yangyu* or foreign taro, *Solanum tuberosm*), acquired only regional importance in areas that were far from the agricultural heartlands. Brought into Asia in the early seventeenth century via Europe rather than directly from Peru, the potato was probably introduced simultaneously by the Portuguese and the Dutch to different parts of Asia.[10] It never caught on in southeastern China even as vegetable; the climate was probably too damp and tropical for its cultivation in most of these areas. Slowly potato cultivation spread northward, and by the late nineteenth century it was being cultivated widely enough to be noted as a significant crop in Shanxi, Gansu, Manchuria, and Inner Mongolia.[11] Three American crops, however—namely, maize, peanuts, and the sweet potato—were to transform the food habits of broad segments of Chinese peasant society, and tobacco quickly added nicotine to the general repertoire of addictive recreational substances.

Maize (*Zea mays, fan mai* or "western barbarian wheat") acquired the appellation "western" apparently not because it was directly identified with the Portuguese but because it came from the western regions of Yunnan.[12] Maize was introduced into China both overland from India and Burma and also through the coastal provinces of Fujian and Zhejiang around 1555. Although maize went on to become a primary food crop in some regions, such as Sichuan, Hunan, Yunnan, and parts of Guizhou in the south and Shanxi in the north by the nineteenth century, it also never caught on as a major staple in the tropical southeast. It was nonetheless known, eaten as a snack of roasted half-ripe cobs, and more often used for chicken-feed and fodder.[13] If, as we see below, sweet potatoes can best be identified with the smallholder economy of the deltaic south, by the nineteenth century maize was to become the staple of poorer residents of the highlands from Sichuan, Hubei, and Shanxi.[14]

Tobacco was the sole non-food crop introduced from the Americas into China in the late Ming. It caught on speedily; so rapidly in fact that the Portuguese were sorely disappointed in their plans for setting up a trade in Brazilian tobacco to China.[15] Although cultivated very widely, it was, however, not as major a cash crop in south China as it was in some northern regions such as Shandong. But it was important in other ways. In Taiwan, for example, tobacco had become an important item of trade with the aborigines as early as the Dutch period in the early seventeenth century.[16] Later, as a special and coveted item, it continued to be used as a gift, along with sugar, salt, and cloth, to the aborigines by mainlanders wanting to negotiate with them.[17] Since the quality of Taiwan tobacco was considered rather mediocre, higher-quality tobacco was additionally imported into Taiwan from the mainland during the early Qing.[18] By the nineteenth century tobacco cultivation was widespread throughout Taiwan and was used extensively both by mainland immigrants as well as by aborigine men and women.[19]

In Guangdong, tobacco became a commercial crop of some importance in some counties of the Pearl River Delta, including Xinhui, Dongguan, and Xin'an, in the eighteenth century. In some cases it was grown on hillsides and fields on higher ground, often in rotation with late-ripening rice.[20] Little attempt seems to have been made to grow tobacco extensively elsewhere in Guangdong until the mid-nineteenth century. Tobacco cultivated in other provinces, from areas such as Jining in Shandong, Lanzhou in Gansu, Pucheng and Longyan in Fujian, and Ruijin in Jiangsu, was famous nationally for its fragrance and flavor. Like that grown in Taiwan, Guangdong tobacco, too, enjoyed no such eminent status, and this may have limited its expansion as major commercial crop.

The peanut (*Arachis hypogaea, luo huasheng,* lit., "falling-flower gives birth"), domesticated originally in Brazil, is considered to be a Portuguese introduction to China because it is found listed as a "local product" as early as 1538 in Changshu county (near Suzhou).[21] The availability of many other types of edible vegetable oils, from varieties of *Brassica* species such as rape and turnip, initially slowed the expansion of peanut cultivation in China. But by the seventeenth century it was being cultivated in Guangdong in the same localities as sugarcane, setting up a long-term pattern of combined use of the two products. Peanut cultivation expanded in the Guangdong delta and Taiwan in the eighteenth century and then increased markedly in the nineteenth and twentieth centuries owing to an increase in world market demands for oil.[22]

Peasants in south China used all the available properties of the peanut. Sugarcane is a voracious consumer of nitrogen, requiring 50 to 200 pounds of nitrogen per acre. The nitrogen-fixing properties of the *Leguminosae* family, which includes the peanut, makes this a most suitable crop for growing in conjunction with cane to prevent soil depletion.[23] Peanut meal (remnants after oil extraction) was, moreover, a highly desirable fertilizer for sugarcane.[24] In China, peanut cake was also valued as a high-protein feed, primarily for hogs but in times of need for humans as well. Growing both sugarcane and peanuts, therefore, illustrates a pattern we see repeated; crop combinations that were advantageous for the soil were accurately selected by peasants; crops from the Americas that met special needs were readily integrated into the existing complex cycle. In addition to cultivation, peanuts and sugar were often also complementary products on the market, for they shared similar types of processing methods. This may have resulted in wealthier families undertaking the processing of both by the nineteenth century. For example, it was said that the Lin family in Tu-cheng, Taiwan, "did well in various small enterprises, including the sugar business, peanut oil pressing and the camphor trade."[25] In Dongguan in Guangdong, a nineteenth-century observer noted, "The production of peanut oil is most abundant in this county. The rich have raised family fortunes with sugar sheds (*tangfang*) and oil presses."[26] Similarly, in Ha Tsuen, Xin'an county, the Deng started up a peanut oil–processing factory and soon added the processing of raw sugar.[27]

The sweet potato (*fanshu* or *ganshu*, *Ipomoea batatas* or *I. batatas edulis*), a Spanish introduction into Asia via Manila, was introduced into mainland China via two routes in the last decades of the sixteenth century: from Vietnam into Dianbai county near the Leizhou peninsula of Guangdong and from there into Dongguan county in the Pearl River Delta, and from Manila into the Changle county of Fujian.[28] It was probably introduced directly from Manila by the Spanish to their colony on Taiwan in the early seventeenth century. By the middle of the seventeenth century the sweet potato had spread throughout Guangdong, Taiwan, and Fujian. Several late-Ming commentators noted, "it is treated like grain in Fujian and Guangdong."[29] Xu Guangqi was a great supporter of varieties of yam (*Dioscorea esculenta*) and the sweet potato and wrote extensively about their virtues in his 1608 composition, the *Ganshu su* (Commentary on the Sweet Potato), and his other encyclopaedic study, the *Nongzheng quanshu*.[30] Many areas of Guangdong continued to cultivate varieties of Chinese yam as well as varieties of taro (*Arum colocasia*) throughout, but the sweet potato emerged as the primary staple in addition to rice.[31] As the 1819 edition of the district gazetteer of Xin'an county points out, "There are several types of yam grown in the county: there is the sweet yam, the mountain yam, the sweet potato, the linen yam, the hairy yam, the red yam, the white yam, and the greater yam. Of all these, the sweet potato is used by the local people as a substitute for rice. It is an extremely nutritious food characteristic of the area."[32] Innovative ways of consuming the sweet potato developed as it became a part of everyday life. Taiwan's Chu-lo county gazetteer of 1717 noted that besides being eaten simply baked, boiled, and made into a gruel and soup, it was also cut and dried into pieces and then made into a flour for noodles, and brewed into a kind of wine.[33] By the third decade of the eighteenth century the sweet potato had become important enough as a primary food crop in Guangdong for the Yongzheng emperor's imperial rescripts to estimate the regional food sufficiency and the food importation requirements of Guangdong in terms of *both* rice and sweet potatoes.[34]

Numerous factors influenced this rapid adoption of the sweet potato. The sweet potato is resistant to drought, relatively immune to locusts, and has low requirements of labor input and soil fertility. And, as Qu Dajun's 1690s description cited at the beginning of this chapter shows, the great advantage of the sweet potato was that it could be readily accommodated within the existing complex matrix of food and non-food crops. It can also be grown on marginal sandy land unsuitable for all other food crops. At least two crops of sweet potato and even three crops could be grown in south China per year without compromising yields. Sweet potato yields in twentieth-century China averaged 278 *jin* per *mu* (almost 370 pounds per one-sixth of an acre) of land or twice that of *gaoliang* (Chinese sorghum), millet, barley, or wheat.[35] In terms of calories provided per *mu*, sweet potatoes are twice as productive as these other dry land crops and provide more calories than white rice or the ordinary potato. While caloric content differs slightly with the gluten content of rice, a cup of cooked white rice provides only 185 calories to the 291 calories provided by a cup of mashed sweet potatoes, in addition, as we now know, to the vitamin A in sweet potatoes. The sweet potato has more dry, starchy, and sugary matter than the ordinary white potato, and chemical analysis shows it to have 10–20 percent sugar and over 16 percent starch content.[36]

The availability of a high-calorie, nutritious, but inexpensive and readily cultivable food crop at a time of expanding cash-crop cultivation arguably freed land and labor that would otherwise have been needed for growing food. The sweet potato need not be transplanted like rice, and although maximum size is obtained by fertilizing the seedlings a little, it can be grown without fertilizers. Planting a new crop is relatively cheap, for one tuber can provide a dozen or so shoots for new plants.[37] Twentieth-century studies in Taiwan show that whereas one crop of rice requires 85.92 male labor days, 18.75 female labor days, and 15.79 animal labor days per hectare (2.47 acres), the sweet potato requires only 9.47 male labor days, 2.47 female labor days, and 2.05 animal labor days per hectare.[38] The cultivation of sweet potatoes requires a minimum of work; only an occasional trimming of the tendrils of the plant to prevent excess leaves and smaller tubers is adequate, and this work was almost completely done by women and children.[39]

These properties helped make the sweet potato ubiquitous in both Guangdong and Taiwan.[40] All the earliest rural surveys available from Guangdong (made in the 1920s) point to the fact that sweet potatoes regularly made up three to four months' worth of the food supply for practically everybody living in the countryside. The poor ate sweet potatoes every day at every meal throughout the year in Guangdong as well as in several other provinces.[41] Intensification of non-food crop agriculture in the Qing was thus based on a subsistence food that required markedly less labor than rice and other cereals, less water, and less fertilizer.

What was the impact of this miracle food on the social and economic structure of the regions where it became a staple in the early Qing? The role of the potato in Ireland has been evaluated for its demographic impact in the eighteenth century, sustaining larger populations and increasing fertility by providing more calories.[42] In Flanders, Jan De Vries and others have argued that the potato encouraged the survival of tiny holdings when peasants switched from bread to potatoes as their staple in the eighteenth century because a larger population could be fed per unit of arable land.[43] Clifford Geertz has argued that in Java the cassava "acted more to dampen structural change in the rural economy than to strengthen it."[44] I suggest the sweet potato had a similar impact in south China. In south China the sweet potato gave the smallholder economy greater tenacity and flexibility in the face of population increases and dwindling landholdings. Extensive cash-crop cultivation and increasing quantities of production for the export market were readily accommodated in the south without devastating subsistence crises and also without a transformation of the existing social-property relations.[45]

Intensification of Pre-Qing Patterns of Commercial Agriculture

The commercialization of agriculture in the Qing in Taiwan and Guangdong was structured around three basic crops: rice, sugarcane, and the mulberry. The climatic conditions of south China permitted at least two crops of rice or one crop of sugarcane, or six to seven crops of mulberry leaves per year, in addition to subsidiary crops.[46] The soil and water requirements of rice, sugarcane, and mulberry are similar, though, as we see below, labor needs vary enormously.

Observers of agriculture in the Pearl River Delta in the twentieth century described it as one of the most efficient and innovative systems of agriculture they had ever studied.[47] Three combinations had evolved in the region from the seventeenth century on: (1) sericulture combined with pisciculture and rice cultivation; (2) sugarcane cultivation, the cultivation of fiber crops like kudzu and ramie, and rice cultivation; and (3) horticulture, aquaculture, and rice cultivation. Variations existed, and it is better to view these patterns as dominant in particular counties rather than inflexible structures. Rice, grown for consumption, rent payment, and sale, was the common crop in all three combinations.

As noted, rice was the only major item of export from Guangdong in the Song period.[48] But the techniques of cultivation left much room for improvement. Zhou Qufei in his book on the southern regions, *Lingwai daida* (Answers to Questions on What Lies beyond the Passes), wrote in 1178 with disapproval: "The farmers of Jinzhou [southernmost Guangdong] are very careless. When tilling they merely break up the clods, and the limit of their sowing technique is to dribble in the seed. Nor do they transplant the rice seedlings. There is nothing more wasteful of seed! Furthermore after sowing they neither weed nor irrigate, but simply leave Nature to take care of the crop."[49]

If this was the norm in Guangdong, techniques had certainly improved dramatically by the Qing. Double plowing and careful terracing had developed along with transplantation of the seedlings. To get rid of weeds such as *bai* (*Echinocloa* spp.), which are particularly troublesome because they look like rice, *huan* fish were first introduced in newly diked fields to eat away the roots of weeds. As an added benefit, fish dung would deposit fertilizer in the soil. After their task was completed, the fish were used to supplement the cultivator's diet.[50] Scores of Asian rice varieties (*Oryza sativa*) were cultivated. Broadly distinguished as *keng* (*O. japonica*) and *xian* (*O. indica*), there were also numerous types of Champa rice as well as the salt-resistant *zhi* (red) rice that could be grown on marshy land in the newly reclaimed areas of the Delta.[51] The 1797 edition of the Dongguan county gazetteer records twelve varieties of rice, distinguishing five varieties that could be grown on hills and three glutinous varieties that were used only in making desserts.[52] Subvarieties of rice that could be grown on hillsides were locally evolved. As Figure 27, also from the 1797 edition of the gazetteer shows, notwithstanding Dongguan's location in the lower reaches of the delta, the terrain was far from flat. Hilly protrusions, ranging from 500 to 1,000 feet, dot the landscape of counties like Dongguan, Xin'an, and Xiangshan, and this had made it necessary to use particular varieties that could be cultivated in the steep terraced fields on mountainsides.

Even though rice yields were high, almost 2,400 pounds an acre on an average,[53] some counties of the Pearl River Delta even in the late seventeenth century produced less rice than required and imported it from other areas. Qu Dajun begins his section on grains and cereals in the *Guangdong xinyu* by saying, "Eastern Guangdong is short of grains and regularly relies on western Guangdong."[54] A memorial from the

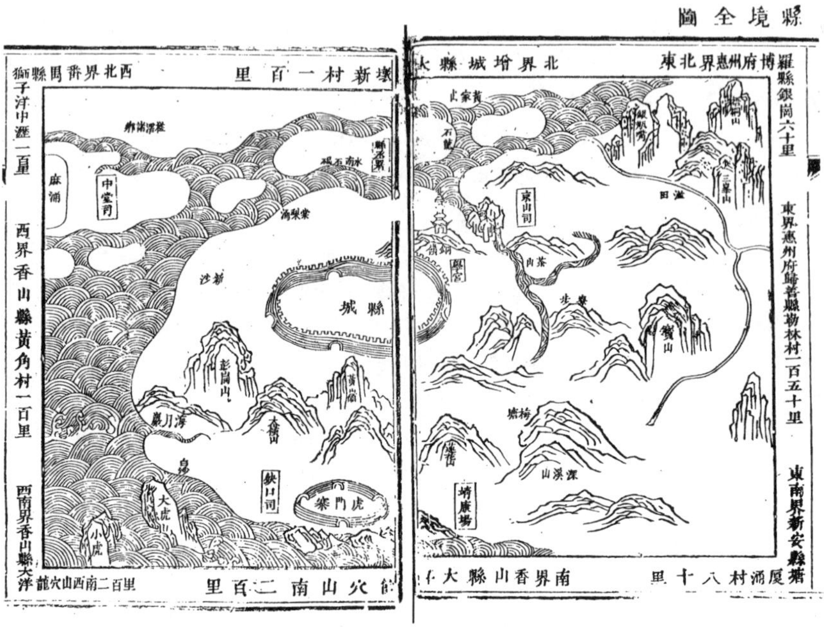

FIGURE 27. Gazetteer map of Dongguan county (*Dongguan xianzhi* [1797]), indicating locations of the county seat, important temples, primary hills, and major polders. Dongguan was known for its numerous temples.

governor of Guangxi in 1727 complained of the extensive purchase of Guangxi rice by the people of Guangdong and attributed the rice shortage in Guangdong to the fact that good farmlands had been devoted to commercial crops such as fruits, sugarcane, tobacco, and indigo.[55] Other sources from the eighteenth century similarly comment on the people of Guangdong cultivating non-food crops and relying on rice imports from Guangxi, a process that made some people rich and rice scarce.[56] Starting in the late eighteenth century, the government began offering inducements to Siamese and then Chinese merchants to bring in rice from Southeast Asia.[57] The imports from abroad included rice from Siam, Cochin China, Indochina, and India in the early nineteenth century;[58] and from Vietnam and Siam in the late nineteenth and early twentieth centuries. By the late nineteenth century annual imports from other provinces, and Southeast and

South Asia were over six million hundredweight (cwt; approx. 267,860 British tons).[59] From the eighteenth century on, various bureaucrats and Qing emperors frequently expressed grave concern that "even in a good year of harvest there is barely sufficient [rice] in Guangdong for six months' consumption." In 1727 the Yongzheng emperor declared:

> The viceroys and governors of these two provinces [Guangdong and Fujian] should do everything in their power to make the people realize that cultivating food is the most important activity for them. The people must concentrate on this vital necessity by devoting their energies to the cultivation of their fields. Agriculture must not be neglected for the sake of profit. Ignoring casual business and working diligently as a farmer brings the greatest merit. Plantations and orchards and so on should be undertaken only when there is extra land and labor.[60]

For obvious reasons there was a tension in bureaucratic circles between producing enough food to ward off famines and peasant unrest on the one hand and cultivating non-staple cash crops to generate the silver for taxes on the other. But the concern of the Qing state that people were no longer producing their food and that the subsistence sector was being eroded has found surprising support from contemporary scholars, who give it a different reading. The trend toward importing rice and increased interregional trade in raw fibers such as cotton has been interpreted as indicative of "a shortage of supplies relative to the size of the Chinese population" presaging the "trapped" economy.[61]

In my opinion, rice imports indicate a potential for growth in the Qing economy. New areas like the Pearl River Delta were able to undertake commodity production, which was vital to the expansion of commercial agriculture, because of an increase in food-crop production in adjacent regions, particularly Guangxi and the Yangzi River valley. The total level of rice imports, eight million pounds, represented only around 3 percent of the total provincial rice production of Guangdong by the nineteenth century.[62] While this was a substantial level of imports by Chinese standards, by the levels of the burgeoning international market in cereal commodity trade it was quite insignificant. Britain, for example, by 1877 regularly imported over 5,708 million pounds of wheat.[63] Although the market in rice expanded in Guangdong, in comparative terms the market in commodities was limited.

Rice exports from Taiwan to the highly commercialized districts of Fujian served a similar function as the rice imports from Guangxi did in the Pearl River Delta. The pattern of commercial agriculture was in many ways far simpler on Taiwan. As we have seen, settlements in Taiwan by the Dutch and the Zheng family were developed for the express purpose of developing export-oriented cultivation of rice and sugar. Cash crop cultivation had therefore begun simultaneously with settlement.[64] Cultivation of both sugarcane and rice expanded through the seventeenth and eighteenth centuries. Table 15 illustrates the increases in acreage for each crop between 1683 and 1735.

Cultivation of both sugarcane and rice expanded steadily through the seventeenth and eighteenth centuries; but as Table 15 shows, at least in the fifty-odd years between 1683 and 1735, the increase in land devoted to sugar was by far more dramatic. By 1735 it was almost two-and-one-half times greater than that devoted to rice. Other commercial crops were cultivated, though not as extensively. The Chu-lo county gazetteer of 1717 notes the cultivation of fruits such as longyan, pears, custard apples, and bananas as well as sesame (around 100,000 piculs or 1.33 million pounds were exported from the one port of Tou-liu-men alone), but above all sugarcane was cultivated as a cash crop in this county.[65] Restrictions against rice exports from Taiwan had been waived by the end of the Kangxi period, and this would account for the general increase in rice cultivation. Throughout the eighteenth century between 500,000 and 1,000,000 *dan* (18,500,000 pounds) of rice were annually exported from Taiwan.[66] By the 1730s, ships from Taiwan to the mainland started carrying wheat, beans, sweet potatoes, and indigo for sale to Xiamen and Shanghai,[67] although rice and sugar were to continue as the primary exports of Taiwan well into the mid-nineteenth century. In this later period tea and camphor wood were added to the list of exports as important items. As demand for tea and camphor soared, more of the upland and mountainous areas necessary

TABLE 15
Land in Taiwan under Cultivation for Rice and Sugarcane, 1683 and 1735
(area in *mu*)

	1683		1735	
County	Rice	Sugarcane	Rice	Sugarcane
Taiwan	43,912	52,839	55,754	89,134
Feng-shan	30,261	26,781	40,296	83,360
Chu-lo	10,961	43,765	18,521	152,200
Chang-hua	–	–	45,042	86,773

SOURCE: Ng Chin-Keong, *Trade and Society*, pp. 103–104; *Chongxiu Fujian Taiwanfu zhi*, pp. 129–162.

for these plants and trees were acquired from the aborigines. Pisciculture, however, which was to become so distinctive a feature of commercialized agriculture in Guangdong's Pearl River Delta, was not a particular feature of Taiwan agriculture during the Qing.

Sericulture, too, had a very different impact on Taiwan. Centered in the Jiangsu-Zhejiang area during the Song and Ming periods, sericulture was introduced into both Guangdong and Taiwan during the seventeenth and eighteenth centuries.[68] But on Taiwan, in many areas like those around An-ping, Chia-i, and Hsin-chu counties where sericulture was introduced by the government in the early Qing, it was soon replaced by a combination of rice, sugarcane, and ramie.[69] This may have been because unlike sericulture these other crops required lower levels of skilled labor, a scarce commodity on Taiwan. In Guangdong on the other hand, sericulture had a major influence on the economy. In the Lower Yangzi and the Lake Tai regions that were at the heart of the established sericultural industry in China, the silkworm-rearing season was relatively short and was limited to the spring. In the Pearl River Delta on the other hand, the southern location allowed silkworms to be reared from April to almost December. Particular counties in the Delta such as Shunde, Sanshui, Nanhai, and sections of Dongguan developed extensive sericulture during the

Qing and many fruit orchards were replaced with mulberry trees in this period. Maintaining the mulberry polders required year-round labor in addition to the labor-intensive process of raising silk worms and silk-reeling. So, in several of these areas, rather than maintaining rice and sericulture, which were both labor-intensive occupations, the peasants turned rice fields into fish ponds and planted mulberry trees on the embankments of these ponds. By the end of the eighteenth century, for example, only 20–30 percent of the land in Jiujiang district (Shunde county) was apparently still being cultivated for rice; the rest had been turned into fishponds and mulberry polders.[70] With the rapid growth of silk exports in the 1860s the economies of these counties became even more structured around sericulture and aquaculture; as one gazetteer noted, "In Jiujiang fishponds occupy half the land. Fish are raised in the ponds, mulberry trees are planted on the dikes. The men sell fish, while the women tend silkworms."[71] But Jiujiang district was an exception. In most areas, rice continued to be cultivated even at the height of the silk-export boom.

Prior to the mid-nineteenth century when mechanization began to change the industry, almost all aspects of sericulture, from growing the mulberry trees to reeling the silk from cocoons, were carried out within the same household.[72] The work was extremely laborious. As C. W. Howard commented in his early twentieth century study of sericulture in south China, "[i]t can be successfully carried out only where there are dense populations who are content to give long wearisome hours for a small money return."[73] The work was indeed exhausting. First, sheets of silkworm eggs with between 200,000 and 240,000 eggs on them were purchased. About 80 percent of the eggs hatched, so there were around 200,000 worms. Once hatched, the newborn worms had to be fed every two hours with mulberry leaves shredded to the thickness of coarse hair. The bits of chewed leaves and the droppings of the worms had to cleaned out continuously. Because the worms were delicate and tiny at this stage, they had to be manipulated by using a goose feather, and a household could end up moving 200,000 worms by hand every day. Altogether there are five stages in the growth of the silkworm from birth to the stage of the cocoon, with each stage lasting about three days when the worms eat voraciously and then rest. To raise worms from one egg sheet, stage 1 required 9–10 pounds of leaves; stage 3, 78–91 pounds; and stage 5, also lasting three days, no less than 2,600 pounds of leaves. The 200,000 worms by this time also required a considerable amount of space; they rested in no fewer than 100 baskets, 4 feet in diameter, which were usually stacked on bamboo shelves one above the other. After eighteen days of this extremely time-consuming feeding and cleaning, the silkworms finally spun themselves into cocoons, whereupon they had to be taken out and placed onto spinning racks.[74] The women continued to work even after the cocoons had formed, as they provided almost all the labor for reeling the silk yarn. In the Pearl River Delta by the end of the nineteenth century peasants raised six to seven rounds of silkworms each year, essentially around-the-clock work each month from the end of February to the first of October. Not surprisingly few families involved primarily in sericulture could afford the labor necessary to cultivate rice; but the income from the sale of silk no doubt gave some of them the means to purchase their food. Counties such as Shunde were therefore among the largest importers of rice.[75] But simultaneously, sweet potato cultivation also continued in these areas.

Unlike sericulture, which developed in Guangdong only in the seventeenth century and later, aquaculture was fairly well established by the late Ming. Gaspar da Cruz of the Order of Saint Dominic, visiting Guangzhou in the winter of 1556, has left a comprehensive account of pisciculture:

There are in the country, a great abundance of sea-fish, in sort that every day all the market-places are newly full of fresh sea fish, which seems a wonderful thing. But it is no longer a wonderful thing, on seeing the wonderful diligence which they use to provide themselves in the following way. You must know that in the end of February, in March, and part of April, when the great flowings are, there cometh great store of fish from the sea to spawn in the mouths of the rivers along the sea, whereby there breedeth infinite small fish of many sorts in the estuaries of the rivers. To get these spawns in this time, all the fishers along the sea coast do meet in their boats. . . . These fishers then, do take a very great quantity of this small fish and cast it in cisterns which they have made with stakes, and a very strong net made of wire, where they do feed them until the end of the fishing time. . . . [He then talks about how people come with baskets lined with oil paper to buy the fish.] Then they carry this fish in these baskets all through the country inward, changing every day the water; and all men of any possibility, within their grounds and enclosures have great store of fish in ponds, for the which they buy the baskets they have need. They bring up this fish in the ponds in a very short time with cow dung and buffalo dung, wherewith it groweth very fast. . . . In this way it can be understood how in the country many leagues distant from the sea, the marketplaces are daily filled with fresh fish of the sea. [76]

The concept of "a fish for every niche" informed piscicultural practice in Guangdong.[77] The earth scooped out in the process of making the ponds was used to build the embankments for planting fruit trees and later mulberry trees. In Xinhui and Xiangshan counties the ponds were used for raising fish in summer, mushrooms in autumn and winter, and rice seedlings in spring.[78]

The interdependent structure of sericulture and pisciculture led to a complex cycle balancing resources and needs. The fish in the pond would be fed the waste produced by the silkworms, and the pond sediment enriched by fish waste would be used as fertilizer for the mulberry trees.[79] Further refinements developed in the nineteenth century included planting various aquatic grasses in the ponds and breeding pigs as a supplementary source of income. The pigs were fed water hyacinths and aquatic grasses, the fish were fed pig and silkworm wastes, and both pig and fish manure were utilized for the mulberry trees.[80] The dung put into the ponds fertilized the algae bloom, which was eaten by the fish or their prey. This complex ecological structure of fish-pig-silkworm-mulberry cultivation therefore utilized all the available assets with a minimum of new inputs. The versatility of this pattern and its adaptability to market conditions is shown by the fact that in some areas vegetables or fruit trees rather than mulberry trees utilized the manure. With the decline of silk prices during the Depression of the 1930s, thousands of *mu* of mulberry trees were converted into sugarcane fields. The same symbiotic pattern obtained, except that now instead of silkworm wastes, the fish were fed bagasse and molasses after the sugarcane had been processed.[81]

Dwight Perkins has argued that over the span of eight centuries, from the twelfth to the twentieth, agricultural output in China was raised in equal measure by expanding the cultivated acreage and by raising the yield per acre. To these two basic techniques for raising output, we must then add a third, namely, the development of interdependent patterns of crop rotation and resource maximization by integrating new crops and combining agriculture with sericulture and pisciculture. Elsewhere Perkins has suggested that the major agricultural innovations occurred long before the Ming and that many of the techniques date back to the Tang and the Song.[82] The question that arises is: Given the proliferation of flexible new patterns of cultivation integrating New World crops and sericulture, were there, in fact, also improvements in agricultural techniques in the late Ming and Qing? A close study of sugarcane cultivation may elucidate this.

Techniques of Sugarcane Cultivation

Sugarcane consists of six species of perennial grasses of the family *Andropogoneae*, which originated in the Old World.[83] All cultivated varieties of cane are hybrids of these six species. The *Qimin yaoshu* (535) is the first pre-Song agricultural treatise to mention the cultivation of sugarcane.[84] It contains a brief reference, but has no information on methods of either planting or harvesting.[85] Fortunately, Wang Zhuo, in his *Tangshuang pu*, was interested enough in cultivation in addition to sugar manufacturing to include particulars; so there is good twelfth-century baseline from which to evaluate later developments. Wang Zhou begins with the species cultivated:

There are four kinds of cane. There is the *du* cane; the Western cane; the *fang* cane, which is referred to as the *di* cane in the *Bencao*;[86] [and] there is red cane, the *kunlun* cane referred to in the *Bencao*. The red cane is only fit for growing for chewing. One can make granulated sugar (*shatang*) from the variety called *fang* cane; crystallized sugar can be also made from Western cane, which is light in color, and the local people do not value it. The *du* cane is purple and tender, and the taste is extremely concentrated. It is specially used for making crystallized sugar.

Storage and planting methods: Select the short ones. [Wang's annotation]: (The buds grow between the joints. On the short ones the joints are closer together and have bud sprouts). Dig a ditch about two *chi* [about two feet] deep, [though] the width is flexible. Cut off the lower end of the canes. Stand the sets in the ditch upside down; cover them with earth. If you don't invert them, the rain water will collect in the leaves [on both sides of the cane stem] and after a while it is bound to rot.[87]

Wang Zhuo then discusses the preparation of the fields for planting, and methods of plowing:

Mix the damp earth and the dry earth together [during plowing] till it is like dough. Dig a ditch that is more than a *chi* (foot) wide and a *chi* and 5 *cun* deep [about a foot and a half]. Pile the earth [from the ditch] on both sides. Some time between the fifteenth day of the first month and the beginning of the second, plant the canes in separate rows. Cover lightly with a mixture of ashes and then with earth, but for no more than 2 *cun* [inches]. [Fertilize] twice, once around Qing Ming [the fifth day of the third lunar month] and once around Duan Wu [the fifth day of the fifth lunar month] with a thin layer of pig and cow manure and ashes. The earth on top should be in such a way as to allow the shoots to be always exposed. Around the middle of the sixth month [fertilize] again with nightsoil and manure. For the remaining months use the same method mentioned previously.

No amount of weeding is too much for the grass, and no addition of [new] soil is too much. But always keep the sprouts exposed. Wait until they are tall enough to form clumps. Using a big hoe turn over the earth on the mounds and cover [the clumps of stalks] completely. Harvest in the tenth month. All cane is extremely dependent on the fertility of the soil. It cannot be planted with other things mixed in. And, that which is a sugarcane field this year should be planted with the five grains [gaoliang, millet, wheat, barley, and rice] the next year in order to replenish the fertility of the land. Those who have extra land should plant something different for the next three years.[88]

Wang Zhuo's emphasis on the need to fertilize the soil frequently is particularly notable in view of the fact that in Brazil, Cuba, and even the Ommelanden in Java, where the use of complex fertilizers in sugarcane fields was not so thorough, soil impoverishment remained a major problem throughout the pre-industrial period. The maximum life of a sugarcane plantation in these regions was estimated to be around forty years, after which the land was abandoned owing to soil exhaustion.[89]

Since the other Song texts do not mention cane cultivation, our next source of information is the imperially sponsored Yuan text *Nongsang jiyao* (1273). Perhaps in a futile effort to promote the cultivation of sugarcane, citrus, and other southern fruits in the north, the text goes into some detail. The *Nongsang jiyao* recommends plowing the land at least four times before planting cane:

The method of planting: Fertilize the ground. Every year during spring, plow four times. More plowings are even better. Get rid of weeds, and make the land clean and ready to plant and turn the soil over. In general, it is right to plant in the third month. Further south, where it is warm early, [planting] can be done within the second month.

Chop each set into approximately five-*cun* [inch] pieces. Those which have joints in them are the right ones. They should have two or three joints for the shoots to grow out of the joints. The furrow [for planting] is a *chi* [foot] wide; and at the place where you plant, build up the earth slightly on the two banks [of the furrows]. Lay down the sets five *cun* apart. Cover them with two *cun* of soil. When the planting is finished, water around [the sets]. Only moisten the roots, don't drown the plant. If the sets get dry, water once every two or three days. If the rain comes in the proper amount, water once every ten days. When the shoots are more than two *chi* [feet], water continuously and extensively. If there are too many weeds, weed with a hoe.

Without flowering [the cane] ripens fully by the ninth month [and] before the frost which comes after. Classify the stalks by taste; the sweet-sour ones are fully ripened. If the taste is bitter, they have not yet ripened. Harvest the ripened stalks including the roots. Then according to the method [given below], boil them, except for the stalks which are going to be set aside for seed. Chop off the useless tips. Dig a deep pit. Line the bottom of the pit with grass. Store the stalks in an upright position [in the pit] and cover the top with a plank. Cover it with earth. Don't let the air through, freezing will destroy them. And so on to the next spring. At the right time, take the stalks out of the pit and cut into pieces according to the previous method. On the whole, those planting cane all use the top half of the stalks, which are all suitable for planting. The fat and juicy bottom [halves] of the stalks are used to make sugar.[90]

The discussion of the care, selection, and storage during winter months of the seed-cane in the *Nongsang jiyao* indicates a far greater knowledge of propagation than is evident from the *Tangshuang pu*. It recommends that the sets be taken from the upper part of the canes, while using the lower sections for making sugar—an important observation. Twentieth-century texts on cane propagation also suggest that sets are best taken from the upper third of the cane.[91] In addition, the call for repeated plowing to prepare the land thoroughly for planting is justified, for while sugarcane does well in heavy soils, compacted earth and waterlogged soils hurt yields. The increased labor input compared to the Song was therefore primarily directed toward better preparation of land.

The *Tiangong kaiwu*, written at the end of the Ming period, indicates a further increase in labor inputs, this time in the preparation and germination of the seed-cane. Song Yingxing recommends that the seed-cane sets be sprouted in a nursery, rather like rice seedlings: "When the sprouts are one or two *cun* tall, water them repeatedly with a clear liquid fertilizer [and] transplant them with a spade when they are six or seven *cun* high."[92] This would aid germination and encourage more rapid growth of the canes after transplanting and raise yields.[93] The *Tiangong kaiwu* also shows that by the early seventeenth century, fertilizer use had increased compared to the twelfth century. Now, the seedlings were not only fertilized repeatedly before transplanting but also afterwards. The recommended frequency of fertilizing after planting remained the same as in the Song (three times), but the types of fertilizer used varied from manure to sesame and rape-seed meal residues after oil extraction.[94]

The *Guangdong xinyu* of the 1690s shows the further maturation of techniques of cultivation. In order to produce more rapid growth of secondary and tertiary shoots, adding to the size of the clump of cane, Qu Dajun recommends planting at an angle instead of laying the set flat and parallel to the ground.[95] That this was indeed common practice is seen from the 1797 Dongguan county gazetteer, which also mentions that sugarcane ratoons were planted at an angle and that this produced more plentiful, sweeter canes.[96] Planting the seed-cane at an angle may have been a Guangdong agricultural innovation, but it was also used in Taiwan.[97] Each stalk of cane continued to receive care. Pehr Osbeck, a student of Linnaeus, visiting China in 1751 with the Swedish East India Company, noted with approval that the clumps of canes were carefully tied together (probably with bamboo supports) to prevent their breaking in strong winds and the typhoons which swept through south China in the late summer.[98]

But if all these Qing developments required more labor, there was also a major labor-saving innovation. Harvesting the cane at ground level leaving the stools from which another crop would grow, or ratooning, had become the norm. This technique may have developed by the late Ming, though the textual reference is oblique. Evidently, the first year the seed-cane would be carefully fertilized and transplanted as described above, but for the second and third years of cultivation, ratoon crops were common. The *Tiangong kaiwu* says, "At the beginning of the ninth month, cover the roots with (more) earth, in order to protect them from frost and snow after the harvest."[99] Qu Dajun is more explicit, "Old roots are sprouted by covering with earth; new ones are soaked in water."[100] Nineteenth-century observers of cane cultivation in Taiwan also found two- and three-year ratoon crops to be the norm, at the end of which the field would be cleared completely, the roots dug out and burned.[101]

There are, then, two distinct tendencies in agricultural practice after the Song. One was greater labor intensity, involving the use of fertilizers, transplanting the seed-cane, and repeated plowing. This aspect has received the most attention from scholars of Chinese agriculture.[102] But the other—ratooning rather than replanting each year—was actually labor saving. Ratooning saves a considerable amount of labor and money, for only a limited amount of replanting of new fields may have to be done each year. On the other hand, there was a very heavy expenditure every third year when the new seed-cane had to be purchased, in addition to the expenses for the extra fertilizer and labor for raising and transplanting the cane sets. Furthermore, the three-year crop cycle that this involved committed the peasant to cultivating a particular cash crop for the duration and placed him at the mercy of market forces for a period longer than an annual cycle.

How widespread was sugarcane cultivation in the Pearl River Delta? Although the sources for Guangdong are less precise than those for Taiwan, there is evidence indicating an expansion of cane cultivation. Qu Dajun in the late seventeenth century writes, "In Panyu, Dongguan, and Zengcheng [counties] every four out of ten are sugar households; in Yangchun it is six out of ten, and the number of cane fields equals that of rice fields."[103] The Dongguan county gazetteer of 1730 indicates that cane cultivation was spreading so rapidly that even the hillsides were being used for it.[104] Li Diaoyuan's 1778 estimate of the number of households involved in sugar manufacturing is the same as Qu Dajun's of almost a century earlier. Han Donggao, writing a decade after Li Diaoyuan, believed the level was even higher in Yangchun, where "seven out of ten households" were reputedly involved in making sugar, while others commented on the extensive cane fields of Xinhui county.[105] Cane cultivation had also expanded in the Chaozhou region and the Leizhou peninsula by the end of the eighteenth century. By the late nineteenth century, some villages in counties such as Panyu seemingly cultivated little rice and put most of their land under cane, a pattern reminiscent of sericulture in Shunde.[106] With the available information, it is not possible to distinguish between those who merely cultivated cane and those who processed it into sugar, an important distinction discussed below. It is clear, however, that the economy in certain counties of the Delta was structured around sugar production by the nineteenth century. But at the same time, sugarcane was seldom grown continuously as the only commercial crop. Throughout south China it was rotated with other crops such as bananas. Multi-crop agriculture, with dozens of crop-combinations as discussed below, was the norm in many parts of China. The Pearl River Delta probably had the most highly developed variation on this basic pattern.

Yields of Sugarcane

The inclusion of sugarcane cultivation in a pattern of intensive agriculture in south China was not inefficient nor detrimental to yields. Plantation-style monocrop cultivation of sugarcane, using pre-industrial technology, did not ensure the highest yields. As Manuel Moreno Fraginals points out in his classic study on Cuba, *The Sugarmill*: "Sugarcane is one of the so-called 'selected' crops which need the most careful attention, fertilization and crop rotation. The intensive method is the natural one, but Cuba preferred the extensive, which is above all a way to cut production costs."[107] In the Chinese system, where the self-employed direct producer's method of accounting emphasized total output rather than labor input as production costs, careful attention to fertilizing, transplanting, weeding, and so on produced high yields.

Estimating the yield of sugarcane per *mu* is, however, an oblique process, given the paucity of information for the eighteenth century. There are no known contemporary records from Guangdong and only one reference from Taiwan. The best one can do, therefore, is provide a very approximate estimate based on yields per acre. The *Chikan bitan* (Jottings from Taiwan, 1724), discussing sugar processing in Taiwan, notes, "In the better plantations (*yuan*) from every *jia* one can boil 60 to 70 *dan* of black (crude) sugar."[108] That works out to a yield of 3,300–3,900 pounds of sugar per acre, an almost unbelievably high figure compared to the 1,064 pounds per acre yield that late-nineteenth-century British surveys of the Taiwan industry turned up.[109] Another 1903 survey in Taiwan recorded a yield of 16,000 stalks per *jia* (2.47 acres) or approximately 6,700 stalks per acre, although in this case we do not know the processing technique or the yield in sugar.[110] In this example, the Taiwan yield also seems oddly low when compared to the output from an early-twentieth-century sample from Leizhou, Guangdong, that gives a yield of 2,000 stalks of cane per *mu* of land or approximately 12,000 stalks per acre. Again, we do not have a figure for the amount of sugar extracted.[111] Fertilizers were not as commonly used in Taiwan as in Guangdong and may have led to lower yields there in the two samples.[112] An early-twentieth-century example, probably from Guangdong or Fujian, where bean-cake fertilizers were used, indicates the yield was 700 *jin* (over 930 pounds) per *mu* or 5,580 pounds (2.49 long tons) per acre.[113] The processing of the cane in this instance was done with machinery and techniques identical to those used in the eighteenth century. Given these estimates, approximate as they are, it is still possible to compare Chinese yields with other parts of Asia. British sources for mid-nineteenth-century Bengal record yields of half this amount or around 2,240 pounds (1 long ton) of crude sugar per acre. Data from Java in 1840 indicate an even lower yield of two tons per hectare or 1,813 pounds per acre.[114] These comparisons show that the yield of crude sugar per acre in China was at least on par with the higher yields in Asia where similar technologies and varieties of cane prevailed. In all probability, yields in the more developed areas of south China were among the highest in Asia.

Crop Rotation and the Rationalization of Resources

The agricultural system of the highly commercialized sections of the Pearl River Delta maximized the use of land and labor resources. In the Qing after the three-year period of the ratoon crop, cane was rotated with bananas and not with the "five grains" that Wang Zhuo recommended. Qu Dajun discusses the cultivation of bananas in Zengcheng county:

> A lot of people grow bananas. They cultivate them for three or four years, then completely cut them down and plant *baizhe* [white cane, a local cultivar]. *Baizhe* can be planted on the land [used for] bananas, where it is extremely profitable, flourishes abundantly and is sweet. Cane is planted for two years and then they return to planting bananas again.[115]

Bananas and cane both require approximately a year from planting to maturity, and the ecological requirements of soil and water are very similar. Both can be grown in two- or three-year cycles as ratoon crops. In addition to the edible banana (*Musa acuminata*), abaca (*Musa textilis*) was also cultivated extensively in the sugarcane-growing regions in Guangdong and Taiwan.[116] The cloth woven from it, commonly known as *bujiao* (banana cloth), was used primarily to manufacture ropes for the fishing industry; the fiber is resistant to humidity and saltwater. In Guangdong a very soft and light fabric was also made from it, though this fabric was not durable unless silk was used for the weft of the cloth.[117] This pattern of rotating varieties and species of *Musa* may have become the dominant pattern through the course of the late seventeenth and early eighteenth centuries. The 1686 edition of the gazetteer of Panyu county, however, records an even more intensive land use: "When the people of this *yi* [county] plant sugarcane, after the cane sprouts are about two to three *cun* high, around the second month they plant cotton in between. By the time the cotton is picked, the cane is already several feet high."[118]

The high fertilizer requirements and other expenses of such a combination point to the large investment capabilities of those engaged in cultivating cotton and sugarcane simultaneously. As we have seen, in the Qing a trade circuit involving an exchange of raw cotton from Zhejiang and sugar from the south developed, making it probably unnecessary to undertake such an intensive regime of cultivation. The combination of a fiber crop and sugarcane continued, however, as the cultivation of fiber crops other than cotton increased.

Sugarcane cultivation is labor intensive during the planting period, and even more so during the harvest. The intermediate period of growth requires regular maintenance labor. There is no evidence of female labor being used extensively at any stage of the cultivation cycle of sugarcane, except in transplanting and weeding.[119] During the processing of cane, female labor was only used for collection of bagasse, not a particularly skilled task and one that could be done by anyone, male or female or children, depending on the availability of labor. The minimal use of female labor in sugarcane cultivation and processing suggests that it was otherwise employed; the old adage "men farm and women spin" (*nan geng nu fang*) reflected the division of labor within the peasant household. In addition to weaving cotton and spinning silk, women in sugarcane-cultivating areas extensively cultivated, processed, and spun ramie and kudzu.[120]

Ramie (*Boehmeria nivea*) and kudzu (*Pueraria thunbergiana*) could be widely cultivated in these counties for the soil, fertilizer, and climatic requirements are almost identical to that of sugarcane.[121] Women worked in the fields in several regions of China; by the twentieth century, female day-laborers outnumbered male day-laborers in Guangdong.[122] In addition to transplanting rice and sugarcane, tending the vegetables and sweet potatoes, one of the major tasks carried out by women was the collection and processing of bast fibers. Up to four crops were harvested each year. We have already seen the labor-intensive requirements of processing ramie. Processing kudzu was no less complicated. After the creepers had been collected, first the green, outer skin was peeled off by hand. Then the strips had to be boiled over a hot fire and the fibers inside the woody stem peeled off and extracted; no tools were used for this and women just used their fingernails. After this the fibers were washed again, pounded with a beater to get rid of the gummy residues, bleached, washed yet again, and dried in the sun before being ready for spinning and weaving.[123] Producing the banana fiber was also time-consuming. The abaca stems were cut lengthwise, spread out, and left to rot and soften. When the gummy matter surrounding the fibers had sufficiently decomposed, the stems were pounded and washed; the fibers were then cleaned again and combed out and dried before spinning. The heavy and continual labor requirements of processing ramie, kudzu, and abaca were then balanced out by sugarcane, which is labor intensive for only short periods. Moreover, ramie, kudzu, and abaca were grown on marginal land, and the yield was much higher than that of cotton.[124] These characteristics made the cultivation of bast fibers compatible with sugarcane cultivation in Guangdong and Taiwan.

In Guangdong, both Qu Dajun and Li Diaoyuan comment on the ramie and kudzu cloth made in Dongguan, Zengcheng, and Yangchun, which were also famous for cane cultivation. There were many varieties of ramie and kudzu cloth (*ge*), depending on the fineness of the fibers and the amount of silk or other fibers woven into the weft. Writing of the cloth that was made for the bride's trousseau and was not for sale as well as the other varieties, Li Diaoyuan (1778) notes:

> In Guangdong and Guangxi the woman-cloth (*nü ge*) of Zengcheng is especially superior. Then there is the "dragon river cloth" (*long jiang ge*) from Guangzhou, which is durable and heavier in quality. It is usable in all weathers. . . . The women of Leizhou make a living weaving *ge* cloth. . . . All the professional weavers are from Dongguan, and their work is quite different from that of the ordinary weavers of ramie. This type of weaving of *ge* cloth is a fine craft.[125]

Both *ge* thread and cloth were sold in Zhejiang and Jiangsu for "several thousand ounces of silver." Guangdong sugar was also sold in these provinces.[126]

Besides the crops mentioned so far, vegetables, oranges, litchees, and longyan were cultivated. Various types of citrus, for example, the "mandarin oranges" and "honey oranges" of Xinhui, were famous nationally. Dried orange peel, candied oranges, fresh and dried longyan, and litchees from the region were sold as far away as Southeast Asia.[127] Cloth, paper, palm fans, reed mats, and incense—the last a nationally famous product from Dongguan—were also widely marketed.[128] In Xinhui, palmyra (*Corypha umbraculifera*) was grown on polders and dykes. The leaves were harvested three to four times a year, dried, graded, and sold to workshops making fans in Jiangmen and Huicheng. The fans were an important item of trade with the rest of China since Ming times, employing up to one-half the population of the county according to one eighteenth-century account.[129]

Map 1 (front endpaper) approximates diagrammatically, with no allowances made for crop rotations, the complexities of the commercial pattern in the Pearl River Delta. As we see, there was a considerable and indeed impressive degree of sub-regional specialization, with counties like Nanhai and Shunde specializing in pisciculture and sericulture, and Panyu and Dongguan specializing in rice and sugarcane. In the interest of clarity, however, the map could not accommodate the almost universal cultivation of sweet potatoes and other vegetables that provided for daily consumption and subsistence needs.

Capital Needs of Commercial Agriculture

Could a peasant household casually acquire the means necessary to initiate cash-crop production? How long would they have to wait for a return on a commercial crop cultivated? What were the initial investments involved? Let us begin with a tabulation of the time required for the maturation of various commercial crops. This factor has been by and large ignored in the literature on commercialization of agriculture.[130] In the absence of information from an earlier period, data from the twentieth century can give us some idea of costs.

Some sources estimated that gross income from sericulture could be ten times that of rice, others three to five times, while yet others claimed that it was the same.[131] Merely producing mulberry leaves for sale in 1923 brought about the same amount of money as growing rice.[132] Faure concludes, on the basis of information on sericulture in Guangdong provided by Howard and Buswell, that in a good year in the 1920s a family of eight working all year, raising both silkworms and fish on 10 *mu* (1.6 acres) of land, was left with a net profit of 338 dollars on an initial investment of 400–500 dollars.[133]

People would, however, have to wait for the returns. Mulberry requires at least a year to reach maturity before the leaves can be picked. In the second year only a handful of leaves can be picked without injury to the plant. People planting mulberry usually waited three years to begin harvesting; six *mu* (one acre) of mulberry trees could provide 24 piculs of leaves per crop in a good year. But if a family of five were to raise silkworms even from two sheets or egg boxes of silkworms, they would require up to 40 piculs of leaves during the fastest period of growth for the worms. It was in this last stage of feeding that peasants invariably ran out of homegrown leaves and had desperately to find other sources or else lose the silkworms.[134] Few farm families had enough land to grow mulberry to feed seven crops of silkworms. In addition, there were expenses for baskets, charcoal stoves used to keep the worms at the right temperature, spinning racks, and so on. All of this could cost another 180-odd dollars.[135]

Ponds had to be dug for raising fish, which were integral to sericulture in this region. Gaspar da Cruz had noted in the sixteenth century that fish ponds were to be found on the grounds of all "men with any possibility." Various lineage estates owned fish ponds.[136] They varied in size from four to twenty *mu* and five to nine feet in depth.[137] In the late nineteenth century, the cost of digging a pond of ten *mu* was 450 taels. Fish hatchlings and fish breeders cost an additional 72 taels. The mulberry seeds for the embankments of a 10 *mu* pond cost 33 taels.[138] A total expenditure of 555 taels was a hefty one, particularly considering that an outlay of 2 taels would purchase enough rice to feed an adult male for 100 days.[139] And the nineteenth-century figure was not an overestimate. Based on the data supplied by Howard and Buswell in 1923, Faure has calculated that an initial outlay of 400 to 500 yuan was needed for an operation of 10 *mu* at a time when the price of rice was 9.5 yuan per picul.[140] Pisciculture was obviously not a feasible avenue of commercialization for the poorer segments of rural society at any time. As in the case of sericulture, it required access to capital, labor, and the ability to wait for returns on investment.

There were similar costs associated with cane cultivation and horticulture. The banana and plantain require eight to ten months to bear fruit, which makes them one of the most rapidly maturing fruit trees;[141] but these ratoon crops were more expensive the first year of planting. A greater initial outlay of capital was therefore required than for crops propagated from seed, such as grains.

Other fruit trees commonly planted in the Delta, such as longyan and litchee, require four to six years of growth before producing fruit. Oranges can produce fruit after two years, but become fully mature only in six.[142] Tea shrubs have to reach a maturity of three years before any leaves can be picked. The coconut palm requires six to seven years of growth before it can flower and bear fruit, with full maturity reached only after ten years.[143] In the first year of cultivation, moreover, citrus and other slower-growing fruit needed a major investment: dikes had to be built, fields leveled, irrigation channels constructed, and seedlings purchased. So, though such fruit trees required less ongoing labor than annual crops, the period spent waiting for returns was much longer, and the grower had to have security of tenure and control over the land to undertake such ventures. A peasant household contemplating growing any of these cash crops had to have the necessary resources, money, security of access to the produce that could take several years to bear fruit, and access to labor power.

Money and labor were also needed for sugarcane, which requires about one year for the crop to mature. Considerable labor power was needed for plowing and digging the furrows. Then the individual sets had to planted by hand, sprouting them first in liquid fertilizer, like rice seedlings, for the best results. Weeding had to be done at least once. Fertilizers had to be applied twice, preferably three times, and the soil of the furrows had to be turned at least once. From all accounts of the 1920s and early 1930s, this labor could be provided by two adults for cane fields of up to fifteen *mu* if the cane was cultivated for crushing and juice-extraction. If the cane was to be grown for eating then two adults could cultivate only six *mu* of land because more weeding and anti-pest care were required to retain an appetizing appearance.[144] Negishi Benji's survey of Guangdong in 1940 found that in general three people worked on one *mu* of land, performing all tasks.[145] In either case we can conclude that cultivating sugarcane required the fairly regular labor input of two adult males.

A major recurrent expense was fertilizer. Sesame, rape seed dregs, and peanut cake seem to have been most popular fertilizers used in sugarcane cultivation from the seventeenth century onward.[146] In the 1880s, Fielde noted in Shantou that the bean-cake fertilizers for sugarcane cost on average 5.6 taels per *mu*, while another early-twentieth-century source puts the cost at 7–9 taels per *mu* for soymeal and bean-cake fertilizers.[147] Twentieth-century budgets for the cultivation of sugarcane on rented land do show that fertilizers were a major expense, taking up approximately 20–25 percent of the total expenditures.[148] Adachi Kenji has suggested that fertilizers such as soymeal, sesame, and rape-seed dregs were typically used only by the rich peasants in the Qing. According to him, poorer peasants, even in the eighteenth century, could only afford to use nightsoil, hair trimmings, ash, and other cheaper fertilizers.[149] It is likely that sugarcane growers had to make prior arrangements for the bean and peanut fertilizers.

Then there were costs associated with the harvesting and processing of cane. Japanese studies conducted in the Guangdong Delta during the late 1930s describe in detail the processing of sugarcane using cane crushers no different from those used in the eighteenth century.[150] These observations, made in Dongguan county, show that each bundle of cane (six to eight stalks) would be passed through the crusher three or four times; with this method 300–360 *jin* of cane could be processed in a day.[151] But the need to work quickly to prevent sucrose fermentation required an investment in readily available labor power to keep the crushers going around the clock.[152] In Zengcheng county, Japanese surveys show cane crushers worked in two shifts, 7.00 A.M. to 4.00 P.M. and 4.00 P.M. to 6.00 A.M.[153] At this site in Zengcheng, 36–40 vats (*huo*) of sugar were produced every day, each vat containing 40–42 *jin* of sugar. On an average, then, approximately 1,560 *jin* (2,080 pounds) were produced every twenty-four hours. This survey does not indicate how many crushing units were in use but based on the estimated yield of around a long ton of sugar per acre referred to earlier, it would have taken twenty-four hours or so to process the yield of an acre.

The *Chikan bitan* provides detailed information on the number of people required to operate one cane-crushing unit in early-eighteenth-century Taiwan: "Two people as sugar masters [to check the boiling of the syrup], two people to oversee the fire [lit. *huogong*, fire artisans to control the temperature of the boiling sugar syrup, a crucial detail], two people to operate the crusher, two people to drive the oxen, seven to cut [and strip] the cane, one person to select the cane, and one person to look after the oxen."[154]

In other words, seventeen laborers were required to process the cane from two *jia* (4.9 acres) of land, suggesting that this was not a venture that could be initiated without the capital for hiring labor and animals. As Figure 28, from a mid-eighteenth century set of paintings of "Scenes from Aborigine Life" shows, the labor estimate given by the writer of the *Chikan bitan* was not an overestimate. As the artist shows, the cane had to be harvested, crushed, and boiled simultaneously.

To ensure the availability of so many laborers, arrangements would have to be made before the harvest commenced, either through cooperative arrangements or by hiring labor. The latter would require ready cash.

The records of the Board of Punishment from the Qianlong period have several references to the use of hired labor on a seasonal basis for manufacturing sugar in Guangdong. There were no written contracts, and the workers were paid either every five days or once a month. In 1741, the daily wage of a laborer working in cane crushing in Guangdong was 25 cash.[155] This was about the going rate for labor wages in Guangdong. In one case from 1741, an agricultural worker was promised a wage of 600 cash per month, and in another dated 1752, a short-term worker was hired for 300 cash.[156] Wages increased only slightly by the end of the century. In 1795, they ranged from 500 to 750 cash per month for sugar-press workers; wages stayed around that level a decade later when seasonal workers in sugar manufacturing received

FIGURE 28. Sugarcane crusher and boiling shed in Taiwan (*Taifan tushuo* [1746]). The commentary reads: "There are sugar processors in every district. The fields are fertile and suitable for cane. Consequently all the inhabitants but the aborigines grow it. Sugar can be made beginning from the ninth month up to the forth or fifth month. Merchants sell it in Jiangsu and Zhejiang. Undoubtedly, it is one of Taiwan's biggest enterprises." Reprinted with permission of the Fu Ssu-nien Library, Institute of History and Philology, Academia Sinica, Nankang, Taiwan.

500 cash per month.[157] By the 1880s in Sichuan, short-term workers crushing sugarcane were getting 60 cash per day and food; laborers in Shantou during the busy season could get around 214 cash a day without food.[158] There may have been a range of wages with "sugar masters" receiving more than workers who cut and stripped cane. The

employer may have had to provide room and board for the seasonal workers.

Twentieth-century surveys show that it took four hours to crush the cane from one *mu* of land.[159] If we accept that 25 cash per day was the standard wage for workers processing cane in 1741 in Guangdong, we see that the cost of hiring seventeen workers to crush the cane from 6 *mu* of land would have been 425 cash per day (with two twelve-hour shifts). Wages were higher in Taiwan than in Guangdong in the eighteenth century, perhaps because labor was still scarce. In the example dated 1724 that we have from Taiwan, the seventeen workers would have to have been hired for a minimum of nine days just to process the cane from 2 *jia* (4.9 acres) of land, even if the operation continued every day in two twelve-hour shifts. In this particular case, the workers were actually hired for the month, probably to help also with the harvesting. The total expenditure for wages is listed as 60–70 taels, a substantial expenditure by any standard.[160]

Then, in addition to wages, there were other costs of production. Typical illustrations of the cane-crushing equipment from the early seventeenth century, such as from the *Tiangong kaiwu*, show only one animal being used. Qu Dajun and later Li Diaoyuan mention three oxen being used to operate the crusher in Guangdong; Figure 28 above from Taiwan shows a pair.[161] Since cane crushing continued day and night, one team of oxen would not have been enough. The description of cane crushing in the *Chikan bitan* notes that, in addition to the labor of seventeen men, twelve oxen were used in teams of four for cane crushing.[162] By the end of the eighteenth century, when many of the crushers were made of stone, more animals were probably needed to turn the heavier rollers. Negishi Benji found cane-crushing units in twentieth-century Guangdong using twelve to sixteen oxen, teams of two to three being used in two-hour shifts.[163] Qu Dajun writes that the owners of cattle used their draft animals to plow fields in the spring and crush cane in the winter,[164] and it is possible that several such families cooperated in cane-crushing ventures. Since many households could not afford to own even a single draft animal, however, such families would have had to arrange to rent one at harvest time.

Other expenses for processing cane included the very large iron pans used to boil the syrup, the ingredients and products to refine and clarify the sugar, and the conical jars used to strain and crystallize the syrup, in addition to animal feed, knives, ladles, and various other tools. Although some of these items would not have been recurrent expenses, they could add up to a considerable initial investment. But the most expensive item of equipment needed was the cane crusher itself.

Prices of cane crushers have to be estimated from nineteenth- and twentieth-century data, for none of the sources give prices for the eighteenth century. But as the data below show, we can safely assume that it was an expensive piece of equipment. In the late nineteenth century, a cane crusher cost 150 dollars (145 taels) in Taiwan.[165] An additional one hundred Taiwan dollars (95 taels) was spent at the beginning of every season to erect the shed to house the cane crusher, renew the wooden fittings on the crusher, and set up the paraphernalia. We can gauge the expenses involved by noting that the average price of rice for one *dan* (approximately 185 pounds) in Taiwan at about the same time varied between 1.68 taels and 1.62 taels.[166] Thus, an initial outlay of 145 taels for a cane crusher and an additional 95 or so taels every year for recurrent costs were clearly substantial expenditures.

Cane crushers were similarly priced in Guangdong. In three of the major sugar-producing counties of Guangdong surveyed in the 1930s, the price of the cane-crushing equipment was well over one thousand dollars. The whole process of setting up the crushing shed and the stoves, aligning the heavy stone rollers on their axles, and so on cost another 1,000 to 2,000 dollars.[167] While allowances have to be made for wartime inflation in noting these dollar amounts, the current price of rice shows that the cane crusher was indeed a very expensive piece of equipment. In Panyu county, for example, one of the counties surveyed, the price of rice varied from seven dollars per *dan* in 1928 to four dollars per *dan* in 1933.[168]

How did peasant producers meet the large expenditures involved in sugarcane processing? Hiring all the equipment and having the money to pay for the laborers was clearly one way; community-based organizations were another. Cooperative cane-crushing arrangements among members of the same economic strata are the most readily identifiable form. Organizations such as these already existed in the seventeenth century; as Qu Dajun comments, "*Shang nong* [upper or rich peasants] each have a crusher; five *zhong nong* [middle peasants] have one; eight to ten *xia nong* [lower or poor peasants] have one."[169] These rich peasants probably also had enough land to justify a cane crusher, for cane from one *mu* of land could be crushed in four hours. Details of how these cooperative associations operated can be gathered from twentieth-century descriptions. Kulp, describing "sugar manufacturing associations" in Phenix village near Shantou in 1920, commented that "the incapacity of the individual to conduct such [sugar] manufacture alone because of the capital needed is compensated for by the collectivity, a form of association common among poor peasants throughout China."[170] In Phenix Village, not all the poor and middle-peasant cultivators of sugarcane in the area joined the association, but as long as several were willing to do so, the association could exist. Work was launched with some ritual observances. Implements, the roller-millstones, knives, pans, and so on were purchased or rented through the funds raised by the association. Stoves for boiling the juice were also constructed, often near the village temple where there was a patch of non-agricultural land. Harvesting and processing were undertaken together by the members. Some associations disbanded after the season with another religious ritual; others continued for several years. These associations were founded on the principle of *ganqing* and the sentiment of reciprocity; but as Kulp noted, none of the members could afford to have the enterprise fail, and the poorer ones in particular worked doubly hard to make sure the sugar was produced. While such interdependent associations enabled those otherwise too poor to undertake commodity production to do so, I suggest they also acted as a buffer against the market. Both labor power and access to the implements of production could be secured through non-market relations; since there was no question of wages paid by the hour, the poorer peasants just put in more of their own labor. The direct producer could also conceivably decide to opt out of commercial production altogether in a particular year.

This is exactly what happened in Phenix Village. Those involved in the first sugar association refused to join another one started some years later to process the cane. Instead, they continued selling their cane as stalk or shifted to cultivating other crops. In due course, they abandoned cane cultivation altogether. Broken cane-crushers and mill-stones and abandoned oven-holes were the only remnants of this cooperative enterprise. Obviously, long-term investments in sugar-cane-processing equipment or technology would not have made sense for these direct producers.

Gross income from cultivating and processing cane varied, of course, according to the yield of land and the amount of sugar extracted. It is difficult to calculate the "profit" from cane cultivation, for which we have data only from the twentieth century, for the self-employed direct producer did not calculate the value of his own labor in monetary terms. A general rule of thumb, which held from the late eighteenth to the mid-twentieth century, was that income from one crop of sugarcane equaled approximately two crops of rice.[171] A 1920s survey of sugarcane cultivation in Guangdong's Jieyang county near Shantou, tabulated by David Faure, suggests that income after rent payment, food for the workers, and seedlings was only 30 dollars, or just enough to buy a little over 3 piculs (around 420 pounds) of rice at current Guangzhou prices.[172] While this was something, it was certainly not a large return for undertaking all the risks of the market. And, if this was the situation in the twentieth century, when by all accounts Chinese producers were even more involved in market relations than they had been in the eighteenth, why did direct producers in the Qing feel compelled to enter the market at all? What were the factors promoting market relations for a peasantry that owned most of its means of subsistence?

Rent, Taxes, and Commercial Agriculture

The expansion of commercial agriculture in the Qing was prefaced by two changes that required the direct producers to have access to cash: one, the Qing state's tax demands that were now payable only in cash;

the other, the landlords' demands for rent and interest payments both in kind and in cash.

Rice was the most common form of rent payment. Depending on the arrangement, this could be a significant portion of the output, for there are examples of sharecropping in which the landlord provided not only the land but also the tools while the tenant provided the labor and the landlord's share of the crop was calculated on the dual basis of land and tools.[173] In both Taiwan and Guangdong, landlords were involved in trading rice received as rent.[174] The gentry-landlords of Shunde and Dongguan of the Mingluntang, one of the largest corporate landlords in Guangdong, sold the rice collected as rent in the intermediate-level markets of the grain-deficit, mulberry-growing districts of Shunde. They also owned shops in Guangzhou and operated granaries, rice mills, and pawnshops in two counties. Cash incomes from the businesses were used for moneylending; the rent grain was also recycled as credit in kind to the peasants, with the interest again collected in kind.[175] These large landlords of Guangdong were similar to their counterparts in Taiwan; the latter were frequently accused of fixing prices. Well over one thousand of them ran businesses milling rice. As several senior officials from governors to censors in Taiwan in the 1720s noted, the landlords received hundreds and thousands of pounds of rice, built warehouses, and hoarded the rice and manipulated prices whenever there was a large purchase to be made for sale on the mainland.[176]

Landlords could also stipulate that peasants pay their rent in particular crops. In Xinhui, the Chen lineage of Waihai near Jiangmen started collecting rent in oranges as early as the Yuan dynasty and continued to do so in the Qing.[177] In Dongguan county, many poor tenants had to cultivate indigo for a living in the Qianlong period.[178] A contract for land rent from Taiwan's Chu-lo county, dated 1771, specifies that "the rent to be paid every year is 208 *dan*, 1 *dou*, and 1 *sheng* [of rice] and 6,941 *jin* of sugar."[179] In Fujian, where small-scale cultivation of tea was common, tenants had to sell their tea to landlords at prices fixed by the latter.[180] When landlords began to collect rent deposits in cash, as in Guangdong in the nineteenth century, smallholders renting land perforce had to cultivate cash crops and enter into market relations. Wu Liangkai has shown that nationwide many commercial crops like sugarcane, tobacco, cotton, oil-seeds, and vegetables were cultivated most often by tenants.[181]

The state also made cash demands on the peasantry. Numerous taxes, such as the cotton tax of the Lower Yangzi region, were increasingly converted into silver beginning in the sixteenth century.[182] The monetization of the land tax, completed through the course of the seventeenth century under the "single-whip" taxation reforms, meant that all direct producers had to sell a certain proportion of their output on the market if they were to retain title to their land.

Officials and emperors were quite ambivalent about the market involvement of the peasantry. On the one hand, they made constant pronouncements about the dangers of cultivating cash crops instead of rice and other food crops. The Yongzheng emperor noted in 1727, "The people of Guangdong seek only money and profit, and plant much of their land with such things as longyan, sugarcane, tobacco and indigo with the result that they have much wealth and no rice."[183] Sharing these sentiments, the Qianlong emperor also wrote, "The small farmers in their ignorance, are eager only to sell their harvest so that they can receive money on the spot. They do not think of laying in reserves [of food grains] for the remainder of the year. The scheming merchants, for their part, are only intent on cornering the crop and do not feel concerned by the food shortages this will cause the people."[184]

On the other hand, not only did the state collect taxes in cash, it also took measures to encourage commercial activities such as sericulture and weaving in all parts of China. In the tradition of Chinese imperial concern with agriculture, the Qianlong emperor undertook the compilation of agricultural treatises. A team of more than fifty collaborators prepared the treatise *Shou shi tong kao* (Complete Investigation of Work and Time, 1742), one of longest in China and far more ambitious than previous imperially sponsored treatises. Extensively illustrated and written in simple language, it exhibits Confucian unease with commercial agriculture and devotes a great deal of attention to rituals. But it also includes sections on horticulture, economic crops, a long section on sericulture, and supplementary sections on cotton and ramie cultivation. Although the treatise drew primarily from previously published works, it popularized works previously available only in limited circulation. The *Shou shi tong kao*, printed and distributed by royal command, was sent to every province and county of China.[185]

Imperial ambivalence regarding commercial agriculture was particularly evident in the sponsorship of sericulture. The state had an active interest in the silk trade and procurement of silk for the imperial household. Zealous officials recruited skilled sericulturists and artisans and sent them out to remote areas, gave out free mulberry seedlings, and even exempted land with mulberry trees from taxation.[186] In Taiwan, where there was no sericulture prior to Qing rule, officials recommended in 1723 that the government sponsor mulberry cultivation and sericulture and teach weaving techniques. This would promote settled communities, for, as the memorial argued, "The land of Taiwan has no cultivation of mulberry, nor cotton and ramie. Therefore its people all roam indolently." Ethnic Han officials, clearly bothered by the scanty clothing of the Taiwan aborigine and their drinking, wrote, "The women devoting their attention to sericulture and weaving will be industrious and will become well mannered, the people will be enriched and the vulgar made gracious."[187] Needless to say, all this spinning and weaving would add to the revenues of the state. Sericulture had been an essential means of paying taxes since the late Ming. The observations of an editor of a Jiangnan gazetteer of 1611 makes the link between cash crop and taxes eminently clear:

> The meeting of both public and private obligations depends largely on the profits from silkworms. Therefore sericulture is most important. Loan contracts are always drawn up with a repayment date at the end of the silkworm season. Therefore, at the time of the quota of the autumn tax assessment, many are unwilling to turn over their saleable rice, thinking that perhaps as the days pass the price of rice will rise. Ordinarily rice is pawned at a pawnshop for silver; after the silkworms have matured, the profits are used to reclaim it. Therefore in paying taxes the people depend on the profit from silkworms; they do not depend on the profit from paddy fields.[188]

Finally, the poorer peasants may have had to engage in market relations in order to round out their subsistence needs. Peasants on exiguous landholdings may have had to produce high-value crops like sugarcane to meet tax and rent demands, but also to purchase grains for their own consumption from time to time; this interpretation can help explain why it has been found that the bulk of the purchases made by Chinese peasant producers both in the nineteenth and the twentieth centuries consisted of food grains.[189] Arguably then, external pressures—landlord compulsion, the state's tax demands, merchant pressures to pay interest on loans—fostered market involvement among all segments of the direct producers. Under these circumstances, a part of the subsistence needs of the peasants themselves became implicated in the logic of market reproduction. But does this necessarily mean that there was a transition to capitalism in Chinese agriculture?

Conclusion: Commercialization without Specialization

Lenin posited a smooth transition from agricultural production for sale to specialization by comparative advantage, and finally to agrarian capitalism. This last stage would see the production of food crops themselves as commodities for the market rather than for direct consumption within the family farm. Furthermore, marginal producers, no longer able to produce commodities competitively, would get out of farming altogether, becoming a rural proletariat dependent entirely on wage-labor for all their subsistence needs.

There was an impressive degree of commercialization in south China, which this and preceding chapters have tried to make clear. But clearly, specialization in agriculture and manufacture remained overwhelmingly micro-regional. Extra-regional specialization and trade was limited to some products, for example, rice, cotton, silk, and sugar. There was little *systematic growth* of specialization by ecological niche. In each county and even within the best-located micro-regions, such the Pearl River Delta or the hinterland of the Yangzi Delta, an elaborate array of crops continued to be grown. Crucially, peasants continued to grow their own food—in Guangdong, sweet potatoes, yams, and possibly even rice. Although it is difficult to ascertain the allocation of labor time within peasant households and whether more labor time and resources were devoted first to subsistence crops and only subsequently to commercial crops, the information on the division of agricultural labor by gender suggests strategic uses of resources. Ultimately, the need to accommodate both commercial agriculture and subsistence agriculture within the household by definition worked against full specialization. Potentially, too, this subtracted from time that could be spent on cash-crop cultivation.

These contradictory pressures on the peasantry of China, particularly on the small and medium peasants of the delta region of south China, are captured in the observations of Arthur Smith on late-nineteenth-century rural China:

> In many parts of China the farmer comes much nearer to independence as regards producing what he needs, than any class of persons in Western lands. This is especially the case where cotton is raised, and where each family tries to make its own clothing from its own crops. . . . No poor family has land enough to raise all that it requires, and every family not poor has a multitude of wants which must of necessity be supplied from without. Besides this, in any district most families have very little reserve capital, and must depend upon meeting their wants as they arise, by the use of such means as can be secured from day to day. The same comparative poverty makes it necessary for a considerable part of the population to dispose of some portion of its surplus products at frequent intervals, so as to turn it into the means of subsistence. The combined effect of these various causes is to make the Chinese dependent upon local markets to an extent which is not true of inhabitants of Occidental countries.[190]

Evidently, the peasant family tried to ensure its subsistence by direct non-market means as best as it could, no matter how deeply it was involved in cash-crop production. Peasant families did not *aim* to have only a subsistence level of income and tried to increase their consumption over subsistence if they could. But the basic logic of production for the market was to enable them to recover consumption needs, to buy small amounts of food, salt, matches, oil, and similar commodities to round out their essential requirements, a pattern that is true of many peasant societies.[191] Production for the market in these circumstances did not reshape all spheres of activity, for, most significantly, the peasant family also tried to keep its labor power out of the market and by and large, they were *able to do so* because of the security of small property in Qing China. To bolster this kind of property structure, small peasants themselves formed, as noted, cooperative associations, which made it unnecessary for them to hire the labor of others at times of acute labor shortages, for example at harvest time and when crushing cane. The interests of the Qing state and the tenacity of peasant institutions also made it altogether unlikely that merchants or gentry could expropriate successfully small peasants en masse. For these reasons—direct non-market access to both subsistence and labor power—agriculture remained incompletely commodified. Thus, while the agriculture of south China was highly commercialized, it was not what one might call a system of generalized commodity production, a compact definition of capitalism.

Peasants, however, did not have the luxury of staying out of the market. In addition to subsistence needs, they had to pay rent, interest, and taxes in cash. Most relevantly, the mechanism of market entry was most often through merchant loans. Merchants imposed, as we shall see, a price in advance with added interest payments, a logical avenue for increasing income and providing security if the crop was not delivered. But by the same token, price-fixing and high interest rates arguably dampened potential increases in productivity, for no matter how efficiently peasants might produce an item, they would get the same return. Peasants did not, in other words, see the profits of enterprise that were subordinated in the first instance to the merchant's profits of alienation and profit by squeeze. Entering the market under these conditions, the peasants of south China could not be profit-maximizers, or "penny capitalists," as Sol Tax's classic term for peasant entrepreneurs would have it.[192] In the next chapter, I turn to a discussion of the mechanisms of market entry and mercantile involvement in commercial agriculture.

SIX

MARKETS AND MONOPSONIES: COMMERCIAL CAPITAL, STRATEGIES, AND STRUCTURES

> Many people are traders and pursue every opportunity. With incense, sugar and boxes of fruit, iron goods, rattan-ware and wax, pepper, sappanwood, and palm products, they go north to Jiangxi, Jiangsu, Zhejiang; in the northwest they go to Changsha and Hankou. The clever and shrewd ones go south to Macao and reach the Dutch, Japan, the Ryukyus, Siam, and Luzon.[1]
>
> —*Guangdong xinyu*

> In spring, the capital in sugar [*tangben*, "sugar capital"] is distributed among those peasants cultivating sugarcane. Then in winter the profits from sugar are realized.[2]
>
> —*Guangdong xinyu*

SEVERAL OBSERVERS OF THE Pearl River Delta from the late seventeenth century on noted the cyclical pattern of merchant loans in sugar manufacturing in Guangdong. Merchant capital in the countryside was nothing new. There were regulations regarding merchant loans as early as the Han.[3] But did the socioeconomic changes of the Qing and the tremendous expansion in foreign trade alter the relationship of merchant capital to the production process? The question here is not whether peasants or merchants were uninterested in increasing their personal wealth, but whether they could independently use the market to do so.[4] To what extent were the choices made outside the market, in families and through other social and political institutions, important?[5] And did the proliferation of markets in the early Qing represent a fundamental change in the type of economic opportunities available to individual entrepreneurs? We begin with an overview of the layout of the southern trade nexus with the national market, for this affected the routes through which merchant capital entered Guangdong and Taiwan, and then move on to a discussion of trading networks, the county-level lower-level markets, and their modes of operation within the existing social formation.

Trade Routes and Commodities

The spatial distribution of commercial routes in the Qing had considerable overlap with the administrative grain-tribute routes and postal routes. As has been pointed out, some of these routes dated back not just to the Ming period, but even earlier.[6] The development of the south during the seventeenth and eighteenth centuries expanded the coastal trade and linked regions as far up north as Manchuria with Taiwan and Guangdong via the Fujian traders and their ships. Altogether, the customs revenues of Fujian and Guangdong accounted for 65 percent of the revenues generated by the customs houses in the coastal trade in 1735, increasing to 79 percent of the revenues by 1812.[7] The unique position of Guangzhou as the primary port of trade for western traders also directed a substantial portion of the trade in silk and tea to the region from the mid-eighteenth century on. But this growth of the coastal trade did not mean a demise of the inland trade routes. The trade in bulk commodities such as salt, rice, and cotton still largely determined the directions of interregional trade.[8] To some extent, from the mid seventeenth century on, sugar and soybeans could be added to this list of bulk commodities. Overall, the assorted manufactured goods described so enthusiastically by Qu Dajun in the *Guangdong xinyu* (see the epigraphs to this chapter), while certainly adding volume and value to this trade, did not establish such large markets so as to form an independent or alternative trade nexus.

Guangdong was integrated into the national market through four major routes determined by the trade in bulk commodities: (1) the West River (Xijiang), which carried the trade southwest to Guangxi, Yunnan, and Guizhou; (2) the coastal route, with links to the Fujian coastal trade north to Shanghai and Tianjin; (3) the Meiling Pass, through Nanxiong prefecture, leading into Jiangsi and the lower Yangzi; and (4) the Zheling Pass, also through the mountains, which connected with Hunan and the middle Yangzi.[9] The Meiling route, despite its rugged terrain, remained a major artery with the increase in tea exports, for, no doubt in order to collect taxes more efficiently, Qing government regulations did not permit tea to be shipped by the coastal route.[10] Similarly, and probably for the same reasons, government restrictions also applied to the silk trade. For although silk could be transported by sea, junks originating in Jiangsu were only allowed to carry less than 400 pounds of silk each, and manufactured silk goods were not allowed.[11] The tea trade to Guangdong via the overland route through the Meiling Pass therefore overlapped with the circuits of the silk trade. Merchants from all the major silk-producing regions in the lower Yangzi such as Zhejiang and Jiangsu channeled both their tea and silk export goods toward Guangzhou via the Meiling route.[12] But, what underpinned this trade was not the burgeoning overseas export market in tea and silk, but the route of salt export from Guangdong. As Fujii Hiroshi has pointed out, interregional trade circuits of the various provinces were fundamentally shaped by the demand for salt, a government monopoly.[13] Guangdong had been an officially designated salt-producing area in the Ming,[14] and this policy was continued in the Qing. By the 1750s over 1,009 tons of Guangdong salt were transported annually to other provinces.[15] The salt trade from Guangdong that was sent over the Meiling route extended to Jiangsu, Hubei, and Jiangxi, where it overlapped with the rice trade from the lower and middle Yangzi regions, including Hunan.

Southward, the other main trade nexus for Guangdong was formed by the rice trade. One major branch of the rice trade went down the West River from Guangxi into Guangdong. Starting in the second half of the eighteenth century, as we have seen, Guangdong increasingly imported rice from Southeast and South Asia. Before these other sources of rice became available, however, Guangxi had been the primary supplier. In the 1730s, for example, average imports of rice from Guangxi into Guangdong ranged from 8,250 tons to 16,500 tons, sometimes rising almost to 25,000 tons when the Guangdong harvest was not good.[16] Raw materials such as lead, iron, and timber were also imported into Guangdong from Guangxi.[17] When rice from Southeast Asia arriving in Guangzhou began to shift the rice trade from Guangxi, the route did not die. On the contrary, expansion of sericulture in the Pearl River Delta set up an alternative demand, namely, that for charcoal for boiling the cocoons. This then led to a major trade in charcoal between those counties of Guangxi province that had extensive timberland and the silk-producing Jiujiang region of Guangdong's Shunde county in the nineteenth century.[18] In this brief review of commodities carried on the Meiling route and the West River route certain patterns emerge. Clearly, at one level, the circuits of trade were discrete. Salt exports from Guangdong had little overlap with rice imports. But, on the other hand, complementary trade nexuses were easily set up; charcoal instead of rice could be loaded on the boats going down the West River, tea and silk were sent south along the same route over which salt, sugar, and iron goods were exported north over the Meiling Pass.

The extent to which interregional commercialization of agriculture developed along complementary lines of trade can be illustrated further by a closer look at the trade in sugar and cotton. Both Guangdong and Fujian evidently had substantial levels of cotton cultivation and textile production in the early Ming. Levies in the Ming included taxes payable in cotton products from these two provinces.[19] By the late seventeenth century, when tea and sugarcane cultivation in Fujian and sugarcane in Guangdong expanded, cotton cultivation was displaced in many counties. Qu Dajun noted, "Winter cloths are all from Jiangsu and Hubei—*lengbu* [a type of textile] from Songjiang, *dabu* from Xianning. The traders come continuously and cotton is the principal commodity. Not enough cotton is cultivated within Guangdong for the ten prefectures together."[20] But the demand for raw cotton still existed, as spinning and weaving for household needs continued.[21] Were the same merchants selling cotton in Guangdong and carrying sugar from Guangdong to the northern regions? The limited information available suggests as much:

Many of the rich merchants in the county buy sugar exactly when it is fully processed. . . . Carrying a lot of capital, they go to each district to buy sugar, or else first give [money] on account for the cane crushers and the sheds for boiling sugar, and then get the sugar in this period. There are those who transport the goods themselves, others who stay for the middleman, waiting till the Third or Fourth Month for a good southern wind to rent oceangoing junks and ships. They load on the bags of sugar and sail, going up on the sea route to Suzhou and Tianjin. Then in autumn when there is the northeastern wind, they carry back cotton and colored cloths for sale to the county, traveling back to Leiqiong and other prefectures. One round-trip and the profits are severalfold; there are many families that have thus risen to riches.[22]

Some of the Guangdong sugar sold in the northern markets and abroad was produced not only in the Pearl River Delta but also on Hainan island and in Chaozhou prefecture, and brought to Guangzhou for transshipment.[23] This raises the question, explored below, of how possible would it have been for merchants engaged in complementary branches of trade to attempt vertical integration across interregional trade circuits?

Taiwan's trade was far more unidirectional than Guangdong's because it was primarily an export trade. While some beans, sweet potatoes, indigo, deer skins, and venison were exported from Taiwan to Xiamen and the mainland ports, sugar and rice had been the primary exports since the Dutch period, and this continued in the eighteenth century. Most of Taiwan's trade to the mainland was channeled through the port of Tainan to Xiamen, which operated as a receiving and distribution point for commodities in Fujian. Beginning in the 1780s, Lu-kang in Taiwan also developed a fairly substantial direct trade with the Han River region on the mainland with supplies intended for Quanzhou and Zhangzhou in Fujian. Annual shipments of rice from Taiwan were around 14,000 tons.[24] Although most of this rice was sold in Fujian, some of it was re-exported to the Chaozhou region of Guangdong.

Taiwan, already a major exporter of sugar by the 1630s, apparently exported around "100 million *jin*" or 60,000 tons to the mainland by the 1720s.[25] In addition to Fujian, sugar from Taiwan was also shipped to Suzhou, Ningbo, Shanghai, and Tianjin. During the eighteenth century, ships plying the Fujian–Taiwan trade were classified according to their destinations as "northern junks" (*beicao*) and as "southern junks" (*nancao*).[26] There were also special junks called *tangchuan*, or "sugar ships," used in this trade. In 1725, the governor of Fujian estimated there were at least 500–700 such ships each with a carrying capacity of 70–140 tons of sugar plying the route between Taiwan and Xiamen.[27] It is not possible to estimate, given the extensive level of transshipment of commodities, how much of the sugar sold by traders from Fujian in the north was produced in Taiwan as opposed to being produced in Fujian itself. One record, based on the receipts of the Fujian customs, suggests that in 1724, about 38 percent of the revenues were collected from the export of Taiwan sugar.[28] Conceivably this may have been the typical level until the nineteenth century, underlining the overall importance of the sugar in the Taiwan–Fujian trade. Between July and October 1731, for example, a total of 53 ships arrived from Fujian in Tianjin. Of these, 45 carried cargoes of sugar, transporting a total of over 4.5 million *jin* or around 2,600 tons.[29]

Similarly, it seems that some of the Taiwanese sugar destined for the international market was also re-exported to Guangdong. For example, *The Chinese Repository* of 1833 noted significant quantities of sugar from Fujian being imported into Guangdong.[30] By the same routes, some of the sugar produced in eastern Guangdong in the Chaozhou region was also exported to Xiamen, ending up in the shipments to Tianjin.[31]

Taiwan's imports from Fujian and the other mainland areas consisted of various types of manufactured goods, including luxury items such as silks, gauzes, and velvets from Suzhou and Zhejiang, as well as the more mundane necessities, such as cotton cloth and raw cotton, tea, medicinal herbs, earthenwares, tiles, iron vessels, and paper.[32] Some of these goods, also brought from the north by the Fujian traders, were for export to Southeast Asia. The picture that then emerges is one of considerable overlap in the commodities trade of Guangdong, Taiwan, and Fujian with one major artery extending north to the Yangzi Delta, Tianjin, and Japan, and the other to Guangdong and Southeast Asia. The domestic trade circuits of Guangdong, Taiwan, and Fujian were therefore interconnected and, as in the case of the international trade networks, crossed macro-regional divides.

In addition to the prominent role of Fujian merchants in the settlement, trade, and local economy of Taiwan, there is also evidence that in the seventeenth and early eighteenth centuries, along with the movement in goods, both mercantile capital and merchants from Fujian began to move into Guangdong as well. This included mercantile families who were to become enormously wealthy; for example, some of the famous merchants discussed earlier, such as Houqua (Wu Guoying and his sons), moved from Fujian to Guangdong during the early Qing.[33] Pan Zhencheng (Puankequa), who traded with Manila and other Southeast Asian ports and the various western companies including the Swedish, was also from Fujian. As early as the Kangxi period, sugarcane manufacturing and the sugar guilds (*tanghang*) in Yanping county were controlled by people from Fujian.[34] The 1758 edition of the *Guangzhou fuzhi* noted, "In eastern Yue [Guangdong] there are sugar guilds everywhere. They were started by people from Min [Fujian]. Now as a result, the profit is similar to that of Min."[35] The Guangdong salt trade, which apparently involved "several thousand" merchants, was also primarily controlled by traders who were from "outside Guangdong" and had relocated there in the seventeenth century.[36] It is not known whether these salt merchants were linked to either the Yangzhou or the Huizhou salt merchants who controlled so much of the long-distance trade in salt throughout China, or whether they, too, had Fujian links. Overall, by the 1730s, the Quanzhou and Zhangzhou merchants of Fujian were said to number well over a thousand in Guangzhou. They were also the most prominent group among the Chinese merchants in Macao at that time.[37]

Given the extensive trade merchants from Fujian had with northern China and Southeast Asia, it seems that many of these merchants relocating to Guangzhou had made their money outside the province and were bringing it to Guangzhou as the new trading opportunities opened up there in the eighteenth century.[38] The presence of Xiamen merchants in Guangzhou and Macao was also noted by British traders. These merchants continued their links with Fujian as well; as one source noted in 1723, "Suqua, Cowlo, & severall of the Merchants arrived here from Amoy. We went and wellcomed them on their arrival, according to Custome, they tell us, i.e. Susqua & Cowlo, that they have built large Hongs at Amoy, in order to live there."[39] It is therefore not surprising that when, in the eighteenth century, the Qing institutionalized foreign trade by authorizing leading merchant houses to regulate and broker it, several of them came from Fujian.[40] Clearly mercantile capital was able to cross provincial boundaries with relative ease. What were the trading structures through which this capital entered the countryside?

Hierarchies of Traders: Cohong Merchants, Shopmen, Brokers, and Traveling Merchants

Chinese mercantile capital was structured in an elaborate hierarchy through individuals involved in managing trading, custom's duties, and brokerage funds.[41] The merchant collective in Guangzhou known to European and American traders as the Cohong (*gonghang*) was at its pinnacle. The base of the trading hierarchy consisted of hundreds and thousands of small brokers (*jingji*), itinerant merchants (*keshang*) who went from county-town to village markets, and local merchants (*zuoshang*) who interacted directly with the peasant producers and often ran the small shops in the county-towns.

The origins of the Cohong can be traced to the Ming mercantile guilds[42] or trade organizations (*qihang*) engaged in foreign trade. Mercantile interest groups (*kegang*) that dominated the foreign trade out of Guangzhou can be traced back at least to 1556.[43] In addition, in both Guangdong and Fujian, there were *hang shang*, or "authorized merchants," who acted as authorized brokers (*yashang*) for foreign trade.[44] These merchants were authorized to board incoming ships and collect the customs duties on behalf of the government. Such trading firms were variously called *yanghuo hang*, *yanghang*, and *waiyang hang* (lit., "foreign" or "overseas trade guilds").[45] In the early days of foreign trade when trade with all Europeans was not yet legal, practical matters such as the location where goods were to be loaded could still be arranged between the foreign traders and their Chinese suppliers to take place presumably anywhere on the coast. As Peter Mundy reported, for example, in 1637, "Wee receaved a lettre from our Merchantts att Cantan wherein they advised thatt they had provided aboutt 5 or 600 tunnes offe sugar, greene ginger, sugar candy and China rootes, and had Fraighted 3 greatt Junckes to lade it in, with which they hoped to come Downe themselves very sodainely."[46] Local officials, not unexpectedly, sought to monitor this and other efforts to evade customs duties and taxes and assigned the authorized merchants to act as guarantors for any breach of laws and regulations. In return for the risks, the *hong* merchants enjoyed preemptive rights of purchase over the goods brought in.[47] Many of these institutions, such as the selection of a group of wealthy and well-connected merchants to act as authorized merchants and the regulations monitoring foreign trade, were initially developed to supervise Chinese traders going to Southeast Asia from Fujian in the late Ming. They were then adapted by Qing officials to deal with the foreign traders coming in ever larger numbers to Guangzhou.[48]

After Qing power was established in Guangdong in 1681, the newly appointed governor-general of Liang-Guang, Wu Xingzuo (1632–1698), became very interested in promoting foreign trade and attempted to form a general association of officials and all major merchants. Various trading agencies were formalized through his official initiative in 1686, and the existing trading guilds were organized into two major categories: the Jinsi hang, dealing with interregional trade, and the Yanghuo hang, dealing with foreign trade.[49] Then, in 1720, the most prominent of the merchants involved in foreign trade were organized into the Cohong. Like their antecedents in Fujian, they were appointed by the government to oversee foreign trade; check weights and measures and the quality and quantity of the transactions; and act as guarantors for their clients to prevent a breach of law.[50] Membership in the Cohong ensured the commercial dominance of these families; at the time of its formation, there were probably as many as forty-five merchants involved. At other times, the Cohong had fewer than thirteen members.[51] Because the first group of Chinese merchants allowed to trade with foreigners in the 1550s had done so at a location near the Western Gate in Guangzhou (Nanhai side) called "Thirteen Guilds" (Shisanhang, sometimes translated as "Thirteen Factories"),[52] the Cohong was often called the "Thirteen Hongs" and the authorized merchants termed "hong merchants" by the European traders. The term "Thirteen" (*shisan*), however, being understood as the cardinal figure of thirteen by many of the European traders, caused numerous problems in the nineteenth century. The East India Company traders, for example, frequently gauged the commercial outlook of the times by the actual number of members in the Cohong and whether there were thirteen merchants present in the collective.[53] There was also a tendency to see the organization itself as a static institution controlled by thirteen mercantile families. Although there was a continuity in its nomenclature, the institution of the Cohong nonetheless evolved and changed through the course of the eighteenth and early nineteenth centuries, particularly after the restriction of most of western trade to Guangzhou in 1757 and the emergence of the English as the largest trading partner. Changes also occurred as the merchants who dominated the Cohong by the beginning of the nineteenth century were engaged in a vastly different world of international trade than their Fujian predecessors who had started out with capital from intraregional and intra-Asian trade in the seventeenth and mid-eighteenth centuries. If there was a point of continuity between the seventeenth-century and the nineteenth-century institution, it came from another source, namely, the relationship of Cohong to the Qing state and its officials.

As the checkered history of the institution shows, there were three groups with conflicting interests in foreign trade, leading to various types of friction. Tensions between the commercial interests of the Cohong merchants, the officials who sought to control the profits of foreign trade for their own ends, and foreign traders such as the British, who sought to circumvent Chinese monopsonies, were clearly evident from the inception of the Cohong. The Cohong was dissolved a year after its formation in 1720, reconstituted again in 1760, only to be dissolved shortly afterward by the Governor-General Li Shiyao

(d. 1788), who apparently accepted a bribe of 100,000 taels from the English traders to do so.[54] Reestablished in 1780–1782, the Cohong then continued to function as the primary institution in Guangzhou overseeing legal foreign trade up to the Opium War.[55]

The Cohong, however, represented only one dimension of the overall structure of the state's involvement in foreign trade. This trade was too lucrative a source of revenue to be neglected by the central government and the emperors. In 1684, quite clearly with the intention of drawing some of the income from foreign trade into the coffers of the central treasury, the Kangxi emperor appointed a representative of the Imperial Household Department (*neiwufu*) to collect customs duties on foreign trade at Guangzhou, and made similar arrangements at Zhangzhou, Xiamen, Ningbo, and Yuntaishan (Jiangsu). This imperial representative or superintendent remitted the monies to the Board of Revenue at Beijing (the *hubu*, and the representative was therefore called "Hoppo" by the Western traders).[56]

The superintendent of each of the customs bureaus had a tax quota to be remitted to the central government, but was also routinely assigned a higher quota, or "excess quota," to be forwarded to the Imperial Household Department. The technical restriction of most officially sanctioned western trade to Guangzhou after 1757, of course, made the situation there unique. Up to the Opium War this was the most lucrative of all the customs bureaus, both in terms of the revenues generated for the state and in terms of the opportunities for personal enrichment through bribes and gifts offered to the superintendent. By the latter half of the eighteenth century the Imperial Household Department itself was directly involved in the foreign trade at Guangzhou. The superintendents not only sent large gifts and bribes to the managers of the Imperial Household Department but also sent hundreds of thousands of taels as "voluntary contributions" to the coffers of the emperor himself.[57] This tripartite interest in foreign trade—those of the Cohong merchants, the provincial administrators, and the central government including the imperial household—resulted in a complex system of checks and balances. Each party was fully aware that they could not do without the other two, but at the same time was most conscious of the funds diverted into pockets other than its own. Different power alignments evolved continuously, frequently showing a commonalty of interests between the provincial gentry-administrators and mercantile community versus those of the central government.[58]

Technically, the trade in high-demand items of export such as silk, tea, nankeens, and sugar, plus a category called "China drugs" or "China roots," which included rhubarb, cassia, camphor, galingal ginger, and similar products, was supposed to be confined to the hong merchants. Specific items of import such as woolens, raw cotton, cloves, pepper, various dyes, sappanwood, ivory, bird's nests, metals, and skins were likewise presumed to be under the purview of hong merchants.[59] These hong merchants, representing the wealthiest mercantile elite, paid a great deal of money for the privilege of membership and the status it brought, including the ninth rank of the mandarinate.[60] As a result, to some extent they were interested in safeguarding their privileged trade status by acting as a collective. They were, however, by no means an unified interest group. Each firm tried to further its own interests at the cost of its rivals. Each hong merchant company traded on its own account and with its own capital for individual profit. The corporate character of the Cohong was evident primarily in its efforts to enforce oversight of foreign trade regulations, and if any member merchant became insolvent, the other merchants had a joint responsibility to repay foreign creditors from a common fund. Therefore, while the hong merchants had a formal trading monopoly on certain commodities, their business structure made it possible and indeed profitable to retain links with the smaller Chinese merchants, called "shopmen" or "outside merchants" by the European traders, and expand their personal opportunities for profit.[61]

By law, the outside merchants were allowed to trade in commodities needed by foreign residents in China, such as food and clothing. They could also sell eight other items, including fans, and umbrellas, leather shoes, and chinaware.[62] As late as 1828, the hong merchants continued officially to push for regulations that would prevent outside merchants from dealing in silk, tea, and sugar. In practice, however, the regulations were ineffectual. As John Phipps commented regarding the regulations of 1828, "It need hardly be said, that the trade with shopmen or outside merchants was carried on with freedom, before this regulation was passed, and that it was but little, if at all, affected by the interference of government. The trade in the above articles is not, in practice, confined to the Hong merchants."[63] The outside merchants had several advantages that allowed them to go on trading and in some instances thereby amass large fortunes.[64] The shopmen did not have to pay all the overhead of foreign trade that the hong merchants were faced with and were therefore in a position frequently to undercut the price-fixing attempted by the Cohong. The volume of trade conducted by these outside merchants also increased as more British traders, "country traders," and Americans started coming to Guangzhou in the early nineteenth century, all of them private merchants chafing under the monopoly privileges of the East India Company. Such private traders, particularly the smaller American traders, found it more profitable to deal with shopmen for silks, nankeens, teas, and sugar than with the structures of formal trade and the Cohong merchants. Many traders from Bombay also sold their cotton and other goods to the outside merchants in China; the lucrative but illegal opium trade was also part of this network. The outside merchants were able to circumvent the formal monopolies of the Cohong with impunity because several less affluent hong members lent their names to the trading activities of such merchants for a fee.[65]

Given this range of commercial interests and deviations from the stipulated regulations, it is difficult to determine precisely who handled the bulk of the sugar export trade. Some of it was certainly handled by the hong merchants. Because the demand for sugar was regular, the trade was attractive to well-known merchants as well as small traders. In 1704, for instance, Leanqua (Chinese name and dates unknown), one of the authorized merchants in Guangzhou, sold copper, tutenague, and sugar for a total of 10,000 taels to an East India Company ship. The business dealings of another hong merchant, Poonqua (Ni Pingfa, dates unknown), suggest he, too, was involved in selling sugar. In 1802, he had run up a large debt to country traders; he could repay only in kind, and most of the repayment was made in sugar.[66] But since shopmen were the ones who most often supplied country traders, and this was the primary export market for sugar, it seems likely that shopmen were the ones who most frequently dealt in the commodity. And, regardless of their formal position, both shopmen as well as the hong merchants operated on the same principles of forward dealing and an advance-credit system to ensure their supplies of commodities.

Without an advance contract, prices fluctuated with every major demand; in 1689, for example, when English traders wanted to buy 1 million *jin* of sugar and 300,000 *jin* of tutenague without prior arrangements, the prices of these commodities rose sharply in the market at Guangzhou.[67] Consequently, arrangements were made far in advance; in 1783, in one instance, we find supercargoes of East India Company ships making advances to the Cohong merchants for one-half the cost of tea, and as much as nine-tenths the cost of raw silk, nine months ahead of the time of delivery. The money was to "enable the Hong Merchants to pay cash to the country dealers and so to secure prompt delivery and to obtain the lowest prices."[68] The implications of an advance-credit system within the existing social formation were manifold. Although substantial amounts of money changed hands well before the time of delivery, the complex commercial hierarchy through which the money then found its way into the hands of the peasant producer added several layers of intermediaries. Through these loans the direct producer who borrowed operating capital in return for forward contracts on his crop became vertically integrated into the world market. The wealthy hong merchants with their official connections, however, remained many steps removed from the immediate process of production, which was left to hundreds, and then thousands, of small producers who operated at the other end of the commodity chain. In spite of the vast amounts of money involved in the silk, tea, and sugar export trade, the hong merchants and shopmen thus essentially remained procurers and brokers. As middlemen to the Europeans and Americans, they simply contracted to deliver stipulated quantities of goods at prearranged prices regardless of market conditions. Each of the mercantile intermediaries handling the loans sought to ensure against losses and increase its margin without assuming the risks of production.

Various types of brokers were crucial to this process of working the money down to the peasant-producer and getting the commodities from them to the national and international markets. Operating as middlemen between buyers and sellers, all brokers were essentially commission agents. The brokers known as *jingji* operated at the lowest level of the marketing hierarchy—the standard market—and did not go through the process of getting a license from the state. In contrast, in the higher- or intermediate-level markets, where market taxes were collected by the government, the brokerage firms were licensed by the provincial treasury, and the brokers were commonly known as *yahang*. By paying a fee for the license, these brokers were authorized to arrange for the sales of commodities such as grain, tea, wine, vegetables, and textiles, and supervise the slaughtering of livestock. For providing these services, the brokers were permitted to charge commission fees, divided between buyer and seller, technically 5 percent or so of the value of the goods.[69] Either the *jingji* or the *yahang* could form the immediate link to the market for the majority of direct producers. Often there was little distinction in the scope of their activities, which could range from functioning at the village level as retail brokers to working as large-scale wholesale dealers. The *yahang* brokers typically bought the goods on account for town- and city-based merchants, provided initial storage and transportation for the commodities, and advanced money for the stipulated sale prices. The larger wholesale dealers were, in turn, the suppliers for national and international markets.

Within these basic categories one can locate many petty traders and merchants with overlapping activities, such as itinerant merchants and local merchants. These small-time merchants picked up commodities at the point of production and delivered them to wholesalers at the market towns. Some invested their own capital in the process and completely circumvented the agency of the middleman-brokers, while other *keshang* operated on a commission basis for *yahang* brokers. The scale of operation of the *keshang* and *zuoshang* also varied enormously; the largest transported goods in their own conveyances to other provinces; some operated small retail outlets in the county-towns and depended on others to pick up the goods.[70] Except for those producers who were wealthy enough to have their own means of transporting produce to the market, or those who were selling such small quantities that they could carry the goods themselves, in Guangdong the *yahang* and the *keshang* typically went down to the village to collect the produce. The common pattern was to find out who had what to sell on the market days, and then to travel down to the villages on "cold" days, that is, days on which no markets were held, to make a bid for the goods or transport the commodities purchased.[71]

Itinerant merchants, brokers, retailers, and wholesalers as well as those involved in interregional trade were all linked through commercial organizations, most commonly trade guilds and guild-like organizations. A range of such organizations existed, and as William Rowe points out, the overlapping terminology reflected organizational flexibility.[72] In addition to *hang*, which usually referred to a trade association in the entire trade of a commodity, terms for mercantile associations such as *bang*, *gongsuo*, and *huiguan* have often been translated as "guild," although there were differences in their range, scope, and function.[73] These guilds and commercial associations could be exclusive to one particular line of trade and commodity or more broadly inclusive and based on place of origin. At the national level, merchant guilds based on place of origin often handled the trade in a variety of products from the same region. Rules, regulations, and the range of trading activities differed from guild to guild. Fukienese merchants from Quanzhou and Zhangzhou had set up three major commercial guilds (known as the Sanjiao) in Taiwan by 1725, which controlled all the trade to and from the mainland. Called Beijiao, Nanjiao, and Gangjiao, each had several tens of business firms affiliated to it. By the late eighteenth century, the Gangjiao had come to be called the Tangjiao (Sugar Guild) and apparently had more than fifty affiliated businesses.[74] In the nineteenth century, if not earlier, members of the Sugar Guild also acted as middlemen for the Beijiao, collecting the sugar from the smaller manufactories via their agents, while the Beijiao controlled all the commodities in the export trade.[75] On the mainland, there were several guilds involved in the sugar trade which operated as local-origin associations (*huiguan*). In Ningbo, for example, Fujian merchants trading principally in salt, fish, and oranges also had a special section dealing with sugar products.[76] Frequently such merchants were involved in trade and credit arrangements in complementary lines of business. The manufacture of salted olives and salted fish in Dongguan during the end of the Qianlong period, for example, was controlled by the salt merchants.[77] Similarly in eighteenth- and early-nineteenth-century Shanghai, merchants from Chaozhou who belonged to the Chaoyang and Huilai *bang* controlled the trade in sugar as well as tobacco from Guangdong.[78] This type of vertical integration of a sector ot the market may have served to increase total profit; at the very least it added to the market strength of these larger traders.

There were more localized *tanghang* (sugar guilds) which had retail outlets in various county-towns and cities. They also operated as wholesalers and quality controllers for the larger merchants. The guilds attempted to regularize the quality of sugar sold and the type of packaging used. The size and weight of the containers in which the sugar was packed was strictly stipulated by the Sanjiao, the export guilds of Taiwan. The Sanjiao regulations also warned against adulterating sugar with sweet potato starch and threatened those who did so with public exposure.[79]

The hierarchies of these various types of merchants and brokers represented a chain of financial arrangements, which Japanese surveys of the traditional sector of sugar manufacturing in Taiwan in the nineteenth century have traced in detail. The money to purchase goods at the village level usually originated as loans from a city-based native bank, the export guild, or a wealthy merchant.[80] At this point, the interest rate was usually around 1.5–2.0 percent per month. Next, either the guild or the export merchants lent the money to other merchants in the sugar guild, who lent it to the broker. The *yahang* then either went down the chain to an unlicensed broker in a standard market or lent the money to a traveling merchant. At each level it was possible to multiply the number of middlemen, as the money moved from the prefectural capital to the county capital, the intermediate market, the standard market, and ultimately to the peasant. The more numerous the intermediaries, the higher the rate of interest and the greater the squeeze on those operating at the lower levels, since the complicated chain of loans increased the risks of business. The sugar guilds, as creditors to the brokers and itinerant merchants, also sought to control the profits. *Yahang* and *keshang* were, for example, entitled to only 30 percent of the export sale receipts, while the urban export guild such as the Beijiao and Kangjiao kept 70 percent.[81]

Given that the guilds and similar commercial organizations exerted such great influence on the logistics of market operations, the question inevitably arises whether the guilds were able to fix prices of commodities as well. Guild regulations certainly tried to control the percentage of the price that members could collect as commission and sought to restrict competition among members in various ways. The regulations of the Sanjiao in Taiwan, for example, stipulated that the merchant buying sugar from producers to resell to shopowners could charge only 2 percent of the price of a sack of sugar as commission and that violations would be punished with a fine.[82] Information on the role of the guilds in controlling market prices is not readily available.[83] The practice was frowned upon by the government, and to an extent the licensed broker (*yahang*) had to ensure that prices were "market-determined" (*shijia*).[84] Nevertheless, price-fixing even at the level of the national market was common. The indigo dyeing guild of Wenzhou, for example, fixed prices twice a year. The Wenzhou millers' guild could fix prices one month ahead of sale, and the cotton and cotton-textile guilds in Ningbo also regularly fixed prices.[85] Other guilds set minimum price levels or stipulated that members should not undercut other members when that particular line of business was experiencing an economic downturn.[86] But, national-level prices of commodities, manipulated through price-fixing or otherwise, had little to do with the prices paid at the level of the peasant-producer. Prices here were determined by the merchants and gentry-landlords, who had the dual position of purchaser and creditor and could, most importantly, bring pressures other than the market to bear on the negotiations. And it is this access to social power that needs to be taken into consideration before evaluating the potential of the market and an expanding commodity economy to generate change in the social relations of production.

Markets without a Market-Driven Economy?

Guangdong does not seem to have had very many markets in the Ming. Hayashi Kazuo has suggested that there were only thirty-six regularly operating markets in the entire area of the Pearl River Delta. Recently, Ye Xian'en and Tan Dihua have revised this figure upward to 166 markets in the region by the end of the Jiajing period (1522–1566).[87] But then, starting in the 1660s, there was a veritable boom in the development of new markets. As we see in Table 16, by 1735 there were as many as 444 markets in Guangzhou prefecture and by the end of the eighteenth century over 540. It is not possible to identify exactly which of these five-hundred-odd markets were "intermediate markets" versus "standard markets," according to the marketing hierarchies proposed by Skinner. The actual number of local-level standard markets may have been slightly higher than the last figures cited above, for the gazetteers, from which these data are compiled, generally only recorded the markets noted by officials. Significantly, as Table 16 shows, the most rapid increase in the number of markets in Guangdong Delta occurred in the seventeenth and eighteenth centuries rather than the nineteenth. Only in some of the core counties involved in sericulture was there a renewed spurt in the development of new markets in the mid-nineteenth century. In others, such as Gaoming county, on the periphery of the Delta, only one new market developed between 1735 and 1911.

Lower-level local markets developed far more slowly in Taiwan. To some extent, this was a reflection of the physical geography of the region, where the nearly unnavigable rivers and mountainous hinterland hampered inland transportation. But more important, immigrants from the mainland often settled around the military garrisons, which functioned as both markets and administrative centers.[88] The pace at which markets developed reflected population shifts. For example, the core area of settlements, Taiwan county, added only seven markets during 1694–1740, while Feng-shan in the south and Chang-hua and Tan-shui in the north, areas to which many of the recent immigrants moved to during this period, added thirty-four. Then, however, during 1740 and 1768, a spate of new markets and settlements developed

TABLE 16

Standard Markets in the Pearl River Delta, 1522–1911

County	Ming Jiajing (1522–1566)	Kangxi (1662–1722)	Yongzheng (1723–1735)	Qianlong (1736–1795)	Jiaqing–Daoguang (1796–1850)	Xianfeng–Tongzhi (1851–1874)	Guangxu–Xuantong (1875–1911)
Panyu	17	73	–	82	–	99	107
Nanhai	19	–	54	46	160	201	244
Shunde	11	43	36	42	–	90	88
Dongguan	12	–	49	–	83	–	–
Xinhui	16	44	45	–	69	–	70
Xinning	8	–	22	–	56	–	72
Kaiping	–	–	15	–	24	–	47
Enping	9	18	18	–	22	–	–
Huiyang	9	–	13	12	–	–	–
Gaoyao	7	–	22	–	39	–	–
Baoan	–	30	31	–	36	–	24
Qingyuan	7	16	7	15	–	–	40
Huaxian	–	9	8	–	–	–	22
Conghua	10	14	13	–	–	–	–
Zengcheng	11	–	26	–	40	–	29
Sanshui	–	10	20	–	23	–	22
Xiangshan	9	12	12	–	32	–	37
Gaoming	11	29	29	–	–	–	30
TOTAL	156	298	420	197	584	390	832

SOURCE: Ye Xian'en and Tan Dihua, "Ming Qing Zhujiang sanjiaozhou nongye shangyehua yu zushi de fazhan," pp. 93–96. Data based on county gazetteers. Information available only for certain reign periods.

in the older settled areas of Taiwan and Chu-lo counties.[89] On Taiwan as in Guangdong, the initial impetus to establish markets came from wealthy local elites and merchants. The collaboration between resident officials and the mercantile elite, for example, is clearly discernible in the establishment and maintenance of major trading centers such as Chang-hua and Lu-kang in Taiwan in the eighteenth and nineteenth centuries.[90] In Guangdong, the cooperation between official and commercial interests reached well below the level of the prefecture. After the evacuation of the coastal regions of Guangdong, for example, numerous government officials worked with the gentry to establish and construct small, local-level standard markets and helped renovate the markets that had been abandoned when the coastal population was moved inland. In Yanjiang county, the magistrate even gave several merchants 3 taels each in 1685 to set up stores in the county town and encouraged them to live there.[91] The rent was collected by the proprietors of the land on which the market was built, "either a fixed amount, or a percentage upon their sale or supposed sale."[92]

Although hopes for enhanced revenues led magistrates to encourage the development of markets, in many cases the resulting monies eluded them. Qu Dajun at the end of the seventeenth century noted the use of strong-arm tactics to protect controlling interests in markets and access to the markets. In some counties, elites built roads and limited access so successfully that there was no official presence to check weights and measures. Qu concludes in his comments on the markets, "The way to wealth has been to guard property, annex and monopolize, settle matters by force, recklessly grab land, and without authority or official sanction control the profits of the land and sea. . . . Commercial taxes and market rents do not get to the prefectures."[93] The firmer establishment of Qing rule in the south in the eighteenth century did not bring a greater measure of state control over these markets. A hundred years after Qu Dajun, the *Dongguan xianzhi* of 1797 tells of the local gentry and village bullies controlling all the marketplaces in the county.[94] A memorial in the 1819 gazetteer of neighboring Xin'an county expressed similar concern over this state of affairs, "There are two major evils. The first is fighting for markets.

On market days the people who go there on behalf of the profiteers commit murder and arson. Cases have been taken to court again and again through the years, but always there have been recurrences soon after."[95] The other "evil" deplored by the memorialist was land grabbing or "fighting for fields," a phenomenon we have discussed earlier. The crisis in gentry incomes and privileges that had resulted in a revitalization of the lineage organizations in the seventeenth century had evidently set in motion diverse strategies for increasing income, including the control of markets. Such control provided additional income that the gentry and elites often invested in developing paramilitary forces that in turn, gave them additional extra-economic control of markets and made further accumulation possible.[96]

Genealogies show that several lineages owed their initial rise to wealth and power to the money made by collecting rents and fees at the markets; others used control of the markets to consolidate their social and economic power. Ancestors of the Rong lineage of Xiangshan, for example, originally salt makers who moved into agriculture when the salt marshes they owned dried up, pooled resources and, during the social turmoils of the mid-seventeenth century, formed a market with twenty other families who belonged to the same *pai* (salt-making team).[97] They also set about investing in all the accoutrements of gentry status, including participating in the examination system. By the end of the century, county officials tried to collect market fees because the market had become lucrative and was providing a great deal of income to the Rongs. Official efforts were nevertheless thwarted when one of the Rong family passed the imperial examinations (*jinshi*) in 1705. From then on the income of the market accrued only to its founders. Having an official connection gave the lineage enough clout to circumvent members of the local bureaucracy who tried to lay down the law.

Such cases can be found all over south China, and the connection between lineage power and control of markets is amply clear. In southern Xin'an county, in the area that was to become the New Territories after 1898, the five major lineages had all set up markets in the seventeenth and eighteenth centuries.[98] Slightly further up the Delta, the Cui lineage of Shatou, the He of Xiaolan, and the Longs of

Daliang had all built markets in Shunde county, and control of these markets was reflected in their local standing.[99] The social power of the lineages and lineage corporations extended well beyond the role of rentiers of the marketplace. For example, the You Gong Tang, the ancestral hall of the Ha Tsuen branch of the Deng lineage founded in 1751, not only managed the market and its piers but also oversaw the maintenance of local waterways and pathways. The ancestral hall also controlled the lineage militia.[100] All the five lineages of southern Xin'an county charged a fee for weighing goods sold in the markets they controlled.[101] The weighing scales were retained by them or hired out to private individuals at a high rent. At the other corner of the Pearl River Delta, the Guans of Kaiping owned half the shops, collected fees, and imposed "unofficial levies" of all kinds in Upper Zhikan market.[102] In the Old Tai Po (Dapu) market, the Dengs collected a fail-proof fee, a "basket tax" that had to be paid by anyone who entered the market carrying a basket.[103] Economic and social power was easily translatable into coercion. As Freedman, in his reconstruction of the history of the Deng lineage notes, "As Masters of the Market [Tai Po], the Tang [Deng] people taxed sellers and, if the stories now told are to be taken as history and not as retrospective justifications of revolt, they harassed buyers by their exercise of the privilege of claiming choice 'goods.'"[104]

Hayashi Kazuo's research identifies several instances of particular villages in Guangdong and their inhabitants being "bonded" or "attached" (*reizoku suru* or *lishu*) to specific markets.[105] Given that lineages and other similar organizations were involved in struggles over the control of markets and lands adjacent to markets, "bonding" or restricting villagers to particular markets would have been a natural extension of elite attempts to garner market fees. As the Rev. William Ashmore noted, "[P]illage on land, and piracy on the rivers made travelling unsafe and dangerous. Every trading boat and every passenger boat had to go armed."[106] Under these circumstances, it is most improbable that individuals could have patronized the markets of rival lineages or associations.

Control of markets was one of the primary causes of inter-lineage and inter-village feuding. Challenges to the dominant lineage often commenced with a struggle over the market. In 1843, for example, the Hakka who rented the marketplace from the Jin lineage of He'ao in Guangdong refused to pay the rent; a feud ensued which continued for six years; then ninety villages joined together in 1850 to "exterminate" the Jin and seize control of another marketplace. The villagers mobilized an army of over 5,000. Ultimately, after a few years of fighting when both sides were exhausted, the Jin lost one market but managed to get an agreement for increased rent from the other.[107] The market at Phenix Village near Shantou was established just half a mile down the road from the Tan lineage village market and in direct competition with them.[108] Talk of the bitter rivalry between the Yuen Long market and the Ha Tsuen market going back centuries was still common in Ha Tsuen village in the 1970s.[109]

The interlinked and symbiotic relationship of powerful gentry lineage elites and local representatives of the state sustained the extra-economic nexus in the operation of markets. About 10 percent of the sales taxes from the larger markets was retained as the prerogative of the local commissioner of education (*xiao li*). "The rest," as Arthur Smith observed, "will be under the control of the village headmen, perhaps for the nominal purpose of paying the expenses of a free school, the funds for which not improbably find their way largely or wholly into the private treasuries of those who manage the public affairs of the village."[110]

Across the straits in Taiwan, the pattern was only slightly different. Lin Shi, the pioneer ancestor of the legendary wealthy Lin family of Wufeng, "summoned merchants to come" and made his fortune by controlling not only rice lands, but the trade in rice at the major marketing center of Ta-li-chi.[111] The overall lower population-to-land ratio and the availability of new lands through arrangements with the aborigines meant the congruence of lineage vicinage and market control was less circumscribed in Taiwan than in Guangdong. Higher-order lineages (e.g., the Hakka in the P'ing-tung plain of southeastern Taiwan) were able to expand and include members in several vicinages and marketing areas.[112] Periodic standard markets on Taiwan were less common, for, as noted, they were often part of garrisons. Indeed such markets may have been even less possible, for the violence was even more endemic as the struggles over land and resources were amplified in a settler colony. Unlike Guangdong and Fujian where inter-lineage feuding dominated, here the violence was generated most often by inter-ethnic rivalry between immigrants from Guangdong versus immigrants from Fujian, or rivalry between immigrants from the two areas of Fujian, Zhangzhou and Quanzhou. The result was that feuds often spilled over into several counties. For example, in 1782, when the ongoing rivalry between immigrants from Zhangzhou and Quanzhou in Taiwan's Chang-hua county escalated into open war over a gambling losses at the marketplace, the feuding started out in Chang-hua county but quickly spread to Chu-lo and other southern counties as well.[113] This particular incidence lasted for almost four years. Commercial guilds could also foment feuds. In the northern area, in 1853, for example, the Upper Guild (Dingjiao) and the Lower Guild (Xiajiao) instigated clashes between the Zhangzhou and Quanzhou immigrants.[114] Merchants guilds routinely financed militia and self-defense corps in cities where they did business.[115] And then there was the usual inter-surname, inter-clan rivalry; even in the 1960s, people recalled how at the turn of the century the Chens of Wang-kang, Chang-hua county, made it virtually impossible for the Hongs from the neighboring village to pass through their territory to go down to trade in Lu-kang, the major port of Taiwan. "Armed expeditions of Hungs [Hongs] would attempt to break through the blockading Chens. Sometimes they were let through in order they could be robbed of their purchases on their return."[116] The state sought to intervene, troops were sent from time to time, officials were exhorted to keep the peace, and numerous decrees of the Qing state with proclamations prohibiting banditry and feuds were carved on stone; they were set up, ironically enough, in the market squares.[117] It has been tabulated that for the 212 years of Qing rule, there were outbreaks of communal violence every 2.7 years on Taiwan.[118] Of necessity, then, access to the market for the direct producers all over south China was mediated through this complex web of social power. And these relations of power were even more evident when it came to the marketing of bulk commodities.

Grain was, as we have noted, the primary bulk commodity on the market. Landlords and merchants made alliances to transport grain collected as rent to the market. The majority of landlords, in Guangdong and Taiwan, collected rents in kind, and many used the agency of the *yahang* brokers to sell the rice collected as rent. This connection with the gentry-landlords was frequently used by the brokers to fix prices in the market.[119] The *yahang* with gentry connections could in effect enjoy monopoly privileges in the local markets and were often accused by officials of manipulating weights, measures, and currency exchange rates. The business of operating as brokers itself became a monopoly, with many getting licenses year after year and passing on the privileges to sons and nephews. Although gentry were legally barred from holding *yahang* licenses, powerful and wealthy families and degree holders were known to acquire them through a variety of ruses such as assumed names and the names of servants. Local strongmen (*haoren*) and powerful families (*haozu*), who opened up land through reclamation projects in Xinhui, collected the rent due entirely in rice, which they sold to grain merchants in the county capital, Huicheng. They then used the income to develop yet other marshes for reclamation (with the tax waiver, of course), which were rented out under similar arrangements of rent in kind.[120] Landlords-turned-brokers were in powerful positions to use the market to further their social and political standing, and these connections extended to trading networks not just for rice but for all sorts of goods. The trading ties of these rentiers with the wholesale merchants was intimate enough for them to use the trade guilds to arbitrate conflicts, and relationships were built up over decades and generations. The regulations of the palm fan guild of Xinhui, for example, stipulated that the head of the guild (*jiashou*) was to have a term lasting no longer than three years. In practice, such positions were held for twenty or thirty years.[121] The list of officeholders of the palm fan guild also illustrates very well how close the relationships between gentry and merchants could be. Two of the chief executive officers of the guild (*shoushi hangzhong*) were gentry from the most prominent lineages, including the main branch of the He lineage, whose clout dated back to the Ming period.[122] The guild also bought influence; it hosted lavish feasts each year with expenditures of 2,000–3,000 taels and invited all the local gentry.

Yet the gentry could also use their access to political power to discipline the merchants when it was in their best interest to do so, as in this example from Foshan. In Foshan township, the famous and extremely wealthy Beidi Ancestral Temple (*zumiao*) was run by the senior members of the local gentry. The Yi, the Huo, the Li, and the Chen—the so-called famous four lineages of Foshan—ran the affairs of the town. Some, like the Chens, had made their money by operating the first market in the area in the Ming and then had acquired gentry status via the examination system in the early Qing. Collectively, as part of the temple administration, the four lineages oversaw the operation of the main ferry-pier of the town and collected the rents from this and other temple properties. In 1787, the Chen wanted to built a road to the pier, and this construction involved the demolition of several shops. When the shopkeepers tried to protest, the magistrate sided with the local gentry and declared the land public property.[123] By the 1830s, even the rice prices in the town were set by the gentry via directives to the merchants.[124]

The development of a highly commercialized agricultural economy and markets during the seventeenth and eighteenth century, predicated on and accompanied by the growth of the smallholder producer sector, has been perceived by some scholars as a social transformation which marked the demise of extra-economic coercion associated with the erstwhile manorial-serf economy.[125] However, as this account shows, the amelioration of extra-economic coercion may have been more apparent than real. Instead of being bonded to specific landlords, the direct producers were now bonded to specific markets by lineage ties. The elites, in the process of regrouping and reorganizing in the Qing, restructured the ways in which their access to the surplus was determined. Their income no longer depended only on access to office and the control of land and labor. Income augmented through direct or indirect commercial activities became crucial for maintaining their privileged positions. Besides the earnings from pawnshops, rent from the property on which businesses were situated, and rent from the shops themselves, they collected various fees, such as for the rental of weighing scales and the use of ferry piers. Part of this income was routinely directed toward supporting lineage militia and self-defense corps, both to ensure control over the markets and to intimidate potential competitors. Other institutions intended to bolster elite power, such as temples, academies, and literary societies, also received shares of commercial income.[126] This overarching gentry-landlord control over local markets and their ability to use it to further specific class interests then defined the limits within which merchants operated and became involved in commercialized agriculture.

Merchant Capital and Commercial Agriculture

Did merchant capital during the Qing become directly involved in production? Or did it simply commission a number of immediate producers to supply certain items that would subsequently be collected and sold by merchants and their agents?

The most frequently encountered references to merchant capital during the seventeenth century refer to loans for sugarcane cultivation.[127] There is some indication that this capital was not local and, as mentioned earlier, could have been from Fujian. The 1822 edition of the *Guangdong tongzhi* (Guangdong Provincial Gazetteer) notes, "People from outside Guangdong (*Guangdong ben wai zhi ren*) only know [how to] aim for large profits. The land is used for planting things like longyan, sugarcane, tobacco, and indigo. This makes people rich, but rice scarce."[128]

It is not clear from the reference whether the same merchants were lending money to produce all the crops referred to above. But by the mid-eighteenth century, there were merchants "who specialized in dealing in sugar as their livelihood" (*fantang shengli*).[129] These merchants typically went into several villages in Guangdong either prior to the planting or just before the sugarcane harvest, when they gave loans to hire extra hands and the equipment needed to manufacture sugar.[130] One of the Board of Punishment Records gives a description of how this system worked when the arrangements were made at harvest time.

In 1751 in Hepu County in southwestern Guangdong, a rich tenant farmer, Chen Daheng, leased extensive lands and cultivated sugarcane with the help of hired laborers. Presumably because he lacked the resources to process the cane, he entered into a contract with a merchant, Lu Dazhen, who "specialized in dealing in sugar as a livelihood." On the second day of the fourth month of 1751, "Lu Dazhen and Chen Daheng traveled by boat to Chenshikang market, where Chen informed Lu that he had sugar to sell and Lu agreed to buy 50,000 *jin* of sugar at 3.5 taels per 10,000 slabs.[131] He furthermore gave 200 cash as down payment to Chen with a contract that on the twelfth of the month the money would be paid in full, with the sugar being released [to the merchant] on the fourteenth."[132] Chen, however, did not honor the contract. He avoided accepting the remainder of the payment on the stipulated day and told the merchant to return later when the sugar was supposed to change hands. But when Lu Dazhen did return, he found that the sugar promised to him had been sold to another merchant for a better price. At that point, the irate merchant "caused a disturbance, started a fight and brought about a death."

These contracts were the local-level examples of the system of forward dealing noted earlier at the level of the hong merchants. For all these merchants, large and small, this was a way of reducing price fluctuations and securing deliveries. Typically, merchants lent money to sugarcane cultivators in the spring and collected the sugar in winter.[133] Such arrangements, including the lapse of several months between the date the money was given and the date of delivery, were not limited to sugar manufacturing, nor were they unique to Guangdong. Merchants also advanced money for the weaving of ramie and *ge* cloth in Jiangxi in the second month, returning in the summer and autumn to pick up the cloth. Others operating in Hubei, Sichuan, and Yunnan gave advances for the purchase of silkworm eggs and mulberry leaves.[134] There were also merchants who after examining the blossoms on the litchee, longyan, and orange trees in Guangdong agreed on a price per picul of harvested fruit: "There are practically as many wholesale fruit dealers as general merchants. The former buy the fruits before the harvest is even ripe; sometimes when the trees are only in bloom."[135]

There was a considerable element of risk in these ventures. If a peasant like Chen defaulted or the quality of the produce was poorer than the agreed-upon price warranted, a merchant could lose his investment. Merchants therefore sought to compensate for these risks, as seen below, by giving the peasants a price considerably lower than the price on the market. Such loans were contracted for individually with each producer, and this also increased the merchant's risk. It seems, however, that this was the primary way in which merchants were involved in commercial agriculture, while their involvement in the immediate process of production is debatable.

Qu Dajun's and Li Diaoyuan's descriptions of sugar manufacturing from the beginning of the eighteenth century suggest that all aspects of processing were carried out by local producers.[136] An effort at documenting other types of mercantile involvement in agriculture by Tan Dihua and Ye Xian'en has yielded a contract entered into by several merchants in Xinhui in 1710.[137] This group of merchants apparently regularly set up twenty or more temporary sugarcane-processing huts in the county capital and got their cane as well as the people working the crushers from the neighboring villages. The enterprise was established enough to draw government attention; the county government, under the guise of registering the workers, extracted a fee of 20 taels per manufacturing unit.[138] But were these merchants buying the cane and processing it themselves in the centralized locations in what may have been an example of an incipient capitalist venture,[139] or were they merely leasing the cane crushers to direct producers, who brought their cane to these locations and who were already indebted to the merchants and were going to turn over the sugar to them at a previously stipulated price? I think the latter interpretation is the more likely, for, as explored below, similar arrangements existed in Taiwan.

These types of arrangements that brought producers to a particular location were also noted by Europeans like George Staunton and Charles Eckeberg traveling through Guangdong in the eighteenth century. Staunton commented, "The cane plantations in China belonging to individuals were of very little extent; and the expence [*sic*] of erecting sugar mills too heavy to have one upon each plantation. The business of extracting the juice of the cane, and boiling it into sugar is therefore a separate undertaking from that of him who cultivated the plant. The boilers of sugar travel about the country, with a small apparatus sufficient for their purpose."[140] Staunton further noticed the use of unpaid family labor: "The boiler of sugar endeavors to enter into an agreement with several planters at a time so that his works erected near the center of their several plantations may serve them all without changing his establishment. During the time he is employed the servants and children of the planter are busily engaged in carrying cane to the mill."[141] The cane crushers that Staunton observed were made of stone. Since the wooden support posts did not have to be buried in the ground for stability as in the case of wooden crushers—the weight of the stone being adequate to provide the necessary stability—these stone crushers could be moved around on boats. Eckeberg, captain of a Swedish East India Company ship that visited Guangzhou around 1751, described a similar process. Eckeberg refers to "sugar-bakers," as he calls them, traveling on the waterways with crushers on board, crushing cane brought to them from some distance, boiling the juice to a preliminary stage, "leaving it to be refined by other sugar bakers . . . into fine and coarse powder-sugar."[142] These descriptions leave many questions unanswered regarding who these individuals were, where they got their capital, and how they were paid. It was probably an alternative arrangement to the village associations, and the portable stone cane crusher may have made it possible to have ambulatory sugar-processors. As a report of 1869 notes, "Itinerant sugar boilers go about the Chekiang sugar districts, carrying with them an iron cauldron and a pair of cylinders. The sugar mills are of the rudest kind, being set up in the midst of the cane plantation, and are sometimes rented out. The juice having been boiled and partly clarified is transformed into a green or black sugar of a pasty description."[143]

Itinerant artisans traveling with cane crushers enabled many more smallholders, who even collectively could not afford to buy a cane crusher, to carry out sugar manufacturing. Such arrangements were also common among hemp, cotton cloth, and ramie producers. Hakka weavers from north-eastern Guangdong came down to Xin'an county annually in the nineteenth century, bringing their looms and tools with them, rented a work-space, and stayed only as long as there was work for them.[144] But this type of arrangement, in itself, could have proved to be a long-term disincentive to permanent investments such as water-mills to drive cane crushers or better and more efficient looms.

Much more information is available about the ways in which sugar processing was organized in Taiwan.[145] There were four types of arrangements, some dating back to the seventeenth century, identified by Japanese and Chinese researchers conducting extensive interviews among sugar producers in the late nineteenth century. The largest of these enterprises were started in the seventeenth century by the *kenhu*, or reclaimer households, who set up sugarcane cultivation and sugar processing as they settled the lands with immigrants; hence they were called *toujia bu* (lit., "head-householder organization"). Since both the Dutch and the Zheng governments were interested in sugarcane cultivation, settlers were often given cane crushers along with cattle.[146] These large but atypical enterprises usually had one major investor, the *toujia*, who provided the bulk of the funds and operated through a salaried manager. The cane was cultivated by tenants on lands owned by the major investor. Rents were collected in sugar by the intermediate landlords (*xiaozu hu*) and the reclaimer households (*dazu hu*). As the power of the merchants involved in the sugar trade increased through the course of the eighteenth and early nineteenth century, they, rather than rentier landlords, tended to provide the capital and nominate the manager. The cane crushers and other equipment purchased for such enterprises were considered indivisible and tied to the land.[147]

Then there were associations called *gongjia bu* (general public organization) that were based on "shares" (*toufen*) and could include members who did not grow sugarcane. The association or organization typically consisted of two to five members, received cane from as many as fifty to one hundred growers who "entrusted" their cane for processing with the arrangement that they would get 40–50 percent of the sugar processed while the association received 50–60 percent. Often, especially in the larger organizations of this sort, a rich merchant who was the middleman for the sugar guild (*tanghang*) lent the money to the association to start the venture.[148] Such associations in Taiwan seem to date back at least to the eighteenth century, with formal contracts drawn up among the shareholders.

In one instance, eight individuals, with eight different surnames, set up a sugar-processing association in 1760 in southern Taiwan. Each individual had shares in the organization and gave money for its operation and construction. The main clauses of the contract were:

1. If any of the oxen used for turning the cane crushers is stolen, every member has to help catch the thief. It is not the sole responsibility of the owner of the ox. If the robber is caught, he has to be taken to the magistrate's yamen; the expenses of the court will be shared equally by all members.
2. Workers (*gongren*) must be sincere and honest and be observed separately. If there is collusion with vagabonds and rebels and the work does not get done, it will be the responsibility of the employer.
3. Anybody, including soldiers, if thirsty, can take up to three stalks of cane from the fields. But if anybody takes more than that, he should be caught and taken to the yamen for punishment.
4. If the cane fields burn up, it is assumed that this must be have been done on purpose by vagabonds and rebels. If the criminal is identified, the owner of the field (*yuan*) that was burned down should be the person to take him to the yamen. But all members of the association will share the expenses.
5. Should there be an accident or an unexpected turn of events in the compound during sugar manufacturing, no matter how big or small, the expenses will be equally shared without making excuses. Any breaches, punishments, and fines will be settled at the sugar association's office in the Da Dongmen [Buddhist] temple in Taiwan prefecture.[149]

The contract lays out the mutual responsibilities of the financiers quite clearly. As the document indicates, the share of investment was really a direct share in the loss or profit. It was not an investment of shares as in a joint-stock enterprise, in which the investors have only limited liability. And although this was clearly a large enterprise, all eight of the financiers were linked to the guild-like organization of the sugar association and subject to its discipline. The "employer" (*guzhu*), who was to be held responsible if the work did not get done, was probably similar to the hired overseers of the sugar guild noted in nineteenth-century enterprises in Taiwan.[150] In the latter cases, they were usually relatives of the investors or persons recommended by their close acquaintances and relatives. The overseer was not allowed to trade on his own account.

In the operation of both types of enterprises, the role of the merchant-investor was to supply the primary capital and appoint the manager. The primary investor then took about 45 percent of the sugar, with the rest going to the cultivators. The merchant tried to acquire the sugar as cheaply as possible, and his profit lay in the price differential between the purchase price and the sale price.[151]

At the other end of the scale were small peasant enterprises, consisting of fifteen to forty peasants, reminiscent of the types of organizations seen in Guangdong. In 1890, Wykeham Myers found agents of moneylenders setting up crushing and processing equipment near sugarcane fields at the beginning of the cane-crushing season.[152] Cultivators who had loans from a particular merchant had to take their cane to their lender's mill. The cultivators were charged 7 percent of the sugar produced from their cane as cost of manufacture, more if they did not provide the two oxen required to operate the mill. A somewhat similar association, called *niuben bu* (lit. "ox-extending organization"), was formed by wealthier peasants who owned cattle. Investment shares in this venture were based on units of three head of cattle provided for one- to two-hour segments. The cooperative not only crushed cane produced by members, but also bought cane produced by non-members with funds belonging to the members.[153]

These different organizations coexisted throughout the sugarcane-growing regions of south and central Taiwan. Although merchant capital was involved directly in the larger organizations, they did not come to dominate sugar production. The larger enterprises seem to date from the early eighteenth century rather than later. On the contrary, available evidence from the end of the nineteenth century indicates that when the sugar trade expanded, the small associations, formed by twenty or so peasants, became predominant. One study tabulates that there were perhaps some 738 cane crushers operating in 1764. By the end of the nineteenth century some 1,400 cane crushers were recorded in use.[154] It is relevant to note that guild monopsonies controlled competition even in the larger and more formal structures, with merchant profits coming from taking the final product for sale to the market.

Was it possible for a peasant-producer to circumvent the local-level merchant and sell the crop to someone else who offered a better price? Could the producer, having sold the crop, then pay off his creditor in cash? Technically this could happen, as in the case of the "rich tenant farmer" Chen Daheng, who marketed his crop independently of the merchant Lu who had given him a loan. But it is unlikely that this was typical practice. In the case of Chen and Lu, the breach of contract was deemed serious enough to end in the death of Chen. And most village studies suggest that breaking a contract was a serious affair. In Xinhui, the palm fan guild controlled a business that involved several hundred thousand taels of silver each season. The guild had its own militia (*weidui*). Financed by the merchants ostensibly to defend against bandits, the militia was used to discipline those who broke contracts.[155] Breaking a contract even with an individual merchant could bring trouble; many traveling merchants and brokers were a tough lot with secret society affiliations. Liu Lichuan was probably quite typical; a sugar broker from Xiangshan county in the 1840s, as well as an opium smuggler, he was best known as the leader of the Guangdong faction of the Triad (Sanhe hui) in Shanghai.[156] Throughout Guangdong small merchants and yamen workers joined Triad societies, along with professional gamblers, smugglers, pirates, and gangsters, for these organizations provided mutual security and protection against more powerful social groups and gave members political clout in addition to business connections.[157] The available information, then, suggests that small peasant producers were not able to set prices any more than they were able to choose which market to sell in.

In cash-crop cultivation, including sugarcane, the direct producer's earnings depended on the arrangements under which loans for cultivation and preemptive purchase had been made. We have already noted how the price of fruits and sugarcane were often determined by merchants who went to the countryside well before the commodity was actually available for sale. In areas of cane cultivation, we have also seen how the seasonal sequence was connected to the sugar-for-cotton trade. But unlike the fruit producers, sugarcane cultivators got loans for cultivating as well as for processing, and the interest was collected in kind. Nineteenth-century sources on the marketing of sugar indicate that in Guangdong guild merchants (*hangshang*) who lent the initial production funds sent out wholesale brokers (*tunzhuang*) to collect the refined or semi-processed sugar. In all these cases, the price at which the cane or sugar would be purchased was negotiated at the time of the loan.[158] There are several references to credit arrangements from the periurban areas around Guangzhou suggesting, "Most peasants borrow money from city merchants and sell their products to the merchant or the moneylender as repayment for the principal loan."[159] At a minimum, this system left the peasant at a disadvantage in terms of the market price. Since agricultural prices are lowest right after the harvest, the loans typically collected soon after the winter harvest would have given the producer the lowest price for the commodity, *even if market prices were being paid.* In this system of forward dealing, however, the merchant had no guarantee that the crop or product would be available in the quantities promised and consequently offered a reduced price (*tuijia*) that was 50 to 200 copper cash less per *jin* (1.3 pounds) than the current market price of sugar, that is, about 10–15 percent below the already low post-harvest price.[160]

These types of practices, in which the advances served both to place a preemptive hold on the finished product and to determine prices, were not limited to the sugar manufacturing sector. Chinese merchants from Guangzhou who sold silk to foreign buyers in the 1770s and 1780s typically first contracted to furnish a determined amount of silk at a negotiated price and then sent out their agents, or *keshang*, to collect the silk. These purchasers were provided with 50–80 percent of the purchase price and were made responsible for the delivery.[161] To ensure delivery, households in the hinterlands of Guangzhou and Foshan were often "bound" exclusively to one specific silk merchant.[162] The arrangements in tea manufacturing and export processing in Guangdong, which had grown substantially during the seventeenth and eighteenth centuries, were very similar to those in sugar and silk manufacturing.[163] Sometimes these advances and pricing arrangements extended beyond one year or one agricultural cycle. In Xinhui county, fan palm merchants gave growers credit for as long as four years in advance to acquire supplies at prices agreed upon at the time of the loan.[164] In this case, in fact, the guild even controlled when the palm could be cut. These types of arrangements were not particular to the south. In Suzhou, Nanjing, and Hangzhou, the heart of the silk-producing region of China, merchant enterprises called account houses (*zhang fang*) distributed raw materials and even looms to weavers' households. "The loom household [weaver's household] was permanently attached to one account house and would not freely switch its association to another. The relationship was sometimes spelled out in a written contract, and it conformed to the practices and regulations of the local guild."[165] Lillian Li concludes, "[A] *chang* [*zhang*] *fang*'s functions, no matter how extensive, remained those of a middleman, handling transactions at various stages in the production process."[166]

So far, we have considered only one aspect of the workings of commercial capital, profits made by buying and selling. But usury was an integral feature of all merchant capital as well, and it is here that the possibilities of profit multiplied. As Chen Han-seng has noted, "To continue rural exploitation, usury capital must work hand in glove with its twin brother, trade capital. In Kwangtung, numerous dealers of unhusked rice, of fruit, of sugar, and of pigs, extort from the peasantry a huge profit through both price and interest."[167] Merchants interested in sugarcane cultivation usually advanced all the necessary items—the seed-cane, the bean-cake or peanut-meal fertilizers, the bamboo supports to protect the cane from high winds during the typhoons, and so on. If twentieth-century practices are any guide to the types of arrangements that existed earlier, merchants usually overvalued the items lent to the peasants by about 10 percent.[168] The interest and principal were both collected in kind.

The perennially capital-deficit peasant entering into these arrangements for cane cultivation often paid a monthly interest of 6 percent or more in Guangdong in the twentieth century. Under Qing law interest was not supposed to exceed 3 percent per month, but the average rate of interest in practice was 5 percent *per month*.[169] Yang Lien-sheng has pointed out that there were numerous instances in which even this illegally high level was exceeded. One form of usury, common in the Qing, was the seal-stamp money (*yinzi qian*), so called because the creditor would stamp a seal in the account book held by the debtor as a record. In these loans, typically the debtor paid back the loan in ten monthly installments equal to 13 percent of the loan. This worked out to paying 3 percent interest the first month, but 30 percent interest by the last month, for a portion of the principal would have been repaid each month.[170]

Conclusion: Commercial Capital and Smallholder Manufacture

Merchants thus profited from the sale of the commodity, the sales commission fee, interest on loans for cane cultivation and processing, above-market prices charged for fertilizers and other material, and below-market prices paid for the commodity. The loans also served to guarantee the merchant certain quantities of the product at prearranged times. The labor process, on the other hand, remained fragmented and consequently outside the control of the merchant, for it continued to be organized by the direct producer within the peasant household or in cooperative arrangements involving other smallholders. Some scholars of China have seen similarities between the types of mercantile activities described in this chapter and the putting-out system in the English cotton industry prior to industrial revolution as pointing to the potential for change in China.[171] There is, however, no linear connection between the existence of a widespread putting-out system and imminent economic transformation that can be readily established. On the contrary, as Dobb notes in his classic study on the development of capitalism in England, the putting-out system as a mature form of moneylending capital may actually have slowed down the process of investment in production.[172] Marx put it even more unequivocally, "This method always stands in the way of genuine capitalist mode of production and disappears with its development."[173]

Commercial capital left the peasant producer nominally independent, undertaking commercialized agriculture at the behest of the merchant. An Imperial Maritime Customs report, typical of many, noted this, "Cane is grown on small holdings . . . under advances from exporting merchants."[174] Such arrangements tied neither the merchant nor the producer to a line of production for any length of time. Indeed, for many crops, terms and types of crops to be cultivated were renegotiated at the end of each harvest. As a result, neither the producer nor the merchant had incentive to invest in long-term improvements in cultivation, extra fertilizers, or in specific technologies of manufacture. Kulp noted that when the merchants purchased the fruit, "on the basis of the quality and abundance of the blossoms, the dealers estimate the probable quality and quantity of the crop and higgle with the gardener [peasant] until a price per picul of harvested fruit is agreed upon. After the bargain is struck *the original owner is no longer responsible for the crop*. . . . Thus the orchards may be brought up by a few dealers who then are in a position to maintain monopoly control of the local products."[175]

Since the impetus for commercialized agriculture was translated into rural production structures primarily via merchant loans, the drying up of loans for any crop, particularly those involving manufacturing like sugar, forced producers to switch to cultivating other crops.[176] For example, when sugarcane prices declined after 1900 and rice prices rose in Guangdong in the 1910s, many sugarcane areas were turned over to rice cultivation within a couple of years. One survey of sugar manufacturing in Panyu, Guangdong, found that after the Revolution of 1911 sugar production almost disappeared in the county because cane growers were unable to set up the cane-crushing sheds without loans from the merchants.[177] Cheaper sugar from abroad replaced Chinese sugar even in China's internal markets. Similarly, in some areas of the Delta there was a shift to sericulture in response to world market demand. Then, in the 1930s when the world silk market collapsed, the mulberry fields were abandoned. With the establishment of local sugar refineries shortly thereafter, cane was once again planted on lands that were previously devoted to mulberry and rice.[178] This flexibility was a key to the survival of the smallholder economy. But it also gave the existing structure of production tenacity, the ability to retreat and expand its links with the market, preventing the dissolution of smallholders in the face of trade and commercial capital.

By the same token, commercial capital, too, could continue to profit under these existing social arrangements. Merchant-gentry who owned land could squeeze peasants through their relationship with them as landlords and moneylenders, relationships that assured them access to the surplus independently of their role as merchants producing sugar. As Takekoshi Yosaburo noted of the sugar enterprises run by merchant-landlords in Taiwan in the late nineteenth century:

> Here sugar was manufactured from the cane grown upon the owners' plantations, or from that brought from elsewhere. The cane was grown by the tenants, or by those who through being heavily indebted to the landowner stood in the same relation as retainers. This is still the system prevailing in the south; under it the master of the sugar factory secures a threefold profit.
>
> 1. As landlord, he claims from his tenants 15–20 percent of the cane as rent.
>
> 2. As capitalist, he secures 14–24 per cent interest on all the money he may have loaned to his tenants.
>
> 3. In order to cover the running expenses of the sugar factory, he as master, appropriates half the cane brought in by his tenants.
>
> These vast profits leave very little for the poor tenants, who have therefore no means of improving the soil, but fall deeper and deeper into debt, until at length they become mere slaves of the sugar factor. This system has proved the greatest hindrance to the growth of the business.[179]

Merchants and landlords thus provided not only the link with the market, but they may have been the closest the peasants ever got to the market in selling their commercial crops. In Guangdong and Taiwan, providing the capital for commercial crop cultivation gave the lenders control over distribution and circulation, without necessitating direct involvement at the level of production. Production structures remained fragmented: a diverse range of producers, middle and rich peasants, smallholder-operators, tenants, wage laborers, was incorporated into the same marketing circuit, but in all these cases the market was controlled by merchants and landlords. This evidence of mercantile involvement also calls into question standard interpretations such as the claim that "both the sugar-cane grower and the silkworm rearer acted as independent farmers who responded directly to the market."[180]

The merchant moneylenders maximized their returns by a combination of mechanisms spelled out above. This made it possible for them to charge high interest rates and to control the bulk of the produce from the commercialized sector of the rural economy. The historical alternative that developed in parts of western Europe, wherein capitalists took control of production, especially rural manufacturing units connected to commercial products,[181] was apparently neither possible, given the security of small property, nor necessary, given the restructuring of extra-economic coercive powers in the marketplace.

It mattered little to the merchant whether the peasant producer spent one week or one day in processing the cane, as long as he received the agreed-upon quantity of sugar at the pre-arranged price. The merchant's indifference to the tempo of production can be explained by the fact that he did not pay for the costs of labor out of potential profits. Technology that increased efficiency and output per unit of production was also not a concern for the merchants, who were not competing with other units producing larger quantities of sugar in shorter periods of time and therefore selling the product more cheaply. On the contrary, mercantile and broker affiliations with guilds and other monopolistic organizations assured them a market for their commodities. The involvement of gentry officeholders in the guild also ensured that commercial interests would receive protection in the courts. Monopsonies were protected, on the one hand, by a range of regulations bolstered by the power of the guild and, on the other, by the control of the markets by the elites.[182] Simultaneously, the direct producers remained independent smallholders, able to decide how family labor and land resources were to be allocated. Their best strategy was to produce as many of their subsistence requirements as possible through the deployment of family labor and to decrease the risks of market involvement by avoiding specialization and by cultivating and processing a range of commodities. They, too, were unlikely to undertake innovations that tied up limited resources, particularly as they had no control over the conditions of their participation in the market.

These arguments can be illustrated by the experience of Wykeham Myers. In 1890, he spent a considerable amount of time and energy trying in vain to get Taiwanese merchants to adopt a vertical two-roller cane crusher with cast iron shells covering the rollers. This was scarcely new technology in the late nineteenth century; as we have seen in Chapter Two, iron-clad rollers had been noted in Brazil by Richard Flecknoe as early as 1648. Myers even went to the trouble of developing a "primer" in Chinese to explain the benefits of the iron-clad mill. When compared to the same design model made of stone and wood commonly used in China, the crusher with iron-clad rollers extracted 18 percent more juice. But to his disappointment and frustration, he noted, "The dominating money-lenders and their agents the mill-owners could not be got to take much interest in the subject, and, indeed, seemed only to fear lest any innovations either from instruction or mechanical aids, might interfere with the arrangements which they said were, as far as they were concerned, sufficiently remunerative to themselves."[183]

Although we do not know the exact price of these roller mills with iron shells as compared to the Chinese ones (which cost approximately 150 Mexican dollars),[184] the additional sugar juice extracted by the more efficient mills would have offset any initial expenditures involved. In the district of Takow (Kaohsiung), where this experiment was being attempted by Myers, he calculated that if the iron mills were used, an additional 108,000 piculs (well over 6,400 tons) of sugar could be produced from the same amount of cane currently cultivated and processed. This, at the contemporary Taiwanese selling price of $2.50 per pound of sugar, Myers argued, would have meant an additional sum of $270,000 for those merchants involved in processing and selling the sugar. He was at a loss to explain their rejection of more efficient technology and higher returns.

What Wykeham Myers failed to take into consideration was that, given the overall structure of marketing, producing more sugar than contracted for was not automatically in the best interests of the merchants or the guild involved. Guilds maintained a high price for commodities by limiting supply. This strategy, logical in the social context of China, would not work on the world market, in which fully capitalist production, based on the logic of productive innovation and lowering the unit cost of production, had already taken a firm hold in western Europe and northern America by the eve of the nineteenth century. The logic of competition and profit that Wykeham Myers assumed, based on his experience of capitalist conditions in the late nineteenth century, also did not apply within the existing social and economic formation of China. Profits were linked to monopsonies that controlled and limited competition. The merchant at each level made profits by buying cheap and selling dear and by charging high interest on loans. Profits of alienation and profit by squeeze dominated at the expense of the profits of enterprise. Producing greater quantities of sugar under these circumstances would simply drive down the prices of sugar and would not be in the interests of any of the parties involved.

But while merchants and brokers in Taiwan favored existing arrangements that were "sufficiently remunerative to themselves," larger events in the world had set in motion fundamental changes that soon rendered those arrangements obsolete. As we see in the next chapter, the Industrial Revolution, the concomitant transformation of manufacturing technologies, and the structure of the world market were to affect the very foundations of society and economy in China.

SEVEN

DIVERGENT OUTCOMES: THE SUGAR INDUSTRY IN GUANGDONG AND TAIWAN

> Sweet is Taiwan sugar, but bitter is the life of a cane farmer.[1]
>
> —1920s Taiwan folk song

> Phenix village, Guangdong: Moreover there are cooperative industrial undertakings such as sugar-manufacture or boat-sailing of a temporary or irregular nature. . . . This [sugar-making] cooperative society lasted for several years and then went out of existence.[2]
>
> —Daniel Kulp, 1923

STARTING IN ABOUT THE LAST QUARTER of the eighteenth century, particularly after 1815, successive technological and organizational developments transformed the world of sugar manufacturing. As Manuel Moreno Fraginals notes, these changes affected sugar producers, merchants, and consumers; modified human and labor relations; and altered age-old habits of consumption.[3] In the pre-industrial cane-sugar-producing nations of the Caribbean, the impact of the Industrial Revolution brought profound changes in the social organization of production. Increasing the output of sugar mills and plantations became a "preoccupation of planters, agronomists and engineers"[4] and, one might add, various governments as well. In the industrialized world, sugar consumption spiraled, while industrial chemistry was harnessed to increase the quantity and quality of the product. New areas of demand and new consumers were created even as other sources of sugar, such as the sugar beet, were discovered. Once again, sugar became a force impelling vast movements of laboring people.[5] In the earlier period, the demands of cane-sugar plantations had brought slave labor from Africa to the Americas; this time labor from China, India, Japan, and the Philippines was drawn into the ambit of sugar. Through the course of the nineteenth century, besides tea, silk, and sugar, Guangdong also exported labor. Tens of thousands of indentured Chinese workers from the Pearl River Delta were brought to Cuba, Jamaica, Trinidad, and Mauritius to work as substitutes for the newly emancipated Afro-Caribbean slaves; over thirty thousand immigrants from Guangdong came to Hawaii to develop new sugar plantations.

Amid all these global changes, established producers like south China still enjoyed certain advantages, even in the mid-nineteenth century. Guangdong remained one of the largest producers in Asia. There was even a potential for expanding the export market, particularly to Japan, where sugar consumption soared during the late nineteenth century. But by the beginning of the twentieth century, areas of the Pearl River Delta that had cultivated cane and produced sugar for almost two thousand years had abandoned cultivation. Only Taiwan, of all the sugar-producing areas in south China, emerged as a leading producer of industrial-grade refined sugar by the early twentieth century. Below I trace the divergent histories of cane-sugar manufacturing in Taiwan and Guangdong and the social responses to the opportunities and constraints provided by the changes of the nineteenth century.

The Industrial Revolution and Cane-Sugar Manufacture

Pre–Industrial Revolution sugar-processing technology confronted several problems: the inefficient extraction of cane juice, the unreliability and slow pace of operation of wind-, cattle-, and water-powered mills, the relatively high and recurrent costs of motive power for the cane crushers including the costs of feeding, housing, and paying for human and animal labor, and the time it took to dry the sugar. On the larger plantations of Cuba and Jamaica and in England, there had been persistent experiments to improve the output of sugar-cane crushers by tinkering with the existing design of the vertical three-roller crusher. First, the seventeenth-century design of wooden cane crushers with iron shells covering the rollers was considerably modified; in 1721 a patent was granted for a sugar mill made entirely of iron with hollow rollers cast in one piece that had an iron gudgeon through them attached to the shell with a spider. Then, all the other remaining wooden parts of the crusher, such as the cogs, came also to be made of iron.[6] The expansion of the British iron industry in the second half of the eighteenth century dramatically increased the quantity and quality of iron available and provided the means to widely implement these changes in the construction of the crusher. Many of the Cuban plantations were among the first to adopt these modifications and use vertical three-roller cane crushers made of iron.

Major innovations came with the use of steam to drive the sugar mill and a fundamental change in the design of the crusher. Part of the general effort to harness the power of steam to drive all sorts of machinery, experiments in altering the motive power of cane crushers had been going on since the mid-eighteenth century. As early as 1767 a patent was granted in London to John Stewart of Jamaica for "a machine or invention to work mills, by the power of a fire-engine, but particularly useful and profitable in grinding sugar canes."[7] As illustrated in the insert in Figure 29, Stewart still used the design of three vertical-rollers in a straight-line for his mill. But a major break with this design had already occurred—the development of a horizontal three-roller mill with their centers at the angles of an isosceles triangle secured in a headstock or housing. This mill was quite different from the medieval two-roller horizontal mill used in parts of the Middle East and the Mediterranean where the axle had been mounted in a straight line. The triangular arrangement of the rollers in this new design was probably first developed in 1754 by John Smeaton in Jamaica.[8] Efforts to improve this design by strengthening the construc-

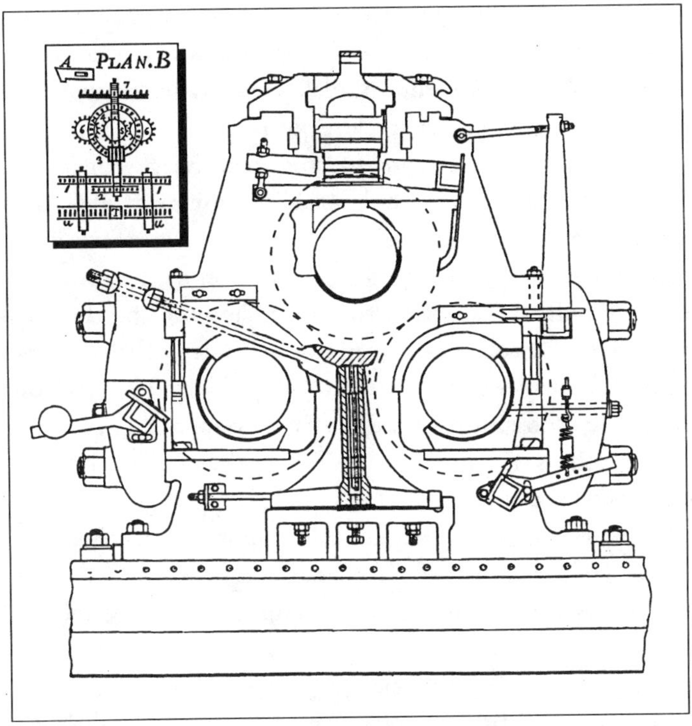

FIGURE 29. Steam-driven sugarcane mills. The ground plan of John Stewart's patent mill (1767) in the insert shows a cog wheel designed to provide power to another mill to grind corn. The industrial mill (drawing adapted from Deerr, vol. 2, p. 543) included an adjustable trash turner and had the top roller as the moving element. The design incorporated several developments from the 1880s and was manufactured ca. 1894.

tion of the headstock, adding a trash-turner, incorporating a weight-and-lever device to allow elasticity in the motion of the rollers, and so on, continued actively in the following decades. Figure 29 illustrates an industrial mill from the mid-nineteenth century; the design includes many of the later modifications to Smeaton's basic model. Made of cast and wrought iron, these new mills began to be produced in commercially in England by the 1790s and were sold soon after to Cuba and Mauritius.[9]

The horizontal, isosceles-triangle placement of the rollers in the design of the new mills had several advantages over the old vertical three-roller mills. In the earlier model, the distance between the rollers could be fixed to bring them closer or farther apart; but once fixed, the pressure exerted on the cane passing through the rollers was constant. The new horizontal mill had a simple spring-and-weight mechanism allowing irregular-sized cane to be processed with equal efficiency. There was also a better distribution of the cane along the length of the roller. In addition to multiplying the speed of crushing, this prevented the problem of wear at one point of the primary roller, a common difficulty with the vertical-roller model. The horizontal design also made it possible to slide the cane down to a board in front of the rotating rollers. A moving belt, to feed the cane to the horizontal mill, was developed around 1840.[10] This speeded up crushing, as the stalks of cane no longer had to fed by hand; it also eliminated injuries to workers, whose hands had often been caught between the rollers.

The new mills and steam-driven machinery did not gain popularity overnight. John Stewart had to spend no fewer than twenty-one pages on the "Utility of the said invention, and answers and explains every objection or doubt of it answering the designs which the writer has heard of."[11] In many places the first response of the planters was to attempt to increase the efficiency of traditional means of motive power, whether it be cattle, wind, or water, or a combination of all three.[12] Up to 1840, even the new iron horizontal mills were not designed exclusively to be driven by steam. Despite the adoption of the new horizontal mill, waterwheels and animal-powered cane crushers continued to operate on several estates in Cuba, largely as a result of the power of cattle ranchers, who pushed for the continued use of animal-powered mills.[13] The line between preindustrial technology and industrial manufacture, however, was firmly crossed in 1816 when the new horizontal mill driven by an 8–12 h.p. steam engine was developed by the English firm of Fawcett, Preston and Company. As early as 1817 one such mill was sent to a plantation in Martinique.[14] The importance of this transition lay not just in the motive power of steam and the use of iron machinery but in the technological complex inaugurated by the Industrial Revolution that unified diverse processes of manufacture, replaced human labor, and henceforth dictated the entire pace of production.

The savings obtained by replacing teams of oxen and the labor necessary to maintain them soon made the steam-driven mill the machinery of choice among the more entrepreneurial plantation owners in Cuba, Mauritius, and Martinique, as well as in the new areas of cane-sugar production, such as Louisiana, where sugar exports rapidly became the cornerstone of the economy.[15] The advantages of steam could not be ignored. In the mid-nineteenth century, three mechanized mills in Cuba, for example, were able to produce 9,299 tons of sugar annually while three animal-driven mills, operating the same number of hours, produced only 1,539 tons. When steam-driven vacuum evaporators were added to process the sugar syrup, these mills yielded 70 percent more sugar from the same weight of cane than an animal-powered mill.[16] By the 1870s, "[t]he steam-engine sealed its triumph over the water-wheel" in sugar manufacturing, no less than in other branches of industry.[17]

The competition from European beet-sugar producers added to the urgency of increasing productivity while cutting manufacturing costs in the cane-sugar industry. Mid-eighteenth-century German and French laboratory experiments had shown that various types of beetroot contained sugar that could be extracted and crystallized. Beet-sugar factories had already been set up by the turn of the eighteenth century under Prussian imperial auspices. Then, during the Napoleonic wars and Continental System (1806–1814), when cane-sugar supplies from the tropics were suspended due to the blockade, the European beet-sugar industry received a further boost. Beet-sugar manufacturing continued to expand in France, Germany, and Austria-Hungary, and its share of world sugar production reached almost 50 percent by 1880 and 59 percent by 1890.[18]

In few industries was the "ever-closer marriage of science and technology" so visible as it was in the sugar industry in the nineteenth century.[19] Advances in organic chemistry and chemical engineering were soon put to work. On cane plantations, chemists replaced the sugarbakers of yore. The possibility of using steam to evaporate liquids had first been explored at the end of the seventeenth century.[20]

But it was not until the early nineteenth century that industrial uses of steam for evaporation became common. Vacuum pans developed in 1818 in the sugar-beet industry for the rapid evaporation of the sucrose solution quickly became standard equipment in the cane-sugar industries of Cuba, Louisiana, and Mexico where the manufacturing processes were already highly mechanized.[21] Unlike the open-pan method, which burned some of the sucrose when boiling off the water at 248°F and caramelized it, the vacuum pan boiled off the water at 140°F leaving behind white sugar crystals. These methods were fuel efficient; beet-sugar houses using even the earlier models around 1828 attained an evaporation of 9 to 10 pounds of water with 1 pound of coal.[22] As the illustration in Figure 30 of a mid-nineteenth-century vacuum-evaporator indicates, the basic design was a closed boiler with a top opening that was hermetically sealed and had a heating surface through which the steam circulated and evaporated the cane juice. Shortly thereafter, the centrifuge that had been invented in France in 1837 to dry textiles was modified for use in separating crystallized sucrose from the dross.

The savings in production time with the combination of the vacuum-evaporator and the centrifuge were immense. The traditional method, in which the thickened sugar syrup was first allowed to crystallize naturally and then washed with a water and clay solution to remove the molasses, took a minimum of 10 to 14 days to get the sugar ready for sun or oven drying. Using a centrifuge, about thirty pounds of sugar could be processed for drying every twenty minutes.[23] By the 1830s, it became common to add sulfuric acid or oxalic acid to clarify sugar juice by neutralizing excessive lime. The use of bone charcoal filters to decolorize sugar was also increasingly prevalent. These developments allowed for the standardization of the end product based on sucrose content. Whereas earlier there had been as many as twenty-one different grades based on the color of the sugar, by the 1880s only a sugar purity of Pol. 95 degrees and above was acceptable for the appellation "refined sugar" for world market trade.[24] This highly refined sugar could be stored indefinitely, which in turn affected sugar prices on the world market. Importers of Caribbean

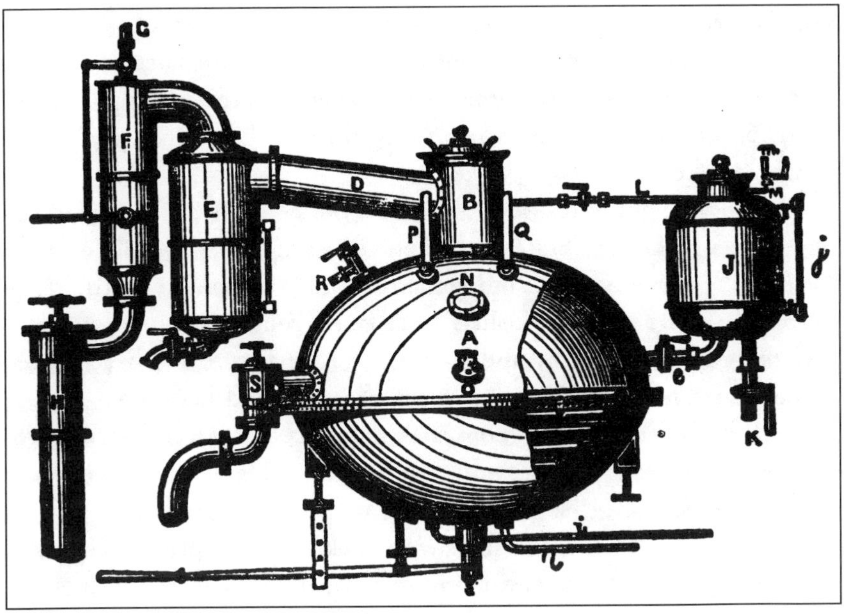

FIGURE 30. Sugar vacuum evaporator, 1850. The use of vacuum pans was patented by Edward Charles Howard in 1813. This model shows the Howard-type closed boiler (Moreno Fraginals, *The Sugarmill*, p. 112). Reprinted with permission of Monthly Review Press.

sugar, for example, built up immense stocks and were able to force lower prices on the producers.[25]

The ability of European firms to build up such large stocks of sugar was a product of the concurrent revolution in transportation and the expansion of the global economy. Widely dispersed agricultural economies were now linked and directly subject to the demands of the industrial world economy.[26] In the eighteenth century, the typical trade ships called East Indiamen took between 5 and 8 months to travel between London and Calcutta and another six to eight weeks to reach China. Clipper ships in the 1830s racing with tea from China to London reduced the trip to 90–105 days. By late 1860s the steamer had shortened the voyage to 68 days. Steamers with up to five times the cargo capacity of sailing ships of the same displacement replaced the latter, and freight rates began to fall.[27] Between 1860 and 1880 with the construction of the Suez Canal (1869), freight rates between major Asian sugar-producing regions, such as Java and the Philippines, and Europe fell as much as 63 percent. Freight rates between America and Europe fell on average 25 percent.

Falling freight rates revolutionized the agricultural commodities market. The United States had exported negligible quantities of grain in the 1840s, perhaps no more than 14 million bushels; by the 1870s more than 300 million bushels were being sold, mostly to Europe.[28] Many areas in Germany and Eastern Europe that formerly produced wheat switched to cultivating sugar beets. World beet-sugar output soared.[29] Governments of countries selling beet sugar sought to promote the industry by providing subsidies and aids to growers and manufacturers. Beet-sugar prices were thus kept artificially low. A combination of increased cane-sugar stocks and low-priced beet sugar led to a dramatic fall in sugar prices on the world market. In England, one of the largest markets, sugar prices fell by 30 percent between 1840 and 1850 and by another 25 percent in the next two decades. By 1900, Caribbean and Brazilian crude sugar producers were getting less than one-fourth the price paid only sixty years earlier.[30] As a result of these momentous changes, only the producers of better-quality sugars at the lowest possible prices could survive as exporters of refined sugar to the world market by the end of the nineteenth century. China's situation, compared with that of the Caribbean economies, was far more secure. China, as the only major sugar producer in East Asia, still enjoyed a relatively closed market in the 1860s and 1870s. But East Asia, too, was entering a period of rapid change in the nineteenth century, as its existing links with the world market were strengthened.

The Post–Opium War Restructuring of Trade in East Asia

Decades before the formal abolition of the British East India Company Charter in 1834, the dynamics of East Asian trade had begun to change with the opening of the Indian trade to European private traders in 1813 and the establishment of Singapore as a free port in 1819.

Thousands of European and American entrepreneurs flooded into Asia, eager to try their hand at the fabled China trade.[31] At Guangzhou, during the early 1830s, increased competition among the newcomers led to overabundant stocks and falling prices in the import trade in legal goods. The "singsong" trade in musical boxes, for example, on which many of the smaller European traders had depended, fell off because Chinese merchants were having them copied for half the cost. Similarly, large imports of pepper from Southeast Asia by American and English traders had glutted the market. British woolens and mercury were also overstocked and sat in warehouses gathering dust.[32] Meanwhile, overall Chinese exports increased substantially after the abolition of the East India Company charter. The value of exports carried by British and American ships from Guangzhou rose from $19,216,215 in 1831–1832 to $34,866,423 in 1836–1837.[33] The intense competition among foreign traders pushed up prices of export goods and actually benefited the Chinese more than the British and American traders could have anticipated. Between 1834 and 1842, the price of tea rose by 55 percent and that of silk by 25 percent, driven to some extent by the crisis of the Opium War (1839–1842).[34]

Imports did not so do so well. Only the volume of imported cotton piece goods increased slightly, and that, too, because the price had been lowered.[35] From the Western traders' point of view, the situation improved somewhat only with the increased frequency of military confrontations. For, in addition to opium, a profitable import had been discovered: "[T]here is recorded for the first time [during the Opium War] the beginning of a line of trade which in later generations grew to large proportions . . . namely the supply of foreign arms, munitions and implements of war to the Chinese."[36]

Changes occurring between 1840 and 1870, as a result of the Opium War treaties (1842–1843) and the treaties of Tianjin (1858) and Beijing (1860), speeded the restructuring of Chinese foreign trade. The opening of additional ports besides Guangzhou to western trade, the abolition of the Cohong, and the liberalization of the opium trade were direct outcomes of the various treaties.[37] Guangdong lost its monopoly over tea and silk exports with the opening of Shanghai in 1842. Since shipping tea and silk from the Yangzi Delta down to Guangzhou had added 35–40 percent to the cost of those items, western traders simply shifted their base of operations when Shanghai became available as a port.[38] For a decade or so after 1842, many western ships had continued to call at Guangzhou and Huangpu (Whampoa) to get the benefits of docking in freshwater and loading coal. Most American and British traders maintained their business houses in Guangzhou during this period, for the important Chinese merchants had not yet moved out. But with the opening of Macao (1845), Japan (1854), and the Philippines (1855) to all Western traders, it became unnecessary for ships to make the slow journey up the bay and the Pearl River estuary for supplies, drinking water, and coal.[39] In the 1850s, the economic and political upheavals of the Red Turban and Taiping rebellions and numerous military confrontations in the environs of Guangzhou also began to shift the trading center of the south China economy away from that city to Hong Kong, especially after 1856 when all the factories or warehouses of the foreign traders in Guangzhou were burned down. Trade was likewise disrupted throughout the Delta counties; the Red Turban Rebellion (1854) burned down most of Foshan and its neighborhood and set back the silk- and cotton-spinning industries there for a considerable time. During the 1870s, the shift of Western and Chinese traders to Hong Kong and Shanghai became permanent. By 1880, Hong Kong handled 21 percent of the value of China's total export trade and 37 percent of the import trade.[40]

The shift from Guangzhou to Hong Kong represented more than just the traditional shift from one entrepôt closed by war to another offering safe harbor for commerce. For, beyond regional wars and imperialist treaties, the years between 1848 and the early 1870s marked the period when, as Hobsbawm puts it, "the world became capitalist and a significant minority of developed countries became industrial economies."[41] The development of Hong Kong was a symbol of the reach of industrial capitalism and the merger of trade and finance capital in its service. There are innumerable examples of the ways in which China was integrated into this burgeoning world market and its "tightening net of economic interchanges."[42] The increase in the volume of foreign trade is but one indicator. In one year alone (1879), overall foreign imports increased by 16 percent; in the same year, silk exports from Guangzhou increased by 30 percent over the previous year.[43]

The electric submarine telegraph was symbolic of this new world market. The construction and laying of submarine cables, begun in 1851 (Dover to Calais), reached a frenzied level in 1870–1872. To the London–Calcutta connection established in 1865, were now added the Bombay–Aden, Singapore–Batavia, Singapore–Penang–Madras lines in 1870; the Far Eastern section linking Shanghai, Hong Kong, Saigon, Penang, Singapore, India, and London was completed in 1871. By 1872 it was possible to send a telegraph from London to Tokyo and Adelaide.[44] As Hobsbawm writes, "this extraordinary acceleration of the speed of communication had one paradoxical result. In widening the gap between the places accessible to the new technology and the rest, it intensified the relative backwardness of those parts of the world where horse, ox, mule, human bearer, or boat still set the speed of transport."[45] The widening gap was to be acutely visible in the contrast between the coastal cities of China, in instant contact with London, and the rural settlements of the inland provinces. The telegraph also made the traditional methods of Western trading in China obsolete and transformed the China trade.

The old, well-established trading companies like Jardine, Matheson and Company or Butterfield and Swire had made a significant proportion of their profits from commission and insurance fees for the long and risky journey of cargoes from Guangzhou and Hong Kong to London. They also took advantage of opportunities for speculation and dealings on the futures market in tea and silk. Now these options were curtailed. The London market knew ahead of time the size and value of shipments. The structure of banking changed; vast quantities of bullion did not have to pass through the hands of the agency houses on a commission basis. As the *Maritime Customs* recorded:

> While rapidity of communication has diminished the chance of large profits, it has also lessened the risk of heavy losses, and tended to reduce the trade to a system of regular shipments for full or partial commissions. . . . [F]oreign merchants began to sell their silk by telegraph "to arrive" in London, and aided by banks immediately entered the market again. The old-fashioned "venture" of a shipment of silk, with the outturn unknown and the proceeds

unavailable till the voyage was ended and the goods actually landed and sold, was completely a thing of the past. The dealer was no longer a true "merchant," but had become a mere link in a trading chain, bound fast to the interests financing him.[46]

Western trading firms, facing reduced profits from the traditional commission agency business in China, were forced to reorganize. The international economic depression of the 1870s also put pressure on these firms by signaling that fortunes in the China trade could no longer be built on the basis of the silk, tea, and opium trades alone. In 1873, Brooke Robertson, British Consul General in Guangzhou, noted:

> Never within the memory of those engaged in the China trade has so much depression existed both in China and in England as during the last twelve months: various causes have contributed to this, not the least among which has been the stagnation of the home market and the high prices paid in China for tea and silk and the two combined have been as disastrous to foreign trade as a war would be, and probably more so.[47]

Established trading firms like Jardine and Matheson, Butterfield and Swire, Agustine Heard and Company, and Russell and Company, rapidly moved from the commodities market into industrial manufacturing and financial enterprises.[48]

Coastal steam-shipping, insurance, banks, and wharf and godown construction were the most lucrative areas of new investment and drew the largest shares of capital. The opening of Taiwan to western traders after 1858 provided opportunities in railway and telegraph line construction contracts to entrepreneurial companies like Jardine and Matheson.[49] Sugar refineries and rice mills, and somewhat later silk filatures and cotton mills, became related investment areas for venture capital on the mainland as well as Taiwan.[50]

Numerous British entrepreneurs from about the 1840s on had become interested in the possibility of developing sugar factories in Asia as a result of the expansion of the world market in sugar and the changes taking place in the British Caribbean cane-sugar-producing economies after the emancipation of the slaves (1834).[51] Some, as we have seen in Chapter Two, moved to India. Others, like John Swire, who founded Butterfield and Swire Company and the Taikoo Sugar Refinery in Hong Kong, had personal links with the sugar-refining business in England.[52] Firms like Jardine, Matheson and Company, having made their money in the import trade, particularly opium, invested in whatever had the potential for profit. In 1869, Jardine started a modern sugar refinery at Huangpu near Guangzhou.[53] There were apparently some Chinese merchants involved in this venture, but little is known about them, for the operation was short-lived. Organized opposition from people involved in small, traditional-style sugar manufacturing in the region closed it down within a year.[54]

Interest in developing sugar refineries was renewed in the 1870s when the agricultural crisis caused by plant diseases and adverse climate in many parts of Europe created a dearth of sugar beets. In 1876 and 1877, the crop failed outright in France, one of the largest producers. The resulting shortage of sugar could not be adequately compensated by cane sugar from the West Indies. The Chinese, in contrast, during these years had bumper cane harvests and the domestic price of sugar remained unusually low because famines in north China had limited the market there. Thus, in the late 1870s, European traders were able to buy sugar cheap in China and sell dear in Europe. This set up an export boom and underlined the potential of the Chinese product.[55]

Industrial sugar refining began in China when Jardine and Matheson founded the China Sugar Refining Company in Hong Kong and started production in 1876. A branch refinery was started up in Shantou in 1878 and remained open until 1886, when financial difficulties at China Sugar forced its closure. While it was in operation, the Shantou branch employed more than a hundred Chinese; in contrast to the opposition encountered by the Huangpu refinery in 1869, it seems have been welcomed locally as a source of profit. In fact, refineries became more than just employers for Chinese. Both China Sugar and the Shantou branch of China Sugar, as well as Butterfield and Swire's sugar refinery set up in Hong Kong in 1881, the Taikoo, had several Chinese investors.[56]

The restructuring of trade had brought a segment of the Chinese mercantile elites into closer collaboration with the European firms. Just as the demise of the British East India Company had opened the way for hundreds of smaller British and American traders to enter the China trade, the abolition of the Cohong and the development of Hong Kong seems to have provided opportunities for some Chinese traders. The *Hong Kong Almanack and Directory for 1846* listed only two compradores. The *Hong Kong Chinese Directory for 1872* lists no fewer than fifty-five general merchants, forty-one marine compradores, and forty-five foreign-firm Chinese compradores in addition to seventy-four other traders.[57] Although the former Cohong merchants continued to be among the largest traders in silk and tea well into the 1860s and sought ways of holding on to their monopolies, several of the smaller merchants emerged as traders and shareholders in the British and American companies.[58] Joint-account trade became common in commodities such as sugar. For example, Jardine and Tucksing (Chinese name not known), "an aggressive merchant from Swatow," shipped peas, bean-cake, and oil from Niuzhuang to Fuzhou and Guangzhou, and shipped back "southern goods" such as sugar and nankeens to Tianjin and Niuzhuang, making a profit of 15 to 20 percent on each shipment in the 1860s and 1870s.[59] Although the sums of money involved and the quantities of commodities carried in this trade were now many times more than those of the two previous decades, this type of joint-account trade between European and Chinese partners was not new. The novel element was the increased number of joint-stock investments made by Chinese merchants in long-term projects. Starting after 1842, and with greater frequency after the Treaty of Tianjin in 1860, Chinese merchants bought shares (*fugu*) in companies, including steamship lines, banks, insurance, electric and power companies, silk filatures, soybean and peanut-oil factories, and sugar refineries.[60] Both the Jardine and the Swire sugar refineries attracted Chinese investors. In 1882, the stock shares of the Swire refinery were valued at $200 each, and there were at least six Chinese investors with about 1,900 shares between them. The total Chinese investment was thus around $380,000, a substantial sum.[61] Xu Run, the compradore of Dent and Company, invested a total of 1,275,000 taels in various industrial enterprises, including the sugar refineries.[62]

It quickly became evident that there was a profitable market in East Asia for refinery-produced sugars, both brown and white. The finished products could be sold in China, Japan, India, Australia, and, for a while, even in California.[63] Jardine and Matheson and Swire's, competitors in many sectors of the emerging industrial economy of the treaty ports, struggled to gain control of the most lucrative of these sugar markets—the Japanese market.[64] There was competition also from the Japanese and Chinese traders in Japan, many of whom bought sugar from Taiwan and the Ryukyus. A letter written in 1888 by the branch manager of the Swire's enterprise in Kobe, who was locked in battle with a consortium of Japanese sugar dealers (dramatically called the "Ring" by the manager), illustrates the intensity of this competition. As the besieged manager noted, "The fight with the Ring is not yet over. These men are putting every obstacle in our way. . . . At our first sale the Ring ran up prices so as to bounce all outsiders from the Market; I hear that they are now underselling us. . . . On Monday & Tuesday I received four anonymous postcards warning us against selling in Osaka."[65]

Western companies were also attracted to Taiwan by the possibility of developing sugar manufacturing. These were, however, still only export companies, rather than refineries. In 1856, an American firm, Robinet and Company, set up an export venture in Kaohsiung with the purpose of exporting sugar from Taiwan to Japan and the Chinese mainland. Taiwan did particularly well in the export of brown sugar, for which there was a market in both China and Japan. The export price of white sugar from Taiwan in the 1867–1868 season was $6.50 a picul, more than two-and-half-times that of brown sugar at $2.50. This price difference probably favored the increased export of brown sugar.[66] In 1873, the Australian company Melbourne Sugar also began to purchase raw sugar from Taiwan.[67]

Peasants and Refineries: Guangdong and the World Market in the Late Nineteenth Century

The industrial refineries set up in Hong Kong by Jardine and Matheson and by Swire's Taikoo were the first such ventures in East Asia.

Jardine's Hong Kong refinery had a daily capacity of 238 tons, while Taikoo could process 714 tons daily by 1884 when it was in full operation. The refineries could hope to return maximum profit only when operating at full capacity. A steady supply of raw sugar and sugarcane were therefore essential. In addition to getting supplies from Guangdong and Fujian, changes in raw sugar manufacturing in Southeast Asia made this a viable project. Steam machinery had been installed in Java around 1838; by 1868 Java had eleven steam-driven mills, fifty-seven water-driven mills, and twenty-nine mills that combined water and steam to operate the crushing equipment. Similarly, the Philippines had installed 239 steam-driven mills by 1887.[68] Almost immediately after beginning operations, Taikoo began purchasing raw sugar from the Philippines and Java. Two steamships were purchased by Taikoo for the specific purpose of transporting raw sugar from these regions to Hong Kong.[69]

Local purchases made by the refineries encouraged increased cane cultivation and the manufacture of semi-processed sugar in several parts of Guangdong, Taiwan and Fujian during 1870–1900.[70] In Guangdong, the counties that were to emerge as the primary cultivators of sugarcane in response to this demand were primarily in the Shantou and Chaozhou districts rather than the Pearl River Delta.

In the Delta, the phenomenal increase in the world market demand for silk from the 1860s on had already altered the pattern of commercialized agriculture that existed prior to the Opium War. Just before the war, the annual average export of raw silk from Guangzhou had been around 500,000 pounds. By 1859, this had increased to almost 7 million pounds.[71] This trend toward increased exports continued as a silkworm blight destroyed silk cocoons in France and caused a severe shortage in the expanding French silk-weaving industry.[72] The American silk-weaving industry also became a major market for Chinese raw silk from about the 1870s on. As a result, the local economies of several counties in the Guangdong Delta, such as Nanhai, Shunde, and Panyu, which were already involved in some sericulture, now began producing additional quantities of silk for the world market. B. C. Henry, traveling through Nanhai in the 1880s, describes the frenetic activity:

> Around the base of these hills, and for miles on all sides, the land is covered with mulberry plantations. . . . Thousands of boys, women and girls are employed to strip them [the leaves] off, and pack them in baskets. Hundreds of men, in little boats propelled by paddles, dart back and forth along the canals, carrying these leaves to the market-places, where they are weighed by men detailed for that purpose, and purchased by the owners of silkworms.[73]

In Dongguan county, once noted for its extensive sugarcane fields, entrepreneurial gentry now purchased mulberry seedlings and even hired instructors from Shunde to teach the locals.[74] By the end of the 1860s, silk exports from Guangdong alone accounted for a total value of $5,850,000.[75] Silk exports from China as a whole increased more than sevenfold between 1870 and 1928.[76] Land that had previously been used for cane cultivation was now turned over to mulberry trees in the Pearl River Delta.

Other changes in the pattern of agriculture and land use were brought about by developments in transportation in the mid-nineteenth century. Faster steamer service brought the north China market within reach of south China's horticultural products. In Dongguan county, for example, sugarcane cultivation was replaced by expanded fruit and banana cultivation.[77] Therefore, although most counties in the Delta continued to cultivate some sugarcane and increases in cultivation took place on the newly developed polders, the more dramatic expansion in cane cultivation, as a result of the demand set up by the Hong Kong refineries, came elsewhere in Guangdong.

The Treaty of Beijing (1860) had given access and treaty port status to Shantou in Chaozhou prefecture in northeastern Guangdong. Although these areas of Guangdong had cultivated some cane in the earlier periods, from the 1870s to the turn of the century there was a veritable sugar boom in the areas around Shantou and the surrounding counties. Shanwei, the regional port closest to Hong Kong, was linked directly to Hong Kong and north China by steamers belonging to both Jardine and Matheson and Swire's. A similar phenomenon occurred in Taiwan, which was also opened to Western trade through the treaties of 1858–1860. The expansion in shipping drew Taiwan into a closer nexus with ports on the mainland and increased Taiwan's trade with Japan. Here, too, cane cultivation spread to new areas, particularly in southern Taiwan.[78] As the figures in Table 17 indicate, export levels from Taiwan fluctuated quite sharply from year to year in the nineteenth century; at times, as in 1875 and 1877, the drop was as much as over 23 tons. But then, beginning with the first years of the twentieth century, the output from Taiwan shows a steady trend upward, while that of Shantou collapses rapidly from a peak of 109,508 tons in 1899 to 29,714 tons in 1909.

Although the expansion in cane cultivation in northeastern Guangdong was related to the development of the refineries, Shantou had also managed to expand its domestic markets during the period 1880–1900. This was partially due to the decline in sugarcane cultivation in the Pearl River Delta. Approximately 15–30 percent of the amount produced in Shantou went to Hong Kong and other foreign areas such as Japan. The bulk of it was sold in the northern ports of China.[79] The growth of guilds from Shantou region (e.g., the Chaozhou *bang* and the Chaohui *bang*) in Hankou and Tianjin during the nineteenth century was probably aided by their control of most of the nation's sugar supply.[80] The output from Taiwan was also sold in these same areas. The *Maritime Customs* reported in the 1880s:

> The interesting feature of this new sugar boom in Chinese sugar was the exceptionally large part taken by sugar from Formosa [Taiwan], in the south of which island new land was being put under sugar cultivation every year, the product of which was rapidly taking the place of sugar from Swatow [Shantou] and other parts of south China. Formosa sugar accounted for nearly two-thirds of the export . . . from China in 1880, whereas in the previous good sugar seasons of 1876–77 it was barely more than one-third of the total.[81]

The export figures given in Table 17 imply a rapid increase of cane cultivation, although survey data on the acreage under cane in the Shantou region are not available for this period. Data for rice imports to Shantou are available, and these show an upward trend. Correlating this import data with sugar-export data, some scholars, such as Fan I-chun, have argued that cane replaced rice lands.[82] This linear equation is somewhat problematical. Sugarcane, as discussed earlier in Chapter Five, took less labor than rice. Adele Fielde, writing her 1888 report

TABLE 17

Exports of Sugar from Shantou and Taiwan, 1867–1910
(weight in long tons, or 2,240 lbs)

Year	Shantou	Taiwan	Year	Shantou	Taiwan
1867	40,041	15,065	1891	99,512	33,843
1870	36,977	35,473	1892	71,339	35,690
1871	58,200	34,666	1893	60,890	30,321
1872	48,590	37,336	1894	55,347	43,674
1873	52,936	30,131	1895	79,269	42,059
1874	59,160	40,747	1896	79,625	42,817
1875	69,150	29,028	1897	80,124	38,396
1876	85,953	52,282	1898	87,406	39,588
1877	63,829	36,103	1899	109,508	30,598
1878	62,183	24,562	1900	82,637	34,000
1879	64,371	45,443	1901	83,196	46,893
1880	74,285	63,183	1902	65,357	32,992
1881	73,305	44,823	1903	60,719	58,968
1882	75,201	36,423	1904	63,932	49,565
1883	87,843	46,059	1905	48,269	63,359
1884	108,205	57,425	1906	33,406	81,448
1885	88,974	33,189	1907	53,411	68,450
1886	77,750	23,165	1908	49,649	122,000
1887	91,379	32,922	1909	29, 714	160,000
1888	83,879	38,930	1910	42,071	256,950
1890	88,813	42,938			

SOURCES: Davidson, p. 457; H. C. Prinsen Geerligs, *The World's Cane Sugar Industry*, p. 75–91; Imperial Maritime Customs, *Decennial Reports, 1861–1911*.

from Shantou, believed that it was this feature together with the possibility of extending cane cultivation to unirrigated lands in the Shantou region that resulted in sugar becoming the primary export. Moreover, although sugar formed the principal item of export, cane did not become the only commercial crop. Rice occupied up to one-half the acreage of many farms, with the rest devoted to cane. In the cane-growing village surveyed by Fielde in the 1880s, peasants cultivated indigo, sesame, peanuts, kudzu, ginger, and wheat in addition to subsistence crops such as sweet potatoes, yams, lentils, and vegetables.[83]

It is possible that the increased rice imports were a reflection of multiple factors: purchases of the grain in growing urban centers, the intensified commercialization of agriculture, including purchases by some peasants who previously had grown all of their own food but now had sufficient cash to buy some of it instead, and the impact of remittances from the increased numbers of relatives in Southeast Asian countries, such as Thailand.

What was the social and economic impact of this increased cultivation on the market in Guangdong? The broader economic changes were greatly mediated through the political shifts under way, which, however, did not undermine the social power of the local elites. On the contrary, the crisis of the Qing state in the late nineteenth century had changed the equation of power between the central state and the gentry. As Philip Kuhn notes, the disintegration of the imperial administration in the late nineteenth century enabled local elites to arrogate to themselves numerous functions of the state and continue their role as "protector of local property relations and the social status quo."[84] Protecting the status quo involved, among other things, strengthening the local militias. Lineages in the Pearl River Delta, as noted earlier, used rents monies to hire *sha fu* (guards of the sands) to protect property on the polders. During times of severe crisis, it was common for several lineages to join together their private guards to form local militia. In the famous Sixteen Sands Polder (Shiliu Sha) of Shunde county, the gentry militia organization, called Gongtong ti (United Organization), was one such example of an alliance of lineages. In the mid-nineteenth century, facing attacks by members of the Red Turban Rebellion, the gentry militia was put in charge of local defense and all tax collection on behalf of the Qing state. It was a simple step for the gentry armed with these powers to remove certain lands from the tax rolls and use their position as collectors of the transit tax levied on trade (*lijin*) to extend their control of the major market towns.[85]

By the second half of the century, there were additions to this configuration of social power in Guangdong. The rural elite now had in their midst an increasing number of local strongmen, middlemen, bandits, and "bandits in uniform"—as Helen Siu calls the leaders of local self-defense corps—sometimes as protégés of the gentry, sometimes as their rivals.[86] These new claimants to power could, however, still deploy the well-known techniques of the old society to establish a foothold in the existing socioeconomic structure. A combination of patronage and intimidation, including protection fees, passage fees, landing surcharges, payments before harvesting, and confiscation of boatloads of harvested produce, enabled these upstarts to control resources and extract surpluses from the direct producers. These activities became adjuncts to violent armed confrontations.

Control of markets had been one of the primary causes of feuding since the seventeenth century. The feuds now escalated. In the struggles over markets between the Ye, Chen, and Yuan alliance and the Lin and their allies, more than four hundred villages in Xinhui county were burned down between 1882 and 1911.[87] Competition for resources also intensified with commercialization. When the inhabitants of a sericulture-dependent village in Shunde awoke one morning "to find their only wealth, the lusang [mulberry] trees denuded of every branch and leaf" and the silkworms of the neighboring village doing suspiciously well, their only recourse was to plan "a retaliatory raid next season."[88] In neighboring Xiangshan county, the litigation and tussles over the control of the fertile polders became ever more aggressive; embankments were destroyed to hamper the enemy and flood their fields and villages. Commercialization and the expansion of the money economy took many forms in the countryside, including increased opium consumption. There was now more at stake than just the control of the market towns; control of opium rings and salt-smuggling networks based in the markets became additional motives for ongoing feuds. Numerous mercenary gangs organized into "banner" or "flag societies" (*qihui*). This was the case in the growth of the Red and Black Flag societies of Haifeng and Lufeng near Shantou; the Black Flag attacks specifically targeted the market town identified with its opponents.[89] The conflicts of the Red Flags and the Black Flags of Haifeng over the control of markets reached their peak during the boom years of the Guangdong sugar trade in the 1880s and 1890s. Attempts by the older elite lineages to control the opportunities to open up new markets at a time of increased world market links in the late nineteenth century may have actually intensified the violence even as increases in population increased competition for resources.

A growing population also made available more able-bodied young men for purposes of warfare. The availability of mercenaries, products of the social and economic dislocation of south China after the Opium Wars, enlarged the scale of operations of feuds, which now involved several counties even in Guangdong.[90] William Ashmore, a missionary, observed near Shantou in 1897, "There would not only be occasional pitched battles, but marauding parties would assail wayfarers and make it perilous, for months and even years, to be out of safe running distance. Roadways would be blocked, fields would be devastated; houses would be plundered and left with doors and roofs battered down."[91] And bringing in the state, in the form of its county or provincial representatives, could add to the problem. Although Ashmore was probably exaggerating somewhat to highlight his own role as an arbitrator in this conflict, the report noted that when the government sent in a General Pang to restore order, Pang burned down some twenty towns and villages, stamped as many as he could to death, and cut off four-thousand heads [he was from a rival lineage]; his force of some three-thousand soldiers then lived off the villagers for months, "ate their rice; chewed their sugar-cane; drank their tea; nibbled their sweetmeats; smoked their tobacco and occasionally their opium; quartered themselves in their dwellings and when out of fuel they pulled down bits of the roof . . . and cooked their rice and sweet potatoes with that."[92] By mid-century, guns and cannon had replaced the spears and swords of local militia, making combat more deadly.[93] Villages throughout the region built watchtowers and cannon emplacements.[94]

The intensity of the conflicts may have also heightened as a result of the additional funds becoming available from commercial agriculture. The levying of the traditional fees and taxes on a larger volume of trade provided additional sums of money usable for supporting the lineage militia. If early-twentieth-century figures on lineage incomes from markets are any indication, these were substantial subsidies. For example, by the 1920s in the Guizhou mulberry-leaf market in Shunde county, the dominant lineage earned no less than $50,000 annually from the market. Most of it went to the lineage militia.[95] More resources also meant that the wealthier lineages and the wealthy within the lineages became more able to protect their own. Poorer members of the lineages "volunteered" to fight as substitutes for wealthier members in return for compensation to their families.[96] Large-scale lineages, despite internal differences, were able to mobilize all the component branches if the interests of one of them was threatened.[97]

Although the older social relations were now subject to many forces well outside their ambit of control, the established elite were, nevertheless, able to seize the initiative and prevent the complete dissolution of their own social nexus of power. For example, the increase in commercialized agriculture in the second half of the century in Guangdong was paralleled by the growth of new markets during the export boom. Thirteen new markets developed in the Shantou region.[98] In the Pearl River Delta, as indicated in Table 16, some counties gained as many as forty markets during the period 1840–1890.[99] But gentry and merchant initiatives were still responsible for starting these markets as in the earlier period. End-of-the-century editions of gazetteers are filled with testimonials about the contributions of merchants who set up new markets in Shunde or gentry who sought to develop sericulture in Dongguan.[100] The mulberry-leaf and silk-cocoon markets in Shunde, the maintenance of dikes, the "protection services," all continued to be organized by gentry and the lineages. And the elite were still able to control the free entry of capital that might have been inimical to their own interests. The ability of merchants and outsiders to move into the established village settlements remained restricted. Among the Guans of Kaiping and the forty villages in which the lineage's members lived, no outsider operated permanent stores even in the 1900s.[101] In the Phenix village market, on the outskirts of Chaozhou city in the 1920s, "outsiders" ran the shops selling meat, beancurd, paper, and other petty businesses. The two essential and profitable shops, rice and opium, were, however, run by lineage members of the single-surname village. Kulp commented on the social status of these "outsiders" in 1923: "The merchants may sell goods and live in the village shops; they may watch ceremonies. They must pay rent and refrain from violating local taboos and from breaking village customs so far as they come in contact with them. Beyond that their rights and duties do not extend."[102]

Industrial manufacture, too, remained subservient to the relations of personal dependence and the social hierarchies of village, community, lineage, and gentry. Capitalists became part of this ambit of power relations rather than being able to reshape the pre-existing social property relations. In the silk industry, for example, steam reeling was started in 1872 by Chen Qiyuan in what was probably the first Chinese-owned and -operated filature. An impoverished schoolteacher who was unsuccessful in the imperial examinations, Chen went to Vietnam with his brother in the 1850s; both made money through trade and pawnbroking and, having studied French silk technology in Hanoi, decided to invest in steam filatures back in their home village in Nanhai. The steam filatures produced good-quality silk but required several workers, and the reeling machines cost about 12,000 taels each.[103] Seen in Figure 31, as illustrated by Chen in his primer on mulberry and silk, the equipment was fairly modest in size and based on the French system of silk reeling à la Chambon. By 1881 there were eleven steam filatures in Nanhai.[104] The same year, over two thousand weavers who saw their livelihood threatened by the owners of the export-market-oriented filatures buying up all the cocoons and driving up the prices of hand-reeled silk (on which they depended), rioted and destroyed one filature. In the ensuing melee, including defense of the filature by some of the villagers, four people died, and the state militia was called in to restore peace. The magistrate, while disciplining the weavers, also disciplined the capitalists. All the steam filatures were ordered closed; Chen and the others moved their factories to Macao for three years.[105]

Capitalists like Chen became new members of the gentry and as such got access to the nexus and the web of extra-economic relationships binding gentry with other village members. When starting his factory, Chen Qiyuan used his village and gentry connections to recruit workers; when confronted with Luddism in the 1881 riot, he

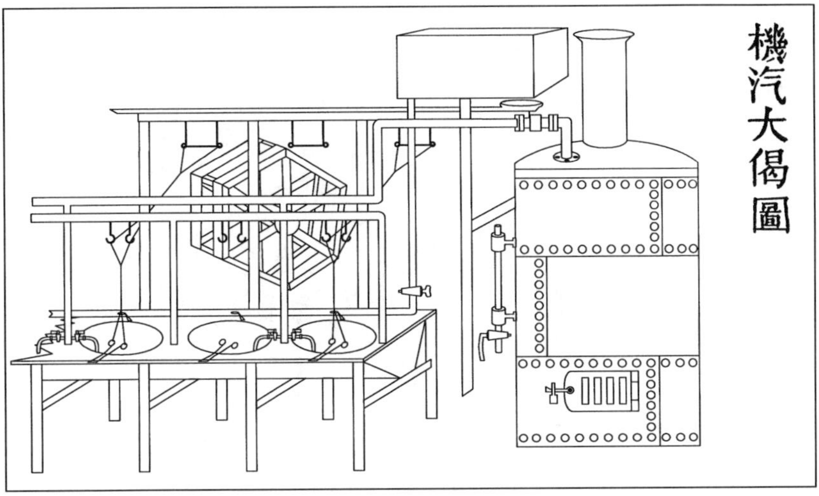

FIGURE 31. The steam-powered silk-reeling machine of the type developed by Chen Qiyuan in 1872, as illustrated in the *Cansang pu*.

could call on the lineage militia to defend his factory.[106] And like the ideal Confucian patriarch, he practiced charity toward the elderly and infirm and contributed to the building of dikes while also setting up rice, meat, and grocery stores in the village.[107] As a capitalist, however, he was not able to discipline his workers, who were members of his own village; an alliance with the lineage was crucial, and such partnerships could take many forms.

In 1898, when Chen wrote his primer on mulberry cultivation and silk reeling, *Cansang pu*, "in simple language so that all may understand," he included the design for a cheap foot-treadle-operated reeler.[108] Illustrated in Figure 32, this treadle-operated reeler produced a somewhat better quality silk and at a faster pace than the hand-turned reeler but was inferior to the steam filature product.[109] Its main virtues were that it cost only about 4 taels and could be operated under non-industrial conditions.[110] Ostensibly he did this out of concern for the common producer of silk in Guangdong.[111] It seems contrary to the interests of a capitalist to promote household manufacture. But the smallholders were not the only ones to benefit from Chen's philanthropy; lineages rented out treadle-operated reelers to

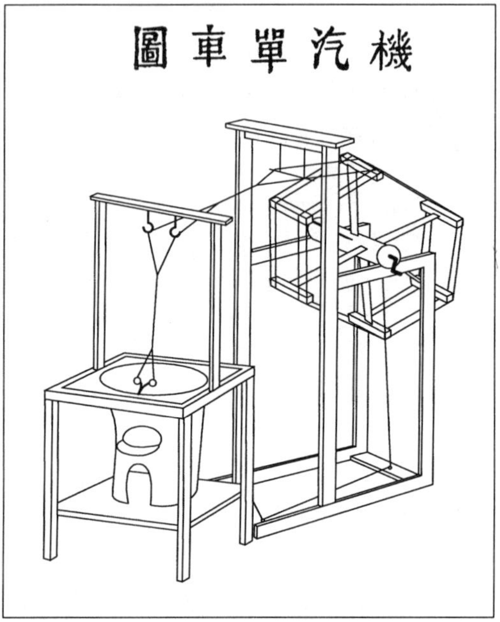

FIGURE 32. Foot-treadle-operated silk reeler developed by Chen Qiyuan in the 1890s adapting the self-crossing system à la Chambon.

producers usually at 10 percent of cost.[112] Silk-reeling workshops using these small machines were sometimes set up in the ancestral halls.[113] As in the case of land reclamation and polder development, lineages and elites were interested in all possibilities of accumulation, including the renting of space for the filatures and investments in filatures. By the twentieth century most of the filatures in Shunde were owned by lineage corporations, and the workers were predominantly daughters from the peasant households of the lineage.[114] The lineage could also discipline workers. Even in 1925, lineage elders and local gentry successfully disciplined women workers involved in a strike by threatening to expel their fathers and brothers from the lineage and excluding them from the ritual feasts.[115] Workers were told, "the whole family will be expelled from the lineage if one of its family members did not go back to work; that the strike leaders would face the most severe form of traditional punishment—[being] drowned to death in a pig cage."[116] In industry as in commercial agriculture, social property relations set the parameters of developmental possibilities.

Through all these changes, production and cultivation of all commercial crops remained in the hands of innumerable small producers. Some legal restrictions on selling land, such as those prohibiting Manchus from selling land to Han Chinese, were relaxed in the late nineteenth century.[117] But there seems to be little evidence that customary jurisdiction over land sales and settlement rights changed in any significant manner to make it easier for "outsiders" to move in. The export of laboring men and their remittances from abroad, in fact, allowed families to maintain their hold on property, engage in moneylending to supplement incomes, and add to the property whenever possible, while building gentry-like residences and constructing ancestral halls.[118]

Did tenants cultivating cash crops pay a higher rent? This was certainly the case by the twentieth century in the Pearl River Delta. Landlords demanded cash rents on sugarcane lands, and these were often 10 percent higher than those on rice land in the same region.[119] Frequently these rents were high, amounting to more than one-half the total cost of cane cultivation per *mu*, leaving little for the fertilizers so necessary for cane cultivation.[120] Even those who owned land spent almost one-third of the money obtained by selling cane on the purchase of fertilizers. Most peasants, like the two brothers interviewed by Fielde, cultivated cane on an unirrigated plot of 3.5 *mu* (approximately 0.5 acre).[121] Such small producers could not afford the expense of processing the cane themselves. They simply sold it to merchants and brokers.[122] In these circumstances, quality control was difficult, and this affected the marketability of such canes for the refineries. Richer peasants who were able to form cooperatives and process the cane or get loans to do so were perhaps in a better position to benefit from the rising prices and steep inflation of the last quarter of the nineteenth century.[123] Yet there is little to suggest that producers were undertaking these ventures independently of trading capital and merchant loans. The necessity of such loans is underlined by the fact that in their absence sugar manufacturing was abandoned. A 1920s investigation into the decline of sugar manufacturing in Panyu county in the Pearl River Delta concluded the main cause had been the unavailability of mercantile capital to the peasant producers.[124] In a few years, the loans became unavailable for silkworms, and the market shifted; all the cultivators switched to sugarcane and rice cultivation.[125]

For the rentiers, incomes from rent did not decline with commercialization; on the contrary they could demand and get higher rents. As the Shunde gazetteer recorded in the biography of a gentry member well known for his deeds of charity: "In the reign of Guangxu [1875–1908] the price of raw silk soared, so He Jiarao talked to his old tenants and told them that he would rather increase the land rent 10 to 20 percent than find new tenants."[126] Similarly, there was no attempt to change the organization of production and undertake commercial cultivation. There does not seem to be a single known case in Guangdong in which the landlord, instead of leasing out to tenants, considered farming it with hired labor.[127] Even the Minglun Tang, the largest corporate landlord in Guangdong by 1940, owning 76,000 *mu* (almost 12,700 acres), still leased out its lands and rented it out in the multi-layered tenancy arrangements examined in Chapter Four.[128] In the initial stages of development, when the land was still marshy, servile tenants like the Danmin could still be brought in. Access to the labor of these temporary tenants was not based on the market; they were "hereditary tenants who look upon the members of the clans [lineages] that harbor them as their masters, and who in addition to farming the fields assigned to them, render additional services as laborers, servants and watchmen, for which they are paid no wage, though here and there their wretched condition is occasionally alleviated by perquisites of various kinds."[129] After the land became productive in about ten years or so, the polders were rented out in multilayered tenancy arrangements.

Household manufacture with many more producers than in the earlier period also could continue under the arrangements of a previous epoch. As demand for silk increased on the export market, more small producers started producing silk: "[C]ertain men more enterprizing than others buy up large quantities of cocoons and reel more silk and we see in many homes 4, 6, 8 10 or more reels with women hired to run them."[130] The persistence of the family workshop is underscored by the fact that twice as much silk overall continued to be spun on treadle-reeled filatures as on steam filatures even at the peak of the export boom.[131] Only the export-quality silk was overwhelmingly produced in the steam filatures.[132] Hand reeling also continued, relying on community and neighborhood associations.[133] Commercial opportunities such as silk reeling at home and work in filatures may have simply strengthened the smallholder's tenacious hold on property by enabling the use of a daughter's labor to earn a cash income while the rest of the family continued to be engaged in agriculture.

In Shunde county, where up to 80 percent of the population was involved with sericulture at the height of the silk export boom, the demand for skilled silk reelers and other wage work gave younger women expanded employment opportunities. Cash incomes allowed some of them, with the support of their families, to adapt marriage patterns that enabled them to continue living with their natal family even several years after marriage, or to conduct only a ritual marriage that did not require them to leave home.[134] Generally, reelers acquired greater esteem within the family; their living conditions and health, including the benefits of reduced child-bearing, were the results of their income. As Howard and Buswell noted in the 1920s, "The reeling women can be recognized in a filature town because they are always dressed better and show a better physical appearance."[135]

But even in Shunde, the massive expansion of sericulture could not transform rural property relations. Like the elites, peasant families, too, adapted to the new economic circumstances while at the same time being able to preserve the pre-existing social relations. A most relevant point is that the interests of both the peasant households and the lineage prevented the complete commodification of labor. For example, a number of families permitted their daughters to remain unmarried through the practice of sworn spinsterhood, or agreed to natolocal marriages and other variations in the local marriage patterns.

Fathers often paid for the ritual ceremonies that marked the transition to the formal designation of spinster. "Her mother wanted her to marry, but her father, who owned a small silk-reeling workshop, wanted her to become a spinster because she was an especially skillful reeler and helped him in his business. . . . Then when she was 22, he held a spinster banquet for her. On that occasion, the informant recalled, her father was a truly happy man."[136] This was the very opposite of proletarianization;[137] the head of the household placed a preemptive bid on his daughter's labor and controlled access to it through non-market means. As Janice Stockard's interviewees recalled, male heads of families who owned silk reeling enterprises paid their daughters one-half the wages of less skillful hired workers,[138] underlining the logic of family manufacturing with its super-exploitation of family labor. And when the daughters did work in factories, they sent money home to the rural family, sustaining their access to the means of subsistence.

Ultimately, the broad array of changes of the late nineteenth and early twentieth centuries could be contained within the established social property relations of rural Guangdong. No crisis of reproduction, as yet, confronted the elites. Opportunities opened up by trade and commercial agriculture strengthened, rather than weakened, the power of lineages and local strongmen and enabled further dominance over weaker groups and minor lineages.[139] Direct producers also still retained products, activities, and relations independent of the system of commodity exchange. Increased commercialization of the agrarian economy may have only made their hold more tenacious.

The World Market and the Transformation of the Taiwan Sugar Industry

Notwithstanding continuities in the Chinese agrarian sector, the conditions of commercial agriculture and production in other parts of the globe had been changing particularly rapidly in the last quarter of the nineteenth century. Under colonial auspices, vast areas were converted into producers of specialized exports to the industrialized societies. In addition to the reorganization of sugar cultivation in Java, Fiji and the

Philippines, jute, indigo, and tea plantations in India, coffee and tea plantations in Sri Lanka, tobacco plantations in Sumatra, and rubber plantations in Malaya and Vietnam are other examples of this phenomenon in Asia.[140] The Japanese colonization of Taiwan and its conversion into the primary sugar producer for the Japanese market was a similar and related development of colonial commodity production for consumption in the home market.

This new wave of colonization in the last quarter of the nineteenth century was part of what has been called "the second period of capitalism."[141] The period also marked a phase of crisis in industrial capitalism, which had a particular impact on the agricultural commodities market. Hobsbawm suggests that the crisis of 1873–1896 was actually a depression: "Historians have doubted the existence of what has been called the 'Great Depression' of 1873 to 1896, and of course it was nothing like as dramatic as that of 1929 to 1934, when the world capitalist economy almost ground to a halt. However, contemporaries were in no doubt that the great boom had been succeeded by a great depression. A new era of history, political as well as economic, opens with the depression of the 1870s."[142]

One of the characteristics of this economic crisis was the rapid fall in prices and, with it, profits. In an effort to stem the fall of prices that resulted from intensified competition between the industrialized economics, nearly every country, with the exception of Britain, established protective tariffs. Cartels and trade agreements soon followed in an attempt to protect specific markets, prevent overproduction in domestic industries by prior agreement among manufacturers, and provide advantages in the export sector.[143]

Sugar was one of the primary commodities to be affected. During 1850–1904, for example, Germany and Austria routinely sold about 60–65 million tons of beet sugar at less than the cost of production through government subsidies in an effort to enter new markets or keep competitors out of other markets.[144] Several sugar-producing nations, such as France, responded by developing high import tariffs to protect domestic producers. Other arrangements between states closed off segments of the commodities market through barter arrangements between governments, for example, the exchange of German beet sugar for grain from the United States.[145] Many of these arrangements developed over the course of the several decades, and attempts were made to regulate the market by establishing treaties and conventions among the industrialized nations. By the late nineteenth century there were essentially four types of markets in cane sugar:[146]

1. *Completely protected domestic markets or duty-free export markets:* for example, United States continental, Hawaiian, and Puerto Rican production; or colonial-possession production for the home market, such as that of the Philippines for the United States and Réunion for France.

2. *Preferential markets:* for example, the United Kingdom and Canadian outlets for sugar produced in British colonial and Dominion countries, or Cuban exports to the United States.

3. *Markets developed through trade and price advantage:* for example, the Javanese sugar trade to India till the 1930s, or the Taiwanese and Javanese sugar trade to China after the turn of the century.

4. *Residual markets:* small consumers such as Iran, Switzerland, Chile, New Zealand and so on.

By the early twentieth century, only markets in the third and fourth categories remained unprotected by tariffs or preferential entry quotas. There was active competition for these markets. And Taiwan, under Japanese colonial control after 1895, was to become the major sugar producer in Asia, competing for all the East Asian markets, including mainland China.

As a Japanese colony after 1895, Taiwan could export sugar to Japan under a preferential customs tariff. But Taiwan was also able to develop a broader market. There was a specialized market in soft brown sugar in China and Japan that had been supplied earlier by Taiwan, continental China, and the Philippines.[147] Starting in the late 1880s, Philippines brown sugar had been sold in increasingly large quantities in both China and Japan. By the twentieth century, however, Taiwan captured not only the Chinese and Japanese markets but also the Philippine market for brown sugar.[148]

Until 1870, Taiwan's sugar exports never exceeded 18,500 tons in any given year.[149] Most of it went to Tianjin and Shanghai via Fujian and to Japan. The trade in sugar was closely affected by the general rise in Taiwanese trade that began when the treaties of 1858–1860 brought an increased Western presence, beginning first in the ports of An-ping and Tan-shui, then those of Keelung and Takow (present-day Kaohsiung). Volume in the primary export commodities—sugar, camphor, and tea—rose sharply up to the 1880s. Although exports leveled off after this period, Taiwanese sugar was entering some new markets.[150] Besides the traditional markets of the mainland, Hong Kong, and Japan, small quantities of Taiwan sugar began to be exported to California and Canada during the 1870s and 1880s as well as Australia, where the newly established refineries did not as yet have steady sources of supplies of raw sugar. Beginning with a shipment of a mere 19.5 tons to Australia in 1870, exports increased to over 8,350 tons by 1879.[151] A peak was reached in 1880 with an export volume of over 63,250 tons.[152] By the 1890s, however, the Australian market was eliminated as the sugar plantations on Fiji developed under the auspices of the Australian-owned Colonial Sugar Refining Company Limited. The California market, too, was restricted by the passage of tariff laws designed to protect the growing American cane- and beet-sugar industries. Only the markets of mainland China and Japan remained as the major importers of Taiwan sugar.[153]

The trajectory of economic change on Taiwan in the 1880s was, to some extent, shaped by political vicissitudes that were the opposite of those in Guangdong; in the last quarter of the century the Qing state became far more directly involved in scrutinizing the power of the local elite while investing in Taiwan's economic development. The interest of western nations in controlling Taiwan had been evident since the 1840s, when Britain had been involved in military activities there during the Opium War. Townsend Harris, the first American consul in Japan and better known for his role in the "opening" of Japan, had recommended the outright purchase of Taiwan from the Chinese government in 1854.[154] After the Treaty of Beijing (1860), which gave privileges to Britain, the United States, France, and Germany in Taiwan, other treaties were concluded by Prussia, Portugal, Denmark, Spain, Belgium, Italy, Austria, and Japan giving them trading privileges in Taiwan. When the Franco-Chinese war broke out in 1884 and

Keelung was attacked by the French, an unusually energetic and reform-minded governor of Fujian, Liu Mingzhuan (1836–1896), was sent to defend the island.[155] Part of a cohort of military men who had acquired imperial recognition for the ruthlessness with which they had dealt with mid-century problems such as the Taiping and Nian rebellions and had then risen to become influential patrons of industrial development, Liu undertook an aggressive program in the six years (1885–1891) of his tenure as governor of Taiwan. Indigenous and overseas Chinese mercantile investments took place in mining, in transportation including a short railway-line, and in manufacturing enterprises. Overseas Chinese from Singapore invested in a commercial steamship line established by Liu, while a group of businessmen from Shanghai, Zhejiang, and Suzhou were persuaded to undertake the development of the city of Taipei.[156] As part of the efforts to raise state revenues and promote the cultivation of export-market crops such as sugar, tea, and camphor, Liu ordered the survey of all agricultural lands in 1886–1888. The cadastral survey tried to simplify the multi-tiered system of landownership rights based on tax liabilities, which, as we have seen, had made the sale of property so extremely complicated.[157] This also served to scrutinize the power of the "big-rent households" (*dazu hu*). Although the cadastre did not by any means eliminate the rentiers as a class, it limited the amount of rent that they could collect solely on the basis of their initial role in opening up lands. The ipso facto landlords, the "small-rent households" (*xiaozu hu*), were now made responsible for tax payments to the government. Recognizing as landlords those who were in direct contact with tenants somewhat simplified tax collection and provided a segment of the population with clearer ownership deeds.

The process of creating yeomen out of rentiers was, however, not that simple. Increased immigration from the mainland and the consequent demand for land seem to have obviated the need for the "small-rent households" to be more closely involved with farming than the earlier "large-rent household" landlords had been. In the short term, rentier incomes were made more secure by the added attention of the state; by 1900 the rent collection rights of the *xiaozu hu* could be sold for three times the 1850s price.[158] The main impact of the increased momentum of commercialized agriculture seems to have been to reduce the permanent or long-term tenancy rights of the direct producers to short-term leases of three to five years.[159] As in Guangdong, the practice of demanding rent deposits continued while rents increased.[160]

Liu's reforms also did not necessitate a fundamental shift in agricultural investment patterns of the established elites. For example, the booming tea trade would seemingly have been an appropriate avenue of investment; tea exports from the port of Tan-shui reached over 16 million pounds by the mid 1880s, and the total value of the Taiwan tea trade (1867–1900) was estimated to have been around 150 million yen.[161] Large landlords like the Lin, one of the wealthiest in Taiwan with vast holdings in tea, camphor, and rice, were said to have owned land with almost 900,000 tea bushes by the late nineteenth century.[162] The Lin do not seem to have tried to organize plantations or centralize processing anywhere in their vast holdings although throughout the 1880s and 1890s British "tea experts" had been actively trying to get Taiwan manufacturers to develop the tea growing, firing, and packing systems that were being used in India.[163] We have already noted similar difficulties faced by Wykeham Myers trying to sell a new type of cane crusher.

The importance of the export sector in the overall economy of Taiwan, however, resulted in some changes in the commercial guilds under the impact of western trade. After 1860, many of the older Taiwanese merchant guilds lost power and influence in the sugar-export business to the compradores working for western traders.[164] The Beijiao guild in Tainan, which had earlier controlled much of the export trade to the mainland, found itself unable to compete with the newly reorganized Yanghang, or Foreign Guild. Some of these guild merchants, especially from the Kaohsiung area, became independent traders selling sugar to the mainland and exporting to Japan.[165] Other local merchants became compradores (*maiban*) for trading firms such as Jardine and Matheson or Russell and Company. In the agricultural sector, however, the terms under which the business was carried out did not differ much from the operations of the earlier Chinese mercantile guilds. In sugar manufacturing they were accommodated within the types of arrangements for cane crushing and cultivation that had existed in eighteenth- and early-nineteenth-century Taiwan.[166] Partial payments were made for an agreed upon volume to be delivered at the current market rate. As a clause of a 1890 contract between "Messers Russell & Company, American Merchants of Taiwanfoo and Sim Tai Hong (Lintai hang) of Taiwanfoo," indicates,

> That the said Russell & Co., hereby agree to pay the said Sim Tai Hong, on and for all Sugars and for produce bought, purchased and contracted for by, through or with the said Sim Tai Hong, advances to the extent of (65%) Sixty five percent, on signing the purchase and for contract note, or as soon after so doing as possible the balance (35%) Thirty five percent, on due full and complete and satisfactory delivery into Godowns at Anping.[167]

Sim Tai operated on the basis of a commission of 1 percent for all sales made by or through the *hang* by Russell and Company. Sim Tai Hong was also a compradore for another British merchant, a David Moncrieff Wright, and sold sugar to him under terms similar to those agreed upon with Jardine. In this case, Sim Tai also bought opium from Wright. Most of the Taiwan compradores supplying western traders with sugar and other local products developed a parallel trade in opium, kerosene, iron and steel tools, and cotton textiles through their connections with the western traders. Others combined trading activities with moneylending to westerners.[168] The compradores also provided warehouses and other necessary facilities to carry out the expanded commodity trade.

As the older guilds lost their export monopolies, the compradores moved into the established commercial networks. With the development of better roads and railway transportation in the 1880s and 1890s, merchants from the sugar guilds and the compradore firms began to travel directly to the villages where contracts for manufacturing sugar had been arranged.[169] The sugar guilds supplying the export merchants could now also lend money directly to the sugar-manufacturing units and circumvent the services of the middleman-merchant, or *keshang*.[170] But the compradores and the merchants of the export guilds did not become directly involved in production.

There is no record of the compradores investing in land and taking over the cultivation of cane.

While the compradores began to travel down to the villages, which was new, there seems to be little evidence that the direct producers could now also travel to distant markets. As larger numbers of small producers entered commercial agriculture and began competing for merchant loans, interest rates went up, and merchants could demand a higher return. The merchant's share in a *toujia bu* (cane-crushing association based on shares), for example, increased from 50–55 percent of the product to 60–70 percent by the 1890s while the level of initial investment remained the same.[171] These changes, minimal and in many ways with an undertow forcing a replication of the relations of production going back to the beginning of the nineteenth century, however, were abruptly and painfully transformed under colonial aegis in the following decade.

The metamorphosis of Taiwan into the major producer of sugar in East Asia followed its colonization by Japan in 1895. The transformation was based on a deliberate policy of developing production for the Japanese market. In 1888, Japan consumed about five pounds of sugar per capita. By 1897, this had risen to ten pounds, and by 1903 to twelve pounds. Domestic sugar production in Japan, a substantial quantity of it from the Ryukyus, met only 18 percent of the demand by the end of the nineteenth century.[172] The rest was supplied by the British refineries in Hong Kong, by Chinese and Japanese traders bringing in sugar from Taiwan, and by imports of German and Hungarian beet sugar. In 1894, Jardine and Matheson's China Sugar refinery in Hong Kong along with Butterfield and Swire's Taikoo refinery provided 54 percent of the sugar demand at Yokohama and 40 percent of the demand at Kobe.[173] But by 1895, demand increased so rapidly that German and Hungarian beet-sugar imports surpassed those from Hong Kong.[174] Sugar imports cost 20–30 million yen a year by the 1890s.[175] Consequently the Japanese government and Japanese businesses were particularly interested in developing industrial manufacture on Taiwan. The figures tell the story. In 1895, the total export of sugar from Taiwan had been just over 42,000 tons. By 1910–1911, the total exported was well over 250,000 tons.[176] The success of the Japanese enterprise in the sugar industry of Taiwan rose directly from the power of the colonial state to change, by fiat, many of the barriers to industrial manufacture arising from the smallholder system of production.

The Japanese government began by launching a land survey. All those failing to comply with the regulations of the survey were to have their lands confiscated. The state was above all interested in generating revenues and had no intention of permitting oversight. Surveys were started in 1898, and by 1903 the Japanese government could declare that both revenues and acreage of cultivated lands were almost double those recorded under the Qing.[177] Some changes in the system of landownership had already been initiated, as we have seen, in the last days of Qing control of the island. The programs of both Liu Mingzhuan and the Japanese colonial government recognized the need to eliminate the non-agricultural rentier class in order to raise productivity. Yet the Japanese government was also aware that outright appropriation of the "big-rent households," numbering about 40,000 in 1890s, would have been tantamount to a social revolution, a step which Baron Gotō Shimpei (1857–1929), as the head of colonial civil administration of Taiwan, was aware would only stiffen resistance. The administration instead resorted to obliging the *dazu hu* to exchange their hereditary rent rights for income-bearing state bonds. The former "little-rent households," the *xiaozu hu*, who had been functioning as landlords were now recognized as the full legal owners of the land.[178] The colonial government saw the role of this class as that of capitalist peasants promoting the cultivation of cash crops. To assure their participation in the agrarian program, the government monetized all aspects of the rural economy. As Takekoshi candidly concludes, "it has also ensured security of landed property, so that capitalists can now invest in Formosan land without any qualms."[179]

The colonial land reform program sought neither to transfer land to the tillers nor to defend the rights of the smallholder. Instead, the state sought to provide clear titles to land, clarify the identity of landlords, and register all lands. To stimulate the land market, the state terminated permanent tenancy and set a twenty-year ceiling on leases.[180] Since the colonial state was interested in promoting capital accumulation, there were no limits on rents and "protection fees" (*fangzu yin* or *aidi yin*), essentially rent deposits, that landlords could demand as guarantee of rent payment.[181] The legal and social power of the new landlords and the colonial state was underlined by a reorganized version of the Ming-Qing institution of the *baojia*, literally a system of group security and tithings. The population was organized into household groupings of 10 and 100 and each group was placed under the authority of the village headman and the local police. As George Barclay puts it, "With a shrewd combination of police force and political guile, they imposed strict political order and penetrated every town and village with a structure of organized control."[182] As seen below, the revitalized *baojia* system of the colonial state was to be a particularly effective mechanism for implementing agricultural policies and "persuading" independent-minded smallholders to cultivate particular varieties of cane and other crops deemed necessary by the government.[183] The unit of cultivation remained the small family-holding. In 1910, the average farm was 4.87 acres and remained so down to 1940.[184] The earliest available surveys, also dating from 1910, indicate 33.7 percent were owner-cultivators, 42.3 percent tenants, and 23.5 percent part-owners and part-tenants.[185] But formal resemblance with the smallholder cultivation of the Qing ends there. For the vast majority of cultivators in the sugarcane-growing areas, though still owning some of their land and farming equipment, were in actuality turned into contract workers for the sugar refineries.

A governmental agency was founded in 1900, with the explicit task of industrializing Taiwanese sugar manufacture. This agency worked closely with the Taiwan Seitō Kabushiki Kaisha (Taiwan Sugar Refining Joint Stock Company), the first industrial mill and refinery established in Taiwan. Founded in 1900 as a colonial venture, it received a government subsidy of 60,000 yen for each of its first five years of operation. The company, organized by Mitsui, was far from being a casual enterprise; its shareholders included the imperial household, a "wealthy Formosan native interested in the sugar industry," and such stalwarts of Japanese industrialization as the Mori, Sumitomo, and Suzuki.[186] Production in the Taiwan Seitō Kaisha refineries began in 1901. The mills had a daily grinding capacity of thirty tons, and the initial projected output per year was to be 4,500 tons. The company found, however, that Chinese cultivators were unwilling to sell it cane; and in the first year of operations, the mill managed to produce considerably less than 2,000 tons.[187] The Taiwan Seitō Kaisha then moved to expropriate the smallholders and other landowners wherever possible. During the Land Survey, those who could not provide landownership records within a certain allotted period of time had their lands confiscated and put on sale. Many of these lands were purchased by the sugar companies. As Zhang Hanyu has pointed out, Japanese capitalists rather than Taiwanese were the direct beneficiaries of changes in the land laws which made it easier to sell land.[188] Eventually, by the 1920s, five Japanese sugar corporations came to own as much as one-fifth of all cultivated land in Taiwan and 70 percent of the land under sugarcane.[189]

Two types of cultivators were directly linked with the refineries, "company tenants" and smallholders who were under contract to sell to the factories and prohibited from selling to others. Having acquired control of the lands, the companies then rented them out to "company tenants," providing them also with seed-cane, implements, and capital.[190] The cane was purchased by the company at a fixed price which did not favor the peasant cultivators.[191] In other areas, to ensure an adequate supply of cane from independent peasants, the government stipulated that the mill must agree to take all the cane planted in the district and set the price at which the cane was to be bought. In addition, if the peasants agreed to cultivate the newer varieties of cane and did so for five years, they were to be provided with fertilizer and seed cane at modest rates.

The "Regulations for the Encouragement of the Sugar Business" issued in 1902 were, as Takekoshi Yosaburo puts it, "sufficient to impress anyone with the earnest desire of the authorities to turn Formosa into another Java."[192] These policies were intended to benefit capitalists investing in sugar cultivation and modern refineries. It provided subsidies to those who developed or bought land with the explicit purpose of cultivating cane, and it underwrote the purchase cost of machinery by 20 percent. The Sugar Bureau enforced other regulations, stipulating that persons wishing to set up a factory had to obtain a license from the director of the government's sugar agency, marking the district in which the factory was to be set up, and allowing no other factory to operate in the district. A state-operated railway connecting several sugar districts was installed, which the sugar company was allowed to use at one-half the regular tariff. At Keelung, a new harbor was constructed to facilitate the export trade. Small irrigation projects were under way by the end of the first decade of the twentieth century; and after 1911, a major irrigation project servicing 370,650 acres of prime sugarcane land was also constructed.

At the same time, the state also moved against the small-scale producers. By 1905, the state prohibited grinding cane on the two-roller buffalo-driven mills. Anyone planting cane in a district where there was a modern factory was prohibited from selling it or transporting it for any purpose outside the district. The entire crop had to be sold to the factory.

Researchers in several agricultural field stations provided the technical underpinnings of this transformation of the sugar industry. One of policy's architects, Nitobe Inazō (1862–1933), set up agricultural experimentation stations as early as 1896. Nitobe's long-range plans for agricultural development and forestry were based on the formula, "rice as the essential 'Formosan crop' (produced principally in the wet northern region) and sugar as the great 'profit crop'—the Japanese crop—produced in the warmer, drier southwest."[193] The policy implications of this formulation were far-reaching. Drawing on various types of research in plant breeding already being done in Japan and elsewhere, experimental farms and agricultural laboratories developed improved high-yield strains of rice, sugarcane, tea, vegetables, and fruits, which were then released for general planting.[194]

The Sugar Research Institute, set up in Tainan, the heart of the traditional cane-cultivating districts of Taiwan, was to become one of the foremost sugar experiment stations in the world. Two primary varieties of cane were cultivated in Taiwan prior to 1895: a green variety that yielded little juice but was hardy, and the more commonly cultivated "Tekchia," which yielded about 8 tons of cane per acre.[195] Nitobe sent students to Germany, Java, and Hawaii to study the sugar industries in these areas, and experimental findings from them were soon implemented in Taiwan. Several new, improved high-yield varieties of cane were imported, such as the Stripped Tanna cane from Java and the Lahaina cane from Hawaii (both of which were rejected because they required great quantities of water and constant care). The Rose Bamboo, also imported from Hawaii, with a medium-high yield but flexible water requirements, was deemed the most suitable for Taiwan.[196] In contrast to the 8 tons of cane per acre and only 1,064 pounds of brown sugar produced from the traditional Tekchia cane, the Rose Bamboo could yield 14 tons per acre and 3,360 pounds of crystallized sugar. Because ratoon crops had a lower sucrose content after the first crop, the Rose Bamboo had to be replanted afresh.[197] The effectiveness of the alliance of the government with the sugar companies was such that within five years of the introduction of the Rose Bamboo variety in 1902, more than 60 percent of the cane-crop area of Taiwan cultivated only this variety.[198] The alacrity with which this single variety was adopted was due to the use of the police and the *baojia* for distributing the new cane seedlings.[199]

By 1908, there were 50 factories using steam-driven machinery and 11 factories with grinding capacities of 500–1,200 tons of cane per twenty-four-hour period. The production capabilities of these refineries, imported from Britain, the United States, and Germany, ranged from 2,400 tons to 39,000 tons.[200] The "Big Six"—Taiwan Seitō, Meiji Seitō, Yensuiko, Tōyō Seitō, Teikoku, and Tainan Seitō—had clear support from the colonial state and dominated the market. Up to 1910, several of the small Chinese refineries and that of a Western trading company, Bain, continued to function. There were also a host of small Japanese companies. After 1911, these smaller enterprises were absorbed by the "Big Six" or forced to close down under government pressure. Of the 147 Chinese companies that engaged in some form of industrial manufacture in the first decade of the century, only 7 survived after 1911.[201]

The transformation of the agrarian sector in the first decade of the twentieth century, even while some of the Taiwanese-Chinese merchants were operating, is underlined when we look at the changes in the contracts between cultivators and merchants from the Sugar Guild. Earlier, as we have seen, the merchant had little recourse if the amount of sugar agreed upon was not available at the time of delivery. Legal guarantees that the merchant could recoup the loan were difficult to implement.

Beginning in 1905, the new contracts stipulated that loans were to be given only against a deposit of security. Part or all of his land was typically the only collateral a peasant had to offer, and the amount of loan was usually set at 80 percent of its market value. The lender also received a copy of the land registration document. In order to reduce registration fees that were based on the value of the land, the lender usually valued the land at 50 to 60 percent below market value. If the peasant failed to produce sugar in sufficient quantity or of sufficient quality, the contracts stipulated that the entire loan had to be paid off in cash or the merchant could cash in the collateral. And it would seem that many did so.[202]

Using this two-pronged approach, the traditional labor-intensive, small-scale production structure was overhauled. By 1911, only 191 buffalo-driven mills remained in operation in all of Taiwan, whereas in 1901 there had been 1,117.[203] The ability of the colonial state to impose its will on the cultivators obviated any need to turn the entire island into plantations. The Taiwan Sugar Corporation did have some plantations, accounting for about 10 percent of all the farmland in Taiwan and providing approximately 20 percent of the cane supply for the mills. The remaining 80 percent of the supply continued to be grown by individual farmers, who were, however, not free to market their cane to buyers other than the stipulated mills. For those who were tenants of the sugar companies, the land was rented only on the condition that particular varieties of cane be grown. The Civil Administrator's Office in Taipei directed local police officials to harass small farmers who were reluctant to sign contracts with the mills at the prices set by the mill owners.[204] Bitter indeed was the life of the cane farmer!

By fiat and by forced transformation of smallholders into workers for the sugar factories on the one hand and the establishment of industrial sugar factories on the other, the Japanese colonial state thus constructed the foundations of the capitalist sugar industry in Taiwan. Once this initial development had taken place, the colonial government found it possible to permit the continuation of the small-scale farm unit for purposes of cane cultivation as long as the marketing of cane and its processing in the refineries were strictly controlled. The control of the state over the small-scale cultivators was further demonstrated when the vast irrigation network called the Kanan or Chia-i–Tainan system was constructed between 1920 and 1930. Providing irrigation and drainage to 370,500 acres, the project was designed to accommodate both sugarcane and rice cultivation in rotation rather than in competition as had been the case before. A system of agricultural associations was set up, integrating some 300,000 farm families into the irrigation network under government control. All cultivators were required to belong to these associations. By adjusting the water supply of this vast irrigation network, Taipei could control the quantitative balance and rotation of crops thought desirable by the central planners. A three-crop, three-year planting cycle combining sugarcane, rice, legumes, and mixed minor crops of vegetables and sweet potatoes was imposed, with the proportion of land devoted to each crop being controlled by different allocations of water supply. Through the agricultural associations, the government organized the distribution of fertilizers, credit, and marketing.[205]

It is clear that small-scale cultivation per se was not inimical to centralized manufacture. The size of the plot of land on which cane was cultivated mattered little as long as the producer and cultivator operated within an industrial framework. The success of the Taiwan sugar industry under the Japanese was a reflection of the fundamental transformation that had occurred in the relations of production, which now directly linked the cultivator and the industrialist. On the mainland, in contrast, this nexus was yet to be established.

Conclusion: The Crisis of Smallholder Production

A conjunction of economic trends in the world market resulted in what may be termed a crisis in the sugar industry in 1900–1914. This was a crisis of overproduction and falling prices as dozens of new producers came on the market. In Asia, in addition to Taiwan, the Philippines was producing around 350,000 tons for export by 1914; Java almost 1,250,000 tons. Refineries like the Dai-Nippon Seitō had also been set up in Japan. With raw sugar from Okinawa (Ryukyus) and Java, Japan began to export sugar, an average of 64,000 tons by 1915.[206] Worldwide, German and Austro-Hungarian beet sugar, Californian beet sugar, Cuban cane sugar after the Spanish-American War, and the expansion of the cane-sugar industry in Hawaii, Fiji, Australia, and Natal all added to the glut. Technological developments of the nineteenth century had affected both the cultivation and processing of cane. Geoffrey Masefield has estimated that as a result of new industrial techniques and improvements in the varieties grown, the yield of sugar per acre increased tenfold between 1850 and 1950, an increase in output unmatched by any other crop.[207] The result was a slump in sugar prices; in London raw sugar prices dropped from 25s. 6d. per hundredweight (112 pounds) in 1872 to 7s. 3d. by 1902 and continued to fall in the first decades of the twentieth century.[208]

In China, by contrast, the price of sugar remained practically constant throughout the period 1834–1881.[209] Initially, this price had been low by world market standards. But once refineries were set up in Hong Kong, processing raw sugars from Java, the Philippines, and China, the prices at which sugar could be imported into China were lower than the domestically manufactured product. Prices fell by almost fifty percent in one decade, 1891–1902.[210] The Maritime Customs report for Shantou reported in 1902:

> The Hong Kong product is so much cleaner than the native article that it is gaining in popularity. . . . The price, too, is in favor of the imported article, as the average price of Swatow [Shantou] brown during the year was Hk. Tls. 3.45 per picul, and that of the Hong Kong variety was Hk. Tls. 3.30. Swatow white was quoted at Hk. Tls. 5.25, and Hong Kong white at Hk. Tls. 4.75 while Hong Kong refined sugar could be laid down here at the same figure as was asked for the local white.[211]

The integrated investments of steamship lines and refineries aided the domination of the refinery-produced sugar. The China Navigation Company, a subsidiary of Butterfield and Swire, for example, retained the right to carry all sugar refined at Taikoo to north China, Japan, India, and Australia, adding considerably to the profits of the parent firm.[212]

As profit-making enterprises, the Hong Kong refineries were interested in obtaining the lowest-priced stocks. Throughout the 1880s and 1890s, there had been continuous problems with securing supplies of cane and raw sugar for Hong Kong. The quality of cane purchased from Shantou was not uniform; supplies varied enormously from year to year; and the slower inland transportation meant that the canes often arrived rotten.[213] Industrial refineries needed a continuous and regular supply of cane to be financially viable; these refineries could not be shut down and started up at random, as frequently happened when the supply of cane was irregular. Under these particular conditions of production and marketing, the small-scale sugarcane cultivator in China could not hope to compete with industrial production on the world market by the end of the nineteenth century. Small-scale cultivation and small-scale manufacture were no longer feasible arrangements. By the decade of 1900–1910, the Hong Kong refineries began getting all their raw stocks from Java and the Philippines at far lower prices than from mainland China.

Prices could not be pushed any lower, for both Chinese independent smallholders and the merchants had a limit below which they switched to producing other crops. Not tied into the market for one particular crop as in Taiwan or Java, producers in Shantou switched to rice, vegetables, and fruits. The cultivation of oil crops increased in most former cane-cultivating areas.[214] Whereas in 1899 Shantou had exported almost 110,000 tons of sugar, by 1911 a report on Shantou by the Maritime Customs noted, "little sugar is exported . . . because of deficient planting methods and little fertilizer."[215] A similar situation existed in the Pearl River Delta. In Jiulong [Kowloon], the Maritime Customs reported cane cultivation was abandoned because it was no longer profitable and merchant loans were no longer forthcoming.[216] And in Dongguan county by 1908, people no longer bothered to make white or refined sugar; most of the sugar-processing sheds were closed, and only some brown sugar was produced.[217] The total number of sugar-processing units in Guangdong declined from 406 in 1912 to 229 in 1913. Throughout China, land under cane declined.[218] Demand, however, remained fairly constant in China. Only the domestic product lost its share of the market. Already by 1911–1913, China imported over 340,000 tons of sugar; by 1925–1928, this was to increase to 500,000 to 700,000 tons.[219] By 1930, overall domestic production in China had declined to an all-time low of 119,048 tons.[220]

This rapid withdrawal from a market at a time of buoyant demand highlights the apparent limitations of decentralized smallholder-based commercialization. For the story of sugar was not unique. The sequence by which China became a net importer of a commodity that it had previously exported to the world market or lost its share of the world market in other commodities was repeated many times. The tea-export trade of Guangdong, for example, showed a similar pattern;[221] tea, like sugarcane, was "produced by millions of independent peasants, from odd shrubs planted in chance corners and brought to market haphazard by thousands of independent dealers operating in different districts."[222] The Maritime Customs report, summarizing the falling percentage of the British market for Chinese tea by the 1880s pointed out, "It must be remembered that tea in China was, as it still is, a sort of agricultural by-product." Indeed, rice and a range of crops continued to be cultivated even in the tea districts most actively involved in the world market.[223]

On the one hand, China's smallholder-dominated agrarian regime was singularly capable of producing impressive volumes of commercial products on a regular basis. On the other hand, neither trade nor demand was sufficient to transform the overall social property system, which was based on peasant possession of the means of production. This meant that the first priority of the peasant household was to protect its subsistence needs and sell only the surplus—if there was any—on the market. Only this explains why, in the early 1930s, even rice from Rangoon, Thailand, and Vietnam was cheaper than locally produced rice in Guangdong.[224] The other actors on the scene, the landlords and merchants, also found it rational to continue established arrangements as long as they were assured incomes from rent, rent deposits, unpaid labor of tenants, and usury through the deployment of their social and economic power. Since the markets functioned through monopsony guilds, there was no competition to force systematic cost-cutting and investment in more efficient machinery over any length of time. The Qing state, in turn, by the end of the nineteenth century had neither the political cohersion nor the concentration of economic clout to accomplish what the Japanese colonial government could do on Taiwan.

CONCLUSION

BY PLACING CHINESE LOCAL HISTORY within a global framework, I have attempted to study long-term economic change and analyze the ways in which the structures of everyday life, foods, and agricultural technologies of rural China were imbricated in international commodity flows, distant economic decisions, and intra-European trade rivalries. A specific tension underlies the approach that I have used; can there be a "China-centered history"[1] even as this history is being shaped in the crucible of world capitalism? I return to this question in the final pages of the conclusion. But first, synthesizing the empirical particularities, I want to draw together the arguments of the various chapters so as to consider their theoretical implications and examine some of the salient debates shaping my interpretations of Qing China.

The Dimensions of Change in Qing China

To iterate briefly the primary dimensions of local society delineated earlier, I have argued that the establishment of Qing hegemony in the seventeenth century coincided with certain notable changes in the structure of Chinese society, namely, the expansion of a small-scale peasant-producer economy comprising the vast majority of the direct producers, including both owner-operators and tenants. Direct producers, who had earlier been bound either by customary or legal status to the land, such as the serf-like *nupu*, through rebellion, uprisings, and support of the state now gained fundamental rights to land, their own labor, and the labor of their families. I have argued that the interests of the Qing state in maintaining a large tax base and preventing rural upheaval not only aided the entrenchment of the smallholder in south China but made it altogether unlikely that the imperial state could accede to the cataclysm that would have resulted from millions of peasants being thrown off the land and stripped of their subsistence rights. While some forms of unfree and bonded labor as well as bonded tenancy continued to exist, the vast majority of direct producers in south China became smallholders with tenacious legal rights to subdivide and inherit their lands, including the right to inherit permanent tenancy rights.

Simultaneously, however, as I have also shown, many of the concessions gained by the direct producers were vitiated by the realignment and regrouping of an elite consisting of gentry-landlords, non-gentry-landlords, and merchants, who now became members of the gentry in larger numbers than ever before. Such elites were able to maintain their access to the surplus through a range of strategies by *concurrently* ensuring a share of the state revenues in the form of salaries and compensation for governmental offices and through their access to institutionalized state power while retaining their individual access to the surplus through rental income from land, income from mercantile activities, and interest payments on loans to peasant producers. Some families clearly withstood the vicissitudes of economic and generational change better than others, but most important, I have argued, there was no *systemic* barrier either to the reproduction of the elites as a class or to the entry of new members to this class. Any potential crisis of reproduction was bypassed by the revitalization of the lineage in the seventeenth century, the establishment of corporate landholdings, the development of local political organizations based on the lineage, and the enhancement of village community rights; these institutions collectively served to ensure a continuation of local elite social power throughout the Qing. At the same time, I suggest, these very institutions also served to defend peasant property from encroachment and peasants from dispossession. Defense of their hard-won rights to land and property necessitated community, village, and lineage alliances—necessities, I argue, that created a symbiotic relationship between the elites and the direct producers and blurred the realities of class stratification. Simultaneously, peasant rights, articulated as settlement rights, rights to collect firewood, draw water, cultivation rights, burial rights, and so on, transmitted in the village community through descent and reiterated through lineage and other similar corporate bodies strengthened these institutions. I propose that ultimately these corporate organizations served to close off a free and unfettered market in land, with fundamental consequences for processes of accumulation, land alienation, and the generalized rise of wage-labor.

The social restructuring of the Qing coincided with a rapid expansion of commercialized agriculture, fostered by the tax demands of the state, now assessed in cash, and the growing world market. This commercialized agriculture was, however, largely based on decentralized, small-scale peasant production. At the same time as the expansion of commercialized agriculture, the peasant household was able to maintain its subsistence sector, perhaps even increase its caloric intake with the availability of foods like sweet potatoes and peanuts introduced from the Americas. As China became more intimately linked to the world market, providing sugar, silk, and tea in ever larger quantities, the role of trade in driving this economic expansion inevitably becomes an important point for discussion. There is much evidence that cash cropping and the market nexus increased social differentiation; some individuals may have become rich peasants and even risen to become managerial landlords.[2] Other peasants, under the imperatives of debt, fragmentation of property through subdivision among agnates, or the higher costs of the fertilizer and labor needed to produce cash crops, may have fallen into the ranks of poor tenants and part-time wage laborers. But, despite this increased social differentiation, the total proportion of the completely landless remained remarkably small. I have shown that most agricultural laborers did not lose possession of, or access to, land and all means of subsistence; production for the cash economy did not shape all social and political relationships. Direct producers could withhold their labor from the market and, at minimum, allocate it first to cultivate their own plots and provide for their household subsistence needs. The persistence of familial and village cooperative arrangements also permitted smallholders to gain access to additional labor and resources without entering the market. This poses a question: Would more trade have produced a systemic pressure toward economic development that led to capitalist transformation? Would the increase in market transactions have acted as a solvent of non-market relations of production? Several scholars of Chinese economic history have argued that this would indeed have been the case.[3]

The Peasant Economy and the Market

The extent to which markets are embedded in the social formation is a subject of considerable and ongoing debate between economists and historians. Few scholars have drawn the opprobrium of neoclassical economists favoring rational-choice theories quite so vehemently as Karl Polanyi.[4] Yet, while there is much that is indeed problematic with Polanyi's historical schema, as Douglass C. North, one of the few economic historians to take Polanyi's work seriously as well as one of his more eloquent critics, writes, "The stubborn fact of the matter is that Polanyi was correct in his major contention that the nineteenth century was a unique era in which markets played a more important role than at any other time in history."[5] And it is this particular dimension of Polanyi's insight that is relevant here:

> The existence of a market is often taken to establish the existence of a market system in the modern sense of price-making markets, and to imply the relevance of the body of economic theory to the analysis of the situation in which the market is found. As a result a modern market is read into the social organizations of many historical and primitive societies where there is no other evidence to support the existence of a system similar to ours except the occurrence of some form of market.[6]

The "modern" or capitalist market is a mechanism which produces prices and, through the function of market prices, regulates the supply of goods in relation to demand. Other than Polanyi's insistence that the contemporary market is a historically specific phenomenon, his interpretation of the modern market is congruent with that of neoclassical economists such as Thomas Rawski, "Economic theory is built around the logical analysis of profit-seeking behavior by large numbers of well-informed, independent individuals in competitive markets governed by legal systems that enforce contracts and ensure the rights of private owners."[7] As Polanyi points out, these "self-regulating" market systems require "independent decision-makers buying and selling and producing for sale with inputs bought on the market, protected by law in their contractual rights, and making their decisions with the objective of a monetary profit or gain. When these conditions and the specific institutions which embody them (such as banks, free wage labor, alienable land) are absent, economic analysis (in the market context) cannot be effective."[8]

It is precisely this problem of transposing the notion of price-making markets on to the precapitalist economy of China that has complicated our understanding of commercial exchange in Ming-Qing China. Ramon Myers, for example, who has contributed extensively to this subject, treats all Chinese markets as if the logic of modern capitalist markets operated:

> These markets [in late Imperial China] were highly competitive, easy to enter and withdraw from, and provided valuable economic information for buyers and sellers alike. Price signals in markets informed farmers about which goods to buy, their value, and what products might be sold at a profit. They also picked up scraps of information about work opportunities. Merchants entered markets with a different attitude: to find suitable goods at prices that could be cheaply purchased and sold elsewhere at a profit.[9]

David Faure, who has likewise written prolifically on the market, also blurs the nexus between social power and economic power in the operation of markets, although he is acutely aware of the social power of the "lords" of the markets. Faure notes:

> In the first place, it must be realized that markets were opened for trade in a manner that is analogous to shops being opened for business. The owners of markets, known sometimes as the 'lords' (*zhu*) of the markets, often owned the land on which the markets were founded. They arranged for the infrastructure that was needed for the market's smooth operation, including standard measures, transport facilities, and agreements with the local yamen. They often commanded advantageous positions in the markets they organized, but as rural entrepreneurs, they also competed among themselves for trade.[10]

Yet, he goes on to conclude, "Moreover it is unwarranted to assume that the sellers of agricultural produce in rural markets were always the weaker parties" and argues that there is little reason to suggest "that rural trade was conducted under virtual monopsonistic conditions." Indeed there was competition; for control of resources and incomes and markets were a primary source of elite and lineage income. But reading "*market* competition," a specific historical phenomenon, into a situation in which markets were evidently controlled by socially powerful lineages and individuals whose efforts to retain monopsonistic controls included intimidation and violence if necessary isolates the reality of economic transactions from the societal context within which these transactions took place. Depending on the formal appearances of a market alone without penetrating "the inner essence and inner structure . . . behind its outer appearance"[11] can camouflage relations of production that are inimical to market forces as understood in the particular sense of capitalist markets. The value of utilizing the market as the sole analytical tool and paradigm[12] with independent and transhistorical explanatory potential is limited by the embeddedness of markets within particular historical social formations.

How "free" were the Qing markets, and how "independent" were the producers involved in buying and selling? In Guangdong and Taiwan, as we have seen, particular dominant lineages and landlords of the locality controlled the local-level market; feuds to control markets and garner market fees were endemic. Clearly, even in some of the most highly commercialized regions of the Chinese empire direct producers could not freely choose in which markets they would buy and sell. Can we write off this evidence simply as "aberrations in modern China"?[13] There was indeed rational choice exercised by the peasants; the choice was to ensure survival, under various forms of extra-economic restraints.

Peasants cultivating cash crops such as sugarcane received advances in cash and kind from merchants prior to the planting and harvesting of the crop; many direct producers did not, and could not, take their crop to a market for sale unless they had access to armed protection. Most grew cash crops to pay rent and taxes while maintaining a direct and non-market access to subsistence needs. While the market for rice was the largest commodity market, the bulk of the rice in circulation was collected as rent payment; most peasants neither ate rice nor purchased it on a regular basis on the market. The lack of price disparities on the major rice markets of China has been cited as evidence for "the free play of the market."[14] Uniformity of prices, however, has been shown to be the result of numerous other factors, such as monetary supplies and state and/or gentry-landlord control. In the early seventeenth century in parts of eastern Europe, for example, the expansion of the grain market by lords brought uniformity in prices but diminished currency circulation in the regions east of the Elbe and intensified the economic isolation of the estates.[15] During the entire first half of the eighteenth century, the movements of wheat prices in Danzig (Gdansk, Poland) and London were very similar.[16] Yet that does not suggest similar social and economic developments were under way in these two regions. The congruence in prices was not the result of the trading activities of the Polish serfs who produced the grain, for the peasant's consumption share of the total volume of grains sold was minimal, but the outcome of the privileged sellers and purchasers, the lords, setting prices. As part of the European market, estate lords expanded grain cultivation, reduced the serfs' subsistence plots, and increased their own share of the surplus, with which they then bought Caribbean sugar, among other luxuries.[17] Similarly, the gentry in Foshan and the landlords of Taiwan determined the price of rice in the eighteenth century; uniformity of prices was possible precisely because the sellers of rice in the markets were landlords,[18] who had non-market access to the peasant surplus and controlled the markets, where they collected dozens of fees in addition to the income from the sale of grains.

The thesis substantiated in this book is that trade and production for exchange within these social parameters were not sufficient to transform the process of production into one in which pressure to innovate, reduce the unit cost of production, and apply available innovations were experienced as a direct objective pressure by each production unit. Trade has been shown to have had divergent outcomes on economic development depending on the social formation. In an agrarian economy based on serf labor, such as that of eastern Europe, the growing demand for grain exports increased the total area of the demesne, but there was a decrease in the yield per unit area. Even when exports accounted for as much as 25–45 percent of the commodities produced, trade did not transform social productive relations.[19] On the contrary, the Baltic trade tended to set in motion a more repressive and ultimately stagnant pattern of overall societal development resting on a class of producers without independent access to the market. In Guangdong and Taiwan, trade and the income from trade enhanced the power of lineages and social elites. At the local level, the merchant-moneylenders who advanced money, raw materials, and even tools to the direct producers did not intervene in the process of production itself. Production was carried out by a multitude of individual peasant households. The merchant's profit did not depend on innovation or reinvestment in improved production techniques, thereby bringing better goods to the market, or goods produced in a shorter time and at a lower cost than his competitors. The merchant's profit was purely the profit of commercial capital made by exploiting the difference between production prices and sale prices. This type of profit-making was common to all levels of trade—from the petty itinerant merchant to the enormously wealthy hong merchants who controlled the export market. The direct producers, the peasant households, remained in charge of organizing the production process, the allocation of labor time to different tasks, and the selection of technologies used for manufacture.

Technology and Society

But the question still remains: Was it a combination of limited trade *and* limited technological development that curtailed the Chinese take-off into sustained economic development? Mark Elvin and Joseph Needham begin their inquires with a similar question: "Why did China not break through to modern economic growth at about the same time as Europe?"[20] "Why did modern science not arise in China?"[21] As A. C. Graham has noted, this question is one "from which Sinologists tend to shrink into their individual compartments, afraid of being caught up in inconclusive generalizations."[22] By asking the question nonetheless, both Needham and Elvin place the Chinese experience in a broad comparative context. Given the overarching tendency of Sinological studies to focus on Chinese exceptionality, any conceptual edifice that encourages a rethinking of fundamental paradigms is laudatory, even if one is not in agreement with all its findings.

Needham and Elvin frame their investigations by analyzing the specificities of Chinese society. Needham, particularly in his earlier writings on the development of modern science and the role of those trained in a cumulative written tradition, argued that "the rise of the merchant class to power, with their slogan of democracy was the indispensable accompaniment and sine qua non of the rise of modern science in the West. But in China the scholar-gentry and their bureaucratic feudal system always effectively prevented the rise to power or seizure of the State by the merchant class, as happened elsewhere."[23] Elvin isolates the role of technological inventions in the Industrial Revolution and proposes that technological stasis, marked by the absence of inventions in China and a paucity of investable surplus, underlay China's "trapped economy."[24]

The premises of Needham's inquiry are quite clear: "Science is a function of the socially acting human mind. Science reveals to us the levels of organization in the universe. But both mind and science are themselves products of the social level, and may be studied like any other phenomenon at the level appropriate to them."[25] Needham's insistence on locating scientific developments within a social matrix arises out of a recognizably Marxist paradigm. This analysis of Needham's closely reflects Marx's views on technology and society: "Technology discloses man's mode of dealing with Nature, the process of production by which he sustains his life, and thereby also lays bare the mode of formation of his social relations, and of the mental conceptions that flow from them."[26] And, despite Needham's focus on China, the genesis of his project was based on his commitment to understanding the rise of modern science as the product of diverse cultural and intellectual contributions.[27] Although the final volumes in the series *Science and Civilisation* will now be completed by others,

Needham's fundamental impulse of locating the historical processes at work in China within a global comparative framework is a legacy that will continue to challenge scholars of the history of technology.

Needham's sociological comments on China are based on the early writings of Karl Wittfogel and on his readings of Marx and Engels on the Asiatic mode of production. Needham used the term "bureaucratic feudalism" as part of a more eclectic formulation than Wittfogel's "Oriental despotism."[28] He also rejected the notion of stagnation associated with the Asiatic mode of production, and was critical of "stages of development" theories. Instead, he proposed that the absence of chattel slavery in China may have been an impetus to the early development of various technologies and labor-saving devices. Many of Needham's formulations regarding the mercantile class and the stifling role of the state bureaucracy are debatable in light of recent research on rural Chinese society.[29] As this book shows, merchants in south China had considerable economic and social power but used it in gentry-like fashion to bolster a range of squeezing mechanisms and extra-economic powers.

There is, however, another dimension to Needham's legacy. Needham's emphasis on Chinese origins and prototypes for myriad technologies and scientific principles arose out of the political context of the 1940s and 1950s when Needham first undertook the project as a means of challenging the marginalization of China; the project then led to a constant privileging of Chinese contributions. This may have had the untoward consequence of bolstering Sinocentric claims to a unique genius[30] rather than promoting a universalist model of the origins of modern science, the initial impetus behind Needham's project.

Elvin's interpretation of the role of technology and science in society gives greater autonomy than Needham's to the intellectual processes that generate invention. For Elvin the intellectual processes are not embedded in the social formation but are co-equal to economic forces in generating technological developments: "We are compelled to conclude that, at least in the case of textiles, the basic obstacle in the way of further technological progress in China after this time was *not* a lack of better scientific knowledge. Rather, it must have lain in a weakening of those economic and intellectual forces which make for invention and innovation."[31] Inherent in Elvin's argument is the formulation that inventions lie at the core of economic growth, particularly the transition to an industrial revolution.

Our understanding of the relationship between technological change and economic transformation can be distorted by this largely erroneous view of the Industrial Revolution. David Landes, in *The Unbound Prometheus,* puts this succinctly: "One of the cherished myths of economic history is the image of a swift and drastic shift from rudimentary hand tools to machines. . . . In fact, as is so often the case with revolutions, the old and the new were not that far apart [in the Industrial Revolution], and the change was slower than usually pictured."[32] Elvin succumbs to the aura surrounding inventions in modern capitalism. In a mature capitalist economy, competition forces a continuous development of new technologies. As a particular technology becomes generalized across the economy, there is a systemic pressure on capitalists to seek new inventions for deployment in the production process so as to increase their productivity and thus their share of the market.[33] Contemporary folklore is particularly rich in tales of inventions, and Elvin's model finds an attractive resonance. But there is a need for caution in superimposing the logic of capitalism on the historical past.

Studies of various types of machinery most commonly associated with the Industrial Revolution make evident that the new technologies were based on concepts developed in the sixteenth century or even earlier. For example, Hargreaves's "spinning jenny" (perfected in 1768) and Arkwright's "water-frame" (developed in 1769), which not only produced finer threads but allowed the application of water and animal power to spinning, were constructed from elements that made up the old spinning wheel. The linking devices which made possible the operation of almost a hundred spindles by a single spinner were also based on mechanisms developed in the sixteenth century. It was their novel application to spinning machinery which revolutionized production.[34] These technological developments in the cotton industry came two or three decades *after* the acceleration in growth rates in the industry. "These inventions did not initiate cotton's explosive expansion. But . . . once they had been made, the rate of expansion could rise to levels that would previously have been quite impossible."[35]

Rather than the machinery involved, it was the entrepreneur's direct supervision of the organization of production that distinguished production under the Industrial Revolution from that of older regimes. As Keith Tribe notes of the Wedgewood factory at Etruria, the innovations were not "some new set of machinery" but rather "a new spatial flow of production." The same held true for the textile factory, where the principal innovation was the inauguration of flow production. The elements of this reorganization were "the creation and disciplining of a skilled labour force; the development of new forms of accounting; the standardization of product quality; the formation . . . of managers to administer the growing complexities of production and sales."[36]

The other fundamental concern that arises with both Needham's and Elvin's approaches is making the European experience the norm against which other societies' historical experiences must be compared. As has been pointed out, a formulation that begins with the negative query of why China did not arrive at the Industrial Revolution can generally only end by demonstrating that China was not following the path of Europe's evolution.[37] Although Needham's work in particular seeks to place the Chinese experience alongside developments in other parts of Asia, epistemological barriers, legacies of area studies, nationalism, and neo-colonial paradigms have slowed efforts to investigate "Asia before Europe"[38] and provide counterpoints to the normative Eurocentric framework. Asian history, however, framed as the history of peoples of a spatial entity, does not exist; there are only the linear histories of modern nation-states anachronistically superimposed on the past. Comparative pre-colonial or even post-colonial Asian histories are yet to be written. If one is to avoid lapsing into some version of an orientalist discourse fetishizing the uniqueness of the "Middle Kingdom," some comparative reference points are necessary; scholarship on Europe has provided that focus of comparison. The questions raised by Needham and Elvin possess the heuristic value of challenging epistemological barriers by forcing us to think farther than national polities.

Beyond questions of technology, however, the theoretical edifice on which Elvin relies for his explanation of economic stasis in late imperial China, "the high-level equilibrium trap," draws heavily on a particular strand of European thought, namely Malthus's model of population growth outstripping resources. Did the potential for transformation in China get derailed by its burgeoning population?

Demography and Social Structures of Production

Population size and its impact on the pattern of Chinese agrarian change have long been subjects of contention. Several scholars, besides Elvin, have assigned demographic growth a central causality in China's historical evolution.[39] Others, particularly Chinese and Japanese scholars working within a Marxist paradigm, have typically sidestepped questions of demographic impact. Their position, broadly defined, has been: "The problem of population and its growth certainly influenced Chinese history, but such influence was not decisive and cannot be used in lieu of class conflicts in the study and interpretations of history."[40] There is an implicit assumption in this formulation that the two dimensions of social relations—demographic and socioeconomic—are separable and do not impinge on each other in shaping the contours of history.[41]

Ho Ping-ti's classic study of Chinese demography provides a long-term perspective on the agricultural and institutional factors affecting the growth of the Chinese population. He has suggested that, "the optimum condition [the point at which 'a population produces maximum economic welfare'] at the technological level of the time" was reached in Qing China between 1750 and 1775, after which it became a negative influence.[42] In many ways Ho Ping-ti's arguments presage Elvin's model of "high-level equilibrium trap" by arguing that population growth absorbed all potential surplus in the Chinese economy, leading to a trapped economy.

Yet, with all the demonstrated interest in questions of demogra-

TABLE 18
Comparative Trends in Population Growth in Europe and China, 1750–1913
(in millions)

Year	Europe	China
1750	120–140	200–250
1800	180–190	295–300
1850	266	410–435
1900	401	385–410
1913	468	430–455

SOURCES: Armengaud, pp. 27–29; Ho Ping-ti, *Studies on the Population of China*, pp. 281–282; Dwight Perkins, *Agricultural Development*, p. 16; Liang Fangzhong, *Zhongguo lidai hukou, tiandi, tianfu tongji.*

phy, it is seldom asked why the estimated doubling of the population of China from approximately 200 million in 1750 to some 400 million in 1850 resulted in slowed growth or a trapped economy, whereas Europe's surging population on the eve of the Industrial Revolution had such a different outcome. The population of Europe, particularly western Europe, also more than doubled between 1750 and 1850. As Table 18 shows, the population of Europe, estimated to be around 120 million in 1750, rose to some 190 million by 1800, increasing to 401 million by 1900. Although there were considerable regional variations even within relatively small areas such as the Netherlands, overall the population of Europe increased 34 percent for the second half of the eighteenth century, 43 percent for the period 1800–1850, and 50 percent for the period 1850–1900.[43] As noted in Table 18, these are comparable to the rates of population growth in China.

The divergent impact of demographic increase in Europe and China underlines the limitations of viewing population trends as a "cause" of either economic stagnation or growth. Demographic increase in an economy where the potential for development of the productive forces is limited by the existing systems of property-relations would undeniably lead to an imbalance between available resources and population size. The relationship of demographic change and the specific structures of production is neither simple nor linear.[44]

A demographic explanation for either growth or stagnation furthermore fits the historical evidence for south China poorly. An intensive pattern of agriculture had developed, even when many areas of Guangdong province were underpopulated in the seventeenth century. As late as the eighteenth century many areas of Guangdong still had potentially arable land awaiting development. This was even more so the case in Taiwan, where the ratio of population to land did not begin to decline until the 1920s, for when sufficient pressure for new lands developed in the Qing, aborigine lands were taken over. The increase in population indeed made possible the opening up of new lands and expanded the output of the land through a regime of intensive agriculture. The initial availability of these lands, made accessible by government tax-waiver initiatives, firmly established the smallholder peasant economy in south China. Once a small-producer rural economy was established, with land and burial rights as the signifiers of membership in a community, it generated, in the context of commercialized agriculture and partible inheritance, a structure of increasing demand for land. Given the vagaries of the labor market, there were pressures to ensure economic reproduction through a demographic strategy of early marriage and, if possible, numerous sons.

It also made sense in this system for landlords to plow back available surplus into the purchase of more land whenever possible, opening up new lands, and creating polders for agriculture. The endemic land-hunger of those operating increasingly small parcels of land ensured greater incomes from rent and rent deposits. On the other hand, there was little incentive for landlords to invest in fixed capital improvements in technology as long as their income could be guaranteed by rents in addition to assorted fees, usury, control of the market, and access to bureaucratic office. The merchant-landlord and the landlord-entrepreneur could readily use their capital to invest in ways that were already familiar, relatively safe, and had established returns.[45]

The inadequacies of the Malthusian model positing the inevitability of crisis predicated on population growth outstripping resources has led to alternative interpretations. Dwight Perkins, developing Ester Boserup's thesis, views the expansion of an intensive regime of agriculture as both made possible by and a response to demographic increase, thus inverting the relationship between demographic growth and economic stagnation or decline.[46] Other scholars, such as Philip Huang, have explored the concept of "involution," a phrase most evocatively applied to peasant society first by Clifford Geertz in his study of "agricultural involution" in Indonesia.

Variations on the Theme of Involution

Geertz used the term "agricultural involution" to describe the intensification of agriculture without subsistence crisis or structural transformation in a small-peasant dominated agrarian economy undergoing rapid population growth. The term "involution" has now become "a standard concept of textbook social science."[47] Reflecting the increased influence of Geertz among contemporary historians, two major recent works on the Chinese peasant economy and agriculture have also employed the term "involution."[48] Both Philip Huang and Francesca Bray employ the term, although in very distinct ways.

Bray's use of the term is closer to Geertz's. Discussing Song and post-Song agricultural and social developments such as the strengthening of the tenants' customary rights, Bray proposes that there was a "social stability of wet-rice systems" and comments that "it is easy to see that such improvements in tenant status as we have just described, together with the considerable degree of social mobility, would tend to reduce friction and antagonism between the landlord and tenant class, acting as a damper on class conflict precisely where changes in agricultural technology and economic development were most pronounced, and reinforcing rather than transforming the relations of production."[49] Her conclusion regarding rice culture acting as a damper on class conflict is problematic. Numerous studies show abundantly the very acute class tensions that existed in rice-growing areas, not only in Guangdong but also in Hunan and Jiangsu.[50] Bray tends to view the social relations of production of small-scale wet-rice cultivation as a purely technical problem which impeded the entrepreneurial spirit:

> Yet even when China's southern-based economy was thriving and expanding, when the country was prosperous and entrepreneurial spirit abounded, the very nature of wet-rice agriculture was such that economic and technological innovation of the type we Westerners associate with 'progress' was virtually impossible. . . . It is clear that the small size of units of production (and of individual fields) suited to efficient wet-rice production is a barrier to economies of scale and thus to technical inventiveness of the type to which we owe the European Agricultural and Industrial Revolutions, that is, a tendency towards mechanization and improved returns to labour.[51]

Bray's argument is not only undermined by the experience of Japan, where rice cultivation empowered the *gōnō*, or rich peasants, and made them allies of the nineteenth-century social revolution, but as has also been amply demonstrated, the breakthrough in English agriculture was not simply a result of "technical inventiveness" but a reflection of the rise of a novel social-property system.[52] In fact, as far as the contents of these new developments and techniques are concerned, they were revolutionary more from a sociological perspective than from a technical one. As one scholar of European agricultural history has pointed out, the onset of the agricultural revolution in Europe "consisted in the accelerated application, in sparsely populated territories, of agricultural techniques that had been gradually developed in regions confronted with the problem of a high-density population."[53] The major facets of this agricultural revolution were the extension and introduction of new crops, the improvement of traditional farm implements (mainly the design of the plow, both in form and in the increased use of iron), and the improvement of arable land through crop rotation and draining, coupled with the increased use of horses for farmwork.[54]

The fundamental transformation in English agriculture occurred with the gradual elimination of fallow land and its replacement by the continuous rotation of crops. The well-known reorganization of landownership that accompanied this change need not be reiterated here.[55]

The mechanical reapers and threshers, the use of non-animal traction for farmwork, and the Industrial Revolution–related mechanization of agriculture were yet to come. These were nineteenth-century developments and mostly originated in the United States, where vast tracts of lands had to be cultivated with a limited labor supply. Bray's focus on mechanization and labor-saving devices as the core of the agricultural revolution in Europe (and by comparison their absence in China) is both historically inaccurate and inverts the causal sequence between the social relations of production and technological change.

Huang's usage of the term "involution" and the concept of "involutionary growth," which he terms "a taxonomic concept," is used to contrast a particular inward-turning type of change, as contrasted with evolutionary change or revolutionary change.[56] Huang uses the term to denote "growth without development." Framing his inquiry within the parameters proposed by A. V. Chayanov, who documented the ways in which "[t]he peasant farm, restrained by its land area, forces up its labor intensity,"[57] Huang has elaborated on the roots of underdevelopment in China. In this sense, Huang's concept of involution distances itself from the notion of techno-economic stasis and yet does not take on Geertz's specific notion of shared poverty and blurred social differentiation.[58]

But problems remain. "Involution" or its modification as "involutionary growth" is a description; neither can suffice to explain how and why this form dominated the Chinese rural economy. Ultimately Huang's model of agricultural commercialization lapses into a demographic explanation: "Agricultural intensification is driven by population increase (Boserup 1965) but at a given level of technology, population pressure will sooner or later lead to diminished return for further labor intensification, or what I, following Clifford Geertz (1963), term involution."[59] As historical demographers have shown, there are different patterns of population growth; David Levine has demonstrated that in Europe in the late eighteenth and nineteenth centuries, population growth occurred not in the countryside but among the proletarianized masses of the urban and periurban areas.[60] In England, after a century of stagnation, population began to increase after the middle of the eighteenth century. This increase has been correlated with a marked change in the percentage of people marrying, the average age of marriage, and fertility rates. Robert Allen suggests that yeoman farmers had delayed marriage and having children until they came into property, resulting in a significant check on fertility; in the late eighteenth and early nineteenth centuries, access to wages in proto-industrial workshops removed these checks on fertility for the landless.[61] Population growth had no effect on the amount of labor available to the agricultural sector and therefore had no implications for labor intensification. On the contrary, the landlord's revolution involved a reduction in labor while pushing output per worker to unparalleled levels in English agriculture.

In China, most of the population growth occurred in the countryside among the landowning peasantry and therefore could have the kind of effect Huang notes. But commercialization of agriculture and agricultural intensification continued not only in Guangdong after depopulation in the seventeenth century but also in the Yangzi Delta after the mid-nineteenth-century depopulation caused by the Taiping Rebellion, where Ho Ping-ti has estimated a population *decline* of more than 19 percent in Zhejiang province, including the Yangzi Delta region, over the period 1850–1953.[62] Without taking into consideration the nature of the social-property relations, it is therefore impossible to generalize causal links between demographic growth and more intensive techniques of cultivation.

The argument developed in this book is that, contra models of agricultural involution, the peasant-producer-dominated economy of south China was the outcome of specific social processes at a historical juncture and represented a particular system of social-property relations. Deviating from the dominant consensus in the field, I am suggesting that the Qing social formation represented a new type of rural society. While the genesis of this society may have lain in the social system of smallholder landownership that partially evolved perhaps as early as the Qin-Han, the casual continuity posited for the last 550 years of imperial China, linking the beginning of the Ming (1368) with the early twentieth century,[63] blurs fundamental changes that occurred during the Qing. It was only during the Qing, and for the first time in imperial China, that the absolute majority of direct producers gained full property rights, including the right to inherit, subdivide, and fragment the land; direct producers were also able to defend their rights to the land and restrict the access of outsiders through their state-sanctioned community organizations. The manorial estates and the ongoing process of enserfment of direct producers, so visible even in the late Ming, were drastically curtailed nationally and eliminated in south China in the Qing. Together, I suggest, these new peasant rights came to constitute the primary barrier between capital and production in the agrarian sector and, in the long-term, set the limits of economic development in the Qing period. As I have shown, the economic arrangements resulting from these social-property relations were incompatible with the requirements of long-term growth and transformation, even with escalating world market demand for the products of south China.

The smallholder economy was able to attain impressive levels of commercialization, produce commodities for export, and support a growing population base through a household-level rationalization of land and labor resources. This took the form mainly of once-for-all changes in technology and periodic switches in cropping patterns; for example, the replacement of rice by the combination of sugarcane, sweet potatoes, and ramie or the combination of sericulture and aquaculture, or the switch to the vertical two-roller cane crusher. Production for subsistence was combined with production for the market in a micro-level specialization on the small unit of production, as opposed to *an expanded and ongoing division* of labor based on specialization within the regional and national economy. Pockets of specialization did not supplant all other crops; raw cotton was imported and sugar was exported, but none of the counties in the Guangdong delta ceased to produce subsistence crops or half a dozen other commercial crops for the same markets. As this agricultural system became entrenched, innovations tended to be those that could be accommodated within the smallholder economy, and innovations usable in a larger scale organization of production were set aside. Ultimately, in Guangdong, the small unit of production was an obstacle to a dynamic response to the world market after the Industrial Revolution had transformed sugar manufacturing in the nineteenth century.

However, this was not the case in Taiwan. Here too, however, the small producer was nominally the owner of productive property. What was the difference?

There were two crucial differences between Guangdong and Taiwan. In Guangdong, under the Qing property structures, the real controller of the immediate process of production was the peasant head of household. The choice of the crop mix and the allocation of family labor-time to farming and to subsidiary occupations such as spinning remained within the control of the head of household; switching to other commercial crops, even temporarily minimizing involvement with the market, remained an option, even if such an option could only be exercised through cutting further into subsistence needs. In Taiwan, under the Japanese, this level of smallholder independence was sharply curtailed and indeed removed over time. Although the Taiwanese peasants who formally owned property carried out the labor process, the real controller of the immediate process of production became the sugar factory owner, the employer who imposed industrial discipline with the help and support of the colonial state machinery. In contrast to Guangdong, in Taiwan the labor of small producers could be harnessed to the needs of industrial capital. Only the formal appearance of property ownership in Guangdong and Taiwan remained the same; the real structures of production were transformed in Taiwan. This was one avenue of capitalist transformation, brutal and ruthless under the aegis of the police and the colonial state. On the mainland, existing social property relations continued to shape the possibilities, but also crucially the constraints, within which economic development could take place in the twentieth century.

By examining the economic trajectory of Chinese history in a broad comparative framework, I have attempted two basic interventions: to go past the artificial dichotomy posed by the juxtaposition of "local" with "global" history, and to reinitiate a dialogue with historians of other parts of the globe concerned with understanding long-term historical change in peasant societies. Such an effort can, I hope, move us beyond the superficial enshrining of difference as a historical category that can so readily fit today's nationalist narratives of East Asian exceptionalism. As I have shown, by the sixteenth century the long journey toward capitalism[64] that had begun in small isolated pockets of western Europe was reshaping concrete material conditions in many parts of the world, including China. In this context the call for writing a "China-centered history" is problematic, and efforts to write such a history can ultimately set "China" apart from the "West" and reinscribe a history of "Middle Kingdom" exceptionalism. Once the disparate economies of Asia were connected to the Americas via the European traders, China, too, was linked to the spatial economy of global capitalism. Self-referential histories, nationalist, and Orientalist historiographies may obscure these connections and cultivate historical amnesia, but quite clearly no country could remain "closed" even if governments sought to impose restrictions, be they *sakoku* in Japan or the "Canton-system" in China; these efforts at autarchy, if they were such, proved malleable and permeable. The introduction of the sweet potato, the flow of Mexican and Peruvian silver into China, and the saga of Japan's successful attempt at "import-substitution" in the eighteenth century in sugar owing to the probable copying in Kii (Wakayama) of a cane crusher developed in the Americas[65] all provide extensive empirical data on the simultaneous unfolding of the New World–meets–Old World drama in both East Asia and Europe. There was no golden moment when time stood still in East Asia while Europe embarked on the road to capitalism.

Yet I have also sought to foreground the local and regional dimensions of this economic trajectory by tracing the webs of social power that shaped daily life. In studies of cross-cultural trade, world systems, and world networks, the local often sits like an abandoned waif at the doorstep of the entrepôt, the company warehouse, and the treaty port. Narratives focussing solely on commodities, trade data, and disembodied mercantile institutions can implicitly erase historical specificity and substitute instead a new transhistorical dichotomy of core and periphery that abrogates local class structures and human agency. I have attempted to show that global trade, and all that it entailed in the form of new crops, technologies, and mercantile opportunities, may affect the rural economy in ways that presage a break with the ancien regime or just as readily help sustain it in its new form. By demonstrating how world trade and the processes of globalization affected local, village-level social and economic life over the long term in south China, I have attempted to put forward a model that, first, interrogates the writing of local histories that privilege contemporary nation-state boundaries to the exclusion of omnipresent global currents and, second, elucidates why global interchange alone could not set in motion the fundamental and systemic social transformation leading to an ongoing process of economic development.

APPENDIX

APPENDIX

WEIGHTS, MEASURES, AND MONEY

Lack of standardization resulted in frequent debates and disputes over weights and measures among traders at Canton, Nagasaki, and Macao. There were also enormous regional differences within China as well as variations in the imperial standard measures during the different dynasties. In the text therefore I have preserved the Chinese terms, and below I have given nineteenth- and twentieth-century equivalents. The figures given below are standard approximate conversions to avoirdupois weight, linear measures, square measures, and currency only to facilitate broad comparisons based on commonly accepted values. Only those weights, measures, and currencies referred to in the text have been entered here.

Weights and Measures of Volume

Chinese Measures of Rice

The term *shi/dan* can indicate both a weight and a measure of capacity. When rice was sold or when it was collected as rent, it was measured by volume or capacity; but there was such great variation in capacity measures that any effort at comparative equivalents are rendered meaningless. Ch'üan and Kraus in their classic study of mid-Qing rice prices therefore opted for a discussion based on the weight of a *shi/dan* of rice. After an exhaustive discussion of a range of sources, they concluded that an imperial *dan* of milled rice weighed between 175 and 195 pounds and settled on 185 pounds as a standard equivalent.[1] I have adopted the same. Adult consumption, during "a reasonably good year" is estimated to have been around 1/100 of a *dan* per day or around 550 pounds per year.[2] In the absence of currency equivalents, I have given the price of 1 *dan* of rice in tables where I have quoted sugar prices or wages in order to give some estimates of the costs of living.

Chinese Measures of Weights and Volumes

Weights and measures varied enormously with the locality. For purposes of simple computation, I have used the following standard ratios of the so-called Customs picul, which was standardized in the nineteenth century by treaty:

16 *liang* (tael) = 1 *jin*
1 *jin* = 1 catty = 1.32 pounds
100 *jin* = 1 Customs picul = 133.3 pounds

The standard subdivisions of measures of volume are:

10 *ge* = 1 *sheng*
10 *sheng* = 1 *dou*
5 *dou* = 1 *hu*
2 *hu* = 10 *dou* = 1 *shi*

Measures of volume have been computed, in terms of twentieth-century units, at:[3]

1 Song *sheng* = 2.4 *shi* : 1.40 pints (dry)
1 Ming *sheng* = 3.9 *shi* : 2.25 pints
1 Qing *sheng* = 3.8 *shi* : 2.19 pints

Chinese Units of Linear Measure

There were major regional differences in linear measurements even in the Qing. One *chi* could vary in practice from 8.6 inches to 27.8 inches, sometimes depending on what was being measured. Even within Guangzhou, a city that had shared jurisdiction between Nanhai and Panyu counties in the Qing, the Nanhai *chi* measured 14.7 inches while the Panyu *chi* measured 14.8 inches.[4] The standard subdivisions of linear measure:

1 *cun* = 1 *chi*
10 *chi* = 1 *zhang*

Seventeenth-century traders measured 1 *zhang* as 141 inches. The official historical variations were:

1 Tang *chi* = 12.24 inches
1 Song *chi* = 12.09 inches
1 Yuan *chi* = 12.09 inches
1 Ming *chi* = 12.24 inches
1 Qing *chi* = 12.60 inches

Chinese Measures of Land

The *jia* was used as a measure of land in Taiwan, and comes from the Dutch *morgen.*

Morohashi Tetsuji in the *Dai kanwa jiten* (Tokyo, 1955–1960), *sub verbo,* gives the *jia* as equivalent to 16 standard *mu,* or 2.3 acres. But in terms of Taiwan's land taxes in the Qing, the rate was calculated at 1 *jia* = 11.3 *mu.* Rather than convert a *jia* to the mainland measure of a *mu,* since a *jia* turns out to be very close to a hectare (1 *jia* = 0.96992 hectares or 10,000 square meters) the standard practice in English-language scholarship on Taiwan is to convert *jia* to hectare. But since the mainland measures are typically converted to acres, for the sake of uniformity I have converted the *jia* to hectare and then converted the hectare figure to acres. The conversion rates used are:

1 *jia* = 1 hectare = 2.47 acres

The "standard *mu*" for the twentieth century is usually computed at 0.1647 acre. The official Qing *mu* was somewhat (8 percent) smaller, being equal to 0.1518 acre though local measurements varied. I have simply used the standard conversion rate of 6 *mu* to an acre for my calculations.

Other Measures of Weight and Volume

1 Japanese *kin* = 1.32 pounds
100 *kin* = 1 customs picul = 133.3 pounds
1 Japanese *koku* of rice = 4.96 bushels
1 U.S. bushel of wheat = 60 pounds

1 U.S. bushel of rice = 45 pounds[5]
1 Dutch *pond* = 1.1 pounds avoirdupois.
1 Portuguese *arroba* = 32 pounds avoirdupois
4 Portuguese *arroba* = 1 *kintal* = 1 Portuguese hundredweight = 130 pounds avoirdupois

Currencies

With some exceptions, as in the Han and Song periods, Chinese governments issued coins only in copper. The currency of account, however, was not a coin but silver by weight in *liang* (1 *liang* = approx. 1 ounce avoirdupois). Although theoretically 10 *liang* of silver were to equal 1 *liang* of gold, gold was not the standard.

Most scholars used the term *tael* as the equivalent for the *liang*. The word *tael* derives from the Indian *tola* (balance scale or weight, as well as a silver coin) and entered Chinese via the trading world of Southeast Asia and the Malay word *tahil*.[6] In terms of foreign trade, according to Peter Mundy, there was a difference of 15 percent in value depending on whether a tael was Spanish silver dollar (regarded as better) or a Japanese silver coin.[7] All silver coins were assayed, weighed, and treated as bullion in China and marked by a "chop" or seal of the Chinese trading house.

Because the tael was the common money of account, for ease of calculation, I have converted all other currencies to the tael at the following exchange rates prior to the Opium War:

1 Chinese *liang* = 1 tael
1000 copper cash (*li*) = 100 conderines = 10 mace. However, between 1644 and 1743, the actual rate of exchange varied at 700–815 cash = 1 *liang*.[8] In 1800 the copper cash to silver exchange ratio technically stood at 1,450–1,650 = 1 *liang*.[9]

Regional Differences

The Canton Tael, at 579.85 grains of silver, was the heaviest mercantile tael in China, although there were about nine different types of taels in circulation in Guangzhou.[10] After the Opium War, the Mexican dollar became the most commonly used silver dollar in south

China. Altogether, by the close of the 19th century, there were some 170 different kinds of taels in circulation in the provinces of China.[11]

In nineteenth-century Taiwan, the Japanese silver yen coin, the Mexican silver dollar, and the "Tamsui dollar" were all in circulation. The Tamsui dollar was valued at 4–5 percent below that of the original silver coin.[12]

Other Currencies

1 Japanese *kan* = 1,000 *mon* or copper coins equal in weight to 2.28 pounds or 100 taels
1 Japanese *momme* = 1 mace
1 Japanese *ryō* = 4.5 *momme*
10 Japanese *momme* = 1 tael
1 Dutch *guilder* = 20 *stuivers*
1590–1636: 3 Dutch *guilders* and 2.5 *stuivers* = 1 tael
1637– 1743: 2 *guilders* and 17 *stuivers* = 1 tael
Spanish *rial of eight* (the silver peso, also known as "rial of plate" or *peso de plata*, was the Spanish coin used as common currency by all traders):
1 Spanish *rial of eight* = 7/10 to 9/10 of 1 tael
Maravedis—a Spanish copper coin and money of account
Pre-Opium War English and American currency:[13]
£1 = 3 taels
£1 = U.S. $ 4.00

REFERENCE MATTER

NOTES

For complete author names, titles, and publication data for works cited here in short form, see the Works Cited, pp. 563–623. For the abbreviations used here, see p. 563.

Introduction

1. *Su Shi shiji* (Beijing: Zhonghua shuju, 1982), juan 24, p. 1269. Poem written in 1074. Wang Zhuo cites the poem as an example of poetic encomia to this remarkable substance. Wang Zhuo, *Tangshuang pu* (preface dated 1142), rpt. in *Congshu jicheng* (Shanghai: Shangwu yinshuguan, 1935–1937), part 2, p. 2. Though this is the standard edition of this work and my citations are to this edition, the *Congshu jicheng* text has some printing errors as pointed out by Shun An, "Baming chaoben *Tangshuang pu*," *Tushu jikan*, n.s. 3:59–62 (1941). Shun An's corrections are based on a Ming manuscript. Other editions consulted include *Meixiu congshu*, 3 *ji*, no. 5 (Shanghai: Shenzhou guoguangshe, 1928–1937), pp. 255–264. The date of the first publication of *Tangshuang pu* is based on the *Meishu congshu* text, as is the reading of the character *tu* (land or soil) given as *shi* (scholar) in the *Congshu jicheng* text.

2. Fernand Braudel, *The Wheels of Commerce*, Sian Reynolds, tr. (New York: Harper and Row, 1982), p. 191. The seemingly organic connection between cane cultivation and plantation culture has become so firmly established in the literature that scholars have even theorized that cane as crop demanded extensive monoculture: for example, Ralph Shlomowitz, "Plantations and Smallholdings: Comparative Perspectives from the World Cotton and Sugarcane Economies, 1865–1939," *Agricultural History* 58:1–16 (1984).

3. Sidney Mintz, *Sweetness and Power* (New York: Viking, 1985), p. xxix and "Production."

4. Imperial Maritime Customs, *Decennial Reports, 1922–1931* Fifth Issue, vol. 2 (Shanghai: Inspectorate General of Customs, 1935), p. 130.

5. Carlo M. Cipolla, *Before the Industrial Revolution* (New York: W. W. Norton, 1976), pp. 3–61; Jan de Vries, *The Economy of Europe in an Age of Crisis, 1600–1750* (Cambridge: Cambridge University Press, 1976), pp. 176–209; Walter Minchinson, "Patterns of Demand 1750–1914" in Carlo M. Cipolla, ed., *The Fontana Economic History of Europe, The Industrial Revolution*, vol. 3 (Harmondsworth: Penguin Books, 1973), pp. 77–186; and William Barber, *A History of Economic Thought* (Harmondsworth: Penguin Books, 1967). A reflection of the continued importance of Adam Smith and his writings on the transformative potential of the market is evident not only in the writings on the economic history of Europe but also among historians of China; e.g., Ramon Myers, *The Chinese Peasant Economy, Agricultural Development in Hopei and Shandong, 1890–1949* (Cambridge: Council on East Asian Studies, Harvard University, 1970); and David Faure, *The Rural Economy of Pre-Liberation China* (Hong Kong: Oxford University Press, 1989).

6. Mark Elvin, in *Pattern of the Chinese Past* (Stanford: Stanford University Press, 1973), argues that a technological standstill contributed to the "high-level equilibrium trap," which then led to economic backwardness.

7. The focus of this study is Guangdong province, particularly the Pearl River Delta, and Taiwan prefecture, later designated a province. Although historically Fujian province and Guangxi province were also considered a part of "Lingnan" or literally "south of the Wuling Range," and hence part of South China, these regions are discussed here only tangentially.

8. Pro-Guomingdang Han nationalist scholarship tended to accept the thesis of stagnation and stasis in the last three centuries while reclaiming a history of dynamic economic growth in the Song and Ming and explaining the stagnation as a result of Manchu conquest: see, for example, Zhou Jinsheng, *Zhongguo jingji shi* (Taipei: Zhongyang tushu chubanshe, 1959).

9. For a detailed analysis of pre–World War II Marxist writings on China on these topics, see Arif Dirlik, *Revolution and History* (Berkeley: University of California Press, 1978), pp. 95–136, 181–225.

10. Nishijima Sadao, *Chūgoku keizai shi kenkyū* (Tokyo: Tōkyō daigaku shuppankai, 1966), pp 805–872. In two very important articles, "Shina shoki mengyō shijō no kōsatsu," *Tōyō gakuhō* 31.2:262–288 (1947), and "Shina shoki mengyō no seiritsu to sono kōzō," *Orientalica* 2:88–141 (1949), Nishijima first explored China's economic development before the impact of Western trade. Nishijima's work was of course part of the larger ongoing debates among Japanese Marxist scholars in the 1930s and 1940s on the question of periodization of Chinese history, as reflected in Suzuki Shun and Nishijima Sadao, eds., *Chūgokushi no jidai kubun* (Tokyo: Tōkyō daigaku shuppankai, 1957).

11. Fujii Hiroshi, "Chūgokushi ni okeru shin to kyū, 'Shokkōtai' no bunseki o meguru shomondai," *Tōyō bunka* 9:21–40 (1952); Imahori Seiji, "Chūgoku ni okeru hōkenteki shōkōgyō no kikō, seisan kankei yori mitaru Naimōko no toshi to nōson," *Tōyō bunka* 3:1–54 (1950); Hirase Minokichi, *Kindai Shina keizaishi* (Tokyo: Chūō kōronsha, 1942); Tanaka Masatoshi, *Chūgoku kindai keizaishi kenkyū josetsu* (Tokyo: Tōkyō daigaku shuppankai, 1973). See also Tanaka Masatoshi's article, "Rural Handicraft in Jiangnan in the Sixteenth and Seventeenth Centuries," Linda Grove, tr., in Linda Grove and Christian Daniels, eds., *State and Society in China* (Tokyo: University of Tokyo Press, 1984), pp. 79–100. Tanaka's essay was first published in 1961.

12. I have translated *ziben zhuyi mengya* as "incipient capitalism" rather than simply "commercialization" as proposed by Frederic Wakeman, *Ming Qing Historical Studies in the People's Republic of China* (Berkeley: Institute of East Asian Studies, 1980), p. 98. As I show in Chapter Five, "commercialization" may not lead to capitalist development, whereas the Chinese scholars, by using the term *ziben zhuyi*, do propose that these were proto-capitalist tendencies.

13. Fu Yiling, *Ming Qing shidai shangren ji shangye ziben* (Beijing: Renmin chubanshe, 1956), and Fu Yiling, *Ming Qing nongcun shehui jingji* (Beijing: Sanlian shudian, 1961); Fu Zhufu and Li Jingneng, *Zhongguo fengjian shehuinei ziben zhuyi yinsu de mengya* (Shanghai: Shanghai renmin chubanshe, 1956); Li Wenzhi, ed., *Zhongguo jindai nongyeshi ziliao* (Beijing: Sanlian shudian, 1957); and also Zhongguo renmin daxue, Zhongguo lishi jiaoyanshi, ed., *Zhongguo ziben zhuyi mengya wenti taolunji*, 2 vols. (Beijing: Sanlian shudian, 1957); Peng Zeyi, *Zhongguo jindai shougongye shi ziliao*, 4 vols. (Beijing: Zhonghua shuju, 1957); Shang Yue, ed., Zhongguo renmin daxue, Qingshi yanjiuso, comp., *Ming Qing shehui jingji xingtai de yanjiu* (Shanghai: Renmin chubanshe, 1957); Nanjing daxue, Lishixi, Zhongguo gudaishi jiaoyanjiushi, ed., *Zhongguo ziben zhuyi mengya wenti taolunji*, 2 vols. (Beijing: Sanlian shudian, 1960); and Zhang Youyi, ed., *Zhongguo nongyeshi ziliao*, 3 vols. (Beijing: Sanlian shudian, 1957). An overview of research trends in economic history in the 1970s in China can be gleaned from Albert Feuerwerker, ed., *Chinese Social and Economic History from the Song to 1900* (Ann Arbor: University of Michigan, Center for Chinese Studies, 1982). For a general discussion of more recent Chinese scholarship on the subject of incipient capitalism, see Philip Huang, *The Peasant Economy and Social Change in North China* (Stanford: Stanford University Press, 1985), pp. 11–23.

14. Fu Yiling, "Ming Qing shidai jieji guanxi de xintansuo," *Zhongguoshi yanjiu* 4:65–74 (1979); Jing Su and Luo Lun, *Qingdai Shandong jingying dizhu di shehui xingzhi* (Shandong: Renmin chubanshe, 1959); Li Wenzhi, Wei Jinyu, and Jing Junjian, eds., *Ming-Qing shidai de nongye ziben zhuyi mengya wenti* (Beijing: Zhong-

guo shehui kexue chubanshe, 1983). Philip Huang, *The Peasant Economy*, p. 12, finds that this volume provides "the richest documentary support and the most sophisticated analytical elaboration to appear since 1949." Regional studies such as Guangdong lishi xuehui, ed., *Ming Qing Guangdong shehui jingji xingtai yanjiu* (Guangzhou: Guangdong renmin chubanshe, 1985); and Ye Xian'en, Li Longqian, Huang Qichen, and Tan Dihua, eds., Ming Qing Guangdong sheng shehui jingji yanjiuhui, comp., *Ming Qing Guangdong shehui jingji yanjiu* (Guangzhou: Guangdong renmin chubanshe, 1987), also explore similar issues.

15. Li Wenzhi, "Ming-Qing shidai Zhongguo nongye ziben zhuyi mengya," in Li Wenzhi, Wei Jinyu, and Jing Junjian, eds., pp. 198–229.

16. *Nupu* is a term that has aroused a fair amount of controversy. Those who seek to differentiate the Chinese experience from that of Eastern Europe prefer to translate the term as "bondservant" rather than "serf." Others would seek to identify the similarity of evolutionary patterns and translate the term as "serf." Mark Elvin, for example, in *Pattern*, pp. 238–245, uses the term "serf," and the gradation of "serfs" as indicated by him goes from "adopted sons" to laborers, the common denominator being bondage to the land where their labor was used. Other scholars, notably Chu Mi, who has written extensively on this issue, prefer the term "bondservant" to "serf": Chu Mi [Wiens], "Lord and Peasant: The Sixteenth to the Eighteenth Centuries," *Modern China* 6.1:3–40 (1980). Fu Yiling uses the term *nupu* in the sense of bonded servants and discusses their uprisings simultaneously with those of servile tenants (*diannong*): Fu Yiling, *Ming Qing nongcun shehui jingji*, pp. 68–153. I have rendered the terms *pu, nupu, nubi, tongpu,* and *jiading* as "serf," although more often in the text I have left the terms in their original. Only the term *nuli* is translated here as "slave."

17. The term "commoner-landlords" is often used in contradistinction to the notion of "gentry-landlords" (e.g., by Li Wenzhi). However, I believe this term is not entirely accurate, for the gentry sans official rank were also commoners, i.e., not hereditary aristocrats. I am using the term "gentry-landlords" to designate those who already held positions in the bureaucracy or had passed the imperial examinations which entitled them to do so, or were immediate relatives of office-holders and enjoyed the tax-exemptions of the office-holder. "Landlord" is used for those who were not office-holders per se but were members of the elite through a combination of their social and economic power.

18. There has been a long debate about whether Chinese peasants were engaged in "class struggle" and exhibiting "class consciousness" when they rebelled against the state and its officials, when they organized against grain hoarding at times of famine, and or when they organized against gentry and landlords. Instead of entering that increasingly sterile polemic, I believe it is perhaps more useful to think of "class" in terms delineated by E. P. Thompson: "Class forma-

tion . . . arises at the intersection of determination and self-activity": Edward P. Thompson, *The Poverty of Theory* (New York: Monthly Review Press, 1978), p. 106. By foregrounding class formation in the process of social struggle and the roles of experience and agency in the production of collective consciousness, we can perhaps hope to move beyond the explanatory limitations imposed by defining "class" only in static and oversimplified economistic terms.

19. Brenner defines this concept in "Social Basis of Economic Development," in John Roemer, ed., *Analytical Marxism* (Cambridge: Cambridge University Press, 1986), p. 26. My general conceptual premises of the argument regarding peasant property relations have been drawn from Robert Brenner's "Agrarian Class Structure and Economic Development in Pre-Industrial Europe," *Past and Present* 90:30–75 (1976); and his "The Agrarian Roots of European Capitalism," *Past and Present* 97:16–113 (1982).

20. G. William Skinner, "Marketing and Social Structure in Rural China," *JAS* 24.1:3–43 (1964), 24.2:195–228 (1965), and 24.3:363–399 (1965).

21. Here I am following the practice suggested by David Landes in defining the terms "industrial revolution" and "Industrial Revolution." The words in lowercase refer to that "complex of technological innovations which by substituting machines for human skill and inanimate power for human and animal force, brings about a shift from handicraft to manufacture and, so doing, gives birth to a modern economy. The words when capitalized denote the development of the above phenomena in the specific historical context of eighteenth century England": David Landes, *The Unbound Prometheus* (Cambridge: Cambridge University Press, 1969), p. 1.

22. William Roseberry, *Anthropologies and Histories: Essays in Culture, History and Political Economy* (New Brunswick: Rutgers University Press, 1989), p. 147. In developing this discussion on anthropology and history, and in trying to use the historically informed village studies of South China conducted by anthropologists, I have drawn on Roseberry's numerous insights from his work on Latin America, particularly those from the section, "Anthropology, History and Modes of Production."

23. Elvin, *Pattern*, p. 315. These standard textbook interpretations of Chinese history have been challenged by many. See, in particular, Nathan Sivin, "Does China's Past Have a Future?" *HJAS* 38.2:449–480 (1978). Ramon Myers, in *The Chinese Economy* (Belmont, Calif.: Wadsworth, 1980), also disagrees with Elvin, but as I point out in the conclusion, his own analysis suffers from an overwhelming optimism in the power of the market and income redistribution via this agency with scant regard for the social and economic power structures that shaped the market.

Chapter 1

1. *Tiangong kaiwu* (preface 1637), Song Yingxing, rpt. in Tao Xiang, comp., *Xiyongxian congshu*, 3 juan, photolithic reproduction (Shanghai: n.p., 1929), juan shang, p. 127. Tao Xiang collated an eighteenth-century Japanese copy of the original Ming edition and the portions of the text reproduced in the Chinese encyclopedia *Gujin tushu jicheng* (1725), Chen Menglei et al., eds. (rpt. Shanghai: Zhonghua shuju, 1934). The Tao edition of the *Tiangong kaiwu* has a supplement and biography of Song Yingxing by Ding Wenjiang. This is the edition used throughout this book with the relevant sections translated by me. *Tiangong kaiwu* has been translated in its entirety by E-tu Zen Sun and Shiou-chuan Sun, *T'ien-kung k'ai-wu: Chinese Technology in the Seventeenth Century* (University Park: Pennsylvania State University Press, 1966). I have benefited much from this earlier translation, though in some instances my punctuation, following Yabuuchi Kiyoshi, ed., *Tenkō kaibutsu no kenkyū* (Tokyo: Kōseisha, 1953), differs from theirs. References to the Sun and Sun translation and their notes are identified by the title *Chinese Technology* in this text; my translations use the title *Tiangong kaiwu*. Other editions consulted in translation include *Tiangong kaiwu zhushi*, Zhong Guangyan, ed. and annot. (Guangzhou: Guangdong renmin chubanshe, 1976); and *Congshu jicheng* (Shanghai: Shangwu yinshuguan, 1935–1937).

2. Mintz, *Sweetness*, p. 15; William Aykroyd, *Sweet Malefactor* (London: Heinemann, 1967), p. 2; Norge W. Jerome, "Taste Experience and the Development of a Dietary Preference for Sweet in Humans," in J. M. Wiffenbach, ed., *Taste and Development: The Genesis of Sweet Preference* (Bethesda, Md.: U.S. Department of Health, Education and Welfare, 1977), pp. 235–248.

3. Om Prakash, *Economy and Food in Ancient India*, part 2 (rpt. Delhi: Bharatiya Vidya Prakashan, 1987), pp. 104, 169–170.

4. Underlining the status value of sugar even at this late date in parts of Europe, the elite in nineteenth-century France went in for elaborate decorative centerpieces for formal dinners that copied classical architectural styles: Stephen Mennell, *All Manners of Food* (New York: Basil Blackwell, 1985), pp. 145–146, for variations in conspicuous sugar consumption.

5. Some economic historians of Europe, such as W. H. Chaloner and W. O. Henderson, point to increasing sugar consumption in the 1840s as "an indication of rising living standards in these years": John Burnett, *Plenty and Want* (London: Thomas Nelson and Sons, 1966), p. 9. Mintz, *Sweetness*, whose arguments are discussed at the end of this chapter, sees the increased consumption of sugar as a more complex issue.

6. S. Cantor and M. Cantor, "Socioeconomic Factors in Fat and Sugar Con-

sumption," in M. Kare and O. Maller, eds., *The Chemical Senses and Nutrition* (New York: Academic Press, 1977), pp. 429–446.

7. *Statistical Yearbook of China, Sample Survey* (Hong Kong: Oxford University Press, 1985), p. 568.

8. United States Department of Agriculture (USDA), Foreign Agricultural Service, *Report on World Sugar Supply and Demand, 1980–1985* (Washington, D.C.: U.S. Government Printing Office, 1977), p. 149.

9. On the use of sugar among the Malaysian Chinese, see Eugene Anderson and Marja Anderson, "Modern China: South," in K. C. Chang, ed., *Food in Chinese Culture* (New Haven: Yale University Press, 1977), p. 353.

10. Mintz, *Sweetness,* chapter 1.

11. Shi Shenghan, *A Preliminary Survey of the Book "Qimin yaoshu," an Agricultural Encyclopedia of the Sixth Century* (Beijing: Kexue chubanshe, 1958), pp. 77–79. Li Qiaoping, *Zhongguo huaxue shi* (Taipei: Taiwan shangwu yinshuguan, 1955), p. 224, has listed the broad range of malt-sugar sweeteners used in the Zhou period.

12. Katō Shigeshi, "Zhongguo de ganzhe yu shatang de qiyuan," Yu Jingrang, tr., *Dalu zazhi* 9.11:337–340 (1954). China does produce beet sugar now, especially in the northern provinces of Inner Mongolia and Heilongjiang, but it was insignificant as a source of sugar till the late 1950s: Dwight Perkins, *Agricultural Development in China, 1368–1968* (Chicago: University of Chicago Press, 1969), pp. 273, 285.

13. Katō Shigeshi, *Shina keizaishi kōshō* (Tokyo: Tōyō bunko, 1953), p. 676. Sugarcane was domesticated in the Pacific, probably in New Guinea. But manufacturing of sugar did not begin there until the nineteenth century. Not all societies which had sugarcane moved to the next step of manufacturing but instead ate the plant as a variety of fruit: Noel Deerr, *The History of Sugar* (London: Chapman and Hall, 1949), vol. 1, pp. 12–15. Routes through which sugarcane may have been introduced from easternmost India to China are discussed in Nagendra Nath Acharya, "Trade Routes and Means of Transport in Ancient India with Special Reference to Assam," in Dineschandra Sircar, ed., *Early Indian Trade and Industry* (Calcutta: University of Calcutta Press, 1972); and Chen Qian, "Chuan, Dian, Mian, Yin, gudao chukao," *Zhongguo shehui kexue* 1:161–180 (1981).

14. J. W. Purseglove, *Tropical Crops* (New York: Halstead Press Division, 1972), vol. 1, p. 219; Kong Qinglai, ed., *Zhiwuxue da cidian* (Shanghai: Shangwu shudian, 1918), p. 318. See also Liang Jiamian, *Zhongguo zhetang shi zheng,* stenciled mimeo. (Guangzhou: Huanan nongxue yuan, 1980).

15. *Nanfang caomu zhuang* (ca. 305), Ji Han, comp., rpt. in *Congshu jicheng*

(Shanghai: Shangwu yinshuguan, 1936), juan shang, p. 3. There is some controversy about the actual date of the work. Some scholars have suggested that it is not a fourth-century work but dates from the Song period, e.g., Ma Tai-loi, "The Authenticity of the *Nan-fang ts'ao mu chuang*," *TP* 64:218–252 (1978); and Dieter Kuhn, *Textile Technology: Spinning and Reeling*, vol. 5, part 9, of Joseph Needham, gen. ed., *Science and Civilisation in China* (Cambridge: Cambridge University Press, 1988), p. 49. However, Needham's own volume in the series, on botany, considers it an authentic work by Ji Han, written in A.D. 304: see Joseph Needham, Lu Gwei-djen, and Huang Hsing-Tsung, *Biology and Biological Technology: Botany*, vol. 6, part 1, of Joseph Needham, gen. ed., *Science and Civilisation in China* (Cambridge: Cambridge University Press, 1986), pp. 541–542. Li Huilin also considers it a work dating to the third and fourth centuries and certainly derived from the original by Ji Han: *Nan-fang ts'ao-mu chuang: A Fourth Century Flora of Southeast Asia* (Hong Kong: Chinese University Press, 1979), p. ix. I am following the conclusions of Needham and Li in this matter.

16. George Watt, *Dictionary of the Economic Products of India* (Calcutta: Office of the Superintendent of Government Printing India, 1893), vol. 6, part 2, p. 66.

17. Chinese descriptions suggest that the cane grown for making sugar was pale green in color with slender stalks and thin but hard outer rinds: *Guangdong xinyu* (preface 1700), Qu Dajun (rpt. Hong Kong: Zhonghua shuju, 1974), juan 27, p. 689; *Nongzheng quanshu* (preface 1628), Xu Guangqi (rpt. Shanghai: Guji qubanshe, 1979), zhong ce, juan 30, p. 815. This description matches those provided by botanists such as in Purseglove, vol. 1, p. 219.

18. *Tangshuang pu*, part 3, p. 2.

19. *Guangdong xinyu*, juan 27, p. 618.

20. Ibid. The *Guangdong xinyu* does not discuss the supposed medical properties that distinguished this variety from other types. While this requires more research, my hypothesis is that the reputation of *kunlunzhe* as *yaozhe* came from its foreign origins, for the description of this cane matches that of cultivars of *Saccharum officinarum*, which in natural hybridization with *Saccharum spontaneum* produced many thick-stemmed cultivars with red and purple culms; these cultivars are common in Southeast Asia: Purseglove, vol. 1, p. 216. As Edward Schafer has pointed out in his discussion of foreign slaves in China, *kunlun* or *kurong* was often used for Southeast Asian people, brought in as slaves in the Tang: Edward Schafer, *Golden Peaches of Samarkand* (Berkeley: University of California Press, 1963), pp. 45–46. Lily Perry, *Medicinal Plants of East and Southeast Asia* (Cambridge: Cambridge University Press, 1980), p. 169, has references to the use of sugarcane in Vietnam, Cambodia, Laos, and the Malay Peninsula for treating wounds, ulcers of the skin, gingivitis, and a range of other ailments. The Chinese may have used the term *yaozhe* for *kunlunzhe* because of this.

21. *Chu ci*, Wang Yi (d. A.D. 158) comp. and annot., rpt. in *Sibu congkan* (Shanghai: Shangwu yinshuguan, 1935), juan 8, p. 40. The information on the circumstances of the poem's composition is based on David Hawkes, *Ch'u Tz'u, The Songs of the South* (Oxford: Oxford University Press, 1959), pp. 101–103. The translation here is that of Hawkes, except for the line "Lightly boiled turtle and roast kid, with cane sauce." In his translation of the line in question, Hawkes reads the word *zhe* as "yam" and so the line reads "Stewed turtle and roast kid served up with yam sauce" (p. 107). However, Dai Guohui, *Chūgoku kansho tōgyō no tenkai* (Tokyo: Asia keizai kenkyūsho, 1967), p. 6, interprets *zhe* as sugarcane. Dai uses Wang Yi's commentary to support his reading of the term. The preface to the oldest collection of the *Chu ci* says the anthology of poems was assembled by Wang Yi, a librarian at the Han court and the present form is attributed to this collection. I am using Dai's interpretation of the term.

22. The character on the bamboo slip is written *tang*, without the rice radical. But the editors of the *Changsha Mawangdui yihao hanmu* materials use Guo Pu's (A.D. 276–324) annotation of the *Fang yan* (comp. 15 B.C.) in the *Er ya* and propose that the character was an earlier form of the term for sugar, which later incorporated the rice radical: Hunan sheng bowuguan and Zhongguo kexueyuan, Kaogu yanjiu suo, ed., *Changsha Mawangdui yihao hanmu* (Beijing: Wenwu chubanshe, 1973), pp. 140, 154. See also Yuan Hanqing, "Wo guo zhitangye de lishi," in Yuan Hanqing, ed., *Zhongguo huaxue shi lunwenji* (Beijing: Sanlian shudian chubanshe, 1956), p. 135.

23. "Ji wen" (ca. 400), Xie Huilian, in *Wen Xuan*, Xiao Tong (ca. 501–531), comp. (rpt. Hong Kong: Shangwu shudian, 1960), juan 67, p. 1310. I am indebted to David Honey for bringing these lines to my attention. See David Honey, "Liturgy or Literature," *Journal of Asian Culture* 5:76–106 (1981).

24. "Ji wen," juan 67, p. 1310.

25. Anderson and Anderson, "Modern China: South," p. 377.

26. *Shuowen jiezi* (ca. 120), Xu Shen, comp. (rpt. Shanghai: Shangwu shudian, 1935), s.v.

27. This is a work extant only in the form of quotations in later texts. The version here is taken from the sixth-century work *Qimin yaoshu* (ca. 535), Jia Sixie, comp.; textual references to the *Qimin yaoshu* are to Shi Shenghan, ed. and annot., *Qimin yaoshu jinshi* (Beijing: Kexue qubanshe, 1957), vol. 4, p. 742. Schafer has suggested that *shimi* was a honey-based sweetener, which is what a literal translation would suggest: Schafer, *Golden Peaches*, p. 153. But as the information from Yang Fu quoted in Jia Sixie indicates, it was clearly a cane-sugar product.

28. Kingdoms such as Funan, located in the southern part of the peninsula, areas now part of Vietnam and Cambodia, had close contacts with ports in the Bay of Bengal by the beginning of the Christian era. It is possible that along

with Brahmin priests, various types of manufacturing technology such as sugar and textile were also imported: A. K. Chakravarti, "Some Aspects of India-China Maritime Trade (A.D. 250–1200)," in *India History Congress Proceedings, 1961* (Calcutta: University of Calcutta, 1963); and his "Early Sino-Indian Maritime Trade and Funan," in D. C. Sircar, ed., *Early Indian Trade and Industry* (Calcutta: University of Calcutta Press, 1972), p. 110. Other routes of possible diffusion include the trade links between Southeast Asia and the Roman world via India: Eric H. Warmington, *The Commerce Between the Roman Empire and India* (Cambridge: Cambridge University Press, 1928). For overland routes between Eastern India and China, see Anthony Christie, "Ta-Ch'in P'o-Lo-Men," *Bulletin of the School of Oriental and African Studies* 20:159–166 (1957).

29. *Sanguo zhi*, Chen Shou (ca. 233–297), comp. (rpt. Beijing: Zhonghua shuju, 1962), juan 48, p. 1154.

30. *Nanfang caomu zhuang*, juan shang, p. 3. Sima Xiangru (179–117 B.C.) was a Han dynasty poet and essayist.

31. Ji Xianlin, who has worked on Chinese transliterations of Sanskrit words, suggests that the term was a phonetic rendering of a type of cane sugar called *suksimira*: Ji Xianlin, "Yizhang youguan Yindu zhitang fa chuanru Zhongguo de Dunhuang canjuan," *Lishi yanjiu* 1:130 (1982).

32. *Sarkara*, the Sanskrit word for granulated sugar after 500 B.C. but meaning gravel or sandy particles earlier in Vedic texts: M. Monier-Williams, *Sanskrit-English Dictionary* (rpt. Delhi: Motilal Banarsidass, 1970), s.v. Shi Shenghan points out that the character for cane sugar was rare in the texts of the period and suggests that this was a Sanskrit borrowing: Shi Shenghan, *Qimin yaoshu jinshi*, vol. 4, p. 744. See also Lallanji Gopal, "Sugar Making in Ancient India," *Journal of the Economic and Social History of the Orient* 7:57–72 (1964). The Sanskrit word is also most likely the basis of the English word "sugar" via the Arabic *shakkar*: *Oxford English Dictionary*, s.v.

33. Gopal, "Sugar Making," p. 63, has suggested that this term may have been used for a variety of concentrated cane-sugar syrup known in India as *phanita*.

34. *Suishu* (ca. 656), Wei Zheng et al., eds. and comps. (rpt. Beijing: Zhonghua shuju, 1975), juan 83.

35. For example, the text in the Pelliot Dunhuang Collection, P3303, dated to ninth–tenth centuries. The discussion of the technology of cane-sugar manufacturing at Dunhuang here, and in Chapters 3 and 4 of this book, is based on this text. Written on the back of a *dharani* or incantation, the text is badly damaged; the writing is poor and has several additions and corrections made on it by clearly a different hand. It is the only known reference to sugar manufacturing at Dunhuang. I am grateful to Mme Kuo Li-ying for arranging for me to

see the microfilm of the original, which is at the Bibliothèque National. A photograph of the fragment, reproduced from Huang Yungwu, ed., *Dunhuang baocang* (Taipei: Xinwenfeng chuban gongsi, 1986), vol., 127, p. 366, was published in Ji Xianlin's article with his corrections. In my translation I have incorporated the readings and corrections proposed by Ji Xianlin of the illegible characters in the fragment.

36. *Qimin yaoshu*, juan 92, p. 742. In the recently published Christian Daniels, *Biology and Biological Technology*, vol. 6, part 3, of Joseph Needham, gen. ed., *Science and Civilisation in China* (Cambridge: Cambridge University Press, 1996), p. 76, Daniels has suggested that Jia Sixie has a recipe for a type of preserved pickled crab made with cane sugar. I think that Daniels is in error, for cane sugar was not generally available in North China and moreover Jia uses the standard character for maltose (*tang* written with a food radical) for this recipe, not the word for cane sugar that he uses elsewhere in the section on "Southern Exotics." The crab *jiang* described by Jia was clearly made using barley or sorghum malt sugar and not cane sugar.

37. Shi Shenghan, *Preliminary Survey*, pp. 77–89.

38. Schafer discusses changes in the Tang diet at considerable length in *Golden Peaches* as well as in "Tang" in K. C. Chang, ed., *Food in Chinese Culture*.

39. The handbook of Hindu priestly rituals, *Purohit Darpan*, reflecting practises from the Gupta period (318–540) recommends sugarcane products for every ritual conceivable: Surendramohan Bhattacharya, *Purohit Darpan*, 1906 (rpt. Calcutta: n.p., 1976), pp. 940–1008.

40. Like Rama, the noble origins of the Sakyamuni's family were traced to the mystical birth of two children in a field of sugarcane (*iksvāku*) who "having been found in a field of sugarcane were called *Iksvāku*": William Rockhill, *The Life of the Buddha and the Early History of His Order* (London: Trubner, 1884), p. 11. The younger of the two children apparently became King Iksvāku, and Gautama the Buddha was born in the 105th generation of this line. Some of these stories parallel contemporary Hindu mythology, so it is hard to tell if the Buddhist versions were elaborating on a Hindu version or vice versa.

41. Schafer, *Golden Peaches*, p. 153.

42. Asvaghosa, *Saundarānanda or Nanda the Fair*, E. H. Johnstone, ed. and tr. (rpt. Delhi: Motilal Banarasidass, 1975); and Deerr, vol. 1, pp. 43–44.

43. Dates of translations of Buddhist texts into Chinese based on Louis Renou and Jean Filliozat, *L'Inde Classique* (Hanoi: Ecole Française d'Extrême Orient, 1953), p. 368.

44. *Tangshuang pu*, part 1, p. 1. The tale is repeated in all Chinese texts discussing the origins of sugar manufacture in China. Wang Zhuo, a native of Sichuan, however, is the first to mention it.

45. The story of a Bodhisattva teaching the people how to make refined sugar is reminiscent of the story of the introduction of tea by Bodhidharma, who apparently fell asleep while meditating. When, in fury he cut off his eyelids and threw them on the ground, tea bushes sprung from them: Lu Yu (d. 804), *The Classic of Tea*, Francis Ross Carpenter, tr. (Boston: Little Brown and Co., 1974). Tea of course enabled later Buddhists to keep awake during meditation. Though tea was used as a beverage in Sichuan as early as the Han period (Yu Ying-shih, "Han," in K. C. Chang, ed., *Food in Chinese Culture*, p. 70), as in the case of sugar, the use of tea in Buddhist monasteries in larger quantities than before validated the legend.

46. Paul Unschuld, *Medicine in China* (Berkeley: University of California Press, 1985), pp. 137–153. The influence of Indic systems on Chinese pharmacology are not included in this discussion by Unschuld, and he is emphatic in pointing out the limited influence of Buddhism on the medicotheoretical premises of Chinese medicine; see, for example, his discussion of Sun Simo, pp. 148–153. But Unschuld inexplicably leaves out the syncretic nature of Sun's philosophy. Sun, though known primarily as a Daoist alchemist and for his writings on medicine, philosophy, and the arts, has also been portrayed as an important Buddhist layman in some traditions: Nathan Sivin, *Chinese Alchemy: Preliminary Studies* (Cambridge: Harvard University Press, 1968), pp. 132, 136–140.

47. Prabodh C. Bagchi, *India and China: A Thousand Years of Cultural Relations* (Bombay: Hind Kitabs, 1950), pp. 171–173. Bagchi notes that one of the texts translated was called the *Zhechan bingbi yaofa*, but I was not able to find the Chinese text.

48. The Codes (*Vinaya*) of the Sarvastivadin school was translated by the monk Kumarajiva in Chang'an in A.D. 401. Several other *Vinaya* texts were also brought back from India by Fa Xian (Fâ-Hien): Kenneth Chen, *Buddhism in China* (Princeton: Princeton University Press, 1964), pp. 91–92. The *Vinaya* codes determine and regulate all aspects of monastic life.

49. Himanshu Ray, *The Winds of Change: Buddhism and the Maritime Links of Early South Asia* (Delhi: Oxford University Press, 1994), p. 129.

50. *Gaoseng zhuan, Taishō Tripitaka, Taishō shinshū Daizōkyō*, Takakusu Jun'ichirō et al., eds. (Tokyo: Taishō issaikyō kankōkai, 1922–1933), vol. 50: ce 2066, juan shang, pp. 2, 4. The monks sending medicinal herbs included Xuan Zhao from Zhejiang and Sengjia Bamo, a Sogdian who lived and worked in China.

51. Paul Demiéville, Jun'ichirō Takakusu, et al., eds., *Hōbōgirin* (Tokyo: Maison Franco-Japonaise, 1931), s.v. "Byō"; Edwin O. Reischauer, *Ennin's Diary* (New York: Ronald Press, 1955), p. 221.

52. Latika Lahiri, *Chinese Monks in India* (New Delhi: Motilal Banarsidass, 1986), pp. 44, 45–46, 68.

53. A dark brown semi-crystallized sugar, sold pressed together in the shape of a ball or *gula* from the Indo-European root *gleu* meaning to make into a ball: T. W. Rhys Davids and W. Stede, *Pali-English Dictionary* (rpt. New Delhi: Oriental Books Reprint Corp., 1975), s.v. Manufactured still today in India, the flatter versions of *gula/guda* look remarkably like chunks of stone and could well have been the source of the Chinese term "stone-honey."

54. *Susruta Samhitā*, Susruta (ca. 300–400), comp. (rpt. K. L. Bhishagaratna, tr., Calcutta: private printing, 1907–1916), chapter 45, pp. 453–454. For discussion of early Indian medicine, see R. C. Majumdar, "Medicine," in D. M. Bose et al., eds., *A Concise History of Science in India* (New Delhi: Indian National Science Academy, 1971), p. 223.

55. *Mingyi bielu* (comp. 510), Tao Hongjing, rpt. in *Congshu jicheng* (Shanghai: Shangwu yinshuguan, 1937), juan 17, p. 22. The *Mingyi bielu* is usually ascribed the date of 510, and attributed to Tao Hongjing. It is extant only in later quotations in the pharmaceutical natural histories and is thought to include commentaries by Tao Hongjing on the *Shennong bencao*, a late first- or second-century work, and two other third-century pharmaceutical texts: see Needham, Lu, and Huang, pp. 248–249.

56. *Xinxiu bencao* (comp. 650–659), Su Gong (Su Jing), Li Ji et al. (rpt. Shanghai: Shanghai hengsheng chubanshe, 1959), pp. 252–253.

57. *Bencao gangmu* (preface 1596), Li Shizhen (rpt. Beijing: Hongbaoji lithograph of *Siku quanshu*, 1885), juan 33, pp. 13a–17b. Li Shizhen also gives a comprehensive list of various texts which refer to uses of cane sugar, and none of these uses predates the *Xinxiu bencao*.

58. Seventh-century Buddhist Pali-Chinese dictionaries giving equivalents for prescriptions, for example, list cane sugar next to embilic and chebulic myrobalans: Prabodh C. Bagchi, *Deux Lexiques Sanskrit-Chinois* (Paris: Librarie Orientalist Paul Geuthner, 1929), pp. 90, 45b. Other uses of sugar and myrobalans can be found in I-Tsing, *A Record of the Buddhist Kingdom*, Junichirō Takakusu, tr. (Oxford: Clarendon Press, 1876), pp. 126, 140. Extant Tibetan texts reflecting Buddhist medical practices and prescriptions from the fourth through the eighth centuries, such as the *rGyud-bzhi* (bshad-rgud), also include many such uses of cane sugar in their section on prescriptions: Rechung Rinpoche, ed. and tr., *Tibetan Medicine* (Berkeley: University of California Press, 1976), pp. 75–77, 79–80.

59. Schafer, "Tang," pp. 96–97.

60. Unschuld, p. 319. Though one of the versions of the *sutra* is easily lo-

cated, Unschuld did not specify the version used; hence it was not possible to track down the original.

61. Ibid. Unschuld does not provide *juan* or page references or edition information on the texts translated, nor are the characters for *ts'ao-chien-lo* (*caojian le*) fruit given in the glossary. Hu Shiu-ying, *An Enumeration of Chinese Materia Medica* (Hong Kong: Chinese University Press, 1980), does not mention the item in her comprehensive Chinese materia medica. I am therefore unable to identify the particular fruit.

62. *Bencao gangmu*, juan 33, pp. 14a, 16a. See also Needham, Lu, and Huang, pp. 308–312.

63. *Gula*, Pali for the Sanskrit *guda*: C. S. Upasak, *Dictionary of Early Buddhist Monastic Terms* (Varanasi: Bharati Prakashan, 1975), p. 83; Gustav Roth, *Viksuni Vinaya* (Patna: K. P. Jayaswal Research Institute, 1970), pp. i–iii. The *Vinaya Pitaka*, dated to the third century B.C. by S. N. Sen, "A Survey of Source Materials," in D. M. Bose et al., eds., *A Concise History of Science in India* (New Delhi: Indian National Science Academy, 1971), p. 39, was one of the most fundamental texts of the Pali canon. It was used for the regulation of monastic life in India and then in China: Kenneth Chen, pp. 91–92.

64. Roth, pp. 40, 81, 294; Upasak, p. 168. *Bhaisajyavastu* (ca. 400–500), rpt. in Nalinaksha Dutta, ed., *Gilgit Manuscripts* (Srinagar: n.p., 1941), vol. 3, p. iii. The Pātimokkha gives a list of the transgressions, as laid out by the *Vinaya*, the penal consequences, and appropriate atonements.

65. I-Tsing noted in the section on "Rules about the Reception at the *upavastha*" that clarified butter and sugar were served in India. The *upavastha* was a day of meditation and confession on which monks were to maintain a fast and then ceremonially terminate the fast. Celebrated on the first day and the fifteenth of every lunar month, monasteries and their patrons took turns providing for these feasts: I-Tsing, p. 40.

66. Aquinas cited in Mintz, *Sweetness*, p. 99. See also Edmund O. von Lippmann, *Geschichte des Zuckers* (Berlin: Julius Springer, 1929), p. 368.

67. Kenneth Chen, pp. 278–279. The distribution of sugared water called *charnamrit*, or "blessed-feet nectar," at the end of Hindu worship is so similar to the ceremony distributing *yu Foshui* that it is possible that this Buddhist ritual was an adaptation of existing Hindu practice.

68. Kenneth Chen, p. 279.

69. The "entire population" of the city turning out for the procession would have meant more than a million people, according to Yi-fu Tuan, *The World's Landscapes* (Chicago: University of Chicago Press, 1969), p. 105. Tuan's figures are accepted as reliable by G. William Skinner, ed., *The City in Late Imperial China* (Stanford: Stanford University Press, 1977), p. 30.

70. Denis Twitchett, "Monastic Estates in Tang China," *Asia Major*, n.s. 5.2:141–142 (1956).

71. *Dongjing menghua lu* (preface 1150), Meng Yuanlao (rpt. Beijing: Zhonghua shuju, 1959), p. 47. The population of Kaifeng on the eve of the Jurchen invasion was around 850,000 and that of Hangzhou just before the Mongol invasion 1.2 million: Skinner, ed., *The City*, p. 30.

72. *Xinxiu bencao*, p. 253; *Jiu Tang shu*, Liu Xu (887–946) et al. (rpt. Beijing: Zhonghua shuju, 1975), juan 198, p. 5312; *Xin Tang shu*, Ouyang Xiu (1007–1072) et al., eds. (rpt., Beijing: Zhonghua shuju, 1975), juan 221, pp. 6239, 6262.

73. *Xin Tang shu*, juan 221, p. 6239. See also Paul Pelliot, "Deux Itinéraires de Chine en Inde a la fin du VIIIe Siècle," *Bulletin de l'Ecole Française d'Extrême Orient* 4:131–413 (1904).

74. There are two possible readings of the location. Beal identifies it as Bactria and notes there were twenty monasteries here and 100 *deva* temples, and apparently "a thousand laymen and priests dwelt here during the rainy season" at the height of its prosperity: Samuel Beal, ed. and tr., *Si-yu-ki: Buddhist Records of the Western World* (London: Trübner & Co., 1884), p. 222. Thomas Watters, *On Yuan Chwang's Travels in India, 629–645 A.D.* (rpt. New York: AMS Press, 1971), p. 103, identifies it with Tokhara, called Tuluoho by Xuan Zang. Major trade routes between China and India via central Asia and from China to the west are discussed in L. Carrington Goodrich, "Trade Routes to China," in J. Labatut and H. J. Lane, eds., *Highways in Our National Life* (Princeton: Princeton University Press, 1950).

75. *Xu gaoseng zhuan*, vol. 50, ce 2060, juan 4, p. 456. Ji Xianlin, pp. 124–136.

76. *Xin Tang shu*, juan 41, p. 1060.

77. *Tangshuang pu*, part 3, p. 3. The different places sending up sugarcane products to the Tang court are mentioned in the *Xin Tang shu*, juan 41 and juan 42, pp. 1051, 1059, 1060, 1063, 1069, 1079, 1081, 1088, 1089.

78. It may be surprising to find cane being cultivated in regions as far north as Dunhuang. Ji Xianlin considers this a puzzle. As Denis Twitchett, "The Monasteries and China's Economy in Medieval Times," *Bulletin of the School of Oriental and African Studies* 19.3:526–549 (1957), has pointed out, Dunhuang was in a well-irrigated oasis, and the climate may have been less arid as well. The other possible explanation is that the cane cultivated there and at Skardo was not the common tropical variety of cane *S. sinense* but the variety *Saccharum barberi*, suited to subtropical and temperate climates, that is known to have been cultivated in parts of China: Purseglove, vol. 1, p. 218.

79. Fa Xian, *A Record of Buddhistic Kingdom*, James Legge, tr. and annot., 1886 (rpt. New York: Paragon Book Reprint Corp., 1965), pp. 7, 24.

80. Twitchett, "The Monasteries," p. 533. Jacques Gernet, *Les Aspects Economiques du Bouddhisme* (Saigon: Ecole Française d'Extrême-Orient, 1956), pp. 138–149. Neither Gernet nor Twitchett, as I have discussed in my dissertation, however, comments on sugar manufacturing in the Dunhuang monasteries.

81. Schafer, *Golden Peaches*, pp. 14–22.

82. Andrew M. Watson, "The Arab Agricultural Revolution and Its Diffusion, 700–1100," *The Journal of Economic History* 34.1:8–35 (1974).

83. Mintz, *Sweetness*, pp. 93–96; al Baghdadi, *Kitab al-Tabikh*, Arthur J. Arberry, tr., as, "A Baghdad Cookery Book," *Islamic Culture* 13.1–2: 21–47, 189–214 (1939); Ahmad Y. al-Hassan and Donald R. Hill, *Islamic Technology* (Cambridge: Cambridge University Press, 1986), pp. 220–224.

84. Jitsuzo Kuwabara, "On Pu Shou-keng, a Man of the Western Regions," *Memoirs of the Research Department of the Tōyō Bunko* 2:37 (1928).

85. Shi Shenghan, *A Preliminary Survey*, pp. 83–85.

86. *Xinxiu bencao*, p. 253.

87. Schafer, "Tang," pp. 108–109.

88. *Rongzhai suibi*, Hong Mai (ca. 1162–1202), rpt. in *Congshu jicheng* (Shanghai: Shangwu yinshuguan, 1936), juan 2, p. 19.

89. *Meng liang lu* (1275), Wu Zimu (rpt. Taipei: Xuesheng shuju, 1966), pp. 242–243.

90. Françoise Sabban, "Sucre candi et confiseries de Quinsai: l'essor de sucre de canne dans la Chine des Song (X^{e}–XIIIe siècle)," *Journal d'Agriculture Traditionelle et de Botanique Appliquée* 35:205 (1988).

91. Ibid.

92. *Tangshuang pu*, part 6, p. 5.

93. *Dongjing menghua lu*, juan 2, p. 75. *Tangshuang pu*, part 6, p. 5.

94. *Meng liang lu*, p. 266; Shinoda Osamu, *Chūgoku shokumotsu shi* (Tokyo: Shibata Shoten, 1974), pp. 161–162.

95. *Gujin tushu jicheng*, juan 301, p. 11.

96. *Tangshuang pu*, part 6, p. 5.

97. Shiba Yoshinobu, *Sōdai shōgyōshi kenkyū* (Tokyo: Kazama Shobō, 1968), p. 216.

98. Katō Shigeshi, *Shina keizaishi kōshō*, vol. 2, pp. 676–687.

99. Shiba Yoshinobu, *Sōdai*, p. 216; Sudō Yoshiyuki, *Chūgoku tochi seidoshi kenkyū* (Tokyo: Tōkyō daigaku shuppankai, 1954), p. 670; Elvin, *Pattern*, p. 129.

100. Shiba Yoshinobu, *Sōdai*, p. 216.

101. Ibid., pp. 343–368.

102. Shiba Yoshinobu, "Commercialization of Farm Products in the Sung Period," *Acta Asiatica* 19:77–96 (1970).

103. Ibid., pp. 329–334; Umehara Kaoru, "Sōdai chihō shōtoshi no ichimen," *Shirin* 41.6: 42 (1958).

104. Kenneth Chen, p. 401. The size of the *sangha* seems to have increased since the Tang.

105. *Su Shi shiji*, juan 24, p. 1269.

106. *Tangshuang pu*, part 2, p. 2.

107. Lu Yu, *Ru Shu ji* (1170), Chang Chun-shu and Joan Smythe, trs. and annots., *South China in the Twelfth Century* (Hong Kong: Chinese University Press, 1977).

108. *Meng liang lu*, p. 270; Shiba Yoshinobu, *Sōdai*, p. 476.

109. Shiba Yoshinobu, *Sōdai*, p. 468; Michael Freeman, "Sung," in K. C. Chang, ed., *Food in Chinese Culture*, p. 174.

110. *Tangshuang pu*, part 6; p. 5. As Richard von Glahn points out, local magnates in Sichuan controlled the trade in various lucrative products, such as the wine monopoly and the rice trade: Richard von Glahn, *The Country of Streams and Grottoes* (Cambridge: Council on East Asian Studies, Harvard University, 1987), pp. 65–66, and 201.

111. Shinoda Osamu, *Chūgoku shokumotsu shi*, pp. 190–195; Frederick Mote, "Yuan and Ming," in K. C. Chang, ed., *Food in Chinese Culture*, pp. 205–207.

112. John de Cora, "Notices," in Henry Yule and Henri Cordier, eds. and trs., *Cathay and the Way Thither, Being a Collection of Medieval Notices of China* (London: Haklyut Society, 1916), vol. 3, p. 99. See also Juvaini Atā Malik al-Din, *The History of the World Conqueror*, John A. Boyle, tr. (Manchester: Manchester University Press, 1958).

113. Karl Wittfogel and Feng Chia-sheng, *The History of Chinese Society, Liao* (Philadelphia: American Philosophical Society, 1949), pp. 170, 176. Some of the Jurchen recipes for sweetmeats and pastries such as "Persimmon Pastry" and "Chestnut Pastry," translated by Herbert Franke and reproduced in Eugene Anderson, *The Food of China* (New Haven: Yale University Press, 1988), pp. 223–225, also use honey as the sweetener.

114. Sergei V. Kiselev, *Derevnii Mongolskii goroda* (Moscow: Akademia nauk SSSR, 1965), pp. 135–167; Sucheta Mazumdar, "Qaraqorum: The Capital of the Mongols," M.A. field paper, 1977.

115. Sugar combined with almonds, rice, and scented waters was used by the elites of the Arab world to manufacture elaborate sculptures. A Persian visitor to the court of the sultan in Egypt in 1040 noted that 73,000 kilograms (161,260 pounds) of sugar were used for the feast of Ramadan to sculpt a tree and other elaborate displays which were eaten at the end of the feast: Mintz, *Sweetness*, p. 88.

116. Marco Polo, *The Description of the World*, A. C. Moule and P. Pelliot, eds. and trs. (London: George Routledge and Sons, 1938), vol. 1, p. 347. The exact location of this city seems to have been a matter of some debate between Henry Yule and Paul Pelliot: see Marco Polo, *The Book of Ser Marco Polo*, Henry Yule, tr. and annot., published 1871, 3rd ed. rev. by Henri Cordier (London: John Murray, 1903), p. 182; and Paul Pelliot, *Notes on Marco Polo* (Paris: Imprimerie National, 1959), vol. 2, p. 875. But both scholars agree that it was a city in Fujian.

117. Polo, *The Description*, vol. 1, p. 347. "Babilonie" is identified as "Egypt" by Pelliot, *Notes*, vol. 1, p. 61, as well as by Noel Deerr, vol. 1, p. 36. The fortress south of Cairo called Babloun is apparently the origin of this name for Egypt.

118. Ibn Battūta (d. 1377), "Travels in Asia and Africa," in Henry Yule and Henri Cordier, eds. and trs., *Cathay and the Way Thither*, vol 4, p. 108. Recent research suggests that Ibn Battūta may not have visited Bengal or China, but got his information from a jurist named Sa'īd from Mogadishu who had: *The Travels of Ibn Battūta, A.D. 1325–1354*, H. A. R. Gibb and C. F. Beckingham, trs. (London: Hakluyt Society, 1994), vol. 4., p. 809.

119. *Nongsang yishi cuoyao* (ca. 1314), Lu Mingshan, rpt. in *Congshu jicheng* (Shanghai: Shangwu yinshuguan, 1936); *Nongshu* (comp. 1313), Wang Zhen (rpt. Beijing: Zhonghua shuju, 1975).

120. *Yinshan zhengyao* (1330), Hu Sihui (Hoshoi), rpt. in *Wan you wenku* (Shanghai: Shangwu yinshuguan, 1935). The ethnic identity of the author is not certain. The *Siku quanshu zongmu tiyao* adopts a different transliteration of his name, indicating that he was either Mongol or of non-Han origin: *Siku quanshu zongmu tiyao* (comp. 1782), Ji Yun (rpt. Shanghai: Shangwu yinshuguan, 1933), juan 22. Joseph Needham and Lu Gwei-djen, who have studied this work in detail as an example of iatro-dietetics, write of Hu Sihui as if he was Han Chinese: Lu Gwei-djen and Joseph Needham, "A Contribution to Chinese Dietetics," *ISIS* 42:13–20 (1951). David Farquhar, in a personal communication, suggested that he was certain that the author of the *Yinshan zhengyao* was Mongol, as does L. Carrington Goodrich, "Brief Communications," *Journal of the American Oriental Society* 60:258–260 (1940).

121. *Yinshan zhengyao*, juan 2, pp. 48, 49, 56.

122. Shinoda Osamu, *Chūgoku shokumotsu*, p. 196; Mote, p. 235.

123. John de Cora, p. 96.

124. Probably written by Huang Zongli (1301); preserved in Ming edition edited by Tian Rucheng (1560); reproduced partially in Shinoda Osamu, *Chūgoku shokumotsu no kenkyū*, p. 201. I was unable to see this rare text in its entirety.

125. Shinoda Osamu, "Mindai no shoku seikatsu," in Yabuuchi Kiyoshi, ed., *Tenkō kaibutsu no kenkyū*, pp. 74–92.

126. In contemporary Europe, consumption of dairy products and meat was generally higher, with copious amounts of meat being eaten by the upper classes. Chaucer's *Canterbury Tales* (ca. 1386) and Langland's *Piers The Ploughman* (ca. 1390) are frequently quoted to describe the fare of the poor in medieval England. This scene, of Piers Ploughman and the peasants trying to appease Hunger, gives an idea of the foods generally available and provides a comparison with that of China:

> 'I haven't a penny left,' said Piers, 'so I can't buy you pullets or geese or pigs. All I've got is a couple of fresh cheeses, a little curds and cream, an oat-cake, and two loaves of beans and bran which I baked for my children. Upon my soul, I haven't a scrap of bacon, and I haven't a cook to fry you steak and onions. But I've some parsley and shallots and plenty of cabbages, and a cow and a calf, and a mare to cart my dung, till the drought is over. And with these few things we must live till Lammas time, when I hope to reap a harvest in my fields. Then I can spread you a feast, as I'd really like to.' Then all the poor folk came with peascods, and brought beans and baked apples by the lapful, and spring onions and chervils and hundreds of ripe cherries, and offered these gifts to Piers, to satisfy Hunger.
>
> Hunger soon gobbled it all up and asked for more. So the poor folk were afraid and quickly brought up supplies of green leeks and peas, and would gladly have poisoned him.

William Langland, *Piers the Ploughman*, J. F. Goodridge, tr. (Harmondsworth: Penguin Books, 1959), p. 89. For further discussion of food in medieval Europe, see Mennell, pp. 40–61.

127. Shinoda Osamu, *Chūgoku shokumotsu*, pp. 236–237. Mote also includes a long discussion of Jia Ming and his text in the section on 'Food and Hygiene' in his essay on Yuan and Ming food and culture: Mote, pp. 227–234.

128. Mote, p. 216.

129. Ibid., p. 254 n. 11.

130. Ibid., pp. 216–217.

131. *Wan shu zaji* (1593), Shen Bang (rpt. Beijing: Xinhua shuju, 1961), pp. 108–114. The amounts given in the text are the levies to be met by Wanping county, the other half being met by Daxing county.

132. He Liangjun, *Siyouzhai congshuo*, cited in Kwan-wai So, *Japanese Piracy in Ming China during the 16th Century* (East Lansing: Michigan State University Press, 1975), p. 131.

133. *Da Ming huidian, Wanli huidian* (1587) (facsimile rpt. Taipei: Dongnan shubao she, 1963), juan 114, p. 1673.

134. Incredible as it seems, all of this food was provided for the 211 people who ate at the feast; the total number of dignitaries invited equals the number of *xi*. The guests and the feasts prepared for them were ranked "upper grade," "up-

per middle grade," and "lower middle grade," and the quantities of each ingredient to be used at each level were specified down to the amounts of soy sauce and vinegar: *Wan shu zaji*, pp. 136–138.

135. Robert Hartwell, "Demographic, Political, and Social Transformations of China, 750–1550," *HJAS* 42.2:366 (1982) p. 366; Gilbert Rozman, *Urban Networks in Ch'ing China and Tokugawa Japan* (Princeton: Princeton University Press, 1973), p. 108; Shiba Yoshinobu graphically demonstrates this in his study "Ningpo and Its Hinterland," in G. William Skinner, ed., *The City*, pp. 401–403.

136. Tsing Yuan, "Urban Riots and Disturbances," in Jonathan Spence and John Wills, eds., *From Ming to Ch'ing* (New Haven: Yale University Press, 1979), p. 283; James W. Tong, *Disorder under Heaven* (Stanford: Stanford University Press, 1991), pp. 148–151. However, I do not agree with Tong's interpretation of these urban populations as "bourgeoisie" and "proletariat," for most, if not all, of the artisans in these imperial kilns and Songjiang silk workshops were bonded laborers.

137. Huang Peijing, "Guanyu Mingdai guonei shichang wenti de kaocha," in Shang Yue et al., eds., *Ming Qing shehui jingji xingtai de yanjiu* (Shanghai: Renmin chubanshe, 1957), pp. 210–213; Skinner, *The City*, p. 29. See also Katō Shigeshi, "Shindai ni okeru sonchin no teiki ichi," *Tōyō Gakuhō* 23.2:1–52 (1936).

138. Li Ding, "Li Changqing ji," excerpt in Xie Guozhen, ed. and comp., *Mingdai shehui jingji shiliao xuanbian* (Fuzhou: Renmin chubanshe, 1980), zhong ce, p. 88. I have simplified the translation here because the original gives the archaic Zhou names of the provinces—many of which covered more than one provincial area in the Ming and Qing—making it awkward in translation to say, for example, "Western Hebei and Northern Shanxi" for "Zhao," etc. The Northern regions named are Yan, Zhao, Qin, Jin, Qi, Liang, Jiang and Huai; the Southern regions named are Man Hai, Min Guang, Yu Zhang, Chu, and Ou Yue. The extent to which the expansion of the market in the late Ming affected elite food consumption can be illustrated by analyzing the various types of foods eaten in the novel *Jin ping mei*. With its emphasis on sensuality the novel provides vivid descriptions of varieties and tastes of foods. While the rich detail includes many a scene in which either cakes (*bing*) or *dianxin* are eaten, there is unfortunately no extended discussion of sugar-based foods. I have, however, only read the standard Egerton translation, *The Golden Lotus*, which as Mote points out is based on the shorter Chongzhen (1628–1644) era version and has fewer details regarding food than the Wanli text: p. 222.

139. *Min bu shu* (1580), Wang Shimao, rpt. in *Congshu jicheng* (Shanghai: Shangwu yinshuguan, 1936), p. 12.

140. Ye Xian'en, ed., *Guangdong hangyun shi* (*gudai bufen*) (Beijing: Renmin jiaotong chubanshe, 1989). See also Evelyn Sakakida Rawski, *Agricultural Change*

and the Peasant Economy of South China (Cambridge: Harvard University Press, 1972), pp. 94–100.

141. A discussion of where and how the "national" market in sugar and goods produced in a specific area such as the Lingnan is taken up in detail in Chapter 6, "Markets and Monopsonies." Here I only wish to suggest in brief outline the scale of commodity exchange in the sixteenth and seventeenth centuries. An overall understanding of the shifts in trade is given in Fan I-chun, "Long-Distance Trade and Market Integration in the Ming-Ch'ing Period, 1400–1850," Ph.D. dissertation, Stanford University, 1993.

142. Martin de Rada's long treatise on the visit to China, *Kingdome of China*, along with the narratives of other contemporary visitors to China, was collated and published by Juan Gonzalez de Mendoza in Rome in 1585; an English version soon appeared: *The History of the Great and Mighty Kingdome of China* (1588), Richard Hakluyt, tr. (rpt. New York: Hakluyt Society, 1853).

143. de Rada, vol. 2, p. 49.

144. Ibid., vol. 1, p. 139.

145. Ibid., vol 2, p. 72; Miguel López de Legaspi (1575), rpt. in Samuel Purchas, comp., *Purchas His Pilgrimes Or Relations of the religions observed* (1613) (rpt. Glasgow: James MacLehose and Sons, 1905–1907), p. 188.

146. Mote, pp. 245–247. For a discussion of conspicuous consumption of the mercantile elite in the late Ming, see also Harriet T. Zurndorfer, *Change and Continuity in Chinese Local History* (Leiden: E. J. Brill: 1989), pp. 105–113.

147. Mintz, *Sweetness*, pp. 88–90.

148. *Tiangong kaiwu*, juan shang, p. 129. Unfortunately Song Yingxing does not explain how the fragile confection would have been unmolded.

149. Vera Y. N. Hsu and Francis L. K. Hsu, "Modern China: North," in K. C. Chang, ed., *Food in Chinese Culture*, pp. 305–306.

150. *Guanglusi zeli* (Beijing: Qinding neibu, 1839), juan 43, pp. 3b–4b.

151. Jonathan Spence, "Ch'ing," in K. C. Chang, ed., *Food in Chinese Culture*, pp. 281–282.

152. *Guanglusi*, juan 42, pp. 1a–5a.

153. Ibid., juan 42, pp. 1a–2b.

154. *Gujin tushu*, juan 301, ce 700, p. 12.

155. Gervase Markham, *The English Hus-Wife* (1615), Michael R. Best, ed. (rpt. Montreal: McGill Queen's University Press, 1994), chapter 2, "Of Cookery."

156. Mintz, *Sweetness*, pp. 91–96. In 1503 Archbishop Wareham, chancellor at Oxford, "at the feast of his inthronisation, ordered to be introduced in the first course a curious dish, in which were exhibited the eight towers of the university. In every tower stood a bedell; and under the towers were figures of the

king, to whom the chancellor Wareham, encircled with many doctors properly habited, presented four Latin verses, which were answered by his majesty": Mintz, *Sweetness*, pp. 91–92. This "first course" was a subtlety, made entirely out of sugar. As Mintz points out, this custom had not entirely been abandoned in later centuries. Mrs. Hannah Glasse's famous cookbooks for the bourgeoisie written in 1747 and 1760 also included elaborate displays, "jumballs," and decorations made of sugar. By then China had become part of the orientalist imagination. The towers of Oxford had given way to quaint and fanciful replicas of Chinese temples, pagodas, and gardens in Mrs. Glasse's book on confections.

157. Cao Xueqin, *The Story of the Stone*, David Hawkes, tr. (Harmondsworth: Penguin Books, 1977), vol. 2, pp. 287–289, 310.

158. Ibid., vol. 2, p. 287.

159. *Shinzoku kibun* (1799), Nakagawa Shundai (rpt. Tokyo: Tōyō bunko, 1965), pp. 19–24.

160. *Suiyuan shidan*, (1797), Yuan Mei (rpt. Shanghai: Xiaocang shanfang wenji, 1824), pp. 14a–14b, 66a–70a.

161. Ibid., p. 67a. This passage has also been translated by Arthur Waley, *Yuan Mei, Eighteenth Century Chinese Poet* (London: George Allen and Unwin, 1956), p. 196. My translation differs considerably from his.

162. Wu Jingzi, *The Scholars*, Yang Hsien-yi and Gladys Yang, trs. (Beijing: Foreign Language Press, 1957), p. 80.

163. Ibid., pp. 112, 169.

164. Ibid., p. 490.

165. Shen Fu, *Six Records of a Floating Life*, Leonard Pratt and Chiang Su-hui, trs. (Harmondsworth: Penguin Books, 1983), pp. 39, 67–69.

166. *Guangdong xinyu*, juan 14, p. 389. I am grateful to Peng Shijiang for sharing his recollections of eating "cow-hide candy" with me.

167. Eugene Anderson, *Food*, p. 153.

168. Mintz, *Sweetness*, pp. 99–108. On the one hand, sugar was so commonly used for medical purposes in Europe that from the thirteenth to the eighteenth century the term "like an apothecary without sugar" came to mean a state of utter desperation. On the other hand, because the majority of remedies involving sugar were introduced into European pharmacopoeia via Islamic influences, Mintz suggests "criticisms of sugar by medical authorities may have even formed part of fashionable, anti-Islamic *partis pris*, common in Europe from the Crusades onwards." Mintz, *Sweetness*, p. 102.

169. P. S. Pittenger, *Sugars and Sugar Derivatives in Pharmacy* (New York: Sugar Research Foundation, 1947). In China, as we have seen, the Buddhists had particular uses of sugar, but overall it was most generally used in bronchial tonics and as a demulcent.

170. *Bencao gangmu*, juan 33, pp. 14b–16b.

171. Ibid., juan 33, p. 15a. According to Li Shizhen, the cane juice after extraction is put into a *zhangmu cao*. Camphor oil is also anti-bacterial, and so it makes good sense. But it is not clear whether Li Shizhen was recommending the use of camphor wood for sugar juice that is to be used for medicinal purposes or just noting common practice.

172. *Bencao qiuzhen* (1773), Huang Gongxiu (rpt. Shanghai: Kexue jixu chubanshe, 1959), p. 219. The translation of the term *xue yu* as blood coagulation is based on Nathan Sivin, *Traditional Medicine in Contemporary China* (Ann Arbor: University of Michigan Press, 1987), p. 241.

173. Hsing-yuan Lowe, *The Adventures of Wu* (1940) (rpt. Princeton: University of Princeton Press, 1983), p. 13.

174. Ibid., p. 13.

175. Martin C. Yang, *A Chinese Village* (New York: Columbia University Press, 1945), p. 33.

176. *Bencao gangmu*, juan 33, p. 14b. Several of these medical uses of sugar and related products are also enumerated in *Gezhi jingyuan* (1735), Chen Yuanlong (rpt. Taipei: Shangwu shudian, 1972), juan 33, pp. 962–963.

177. Shinoda Osamu, *Chūgoku shokumotsu*, p. 330.

178. *Taiwan jishi*, (preface 1875), Wu Ziguang, rpt. in *Taiwan wenxian congkan* (Taipei: Taiwan yinhang, 1959), p. 10. The term used for this wine was *tangjiu*, but it is unclear if it was a distilled spirit like rum or merely fermented.

179. Ji Xianlin, p. 134; *Gujin tushu*, juan 301, p. 10.

180. A population of 295,273,311 to be exact, according to Liang Fangzhong, *Zhongguo lidai hukou, diandi, tianfu tongji* (Shanghai: Renmin chubanshe, 1980); and Ho Ping-ti, *Studies on the Population of China* (Cambridge: Harvard University Press, 1959). The figures for total population size here and elsewhere in this book are based on Liang Fangzhong and Ho Ping-ti. Unless there is a marked divergence in the numbers given between these two sources, I have not entered into a discussion.

181. Estimate based on daily budgets of workers, merchants, and compradors in Shanghai and Tianjin: Tōa dōbunkai, *Shina keizai zensho* (Osaka: Maruzen, 1907), vol. 1, pp. 345–446. Chung-li Chang, *The Income of the Chinese Gentry* (Seattle: University of Washington Press, 1962), p. 311, estimates a total national consumption of 750,000,000 *jin* in the late Qing.

182. Fernand Braudel, *The Structures of Everyday Life*, Sian Reynolds, tr. (New York: Harper and Row, 1982), p. 226. In many areas of rural France at the end of the eighteenth century, Braudel records that the only sugar ever seen (rather than tasted) was the sugar loaf hung over the table of peasant households with the instruction, "hold your glasses up to it briefly so that the sugar can melt into it."

183. International Sugar Council, *The World's Sugar Economy* (London: Brown, Wright and Tuscott, 1963), p. 22; See also Mintz, *Sweetness*, p. 197.

184. Mintz, *Sweetness*, pp. 143–149.

185. Ibid., p. 108

186. Ibid., p. 167.

187. Minchinson, p. 138; USDA, pp. 149, 211.

188. Eric J. Hobsbawm, *Industry and Empire* (Harmondsworth: Penguin Books, 1968), p. 42.

189. Carole Shammas, *The Pre-Industrial Consumer in England and America* (Oxford: Clarendon Press, 1990), pp. 1–4 and chapter 5. In discussions of "tea and sugar as stimulant," the use of opium, also an imported product, is often neglected. Until the 1860s, and the wider campaign to control the open sale of opium in Britain, culminating in the Pharmacy Act of 1868, the lack of access to medical care and frequency of self-medication among the poor led to a remarkable increase in the use of opium combined with sugar. Morphine-laced throat lozenges, and "soothing syrups" which were nothing but opium and sugar were some common uses; actual home consumption of opium ranged from 1.3 pounds to 3.6 pounds per thousand population: see Virginia Berridge and Griffith Edwards, *Opium and the People* (New Haven: Yale University Press, 1987), table 2, p. 274.

190. Shammas, pp. 27–28.

191. Jeffrey G. Williamson, "Why Was British Growth So Slow during the Industrial Revolution?" *Journal of Economic History* 44:687–712 (1984).

192. Robert C. Allen, *Enclosure and the Yeoman* (Oxford: Clarendon Press, 1992), pp. 290–300.

193. For a discussion of wages and demand in Europe, see Minchinson; and Peter Kriedte, *Peasants, Landlords, Merchants and Capitalists* (Cambridge: Cambridge University Press, 1983), p. 147. Figure on British consumption from Deerr, vol. 2, p. 532.

194. Burnett, *Plenty and Want*, pp. 37–38, emphasis added.

195. Mintz, *Sweetness*, p. 143, of course sees the increased use of sugar as problematic. But as Burnett points out, the conclusion that condensed milks and sweet jams were nutritionally inferior to their nineteenth-century predecessors is somewhat anachronistic. In many cases these newer products were additions rather than substitutions in the diet, suggesting a higher caloric intake: John Burnett, *A History of the Cost of Living* (Harmondsworth: Penguin Books, 1969), pp. 268–273, provides several menus of working-class meals from 1900 and 1901 that illustrate the increased use of sugar along with other changes in the diet.

196. Burnett, *A History*, p. 193.

197. Skinner, *The City*, p. 28.

198. An overview of economic development of the region is given in Liu Shiji, "Ming Qing shidai Jiangnan diqu de zhuanye shizhen," *Shihuo* 8.6:274–291, 8.7:326–337, and 8.8: 365–380 (1978).

199. Kang Chao, *Man and Land in Chinese History* (Stanford: Stanford University Press, 1986), p. 60; Skinner, *The City*, p. 225; Elvin, *Pattern*, p. 178. Dwight Perkins, *Agricultural Development*, pp. 290–295 suggests only 4 percent of the population lived in cities by 1900.

200. Chao, *Man and Land*, pp. 58–60.

201. Chen Zhen and Yao Luo, *Zhongguo jindai shougongye shi ziliao* (Beijing: Sanlian shudian, 1957–1961), vol. 1, p. 21. The industrial proletariat increased to 661,000 by 1912: Dwight Perkins, *Agricultural Development*, p. 212. Both figures excluded Taiwan.

202. de Vries, p. 178.

203. Here I am drawing on Jairus Banaji, "Modes of Production in a Materialist Conception of History," *Capital and Class* 3:5–7 (1977). As Marx points out, there is an important and necessary distinction to be made between the simple category, the commodity labor-power, and "capital positing, capital-producing labour, i.e. living labour which produces both the objective conditions of its realization as an activity, as well the objective moments of its being as labour *capacity*, and produces them as alien powers opposite itself, as *values for themselves, independent* of it": Karl Marx, *Grundrisse*, Martin Nicolaus, tr. (rpt. New York: First Vintage Books, 1973), p. 463 (emphasis in original).

204. Diego de Pantoia (1602), rpt. in Samuel Purchas, comp., *Relations of the religions*, vol. 12, p. 371. For discussion of currency and weights, see the Appendix.

205. See the Appendix for the conversion rate of maravedis into taels.

206. The price paid by the foreigners for necessities such as rice was not higher than the domestic price. In the few instances where the domestic price for rice and the comprador's contract for provision are both available for a particular year, it seems that the price paid by the foreigners was even a bit lower than the domestic price. For example, in 1733, rice sold in Guangzhou at between 1.20 to 1.00 taels per *shi*: Ch'üan Han-sheng and Richard Kraus, *Mid-Ch'ing Rice Markets and Trade* (Cambridge: Harvard University Press, 1975), p. 159. The same year and in the same season rice was purchased by foreign traders at 0.90 taels per picul: Hosea B. Morse, *The Chronicles of the East India: Company Trading to China, 1635–1884* (Oxford: Oxford University Press, 1926–1929), vol. 1, p. 219.

207. *Guanglusi*, juan 59, pp. 6a–10a. I am assuming 1,000 cash (*li*) to the tael (*liang*) for the 1790s.

208. George Macartney, *An Embassy to China, Being the Journal Kept by Lord Macartney* (1807), J. L. Cranmer-Byng, ed. (rpt. Hamden, Conn.: Archon Books, 1963), p. 244.

209. Dwight Perkins, *Agricultural Development*, pp. 247–248.

210. Peng Zeyi, ed., *Zhongguo jindai shougongye shi ziliao* (Beijing: Zhonghua shuju, 1957), vol. 1, pp. 396–414.

211. Macartney, *An Embassy*, p. 244. Agricultural wages based on Zhongguo remin daxue Zhongguo lishi jiaoyanshi, eds., *Zhongguo ziben zhuyi mengya wenti taolunji* (Beijing: Sanlian shudian, 1957), pp. 652–653. The typical agricultural wage worker spent more than half his/her income on grain alone if the wage was the sole support of a family of two adults and a child. Susan Naquin, *Millenarian Rebellion in China* (New Haven: Yale University Press, 1976), Appendix 3, pp. 281–282, gives prices of some goods in 1810: knife, 500 cash; one foot of white cotton cloth, 100 cash; 14-year old boy, 4,000 cash; 11-year old boy, 1,000 cash; woman: 10,000 cash.

212. D. J. MacGowan, *Sidelights on Chinese Life* (London: Kegan Paul, 1907), p. 300.

213. Gilbert Rozman et al., *The Modernization of China* (New York: Free Press, 1981), p. 122; Chang Chung-li, *Income*, pp. 372–378.

214. Shammas, p. 81.

215. Mintz, *Sweetness*, p. 184. But as the data from Burnett show, the year 1840, when sugar was the most expensive in the fifty years studied, corresponds with the lowest consumption, while 1848, with the lowest prices, had the highest consumption level for thirty years: Burnett, *A History*, p. 10.

216. Deerr, vol. 2, pp. 530–532.

217. Burnett, *A History*, pp. 254–267.

218. Perhaps the greatest weakness of Mintz's model comes from his ignoring this link between beet-sugar production in continental Europe and increased consumption in Britain. It was cheap sugar from Europe and not the former British colonies that supported the growing English demand for sugar: see Deerr, vol. 2, pp. 504–505, for figures on European imports.

219. *Guanglusi*, juan 43.

220. Wu Chengming, *Zhongguo ziben zhuyi yu guonei shichang* (Beijing: Zhongguo shehui kexue chubanshe, 1985), p. 263.

221. Fan I-chun, "Long-Distance Trade," p. 120.

222. Much of this literature has been surveyed and summarized in Susan Naquin and Evelyn Rawski, *Chinese Society in the Eighteenth Century* (New Haven: Yale University Press, 1987).

223. Wu Chengming, p. 253.

224. Evelyn Rawski, *Agricultural Change*, p. 97.

225. Wang Yeh-chien, "The Secular Trend of Prices during the Ch'ing Period (1644–1911)," *JCICUHK* 5.2:360–361 (1972). Mio Kishimoto finds a similar pattern of deflation and a slump in prices during the period 1662–1722 to rising prices in the eighteenth century: Mio (Nakayama) Kishimoto, "On the Fluctuation of the Price of Rice in the Chiang-nan Region during the First Half of the Ch'ing Period (1644–1795)," *Memoirs of the Research Department of the Tōyō Bunko* 37:55–90 (1979).

226. Sidney Gamble, "Wages of Unskilled Chinese Laborers, 1807–1902," *Far Eastern Quarterly* 3.1:73 (1943).

227. Evelyn Sakakida Rawski, *Education and Literacy in Ch'ing China* (Ann Arbor: University of Michigan Press, 1979), p. 60.

228. In this I am following standard practice, for as Keith Tribe says, "It is usual . . . to nominate Smith as the originator of modern economics": Keith Tribe, *Land, Labor and Economic Discourse* (London: Routledge S. K. Paul, 1978), p. 6. See also Barber, p. 17; Adam Smith, *An Inquiry into the Nature and Causes of the Wealth of Nations* (1776), Edwin Cannan, ed. (rpt. New York: Modern Library, 1937), p. 7; and Brenner, "The Social Basis," pp. 23–24.

229. Karl Marx, *Capital* (1867), Ben Fowles, tr. (rpt. New York: Vintage Books, 1977), vol. 1, p. 247.

230. Classics in the field of economic history such as Henri Pirenne, *Economic and Social History of Medieval Europe* (London: Kegan Paul, Trench, Trubner, 1936); and Paul Sweezy, "A Critique," in Rodney Hilton, ed., *The Transition from Feudalism to Capitalism* (rpt. London: Verso, 1978), have used a trade-centered explanation, as have more recent scholars such as Carlo Cipolla, *Before the Industrial Revolution* (New York: W. W. Norton, 1976), and Jan de Vries.

231. There are several collections from the 1950s cited here earlier, including Zhongguo renmin daxue, Zhongguo lishi jiaoyanshi, ed., *Zhongguo ziben zhuyi mengya wenti taolunji*.

232. David Faure, *The Rural Economy of Pre-Liberation China* (Hong Kong: Oxford University Press, 1989), p. 27. Other scholars who have emphasized trade as the primary factor in initiating development include Evelyn Sakakida Rawski, *Agricultural Change*.

Chapter 2

1. Peter Mundy, *Travels of Peter Mundy in Europe and Asia, 1608–1667*, R. C. Temple and L. Anstey, eds. (rpt. London: Hakluyt Society, 1919), vol. 3, pt. 1, p. 286.

2. William Courteen, a Crown lender and one of the "new merchants" who challenged the monopoly privileges of the East India Company, sponsored a major trade voyage to Goa, Malabar, China, and Japan. The efforts of mer-

chants like Courteen and others were to bring the English East India Company to the point of collapse by the 1640s. See Robert Brenner, *Merchants and Revolution* (Princeton: Princeton University Press, 1993) for the politics of London's merchant groups and the restructuring of the East India Company.

3. Though an earlier generation of scholars like Charles R. Boxer, discussed below, wrote extensively about Chinese traders and their political power in the southern maritime provinces and in Southeast Asia, only a few of the recent scholars have taken up this subject, most notably: Leonard Blussé, *Strange Company* (Dordrecht: Foris Publications, 1986); Jennifer Cushman, *Fields from the Sea* (Ithaca: Cornell University Press, 1990); Chang Pin-tsun, "Chinese Maritime Trade: The Case of Sixteenth Century Fu-chien" (Ph.D. dissertation, Princeton University, 1983); and Ng Chin-keong, *Trade and Society* (Singapore: Singapore University Press, 1983). The predominant tendency in scholarship on Chinese trade is, however, to focus on Western trading companies, for in many ways the field was shaped by scholars such as Hosea B. Morse, *The Chronicles of the East India Company*; and John Fairbank, *Trade and Diplomacy on the China Coast* (1953; rpt. Stanford: Stanford University Press, 1969). See also, for example, John E. Wills, *Pepper, Guns and Parleys* (Cambridge: Harvard University Press, 1974) and others cited below. Louis Dermigny's multi-volume *La Chine et l'Occident: Le Commerce à Canton au XVIIIe siècle, 1719–1833* (Paris: S.E.V.P.E.N., 1964), one of the very few studies to focus on all the various European companies involved in trade, nevertheless focuses only on Western trade at the port. Consequently we do not get a sense of the extent of Chinese maritime trade in Southeast Asia or the Chinese use of the European traders in the port of Canton from Dermigny's work. Unfortunately, scholars of South Asia who have focussed extensively on "Asia before Europe" have also not integrated a discussion of the Pacific trade with the Indian Ocean trade, and the two trading worlds remain more or less discrete and unconnected entities, even when China and India are discussed. See, for example, essays in Ashin K. Das Gupta and Michael N. Pearson, eds., *India and the Indian Ocean, 1500–1800* (Calcutta: Oxford University Press, 1987); and K. N. Chaudhuri, *Trade and Civilization in the Indian Ocean* (Cambridge: Cambridge University Press, 1985).

4. Chinese and Japanese scholars, (e.g., Ts'ao Yung-ho, Iwao Seiichi, Nagazumi Yōko, and dozens of others cited below) have looked at the earlier period in great detail, but there has been very little overlap in the research findings of these scholars and the majority of Western scholars involved in working on Chinese trade. There has been a predilection among Western scholars, under the influence of the Hosea B. Morse and John K. Fairbank paradigm, to subsume all non-Western trade in China under the rubric of "tribute" and write trade history in congruence with the official view from Beijing, suggesting pri-

vate trade was strictly controlled and very limited; see, for example, various essays in John K. Fairbank, ed., *The Chinese World Order* (Cambridge: Harvard University Press, 1968); and the echoes of this framework found in the essays in John K. Fairbank, ed., *Late Ch'ing, 1800–1911*, vol. 10 in John K. Fairbank, gen. ed., *The Cambridge History of China* (Cambridge: Cambridge University Press, 1978–1985); John King Fairbank and Kwang-ching Liu, eds., *Late Ch'ing, 1800–1911*, vol. 11 in John K. Fairbank, gen. ed., *The Cambridge History of China* (Cambridge: Cambridge University Press, 1978–1985); John E. Wills, *Embassies and Illusions* (Cambridge: Council on East Asian Studies, Harvard University, 1984). Sarasin Viraphol's innovative study on Sino-Siamese trade, *Tribute and Profit* (Cambridge: Council on East Asian Studies, Harvard University, 1977), one of the few works in English to deal with the seventeenth and eighteenth centuries in detail, is so caught up trying to understand what was obviously extensive private trade as tribute trade that it detracts from the value of the work.

5. Adam Smith, p. 645.

6. Classic works in the field have to a great extent accepted the culturalist arguments of the contemporary British "free traders" that the Chinese were not interested in foreign trade and that there was an effective monopoly on foreign trade exercised by the Cohong. See, for example, Hosea B. Morse, *The Trade and Administration of China* (Kelly and Walsh, 1921); Michael Greenberg, *British Trade and the Opening of China, 1800–1842* (New York: Monthly Review Press, 1951); Fairbank, *Trade and Diplomacy*; Masataka Banno, *China and the West, 1858–1861* (Cambridge: Harvard University Press, 1964); Hsin-pao Chang, *Commissioner Lin and the Opium War* (Cambridge: Harvard University Press, 1964); Immanuel Hsu, *China's Entry into the Family of Nations* (Cambridge: Harvard University Press, 1960). Research on the clash between "Western" and "Chinese" notions of the world order has received far more attention than efforts at quantitative evaluations of Chinese foreign trade conducted by Chinese traders. The theme of successful political control by Beijing (in contrast to the Mughals) is omnipresent even in works which have consciously sought to re-examine this paradigm: see, for example, Roderich Ptak and Dietmar Rothermund, eds., *Emporia, Commodities and Entrepreneurs in Asian Maritime Trade, C 1400–1750* (Stuttgart: Franz Steiner Verlag, 1991). And as recent an article as John E. Wills, "Maritime Asia, 1500–1800: The Interactive Emergence of European Domination," *AHR* 98:1:101–103 (1993), focuses on the fear of "cultural contamination" and a "defensiveness regarding foreign contacts" of the Qing and ignores the literature on the economic and political underpinnings of the imperial state policy.

7. For a framework based on dependency theory, see Francis Moulder, *China, Japan and the Modern World Economy* (Cambridge: Cambridge University Press, 1977). For applications of Wallerstein's world-systems theory to China,

see Alvin So, *The South China Silk District* (Albany: State University of New York Press, 1986); Rhoads Murphey, *The Outsiders* (Ann Arbor: University of Michigan, Center for Chinese Studies, 1977); and Dilip Basu, "The Peripherialization of China," in Walter Goldfrank, ed., *The World-System of Capitalism: Past and Present* (Beverly Hills: Sage Press, 1979).

8. Braudel, *Wheels*, p. 191.

9. Ibid., p. 190. For a discussion of these changes in the use of sugar among wealthy commoners in Europe in the sixteenth century, see Mennell; Reay Tannahill, *Food in History* (New York: Stein and Day, 1988); and Mintz, *Sweetness*.

10. Frederic C. Lane, *Venice, A Maritime Republic* (Baltimore: Johns Hopkins University Press, 1973), pp. 138–144; Deerr, vol. 1, pp. 73–100, vol. 2, p. 451.

11. Lane, p. 297.

12. For the expansion of the sugar industry in the Azores, Madeira, São Tomé, and Brazil, see Frédéric Mauro, *Le Portugal et l'Atlantique au XVIIe siècle (1570–1670)* (Paris: S.E.V.P.E.N., 1960), pp. 183–204.

13. Columbus's early employment included shipping sugar for a Genoese merchant from Madeira, where he had married the daughter of a Madeiran landowner. For a history of the initial period of sugar cultivation in the Caribbean and the Americas, see Mervyn Ratekin, "The Early Sugar Industry in Española," *Hispanic American Historical Review* 34.1:1–19 (1954); and J. H. Galloway, *The Sugar Cane Industry* (Cambridge: Cambridge University Press, 1989), pp. 48–70.

14. Deerr, vol. 1, p. 116.

15. The rapid diffusion of the sugarcane in the Americas and its presence in the Amerindian diet has led some scholars to the erroneous conclusion that it had been introduced prior to the arrival of Columbus. The various theories suggesting this have been examined in Galloway, pp. 62–63.

16. Deerr, vol. 1, p. 102; Braudel, *Wheels*, pp. 190–193.

17. In sugar-producing areas like Sicily, not directly affected by Turkish rule, the developing New World competition combined with high local taxes on sugar led to an abandonment of many sugar-manufacturing houses in mid-century: Deerr, vol. 1, pp. 78, 86, 94. The Sicilian industry partially recovered by the end of the sixteenth century but remained only a regional supplier. The days of Sicilian and Mediterranean monopolies were over with the arrival of Madeiran and then Brazilian sugars, a trend accentuated when Portugal came under Spanish rule in 1580 and Brazilian sugar could freely enter Spanish dominions: Carmelo Trasselli, *Storia dello zucchero siciliano* (Caltanisseta: S. Sicascia, 1982), pp. 245–246.

18. In 1522, when Del Cano brought one of Magellan's ships back to Spain, the wind system of the Pacific was also charted: Philip Curtin, *Cross-Cultural Trade in World History* (Cambridge: Cambridge University Press, 1984), p. 136.

19. Michael N. Pearson, "India and the Indian Ocean in the Sixteenth Century," in Das Gupta and Pearson, eds., p. 84; and Curtin, pp. 142–143. The realities of the Portuguese enterprise make it surprising that historians like Kavalam M. Panikkar have suggested that there was a "Vasco da Gama epoch" during which Asia fell quickly to Western dominance: K. M. Panikkar, *Asia and Western Dominance: A Survey of the Vasco da Gama Epoch of Asian History* (London: Allen and Unwin, 1953). More recently, Carlo M. Cipolla, *Guns and Sails in the Early Phase of European Expansion, 1400–1700* (London: William Collins, 1965), has argued that guns and mounted artillery on sailing ships fitted with iron nails left Asians unable to resist the onslaught, and European domination was a foregone conclusion. It is forgotten that the success of the Portuguese in East Africa, coastal India, and Southeast Asia, such as it was, was not repeated in East Asia. But because the literature on the Portuguese in South Asia is both voluminous and centered on the Indian Ocean rather than the Pacific, it further tends to exaggerate their achievements.

20. Braudel, *Wheels*, p. 193.

21. This brief discussion on the subject of the rise of Amsterdam as an entrepôt draws on Jonathan Israel, *Dutch Primacy in World Trade* (Oxford: Clarendon Press, 1989); Ralph Davis's classic, *The Rise of the Atlantic Economies* (Ithaca: Cornell University Press, 1973); and Michel Beaud, *A History of Capitalism, 1500–1980*, Tom Dickman and Anny Lefebvre, trs. (New York: Monthly Review Press, 1983), pp. 17–42.

22. The sugar refineries, located on canals for ease of transportation, were enormous multi-storied warehouses with separate floors with heated chambers devoted to drying the processed sugars at different temperatures: J. J. Reesse, *De suikerhandle van Amsterdam van het begin der 17de eeuw tot 1813* (Haarlem: J. L. E. I. Kleynenberg, 1908), pp. 104–150. As discussed in the next chapter, this type of centralization of manufacture never occurred in China.

23. Reesse, p. 107; Deerr, vol. 2, p. 453. Charles R. Boxer, *The Dutch in Brazil, 1624–1654* (Oxford: Oxford University Press, 1957), p. 21.

24. Boxer, *The Dutch*, p. 3, gives the estimate of the sugar trade provided by Willem Usselincx (1567–1647), architect of the Dutch West India Company. Total output of Brazil based on Mintz, *Sweetness*, p. 38; and Deerr, vol. 1, p. 112.

25. Leonard Blussé and Femme Gaastra, eds., *Companies and Trade* (Leiden: Leiden University Press, 1981), p. 4; Gaastra, "The Shifting Balance of Trade in the Dutch East India Company," in Blussé and Gaastra, eds., p. 50; Om Pra-

kash, "The Dutch East India Company in the Trade of the Indian Ocean," in Das Gupta and Pearson, eds., p. 186.

26. C. J. A. Jorg, *Porcelain and the Dutch China Trade* (The Hague: Nijhoff, 1982), p. 17.

27. Kristof Glamann, *Dutch Asiatic Trade, 1620–1740* (The Hague: Nijhoff, 1958), p. 154.

28. Deerr, vol. 1, p. 106; Boxer, *The Dutch*, p. 40. The governor and commander in chief of the Portuguese operations in Brazil, Mathias de Albuquerque, destroyed so many sugar warehouses in Recife that he claimed he had deprived the Dutch of a booty worth 1,600,000 cruzados.

29. Fernand Braudel, *Perspective of the World*, Sian Reynolds, tr. (New York: Harper and Row, 1984), pp. 232–233.

30. Wang Gungwu, "The Nanhai Trade," *Journal of the Malayan Branch of the Royal Asiatic Society* 31.2:1–135 (1958).

31. Zhao Rugua, *Zhufan ji*, Frederich Hirth and William Rockhill, trs. and annots., *Chau Ju-kua: On the Chinese and Arab Trade* (St. Petersburg: Printing Office of the Imperial Academy of Sciences, 1911), pp. 49, 61, 69. See also Paul Wheatley, "Geographical Notes on Some Commodities Involved in Sung Maritime Trade," *Journal of the Malayan Branch of the Royal Asiatic Society* 32.2:5–139 (1961).

32. Arab traders, for example, came to both Palembang and Beranang: Zhao Rugua, p. 70, n. 3. While porcelain was also exported from Thailand, and kilns have been found dating back to the tenth century, it is unclear whether the finer grades produced for export were available prior to the arrival of Chinese potters at the very end of the thirteenth century: Charles N. Spinks, *The Ceramic Wares of Siam* (Bangkok: Siam Society, 1965), pp. 14–17; Anthony Reid, *Southeast Asia in the Age of Commerce, 1450–1680* (New Haven: Yale University Press, 1988), pp. 104–105.

33. Mori Katsumi, "The Beginning of Overseas Advance of Japanese Merchant Ships," *Acta Asiatica* 23:13 (1972).

34. Feng Chengjun, *Zhongguo Nanyang jiaotong shi* (Shanghai: Shangwu yinshuguan, 1937), pp. 78–90; Zhang Xinglan, *Zhong-Xi jiaotong shiliao huibian* (Beijing: Xinmin yinshuguan, 1930), vol. 6, pp. 489–492; overview based on Fang Hao, *Zhong-Xi jiaotong shi*, 5 vols. (Taipei: Zhonghua wenhua chuban, 1954); and William W. Rockhill, "Notes on the Relations and Trade of China with the Eastern Archipelago and the Coasts of the Indian Ocean during the Fourteenth Century," two parts, *TP* 15:419–447 (1914); 16:61–159, 236–271, 374–392, 435–467, 604–626 (1915).

Other scholars have focused more on the political and military aspects of the links with Southeast Asia during the thirteenth and fourteenth centuries: see

Wang Gungwu, "China and South-East Asia, 1402–1424," in Jerome Ch'en and Nicolas Tarling, eds., *Studies in the Social History of China and South-east Asia* (Cambridge: Cambridge University Press, 1970); and Lo Jung-pang, "The Emergence of China as a Sea Power during the Late Sung and the Early Yuan Periods," *Far Eastern Quarterly* 14.4:489–503 (1955).

35. Li Donghua, "Song, Yuan shidai Quanzhou haiwai jiaotongde shengkuang," in *Zhongguo haiyang fazhanshi lunwenji* (Taipei: Zhongyang yanjiu yuan, 1984), vol. 1, pp. 1–40. Li Donghua has tabulated the exports listed in Zhao Rugua and Wang Dayuan's *Daoyi zhilue*, pp. 33–38. Major sections of the *Daoyi zhilue* have been translated in part 2 of the essay by William Rockhill, "Notes on the Relations."

36. M. A. P. Meilink-Roelofz, *Asian Trade and European Influence* (The Hague: Nijhoff, 1962), pp. 16–19.

37. Rockhill, "Notes on the Relations," part 2, p. 129.

38. Marco Polo, *The Book*, vol. 2, pp. 234–235.

39. Ibid., p. 250. Origin of "junk" from *O.E.D.*, s.v. In the later literature the term was used for all Chinese ships in the intra-Asian trade.

40. J. C. Van Leur, *Indonesian Trade and Society* (The Hague: Nijhoff, 1955), p. 209.

41. Shunzo Sakamaki, "Ryukyu and Southeast Asia," *JAS* 23.3:387 (1964).

42. Feng Chengjun, p. 78; Zhang Xinglang, p. 479.

43. Ts'ao Yung-ho, "Pepper Trade in East Asia," *TP* 68.4–5:232–233 (1982).

44. Wang Yi-t'ung, *Official Relations between China and Japan, 1368–1549* (Cambridge: Harvard University Press, 1953), p. 15.

45. Wills, *Pepper*, pp. 4–5. A closely related interpretation of the trade restrictions as a Ming revival of the conventional tributary system with Southeast Asia is also offered by Wang Gungwu, "Early Ming Relations with Southeast Asia: A Background Essay," in John Fairbank, ed., *The Chinese World Order*, pp. 34–62. The complicated history of Ming maritime trade and foreign relations has a daunting body of scholarship. Xie Guozhen, *Wan Ming shiji kao* (Beijing: Beijing daxue tushu guan, 1932), is still a valuable introduction.

46. Ts'ao, "Pepper Trade" p. 233. A more detailed discussion of his view that the desire of the Ming government to curb private trade was behind the trade regulations and that the commercial aspect of the tribute missions has been underestimated can be found in his essay "Shilun Ming Taizu de haiyang jiaotong zhengci," in Sanmin zhuyi yanjiu suo, ed., *Zhongguo haiyang fazhanshi lunwenji* (Taipei: Zhongyang yanjiu yuan, 1984), vol. 1, pp. 41–70.

47. Ts'ao, "Pepper Trade," p. 242. Several envoys of various Korean tribute missions, for example, were found to be smuggling pepper to Beijing.

48. Sakamaki, pp. 387–388. The finances of the Ming state did not permit

this bounty of ships after the mid-fifteenth century; in addition the Ryukyuans started building their own ships.

49. Elvin, *Pattern*, pp. 217–222, for example, interprets the restrictions on trade as symptomatic of the Ming state's isolationistic bent.

50. *Da Ming huidian Wanli* (1587) palace edition (rpt. Taipei: Dongnan shubaoshe, 1963), vol. 3, p. 1587b; Ts'ao Yung-ho, "Pepper Trade," p. 236. The descendents of these Chinese navigators were noted living near Naha port in the fifteenth century: Chang Pin-tsun, "The First Chinese Diaspora in Southeast Asia," in Ptak and Rothermund, eds., p. 20.

51. Ts'ao, "Pepper Trade," p. 242.

52. The dates of the various Zheng He missions are given in J. J. L. Duyvendak, "The True Dates of the Chinese Maritime Expeditions in the Early Fifteenth Century," *TP* 34:341–412 (1939); see also Wang Gungwu, "China and South-East Asia," p. 394, for the missions from Southeast Asia. The increased overall contact with Southeast Asia has been better studied than the impact of these voyages on contacts between China and South Asia. The Zheng He voyages had a greater impact on opening up trade and tribute missions from India and East Africa. The Sultans of Bengal, for example, sent no less than seven tribute missions to China, starting in 1408 and ending in 1439. At least two of the missions of the Southeast Asian states to the Yongle court, that from Samudra in 1411 and 1412, as well as one from Malacca in 1412, actually came on Bengali ships. These missions were substantial affairs; the mission of 1409 contained over 230 people. Of all the tribute missions recorded and the gifts they brought, only Bengal sent crystallized sugar to the Ming court, perhaps continuing a practice from the Tang period. Other items from Bengal included horses, saddles, incense, pepper, textiles and pearls and precious stones: *Ming shilu, Chengzu* (comp. 1430), Yao Guangxiao et al., eds. (rpt. N.p.: Zhongyang yanjiu yuan, 1940), juan 129, p. 1a, juan 88, p. 2–4b; Prabodh C. Bagchi, "Political Relations between Bengal and China," *Vishva Bharati Annals* 1:96–134 (1945). Zhang Weihua has painstakingly tabulated gifts sent to the Ming court as mentioned in the *Xingcha shenglan* (1436), *Yingyai shenglan* (1451), *Ming huidian Wanli* (1587), and the *Dong-Xi yangkao* (1617): Zhang Weihua, *Mingdai haiwai maoyi jianlun* (Shanghai: Renmin chubanshe, 1956), p. 65–68.

53. *Ming shilu, Taizu* (comp. 1418), Zhongyang yanjiu yuan, Lishi yuyan yanjiu suo, ed. (rpt. Taipei: Zhongyang yanjiu yuan, 1962–1967), vol. 6, p. 2761.

54. Ts'ao, "Pepper Trade," p. 241. Though, as discussed below, many of the pirates were Chinese rather than Japanese, in this case they probably were Japanese, for the envoy of the lord of Tsushima nonchalantly presented some pepper, peacocks, and sappanwood to the rulers of Korea in 1406, telling them that these had been seized from a Namban (Southern Barbarian) ship.

55. The commercial center of the once powerful state of Srivijaya, the site of the later state of Palembang on the island of Sumatra, for example, was controlled by Chinese pirates from Fujian and Guangdong as early as the fourteenth century: Meilink-Roelofsz, pp. 18, 22; George Coedès, *Les états hindouises d'Indochine et l'Indonesie* (Paris: E. de Boccard, 1948), p. 405.

56. Kwan-wai So, p. 1.

57. Ibid., pp. 19–22. There is an entire subfield of *Wokou* studies, a substantial body of scholarship, which though broadly relevant to the theme of international trade, cannot be entered into here. Zhang Weihua has also made a close study of the subject, as has Lin Renchuan, "Ming dai siren haishang maoyi shangren yu 'wokou,'" *Zhongguo shi yanjiu* 1:1–19 (1981).

58. On the volume of silver, see William S. Atwell, "Notes on Silver, Foreign Trade and the Late Ming Economy," *Ch'ing-shih wen t'i* 3.8:1–33 (1977). Evelyn Rawski discusses the early switch to silver rents and the monetization of the economy in the counties of Fujian most intimately involved with foreign trade: *Agricultural Change*, pp. 76–85.

59. Cited in Kwan-wai So, p. 214. The extent of trade at Guangzhou, despite these regulations, is also noted in Chang Teh-ch'ang, "Maritime Trade at Canton during the Ming Dynasty," *Chinese Social and Political Science Review* 17.2:264–282 (1933).

60. Ma Huan, *Yingyai shenglan* (1433), J. V. G. Mills, tr. (Cambridge: Cambridge University Press, 1970), p. 113.

61. Tomé Pires, *Suma Oriental* (1512–1515), Armando Cortesao, ed. and tr. (London: Hakluyt Society, 1944), vol. 2, p. 287. Meilink-Roelofz, pp. 60–88, agrees with Pires and collates his information with that of other contemporary sources.

62. Meilink-Roelofsz, p. 89; Wada Sei, "The Philippine Islands as Known to the Chinese before the Ming Period," *Memoirs of the Research Department of the Tōyō Bunko* 4:121–166 (1929). In the pre-Spanish days there was already a small community of Chinese in the Philippines who had married local women, although it is not known if these men were the traders who went to Malacca: Shao-hsing Chen, "The Migration of Chinese from Fukien to the Philippines under the Spanish Colonization and to Taiwan under the Dutch: An Analysis of Their Pattern of Development and Correspondences," *International Association of Historians of Asia, Second Biennial Conference Proceedings* (Taipei, 1962), p. 461. Although it is anachronistic to identify these islands as the "Philippines" prior to the arrival of the Spanish, I am following common usage. Reid, pp. 90–119, also discusses the intra-Asian trade at Melaka. But his reluctance to accommodate the Chinese traders as an integral part of Southeast Asia leaves unanswered how

some of the goods were brought to the port from the various islands including the Philippines.

63. Pires, vol. 1, p. 125.

64. Ibid., vol. 1, p. 123. The early trade of the Portuguese and their efforts to increase their trade in China is usefully summarized in Chang T'ien-tse, *Sino-Portuguese Trade from 1514 to 1644* (Leiden: E. J. Brill, 1934).

65. John Saris, "English Voyages, 1605–1613," rpt. in Samuel Purchas, comp., *Purchas His Pilgrimes: or, Hakluytus Posthumus* (1625) (rpt. Glasgow: James MacLehose and Sons, 1905–1907), vol. 3, pp. 506–518. See also Arun Das Gupta, "The Maritime Trade of Indonesia: 1500–1800," in Das Gupta and Pearson, eds., p. 248. The Chinese traders in Southeast Asia, however, brought considerable amounts of Indian "Coromandal cloth" for the intra-island trade as did the Ryukyuans. Bengal textiles sent to China either as part of the tribute missions or purchased in Southeast Asia in the Ming are discussed by Haraprasad Ray, "Bengal's Textile Products Involved in Ming Trade during Cheng Ho's Voyages to the Indian Ocean and Identification of the Hitherto Undeciphered Textiles," in Ptak and Rothermund, eds., pp. 82–93.

66. Ma Huan, pp. 92, 112, 118. Ma Huan repeatedly notes the existence of the sugarcane plant in Java, Samudra, and Malacca and other Southeast Asian countries in the fifteenth century, but there is no mention of sugar manufacturing. Of all the local products listed as available in the ports where the Chinese traded in the sixteenth century, only Semudera (on Sumatra) is listed as having *shimi: Dong-Xi yangkao* (preface 1618), Zhang Xie (rpt. Taipei: Siku quanshu zhenben jiuji, 1979), vol. 163, juan 4, p. 10a. However, this "stone honey" could have been made from palm sugar rather than cane sugar. Taiwan, too, did not manufacture cane sugar: William Campbell, ed., *Formosa under the Dutch, Described from Contemporary Records* (1903) (rpt. Taipei: Ch'eng Wen, 1967), p. 10; Deerr, vol. 1, p. 213. Although both wild and cultivated varieties of sugarcane were known in Southeast Asia from very early times, and, as we have seen, sugarcane syrup was exported to China by the third century from Funan, there is little evidence of widespread manufacture of cane sugar until the seventeenth century and the coming of the Dutch along with increased Chinese migration. Cane was grown to be eaten only as a variety of fruit, probably because a ready source of sugar, made simply by boiling the sap of the *arenga* or sugar palm, was available throughout the region: Reid, p. 31. This availability may have led to a slower development of commercial manufacturing of other sweeteners in Southeast Asia.

67. The available information is somewhat confusing for the early sixteenth century. Pires mentions Chinese sugar being brought to Melaka and says nothing about sugar from Bengal; Meilink-Roelofsz, summarizing Pires, mentions

sugar as part of the cargo from Bengal, but does not give an alternative source. William Moreland, in his detailed research on Indian trade in Southeast Asia, includes the Burmese region Pegu and Arakan as a purchaser of Bengali sugar: William Moreland, *From Akbar to Aurangzeb* (rpt. Delhi: Atma Ram, 1962), p. 54; Meilink-Roelofsz, pp. 68–69, 76. By the mid-seventeenth century clearer information is available. Om Prakash, who has tabulated this information from Dutch sources, clearly shows the importance of Bengali sugar exports to the west coast of India, Gujarat, and the Persian Gulf and Red Sea, and its absence in transactions in Southeast Asia: Om Prakash, *The Dutch East India Company and the Economy of Bengal, 1630–1720* (Princeton: Princeton University Press, 1985), p. 28.

68. *Dong-Xi yangkao*, vol. 163, juan 4, p. 4b.

69. John Saris records trying to buy pepper at Bantam and having to deal entirely with "Kewee, the chiefe Merchant of the Chinese," who obviously set the price: Saris, pp. 484–85.

70. Meilink-Roelofsz, pp. 243–244.

71. Saris, p. 508.

72. L. Carrington Goodrich and Chaoying Fang, eds., *Dictionary of Ming Biography, 1368–1644* (New York: Columbia University Press, 1976), vol. 1, pp. 919–922.

73. Ibid., vol. 1, pp. 372–375.

74. Chang Pin-tsun, "Chinese Maritime Trade," pp. 180–181.

75. *Dong-Xi yangkao*, vol. 164, juan 7, pp. 2a, 2b. It is not possible to estimate the tonnage of these ships. The smallest junks used around this time, e.g., for the trade to Java, had a carrying capacity of 50 tons. The largest junks could load up to 300 tons: Meilink-Roelofsz, p. 245.

76. Gaspar da Cruz (d. 1570), *South China in the Sixteenth Century*, C. R. Boxer, ed. and tr. (rpt. London: Hakluyt Society, 1953), p. xxi.

77. Antonio Bocarro, *Livro do Estado da India Oriental*, cited and tr. in Charles R. Boxer, *The Great Ship from Amacon* (Lisbon: Centro de Estudos Históricos Ultramarinos, 1959), p. 169.

78. Pires, vol. 1, p. 131.

79. Boxer, *The Great Ship*, p. 2.

80. da Cruz, *South China*, p. xxxii; Iwao Seiichi, "Japanese Foreign Trade in the 16th and 17th Centuries," *Acta Asiatica* 30:5 (1976).

81. da Cruz, *South China*, pp. xxxiii–xxxiv. The Portuguese, for their bit, tried to suggest in 1565 that as traders from Pudulijia, they were not subject to the same restrictions as the Folangji (Franks). The Ming officials quickly saw through this ruse: Carrington and Fang, eds., vol. 2, p. 1207.

82. Luis Frois (1532–1597), letter translated in Boxer, *The Great Ship*, p. 21.

83. Initially the Portuguese called at several ports in western Kyushu, including Satsuma, Hizen, and Bungo. Hirado, an island off northwestern Kyushu, was a favorite lair of Chinese pirates and had a convenient harbor. The ruling Matsura daimyo was, however, staunchly anti-Christian and had driven the Portuguese off to look for another port. Later when the daimyo of Hirado heard of the arrival of the "heretic" Dutch and then the English, he encouraged them to set up "factories" in 1609 and 1613, respectively. Nagasaki, just a bit further to the east, was under the control of Omura Sumitada, the first Christian daimyo. He was willing to help the Portuguese and developed the port at the behest of the Jesuits in 1571: Grant K. Goodman, *Japan: The Dutch Experience* (London: Athlone Press, 1986), p. 239, nn. 4, 6.

84. Boxer, *The Great Ship*, p. 3.

85. Pierre Chaunu, *Les Philippines et le Pacifique des Iberiques (XVIe, XVIIe, XVIIIe siècles)* (Paris: S.E.V.P.E.N., 1960), pp. 268–269.

86. John J. Tepaske, "New World Silver, Castile and the Philippines, 1590–1800," in J. F. Richards, ed., *Precious Metals in the Later Medieval and Early Modern Worlds* (Durham: Carolina Academic Press, 1983), p. 435.

87. Juan Gonzalez de Mendoza, *The History of the Great and Mighty Kingdome of China* (1588), George Staunton, ed. (London: Hakluyt Society, 1853), vol. 1, p. 95.

88. Letter to Felipe II dated 1585, in Emma Blair and James Robertson, eds. and trs., *The Philippine Islands, 1493–1898*, section on "Measures regarding Trade with China" (Cleveland: Arthur H. Clark Company, 1953), vol. 6, pp. 279–281.

89. Tepaske, p. 436. I have converted the figures given in kilograms to avoirdupois.

90. One of the causes of the frequent galleon wrecks on the return voyage to Mexico was that they were grossly overloaded and, in addition, often dragged loaded unofficial flotillas behind them: W. M. Cheong, "Canton and Manila in the Eighteenth Century," in Jerome Chen and Nicholas Tarling, eds., pp. 237–238, n. 5.

91. Tepaske, pp. 434–436.

92. Cited in William Lytle Schurz, *The Manila Galleon* (New York: E. P. Dutton, 1939), p. 70.

93. de Mendoza, vol. 2, p. 265. The price of sugar in Manila is given as "foure roues for sixe rials" on p. 266. See also George B. Souza, *The Survival of Empire* (Cambridge: Cambridge University Press, 1986), p. 65.

94. Chaunu, pp. 168–180.

95. John Davis, "Diaries," in Purchas, comp., *Purchas His Pilgrimes*, vol. 2, p. 315.

96. Iwao, "Japanese Foreign Trade," pp. 8–10; Iwao Seiichi, "Reopening of

the Diplomatic and Commercial Relations between Japan and Siam during the Tokugawa Period," *Acta Asiatica* 14:1–31 (1963); M. T. Paske-Smith, "The Japanese Trade and Residence in the Philippines before and during the Spanish Occupation," *Transactions of the Asiatic Society of Japan* 42.2:695 (1914).

97. *Dong-Xi yangkao*, vol. 164, juan 7, p. 2b.

98. Iwao, "Japanese Foreign Trade," pp. 3, 11.

99. Goodrich and Fang, eds., vol. 1, p. 872. The loan was probably made around 1613. Li Dan's son, Li Yiguan, better known as Iquan, was to become a major business partner of the British and the Dutch.

100. Saris, vol. 3, p. 448.

101. *Generale Missiven van Gouverneurs-Generaal en Raden aan Heren XVII der Verenigde Oost-Indische Compagnie*, W. Ph. Coolhaas, ed. (The Hague, Nijhoff, 1960–1979), vol. 1, p. 137.

102. Nagazumi, p. 330; Iwao Seiichi, "Edo jidai no satō bōeki ni tsuite," *Nihon Gakushūin kiyō*, 31.1:1–33 (1973). The data from Nagazumi Yōko and Iwao Seiichi, based on Dutch archival sources at Nagasaki, do not always match, but together they provide a very full record of Chinese trade to Japan.

103. Robert LeRoy Innes, "The Door Ajar: Japan's Foreign Trade in the Seventeenth Century" (Ph.D. dissertation, University of Michigan, 1980), p. 504. See also C. R. Boxer, *Jan Compagnie in Japan, 1600–1850* (The Hague: Nijhoff, 1950).

104. Iwao, "Japanese Foreign Trade," p. 4.

105. Iwao, "Edo jidai no satō," p. 13.

106. Iwao Seiichi, "Kindai Nisshi bōeki ni kansuru sūyrōteki kōsatsu," *Shigaku zasshi* 62:32 (1953).

107. For a discussion of various factors pertaining to urbanization in Tokugawa Japan and Qing China, see Rozman, *Urban Networks*. Rozman points out that Japan was twice as urbanized as China by the eighteenth century. The national market was also more completely integrated in Tokugawa Japan, and the range of urbanization extended from 12.6 percent in the Tōhoku region to 23.6 percent in the Kinki region: ibid., pp. 103, 272–273.

108. Takekoshi Yosaburo, *Japanese Rule in Formosa*, George Braithwaite, tr. (London: Longmans, Green, 1907), p. 242.

109. Nagazumi, p. 11.

110. Iwao, "Edo jidai no satō," p. 12. For *momme* conversion rates, see the Appendix.

111. Boxer, *The Great Ship*, p. 181. See also Souza, p. 52.

112. Boxer, *The Great Ship*, pp 168–169. The investors, many of whom seem to have been Cantonese, divided "risk and profit on a pro rata basis." There was apparently some effort made by the Portuguese to get Zheng Zhilong (Iquan)

to invest in this deal. Perhaps returning the favor, Iquan allowed the Portuguese to send a considerable cargo to Japan on his ships in 1644 after they were banned from the trade.

113. Both Boxer, *The Great Ship*, p. 131, and Souza, pp. 60–61, point to the extent of Portuguese indebtedness to the Chinese. Throughout 1630–1632, Portuguese Crown administrators and solvent merchants were involved in settling bad debts of compatriots by the hundreds of thousands of taels. In spite of their efforts, by the mid-1630s Portuguese merchants declared bankruptcy in Nagasaki. This, in addition to the proselytizing of the Portuguese, created ill-will among the Japanese authorities: see Boxer, *The Great Ship*, p. 169, for details on Portuguese debts of 1,500,000 to 2,000,000 guilders to the Chinese. Figures cited in guilders converted into taels according to ratio given in the Appendix.

114. Souza, chapters 5 and 6, has an extensive discussion of this realignment of Portuguese trade. To some extent Portuguese involvement in the export of Chinese goods such as silks, porcelains, and sugar to South and Southeast Asia had continued even during the heyday of the Macao-Nagasaki trade. The "Great Ship from Amacon," as the carrack was called, typically carried Chinese products for sale on the west coast of India. A memorandum dated 1600 for the lading of this ship at Macao for Goa noted, "It will carry 10,000 or 12,000 pieces of silk damasks and taffetas of all colors. . . . 3 to 4 piculs of gold. . . . It will take 2 or 3 (?hundred) piculs of sugar, and the money will be doubled or gained once and a half over": Boxer, *The Great Ship*, pp. 181–182. This shipment may well have been the first consignment of Chinese sugar sold in India.

115. Boxer, *The Great Ship*, p. 170.

116. Katō Eiichi, "The Japan Dutch Trade in the Formative Period of the Seclusion Policy—Particularly on the Raw Silk Trade by the Dutch Factory at Hirado, 1620–1640," *Acta Asiatica* 30:34–84 (1976).

117. Morse, *The Chronicles*, vol. 1, p. 5; Campbell, p. 1.

118. Wills, *Pepper, Guns and Parleys*, pp. 21–22. See also Goodrich and Fang, eds., vol. 1, p. 873, and vol. 2, pp. 1086–1087.

119. Saris, pp. 498–499.

120. Ibid., p. 493. The "Carracke" of the Dutch was the Portuguese *nao Santo Antonio*, captured by Admiral Wybrant Van Warwyck in Patani, when it was bound from Macao to Malacca: Charles R. Boxer, *Fidalgos in the Far East, 1550–1770* (rpt. Hong Kong: Oxford University Press, 1968), p. 51.

121. Reesse, p. 160.

122. Glamann, p. 19.

123. Ibid., p. 153. The actual figures given are 1622, 96,244 *ponds*; 1631, 400,000 *ponds*; 1633, 600,000 *ponds*; 1636, 1 million *ponds*.

124. Ibid. Actual figure given is 3.75 million *ponds*.

125. Ibid., p. 157.

126. Reesse, bijlage F, p. CXIII. Actual figure given is 1,964,941 *ponds*.

127. Reesse, p. 163.

128. Glamann, p. 155.

129. Dai Guohui, pp. 139–152.

130. Reesse, p. 166. Braudel, *The Structures*, pp. 220–224, discusses the declining demand for pepper in Europe. By the early eighteenth century, the Dutch were reduced to burning cargoes of pepper and nutmeg to protect prices.

131. Immanuel Wallerstein, *The Modern World-System II* (New York: Academic Press, 1980), pp. 162–164, suggests that the Dutch were able to benefit from their role of providing middleman services at a point when English overseas trade was dislocated by civil war at home, and that the expansion to Barbados and the other islands would have occurred more slowly had the Dutch not been expelled from northern Brazil. Once established, the islands proved to be havens for sugar planters, because they were easier to defend and closer to Europe than Brazil, and it was easier to control slave insurrections and prevent escape.

132. Glamann, pp. 159; 162; 174.

133. Ibid., pp. 159–160. Actual figures given are 1658, 2,044,545 *ponds*; 709,090 *ponds* sold to Japan. Some of the sugar sold to Persia at this time included Bengali sugar picked up by the Dutch in Bengal.

134. Moreland, p. 63.

135. Prakash, *Dutch East India Company*, p. 16.

136. *Generale Missiven*, vol. 1, p. 229. "Simsou" has been identified by Ts'ao Yung-ho as probably the transliteration of Xu Xinsu, a major merchant and competitor of Zheng Zhilong, killed in 1627 by Zheng in the invasion of Xiamen: Ts'ao Yung-ho. "Chinese Overseas Trade in the Late Ming Period," in *International Association of Historians of Asia, Biennial Conference Proceedings* (Taipei: Academia Sinica, 1962), p. 441.

137. Prakash, *Dutch East India Company*, p. 22; *Generale Missiven*, vol. 1, pp. 121, 204–205.

138. Prakash, *Dutch East India Company*, p. 122; Yamawaki Tejirō, "The Great Trading Merchants, Cocksinja and his Son," *Acta Asiatica* 30:112 (1976).

139. Prakash, *Dutch East India Company*, p. 123

140. See Glamann, p. 165, for the distribution of the export of powdered sugar from Batavia, 1713–1735. The usual Dutch shipments to Japan ranged from around 675,000 *ponds* to 902,000 *ponds*.

141. Kirti N. Chaudhuri, *The Trading World of Asia and the English East India Company, 1660–1760* (Cambridge: Cambridge University Press, 1978), pp. 207–

208; Sinnappah Arasaratnam, "India and the Indian Ocean in the Seventeenth Century" in Das Gupta and Pearson, eds., p. 112.

142. Prakash, "The Dutch East India Company in the Trade of the Indian Ocean," p. 197.

143. Prakash, *Dutch East India Company*, pp. 145–161. There has been relatively little attention paid to this increase in opium trade in the late seventeenth and early eighteenth centuries. Opium brought by Chinese traders may have been first introduced to Fujian and Taiwan via Batavian trade contacts. Om Prakash points out that the principal Bengal commodity sold by the VOC in the Indonesian archipelago was opium and that part of the 145,000–185,000 pounds of opium auctioned annually there found its way to China.

144. Arasaratnam discusses in detail the problems confronting the South Asian traders.

145. Tapan Raychaudhuri and Irfan Habib, eds., *The Cambridge Economic History of India, 1200–1750* (Cambridge: Cambridge University Press, 1982), vol. 1, pp. 374–376.

146. Glamann, p. 160: by the 1686–1687 trading season Bengali powdered sugar was sold at Surat at 15.31 florins per 100 *ponds*, while Javanese powdered sugar sold at 12.34 florins per 100 *ponds*. Yet as recently as 1680 Bengali powdered sugar had been 3.36 florins cheaper than Batavian sugar per 100 *ponds*.

147. N. P. Van den Berg, *Uit De Dagen Der Compagnie: Geschiedkundige Schetsen* (Haarlem: H. D. Tjeenk Willink and Zoon, 1904), p. 320; Leonard Blussé, *Strange Company*, pp. 90–95. The actual figures given are 1652, 1.5 million *ponds*; 1710, 8.8 million *ponds* with production capability of 13 million *ponds*.

148. Glamann, p. 263.

149. As cited in Yamawaki, "The Great Trading Merchants," p. 111.

150. Data from Nagazumi, p. 79.

151. Nan Qi, "Taiwan Zhengshi wushang zhi yanjiu," *Taiwan yanjiu congkan* 90:43–51 (1966).

152. *Generale Missiven*, vol. 2, p. 824; Viraphol, pp. 58–63. Viraphol underestimates the extent of Sino-Siamese trade with Japan prior to the 1650s. See Iwao, "Kindai Nisshi bōeki," and Iwao, "Reopening."

153. Yamawaki, "The Great Trading Merchants," pp. 109, 112; Ng Chinkeong, *Trade and Society*, p. 49.

154. "Letter of Captain Limbrey on Trade in Taiwan 1672," published in C. R. Boxer, *Papers on Portuguese, Dutch and Jesuit Influences in 16th and 17th Century Japan*, in Michael Moscato, comp., *Writings of C. R. Boxer* (Washington, D.C.: University Publications of America, 1979), Appendix 1, p. 183.

155. Iwao, "Edo Jidai no satō," p. 12; Yamawaki, "The Great Trading Merchants," p. 115.

156. *Ming Qing shiliao ding bian* (rpt. Taipei: Zhongyang yanjiu yuan, 1972,) Series D, p. 155a, gives the full text of the edict.

157. Iwao, "Kindai Nisshi bōeki," pp. 12–13.

158. Nagazumi, p. 95. Nagazumi Yōko's data have a gap between 1666 and 1682. But Iwao Seiichi provides a set of data for silk and sugar imports during these years in "Kindai Nisshi bōeki."

159. *Generale Missiven*, vol. 1, pp. 172, 240–241.

160. Ts'ao, "Chinese Overseas Trade," pp. 433–435.

161. Guangdong and Fujian were first given permission by the Kangxi emperor to begin trade by the spring of 1685, while the other coastal regions of Beijing, Shandong, Nanjing, and Zhejiang were given permission by the middle of the year.

162. *Xiamen zhi* (1839), Zhou Kai, comp., juan 5, p. 16a; Ng Chin-keong, *Trade and Society*, chapter 4, "Merchants," discusses the process of getting the permits and the expenses.

163. *Xiamen zhi*, juan 15, p. 5b; Ng Chin-keong, *Trade and Society*, pp. 153–158, gives details on this system.

164. *Gongzhongdang Kangxi chao zouzhe* (Taipei: Guoli gugong bowuyuan, 1976), vol. 6, p. 590.

165. This is a distinction often ignored. Because the Qing emperors were, however, concerned that the overseas Chinese communities not become centers of opposition to Manchu rule, from time to time overseas trade to particular areas was indeed banned. As closer studies of these various Kangxi and other edicts have shown, these restrictions were full of loopholes and were easily circumvented: see Blussé, *Strange Company*; and Ng Chin-keong, "The Case of Ch'en I-lao: Maritime Trade and Overseas Chinese in Ch'ing Policies, 1717–1754," in Ptak and Rothermund, eds., pp. 373–400.

166. For a full discussion of the Pan lineage and its links to the copper and salt trade, see Ho Ping-ti, *The Ladder of Success in Imperial China* (New York: Columbia University Press, 1962), pp. 283–286; and Wei Qingyuan and Wu Qiyan, "Qingdai zhuming huang Fan shi de xingshuai," *Lishi yanjiu* 3:127–144 (1981). As the lineage history shows, during the lifetime of Fan Yubin, the international trade links of the family were a key to their wealth. The family had business connections and establishments in Inner and Outer Mongolia, Manchuria, Japan, and Indochina, in addition to Zhili, Hubei, and Guangzhou.

167. *Da Qing lichao shilu, Sheng Zu* (rpt. Taipei: Huawen shuju, 1964), juan 116, 3b–4a. Viraphol, chapter 5, discusses the various aspects of the "encouragement plan" undertaken during the Qianlong period to encourage trade in certain commodities such as rice.

168. Ronald Toby, *State and Diplomacy in Early Modern Japan* (Princeton: Princeton University Press, 1984), pp. 57–64, 139.

169. Hayashi Shunsai and Hayashi Nobuatsu, eds., *Ka-i-hentai* (Tokyo: Tōyō Bunko, 1958–1959), vol. 1, p. 532.

170. In 1686 even the reduced revenue from the Guangdong Maritime Customs was 40,000 taels: Lo-shu Fu, *A Documentary Chronicle of Sino-Western Relations (1644–1820)* (Tucson: University of Arizona Press, 1966), vol. 2, p. 469, n. 222. See also Preston Torbet, *The Ch'ing Imperial Household Department* (Cambridge: Council on East Asian Studies, Harvard University), pp. 98–99; Lo-shu Fu, vol. 1, p. 86; Ng Chin-keong, *Trade and Society*, p. 191. These revenues were always a point of contention between local and provincial officials and the officials at Beijing.

171. Lo-shu Fu, vol. 1, p. 110.

172. Nagazumi, pp. 18–19, 91–96; Iwao, "Japanese Foreign Trade," pp. 12–13. For conversion of *kan*, see the Appendix.

173. Silver and other goods continued to be exported to China via this route and through Satsuma's trade with Fujian via the Ryukyus despite the Bakufu regulations at Nagasaki till the mid-eighteenth century: Tashiro Kazui, "Tsushima-han's Korean Trade, 1684–1710," *Acta Asiatica* 30:105 (1976). See also Tashiro Kazui, "Foreign Relations during the Edo Period: *Sakoku* Reexamined," *Journal of Japanese Studies* 8.2:294–298 (1982) for a discussion of export silver.

174. Tashiro, "Foreign Relations," p. 299.

175. Innes, p. 355.

176. Torbet, p. 96; Yamawaki Tejirō, "Shindai enshō to Nagasaki bōeki no dokusen," *Shigaku zasshi* 67.8:67 (1958).

177. Innes, p. 508. The rest was imported by the Siamese.

178. Morse, *The Chronicles*, vol. 1, p. 7. Although the focus here is the East India Company's trade with China, private trade in high value goods continued despite the East India Company's efforts to eliminate this trade: E. H. Pritchard, "Private Trade between England and China in the Eighteenth Century (1680–1833)," *Journal of the Economic and Social History of the Orient* 1.1:108–256 (1957).

179. Morse, *The Chronicles*, vol. 1, p. 26.

180. Ibid., vol. 1, p. 31.

181. Ibid., vol. 1, p. 99.

182. Jacques Savary des Bruslon and Philemon-Louis Savary des Bruslon, *A Dissertation on the Plan, Use and Importance of the Universal Dictionary of Trade and Commerce*, Malachy Postlewayt, tr. (London: John and Paul Knapton, 1749), s.v. "China."

183. Holden Furber, *Rival Empires of Trade*, p. 41; P. J. Marshall, "Private British Trade in the Indian Ocean before 1800," in Das Gupta and Pearson, eds., pp. 277–279.

184. See P. J. Marshall, *East Indian Fortunes* (Oxford: Oxford University Press, 1976), pp. 96–97; Greenberg, *British Trade*, p. 78; and Holden Furber, *John Company at Work* (Cambridge: Cambridge University Press, 1951), pp. 20–22. The role of Benkulen and the Sumatran pepper trade with China and a firmer control of Coromandal cotton piece-goods for the Malayan trade were two factors that aided this growth: Furber, *Rival Empires*, pp. 237–238; and Marshall, "Private British Trade," pp. 281–284. Bengal opium was sold in the Malayan and Sumatran ports by British and Gujarati traders, as well as in Batavia by the Dutch, and this was purchased by Chinese merchants from Guangdong and Fujian.

185. Chaudhuri, *The Trading World*, p. 175.

186. William Hedges, *The Diary of William Hegdes, Esq.*, Henry Yule, ed. (London: Hakluyt Society, 1888–1889), pp. lxxx–lxxxi. Americans began to move into this trade by the end of the eighteenth century; several American fortunes were made in this same trade, including that of Elihu Yale, founder of Yale University, who traded out of Madras.

187. Morse, *The Chronicles*, vol. 1, p. 157.

188. Ibid., vol. 1, pp. 157, 172, 176, 177, 179, 213, 271.

189. Ashin Das Gupta, *Malabar in Asian Trade, 1740–1800* (Cambridge: Cambridge University Press, 1967), pp. 98–99. The Portuguese, who had continued to import small quantities of Chinese sugar to India throughout the seventeenth century, now stepped up imports to around 1,400 piculs by the 1760s as exports of Bengali sugar began to decline further: Souza, pp. 158–164.

190. See Ashin Das Gupta, "Introduction: The Story," in Das Gupta and Pearson, eds., pp. 40–41.

191. This point has been detailed by Furber in *Rival Empires*, pp. 273–276.

192. Blussé, *Strange Company*, pp. 128–138.

193. Ibid., p. 156.

194. The Sultan of Kedah entered into an agreement with the British in 1786 allowing them to acquire the island of Penang (Pinang), off the coast of western Malaya. This allowed the British to eventually acquire greater territorial control in various parts of the Malayan peninsula. Batavian Dutch efforts at hindering British expansion in Southeast Asia through various alliances with Malayan kings also met with little support from Holland, particularly after 1794, when back in Europe the Dutch and the British allied to resist the Napoleonic invasion of the Netherlands: David Joel Steinberg et al., eds., *In Search of Southeast Asia* (New York: Praeger Publishers, 1971), pp. 78–79, 134–138; see also Marshall, *East Indian Fortunes*, pp. 96–105; and Blussé, *Strange Company*, p. 154.

195. Dermigny, vol. 1, p. 204.

196. Xiamen remained open to the Spanish trading out of Manila.

197. Morse, *The Chronicles*, vol. 1, pp. 130–133.

198. N. K. Sinha, *Economic History of Bengal* (Calcutta: University of Calcutta Press, 1956), vol. 1, pp. 97–113; George Watt, *The Commercial Products of India* (London: John Murray, 1908), pp. 1021–1023.

199. Irfan Habib, *The Agrarian System of Mughal India* (Bombay: Asia Publication House, 1963), p. 41.

200. For details on the trade circuit of raw cotton prior to the importation of Indian cotton, see Nishijima, "Shina shoki mengyō shijō no kōsatsu."

201. *Mu mian pu*, Chu Hua (fl. 1784), first published ca. 1800; rpt. in *Congshu jicheng* (Shanghai: Shangwu yinshuguan, 1935), ce 90, p. 17b.

202. Kang Chao, *The Development of Cotton Textile Production in China* (Cambridge: Council on East Asian Studies, Harvard University, 1977), p. 103.

203. Dermigny, vol. 2, pp. 803–805.

204. William Milburn, *Oriental Commerce* (London: Black, Parry and Co., 1813), p. 483; John Barrow, *Travels in China* (London: T. Cadell and W. Davies in the Strand, 1806), p. 560.

205. Greenberg, p. 81. The issue of opium has so dominated studies of the India-China trade that the extent of the cotton trade is largely ignored by scholars who have looked at this trade, such as Dilip Basu and Tan Chung; see, for example, Tan Chung, "The British-China-India Trade Triangle, 1771–1840," *India Economic and Social History Review* 11.4:411–31 (1974).

206. Imperial Maritime Customs, *Decennial Reports, 1922–31*, fifth issue, vol. 1 (Shanghai: Inspectorate General of Customs, 1935), p. 100; Chao, *The Development of Cotton*, pp. 102–104; Fang Xianting, *Zhongguo zhi mianfangzhi ye* (Shanghai: Shangwu yinshuguan, 1934), Table 11.

207. By 1834–1835, in addition to 82,000 bales of cotton, Calcutta was also exporting rice to China: John Phipps, *A Practical Treatise on the China and Eastern Trade* (Calcutta: Baptist Mission Press, 1835), p. 255; Rudrangshu Mukherjee, "Trade and Empire in Awadh," *Past and Present* 94:97 (1982).

208. Greenberg, p. 82.

209. Morse, *The Chronicles*, vol. 4, pp. 120, 141, 160, 183, 197, 250, 273.

210. Tyler Dennett, *Americans in Eastern Asia* (New York: Barnes and Noble, 1922), p. 58.

211. Benjamin Shreve Letters, Canton Brig, 1816–1817, file #7; Manuscript Collection, Peabody Museum, Salem, Mass.

212. Morse, *The Chronicles*, vol. 4, p. 385; Phipps, p. 314.

213. Deerr, vol. 1, p. 252: "The first manufacture of sugar in these islands [Hawaii] was by a Chinese, who set up a stone mill on Lanai in 1802, and re-

turned with his plant the next year to China." The first shipment of sugar to the mainland was made from Waimea, Kauai, in 1836, where Chinese operated the stone-roller mills; see Deerr, p. 254. Only later, after the 1850s, did the Chinese become important as laborers in the Hawaiian sugar plantations.

214. As a memorial from the Parsee merchants pointed out to the Select Committee of the East India Company in 1829, "Cotton is at present almost a dead weight in the Canton market; some of the Hong merchants have Cotton now in their possession purchased two years ago. The foreign [Indian] Cotton is principally consumed as we understand in the Province of Canton, and the market is of course very materially affected by the importation of manufactured Cotton Goods and Cotton Yarn from Great Britain": Morse, *The Chronicles*, vol. 4, p. 186.

215. Deerr, vol. 1, p. 56; Mintz, *Sweetness*, p. 63. The world sugar market was restructured during the 1830s and 1840s under the dual impetus of capitalist developments in Europe and the emancipation of slaves in much of the Caribbean. We shall return to this theme in Chapter Seven.

216. Henry Yule and Arthur C. Burnel, eds., *Hobson-Jobson* (London: J. Murray, 1903), s.v. See also Thomas Williamson, *The East India Vadomocum*, 2 vols. (London: Parry and Kingsbury, 1810) s.v.

217. Yen-p'ing Hao, *The Commercial Revolution in Nineteenth Century China* (Berkeley: University of California Press, 1986), pp. 22–24.

218. British Parliamentary Papers, *Select Committee Report on the East India Company and Trade with China, 1821–31*, Area Studies Series, China (Shannon: Irish University Press, 1972), vol. 36, pp. 66–72; British Parliamentary Papers, *Report from the Select Committee on the Affairs of the East India Comapny and Trade between Great Britian, the East Indiaes and China, 1830*, Area Studies Series, China (Shannon: Irish University Press, 1972), vol. 37, pp. 482–500.

219. Greenberg, p. 175.

220. Blussé, *Strange Company*, pp. 137–153. The decline of the junk trade at Batavia is most clearly visible in the decline in the value of the tea trade in Batavia, which fell from 149,023 rixdollars in 1731–1740 to zero by 1751–1760.

221. Furber, *Rival Empires*, pp. 271–282, lists various commodities.

222. *Gongzhongdang Yongzheng chao zouzhe* (Taipei: Guoli gugong bowuyuan, 1977), vol. 11, p. 70. This trade in rice is discussed in Chapters Five and Six.

223. Viraphol, pp. 85–107.

224. Phipps, pp. 176–255.

225. *Guangzhou fuzhi* (1879), Dai Zhaochen et al., eds. (rpt. Taipei: Chengwen chubanshe, 1966), juan 162, p. 35b. Viraphol, p. 96.

226. For example, Chinese trade with the Bugis, who started out as pirates at Riau and at Kedah in Malaya, compensated for the loss of the Chinese mar-

ket at Batavia. Closer to home, it is difficult to estimate how much of the Chinese trade was dislocated by the rise of piracy in the South China seas in the period 1790–1810. Several scholars have suggested that Chinese overseas trade never recovered from the dislocation of this period: Jane Leonard, *Wei Yuan and China's Rediscovery of the Maritime World* (Cambridge: Council on East Asian Studies, Harvard University, 1984), pp. 81–82; Diane Murray, *Fields from the Sea* (Stanford: Stanford University Press, 1987); Tian Rukang, "Shiqi shiji zhi shijiu shiji zhongye Zhongguo fanchuan zai Dongnanyazhou hangyun he shangye shangde diwei," *Lishi yanjiu* 8:1–21 (1956). However, as I show below, Chinese shipping seems to have recovered by the late 1820s and 1830s.

227. Ng Chin-keong, *Trade and Society*, pp. 58–61. Both Viraphol and Fu Yiling, *Ming Qing shidai shangren ji shangye ziben* (Beijing: Renmin chubanshe, 1956), p. 203, argue that the Qianlong decree resulted in the decline of Xiamen. But the more recent research of Ng Chin-keong suggests this was not so. I believe Ng's is the more accurate interpretation, for otherwise the continued prominence of ships from Xiamen in Southeast Asia and in new ports like Singapore in the 1830s cannot be explained. See Phipps, pp. 281–283, for Chinese trade at Singapore.

228. British Parliamentary Papers, *Select Committee Report*, p. 75.

229. Hao, *The Commercial Revolution*, pp. 16–17.

230. British Parliamentary Papers, *Select Committee Report*, p. 73.

231. John Crawfurd, *Journal of an Embassy* (London: Henry Colburn and Richard Bentley, 1830), pp. 109–110, 159. Phipps, pp. 202–203.

232. Crawfurd, p. 159.

233. Viraphol, p. 186.

234. At least in the case of Siam, as documented by Viraphol, chapter 8, there was extensive overlap in Chinese personnel involved in trade from both countries.

235. Crawfurd, pp. 177–178.

236. Tian, p. 16.

237. The total tonnage for East India Company ships for the years 1821–1833, given in Morse, *The Chronicles*, vol. 4, appendix following p. 372, tabulated by me. The data show that most years the total tonnage was around 25,000–26,000 tons.

238. G. William Skinner, "Regional Urbanization in Nineteenth Century China," in G. William Skinner, ed., *The City*. In this framework traditional China is seen as consisting of eight macroregions, Guangdong and Guangxi are grouped as one macroregion (Lingnan), and Fujian is separated from them as part of the Southeast Coast macroregion.

239. Greenberg, p. 16.

240. Phipps, pp. x–xi.

241. Crawfurd, vol. 1, p. 269, noted the arrival of junks from Singapore and Penang in 1822, and commented that though the Chinese junks came in after the English and American vessels, they were able to dispose of their goods more rapidly and take advantage of the best prices.

242. Phipps, p. 271.

243. Immanuel Wallerstein, *The Modern World-System*, vol. 3 (New York: Academic Press, 1974), p. 167.

244. For example, Tan Chung, pp. 411–431. This approach also neglects the revival of the Indian cotton export trade to China and Japan in the nineteenth century.

245. The "hong" and "Cohong" are discussed in detail in Chapter Six. The "qua" in the names of these merchants comes from the corruption of the person's name with the addition of the Mandarin Chinese "guan" (lit. official) pronounced "qua" in Cantonese but used as an honorific like "Sir." Thus, Wu Haoguan became transliterated as "Houqua": see Fairbank, *Trade and Diplomacy*, p. 249. Since western traders used the same name even when referring to different generations of a particular family, it adds to the confusion. I have sought to distinguish them by using their Chinese names.

246. Liang Jiabin, *Guangdong shisanhang kao* (Shanghai: Guoli bianyiguan, 1937), p. 126.

247. Morse, *The Chronicles*, vol. 1, pp. 291–294.

248. Liang Jiabin, pp. 205–215.

249. Ibid., pp. 300–305, 412; Morse, *The Chronicles*, vol. 2, p. 262; Morse, *The International Relations of the Chinese Empire*, vol. 1, *The Period of Conflict, 1834–1860* (Shanghai: Longmans, Green, 1910), p. 86.

250. Arthur W. Hummel, *Eminent Chinese of the Ch'ing Period* (Washington, D.C.: U.S. Government Printing Office, 1943), vol. 1, pp. 501–502.

251. Dennett, p. 57. The merchant's name was sometimes also written as "Conseequa" and as "Ponseequa."

252. William Hunter, who worked as the Chinese interpreter for Russell and Company, and therefore saw a lot of Wu Bingjian, notes several instances of unusual generosity and close working relations between the two: William Hunter, *The Fan Kwae at Canton* (London: Kegan Paul, Trench and Co., 1882), pp. 42–48. For details on Cushing's business enterprise, see Henrietta Larson, "A China Trader Turns Investor—A Biographical Chapter in American Business History," *Harvard Business Review* 12.2:345–358 (1933–1934).

253. M. S. Hooper, "Papers and Journal, 1840–1842," Duke University Library, Special Collections, p. 39.

254. Carl T. Smith, "Early American Trade in China and Hong Kong, Russell and Company and the Howqua Family," *Hong Kong Amcham* 7:14–17 (1976).

255. John Murray Forbes, Letterbooks and Journals: "History of Business done by John Murray Forbes for Houqua, 29 Dec., 1832," Forbes Collection, Baker Library, Harvard University.

256. Letter from Houqua to Jamsetjee Jeejeebhoy, 10 July 1829, Commercial Department, 1830, vol. 50, p. 143, Maharastra State Archives, cited in Asiya Siddiqi, "The Business World of Jamsetjee Jejeebhoy," *Indian Economic and Social History Review* 19.3–4:301–325 (1982); William Hunter, p. 49, discusses the draft.

257. Canton, China Collection, Foreign Marketing, "Houqua Letters" MSS: 766, 1841–1843, Baker Library, Harvard University.

258. Ibid.

259. Liang Jiabin, pp. 300–305; Morse, *The Chronicles*, vol. 2, p. 262; Morse, *The International Relations of the Chinese Empire*, vol. 1, p. 86; Hao Yen-ping, "Chinese Teas to America—A Synopsis," in Ernest R. Mays and John K. Fairbank, eds., *America's China Trade in Historical Perspective* (Cambridge: Committee on American–East Asian Relations, 1986), p. 30.

260. John Murray Forbes, Letterbooks and Journals, "American Stock Investment Company Account," Box 1, Forbes Collection, Baker Library, Harvard University.

261. Carl Smith, "Early American Trade," pp. 14–17. Carl Smith has made a study of wills and bankruptcy notices pertaining to Hong Kong history, and I am indebted to him for showing me this particular material in 1993.

262. Thomas Handasyd Perkins, Papers, Box I. Massachusetts Historical Society, Boston. I was not able to figure out Yeshing's Chinese name.

263. Dennett, pp. 85–86; Lo-shu Fu, vol. 1, pp. 391–393.

264. The many such cases of Chinese litigants in the courts of Philadelphia, Salem, Providence, and Boston have been studied by Frederic D. Grant, "Litigation Brought by and against Hong Merchants in the American Courts, 1800–1825," paper presented at the annual conference of the Association of Asian Studies, 12 April 1987. I am grateful to Frederic D. Grant for giving me a copy of his paper.

265. Edward Delano, Diary, 9 August 1841, Franklin D. Roosevelt Library, Hyde Park, New York. I am indebted to Frederic Grant for this reference.

266. Issac Smith Homans, *A Historical and Statistical Account of the Foreign Commerce of the United States* (New York: Putnams, 1887), p. 181. Dennett, pp. 20–21, gives the higher figure of U.S.$180 million; the port records show U.S.$70 million was shipped between 1805 and 1818. This figure is higher than those calculated by Morse, *The Chronicles*, vol. 4, p. 386. But Dennet's and Homan's figures are considered to be more reliable by Hao Yen-p'ing, and I agree with Hao.

267. Hunter, pp. 43–44. The date of this incident is not clear. But given the context of the other issues discussed by Hunter in these particular pages, it was probably in the late 1830s.

268. The shortage of capital, and surplus available for investment, underlies the framing of Elvin's thesis of the "high-level equilibrium trap," in *Pattern*, pp. 312–314, although elsewhere in his book he suggests that there was a surplus available for small investments.

269. Ibid., p. 284.

Chapter 3

1. *Kaogong ji*, compiler unknown, extant portions incorporated into the *Zhouli*, 140 B.C.: E. Biot, tr., *Le Tcheou-li*, 1851, 2 vols. (rpt. Beijing: Wentienko, 1930). My translation is based on the discussion of the passage by Yoshida Mikutuni, "The Chinese Concept of Technology: A Historical Approach," *Acta Asiatica* 36: 50 (1979). There is some debate about the date of the original compilation of the *Kaogong ji*. Guo Moruo considered it to be a text from the Chun Qiu period: Guo Moruo, *Shi pipan shu* (Chongqing: Qunyi shushe, 1945). This is, however, questioned by Yang Lien-sheng, *Studies in Chinese Institutional History* (Cambridge: Harvard University Press, 1961), p. 103.

2. For example, even Joseph Needham's pathbreaking work on Chinese science and technology focuses almost exclusively on inventions and the question of whether China was the first to invent a particular technology. The formulation that inventions equal breakthroughs in economic development is most evident in the work of Mark Elvin. As discussed in the conclusion to this book, Elvin overlooks the actual history of inventions in the Industrial Revolution and develops his framework of the "high-level equilibrium trap" in China based on the absence of inventions and inventors: Elvin, *Pattern*, p. 314.

3. Chinese popular texts and books for young adults on technology have imaginary portraits of the famous such as Sun Simo, Wang Zhou, Li Shizhen, Song Yingxing, and others; little clay statues of some of the inventors are available: see Zhang Runsheng, Chen Shijun, and Cheng Huifang, *Zhongguo gudai keji mingren zhuan* (Beijing: Zhongguo qingnian chubanshe, 1981). This retrospective discovery of inventors is common throughout the globe; consider, for example, the popular U.S. television series by James Burke entitled *The Day the World Changed*.

4. George Basalla, *The Evolution of Technology* (Cambridge: Cambridge University Press, 1988), p. 208.

5. The complex debate regarding whether New World slave plantations were pre-capitalist or capitalist and the necessity of locating slave-labor within a

framework of the world economy have been discussed by Sidney Mintz, "Was the Plantation Slave a Proletarian?" *Review* 2.1:81–98 (1978).

6. C. G. W. Lock, B. E. R. Newlands, and J. A. R. Newlands, *Sugar: A Handbook for Refiners and Planters* (London: E. & F. N. Spoon, 1888), p. 116. I have used this text for referring to some of the problems faced by pre-industrial sugar manufacturers that are not discussed in more recent texts on sugar manufacturing.

7. Ibid., pp. 294–295. Prior to the nineteenth-century development of vacuum pans, cane juice was universally boiled in open pans under normal atmospheric pressure. The resultant boiling point of no less than 230° F led to significant "inversion loss" from the conversion of molecules of sucrose into uncrystallized molasses.

8. I am indebted to the gur makers near Bagpat, India, for patiently demonstrating this to me in December 1979, and to Sonu Kishen for taking me there.

9. I am following Joseph Needham, *Mechanical Engineering*, in Joseph Needham, gen. ed., *Science and Civilisation in China* (Cambridge: Cambridge University Press, 1965), vol. 4, part 2, p. 172. My own extensive digging in various agricultural treatises has also failed to yield an illustration earlier than the *Tiangong kaiwu*.

10. Mark Elvin, in his translation of Shiba Yoshinobu, *Commerce and Society in Sung China* (Ann Arbor: University of Michigan, Center for Chinese Studies, 1970), translates the passage on sugar production in the Song as: "Oxen were used to work crushing rollers." The translation of the crushing mechanism as "rollers" is problematic. In the original, Shiba Yoshinobu uses the word *nian*, which, as discussed below, was not a two-roller cane crusher: Shiba, *Sōdai*, p. 217. While the word *nian* (also written 輾) is used by Wang Zhuo to describe the cane crusher, as is evidenced from the *Taiping yulan* usage, the word does not mean "rollers" but is used to describe crushing and grinding devices: *Taiping yulan* (A.D. 983), Li Fang, comp. (rpt. Shanghai: Zhonghua shuju, 1960), vol. 4, juan 762, p. 3385. In English the more appropriate translation of *nian* is simply "mill," as used by Needham in *Mechanical Engineering*, pp. 178–179, and by Twitchett in "The Monasteries," p. 534. Elsewhere, Joseph Needham did not discuss any other type of cane crusher in China except the vertical two-roller design found in the *Tiangong kaiwu*: Needham, *Mechanical Engineering*, p. 204.

11. Pelliot Dunhuang Collection, Manuscript no. P3303.

12. For example, Song Yingxing discusses only small wooden and stone mortars with wooden handheld pestles for pounding rice and other grains in his chapter on the preparation of grains: *Tiangong kaiwu*, juan shang, part 4.

13. Hendrik C. Prinsen Geerligs, *The World's Sugar Cane Industry* (Manchester: Norman Rodger, 1912), p. 51; Needham, *Mechanical Engineering*, p. 203.

Termed *kolhu* in the current vernacular, the word is from the Prakrit word *kutala*: John T. Platts, *A Dictionary of Urdu, Classical Hindi and English* (London: W. H. Allen, 1884), p. 864.

14. Although the history of this mill in India cannot be traced exactly, the earliest textual references to a cane mill in India date from approximately A.D. 100. Various Buddhist Jataka stories and sutras contain references either to cane mills or to the occupation of those connected with extracting juices and oils: Prakash, *Economy and Food*, pp. 104–105, 139–141; Deerr, vol. 1, p. 44; Gopal, "Sugar Making," pp. 60–61. Archaeological finds dated from areas near present-day Allahabad in Northern India have also revealed stone mortars of 5′ 3″ in height with an inner ring hollowed out to 1′ 3.5″ and with a ladle-shaped slit in the wall of the mortar for conveying the expressed liquid into other vessels. These were used for crushing oil-seeds as well as sugarcane: Gopal, "Sugar Making," p. 61. Vertical-roller mills are not among the agricultural implements described in *Amarakosa* (compiled by the north Indian Buddhist monk Amara between the sixth and eighth centuries and regarded as one of the most complete sources of information on contemporary agriculture and commerce), but the annular mortar-and-pestle mill is: S. P. Raychaudhuri, L. Gopal, and B. V. Subbarayappa, "Agriculture," in Bose, ed., *A Concise History of Science in India*, p. 360.

15. John Gerard, *The Herball or Generall Historie of Plants* (first published 1597) (rpt. New York: Dover Publications, 1974), chapter 25, p. 35.

16. In the Xinghua county gazetteer of 1503, cited in C. Daniels, *Biology*, p. 460.

17. *Tangshuang pu*, part 4, p. 3.

18. *Nongshu*, Wang Zhen, comp., juan 16, pp. 76a–78b; *Tiangong kaiwu*, juan shang, p. 97; *Nongzhen quanshu*, juan 23, p. 573. Needham believes that the illustration reproduced above as Figure 4 is the earliest extant picture of an edge-runner mill: Needham, *Mechanical Engineering*, p. 198.

19. *Nongshu*, Wang Zhen, comp., juan 16, pp. 76a–78b.

20. *Tangshuang pu*, part. 4, p. 3.

21. Professor Nathan Sivin, personal communication.

22. John Daniels and Christian Daniels, in a recent and very important study, "The Origin of the Sugarcane Roller Mill," *Technology and Culture* 29.3:499–500 (1988) and 500 n. 27, have suggested that the mill described by Wang Zhuo was an edge-runner mill, and I concur. In my dissertation, "A History of the Sugar Industry in China" (UCLA, 1984), pp. 96–99, I initially interpreted Wang Zhuo's description of the cane crusher as a version of the Indic annular mortar-and-pestle mill. But upon rereading the texts, I agree that the mortarium size of 10 feet given by Wang Zhuo was too large for an annular mill.

23. Rudolph Hommel, *China at Work* (1937; rpt. Cambridge: MIT Press, 1969), p. 86, describes an oil mill where the diameter measured from the edges of the trough was 16 feet. But in the illustration, in Hommel, the radius between the mill-post and the inner edge of the trough is given as 4 feet, which is very close to the measurements given by Wang Zhuo: see Hommel, p. 88, Figure 133.

24. Needham noticed several edge-runner mills with only one running stone in Sichuan in the mid-twentieth century, while two-wheeled or bogie-wheeled edge-runners seem to have been more common elsewhere in China: Needham, *Mechanical Engineering*, p. 403. Oil mills with one very large roller have been noted also in Persia: al-Hassan and Hill, p. 224, Figure 8.21.

25. Needham, *Mechanical Engineering*, pp. 203–204.

26. *Arthashāstra* (comp. ca. 350 B.C.), Kautilya, R. Shamasastry, tr. (Mysore: Mysore Print and Publication House, 1961), p. 102. The *kolhu* was used for crushing both cane and oil seeds. Gopal, "Sugar Making," p. 60 n. 9, discusses similar references from Varāhmihira's *Brhatsamhitā* (A.D. 530).

27. al-Hassan and Hill, p. 223, summarizes the early-fourteenth-century work of Da'ud al-Antaki and his description of oil processing in Syria. The history of diffusion of the crop has been traced in Andrew Watson, *Agricultural Innovation in the Early Islamic World* (Cambridge: Cambridge University Press, 1983), pp. 24–30. See also A. G. Drachmann, *Ancient Oil Mills and Presses* (Copenhagen: Levin and Munksgaard, 1932), p. 42.

28. Deerr, vol. 1, p. 80; and von Lippmann, p. 229. Trasselli and Daniels and Daniels also provide insights into the early Mediterranean industry.

29. Deerr, vol. 1, chapter 8, discusses the sugarcane industry of the Mediterranean, though, as John Daniels and Christian Daniels point out, his discussion of the Sicilian sugar industry, which is based on a painting by Stradaus (1585), is inaccurate: Daniels and Daniels, pp. 500–501. The earliest and most complete description of the Egyptian sugar industry is from al-Nuwairi (1380–1432). Here, too, as in other areas where the edge-runner mill was used, the cane was cut into small pieces by placing the harvested and cleaned cane on special grooved tables. Next, however, two presses (not one as elsewhere) were used. First the cane was crushed in a "rotating stone press," which was perhaps similar to a millstone. The crushed cane then were put in a basket to be crushed again in a "platform wheel press": al-Hassan and Hill, pp. 221–222. Deerr also translates the relevant section of al-Nuwairi: vol. 1, pp. 88–91. The edge-runner mill was used in Morocco, followed by pressing in a stationary press: Paul Berthier, *Un épisode de l'histoire de la canne à sucre* (Rabat: Imprimeries Françaises et Marocaines, 1966), vol. 1, p. 143.

30. *Tangshuang pu*, part 4, p. 3.

31. Ibid.

32. See Hommel, p. 108, for a discussion of these presses. For other presses used in China such as the tackle-and-weight press to extract liquids, see Needham, *Mechanical Engineering*, pp. 209–210.

33. Hendrik C. Prinsen Geerligs, *Cane Sugar and Its Manufacture* (London: Norman Rodger, 1924), p. 52, commenting on the twentieth-century manufacture of sugar in India.

34. *Tangshuang pu*, part 4, p. 4.

35. Prinsen Geerligs, *The World's Cane Sugar*, pp. 217–218.

36. P3303.

37. Ji Xianlin, p. 125.

38. *Tangshuang pu*, part 4, p. 4.

39. Deerr, vol. 2, p. 583. Though a seemingly minor procedure, this twelfth-century Chinese method was conceptually similar to a process patented in Europe in the mid-nineteenth century; seeding does not seem to have been common before that.

40. *Tangshuang pu*, part 5, p. 4.

41. Shi Shenghan, *A Preliminary Survey*, p. 74.

42. Aizawa Takushi, "Sōdai kansho tōgyō no kōsatsu," *Bunka* 34.4:364–382 (1971).

43. Wang Zhen, the author of the *Nongshu*, was from Tong-ping county, Shandong, and spent his career in the northern areas. Lu Mingshan was an Uighur official of the Yuan government. They themselves may not have been familiar with sugarcane.

44. *Nongsang jiyao*, imperially commissioned (first published 1286), rpt. in *Congshu jicheng* (Shanghai: Shangwu yinshuguan, 1937), juan 6, p. 29.

45. Needham, *Mechanical Engineering*, p. 184. Francesca Bray, *Agriculture*, vol. 6, part 2, in Joseph Needham, gen. ed., *Science and Civilisation in China* (Cambridge: Cambridge University Press, 1984), pp. 501–502, does not discuss the pedal tilt-hammer or its origins for decorticating rice in her broader discussion on the subject of rice and simply refers to the source used here from Needham. The use of this equipment from the plains of India to Southeast Asia to China and Japan suggests that the pedal tilt-hammer may have spread along with rice cultivation very early throughout Asia.

46. *The China Trade, 1600–1860*, catalogue of the exhibit by Patrick Conner (Brighton: Royal Pavilion, Art Gallery and Museums, 1986), p. 66, plate 82, shows a Chinese "export painting" depicting the manufacture and preparation of porcelain. This painting is discussed below in connection with the use of the waterwheel. Here it is relevant to note that a row of trip-hammers are shown pounding clay. *Tiangong kaiwu* also has an illustration of water-powered multiple pedal-tilt hammer mills for polishing and pounding rice: Sun and Sun, p. 93.

47. *Nongshu*, Wang Zhen, comp., juan 16, p. 3a; *Nongzheng quanshu*, juan 23, p. 570. Hommel, p. 100, fig. 155, shows a small *dui* for polishing rice. Though water-driven trip-hammers were used in the Mediterranean as well as early as the Roman period, their uses for industrial manufacture were slow to develop in Europe: Lynn White, *Medieval Technology and Social Change* (Oxford: Oxford University Press, 1962), pp. 81–84.

48. Polo, *Description*, vol. 1, p. 347. This passage has already been quoted in full in Chapter One here. The only detailed information besides Polo's regarding methods of sugar manufacture used in Egypt comes a century or so after Marco Polo's visit to China from the writings of al-Nuwairi: Deerr, vol. 1, pp. 88–91. Al-Nuwairi, however, does not mention the use of wood ashes. The Egyptians apparently strained the thick boiled massecuite through woolen cloth, poured it into conical molds, and after crystallization, reboiled the sugar crystals with milk, recrystallizing it to produce a white refined sugar. These techniques bear little resemblance to the Chinese methods.

49. von Lippman, p. 160.

50. *Bencao gangmu*, juan 33, p. 14b.

51. In the Dunhuang text, there is a partial sentence: "[when the juice is being boiled,] place with chopsticks a little." Ji Xianlin, in his reconstruction of the fragment, has suggested it should read "place with chopsticks a little lime": Ji Xianlin, p. 182. But although lime was already being used in India to clarify cane juice and it is possible that the artisans at Dunhuang were using a similar method, the fact that neither Wang Zhuo nor any of the Song and Yuan texts mention it suggests that, even if known, the technique did not come into general use until the late Ming in the main sugar-producing regions of China.

52. *Nongsang jiyao*, juan 6, p. 119.

53. Song Yingxing was probably aware of the problems of adding too much lime, which redissolved the scum, for he is very precise in his recommendation about how much lime to add: "To each *dan* of sugarcane juice [when boiling] five *ge* of lime is mixed in": *Tiangong kaiwu*, juan shang, p. 129. Whether this lime was to be added in liquid (slaked) form or otherwise is not specified. In Guangdong, since limestone deposits were limited, oyster-shell lime, prepared by the calcination of oyster shells, was more commonly used for clarifying sugarcane juice: Peng Zeyi, ed., *Zhongguo jindai shougongye shi ziliao*, vol. 2, p. 355.

54. The process of boiling the juice with the fire outside a partition seems inexplicable until one remembers that the Yuan procedure being described was utilizing a stove similar to the Chinese kitchen stoves photographed as late as the twentieth century: see Hommel, pp. 147–148. This stove clearly has a "partition"—a wall between the back of the stove, where the openings for supplying the fuel are located, and the front, which consists of the actual platform with in-

dented openings for placing the cooking vessels. Hence the *Nongsang jiyao* recommends that there be a person solely watching over the fuel supply to prevent a smoky fire, for the partition would have cut off the visibility of this person vis-à-vis the person stirring the boiling syrup.

55. *Nongsang jiyao*, juan 6, p. 119.

56. von Lippman, pp. 160–161, suggests that the Nestorians in Persia developed this.

57. Derived from *menos* (less) and *acabado* (finished).

58. Mauro, plate III, opposite p. 204; see also Françoise Sabban, "L'industrie sucrière, le moulin a sucre et les relations Sino-Portugaises aux XVIe–XVIIIe siècles," *Annales, Economies, Sociétés, Civilisation* 49.4:823 (1994); and C. Daniels, *Biology*, p. 333. The manuscript is now deposited in the Ajuda Palace, Portugal.

59. Pedro de San Buena Ventura, *Vocabulario de Lengua Tagala* (Pila: Thomas Pinpin et Domingo Loag, 1613), passage cited and translated in C. Daniels, *Biology*, p. 419. As discussed below, there is a problem with the reference to the citation and pagination given by Daniels.

60. Both von Lippmann and Deerr have suggested that the vertical three-roller mill was invented in Sicily by Pietro Speciale in 1449: von Lippmann, p. 338; Deerr, vol. 2, p. 536. This is a reflection of the tendency to assign a major technical development to a particular individual and to focus on the invention rather than the diffusion and uses of the technology that is typical of many scholars of technology. In this particular case, even the data presented to support this invention were not very convincing. But because of the impressive contribution made by these two scholars to the study of the history of sugar and the frequency with which their work is used by all researchers, their interpretations regarding Speciale gained uncritical acceptance. See, for example, Ratekin, p. 7; and Eliyahu Ashtor, "Levantine Sugar Industry in the Late Middle Ages," in G. L. Udovitch, ed., *The Islamic Middle East, 700–1900* (Princeton: Princeton University Press, 1981), p. 106. But several other scholars have expressed reservations about this genealogy of the three-roller cane crusher, e.g., Mintz, *Sweetness*, p. 234 n. 34; and Mauro, p. 304. Daniels and Daniels, pp. 493–535, have explored this issue in detail based on the work of Carmelo Trasselli. More recently, this issue has been also critically examined by Sabban, "L'industrie sucrière," pp. 817–861.

61. *Bencao gangmu*, juan 33, pp. 13a–13b.

62. *Tiangong kaiwu*, juan shang, pp. 2b–3a. The entire text is one continuous paragraph in the original.

63. In my dissertation, I suggested that these were helical gears, misrepresented by the artist: Mazumdar, "A History," p. 106. But I stand corrected by Daniels and Daniels, who provide the information that helical gears were not

traditional Chinese gearing, and though used in India, they do not seem to have made it across the Himalayas: Daniels and Daniels, pp. 523–524. However, contra Daniels and Daniels, other types of helicoidal forms were used in China: see Needham, *Mechanical Engineering*, p. 124.

64. In my dissertation, I discussed a Mathura Jain manuscript with a painting in the private collection of Dr. Saryu Doshi that I saw presented at a slide lecture at UCLA in Spring 1979: Mazumdar, "A History," p. 110. The illustrated manuscript, apparently an uncataloged item in Dr. Doshi's private collection, was dated 1532 by Dr. Doshi in this public lecture when I showed a particular interest in the illustration. It showed the Tenth Tirthankara drinking sugarcane juice to break his fast, with a drawing of a vertical two-roller cane crusher in the background. But oddly, despite numerous efforts that evening, and since, requesting a copy of the slide from Dr. Doshi, I was unable to get a copy of the illustration. Another illustration from 1540, provided by Saryu Doshi to J. Daniels and C. Daniels from the Jaipur Digambara Jain Bada Mandir collection, shows a scene of cane being crushed in a *kolhu* near Palam; it is reproduced on p. 509 of their article, and in C. Daniels, *Biology*, p. 289. But this is not the illustration that was presented at the lecture in 1979, which had the Tenth Tirthankara standing in the foreground with the equipment behind. The lecture specifically discussed Mathura and not Palam, a distance of some 125 miles. Therefore, until I can find further verification, along with many other scholars, I consider the manuscript from Peru as providing the earliest illustration of a vertical-roller cane crusher.

65. Surendranath Sen, *Indian Travels of Thevenot and Careri* (New Delhi: National Archives of India, 1949), p. 169. Irfan Habib, in "Capacity of Technological Change in Mughal India," in Anniruddha Roy and S. K. Bagchi, eds., *Technology in Ancient and Modern India* (New Dehli: Sundeep Prakashan, 1986), p. 2, and in his other detailed study of sugarcane technology in India, "Technology and Barriers to Social Change in Mughal India," *Indian Historical Review* 5.1–2:156 (1978–1979), also discusses this passage in connection with the development of cane-sugar-milling technology in India. Other contemporary travelers like Francois Bernier, an astute observer on many economic and social matters, do not discuss the cane crusher: François Bernier, *Travels in the Mughal Empire, 1656–1668*, A. Constable, ed. (rpt. New Delhi: S. Chand, 1891).

66. Watt, *Dictionary*, p. 195. That one of the areas noted by Watt as having this mill included the tribal area of Chattisgarh in central India is interesting and unexpected, for the region is fairly remote. William Crooke, *A Glossary of North Indian Peasant Life* (first published 1879), Shahid Amin, ed. (rpt. Delhi: Oxford University Press, 1989), illustration no. 3 from H. M. Elliot, ca. 1840, shows a vertical three-roller cane crusher near Meerut. But, as Shahid Amin

comments, it is somewhat surprising to find this three-roller mill, for there are no other descriptions of vertical-roller mills from western Uttar Pradesh for this period: Crooke, p. xlvii. Illustrations of both the three-roller mill and a *kolhu* are provided in Crooke, plates 3 and 4. The three-roller crusher, from an 1838 drawing, is shown with helical gears. Amin, in his introduction to the Crooke volume, points out that even the *kolhu* was too expensive for one household and was jointly owned by three to six peasant households: Crooke, p. xlix. The ways in which the financial limits of the household determined these arrangements are explored in detail in Shahid Amin, *Sugar and Sugarcane in Gorakpur* (Delhi: Oxford University Press, 1984). J. Daniels and C. Daniels are mistaken in their suggestion that the typical India two-roller cane crushers were 8″ in diameter, and therefore the mills with larger diameters, such as those noted by Watt near Poona (not Goa, as in Daniels and Daniels, p. 527), were closer to the Chinese model and hence may have been introduced from China. The size of the rollers in India varied from locality to locality based on the type of wood used. Frequently the straight part of the trunk of the babul tree (*acacia arabica*) was used, with gears chiseled on: Watt, *Dictionary*, pp. 152, 207, 222, 237. See also P. C. Patil, *Sugarcane Mills and Small Power Crushers in the Bombay Presidency* (Poona: Department of Agriculture, 1927), p. 5.

67. Crooke, p. xlvii.

68. The Japanese vertical three-roller cane crusher discussed and illustrated below is from *Satō seikakuki*, Kimura Yoshiyuki (Edo: n.p., 1797); K. Ota, "Manufacture of Sugar in Japan," *Transactions of the Asiatic Society of Japan* 8:462 (1880). Daniels and Daniels, p. 526 n. 112, has an elliptical reference to a Japanese source referring to a two-roller cane crusher in the Ryukyus in 1590 from "*inland* China." I have not been able to verify the source myself and have therefore accepted the *Tiangong kaiwu* as the first recorded reference to the vertical two-roller cane crusher.

69. George Staunton, *An Authentic Account of an Embassy from the King of Great Britain to China to the Emperor of China* (London: W. Blumer and Co., 1798), vol. 1, p. 388. On Java, the vertical two-roller cane crusher made of stone seems to have been the norm: Van den Berg, p. 329. Though Blussé, in *Strange Company*, has looked at several important aspects of the Chinese–Dutch interaction on Java, he does not address questions of technology and the diffusion of technology to China from Brazil via Batavia.

70. This is the crux of the position put forward by C. Daniels, *Biology*, particularly pp. 322–341. However, as discussed below, my position is considerably at odds with his. Furthermore, the textual evidence for a Chinese invention is absent; Daniels provides only a hypothesis supporting the claim for a Chinese invention.

71. Lynn White, *Medieval Technology*, pp. 83–84; Peter L. Eisenberg, *The Sugar Industry in Pernambuco, 1840–1910* (Berkeley: University of California Press, 1974), p. 38.

72. Irene Wright, "History of Sugar," *Louisiana Planter and Sugar Manufacturer* 55:173–174 (1915), letter dated 5 April 1548. This volume contains a series of summaries and extracts made by Irene Wright from documents in the Archive of the Indies in Seville concerning the sixteenth-century Caribbean sugar industry.

73. Daniels and Daniels, p. 518, use Theodor de Bry's illustration and suggest in their comment that the overshot waterwheel was "probably driving a horizontal two-roller sugarcane mill concealed in the shed." I do not agree with this extrapolation, because given the detailed depiction of the cane-crushing equipment and the processing in the engraving, why would the artist conceal other types of cane crushers if they were in use? Moreover, the cane is shown being carried toward the edge-runner mill, away from the shed.

74. Initial expenses for setting up at least one sugar hacienda in Peru in 1632–1634 show the purchase of "six large grinding stones": Nicholas P. Cushner, *Lords of the Land* (Albany: SUNY Press, 1980), p. 37.

75. Richard Flecknoe, *A True and Faithful Account* (London: William Crook, 1665), pp. 79–80.

76. Mauro, p. 204, traces the development of the three-roller cane crusher and refers to the writings of Rodrigues Palha Vincente do Salvadore, author of *Historia do Brazil, 1500–1627*. The original illustrations in this work, first published in 1627, have unfortunately been lost.

77. Galloway, p. 75.

78. See illustration, for example, by Frans Post, in Braudel, *The Wheels*, p. 192.

79. See illustrations in Reesse, Plate 12, originals in the Bodel Nijenhuis Museum, Leiden. Visscher's engraving "quotes" extensively from Theodor de Bry's illustration. Both Kaspar van Baerle and Frans Post were part of the entourage of forty-six scholars, scientists, artists, and craftsmen assembled by Johan Maurits, governor of Brazil, 1637–1644, to record the scenes and sights of the Americas: Charles R. Boxer, *The Dutch in Brazil, 1624–1654* (Oxford: Clarendon Press, 1957), pp. 112–113.

80. Pierre Pomet, *Histoire générale des drogues* (Paris: J. B. Loyson, 1694), p. 94.

81. Galloway, pp. 78–79.

82. Cushner, p. 71. The information, dating from 1634, on p. 197 nn. 20 and 21, indicates that the equipment described was common to all the estates.

83. C. Daniels, *Biology*, p. 332, suggests that a *trapiche* erected at Surco, Peru,

in 1581 was a vertical-roller mill, but gives no explanation as to why he considers this would have derived from a Chinese source.

84. Sabban, "L'industrie sucrière," pp. 826–831, has argued that the three-roller version represented a fundamental conceptual difference, for these rollers worked on the principle of utilizing symmetrical pressure rather than asymmetrical pressure. On the one hand, Sabban's argument that the three-roller mill used symmetrical pressure further supports my hypothesis that the Italian rolling mills and the cane crushers were related developments. I am, however, not convinced that this distinction proposed by Sabban provides enough evidence for a thesis positing the separate but concurrent evolution of the vertical cane crushers in China and the Americas, for as discussed by Needham, and elaborated here in the following pages, the technical principle of all these mills was the same.

85. C. Daniels, *Biology*, p. 331, writes: "The question now arises as to whether China or the New World has priority for the two-roller vertical mill. The problem is not likely to be solved easily. . . . However, we believe that the appearance of the earliest documentary evidence for the Chinese two-roller vertical sugarmill in the Philippines in +1613, twenty-four years prior to the first Chinese source of +1637, indicates its presence in China, or more precisely Fukien during the second half of the +16th century; it must have been there for the Chinese to have taken it overseas." Two crucial questions, however, remain unanswered in this interpretation: Why should it be assumed that the Philippines mill was of Chinese origin, and why should the Chinese first take it overseas but not use it at home?

86. Lynn White, "Tibet, India and Malaya as Sources of Western Mediaeval Technology," *American Historical Review* 65:515 (1960).

87. Needham, *Mechanical Engineering*, p. 92

88. Basalla, p. 49.

89. Although most horizontal-roller cane crushers had only two rollers, see illustration of three-roller horizontal cane crusher from J. B. Labat, *Nouveau voyage aux Isles de l'Amerique* (1724) reproduced in Sabban, "L'industrie sucrière," p. 829.

90. The standard date of 1100 used for the appearance of the cotton gin in India is based on D. Schlingloff, "Cotton Manufacture in Ancient India," *Journal of the Economic and Social History of the Orient* 17:81–90 (1974). However, Ishrat Alam, "Textile Tools as Depicted in Ajanta and Mughal Paintings" in Roy and Bagchi, eds., p. 130, takes issue with Schlingloff's dating and his interpretation of cotton technology depicted in an Ajanta painting from the sixth century. Schlingloff had interpreted this painting as a bow-string device. The painting reproduced by Alam clearly shows a device with two slender rollers, though a

problem arises in that the rollers are shown as widely separated with no meshing device to separate the seeds from the fibers. The issue is yet to be resolved, but I am accepting Alam's interpretation on this issue because the evidence of the Indic cotton gin in use in Cambodia by 1000 clearly undermines Schlingloff's chronology. Irfan Habib, in his essay in the same volume, also accepts Ishrat Alam's interpretation. See Habib, "Capacity of Technological Change," p. 11, n. 1.

91. Henry Pottinger noted water-powered horizontal rollers in the area around Bela, Baluchistan, in 1810: Henry Pottinger, *Travels in Beloochistan and Sinde* (1816) (rpt. Karachi: Indus Publications, 1976), p. 26. I am indebted to Harbans Mukhia for pointing this reference out to me. Elsewhere, from a nineteenth-century photograph, we see that manual labor was used: Deerr, vol. 1, p. 56.

92. C. Daniels, *Biology*, p. 315, is mistaken when he suggests that the Careri reference is to a *horizontal* roller mill.

93. *Satō seikakuki*, pp. 9a–9b; Ota, p. 465.

94. Habib, "Capacity of Technological Change," p. 2.

95. Reid, p. 31.

96. Needham, *Mechanical Engineering*, p. 122; Dieter Kuhn, *Textile Technology*, pp. 192–195; *Nongshu*, Wang Zhen, comp., juan 21.

97. This issue has been covered at length in Daniels and Daniels, pp. 506, 508–522. Because Daniels and Daniels depend on Schilingloff's dating regarding the appearance of the cotton gin for their chronological framework, they are puzzled by the appearance of the cotton gin in Europe in 1100. However, as seen above in note 90 to this chapter, Schilingloff's chronology is disputed.

98. Daniels and Daniels have strongly argued for a Chinese origin for the vertical two-roller cane crusher based on the interpretation that though this cane crusher was based on the generic technology of the horizontal cotton gin, "a vertical axis is the typical Chinese way of arranging machinery": Daniels and Daniels, p. 523. But surely they mean a *horizontal* axis is the typical Chinese way of arranging machinery, as is discussed in detail by Needham, *Mechanical Engineering*, pp. 546–547, and reiterated on p. 555. As such, the argument in favor of a Chinese origin for the vertical roller posited by Daniels and Daniels based on the design of the equipment alone is considerably weakened.

99. The big cotton reel frame (*mu mian kuang chuang*) and ginning and carding spread from the south, namely Fujian, into the Songjiang area: Dieter Kuhn, p. 219. The cane crusher, introduced from the Philippines, perhaps followed a similar route.

100. Daniels and Daniels preface their detailed discussion of the two-roller horizontal mill with, "We hypothesize that after 1510 the concept of the two-roller horizontal mill evolved in the area [the Mediterranean and Atlantic colo-

nies] or was transmitted from Asia to the Canaries and from there to the New World": Daniels and Daniels, p. 516.

101. al-Hassan and Hill, p. 181; Braudel, *The Structures of Everyday Life*, p. 326.

102. Maureen Fennell Mazzaoui, *The Italian Cotton Industry in the Later Middle Ages, 1100–1600* (Cambridge: Cambridge University Press, 1981), p. 74. The North Indian vernacular term *charka/churka/carkhi*, or spinning wheel, has been mistranslated as "cotton gin" by several scholars: Mazzaoui, p. 74; Daniels and Daniels, p. 506; Schlingloff, p. 81. This has added considerable confusion to the history of the cotton gin.

103. Lane, pp. 143–146; Mazzaoui, pp. 41–42.

104. Jean-Pierre Berthe, "Sur l'histoire sucrière Américaine," *Annales, Economies, Sociétés, Civilisation* 14.1:137 (1959).

105. For Peru and Brazil, see Mauro, p. 204. For the Caribbean, see Ratekin, pp. 4–5. For the Middle East, see Deerr, vol. 1, plate 7. The cotton industry in Hispaniola is discussed in an extract dated 22 January 1518, reproduced in Wright, p. 189.

106. Basalla, p. 25.

107. For example, for a discussion of several types of flour-grinding rolling mills from this period, see R. J. Forbes, "Food and Drink," in Charles Singer, E. J. Holmyard, A. R. Hall, and Trevor I. Willimas, eds., *A History of Technology* (Oxford: Clarendon Press, 1957), vol. 3, pp. 16–19.

108. Basalla, p. 69; Agostino Ramelli, *The Various and Ingenious Machines*, Martha Teach Gnudi and Eugene S. Ferguson, trs. and annots. (Baltimore: Johns Hopkins Press, 1976), p. 37.

109. James Lockhart, *Spanish Peru* (Madison: University of Wisconsin Press, 1994), p. 110. See also various biographical entries in José M. López Piñero et al., eds., *Diccionario histórico de la ciencia moderna en España* (Barcelona: Ediciones Península, 1983), illustrating the presence of a very large number of engineers, metallurgists, and botanists in Peru in the sixteenth century.

110. Lockhart, *Spanish Peru*, p. 143.

111. As discussed above, Needham points out the preference for vertical mountings in many mechanical designs originating in Europe: Needham, *Mechanical Engineering*, pp. 153, 158, 367, 546, 585.

112. For example, see Donald Lach, *China in the Eyes of Europe in the Sixteenth Century* (Chicago: University of Chicago Press, 1968); Matteo Ricci, *The Journals of Matteo Ricci, 1583–1610*, J. L. Gallagher, ed. and tr. (Cambridge: Cambridge University Press, 1959); C. Daniels, *Biology*, p. 332.

113. For example, see various letters in Wright, pp. 42–46.

114. de Mendoza, vol. 2, pp. 207–339, gives the itinerary of Martin Ignatius and the Franciscan friars.

115. M. Romanet du Caillard, *La colonization Espagnole dans le nord de l'île de Formose, 1626–1642* (Paris: Association Française pour l'Advancement des Sciences, 1890), pp. 4–5; Hsu Wen-hsiung, "From Aboriginal Island to Chinese Frontier: The Development of Taiwan before 1683," in Ronald Knapp, ed., *China's Island Frontier* (Honolulu: University of Hawaii Press, 1980), pp. 12–14.

116. de Mendoza, vol. 2, p. 267; comments written in 1588. Schurz also notes the comments of Pedro Chirino, a Jesuit, writing in 1604, "From China come those who supply every sort of service, all dexterous, prompt, and cheap, from physicians and barbers to burden-bearers and porters. They are the tailors and the shoemakers, metal-workers, silversmiths, sculptors, locksmiths, painters, masons, weavers, and finally every kind of servitors in the commonwealth": Schurz, p. 92 n. 7.

117. Letter from Fray Domingo to Felipe II dated 1590, in Blair and Robertson, vol. 7, pp. 226–227.

118. Zephyrin Englehardt, *The Missions and Missionaries of California* (Santa Barbara: Mission Santa Barbara, 1929), vol. 1, pp. 32–40.

119. Silvio Zavala, *The Colonial Period in the History of the New World*, Max Savelle, tr. (Westport: Greenwood Press, 1983), p. 93.

120. de Mendoza, vol. 1, p. 95; Blair and Robertson, eds., vol. 6, pp. 279–281.

121. Eugene Anderson, *The Food of China*, p. 97.

122. The life and times of Jan Con have been traced in Blussé, pp. 52–64.

123. Discussed in detail in Needham, *Mechanical Engineering*, pp. 547–549.

124. Tepaske, p. 435.

125. Schurz, p. 32. See also Sha Ding and Yang Dianqiu, "Zhongguo he Lading Meizhou de zaoqi maoyi guanxi," *Lishi yanjiu* 4: 107–127 (1984).

126. Zavala, p. 95.

127. Schurz, p. 373. The continuing trade connections between Manila and south China are also elaborated in Chrétien L. J. de Guines, *Voyages à Pékin, Manille et l'Ile de France*, 3 vols. (Paris: Imprimerie Imperial, 1808).

128. Schurz, p. 373.

129. T. Volker, *Porcelain and the Dutch East India Company* (Leiden, E. J. Brill, 1954), pp. 27, 37, 43.

130. Ibid., p. 48.

131. This point is particularly forcefully put forward by Daniels and Daniels, pp. 527–528; C. Daniels, *Biology*, pp. 420–421; and Galloway, pp. 204–208. Galloway, however, does not enter into a discussion of the technical details and disposes of the discussion with, "Almost certainly, this Chinese roller mill, probably of Indian derivation, was in turn the inspiration of the three-roller mill of the colonial American industry": Galloway, p. 206.

132. C. Daniels, *Biology*, p. 419–420. On p. 419, Daniels gives the citation to the de San Buena Ventura text as p. 420 and the entry is under the word *Alilisan*. This text, *Vocabulario de Lenua Tagala*, compiled by a priest Pedro de San Buena Ventura and published in 1613, is an extensive compilation of items, terms, and place-names in the various Filipino languages. This is a reference supplied to Daniels by Willaim Henry Scott. However, there is no entry in the de San Buena Ventura text for this word, the page reference is inaccurate, and despite a fairly lengthy search I was not able to figure out the original word and entry that Scott had translated for Daniels. But given the entry under the term *palos* that I was able to locate, I am accepting that a type of vertical two-roller cane crusher was being used in the Philippines by 1613.

133. de San Buena Ventura, p. 462. See also p. 60.

134. Wu Ching-hong, "The Rise and Decline of Chuanzhou's International Trade and Its Relation to the Philippine Islands," *International Association of Historians of Asia, Second Biennial Conference Proceedings* (Taipei, 1962), pp. 469–483.

135. C. Daniels, *Biology*, p. 420.

136. The introduction of New World crops into China is discussed in Chapter Five.

137. Even in Sichuan, Neijiang county, the area where Wang Shao had first written about sugar manufacturing, the only "old method" of grinding cane was the two-roller crusher: an illustration of the equipment is provided in Tan Danqiong, "Sichuan Neijiang de jiufa zaotang," *Dalu zazhi* 12.6:176–183 (1953).

138. Charles Gustavus Eckeberg, "A Short Account of the Chinese Husbandry" (1771), in Pehr Osbeck, comp., *A Voyage to China and the East Indies by Peter Osbeck* (1757), J. R. Forester, tr. (London: B. White, 1771), vol. 2, p. 297.

139. *Guangdong xinyu*, juan 27, p. 690; *Nanyue biji* (1778), Li Diaoyuan, rpt. in *Congshu jicheng* (Shanghai: Shangwu yinshuguan, 1936), juan 14, p. 178; Staunton, *An Authentic Account*, vol. 2, p. 396; Osbeck, vol., 2, p. 350.

140. Staunton, *An Authentic Account*, vol. 2, p. 461; E. H. Parker, *Up the Yangtze* (Shanghai: Kelley and Walsh, 1899), p. 186.

141. Wykeham Myers, *British Consular Report for Tainan, 1890*, in J. W. Davidson, *The Island of Formosa: History, People, Resources and Commerical Prospects* (London: Macmillan, 1903), p. 450; William F. Mayers et al., *The Treaty Ports of China and Japan* (London: Trubner, 1867), p. 239. Hommel, p. 112, mentions rollers with the cogs also worked out of solid stone. But a number of the cogs had broken off and had been replaced by wooden ones inserted into holes directly onto the cylinders. The rollers in Taiwan were 30 inches in height and 25 inches in diameter or about the same size as the Ming ones.

142. Peng, *Zhongguo jindai*, vol. 2, p. 355; Hommel, p. 113.

143. In Cuba, for example, this was a major problem for most of the eighteenth century, and almost up through the mid-nineteenth: Manuel Moreno Fraginals, *The Sugarmill: The Socioeconomic Complex of Sugar in Cuba* (New York: Monthly Review Press, 1976), p. 20. Elsewhere, Moreno Faginals, p. 39, comments that the adoption of the "Jamaican train" as these stoves with ten–fifteen openings were called was a "step backward"; indeed it was a step backward in terms of the continued dependence on slave labor, rather than the switch to steam and mechanization, the focus of the passage in Moreno Fraginals. In reading this passage, C. Daniels, *Biology*, pp. 361–362, however, misunderstands Moreno Fraginals and goes on to suggest that the Jamaica train was "backward" because it was less efficient to boil sugar in a single linear arrangement of pans rather than the clover-leaf shape as was done in China.

144. Although in the Yuan, at least as described in the *Nongsang jiyao*, copper cauldrons of cane juice were still boiled individually, multiple-aperture brick stoves are very old in China, going back to the Han: Yu Ying-shih, p. 59.

145. *Tiangong kaiwu*, juan shang, p. 129.

146. Mayers et al., p. 240. Twentieth-century examples of "old-style sugar manufacturing" in Sichuan also show multiple vessels of juice being boiled on rectangular brick or masonry stoves with multiple apertures for simultaneous boiling; Tan Danqiong, *Zhonghua minjian gongyi tushuo* (Taipei: Zhonghua congshu weiyuan hui, 1956), pp. 145–146.

147. Mayers et al., p. 240.

148. I have discussed this in detail in Mazumdar, "A History," pp. 146–147.

149. Deerr, vol. 2, p. 556. Prior to this, illustrations show cane juice being boiled on open fires both in the Mediterranean and in Brazil.

150. C. Daniels, *Biology*, p. 364.

151. *Hun*, the word translated as "chamber," is used of pigsties and privies. *Wo*, or "pot," literally means "nest" or "hole."

152. Excerpt from Hongzhi period (1488–1505) gazetteer for Xinghua county cited in Dai Guohui, p. 105.

153. Deerr, vol. 2, p. 451.

154. But a detailed description of the operation is provided by Henri Duhamel de Monceau (1700–1782), a noted French botanist and agriculturist, in his work *L'Art de Raffiner le Sucre* (1764), cited in Deerr, vol. 2, p. 464. The basic procedures followed are identical to the process suggested by the *Tiangong kaiwu*, including the refining of the crystallized sugar by remelting, clarifying with the use of egg albumin (or blood), and then pouring the reboiled massecuite into cones for claying.

155. *Min bu shu*, p. 4a.

156. This was to remain the method most commonly used in India to produce the highest grade of refined sugar, called *khand*: Watt, *Commercial Products*, p. 952. Staunton, *An Authentic Account*, vol. 1, p. 388, notes the use of slices of the trunk of plantain trees (which contain a lot of water) being used in Cochin-China.

157. Sabban, "L'industrie sucrière," pp. 849–853, discusses the writings of Liu Ji and an encyclopaedia compiled by him at the end of the Yuan and printed in 1540, but I have not been able to examine the original. See also C. Daniels, *Biology*, pp. 390–391.

158. Liu Xianting quotes from the writings of a late-Ming dynasty *jinshi* of Fujian, Lin Zhifan (studio name Han Zhai), whose own writings have not survived. Liu's own writings were also lost, but his student Huang Hu collected his miscellaneous notes under the title *Guangyang zaji*.

159. *Guangyang zaji*, (ca. 1650), Liu Xianting, comp., rpt. in *Congshu jicheng* (Shanghai: Shangwu yinshuguan, 1937), juan 2, p. 95.

160. The work is better known in the Spanish translation by Francisco Ximenez in his *Quatro Libros de la Naturaleza y Virtudes de la Plantas*, published in Mexico City in 1615. The error of Deerr and von Lippmann, who treat the work of Ximenez as an original rather than a translation, has been pointed out by Daniels and Daniels, p. 513 n. 72.

161. Wykeham Myers, p. 450; Franklin H. King, *Farmers of Forty Centuries* (1911) (rpt. New York: St. Martin's Press, 1988) pp. 173–174.

162. *Tiangong kaiwu*, juan shang, p. 131.

163. I think that the "yellow mud water" referred to by Song Yingxing in the passage was a mixture of some type of Fuller's earth and water. Fuller's earth can be yellowish in color and is known generally for its absorbent properties. The mud and water mixture had to be pastelike. Although in their translation of *Tiangong kaiwu*, Sun and Sun, p. 132 n. 9, suggest the mud itself percolated through the sugar crystals, "Therefore the slurry of yellow mud, on passing through the dark raw-sugar granules, removed the color and odor," this could not have been the case. Descriptions of the Chinese sugar industry from the nineteenth and twentieth centuries indicate that the clay placed on top was pastelike and used to cover the surface sugar in the conical drainage jars, which were then set aside for several days; Wykeham Myers, p. 450; Hommel, p. 113.

164. Wykeham Myers, p. 450.

165. Hommel, p. 113, found that it took 30–40 days for the sugar to crystallize and be available for sale. The methods used were identical to that of the late Ming.

166. *Guangdong xinyu*, juan 27, p. 690. The sudden appearance of this technique of claying in China, the use of the conical shape for the draining vessel,

combined with Song Yingxing's reference to *yang tang*, and the white sugar of the "Western Oceans" has suggested to some scholars, most notably Li Zhihuan, that these techniques were introduced into China through Fujian by Europeans: Li Zhihuan, "Cong zhitangshi tan shimi yu bingtang," *Lishi yanjiu* 2:152 (1981). But direct documentary evidence for this supposition is not available. Li Zhihuan does not indicate any specific region in Europe from which he thinks these techniques may have been introduced. The conical shape of the drainage jar, though clearly not common in China as Song Yingxing's comment indicates, was not a recent innovation nor was it European in origin. It was apparently first developed in the tenth century in the community of Nestorian Christians in Gondev-Shapur in the delta of the Euphrates on the Persian Gulf: Deerr, vol. 2, p. 450. So it is possible that it was introduced via an overland route during the Yuan.

167. Mayers et al., p. 241. Unfortunately Rev. John Scarth does not seem to have published under his own name. Only his notes survive as part of the compilations from the mid-nineteenth century, such as in Mayers et al.

168. The data on the organization of production in Guangdong in the Qing are discussed in Chapter Five.

169. Daniels and Daniels, p. 528, argued that the two-roller cane crusher was probably more efficient than the three-roller version because it did not break down as often and could be kept loaded with fresh cane all the time. But the argument is not convincing. Wykeham Myers, p. 450, reported that the two-roller crushers in Taiwan broke down frequently. There is also plenty of evidence to show that the areas with three-roller cane crushers were more efficient producers of sugar. Moreover, since cane was always crushed at least twice, and usually three times, surely a mill that used the same motive power as a two-roller, but multiplied the number of rollers for the same amount of power was more efficient in its use of both time and labor.

170. Imperial Maritime Customs, *Decennial Reports, 1922–31*, "A History of the External Trade of China, 1834–81," fifth issue, 2 vols. (Shanghai: Inspectorate General of Customs, 1935), pp. 130–131; Innes, p. 523.

171. Galloway, p. 105.

172. Wykeham Myers, p. 460, and his comments on the Taiwan sugar industry, where this problem is referred to in some detail.

173. In response to my earlier work in the dissertation, C. Daniels, *Biology*, p. 336, has argued that the Chinese mill had an advantage over the American three-roller mills, for "transportation of the whole mill proved easier because of the lightness of the two-roller mill." I fail to see how stone rollers could have been lighter than wooden ones.

174. Watt, *Dictionary*, pp. 267–270.

175. Based on Staunton, *An Authentic Account*, vol. 1, p. 388; Ellis, p. 281; Scarth, in Mayers et al., p. 241; Wykeham Myers, pp. 449–451; Hommel, p. 114. The details of the Chinese organization of production are taken up here in Chapter Seven.

176. *Canon Pietro Casola's Pilgrimage to Jerusalem, 1494*, M. Margaret Newett, tr. (Manchester: University Press, 1907), p. 216.

177. Deerr, vol. 2, pp. 451–453.

178. Reesse, pp. 104–150.

179. Dale W. Tomich, *Slavery in the Circuit of Sugar* (Baltimore: Johns Hopkins University Press, 1990), p. 183.

180. Cushner, p. 37; Moreno Fraginals, pp. 24–37, 101. Moreno Fraginals shows that in late-eighteenth-century Cuba, the Cuban sugarocracy quickly turned to the latest innovations and were among the first to comprehend the implications of steam-operated mills.

181. Eisenberg found that 80 percent of the mills in Pernambuco, Brazil, used animal-power in 1854; an 1857 count showed this had decreased to 66 percent, with approximately 31 percent using water-power. The rest had already shifted to steam-powered machinery: Eisenberg, p. 38.

182. *Guangdong xinyu*, juan 27, p. 690.

183. *Xuxiu Taiwan fuzhi* (preface 1774) (rpt. Taipei: Taiwan yinhang, 1962), juan 17, p. 593.

184. In the twentieth century during 1914–1918 and 1931–1937, oxen and water-buffaloes numbered between 23,000,000 and 37,000,000 in a human population that is estimated at 430,000,000–503,000,000 and a cultivated acreage of 1,471,000,000 *shi mu* in 1933: Dwight Perkins, *Agricultural Development*, pp. 212, 236, 287. Data for number of livestock in earlier periods do not seem to be available.

185. Taking up the discussion on this topic of the absence of water-driven sugar mills in Guangdong that I had presented in my dissertation, Christian Daniels has proposed that the reason lay in the local climatic environment of seasonal monsoons: C. Daniels, *Biology*, pp. 319–320, 335–337. But this is a spurious argument. As any standard geography textbook indicates, even the winter months have at least 1–2 inches of rainfall and the profusion of streams and waterways in the region is well known. Moreover, as I argued in the dissertation, and show in some detail here, water-power was used in the same region for operating other types of mills. The question then still remains: Why was it not used for grinding sugarcane?

186. Ratekin, p. 10. Mintz, *Sweetness*, p. 34, also cites this information from Ratekin. Weight given by American authors, so I am assuming the short ton.

187. Deerr, vol. 1 , p. 108; Boxer, *The Dutch*, p. 141.

188. Ts'ao Yung-ho, "Ming Hongwu chao de Zhong Liu guanxi," in Zhang Yanxian, ed., *Zhongguo haiyang fazhanshi lunwenji* (Taipei: Zhongyang yanjiu yuan, 1988), vol. 3, p. 281.

189. Higuchi Hiroshi, *Nihon tōgyō shi* (Tokyo: Naigai keizaisha, 1956), pp. 20, 23. C. Daniels, *Biology*, p. 448, seems to question this date but provides no evidence.

190. Kinjō Isao, *Kindai Okinawa no tōgyō* (Naha: Hirugisha, 1985), pp. 276–281.

191. Robert Sakai, "The Ryukyu (Liu-Ch'iu) Islands as a Fief of Satsuma," in John K. Fairbank, ed., *The Chinese World Order* (Cambridge: Harvard University Press, 1968).

192. George Kerr, *Okinawa, The History of an Island People* (Tokyo: Tuttle, 1964), pp. 151–182, discusses in detail the origins and control of Satsuma over the Ryukyus.

193. Sakai, "The Ryukyu," p. 131.

194. Higuchi, p. 61.

195. Higuchi, p. 60; Innes, pp. 509–513. Tribute amount owed to Satsuma based on information in Kerr, *Okinawa*, p. 179.

196. A *kan* is a unit of weight equal to 2.28 pounds. See the Appendix for details of currency conversions. In 1630, the debt was perhaps as much as 20,000 *kan* of silver. The funds were borrowed to finance the *shinko-sen*, or tribute missions to China, in which Satsuma had a major commercial interest. The large official Chinese delegations sent by the Ming and Manchu governments to the Ryukyus during investiture missions, of which there were ten during the Tokugawa period, also added to the debt of the Ryukyuan government: Robert Sakai, "Satsuma, Ryukyu Trade and the Tokugawa Seclusion Policy," *JAS* 23.3:393–395 (1964).

197. Higuchi, pp. 61–69.

198. Innes, p. 515.

199. Kerr, *Okinawa*, p. 198; Innes, p. 511; C. Daniels, *Biology*, p. 453.

200. Kerr, *Okinawa*, pp. 205–207.

201. Matsushita Shirō, *Kinsei Amami no Shihai to shakai* (Tokyo: Daiichi Shobō, 1983), p. 63; Sakai, "The Ryukyu," p. 313 n. 50.

202. Innes, pp. 510–511; Matsushita, p. 106.

203. Higuchi, p. 20.

204. Innes, p. 515.

205. Here again, C. Daniels, *Biology*, p. 453, makes the error of suggesting that the three-roller sugarcane crusher hooked up to a horizontally mounted waterwheel in Amami was not possible in China due to preferences for *vertical* mountings; inexplicably the illustration proving this point (Fig. 86) is from the

Japanese work *Satō seikakuki*. As explored below, similar types of mountings were used by the Chinese, and the fact remains, as acknowledged by Daniels on the same page, that hydraulically powered mills ground more than twice as much juice than animal-powered ones.

206. Oba Osamu: "Nagasaki and the Importation of Chinese Books to Japan in the Edo Period," *Sino-Japanese Studies Newsletter* 1.1:24–32 (1988). Yoshimune's interests, along with those of several daimyo, resulted in a lively book trade at Nagasaki, where orders were made annually through shipping agents.

207. Higuchi, pp. 74–75.

208. Ibid., pp. 97–114.

209. *Butsurui hinshitsu* (1763), Hiaraga Gennai (rpt. Tokyo: Nihon kōten zenshō, 1928), pp. 178–179. The illustration in the *Butsurui hinshitsu* is that of a Japanese using a two-roller mill.

210. Higuchi, pp. 73–77.

211. Ota, p. 465, records the use of a horizontal cane crusher in the late nineteenth century, but suggests it was used only rarely, when small quantities of cane were to be crushed.

212. *Satō seikakuki*, pp. 8a–8b.

213. Ibid., pp. 7a, 17b.

214. Ibid., p. 17a

215. C. Daniels, *Biology*, p. 461, citing the research of Katsura Masaki, supports the latter's interpretation that the thinner roller diameters seen in the Ryukyus, Satusma, Tosa, Edo, and so on were not derived from China. But both authors propose other locations in Asia as the source, even when they cannot find any evidence, rather than accede to the obvious possibility of an introduction from the Americas.

216. C. Daniels, *Biology*, pp. 459–460. Daniels does not comment on the technical aspect of the size of the rollers, etc.

217. *Tiangong kaiwu*, juan shang, p. 2b.

218. Jean Baptiste Labat, *Nouveau Voyage aux Isles de l'Amerique* (Paris: P. Husson, 1724), vol. 2, p. 242.

219. This design has been noted in the three-roller crushers in both the Ryukyus and southwestern Japan: C. Daniels, *Biology*, pp. 454, 461.

220. Ibid., pp. 448–450, documents this most clearly.

221. Sakai, "Satsuma, Ryukyu," p. 396.

222. *Satō seikakuki*, p. 2a; see also Ota, p. 462.

223. Higuchi, pp. 94–95.

224. Ota, pp. 465–466. This data is supported by C. Daniels, *Biology*, pp. 340, 460.

225. Needham, *Mechanical Engineering*, p. 401.

226. Ibid., pp. 396–405. Water-power was used in China when there was sufficient centralization of production, as on the monastic and other private estates in the Tang and Song: Denis Twitchett, "Monastic Estates in Tang China," *Asia Major*, n.s. 5.2:140 (1956); Sudō Yoshiyuki, "Nan-Sō inasaku no chi-iku," *Shigaku zasshi* 70.6:32–36 (1961).

227. *Nongshu*, Wang Zhen, comp., juan 16, pp. 2b–3a; juan 19, pp. 20b–21a. Needham, *Mechanical Engineering*, pp. 339–352.

228. *Tiangong kaiwu*, juan shang, p. 76.

229. C. Daniels, *Biology*, p. 3, has a reference to the Tai people of Sip Song Panna of Yunnan using water-powered cane crushers. This example of the use of water-power to turn cane crushers from Yunnan is similar to the observations made by Henry Pottinger in Baluchistan and cited above. Both these regions were tribal aborigine areas, with relations of production that set them apart from the small-holder dominated economies of the plains.

230. *Min bu shu*, p. 14a.

231. Needham, *Mechanical Engineering*, pp. 410–411.

232. *The China Trade*, p. 66. Scenes of Chinese life painted for export, 1810.

233. Hommel, pp. 81–87.

234. Lillian Li, *China's Silk Trade* (Cambridge: Harvard University Press, 1981), pp. 37–61, has looked at this question in detail. This link between the state and silk manufacture is crucial in the period prior to the Opium War and has to be understood in evaluating the types of large drawlooms used in weaving by households that operated under contract to the Imperial Factories. Failure to sufficiently account for this particular aspect of the organization of production in the silk industry has led to errors of interpretation among several scholars, who have used examples from the silk-manufacturing sector to suggest incipient capitalism. See, for example, Liu Yongzheng, "Shilun Qingdai Suzhou shougongye hanghui," *Lishi yanjiu* 11:21–46 (1959); and Elvin, *Pattern*, p. 283.

235. Discussion of the "household" and the social organization of production is taken up in detail in the next chapter. But for the purposes of this study, a household is defined as the primary unit of production and was made up of persons who ate together and shared a common budget: Rubie Watson, *Inequality among Brothers* (Cambridge: Cambridge University Press, 1985), p. 78. In the double-cropping rice area, which includes the areas of South China cultivating sugarcane, households in the early twentieth century were composed of an average of 5.9 people: John L. Buck, *Land Utilization in China* (Shanghai: Commercial Press, 1937), p. 38.

236. Chao, *The Development of Cotton*, p. 10.

237. *Nongshu*, Wang Zhen, comp., juan 21, pp. 27b-28a.

238. This discussion of the technology of cotton manufacture is based on *Nongzheng quanshu*, zhongce, juan 35, pp. 975–981; Chao, *The Development of Cotton*, pp. 56–80; Dieter Kuhn, pp. 190–193.

239. *Nongzheng quanshu*, zhongce, juan 35, p. 971, illustration of the smaller gin is on p. 976; see also Chao, *The Development of Cotton*, p. 79.

240. Chao, *The Development of Cotton*, pp. 79–80.

241. Hommel, p. 161.

242. Chao, *The Development of Cotton*, p. 57.

243. *Nongzheng quanshu*, zhongce, juan 36, pp. 1001–1002. Chao, *The Development of Cotton*, pp. 59, 67, 330 n. 4, discusses the potential of this spinning frame for developing the spinning jenny. Elvin has also discussed the large spinning frame and its potential for use in cotton spinning: see Elvin, *Pattern*, pp. 194–199; and Mark Elvin, "The High-Level Equilibrium Trap," in W. E. Willmott, ed., *Economic Organization in Chinese Society* (Stanford: Stanford University Press, 1972), pp. 139–148. Dieter Kuhn, pp. 231–236, points out some of the problems with Elvin's understanding of the operations of the ramie spinning frame.

244. Dieter Kuhn provides an example from the twentieth century on p. 224, n. a.

245. Ibid.

246. Ibid., pp. 221–222.

247. Ibid., pp. 224–225; data converted from grams to ounces.

248. Hommel, pp. 169–171.

249. Sun and Sun, pp. 55–56; Chao, *The Development of Cotton*, pp. 72–75.

250. Chao, *The Development of Cotton*, pp. 73–74.

251. Craig Dietrich, "Cotton Culture and Manufacture in Early Ch'ing China," in Willmott, ed., pp. 127, 130. Hommel discusses the ribbon loom and tape loom and mentions seeing in some areas such as in Datong, Anhui, a very primitive type of loom used for weaving patterned belts: Hommel, pp. 186–188.

252. *Tiangong kaiwu*, juan shang, p. 39. We shall return to these crops in the discussion of commercial agriculture, Chapter Five. Dieter Kuhn, pp. 15–51, has a very full chronological discussion of these fiber crops in China.

253. Dieter Kuhn, p. 38.

254. This was a difficult problem. A report from Taiwan shows that despite repeated attempts to produce machinery for decorting and separating the inner white fiber, nothing had worked even as late as 1890: British Parliamentary Papers, *General Correspondence, dispatches and reports*, Area Studies Series, China, vol. 39 (Shannon: Irish University Press, 1972), p. 12.

255. *Nongzheng quanshu*, zhong ce, juan 36, p. 994. *Tiangong kaiwu*, juan shang, p. 39.

256. In late-nineteenth-century Taiwan, a bamboo-and-iron scraper was used, which had evidently speeded up the process of decorting, and eight pounds of fiber could be produced in a ten-hour working day: British Parliamentary Papers, *General Correspondence, dispatches and reports*, p. 13.

257. *Tiangong kaiwu*, juan shang, p. 39, gives the output of a day's work; *Nongshu*, Wang Zhen, comp., juan 22, p. 7b–8a. Elvin suggests that these large water-powered spinning frames "were owned by manor lords or other well-to-do persons who made them available to the peasantry for a cash fee or percentage of the yarn," but he does not cite any documentary evidence: Elvin, "High-Level Equilibrium," p. 156. Similarities with European arrangements for mills grinding flour, etc., come to mind, but it is not clear that such arrangements existed in China.

258. *Tiangong kaiwu*, juan shang, p. 39, does not describe the multi-spindle frame and indicates that the treadle spinning wheel and the hand spindles were commonly used for spinning ramie. The *Nongzheng quanshu* describes the multi-spindle spinning frame in the 1639 text, juan 36, p. 1001. But as in the case of Xu's description of sugarcane crushing, it is difficult to determine if he is describing current practices or simply repeating information from Wang Zhen's *Nongshu* of 1313.

259. Chao, *Man and Land*, p. 224.

260. Oyama Masaaki, "Large Landownership in the Jiangnan Delta Region during the Late Ming–Early Qing Period," Christian Daniels, tr., in Grove and Daniels, eds., p. 145; King, pp. 78–79; Hommel, pp. 52–54; Needham, *Mechanical Engineering*, pp. 339–350.

261. Chao, *The Development of Cotton*, p. 80, has argued that available technology was more advanced than the "backward production institution" in China. This understanding abstracts technology from its social bearings and makes it a force on its own.

262. The suggestion that the Chinese used "management solutions" rather than "technical solutions" put forward by C. Daniels, *Biology*, p. 336–337, is also problematic. "Management solutions" is a term and organizational principle drawn from late capitalism. To apply this to pre–industrial revolution China is anachronistic; it also does not explain why the Chinese would have preferred a lower level of output—the issue that we are concerned with here.

263. Eric Hobsbawm, *The Age of Revolution, 1789–1848* (New York: New American Library, 1962), pp. 56–57.

264. In Hebei, for example, several families would construct a communal cellar in which to spin cotton to counteract the region's low humidity. "But this

was nothing more complex than a group of independent family operations working under one roof": Dietrich, p. 130.

265. The sharing of cane-crushing equipment among poor peasants is discussed in Chapter Four and Chapter Five. When particular aspects of manufacturing became highly specialized activities in specific localities and were removed from the agrarian sector, such as dyeing and calendering cotton cloth in Suzhou township, efforts were made to centralize manufacture and bring together several tens and even thousands of artisans. Dietrich provides a graphic commentary on how this putting-out system operated on pp. 130–131.

Chapter 4

1. King, pp. 60, 65.

2. In studies of pre-nineteenth century China these ideas have been most clearly articulated by Francesca Bray and Mark Elvin.

3. Edward H. Schafer, *The Vermilion Bird* (Berkeley: University of California Press, 1967), p. 34.

4. Ch'ü T'ung-tsu, *Han Social Structure* (Seattle: University of Washington Press, 1972), p. 140.

5. Schafer, *Golden Peaches*, p. 15. Zeng Huaman, *Tangdai Lingnan fazhande hexinxing* (Hong Kong: Zhongwen daxue chubanshe, 1973).

6. Kuwabara, pp. 3–20; Zhao Rugua, pp. 19–20, 190. All official titles and names of offices are translated according to Charles O. Hucker, *A Dictionary of Official Titles in Imperial China* (Stanford: Stanford University Press, 1985).

7. *Tangshuang pu*, part. 1, p. 1. For discussions of cane sugar prior to the Song, see Chapter One above.

8. Shiba, *Sōdai*, pp. 162–163; *Meng liang lu*, p. 269. Rice shipments to Southeast Asia may have functioned as ballast for the ships.

9. Other genealogies, such as that of the Xu lineage of Xiangshan, *Guangdong Xiangshan Xushi zongpu* (1882), and the Li lineage who settled in Panyu, *Guangdong Taijingtou-xiang Lishi puxi* (1975), suggest the late Song political disorders forced them to migrate further south. See also *Xinhui xiangtu zhi* (1908) (rpt. Hong Kong: Gangzhou xuehui, 1970), part 7, pp. 83–85. Helen Siu and Wolfram Eberhard note similar sections in the genealogies they have worked with: Helen Siu, *Agents and Victims in South China* (New Haven: Yale University Press, 1989), pp. 43–44; Wolfram Eberhard, *Social Mobility in South China* (Leiden: E. J. Brill, 1962), pp. 61–65.

10. Rubie Watson, *Inequality among Brothers*, p. 18. Sections of the Deng genealogy and that of the "five great lineages" of the Hong Kong region have been extracted in Kwok-kin Siu and Siu Kwok-kwan, *Zupu yu Xianggang difangshi yanjiu* (Hong Kong: Xianchao shushi chuban, 1982). Sung Hok-p'ang, "Legends

and Stories of the New Territories, Kam T'in," *JHKBRAS* 13:111–132 (1973) and 14:160–185 (1974), is based primarily on details from the Deng genealogies.

11. *Lineage*: Definition of the *zu* and other associated institutions including non-localized lineages have been elucidated by James Watson, "Chinese Kinship Reconsidered: Anthropological Perspectives on Historical Research," *China Quarterly* 92:589–622 (1982). This is the typology followed here, and it is discussed below in the section on lineage organization. When quoting from the works of authors who have used the word *clan* rather than *lineage* to translate *zu*, I have retained the authors' usage: for example, Hsiao Kung-chuan, *Rural China* (Seattle: University of Washington Press, 1962). I have used the term *lineage* to indicate demonstrated agnatic descent and *clan* for lineage-like associations that fictionalized descent but operated as a corporate body much like the lineage.

12. David Faure, *The Structure of Chinese Rural Society* (Hong Kong: Oxford University Press, 1986), p. 17, does not elaborate but expresses reservations regarding Song settlements in the region of the New Territories and Hong Kong. As Maurice Freedman concludes in *Lineage Organization in Southeastern China*, London School of Economics Monographs on Social Anthropology (London, 1958), p. 7, the common history of migration in the Song may be "either a reflection of some historical reality or a conventional idiom of descent." The "invention" of a genealogy substantiating a lineage's myths of origin and settlement are most fully articulated in David Faure, "Lineage as a Cultural Invention: The Case of the Pearl River Delta," *Modern China* 15.1: 4–36 (1989).

13. Matsuda Yoshirō, "Minmatsu Shinsho Kanton Jukō deruta no saden kaihatsu to kyōshin shihai no keisei katei," *Shakai keizai shigaku* 46.6:62 (1981).

14. Herold J. Wiens, *Han Chinese Expansion in South China* (rpt. Hamden, Conn.: Shoe String Press, 1967), pp. 194–195; H. F. Schurmann, *Economic Structure of the Yuan Dynasty* (Cambridge: Harvard University Press, 1956), p. 30.

15. *Zhujiang sanjiaozhou nongyezhi*, Foshan dichu geming weiyuan hui, eds. (neibu, 1976), vol. 1, pp. 72–73.

16. Liang Fangzhong, *Zhongguo lidai hukou*, p. 332, Table 29; Ho Ping-ti, *Studies on the Population*, pp. 5, 9. Adult sons and grandsons were counted as members of the same "household" unless the common property had been divided up and the individuals lived under separate roofs.

17. Liang Fangzhong, *Zhongguo lidai hukou*, p. 332, Table 29.

18. Sung Hok-p'ang, pp. 122–125.

19. *Zhujiang sanjiaozhou*, vol. 1, p. 71; Ye Xian'en and Tan Dihua, "Lun Zhujiang sanjiaozhou de zutian," in Guangdong lishi xuehui, ed., *Ming Qing Guangdong shehui jingji xingtai yanjiu* (Guangdong: Guangdong chubanshe, 1985), p. 26. Lineage estates are discussed below.

20. Katō Shigeshi, *Shina keizaishi kōshō*, vol. 2, pp. 338–370, has suggested

that nationally 60 percent or more of the rural population were independent free peasants by the end of the Song. Both Niida Noboru and Sudō Yoshiyuki have questioned this; see Denis Twitchett, *Land Tenure and Social Order in T'ang and Sung China* (London: School of African and Oriental Studies, 1962), pp. 28–30.

21. Faure, *The Structure*, p. 150. Examples of peasants entering into bondage are given by Schurmann, *Economic Structure*, p. 30; and Matsuda Yoshirō, p. 60.

22. The He family did not do well after the death of the patriarch, for several of the sons were executed by imperial order in a case of suspected treason. Much of this early history is covered in Lo Hsiang-lin, *Hong Kong and Its External Communications before 1842* (Hong Kong: Institute of Chinese Culture, 1963); also Faure, *The Structure*, pp. 149–150. Originally from Dongguan, He Zhen settled in Huizhou, Guangdong.

23. *Zhujiang sanjiaozhou*, vol. 1, p. 74. An individual named He, for example, forcibly occupied six polders in 1233 and began cultivating them. Similar examples are noted by Schurmann, *Economic Structure*, p. 30.

24. Helen Siu, p. 52.

25. Faure, "Lineage," p. 25.

26. Goodrich and Fang, eds., p. 156, for date of He Xiongxiang. A local cadre repeated the popular tale behind the name "Ninth Son Sands" during my visit to the region in 1984.

27. Ye Xian'en and Tan Dihua, "Lun Zhujiang sanjiaozhou," p. 26.

28. Sung Hok-p'ang, p. 111.

29. I have used the term *gentry-landlords* as the equivalent for *shenshi*—those who had degrees, were scholars, and either held or were retired from public office. This would include both *scholar-gentry*, the term used by Ch'ü T'ung-tsu, *Local Government in China under the Ching* (Cambridge: Harvard University Press, 1962), and the *xiangshen* (literally, "official living in his hometown") found in Ho Ping-ti, *Studies on the Population*.

30. Ho Ping-ti, *Studies on the Population*, p. 117.

31. Liang Fangzhong, *Zhongguo lidai hukuo*, p. 335, Table 30.

32. Ho Ping-ti, *Studies on the Population*, pp. 12, 14, 122. The Ming *ding* registered male adults between 16 and 60, liable for labor service.

33. Liang Fangzhong, *Zhongguo lidai hukuo*, p. 341, Table 32.

34. Miyazaki Ichisada, "Mindai So-Shō chihō no shidaifu minshū," *Shirin* 37:1–33 (1954). Frederic Wakeman, *The Great Enterprise* (Berkeley: University of California Press, 1985), pp. 604–624, summarizes much of the recent research on the subject. His term "scholar-official turned entrepreneurial-estate manager" is on p. 610. Though cumbersome, the term does encompass the attributes of this class, which are distinct from that of the "commoner managerial landlords" of the Qing discussed below.

35. Goodrich and Fang, eds., p. 1113.

36. *Pang shi jiaxun* (1572), Pang Shangpeng, rpt. in *Lingnan gui shu* (Guangzhou: n.p., 1849), no. 32, pp. 10a–11a. A section of this passage has also been cited in Robert Marks, *Rural Revolution in South China* (Madison: University of Wisconsin Press, 1984), p. 11.

37. Fu Yiling, *Ming Qing nongcun*, pp. 1–19. The actual status of the *shipu* could range from that of chattel slaves to that of bondservants who could rise to becoming bailiffs and estate managers; Joseph McDermott, "Bondservants in the T'ai-hu Basin during the Late Ming: A Case of Mistaken Identities," *JAS* 40:691–692 (1981). In Guangdong, the category of domestic slaves *sai man* (*xi min*, or lower people), studied by James Watson in the twentieth century, would seem to be very similar to the *shipu*: James Watson, "Transactions in People: The Chinese Market in Slaves, Servants and Heirs," in James Watson, ed., *Asian and African Systems of Slavery* (Berkeley: University of California Press, 1980), pp. 236–240. For the status of *shipu* in Anhui, Huizhou, in the Ming and Qing periods, see Ye Xian'en, *Ming Qing Huizhou nongcun shehui yu dianpu zhi* (Anhui: Anhui renmin chubanshe, 1983), p. 299.

38. Fu Yiling, *Mingdai Jiangnan shimin jingji shitan* (Shanghai: Shanghai renmin chubanshe, 1963), pp. 66–68.

39. Mundy, p. 263.

40. As the profusion of terms suggests, there were marked local differences in practices. Fu Yiling uses the terms *nupu* and *diannong* (servile tenant) and discusses them simultaneously in his account of peasant struggles: Fu Yiling, *Ming Qing nongcun*, pp. 68–153.

41. James W. Tong, *Disorder under Heaven* (Stanford: Stanford University Press, 1991), p. 181.

42. Jing Junjian, "Ming Qing liangdai 'gugong ren' de falü diwei wenti," in Li Wenzhi, Wei Jinyu, and Jing Junjian, eds. This essay sums up much of the recent scholarship on the subject.

43. Xie Guozhen, ed. and comp., *Mingdai nongmin qiyi shiliao xuanbian* (Fuzhou: Fujian renmin chubanshe, 1981), p. 229.

44. Wakeman, *The Great Enterprise*, pp. 621–622.

45. McDermott, pp. 675–702.

46. Lin Xiyuan (*hao* Ciyai) cited in Shigeta Atsushi, "The Origins and Structure of Gentry Rule," Christian Daniels, tr., in Grove and Daniels, eds., p. 359. Information on Lin Xiyuan from Goodrich and Fang, eds., pp. 919–922.

47. Niida Noboru, "State Power and Serfdom in China," *Acta Asiatica* 8:68 (1965), suggests that in Jiangsu and Zhejiang, which were more developed and had higher populations, there was no need for the landlords to keep serfs bonded to the land; the opposite being the case in Sichuan and Hubei. Brenner,

"The Agrarian Roots of Capitalism," *Past and Present* 97:20–24 (1976), comes to a similar conclusion and points out the link between the Black Death in Eastern Europe and enserfment of the population in regions that had low population densities.

48. Tong, p. 184.

49. Fu Yiling, *Ming Qing nongcun*, pp. 89–90.

50. The frequency of the uprisings in Guangdong has been tabulated in Tong, pp. 37–42.

51. Many of the scholars engaged in this enterprise are represented in Geoffrey Parker and Lesley Smith, eds., *The General Crisis of the Seventeenth Century* (London: Routledge and Kegan Paul, 1978). See also Roland Mousnier, *Peasant Uprisings in the Seventeenth Century: France, Russia and China*, Brain Pearce, tr. (New York: Harper and Row, 1970).

52. François M. A. de Voltaire, "De l'empire Ottoman au XVIIIe siècle," in his *Essai sur les moeurs* (Paris: Editions Garnier Frères, 1963), vol. 2., pp. 756–757.

53. Chinese scholarship on the subject is voluminous, ranging from Fu Yiling, *Ming Qing nongcun*, to more recent works such as Li Wenzhi, Wei Jinyu, and Jing Junjian, eds., *Ming Qing shidai de nongye*, which provides an overview of the research of the past three decades, as do various essays by Liu Yongcheng, Wu Liangkai, Han Hengyu, and others in *Qingshi luncong*, vols. 1–4 (Beijing: Zhonghua shuju, 1979–1982). Linda Grove and Joseph Esherick summarize the debates on this subject in "From Feudalism to Capitalism: Japanese Scholarship on the Transformation of Chinese Rural Society," *Modern China* 6.4:397–438 (1980). Grove and Daniels, eds., *State and Society in China*, also includes several essays by Japanese scholars on this theme.

54. Such a large body of literature exists on this subject that it is not necessary to reiterate the material here. Wakeman has discussed these aspects at length in *The Great Enterprise*, pp. 225–267.

55. Tong, p. 122.

56. Frederic Wakeman, "The Shun Interregnum of 1644," in Jonathan Spence and John Wills, eds., *From Ming to Ch'ing* (New Haven: Yale University Press, 1979), p. 44.

57. Tong, following Charles Tilly's work on the French Revolution, questions whether there was an element of class struggle in the peasant rebellions that broke out all over China during the Ming-Qing transition: see pp. 169–191. Tong settles in favor of a curiously outmoded orthodox Marxist position that suggests peasants are incapable of collective class action. He ascribes the uprisings of the *nupu* (translated by him as "bondsmen") to the general anarchy accompanying dynastic change and cites Fu Yiling's work on the Yuan-Ming transition in support of his own argument: p. 183. But a distinction needs to be made

between the Ming-Qing transition and the Yuan-Ming transitions. As Meng Siming and others have pointed out, in the case of the peasant rebellions at the end of the Yuan, these struggles eventually came to be dominated by the anti-Mongol sentiments of the gentry class, and ethnic issues instead of class issues emerged at the forefront: Meng Siming, *Yuandai shehui jieji zhidu* (1938) (rpt. Hong Kong: Longmen shudian, 1967); Wu Han, "Yuan diguo zhi bengkui yu Ming zhi jianguo," *Qinghua xuebao* 9.2:359–423 (1936). When this research is considered, which Tong does not do, the contrast with the Ming-Qing rebellions is clearer.

58. James Parsons, *Peasant Rebellions of the Late Ming Dynasty* (Arizona: University of Arizona Press, 1970), pp. 206–216, discusses the support of some lower gentry for the rebellions. But this was not unique; the use of mass discontent by lower-ranking officials, for example, such as those holding magistrature during the Fronde in France, has been touched upon in Perry Anderson, *Lineages of the Absolutist State* (London: Verso, 1974), pp. 98–99.

59. *Mingji yiwen* (preface dated 1657), Zou Yi, rpt. in *Taiwan wenxian congkan*, no. 112 (Taipei: Taiwan yinhang, Jingji yanjiushi, 1961), p. 21. Also translated and cited in Wakeman, "Shun Interregnum," p. 46. There is a vast body of scholarship on the politics of the popular revolts at the end of the Ming. Li Wenzhi, one of the most prominent scholars on the subject, identifies this period as marking a new phase in property relations in China, as do I. But there is considerable difference in our respective evaluation of the outcome of these peasant struggles, as is discussed in the conclusion of this chapter. Mark Elvin, drawing on Japanese scholarship, has presented some of this information in chapter 15 of *Pattern*. But with his focus on the elite, he interprets this research very differently and does not see the peasant struggles as having had much to do with the disappearance of serfdom; he declares that "there is no justification for characterizing these north-western movements [i.e., Li Zicheng] as 'peasant rebellions'" (p. 247), a conclusion that is untenable in view of the considerable research suggesting otherwise.

60. Li Wenzhi, "Qingdai qianqi de tudi zhanyou guanxi," *Lishi yanjiu* 5:78 (1963). See also Wakeman, *The Great Enterprise*, p. 1109; Parsons, p. 220.

61. *Yantang jianwen zalu* (ca. 1664), Wang Jiazhen, cited in Chu Mi, "Lord and Peasant," pp. 27–28. Similar sentiments by were expressed by *nupu* and *dianpu* in Huizhou, Anhui: Zurndorfer, pp. 212–215; Ye Xian'en, *Ming Qing Huizhou*, pp. 284–288.

62. Tanaka Masatoshi has collated the information on all the *nupu* and other popular uprisings mentioned in Fu Yiling and collections such as *Zhongguo neiluan waihuo lishi congshu* and marked the sites on a map: Tanaka Masatoshi, "Ru-

ral Handicraft in Jiangnan," in Grove and Daniels, eds., p. 180. An evaluation of the background of the participants in the various rebellions is given on p. 198.

63. Tanaka Masatoshi, p. 180. Tong is in error when he claims that "such rebellions rarely occurred before the fall of the dynasty in the third month of 1644": Tong, p. 190.

64. Fu Yiling, *Ming Qing nongcun*, p. 120.

65. Li Wenzhi, Wei Jinyu, and Jing Junjian, p. 71.

66. *Tianxia junguo libing shu* (preface dated 1662), Gu Yanwu, rpt. in *Sibu congkan* (Shanghai: Shangwu yinshuguan, 1919–1937), juan 40, pp. 2b–3a.

67. Xie Guozhen, ed., *Qingchu nongmin qiyi ziliao jilu* (Shanghai: Xin zhishi chubanshe, 1956), pp. 310, 323. Marks, *Rural Revolution*, pp. 15–18, has also discussed many of these instances.

68. Li Cai (1520–1606), cited in Tong, p. 83.

69. Fu Yiling, *Ming Qing nongcun*, pp. 119, 137–141; Niida Noboru, "State Power," p. 71.

70. Fu Yiling, *Ming Qing nongcun*, pp. 75–77.

71. Enumeration of events recorded in county gazetteers by Tong, pp. 41–42.

72. Among the literati and gentry proscribed for pro-Ming sympathies, the most prominent were Chen Gongyin and his four sons, Chen Zizhuang, Qu Shisi, and Qu Dajun: Hummel, vol. 1, pp. 88, 102, 199, 201; see also Lynn Struve, "A Sketch of Southern Ming Events Affecting the Canton Delta Area," Canton Delta Seminar, University of Washington, April 1973, unpublished paper; and Lynn Struve, *Voices from the Ming-Qing Cataclysm* (New Haven: Yale University Press, 1993).

73. *Shunde xianzhi* (1853), Guo Rucheng, comp. (rpt. Taipei: Chengwen chubanshe, 1978), juan 6, pp. 1a–10b. *Guangdong tongzhi* (1864), Ruan Yuan, ed. (rpt. Taipei: Huawen shuju, 1968), juan 257. Although this is the official figure, given the level of both chaos and corruption, the population data could well have been underestimated.

74. Xie Guozhen (Hsieh Kuo-ching), "Removal of Coastal Population in the Early Tsing Period," *Chinese Social and Political Science Review* 15.4:590 (1932). The evacuation was carried out in two phases.

75. *Guangdong xinyu*, juan 2, pp. 57–58.

76. Sung Hok-p'ang, p. 173.

77. *Conghua xianzhi* (1730), Guo Yuxi, comp. (rpt. Taipei: Chengwen chubanshe, 1974), juan 3.

78. *Xin'an xianzhi* (1819), Wang Chongxi et al., eds. (rpt. Taipei: Chengwen chubanshe, 1974), juan 8, p. 272; Peter Y. L. Ng and Hugh Baker, trs., *New Peace County: A Chinese Gazetteer of the Hong Kong Region* (Hong Kong: Hong Kong University Press, 1983); *Shunde xianzhi* (1853), juan 31, 8a–14b.

79. Struve, *Voices*, p. 207. Yang Ying, revenue officer for Zheng Chenggong, commenting on Zheng's conversation with his generals on the eve of his Taiwan campaign.

80. The slower development of Taiwan may have also been a result of the difficult crossing of the Taiwan Straits, where fast currents could easily sweep smaller vessels out into the Pacific: Lawrence C. Thompson, "The Junk Passage Across the Taiwan Strait," *HJAS* 28:170–194 (1968).

81. This section is based on Hsu Wen-hsiung, "From Aboriginal Island," pp. 3–11; John Robert Shepherd, *Statecraft and Political Economy on the Taiwan Frontier, 1600–1800* (Stanford: Stanford University Press, 1993), pp. 27–37; and Campbell.

82. Here I am omitting details for the sake of brevity, for as Shepherd has pointed out the process of colonization was quite complicated and involved numerous rounds of negotiations with different aborigine groups: see Shepherd, *Statecraft*, pp. 47–59.

83. See Bluss for several references to Bencon in Batavia; and also Charles R. Boxer, "Notes on Chinese Abroad in the Late Ming and Early Manchu Periods from Contemporary European Sources (1500–1750)," *Tien Hsia Monthly* 9.5: 462–465 (1939). Following the Portuguese system of assigning traders a "captain" (*capitâo*) who represented them in all dealings with the authorities, the Dutch, Chinese, and the English also had "captains" in all the ports.

84. Lian Heng, *Taiwan tongshi* (1916), rpt. in *Taiwan shiji congshu* (Taipei: Yushi wenhua shiye gongsi, 1977), juan 26, p. 503.

85. Shepherd, *Statecraft*, p. 87; Hsu Wen-hsiung, "From Aboriginal Island," p. 18; Zhou Xianwen, *Qingdai Taiwan jingji shi* (Taipei: Taiwan yinhang, 1957), p. 27.

86. *Generale Missiven*, vol. 1, p. 708.

87. George Candidus, "Account of the Inhabitants" (1744), rpt. in Campbell, ed., pp. 9–25; Wang I-shou, "Cultural Contact and the Migration of Taiwan's Aborigines: A Historical Perspective," in Knapp, ed., pp. 32, 36.

88. See the Appendix for conversion of Dutch figures given in *morgen* to hectares and acres.

89. Campbell, ed., p. 396. Chen Shaoxing, *Renkou bian* in *Taiwan sheng tongzhi gao: "Renmin zhi"* (Taipei: Taiwan sheng wenxian weiyuanhui, 1950–1952), vol. 2, part 1, pp. 106–111.

90. Ts'ao Yung-ho, Lai Yung-hsiang, and Chou Hsueh-p'u, comps., *Shiqi shiji Taiwan Yingguo maoyi shiliao* (Taipei: Taiwan yinhang, 1959), p. 139. The population fluctuated considerably depending on swings in the Zheng fortunes

of war; population levels have been discussed in detail in Hsu Wen-hsiung, "From Aboriginal Island," pp. 22–23, and Shepherd, *Statecraft*, pp. 94–99.

91. Hsu Wen-hsiung, "From Aboriginal Island," pp. 25–26.

92. Harry Lambley, "Subethnic Rivalry in the Ch'ing Period," in Emily Martin Ahern and Hill Gates, eds., *The Anthropology of Taiwanese Society* (Stanford: Stanford University Press, 1981), p. 291. Up to 1895, 98 percent of Taiwan's Chinese immigrants came from two areas of the mainland: 80–82 percent were Hoklo (*Fu lao*), as the immigrants from Fujian were called, and 16 percent were Hakka from eastern Guangdong.

93. Shepherd, *Statecraft*, p. 155.

94. *Chu-lo xianzhi* (1717) (rpt. Taipei: Taiwan yinhang, 1962), p. 133.

95. Shepherd, *Statecraft*, p. 386.

96. *Taiwan xianzhi* (1720), Chen Wenda, comp. (rpt. Taipei: Taiwan yinhang, 1961), p. 55. On this subject see also Arthur Wolf and Huang Chieh-shan, *Marriage and Adoption in China, 1845–1945* (Stanford: Stanford University Press, 1980), p. 37.

97. Lambley, "Subethnic Rivalry," p. 297.

98. Okamatsu Santaro, *Provisional Report on Investigations of Laws and Customs in the Island of Formosa* (1900) (rpt. Taipei: Chengwen, 1971), p. 53.

99. Wang Yeh-chien, *Land Taxation in Imperial China* (Cambridge: Harvard University Press, 1973), p. 9. The famous *Huangce* (Yellow books) and the *Yulin tuce* (Fish-scale illustrated book) contain the results of surveys, carried out at the beginning of the Ming, on which this system was based: Liang Fangzhong, *The Single-Whip Method of Taxation in China* (Cambridge: East Asian Research Center, Harvard University, 1956), p. 10. As Liang Fangzhong writes, "The main item in the *Yellow Books* was the household, population was treated as the warp, land as the woof, and the household was recorded under the name of its owner. . . . The main item in the *Fish-scale Illustrated Book* was the land; here land was treated as the warp, population as the woof."

100. Wang Yeh-chien, *Land Taxation*, p. 80. In addition there was a grain tax, the salt tax, a customs tax, and various miscellaneous taxes. The Qing taxation system, with its commutation of labor into silver, was not uniformly applied in all provinces till the early eighteenth century. Areas like Guangdong, however, had begun the transition to commuting labor taxes into silver even before the end of the Ming.

101. Memorial by Xu Guoxiang, cited in Oyama, p. 117. See also Fu Yiling, *Ming Qing nongcun*, p. 149.

102. *Qing shilu jingji ziliao jiyao*, Nankai daxue, Lishixi, comp. (Beijing: Zhonghua shuju, 1959), pp. 10–22.

103. Xie Guozhen, "Removal of Coastal Population," pp. 579, 582.

104. The magistrate of Haifeng county, cited in Marks, *Rural Revolution*, p. 37.

105. *Huangchao jingshi wen bian* (Preface dated 1826), He Changling (rpt. Taipei: Guofeng chubanshe, 1963), juan 32, p. 31a–34b; Michael J. E. Palmer, "The Surface-Subsoil Form of Divided Ownership in Late Imperial China: Some Examples from the New Territories of Hong Kong," *Modern Asian Studies* 22.1:119–20 (1987), for information on lineage confiscation of unregistered but cultivated land.

106. *Yongzheng zhupi zouzhe xuanji*, rpt. in *Taiwan wenxuan congkan* (Taipei: Taiwan yinhang, 1965), no. 300, p. 44.

107. *Da Qing huidian, Yongzheng huidian* (1732), juan 27, pp. 25a–25b.

108. Shepherd, *Statecraft*, pp. 235–236.

109. Memorial of Governor Wang Anguo, cited in Thomas Buoye, "From Patrimony to Commodity: Changing Concepts of Land and Social Conflict in Guangdong Province during the Qianlong Reign (1736–1795)," *Late Imperial China* 14.2:42 (1993).

110. *Qing shilu jingji*, pp. 68–95, 141.

111. Ho Ke-en, "The Origins of the *Dan jia* or Boat People of South China," in Frederick S. Drake and Wolfram Eberhard, eds., *South-east Asia and the Hong Kong Region* (Hong Kong: Hong Kong University Press, 1967).

112. *Xin'an xianzhi*, juan shou, p. 35. Eugene Anderson, *Essays on South China's Boat People* (Taipei: Oriental Cultural Service, 1972) for overall discussion of Tanka. See Helen Siu, *Agents and Victims*, p. 46, and Peter Ng and Baker, trs., p. 75, for references to Xinhui *danmin*.

113. In some communities, such as Chakeng, the lines between Danmin origin and the position of hereditary "tenants" known as *xiafu* (*hafu*) and *ximin* (*sai man*), literally "the mean people," had considerable overlap. Several of the twentieth-century studies by anthropologists working on the Pearl River Delta have identified villages in which the positions of these tenants ranged from hereditary servants to "slaves"; they lived in huts on the edges of villages and performed assigned duties from generation to generation such as gathering firewood, clearing nightsoil, herding ducks in the marshes, carrying coffins, etc., all without pay.

114. Palmer, p. 54. Burton Pasternak, *Guests in the Dragon* (New York: Columbia University Press, 1983), p. 15. Ho Ping-ti, *Studies on the Population*, p. 166.

115. Liu Yongcheng, "Qingdai qianqi diannong kangzu touzheng de xinfazhan," in *Qingshi luncong*, vol. 1, p. 69.

116. *Kang Yong Qian shiqi chengxiang renmin fankang douzheng ziliao*, Zhongguo renmin daxue, Qingshi yanjiusuo, comp. (Beijing: Xinhua shuju, 1979), p. 126.

117. Niida Noboru, "Shina kinsei no ichiden ryōshu kankō to sono seiritsu,"

Hōgaku kyōkai zasshi 64.3:129–154 and 64.4:241–261 (1946); Maeda Katsutarō, "Shindai no Kanton ni okeru nōmin tōsō no kiban," *Tōyō gakuhō* 51.4:457–494 (1969); Han Hengyu, "Shilun Qingdai qianqi diannong yongdian quan de youlai jiqi xingzhi," in *Qingshi luncong*, vol. 1, pp. 37–39; Buoye, "From Patrimony to Commodity," p. 48. Other scholars discussing these rights in other provinces include Evelyn Sakakida Rawski, *Agricultural Change*, pp. 14–24; Edgar Wickberg, "Continuities in Land Tenure," in Ahern and Gates, eds., pp. 213–214; and Tanaka Masatoshi, "Rural Handicraft," p. 209; The subject and the literature on Guangdong have received a very full discussion in Palmer and need not be reiterated here.

118. Wakeman, *The Great Enterprise*, pp. 158–161, discusses in passing gentry resistance to a new land survey. Detailed information on local opposition to any efforts by the state to survey the land on this direction is available in Hilary Beattie, *Land and Lineage in China* (Cambridge: Cambridge University Press, 1979), pp. 74–75; and Jerry Dennerline, "Fiscal Reform and Local Control," in Frederic Wakeman and Carolyn Grant, eds., *Conflict and Control in Late Imperial China* (Berkeley: University of California Press, 1975), pp. 104–120.

119. Dennerline, p. 111; Wakeman, *The Great Enterprise*, pp. 1068–1069.

120. Hsiao, pp. 127–128.

121. Philip Huang, *The Peasant Economy*, p. 87. During the Shunzhi period (1644–1661), for example, some 400,000 *ding* of serfs and 20,000,000 *mu* were granted to the estates of the court's beneficiaries such as princes, meritorious officials, and bannermen. The land attached to such estates in North China ranged from the imperial estate of 4,000,000 *mu* to estates of anywhere from 30 to 720 *mu* for other beneficiaries. In Anhui, bonded labor relationships continued well into the twentieth century: Ye Xian'en, *Ming Qing Huizhou nongcun shehui yu dianpu zhi* (Anhui: Anhui renmin chubanshe, 1983).

122. Cited and translated in Hsiao, p. 390 from the *[Qinding] liubu chufen zeli* (1877), juan 15, p. 29a. This edict is not given in the *Qingshi lu*.

123. Fu Yiling, *Ming Qing nongcun*, p. 150. By 1744 even the imperial household estates had divested themselves of serfs, and former serfs were listed as commoners (*liangmin*): Philip Huang, *The Peasant Economy*, p. 87.

124. James Watson, "Hereditary Tenancy and Corporate Landlordism in Traditional China: A Case Study," *Modern Asian Studies* 11.2:162 (1977); Woon Yuen-fong, *Social Organization in South China, 1911–1940* (Ann Arbor: Center for Chinese Studies, University of Michigan, 1984), p. 25.

125. *Gongzhongdang Kangxi chao zouzhe*, vol. 1, pp. 537–538.

126. Niida, "State Power and Serfdom," p. 72.

127. *Kang Yong Qian shiqi*, p. 74; *Baling xianzhi*, excerpted in Li Wenzhi, ed., *Zhongguo jindai nongyeshi zhiliao*, vol. 1, p. 78.

128. Jonathan Spence, *Emperor of China* (New York: Knöpf, 1974), p. 55. See Wakeman, "Shun Interregnum," for the conceptual synthesis of national welfare and peoples' welfare proposed by Dorgon. Similar sentiments of the Yongzheng and the Qianlong emperors are discussed in Chang Chun-shu, "Emperorship in Eighteenth Century China," *JCICUHK* 7.2: 551–570 (1974); and Harold Kahn, *Monarchy in the Emperor's Eyes* (Cambridge: Harvard University Press, 1971).

129. Hsiao, pp. 186–188, 392.

130. Wang Yeh-chien, *Land Taxation*, p. 29.

131. Shigeta Atsushi, *Shindai shakai keizaishi kenkyū* (Tokyo: Iwanami Shoten, 1975), pp. 137–154.

132. *Gongzhongdang Yongzheng chao zouzhe*, vol. 7, p. 29. Ho Ping-ti, *Studies on the Population*, p. 164, also cites Lan Dingyuan's (1680–1733) comment that several hundred thousand workers annually came from Guangdong to Taiwan and were therefore known as *kezi*, or "guest people."

133. James Watson, "Chinese Kinship," p. 591. Chen Han-seng, surveying the Pearl River Delta in the early 1930s, concluded that four out of every five peasants in Guangdong lived in villages with some form of corporate structure: Chen Han-seng, *Agrarian Problems in Southernmost China* (Guangzhou: Lingnan University, 1936), p. 37.

134. James Watson, "Anthropological Overview: The Development of Chinese Descent Groups," in Patricia B. Ebrey and James Watson, eds., *Kinship Organization in Late Imperial China* (Berkeley: University of California Press, 1986), p. 275.

135. For example, in the twentieth century the Poon (Pan) surname group, hereditary tenants of the Man lineage, had only a dilapidated ancestral hall, no written genealogy, and no recognizable ancestral grave sites, although like their wealthy neighbors, the Poon were linked by the belief that they were descended from a common ancestor. Only one mile away from the Poon were the Man (Wen) lineage, one of the "five great clans" of the Hong Kong region, with extensive landholdings of almost 6,000 mu (1,000 acres), elaborate ancestral halls where the ancestral tablets were placed, ancestral graves, written genealogies, lineage schools and educational benefits for its members, and a membership of nearly 2,000 males living in a single-lineage village cluster: James Watson, "Hereditary Tenancy," pp. 162–82; and his "Chinese Kinship," p. 606.

136. James Watson, "Chinese Kinship," p. 594. Emphasis in original.

137. Faure, "Lineage," p. 22.

138. James Watson, "Chinese Kinship," p. 610. One of the "clan" genealogies I have looked at, for example, the *Xinhui Chaolian Lubian Lushi zupu*, follows conventional idioms of descent in every way in its genealogy with the caveat, "the sites of the grave of the ancestors will not be revealed in order to prevent squab-

bling among the descendents": *Xinhui Chaolian Lubian Lushi zupu* (comp. 1947) (Hong Kong: private printing, 1947), p. 28b. The compilers could thus ingeniously sidestep the problem of finding common ancestors. I am indebted to Stevan Harrell and his seminar on Chinese genealogies for introducing me to the complexities of deciphering "real" and "fake" genealogies.

139. James Watson, "Chinese Kinship," p. 611; Hsu Wen-hsiung, "Frontier Social Organization and Social Disorder in Ch'ing Taiwan," in Knapp, ed., pp. 88–89. Stevan Harrell, "Social Organization in Hai-shan," in Ahern and Gates, eds., pp. 135–136, discusses Ploughshare village with various other types of alliances; Jack Potter, "Land and Lineage in Traditional China," in Maurice Freedman, ed., *Family and Kinship in Chinese Society* (Stanford: Stanford University Press, 1970), pp. 120–138, discusses the various conditions that may have given rise to higher-order and more powerful lineages.

140. The attempt at definitions has not been rendered any easier by the variety of terms for kin groups used in the Chinese historical documents and writings, such as *zu, zong, fang, shi, xing*. But as James Watson writes, with the knowledge of an insider, "The anthropological preoccupation with definitions can, at times, be taken to such extremes that the original purpose (analysis) is lost in a blizzard of qualification and detail": James Watson, "Chinese Kinship," p. 606.

141. E.g., in Anhui province, Tongcheng county; see Beattie, pp. 128–129; and Ye Xian'en, *Ming Qing Huizhou*, pp. 155–186.

142. Rubie Watson, "The Creation of a Chinese Lineage: The Teng of Ha Tsuen, 1669–1751," *Modern Asian Studies* 16:95 (1982); Li Wenzhi, "Lun Ming Qing shidai de zongzu zhi," *Jingji yanjiu suo jikan* 4:278–338 (1983). Other studies of the formation of lineages in Guangdong during the Ming-Qing transition include Hugh Baker, *A Chinese Lineage Village, Sheung Shui* (London: Frank Cass and Co., 1968), p. 41; and Alvin So, *South China*, pp. 36–37.

143. *Da Qing huidian shili*, juan 397, p. 2b. Of course, as the *xiedou* increased, the Qianlong Emperor saw the lineage institutions in quite another light. This has been discussed in Hsiao, chapter 8. The ideological role is vividly illustrated in the many lineage regulations compiled in Hu Hsien-chin, *The Common Descent Group in China and Its Functions* (New York: Viking Fund Publications in Anthropology, 1948), pp. 151–156.

144. Faure, "Lineage," p. 20.

145. *Guangdong xinyu*, juan 17, p. 464.

146. Faure, "Lineage," p. 28, ignores this dimension of rural life and is therefore hard put to explain why the economic transformation of Guangdong in the mid-to-late Ming allowed the lineage to become so conveniently an instrument of land development.

147. In the 1660s and 1670s alone there were at least six major revolts and uprisings of the various aborigine tribes: the Dadu revolted in 1661 and 1665; the aborigines of Sha-lu in 1670, and there were three revolts by the tribes from the Pazeh groups. See Shepherd, *Statecraft*, pp. 91–104, for details.

148. *Xin'an xianzhi*, juan 13, p. 365. Qu Dajun writing in the 1680s and 1690s gives a very graphic description of piracy: *Guangdong xinyu*, juan 18, p. 486. Anthony Siu Kwok-kin, "The Hong Kong Region before and after the Coastal Evacuation in the Early Ch'ing Dynasty," in David Faure, James Hayes, and Alan Birch, eds., *From Village to City* (Hong Kong: Hong Kong University, Asian Studies Center, 1984), pp. 3–4, also discusses late Ming piracy in Guangdong at some length.

149. *Guangdong xinyu*, juan 2, p. 52. Qu Dajun, who was quite prejudiced when it came to the *danmin*, believed that the robbers and pirates were from their ranks: *Guangdong xinyu*, juan 18, p. 486.

150. Hsiao, pp. 366–367; Myron Cohen, "Agnatic Kinship in South Taiwan," Ethnology 8.2:168 (1969).

151. See Philip Kuhn, *Rebellion and Its Enemies in Late Imperial China* (Cambridge: Harvard University Press, 1970), pp. 32–37, for a discussion of militia institutions born of the needs of local social units.

152. *Gongzhongdang Yongzheng chao zouzhe*, vol. 9, p. 573; vol. 12, p. 677.

153. Cited in Hsiao, pp. 354–355.

154. *Dongguan xianzhi* (1911), Chen Botao et al., eds. (rpt. Taipei: Xuesheng shuju, 1968), juan 36, p. 3b. The literature on *xiedou* is vast, for every powerful lineage in Guangdong and Taiwan was involved in some version of it. See Hsiao, pp. 364, 366–367; Faure, *Rural Society*, p. 35; Pasternak, *Guests*, p. 19; Pasternak, *Kinship and Community in Two Chinese Villages* (Stanford: Stanford University Press, 1972), p. 145; Hugh Baker, "The Five Great Clans of the New Territories," *JHKBRAS* 6:40–41 (1966); Johanna Meskill, *A Chinese Pioneer Family* (Princeton: Princeton University Press, 1979), pp. 54, 62, 210; and Lambley, "Subethnic Rivalry." See also M. C. Haguenauer, "Formose depuis les origines jusqu'a son annexion par le Japon," *Bulletin de la Maison Franco-Japonaise* 2:3–4: 45 (1930).

155. Suzuki Seiichirō, *Taiwan kyūkan kankon sōsai to nenjū gyōji* (1934), Feng Zuomin, tr. (rpt. Taipei: Zhongwen tushu gongsi, 1981), pp. 8–13, has detailed all the various types of feuds that erupted on Taiwan. See also Lambley, "Subethnic Rivalry," pp. 303–304.

156. Myron Cohen, *House United, House Divided* (New York: Columbia University Press, 1976), p. 5; and Pasternak, *Kinship and Community*, pp. 142–145. The size of these paramilitary forces could be very large; for example, the *yimin* (Righteous Volunteers) of 10,200 Hakka from Hsia Tan-shui Valley (P'ing-

tung Plain) of southern Taiwan, who joined government troops to help put down the Zhu Yigui Rebellion (1721), formed the core of the Liudui paramilitary organization. The military assaults undertaken were more in keeping with the type of total looting and pillage associated with clan and lineage feuding than state military maneuvers. These issues have been further elaborated in Burton Pasternak, "Economics and Ecology," in Ahern and Gates, eds., particularly pp. 164–165; and Burton Pasternak, "The Role of the Frontier in Chinese Lineage Development," *JAS* 28.3:560 (1969).

157. William Ashmore, "A Clan Feud near Swatou," *Chinese Recorder* 28.5: 214 (1897).

158. *Chinese Repository*, 4:560–561 (1836).

159. *Huang Juezi zousu* (1850), Xu Naiji, comp. (rpt. Beijing: Zhonghua shuju, 1959), pp. 121–122.

160. Adele M. Fielde, *A Corner of Cathay* (New York: Macmillan, 1894), p. 128. In Hsin-hsing, a Hokkien village on the Chang-hua plain in Taiwan, a similar situation of banditry almost wiped it out in the late nineteenth century until the peasants organized a mutual protection group: Bernard Gallin, *Hsin Hsing, Taiwan* (Berkeley: University of California Press, 1966), p. 16.

161. Eugene Anderson, *Essays*, p. 6; Harrell, pp. 135–136. Although in a more recent article, Pasternak ("Economics," pp. 163–164) downplays the role of property in the formation of lineages and seeks an explanation in ecology for the absence of such organizations, his earlier work also suggests that changes in land use and access to property and other resources could result in the decline of the lineage: Burton Pasternak, "Agnatic Atrophy in a Formosan Village," *American Anthropologist* 70:93–96 (1968).

162. In the course of a conflict between the Liu and the Hau over irrigation rights in Sheung Shui, Xin'an, for example, gentry members from each side obtained the services of either imperial troops from the county capital or from the provincial capital: Hugh Baker, "The Five Great Clans," pp. 40–41. See also Hsiao, pp. 368–369, for further examples from the eighteenth and nineteenth centuries. Having as many degree-holders in a lineage as possible was clearly vital under these conditions; the Guan of Kaiping did not allow those without degrees even to collect the proceeds of corporate property: Woon, p. 31.

163. *Chinese Repository*, 4:413 (1836).

164. Ibid.

165. Hu Hsien-chin, pp. 151–156.

166. Jing Junjian, "Legislation Related to the Civil Economy in the Qing Dynasty" in Kathryn Bernhardt and Philip C. C. Huang, eds., *Civil Law in Qing and Republican China* (Stanford: Stanford University Press, 1994), p. 44.

167. For example, *Nanhai Xuezheng Huangshi jiapu jieben* (comp. 1910), xiang-

gui section, p. 16b. The Guan of Kaiping founded their lineage trust in the eighteenth century. Only a massive crisis—the need to buy ammunition to resist the Japanese invasion—forced them to auction off its corporate properties in 1944: Woon, p. 28; see also Chen Han-seng, p. 28; and Hu Hsien-chin, p. 67. Rubie Watson, *Inequality*, pp. 70–71, discusses corruption and control of estate managers in Ha Hsuen who were also caught when trying to sell lineage land.

168. In the Shandong famine of the 1870s, apparently such sales had occurred. Land had been bought up by speculators, who were then forced by the state to return it with a very small refund of the purchase money: George Jamieson et al., "Tenure of Land in China and the Condition of the Rural Population," *Journal of the North China Branch of the Royal Asiatic Society of Great Britain and Ireland*, 23:72 (1888).

169. James Watson, "Chinese Kinship," p. 608.

170. In my dissertation, "A History," chapter 4, I have dealt at length with the logistics of land reclamation, such as time, money, and labor power expended. It was impossible for individual families to have undertaken these projects. As Nishikawa Kikuko, "Shindai Shukō karyū shaden ni tsuite," *Tōyō gakuhō* 63.1–2:93–135 (1981), has also pointed out, to even start the process of building a polder, large rocks had to be transported and placed in the riverbeds; the process took anywhere from 20 to 30 years to complete. This labor-intensive work was undertaken by a contractor, who then rented out the lands to tenants.

171. By the 1930s lineages and clans, "collective landlords" as Chen Han-seng calls them, owned four-fifths of all reclaimed polder lands (*sha ku*) in Guangdong: Chen Han-seng, p. 31. A 1937 record shows the total area of the polders was 4,000,000 *mu* (almost seven million acres): Helen Siu, p. 25. Chen Han-seng's study is still the most detailed on the subject; recent publications such as Ye Xian'en and Tan Dihua, "Lun Zhujiang sanjiaozhou," have supplemented this considerably with research on the holdings of particular ancestral estates, although Chen's overall figures still hold.

172. Ji Cheng, "Dongguan Minglun Tang shilue," *Guangdong wenshi ziliao* 16:22–32 (1964), gives the figure as 60,000 *mu*; *Dongguan xian Wanqingsha diaocha baogao*, in *Guangdong sheng difang diaocha baogao ji* (Guangzhou, 1943), p. 2, considered to be the more reliable source, gives the total as 76,000 *mu*. In the lineage villages studied by Potter, 93 percent of the land in Hang Mei hamlet was owned by the ancestral estates: Jack Potter, *Capitalism and the Chinese Peasant: Social and Economic Change in a Hong Kong Village* (Berkeley: University of California Press, 1968), pp. 96–97.

173. Tan Dihua and Ye Xian'en, "Fengjian zongfa shili dui Foshan jingji de kongzhi jiqi chansheng de yingxiang," in Guangdong lishi xuehui, ed., *Ming Qing*

Guangdong shehui jingji xingtai yanjiu (Guangzhou: Guangdong renmin chubanshe, 1985), p. 148.

174. James Watson, "Chinese Kinship," p. 608. Rubie Watson, *Inequality*, p. 51, shows how the Deng shareholders fared in the first generation. Johanna Meskill, pp. 243–245, also gives information on the Lins and their estate formation.

175. For example, in Huicheng, the county capital of Xinhui, the Xi'nan Academy (*shuyuan*) held 703 *mu*; the Xinhui Academy 1,583 *mu*; the *Dongbei gongju*, a local militia body organized in the 1850s, 1,516 mu; and the Palm Fan Guild of Xinhui 277 *mu*: *Xinhui xian Xinhui shuyuan, Xi'nan shuyuan, Dongbei gongju changtian cehuitu* (Xinhui: Changchan zhengli weiyuanhui, 1946). Endowments of other Guangzhou area academies and gentry-supported educational institutions ranged from 200 *mu* to 15,000 *mu*: Frederic Wakeman, *Strangers at the Gate* (Berkeley: University of California Press, 1966), p. 189. Rents received from agricultural lands financed most of the operations of the academies.

176. Chen Han-seng, p. 32; James Watson, *Emigration and the Chinese Lineage* (Berkeley: University of California Press, 1975), p. 36; Rubie Watson, *Inequality*, p. 69. Information on the thirteenth century cited earlier in section on Guangdong's pre-Qing history.

177. The Ui lineage had almost 50 percent of the paddy land in corporate ownership: Emily M. Ahern, *The Cult of the Dead in a Chinese Village* (Stanford: Stanford University Press, 1973), p. 23. For holdings of the Lin lineage, see Johanna Meskill, pp. 243–246. Additional data on lineage holdings in Taiwan are given in Myron Cohen, "Shared Beliefs: Corporations, Community and Religion among the South Taiwan Hakka," *Late Imperial China* 14.1: 2, 20–21 (1993).

178. I am drawing on the definitions used by Ebrey and Watson, pp. 4–5; and Rubie Watson, *Inequality*, p. 78. This definition used by the anthropologists is the closest to the legal definition of the household used in the Qing, "that it is a co-residential kinship group of varying composition, sharing in certain ritual practices and having a common budget—that is dividing productive tasks among its members, pooling income and sharing its consumption": Sybille van der Sprenkle, *Legal Institutions in Manchu China* (London: Althone Press, 1962), p. 14. The Chinese "family" versus "economic family" (*jia* vs. *fang*) in its various manifestations has been the subject of considerable debate. See Myron Cohen, "Developmental Process in the Chinese Domestic Group," in Freedman, ed., *Family and Kinship in Chinese Society*, for an overview of many of these debates.

179. See Dai Yanhui, "Qingdai Taiwan zhi jiazhi ji jiachan," *Taiwan wenxian* 14.3:12 (1963), for an analysis of Qing laws of inheritance. But as Rubie Watson has pointed out, there were on occasion strategies used to eliminate "illegiti-

mate" sons, such as those born of mistresses living in other villages and not recognized by ritual or legal function: Rubie Watson, *Inequality*, pp. 114–115. A powerful lineage, like the Man, could also impose primogeniture or at least unigeniture on their hereditary tenants, the Poon, by restricting the tenancy rights to one son, typically the eldest. There were also types of adoption, common on Taiwan, where the adopted son did not have rights to property; see Johanna Meskill, p. 79; and Myron Cohen, *House United*, p. 71. But in most cases division of property, or at least land, among the sons seems to have been the norm, though not all sons received houses and some had to live with other married brothers: Faure, *The Structure*, p. 51.

180. Jing Junjian, "Legislation Related," p. 53.

181. Ho Ping-ti, *Studies on the Population*, p. 306, n. 9, gives an example of property division in Fujian and suggests that it was quite common. But Niida Noboru, *Tō Sō hōritsu bunka no kenkyū* (Tokyo: Tōhō bunka gakuin, 1952), p. 559, indicates that there were penalties in the Ming, and certainly earlier, if property was divided while the father or grandfather was alive.

182. See Shiga Shūzō, "Family Property and the Law of Inheritance in Traditional China," in David Buxbaum, ed., *Chinese Family Law and Social Change* (Seattle: University of Washington Press, 1978). Twentieth-century practice reflected Qing law. As Myron Cohen observes of Taiwan, "The basis of the jural equality of married men in a family is that each is a coparcener to the estate and can demand its partition": Cohen, *House United*, p. 99.

183. Okamatsu, deed no. 88 (1854), p. 84, and deed no. 89 (1877), pp. 86, 87. This tallies with the information given by anthropologists; maternal uncles and cousins were called in probably because maternal relatives are considered to be more impartial in matters of agnatic property division.

184. van der Sprenkle, p. 108. As Niida Noboru has pointed out, the importance of the middleman in all transactions left an area in which the assertion of all rights was open to mediation and arbitration: Niida Noboru, *Chūgoku hōsei shi* (Tokyo: Iwanami shoten, 1952), p. 350.

185. See also Peter Perdue, *Exhausting the Earth* (Cambridge: Council on East Asian Studies, Harvard University, 1987), pp. 146–150, for a discussion of local custom and ambiguous property claims. I agree with Perdue that Ramon H. Myers and Chang Fu-mei (Chen), "Customary Law and the Economic Growth of China during the Ch'ing period," *Ch'ing-shih Wen-t'i*, 3.5:1–32 (1976) and 3.10:4–27 (1978), exaggerate the clarity of customary law.

186. Evelyn Sakakida Rawski, *Agricultural Change*, p. 30. Shiga, pp. 114–115. This is simply repeating a preconceived notion, because Shiga's own research, following this introduction, points to the numerous barriers to sale as per family law. Han Hengyu, for example, one of the major scholars on the subject of in-

cipient capitalism, has discussed the development of private property extensively in her essay, "Shilun Qingdai qianqi diannong yongdian quan," pp. 37–53.

187. van der Sprenkle, p. 105; H. F. Schurmann, "Traditional Property Concepts in China," *Far Eastern Quarterly*, 15:507–516 (1956).

188. *Ming Qing qiyue*, Guangdong shehui kexue yuan manuscript collection of Pearl River Delta land deeds, and the Taipei Palace Museum facsimile edition of land-deed manuscripts, *Taiwan gong si cang gu wenshu ying ben*, vol. 2.

189. Writing in 1900 about Taiwan, Okamatsu, p. 37, suggests that this term did not have any actual clout. It is conceivable that this was indeed the case in Taiwan by the end of the nineteenth century. The reforms in landownership rights initiated by the last Qing governor of Taiwan, Liu Minquan, and then by the Japanese, made transactions of land part of the broader commercial development of Taiwan. But Jamieson, writing about the mainland, gives a different picture. Although he notes that there was private property, he includes cases that show the limited application of this term: Jamieson et al., pp. 72, 74, and 149. As Duara shows, the authority of the lineage was most clear in the case of land transactions even in twentieth-century north China. In the 1930s in North Brushwood, if a lineage member sold land to an outsider before offering it to the lineage and did not get the permission of the lineage, the sale contract could be annulled: Prasenjit Duara, *Culture, Power and the State* (Stanford: Stanford University Press, 1988), pp. 94–95.

190. Jamieson et al., p. 74.

191. Peter Hoang, "A Practical Treatise on Legal Ownership," in Jamieson et al., pp. 121–127. Cases of homicide arising out of conflicts in land sales have been studied in Thomas Buoye, "Violent Disputes over Property Rights in Guangdong during the Qianlong Reign" (Ph.D. dissertation, University of Michigan, 1991), pp. 178–184.

192. S. Wells Williams, *The Middle Kingdom* (New York: Scribner's, 1883), vol. 1, pp. 280–281. Hsiao, p. 16, has also used Williams's work and, independently tabulating the population of a Pearl River Delta *xiang*, has found that Williams's evaluations were accurate.

193. James Watson, "Chinese Kinship," p. 606.

194. The Meinung community in Taiwan was, for example, made up of nine units and had 10,000 people at the end of the Qing: Myron Cohen, *House United*, pp. 6–9, 17.

195. *Guangdong xinyu*, juan 6, gives descriptions of various local gods, the circumstances of their installation in villages during the seventeenth century, and the protective powers attributed to them. Jamieson et al., pp. 75–76; Faure, *The Structure*, pp. 70, 89; Helen Siu, pp. 77, 312 n. 14; and Rubie Watson, *Inequality*, p. 43, all provide information on various aspects of community activity and the

reiteration of community rights. For Taiwan, see the *bai bai* for the god Co Su Kong as part of the Thai Ti Kong festival studied by Emily M. Ahern in "The Thai Ti Kong Festival" in Ahern and Gates, eds., pp. 397–426.

196. Faure, *The Structure*, p. 34. Example from Tai Wai, a multi-surname village in Xin'an county, later the New Territories.

197. Woon, p. 27.

198. James Watson, *Emigration*, p. 25.

199. Lambley, "Subethnic Rivalry," pp. 282–318.

200. Woon, p. 28.

201. Tenancy deed translated and reproduced in Faure, *The Structure*, pp. 36–37.

202. Bernard H. K. Luk and David Faure, "Xiangdong cun Dushi diqi jianjie," *JCICUHK*, 11:141–161 (1980). Thirty-one deeds are reproduced; the collection is unique because the deeds are all from one village, form a series, and have been kept together. One of the major problems with the other collections I have used is that they are culled from different sites from within a county, and it is difficult, if not impossible, to reconstruct the sequence of sale. Nor is it possible to tell from the documents whether the village in question was a multi-surname village or a single-lineage village.

203. James Watson, "Hereditary Tenancy," p. 170.

204. As noted above, the thirty-one land deeds from Bao'an in Luk and Faure are included in one of the very few collections that allow us this type of analysis because all the deeds pertain to the same village.

205. David Faure (Ke Dawei), Wong Wing-ho (Huang Yonghao), Hamashita Takeshi et al., eds., *Guangdong zongzu qiju huilu* (Tokyo: Tōkyō daigaku, Tōyō bunka kenkyūjo, 1988), p. 13.

206. A similar phenomenon has been noted in Chao, *Man and Land*, pp. 122–123. The location of these sales is not given in this book by Chao. But in his article "New Data on Land Ownership Patterns in Ming-Ch'ing China—A Research Note," *JAS* 40.4:731 (1981), he points out that in Quzhou prefecture, Zhejiang, land sales involved very small parcels.

207. Buoye, "Violent Disputes," p. 193; Byoye, "From Patrimony to Commodity," p. 47.

208. See Melissa A. Macauley, "Civil and Uncivil Disputes in Southeast Coastal China, 1723–1820" in Bernhardt and Huang, eds., pp. 88–89, in particular for a discussion of the frequency and volume of civil disputes over land, inheritance and so on.

209. Fujii Hiroshi, "Ichiden ryōshu sei no kihon kōzō," *Kindai Chūgoku* 5–10.67–134 (1979); Palmer, pp. 13–14.

210. Buck, *Land Utilization*, pp. 194–195; Jamieson et al., pp. 97–113; Wick-

berg, "Continuities in Land Tenure," p. 214. Kang Chao's failure to consider corporate landlords, particularly in South China, I believe, distorts his conclusions regarding landlords and land distribution: Chao, *Man and Land*, pp. 125–128. See also John Robert Shepherd, "Rethinking Tenancy: Explaining Spatial and Temporal Variation in Late Imperial and Republican China," *Comparative Studies in Society and History* 30.3:403–431 (1988).

211. Hoang, pp. 121–127; and Jamieson et al., p. 71.

212. Jing Junjian, "Legislation Related," pp. 68–70.

213. For example, deed 025, from Xiangshan County, dated 1817, facsimile in *Taiwan gong si cang gu wenshu ying ben*.

214. In this discussion of the rentier class, here and in later sections of this book, I have drawn on the discussion of the various types of rents by Pierre Gourbert, *The Ancien Regime* (New York: Harper and Row, 1969), especially chapter 6.

215. Chen Shaoxing, vol. 2, part 1, pp. 117, 164–166; Hsu Cho-yun, "The Chinese Settlement of the I-lan Plain," in Knapp, ed., p. 69. Shepherd, *Statecraft*, pp. 137–177. Even in the twentieth century new lands were available: Samuel Ho, *Economic Development of Taiwan, 1860–1970* (New Haven: Yale University Press, 1978), p. 17 n. 25. Ch'en Ch'iu-k'un's point is relevant here in that although the population was small, land controlled by the aborigines was not as readily available as a simple population-to-land ratio would suggest: Ch'en Ch'iu-k'un, *Qingdai Taiwan tuzhu diquan* (Taipei: Zhongyang yanjiu yuan, 1994), pp. 180–181. In the longer term, however, the Han settlers, through military means, support from the state, and negotiations with the aborigines, did have more land available than smallholders on the mainland.

216. Zhongguo diyi lishi dang'an guan, "Qingdai chakan Taiwan guanzhuang mindi dianzu shiliao," *Lishi dang'an* 1:28–35 (1987).

217. The meltage fee was added to the tax to provide for the loss of silver that occurred when the silver collected as tax from various localities was melted down to make the ingots sent to the central government. For a discussion of the opportunities this provided for local-level corruption and surcharges, see Madeline Zelin, *The Magistrate's Tael* (Berkeley: University of California Press, 1984), pp. 72–115.

218. Ch'en Ch'iu-k'un, p. 108. John Shepherd, "Plains Aborigines and Chinese Settlers on the Taiwan Frontier in the Seventeenth and Eighteenth Centuries" (Ph.D. dissertation, Stanford University, 1981), has also discussed several of these types of arrangements.

219. Okamatsu, deed no. 19, pp. 17–18;

220. Shepherd, *Statecraft*, pp. 256–267.

221. The pace at which the aborigines accepted encroachments on their

lands and settled for rents as rentiers varied according to their location in the plains versus the mountains. A detailed case study of the upland Anli tribe and their relations with their Han tenants via the offices of their interpreter Zhang Dajing has been discussed in Ch'en Ch'iu-k'un, pp. 50–66.

222. *Zhongguo jin sanbai nian shehui jingji taolunji*, Cuncui xueshe, comp. (Hong Kong: Congwen shudian, 1972), vol. 1, p. 45; see also pp. 49, 53.

223. Ho Ping-ti, *Studies on the Population*, p. 257. These are judged to be more reliable than data from any other period.

224. Liang Fangzhong, *Zhongguo lidai hukou*, p. 277. The population of Guangzhou prefecture had increased to 5,799,261 individuals by 1820. The magnitude of this increase in population can be gauged by comparing this figure (close to 6 million individuals in the Pearl River Delta region alone) with the available population estimates for the whole of Guangdong province in 1578, when it reputedly had only a little over 2 million individuals. Dwight Perkins, *Agricultural Development*, pp. 206–214, rejects these figures of fantastic growth and proposes that the provincial totals for Guangdong as a whole begin from an "improbably low base and rise at too rapid a rate." He believes that these figures reflect little more than arbitrary guesses by officials and that the adjusted population data may have been lower by 7 million individuals in 1851. But even if one were to accept the adjustments in calculations proposed by Perkins, the fact remains that the population of Guangdong province had increased dramatically in the first two hundred years of Qing rule.

225. Liang Fangzhong, *Zhongguo lidai hukou*, information from tables on pp. 204, 258, 341, 380, 391–394, 400–401.

226. *Guangdong xinyu*, juan 27, p. 690; juan 21, p. 533. Zhang Jiancun, cited in Adachi Kenji, "Daizu kasu ryūtsū to Shindai no shoyōteki nogyō," *Tōyōshi kenkyū* 37.3:36 (1978). This categorization, and the land needed for subsistence, is strikingly similar to the findings of C. K. Yang, who investigated landholding patterns in the Pearl River Delta in the 1940s. Yang found the minimum amount of land needed to meet the subsistence needs of a household in the Canton area was 10 *mu* (1.6 acres), of which, by then, the peasant typically owned only 30 percent and rented 70 percent. A household cultivating 10 *mu* was considered to be in the "middle peasant" stratum: C. K. Yang, *Chinese Communist Society: The Family and the Village* (Cambridge: M.I.T. Press, 1965), pp. 58–60.

227. See Li Wenzhi, Wei Jingyu, and Jing Junjian, p. 179, for a discussion of Lenin and evolution of the Chinese debate on incipient capitalism. V. I. Lenin, *The Development of Capitalism in Russia* (rpt. Moscow: Foreign Languages Publication House, 1974), pp. 240–251, discusses the significance of hired labor in agriculture.

228. Wu Liangkai, "Qingdai Qianlong shiqi nongye jingji guanxi de yanbian

he fazhan," in *Qingshi luncong*, vol. 1, pp. 6–9; Jing Junjian, pp. 243–260. Chao, *Man and Land*, pp. 145–147, has disputed the understanding of the term *gugong ren* by Li Wenzhi and others, and proposed that an ambiguity in the reading of the law may give a false impression of increase in the numbers of the *gu gongren* in the early Qing.

229. C. K. Yang, p. 51; Chen Han-seng, p. 131, Table 20; Philip Huang, *The Peasant Economy*, pp. 59, 199. Huang found only four out of twenty-three (17 percent) were clearly landless for the second generation. Kang Chao has also pointed out some of the problems of interpretation of the data drawn from the Qing homicide cases, which may have artificially inflated the number of agricultural laborers. The ratio of farmworker households to total rural households, compiled by Kang Chao and Chen Chung-i, is a ratio of 8:9 for Guangdong, higher than the figure cited by the Land Commission (Tudi weiyuanhui), *Quanguo tudi diaocha baogao gangyao*: see Chao, *Man and Land*, pp. 144–149.

230. Richard Lachmann, *From Manor to Market* (Madison: University of Wisconsin Press, 1987), pp. 16, 128; based on data drawn from Hilton, Tawney, Kerridge, and others. Lachmann, pp. 111–118, also shows why it was possible at this particular juncture in English history for resident landlords to subvert peasant unity and why peasant rebellions after 1549 were confined to areas where landlords were disorganized at the county level.

231. *Kang Yong Qian shiqi*, pp. 124–125.

232. John Kamm, "Two Essays on the Ch'ing Economy of Hsin-an Kwangtung," *JHKBRAS* 17: 63 (1977), citing the "Report on the New Territories" presented to both Houses of Parliament, November 1900. See also Liu Yongzheng, "Qingdai qianqi," pp. 57–59.

233. *Chu-lo xianzhi*, pp. 95–96.

234. See, for example, Liang Qichao's description of his home village, Chakeng, Xinhui: Liang Qichao, *Yinbingshi wenji*, in *Yinbingshi heji*, rpt. in *Zhongguo wenhuashi*, vol. 86 (Shanghai: Zhonghua shuju, 1937), pp. 58–60. The "Ten Big Offenses," according to the Criminal Code of the Qing, started with "rebellion"; the lineage undertook "to detect and punish, and hand over to the authorities, members who enter outlaw organizations against the state": Hu Hsien-chin, pp. 57, 61, and Appendixes nos. 29 and 30, giving extracts from lineage regulations in Jiangsu and Hubei. Rubie Watson, *Inequality*, pp. 42–43, has discussed the significance of ritual pork. The lineage council could also whip members for misdemeanors.

235. Liang Qichao, p. 59; see also examples in Hu Hsien-chin and discussion of this in van der Sprenkle, pp. 85–89. Individual gentry members were not allowed to use corporal punishment, but the lineage council could do so.

236. Liang Qichao, p. 60.

237. Work on such projects occurred during the slack agricultural season; as Chang Chung-li notes, "By using the seasonally underemployed labor force on construction projects, capital formation was increased without reducing agricultural output." Many of these activities were grouped under "gentry charitable activities" and received active state support and rewards for the elite in the form of official rank: Chang Chung-li, *The Income*, p. 47.

238. As David Faure puts it in *The Rural Economy*, p. 201, "In other words the tenant who had the right to settle in the village must be treated very differently from the tenant who did not have such rights in any village. This is not to say that landlords necessarily could not enforce their will on the land that they owned, but in the webs of power relationships in the countryside, few of them could ride roughshod over their tenants on the strength of land ownership alone." Faure, however, does not develop his argument to show what, then, were the means of surplus extraction. How did the landlord "enforce his will" on the tenant? Faure also does not explore the necessity of extra-economic coercion, which is my focus here.

239. Children were often kidnapped and sold. As James Watson has pointed out, "Until the foundation of the People's Republic in 1949, China had one of the largest and most comprehensive markets for the exchange of human beings in the world. . . . A unique feature of the Chinese market was its concentration on children, especially those under the age of ten." James Watson, ed., *Asian and African Systems*, p. 223.

240. The specifics of rent are discussed below. Mark Elvin is in error when he states in *Pattern*, pp. 248–250, that people with money were no longer putting it into land. By the twentieth century, 8.5 percent of all cultivated land in Guangdong was polder lands. Matsuda Yoshirō has tabulated that most of this was developed during the late Ming–early Qing period and in the nineteenth century: Matsuda, p. 62.

241. David Faure, "The Rural Economy of Kiangsu Province," *JCICUHK* 9.2:402 (1978).

242. Thomas Metzger, "On the Historical Roots of Economic Modernization in China," in Hou Chi-ming and Yu Tzong-shian, eds., *Modern Chinese Economic History* (Taipei: Institute of Economics, Academia Sinica, 1979), p. 9. See also Marks, *Rural Revolution*, p. 43; Hsiao, p. 391; and Oyama, p. 148.

243. Ch'ü, p. 132. In all other provinces, except for Guangdong, Yunnan, and Guizhou, tax collection began in the Second Month, was suspended between the Fifth and Seventh months, and not resumed till the end of the Eleventh Month. Technically in these other provinces, taxes were to be collected in two lots, making it easier for the peasants. In Guangdong it was collected at one time.

244. Rev. Krone, "A Notice of the San On District," *Transactions of the China Branch of the Royal Asiatic Society* (1859), rpt. in *JHKBRAS* 7.119 (1967).

245. Guangdong and Taiwan (as part of Fujian) did not have to pay the grain tax that was paid in kind as "grain tribute" in Shandong, Henan, Hunan, Hubei, Jiangxi, Jiangsu, Anhui, and Zhejiang. The tax rate, at least as far as imperial intentions were concerned, was not supposed to be onerous. But in practice, at the "nonstatutory or informal" level of government, as Wang Yeh-chien calls it, where taxes were determined in actuality, the tax rate was a major cause of impoverishment and sale of property, especially in the nineteenth century. All taxes could technically be paid in copper, at a conversion rate of copper to silver fixed by the highest provincial authority. Local magistrates usually used their own conversion rates, often 142–175 percent higher than the market rate: Ch'ü, p. 135. The severe deflation starting around 1810 resulted in peasants' having to surrender more of their crops to pay the same amount of taxes as before, and it also reduced sharply their incomes from cash crops and wage-labor. The result was that by the 1870s people paid in effect 100 percent more than they did in 1820, and taxes were three times as heavy as they had been in the eighteenth century: Wang Yeh-chien, *Land Taxation*, pp. 114–115. Land deeds in any collection of land sales documents attest to this. Over 50 percent of the 200 documents I have examined cite the inability to meet tax payments as the reason for the sale of property.

246. Katayama Tsuyoshi, "Shindai Kanton-shō Jukō deruta no tokōsei ni tsuite," *Tōyō gakuhō* 63.3–4:261–262 (1982); Hsiao, p. 532. The number of households in each *tu* in Nanhai ranged from 9 to as many as 133 households.

247. Ye Xian'en and Tan Dihua, "Lun Zhujiang sanjiaozhou," pp. 37–52; Helen Siu, pp. 73–76, discusses tax-farming and the struggle for control of the funds in the 1940s.

248. *Nanhai xianzhi* (1911), juan 4, p. 24a.

249. *Dongguan xianzhi* (1921), juan 51, p. 4a. The *Dongguan xianzhi* (1797), Peng Renjie et al., eds., juan 10, pp. 10b–11a, discusses this problem and the efforts made by a magistrate during the Yongzheng period to rectify the situation. But as the 1921 edition shows, the resolution of the problems was only temporary. See also Rubie Watson, *Inequality*, p. 56; Wang Yeh-chien, *Land Taxation*, p. 42; Kamm, pp. 74–75; and Hsiao, p. 119 for discussions of *baolan*.

250. Kang Yong *Qian shiqi*, vol. 1, p. 125. Because there were so many variations, it is difficult to come to any conclusion whether lineage membership enabled some peasants to rent lands at cheaper rates than non-members. For the Dengs of Ha Tsuen, Guangdong, the Lins of Wufeng, and the Chens of Tatieh in Taiwan, this was indeed the case in the twentieth century: see Rubie Watson, *Inequality*, p. 69; Pasternak, *Kinship*, p. 77; and Johanna Meskill, p. 290, n. 11.

Freedman, *Lineage Organization*, p. 127, has argued that "when being a member of such a group meant having a prior right to tenancy, the poorer people had every reason to stay in the community than go and try their luck elsewhere. . . ." But the obverse was also true; the lineage tenants were scarcely free to go and try their luck elsewhere in a hostile world made more so by intra-lineage feuding.

251. Alice N. H. Ng, Bernard H. K. Luk, and David Faure, "Notes and Queries," *JHKBRAS* 19:194 (1979).

252. Liu Yongcheng, "Qingdai qianqi diannong kangzu," pp. 55–58. As Chang Chung-li has pointed out, "land was considered a secure investment largely because the government upheld the right of landowners to collect rent in full": Chang Chung-li, *The Income*, p. 13.

253. Liang Qichao, p. 59.

254. Okamatsu, p. 86.

255. Ibid., pp. 86–89; Ramon Myers, "Taiwan under Ching Imperial Rule, 1684–1895," *JCICUHK*, 5.2:385; Dong Jiasheng, "Qingdai Taiwan zhi dizu guanxi," in *Taiwan jingji shi (erji)* (Taipei: Taiwan yinhang, 1955), p. 69. Rice sold at 1.5 taels per *dan* in Guangdong in 1845: Wang Yeh-chien, "The Secular Trend," p. 354. So the income of the *dazu hu* was not negligible.

256. Faure, *The Structure*, p. 190, n. 25. Interview in 1982 with villager of Lung Yeuk Tau whose granduncle was involved in rent collection in Xiangshan, Dongguan, and Zengcheng counties of Guangdong.

257. The types of rent bursaries noted by Muramatsu in the Jiangnan, for example, did not operate in Guangdong: Muramatsu Yuji, "A Documentary Study of Chinese Landlordism in Late Ch'ing and Early Republican Kiangnan," *Bulletin of the School of Oriental and African Studies* 29.3:566–599 (1966).

258. *Guangdong xinyu*, juan 17, p. 464.

259. Rubie Watson, *Inequality*, p. 64, notes that even in the twentieth century, the large landlords among the Dengs did not cultivate land, but continued to reside in the village; one landlord who had a house in the market town nevertheless kept a house in the village, where his principal wife lived and where his sons were raised.

260. Liu Yongcheng, "Qingdai qianqi," p. 55. Dwight Perkins, *Agricultural Development*, p. 106, notes the economic implications of fixed rents.

261. Kō-a-in Kanton hakenin jimusho, *Kanton shō nōson chōsa hōkoku* (Guangdong: Nihon sōryōjikan, 1943), p. 6, suggests that in the 1940s leases on paddy fields were being renewed every year in Dongguan county, and only the polder land was being rented out on relatively longer leases of 10–20 years.

262. Han, p. 43.

263. Wages were 8–10 cents a day with noonday meal, 10–20 cents a day with 5 meals during harvest time, or 30 cents a day without meals in the survey

carried out in 1888: Adele M. Fielde, "Report from the American Baptist Mission, Swatou, Guangdong" in Jamieson et al., p. 112.

264. Li Wenzhi, Wei Jinyu, and Jing Junjian, pp. 216–217.

265. In his study of managerial farming in Hebei in the 1930s, Philip Huang found that most farms remained under 200 *mu* (approx. 33 acres) because that was the maximum an individual peasant could hope to oversee: Philip Huang, *The Peasant Economy*, p. 172. See also Philip Huang, *The Peasant Family and Rural Development in the Yangzi Delta, 1350–1988* (Stanford: Stanford University Press, 1990), p. 58.

266. *Kang Yong Qian shiqi*, vol. 1, pp. 130, 135. Since both these are documents from the Board of Punishments (*xingke*), the cases ended in violence.

267. Hoang, p. 137; Ye Xian'en and Tan Dihua, "Lun Zhujiang sanjiaozhou," pp. 49–50; Robert Eng, "Institutional and Secondary Landlordism in the Pearl River Delta, 1600–1949," *Modern China* 12.1:21 (1986); Palmer, p. 27.

268. Ye Shaohua, "Wo suozhidao de Dongguan Minglun Tang," *Guangdong wenshi ziliao* 16:1–21 (1964); Woon, p. 29.

269. Fielde, *A Corner of Cathay*, p. 114. See also Ye Xian'en and Tan Dihua, "Luelun Ming Qing Zhujiang sanjiaozhou de gaolidai ziben," in Ye Xian'en et al., eds., *Ming Qing Guangdong shehui jingji yanjiu* (Guangzhou: Guangdong renmin chubanshe, 1987), p. 185; Hayes, "Land and Leadership in the Hong Kong Region of Kwangtung in the Nineteenth Century," *JHKBRAS* 7:94 (1967).

270. *Nanhai xianzhi* (1911), juan 17, 8a.

271. Hartwell, "Demographic, Political and Social Transformations," p. 420. When merchants acquired gentry status, many of them became full-time officials and took new names in keeping with their new status.

272. Li Wenzhi, "Lun Zhongguo dizhu jingjizhi yu nongye ziben zhuyi mengya," *Zhongguo shehui kexue* 1:143–160 (1981), discusses the differences between "gentry-landlord" (*jinshen dizhu*) and "commoner-landlord" (*shumin dizhu*) and the rise of the "managerial landlords" from the ranks of the latter. But this is a framework not quite applicable to Guangdong, where gentrification had been often linked to mercantile wealth and where mercantile commoners had rapidly acquired gentry status in significant numbers from the eighteenth century onwards. See also Ng Chin-keong, *Trade and Society*, p. 163, on status of the merchant-landlords in Taiwan. Success in business was often the first step in gentrification and lineage building. Local gazetteers are full of such instances.

273. Wu Chongyue's library was known as the Yueya tang, and the 200 rare works dating from the Tang to the Qing were published by him in the collectanea *Yueya tang congshu*. He also sponsored and printed the collectanea *Lingnan*

yishu, which consists of fifty-five Ming and Qing works by natives of Guangdong: *Nanhai xianzhi,* juan 14, p. 48a.

274. *Qing shilu jingji,* p. 372; Thomas Grimm, "Academies and Urban Systems in Guangdong," in Skinner, ed., *The City in Late Imperial China,* p. 496, gives information on the backgrounds of the headmasters. Given this type of interaction, the level of antagonism between gentry and merchants seems to be overstated in Edward J. M. Rhoads, "Merchant Associations in Canton, 1895–1911," in Mark Elvin and G. William Skinner, eds., *The Chinese City between Two Worlds* (Stanford: Stanford University Press, 1974).

275. Perry Anderson, p. 33.

276. Chang Chung-li, *The Chinese Gentry,* pp. 82 n. 54, 24, 91, 105, 184.

277. *Taiwan sheng tongzhi gao,* Li Ruhe et al., eds., *Renwu zhi* section (Taipei: Taiwan wenxian weiyuan hui, 1962), vol. 3, juan 7, pp. 155–218. The Qing examination system in Taiwan has been analyzed in detail in Shepherd, *Statecraft,* pp. 208–214.

278. Liang Jiabin, p. 412. The quotas at both the *shengyuan* and *juren* levels were aids to mercantile mobility into upper gentry status, for those holding *juren* degrees were given official positions.

279. Perry Anderson, p. 34, with reference to Absolutism in western Europe, particularly France.

280. Zhou Xianwen, *Qingdai Taiwan jingji shi* (Taipei: Taiwan yinhang, 1957), p. 27. The biographies of the Shi family are also included in the *Changhua xianzhi* (*Renwu zhi* section), juan 10, pp. 13–15. See also Dong Jiasheng, "Qingdai Taiwan zhi dizu guanxi," pp. 64–65.

281. Hsu Cho-yun, p. 83.

282. *Guangdong xinyu,* juan 2, p. 29.

283. Kō-a-in Kanton Hakenin Jimusho, p. 22, survey of Dongguan county on Wanqingsha; see also Chen Han-seng, p. 48; Eng, "Institutional and Secondary Landlordism," p. 20.

284. An example from Guangdong is found in Li Wenzhi, Wei Jinyu, and Jing Junjian, p. 169; Liu Yongcheng, "Qianlong xingke tiben yu Qingdai qianqi nongcun shehui jingji yanjiu," *Lishi dang'an,* 2.89 (1981).

285. The examples of famous merchants who acquired gentry status in Guangdong are too numerous to be repeated in full. In "A History," pp. 231–236, I have identified fifty-five biographies in Hummel that deal with such cases.

286. Chang Chung-li's classic study *The Income of the Chinese Gentry* is yet to be surpassed for its comprehensive treatment of the sources of gentry-landlord income.

287. Hummel, vol., 2, p. 867,

288. See Peng Zeyi, ed., *Zhongguo jindai shougongye shi ziliao,* vol. 2, p. 109, for

the extent of land under tea bushes and rice owned by the Lins; see also Johanna Meskill, p. 245. For contributions sent, see Hsu Cho-yun, p. 83.

289. See lineage regulations of the Fan lineage in Sichuan, in Hu Hsien-chin, p. 155. The family emigrated from Guangdong.

290. Morton Fried, *The Fabric of Chinese Society* (rpt. New York: Octagon Books, 1969), pp. 117–119.

Chapter 5

1. *Guangdong xinyu*, juan 14, pp. 370–371.

2. Philip Huang, *The Peasant Family*, and his concept of "involutionary growth" are discussed in the conclusion. Huang suggests a continuity spanning the last seven centuries of Chinese history. Eugene Anderson, *The Food*, posits a continuity and also uses the term "involution" to describe the last several centuries. Similar ideas of continuity are indicated by Ramon Myers, *The Chinese Peasant Economy*. In a more recent study, Myers suggests a continuity from Song to Qing extending to marketing structures: Ramon Myers, "Customary Law, Markets and Resource Transactions in Late Imperial China," in R. L. Ransom, R. Sutch, and G. M. Walton, eds., *Explorations in the New Economic History* (New York: Academic Press, 1982), chapter 13. Francesca Bray, as well as Dwight Perkins, *Agricultural Development*, also suggests a continuity in agricultural patterns and techniques.

3. Curiously, in *The Peasant Family*, Philip Huang completely ignores the impact of New World crops on Chinese commercialization, including the role of the sweet potato in maintaining the subsistence sector.

4. Elvin, *Pattern*, p. 167. Ramon Myers suggests that Chinese peasants were "farmers" availing themselves of all market opportunities. These ideas are most fully developed in Myers, *The Chinese Economy*. David Faure also prefers the term "farmer" to peasant: see "The Plight of Farmers," *Modern China* 11.1: 2–38 (1985). Reflecting a certain optimism in the potential of trade, Faure tends to read opportunities for the direct producers: "As long as the farm is looked upon as an independent unit of operation, and the farmer a free agent capable of making decisions in the light of market conditions": Faure, *The Rural Economy*, p. 7.

5. See Skinner, *The City*, p. 234, for factors which promoted the development of markets.

6. Zhongguo renmin daxue, Zhongguo lishi jiaoyanshi, ed., *Zhongguo ziben*, and several studies since.

7. Lenin, p. 317. Li Wenzhi, Wei Jingyu, and Jing Junjian, eds., p. 179, discusses the influence of Lenin's work on the Chinese debate on incipient capitalism.

8. James A. Robertson, "Spaniards Brought Animals, Fruits, Vegetables and All Manner of Plants," in Lewis Hanke, ed., *History of Latin American Civilization* (Boston: Little, Brown and Co., 1973), pp. 36, 40.

9. Ho Ping-ti, *Population*, pp. 183–195; Ho Ping-ti, "The Introduction of American Food Plants into China," *American Anthropologist* 57.2:191–201 (1955); Bray, pp. 456, 518, 530; Hsu Wen-hsiung, "From Aborigine Island," p. 18; Zhou Xianwen, p. 27.

10. The Dutch connection seems most clear in Japan, where it is known as *orando imo* (Holland yam) and *jakaruta* [Jakarta] *imo*. The disparate terms in India, where on the west coast the Portuguese *batatas* is used while on the east coast it is called *bilati alu*, or "European yam," also suggest separate introductions; Watt, *Dictionary*, p. 1028.

11. For the history of the potato and its introduction to Europe, see Redcliffe Salaman, *The History and Social Influence of the Potato* (Cambridge: Cambridge University Press, 1987). As Salaman has illustrated in his classic study, the ready acceptability of the potato in Ireland occurred "because it fitted so readily into the economic structure of their life": Salaman, p. 191. The slow introduction of the white potato in China is discussed by both Ho Ping-ti, *Studies on the Population*, p. 189; and Bray, p. 532, n. "e." Bray is, however, incorrect in suggesting the potato was not introduced till the nineteenth century.

12. Amano Motonosuke, *Chūgoku nōgyōshi kenkyū* (Tokyo: Nōgyō sogo kenkyūjo, 1962), p. 929, points out that Anhui, Henan, Zhejiang, and Fujian were all cultivating maize by the early sixteenth century. Ho Ping-ti, *Studies on the Population*, p. 187, based on the evidence of the 1574 edition of the provincial gazetteer, points to its cultivation in Yunnan. Bray, pp. 456–459, 530, has looked at maize and its cultivation in detail. See also Watt, *Dictionary*, pp. 686–687, 1132. The foreign origin of many fruits and vegetables is indicated in Chinese by the prefix *fan*, "western" or "barbarian," e.g., *fanqie*, or "foreign eggplant," for tomatoes.

13. Bray, pp. 458–459; Perdue, p. 126. Maize was used mostly for fodder and chicken feed in the rice-growing regions of the southeast coast.

14. Ho Ping-t'i, *Studies on the Population*, pp. 149–150.

15. André João Antonil, *Cultura e opulencia do Brasil por suas drogas e minas* (1711), Andreé Mansuy, ed. (Paris: Institute des Hautes Etudes de l'Amérique Latine, 1968), p. 133.

16. Campbell, ed., p. 168.

17. Shepherd, *Statecraft*, p. 275.

18. *Taihai jianwen lu* (1751), Dong Tiangong, rpt. in *Taiwan wenxian congkan*, vol. 129, pp. 21–22, mentions tobacco as among the imports from Xiamen to Taiwan.

19. British Parliamentary Papers, *General Correspondence*, p. 19.

20. Ho Ping-ti, *Studies on the Population*, p. 203; *Zhujiang sanjiaozhou*, vol. 5, p. 77.

21. In India, the peanut apparently entered by several different routes including China: via Africa to western India; via China to Bengal, where it is still called Chinese nuts (*chinebadam*); and via Manila to south India, where it is known as *manila kottai*: Watt, *Commercial Products*, p. 74.

22. *Zhujiang sanjiaozhou*, vol. 5, p. 66.

23. Purseglove, vol. 1, pp. 199, 236. Many species of legumes have nodules on their roots containing bacteria with the property of fixing atmospheric nitrogen, which is then available to the host plant. Further nitrogen is added to the soil as these nodules slough off and disintegrate.

24. Negishi Benji, *Minami shina nōgyō keizairon* (Taipei: Noda shobō, 1940), p. 122.

25. Johanna Meskill, p. 74.

26. *Zhujiang sanjiaozhou*, vol. 5, p. 66.

27. Rubie Watson, *Inequality*, p. 75.

28. Liang Jiamian and Qi Jingwen, "Fanshu yin zhong kao," *Huanan nongxue yuan xuebao*, 1.3:74–78 (1980); Liang Fangzhong, "Fanshu shuru Zhongguo kao," in *Liang Fangzhong jingji shi lunwenji bubian* (Henan: Zhongguo guji chubanshe, 1984), pp. 227–229. The introduction into Fujian is the better recorded and has therefore received more attention than the introductions into Guangdong. Ho Ping-ti has suggested that there was an overland route for the sweet potato from India into Yunnan in the 1560s and 1570s. But this is difficult to establish, particularly because in Bengal, the closest point of contact with the New World via the Portuguese, the sweet potato is known as *chine alu* "Chinese potato," *chini* being the word for "white sugar" as well as "Chinese sugar." The introduction into Yunnan may have been the *Dioscorea fasciculata*, a reddish kidney-shaped yam from Burma called the "Karen potato."

29. Several such comments are compiled in Li Wenzhi, Wei Jingyu, and Jing Junjian, eds., pp. 21–22.

30. *Nongzheng quanshu*, juan 27, zhong ce, pp. 688–695, and juan 51, xia ce, p. 1517. The *Ganshu su* is now lost. Although Xu correctly identified the *Ipomoea batatas* as a new introduction by the Portuguese, he uses the term *ye shan yao* rather than the term *fanshu*.

31. British Parliamentary Papers, General Correspondence, pp. 10–11.

32. *Xin'an xianzhi*, juan 3, p. 122; and Peter Ng and Hugh Baker, p. 38. See also Ho Ping-ti, *Studies on the Population*, p. 187.

33. *Chu-lo xianzhi*, *Wuchan zhi* section, p. 193.

34. Ho Ping-ti, *Studies on the Population*, p. 187.

35. Dwight Perkins, *Agricultural Development*, p. 48, is inaccurate when he suggests that sweet potatoes were only a hedge against disaster. The survey data used by him did not record the output of marginal lands, which is where the potatoes were grown.

36. Watt, *Commercial Products*, p. 688. The common misconception that the sweet potato is nutritionally deficient comes from the fact that all entirely starch-based diets lead to vitamin deficiencies, and the dietary deficiencies noted among the Chinese poor came from eating very little besides sweet potatoes. But acre for acre the sweet potato provides more calories than rice.

37. Purseglove, vol. 1, p. 98; British Parliamentary Papers, *General Correspondence*, p. 10. Martin Yang, however, suggests that the seedlings were first raised in a nursery bed and then replanted: Martin Yang, p. 20.

38. Lu Nien-tsing, ed., *Statistics of Crop Cultivation Survey in Taiwan* (Taipei: Taiwan tudi yinhang, 1962), Appendix 1, p. 487. Discussion of crop rotation in Taiwan based on Chen Chung-min, *Upper Camp: A Study of a Chinese Mixed Cropping Village in Taiwan* (Nangang: Institute of Ethnology, Academia Sinica, 1977).

39. Rubie Watson, *Inequality*, p. 77; King, p. 229.

40. British Parliamentary Papers, *General Correspondence*, p. 10. The widespread cultivation of the sweet potato on the mainland in the first decade of the twentieth century is also noted by King, p. 229.

41. Guoli Zhongshan daxue, Nongke xueyuan, *Guangdong nongye gaikuang diaocha baogaoshu* (Guangzhou: n.p., 1925–1933), vol. 1, pp. 7, 25; vol. 2, pp. 59, 119, 297; vol. 3, pp. 5, 9. Overall acreage data for sweet potatoes are not available, for as has been pointed out, there are few reliable rural surveys giving agricultural yields and actual acreage of crops for most regions of China prior to the 1920s: David Faure, "Neglected Historical Sources on the Late Ch'ing and Early Republican Rural Economy," *Ch'ing-shih wen-t'i* 4.1:59 (1979).

Rubie Watson, *Inequality*, p. 78, found many who recalled the past as "the time when we ate sweet potatoes." A 78-year-old woman remembered that when she married into a poor household in Ha Tsuen in 1918, the family ate nothing but sweet potatoes at every meal. In the north, in Taitou village in Shandong, not only did the peasants eat sweet potatoes every day at every meal throughout the year, the sweet potato was so vital to the domestic economy that the even the architecture of the peasant huts was organized around platforms for drying sweet potatoes: Martin Yang, p. 35.

42. K. H. Connell, "The Potato in Ireland," *Past and Present* 23:62–63 (1962).

43. de Vries, p. 74.

44. Clifford Geertz, *Agricultural Involution* (rpt. Berkeley: University of California Press, 1968), p. 91.

45. Contrast, for example, the devastating subsistence crisis of mid-eighteenth-century Zhili and the various other famines that occurred in north China, where the sweet potato made a slower entry: see Pierre-Etienne Will, *Bureaucracy and Famine in Eighteenth Century China*, Elborg Foster, tr. (Stanford: Stanford University Press, 1990).

46. E-tu Zen Sun, "Sericulture and Silk Textile Production in Ch'ing China," in Wilmott, ed., p. 93.

47. George Trewartha, "Field Observations on the Canton Delta of South China," *Economic Geography* 15. 1:1–10 (1939).

48. Ch'üan Han-sheng, "Production and Distribution of Rice in Southern Song," E-Tu Zen Sun and John De Francis, eds. and trs., *Chinese Social History* (Washington, D.C.: American Council of Learned Societies, 1956).

49. Zhou Qufei, cited and translated in Bray, p. 510. As Ho Ping-ti points out, many of the newer varieties of rice were first introduced in the Yangzi Delta region, not in the regions further south: Ho Ping-ti, "Early Ripening Rice in Chinese History," *Economic History Review*, 2nd ser. 9.2:200–218 (1956).

50. Mark Elvin, "Skills and Resources in Late Traditional China," in Dwight Perkins, ed., *China's Modern Economy in Historical Perspective* (Stanford: Stanford University Press, 1975), p. 94; Bray, p. 502.

51. Bray, pp. 489–495. As Bray points out, China had an enormous range of rice varieties; the *Shou shi tong kao* gives over 3,000 names. Red rice was planted by the Man on newly reclaimed land even in the twentieth century; James Watson, *Emigration*, p. 30.

52. *Dongguan xianzhi* (1797), juan 4, p. 1a.

53. *Bunong shu* (preface dated 1620), Zhang Luxiang, comp. (rpt. Beijing: Zhonghua shuju, 1956); Chen Hengli and Wang Dacan, *Bunongshu yanjiu* (Beijing: Zhonghua shuju, 1958), pp. 26–34. Faure, *The Rural Economy*, pp. 46–48, points out that the average yield of 300 *jin* per *mu* was not uncommon in the twentieth century, and in one experimental farm in Dongguan county yields of 400 *jin*, a whopping 532 pounds per *mu*, was recorded.

54. *Guangdong xinyu*, juan 14, p. 371.

55. Fujii Hiroshi, "Shin'an shōnin no kenkyū," *Tōyō gakuhō* 36.1:44 (1953).

56. *Zhujiang sanjiaozhou*, vol., 6, p. 14

57. Viraphol, pp. 74–83. Viraphol suggests that population pressure forced such imports; but that seems unlikely, for the poor seldom ate rice. Population pressure seems to have led to an increase in sweet potato cultivation rather than rice.

58. Phipps, pp. 176–255. By the 1830s rice from Bengal was being imported into China by British, American, and Indian traders in addition to rice from Manila.

59. Loren Brandt, "Chinese Agriculture and the International Economy, 1870–1930s: A Reassessment," *Explorations in Economic History* 22:170 (1985).

60. *Xin'an xianzhi*, p. 30.

61. Elvin, *Pattern*, pp. 210–211, 214–215. The argument that cash-crop cultivation led to a shortage of food and that rice imports were indicative of this shortage is an argument also taken up in Guangdong jingji nianjian bianzhuan weiyuanhui, comp., *Ershijiu niandu Guangdong jingji nianjian* (Guangzhou: Guangdong sheng yinhang jinji yanjiushi, 1941).

62. Brandt, "Chinese Agriculture," p. 170.

63. Burnett, *Plenty and Want*, p. 100. Figure given as 50.97 million hundredweight, converted at 112 pounds per hundredweight.

64. Wickberg, in "Continuities," p. 214, is incorrect in assuming "commercialization in Taiwan itself was largely a phenomenon of the last four decades of the nineteenth century." Chang Han-yu and Ramon Myers, "Japanese Colonial Development Policy in Taiwan, 1895–1906," *JAS* 22.4:433 (1963), also suggests Taiwan had only a subsistence economy. However, in later writings on Taiwan, Myers has pointed out the extensive commercial agriculture: Myers, "Taiwan under Ch'ing."

65. *Chu-lo xianzhi*, *Fengsu zhi* section, p. 134.

66. *Fujian tongzhi* (1871), Sun Erzhun et al., comps., juan 270, p. 11a. Ch'üan and Kraus, as well as Ng Chin-keong, discusses rice exports from Taiwan at some length, though Ng considers the 1 million *dan* given by the former a somewhat high figure and suggests it was probably around 800,000 to 900,000 *dan*: see Ch'üan and Kraus, p. 67; and Ng Chin-keong, *Trade and Society*, p. 117. Converted at the rate 185 pounds to 1 *dan*.

67. *Taihai jianwen lu*, p. 20, mentions the trade with Shanghai, and *Taihai shichalu* (1736), Huang Shujing, rpt. in *Taiwan wenxian congkan*, p. 48, mentions the other commodities being exported to Xiamen.

68. *Zhujiang sanjiaozhou*, vol. 4, p. 7.

69. Lian, juan 26, p. 498.

70. *Zhujiang sanjiaozhou*, vol. 3, p. 19.

71. *Guangzhou fuzhi* (1879), Dai Zhaochen et al., eds. (rpt. Taipei: Chengwen chubanshe, 1966), juan 15, p. 20b. Of course, this did not mean that sweet potatoes were no longer cultivated.

72. As counties such as Shunde began to specialize in silk yarn manufacture, special markets developed, and there was a division of the labor process by the twentieth century. Trewartha, p. 7, notes there were those who raised mulberry seedlings exclusively, others who sold only leaves, and yet others who sold only silkworm eggs.

73. C. W. Howard, *The Sericulture Industry of South China* (Guangzhou: Canton Christian College, 1923), p. 12.

74. C. W. Howard and K. P. Buswell, *A Survey of the Silk Industry of South China* (Hong Kong: Commercial Press, 1925).

75. Alvin So, p. 79, suggests that by the 1920s Shunde apparently produced only enough rice for a fifteen-day supply of food for its population. This is assuming that everybody ate only rice, though sweet potatoes were still cultivated.

76. da Cruz, pp. 135–136.

77. Eugene Anderson and Marja Anderson, *Mountains and Water: The Cultural Ecology of South Coastal China* (Taipei: Oriental Cultural Service, 1973), pp. 57–62, explore this logic of "a fish for every niche." The species raised primarily included mullet and varieties of carp. The big-headed carp and the silver carp eat algae and plankton found near the surface of the water; they can therefore be raised along with the grass carp, which eat grass and large plants, as well as with the common carp which eats insects and waste matter near the bottom. The mud carp and the mullet scavenge and eat from the mud itself.

78. *Zhujiang sanjiaozhou*, vol.3, p. 21.

79. Ibid., vol. 4, p. 58.

80. Ibid., vol. 5, p. 98.

81. Ibid., vol. 3, p. 48. See also Li Weishi, "Guangdong sheng cansiye de maoyi jiqi shuailuo," *Guangdong wenshi ziliao* 16:7–78 (1964).

82. Dwight Perkins, *Agricultural Development*, p. 13. D. Perkins, "Discussion of Liu-Hwang and Fei-Liu," in Hou Chi-ming and Yu Tzong-shian, eds., p. 92.

83. Purseglove, vol. 1, p. 214; Deerr, vol. 1, pp. 13–14.

84. Shi Shenghan, introduction to *Qimin yaoshu*.

85. *Qimin yaoshu jinshi*, juan 10, pp. 741–742.

86. Probably referring to the Tang *Xinxiu bencao*.

87. *Tangshuang pu*, part 3, p. 2. The *Congshu jicheng* edition has a word missing here. Correction based on a Ming handcopied version; Shun An, p. 60.

88. *Tangshuang pu*, part 3, p. 2.

89. Moreno Fraginals, *The Sugarmill*, p. 20; Blussé, p. 26. In addition to declining fertility, deforestation caused by the massive use of wood for boiling the sugar was also a problem forcing relocation.

90. *Nongsang jiyao*, juan 6, pp. 118–119.

91. Purseglove, vol. 1, p. 230.

92. *Tiangong kaiwu*, juan shang, p. 127.

93. Purseglove, vol. 1, p. 233, points out that transplanting cane raised yields in the twentieth century.

94. *Tiangong kaiwu*, juan shang, p. 118.

95. *Guangdong xinyu,* juan 27, p. 689. The validity of this claim is seen in twentieth-century experiments: Purseglove, vol. 1, pp. 224, 231.

96. *Dongguan xianzhi* (1797), juan 4, p. 1b.

97. British Parliamentary Papers, *General Correspondence,* p. 21

98. Osbeck, p. 350. Osbeck's account is so full of rich observations on Chinese botany and agricultural practices that Linnaeus wrote to congratulate him; the letter is appended to Osbeck's text.

99. *Tiangong kaiwu,* juan shang, p. 118.

100. *Guangdong xinyu,* juan 27, p. 689.

101. Davidson, p. 449.

102. For example, the entire logic of Philip Huang's *Peasant Family* and his use of the concept of "involution" are premised on this observation of steadily increasing labor inputs.

103. *Guangdong xinyu,* juan 27, p. 689.

104. *Zhujiang sanjiaozhou,* vol. 5, p. 37.

105. *Nanyue biji,* juan 14, p. 178; *Zhujiang sanjiaozhou,* vol. 5, pp. 37–38. Li Diaoyuan copied extensive sections of Qu Dajun's *Guangdong xinyu* into his own *Nanyue biji,* for Qu's works were banned in the Qing because of his Ming loyalties and Li was committed to preserving Qu's work. In some instances, such as this particular segment on cane cultivation, it is unclear whether Li is simply copying the text from Qu or putting down his own observations and indicating his agreement with Qu's observations by using the same wording.

106. Peng, ed., *Zhongguo jindai,* vol. 2, p. 114.

107. Moreno Fraginals, *The Sugarmill,* p. 89.

108. Author unknown; reproduced in *Xuxiu Taiwan fuzhi,* juan 7, p. 592.

109. Prinsen Geerligs, *The World's Cane Sugar,* p. 82. The figure given is "9.5 cwts. per acre." Dai Guohui and Ramon Myers have uncritically accepted the *Chikan bitan* figure for 1724 as realistic: Dai, pp. 164–165; and Ramon Myers, "Taiwan under Ch'ing," p. 387. But I think they are too high for the period given the level of technology.

110. Dai Guohui, p. 164.

111. Li Wenzhi, ed., *Zhongguo jindai nongyeshi,* p. 355.

112. Lin Manhong, *Cha, tang, zhangnaoye yu wan Qing Taiwan jingji shehui zhi bianqian* (Taipei: Taiwan yinhang, 1978), p. 43.

113. Samuel Couling, *The Encyclopaedia Sinica* (Shanghai: Kelly and Walsh, 1917), p. 530. Yields of mechanical industrial processing in Guangdong in 1932 were 1,960 *jin* per *mu.* Some areas of Jiangxi, however, managed to extract 3,210 *jin* per *mu:* Dwight Perkins, *Agricultural Development,* p. 284.

114. Watt, *Commercial Products,* p. 939; Purseglove, vol. 1, p. 242.

115. *Guangdong xinyu,* juan 27, p. 688.

116. Purseglove, vol. 2, pp. 357, 377. *Guangdong xinyu*, juan 27, p. 688; *Chu-lo xianzhi* (1717), *Wuchan zhi* section, p. 189.

117. *Nanyue biji*, juan 5, p. 81.

118. *Zhujiang sanjiaozhou*, vol. 5, p. 46.

119. Negishi Benji, pp. 122, 132.

120. This type of interdependent manufacturing was typical of what Medick calls "proto-industrialization." This "functional interrelationship between family economy and merchant capital, and the peculiarly stable and at the same time flexible character of this configuration, constituted a comprehensive set of social relations of production": Hans Medick, "The Proto-Industrial Family," *Social History* 1.3:296 (1976).

121. Purseglove, vol. 2, p. 621.

122. Hsiao, p. 377; Chen Han-seng, p. 104. It is a common misconception that Chinese women did not do farmwork.

123. *Nongzheng quanshu*, zhong ce, juan 36, p. 994.

124. *Nanyue biji*, juan 14, p. 10, suggests that in fact growing *Musa textilis* on dry soil produces a soft but strong fiber whereas irrigated soil produces a weaker fiber; see also Purseglove, vol. 2, p. 621. The yield in the 1960s in China was about 800 pounds of ramie fiber per acre per annum, much higher than cotton, which in 1957 was around 300 pounds per acre on average: Dwight Perkins, *Agricultural Development*, p. 283.

125. *Nanyue biji*, juan 5, p. 81.

126. *Zhujiang sanjiaozhou*, vol. 5, p. 55.

127. Ibid., vol. 6, pp. 74–75.

128. *Nanyue biji*, juan 5, p. 84, and juan 6, p. 96.

129. *Zhujiang sanjiaozhou*, vol. 5, p. 48; see also Helen Siu, pp. 31–32.

130. In *The Rural Economy*, Faure has collated the most data on the subject, but does not, for example, factor the time needed for maturation in tabulating the estimates of costs and investments.

131. Shih Min-hsiung, "Production and the Trade of Silk in the Late Ch'ing Period," in Hou Chi-ming and Yu Tzong-shian, eds., p. 366; Li Wenzhi, ed., *Zhongguo jindai nongyeshi*, p. 431; Alvin So, p. 84.

132. Howard and Buswell, p. 113.

133. Faure, *The Rural Economy*, pp. 154–156; Howard and Buswell, pp. 112–115. Neither Faure nor Howard and Buswell considers the rate of interest that would have to have been paid for the initial investment.

134. Howard and Buswell, pp. 94–95; Alvin So, pp. 85–89; Trewartha, p. 7; Shih Ming-hsiung, "Production and the Trade," p. 365.

135. Faure, *The Rural Economy*, p. 154.

136. *Zhujiang sanjiaozhou*, vol. 3, p. 8.

137. Ibid., vol. 4, p. 59.

138. Alvin So, p. 86. Cost of ponds in the twentieth century from *Guangdong sheng canye diaocha baogaoshu* (Guangzhou: Guangdong sheng difang nonglin shixianchang, 1922), p. 21.

139. Dwight Perkins, *Agricultural Development*, p. 298, grapples with the question of daily consumption of rice in the nineteenth century. Rations for People's Liberation Army men in contemporary China range from 500 to 750 *jin*. The price of rice in the nineteenth century ranged from 2.15 taels per *dan* (1.4 piculs or 150 jin) to 1.89 taels per *dan*: Wang Yeh-chien, "The Secular Trend," p. 359, n. 21.

140. Faure, *The Rural Economy*, p. 156; the price of rice is given on p. 65.

141. Leslie S. Cobley, *Introduction to the Botany of Tropical Crops* (London: Longman, 1976), pp. 153–159.

142. Purseglove, vol. 2, p. 644.

143. Cobley, p. 308. One of the best descriptions of tea cultivation in China is given in Robert Fortune, *Two Visits to the Tea Countries of China and the British Tea Plantations of the Himalayas*, 2 vols. (London: Murray, 1853).

144. Chen Han-seng, p. 47.

145. Negishi Benji, p. 122.

146. *Guangdong xinyu*, juan 27, p. 689; *Lingnan congshu* (1830), Deng Chun, comp. (Guangzhou: Yangzhuo shanfang cangban, 1830), juan 41, p. 4a; *Zhujiang sanjiaozhou*, vol. 5, p. 66.

147. Fielde, *A Corner of Cathay*, p. 111; figure given in dollars converted into taels at the ratio of 1 tael:1.4 dollars, ratio worked out by Wang Yeh-chien, "The Secular Trend," p. 359, n. 18. See also Couling, p. 530.

148. Chen Han-seng, p. 63.

149. Adachi Kenji, "Daizu kasu," pp. 36–38.

150. Negishi Benji, pp. 132–133.

151. Ibid., p. 133.

152. Zhongguo renmin daxue, Zhongguo lishi jiaoyanshi, ed., *Zhongguo ziben*, vol. 1, p. 414. Examples show this was the case in the early nineteenth century as well as in the twentieth.

153. Negishi Benji, p. 133.

154. *Xuxiu Taiwan fuzhi*, juan 17, p. 593.

155. Zhongguo renmin daxue, Zhongguo lishi jiaoyanshi, ed., *Zhongguo ziben*, vol. 1, p. 256; this was not a very substantial wage when we consider that the price of rice in the environs of Guangzhou varied between 3 and 5 taels per *dan*, dropping to below 1 tael only when there was a very good harvest: Ch'üan and Kraus, pp. 154–160, for rice prices during this period.

156. *Kang Yong Qian shiqi*, vol. 1, p. 273.

157. Zhongguo renmin daxue, Zhongguo lishi jiaoyanshi, ed., *Zhongguo ziben*, vol. 1, p. 266; Peng, *Zhongguo jindai*, pp. 396–414.

158. E. H. Parker, p. 186; Fielde, "Report," p. 112; cents converted into cash at the rate of 1 tael = 1.4 dollars, accepting 1,000 cash to the tael.

159. Negishi Benji, p. 133.

160. *Xuxiu Taiwan fuzhi*, juan 17, p. 593. The price of rice in Taiwan during that period was close to the level of rice prices on the mainland: Ch'üan and Kraus, p. 67. This suggests that the high cash wages on Taiwan were the result of limited labor availability.

161. *Guangdong xinyu*, juan 27, p. 690; *Nanyue biji*, juan 14, p. 179.

162. *Xuxiu Taiwan fuzhi*, juan 17, p. 593.

163. Negishi Benji, p. 133.

164. *Guangdong xinyu*, juan 21, p. 533.

165. Wykeham Myers, p. 450. In commenting on this section Davidson simply uses the symbol for the dollar ($) and says, "$150 in local currency" with no explanation. Elsewhere (p. 618), he explains the currency, indicating that the Japanese silver yen coin, the Mexican (also known as the Spanish) silver dollar, and the "Tamsui dollar" were in circulation; see Appendix for conversion rates. Here it is not clear whether he is referring to the Tamsui dollar or the Mexican silver dollar (he does clearly indicate when he is referring to the yen). I have assumed he is referring to the Tamsui dollar, the only "local currency" at the time.

166. Ramon Myers, "Taiwan under Ch'ing," p. 401. Conversion rate of "official *dan*" to 2.94 U.S. bushels is based on Ch'üan and Kraus, p. 211 n. 54. In this I am following Faure, *The Rural Economy*, p. 215.

167. Negishi Benji, p. 132.

168. Chen Han-seng, p. 133. The fall in rice prices was due to the Great Depression.

169. *Guangdong xinyu*, juan 27, p. 690.

170. Daniel Kulp, *Country Life in South China* (New York: Columbia University Press, 1925), pp. 88, 203–204. See Dietrich, p. 130, for collective cotton spinning in communal cellars in Hebei to counteract the problems of the region's low humidity. Crop-watching societies were common in most villages.

171. Staunton, vol. 2, p. 396. Ch'en Cheng-hsiang, *Taiwan: An Economic and Social Geography* (Taipei: Fu-min Geographical Institute, 1963), p. 315, notes that the ratio of production costs of sugarcane to rice in the 1930s was 2:1.

172. Faure, *The Rural Economy*, pp. 65, 157–158.

173. Lin Manhong, p. 57, notes this form of rental was commonly found in the Takuu region.

174. Examples of Guangdong landlords collecting rent in rice with the market in mind, leading to tensions with the tenants, have been discussed by

Palmer, pp. 65, 86; and Kamm, p. 63. Ye Shaohua recalled that gentry-landlords in Shunde who owned polders in the Pearl River Delta collected rent in rice from tenants and shipped it to Chencun market, where it was sold to peasants cultivating mulberry. Ng Chin-keong, *Trade and Society*, p. 163, discusses the number of rice merchants in the Amoy-Taiwan trade network who were collecting rent in rice from their lands in Taiwan. See also Johanna Meskill, for the Lins in Wufeng and the profits from rice trade.

175. Ye Shaohua, p. 13.

176. Several such memorials have been discussed by Ng Chin-keong, *Trade and Society*, pp. 163–165.

177. *Zhujiang sanjiaozhou*, vol. 4, pp. 64–69.

178. *Kang Yong Qian shiqi*, vol. 1, p. 45.

179. Rinji Taiwan kyūkan chōsakai, comp., *Taiwan tōgyō kyūkan ippan* (Tokyo: Rinji Taiwan kyūkan chōsakai, 1909), p. 67. Contract given in Liu Yongcheng, "Qianlong xingke," Dang'an record, p. 91; the area of land rented not specified. Guangdong survey, Zhongguo renmin daxue, Zhongguo lishi jiaoyanshi, ed., *Zhongguo ziben*, vol. 2, pp. 324–325.

180. Robert Gardella, "The Boom Years of the Fujian Tea Trade," in Ernest R. May and John K. Fairbank, eds., *America's China Trade in Historical Perspective* (Cambridge: Harvard University Press, 1986), p. 58.

181. Wu Liangkai, "Qingdai Qianlong shiqi nongye jingji guanxi de yanbian he fazhan," in *Qingshi luncong*, vol. 1, p. 26.

182. Nishijima, *Chūgoku keizai*, and his "Shina shoki mengyō shijō." See also Tanaka, "Rural Handicraft," pp. 79–100.

183. *Xin'an xianzhi*, p. 35; see also Peter Ng and Baker, p. 76.

184. As cited in Kataoka Shibako, "Minmatsu Shinsho no Kahoku ni okeru nōka keiei," *Shakai keizai shigaku* 25.3:96 n. 6 (1959); see also Will, p. 181.

185. *Shou shi tong kao* (1742), Ou Ertai et al., comps. (Beijing: Palace edition, 1847). The compendium has 78 juan and is only slightly shorter than the *Nongzheng quanshu*, which is the longest of the Chinese agricultural treatises. On the wide distribution of the *Shou shi tong kao*, see Bray, pp. 73–75. For peasant literacy levels and the fact that such agricultural texts were readily accessible and widely read, see Evelyn Rawski, *Education and Popular Literacy*.

186. Shih Min-hsiung, *The Silk Industry in China*, E-tu Zen Sun, tr. (Ann Arbor: Center for Chinese Studies, University of Michigan, 1976), pp. 6–7.

187. Lian, *Gongyi zhi* section, p. 498.

188. Tanaka, "Rural Handicraft," p. 87.

189. Philip Huang, *The Peasant Family*, pp. 95–98; Faure, *The Structure*, p. 23; Kulp, pp. 93–96. Wu Chengming shows not only that the grain trade domi-

nated but that grain purchases accounted for 20 to almost 50 percent of all purchases made: Wu Chengming, *Zhongguo zibenzhuyi*, pp. 247–263.

190. Arthur H. Smith, *Village Life in China* (New York: F. H. Revell, 1899), p. 146; emphasis mine.

191. Jairus Banaji, "Chayanov, Kautsky, Lenin: Considerations Towards a Synthesis," *Economic and Political Weekly* 11:1594–1607 (1976).

192. Sol Tax, *Penny Capitalism* (Chicago: University of Chicago Press, 1963).

Chapter 6

1. *Guangdong xinyu*, juan 14, p. 371.

2. Ibid., juan 14, p. 389.

3. See, for example, Nancy Lee Swann, *Food and Money in Ancient China* (Princeton: Princeton University Press, 1950), pp. 413–464.

4. Myers and Elvin, for example, take the mere existence of markets as a sufficient condition for greater economic opportunities for peasants: Myers, "Customary Law, Markets and Resource Transactions," pp. 73, 277–279; and Elvin, *Pattern*, pp. 167, 269. Approaching the issue of market development from a very different perspective, that of the extent of commercialization of agriculture as a prelude to the development of capitalism, Chinese scholars such as Ye Xian'en and Tan Dihua have also overlooked the barriers to peasant involvement in the market: Ye Xian'en and Tan Dihua, "Ming Qing Zhujiang sanjiaozhou nongye shangyehua yu xushi de fazhan," in Ye Xian'en et al., eds., pp. 58–68.

5. Even rational-choice economists, such as Donald McCloskey, acknowledge the importance of institutions outside the market: Donald McCloskey, "The Economics of Choice," in Thomas G. Rawski et al., eds., *Economics and the Historian* (Berkeley: University of California Press, 1996), p. 125. The "market" and its implications are discussed more fully in the Conclusion.

6. These routes have been studied in detail by Fan I-chun, "Long-Distance Trade," especially pp. 14–61, 234–238.

7. Ibid., p. 241.

8. I agree with William Rowe, *Hankow* (Stanford: Stanford University Press, 1984), pp. 60–62, that the extent of the national market prior to the end of the nineteenth century has been underestimated in G. William Skinner's claim that there was no national market in bulk goods: G. William Skinner, "Regional Urbanization in Nineteenth-Century China," in Skinner, ed., p. 217.

9. Fujii, "Shin'an shōnin," pp. 30–33.

10. *Yuehaiguan zhi* (1838), Liang Tingnan and Fang Dongshu (rpt. Taipei: Wenhai chubanshe, n.d.), juan 18, pp. 3b–4b.

11. Ibid., juan 18, pp. 9b–10a.

12. *Chinese Repository* 2:290 (1833).

13. Fujii, "Shin'an shōnin," pp. 88–89.

14. *Ming shi shihuozhi*, Li Xunjiao, annot. (Beijing: Zhonghua shuju, 1982), p. 143.

15. Volume of salt trade based on Ye Xian'en, ed., *Guangdong hangyun shi*, p. 177. Figure of 170 *wan jin* converted to pounds.

16. Ch'üan and Kraus, p. 71. Figures given as 1 and 2 million *dan*, rising to 3 million *dan* of rice.

17. *Chinese Repository* 2:290 (1833).

18. Ye Xian'en, *Guangdong hangyun shi*, p. 172.

19. Chao, *The Development of Cotton*, pp. 20–23.

20. *Guangdong xinyu*, juan 15, p. 426.

21. We have already seen how by the end of the eighteenth century and the first half of the nineteenth when cotton from northern and central China was no longer readily available for south China, the same circuit of sugar-for-cotton was transferred to the Sino-Indian trade nexus; see also Nishijima, "Shina shoki mengyō shijō," pp. 262–288.

22. *Chenghai xianzhi* (1764), Jin Tinglie, ed., juan 19, p. 8.

23. Ye Xian'en, *Guangdong hangyun shi*, p. 189.

24. *Taihai shichalu*, p. 48, Ng Chin-keong, *Trade and Society*, pp. 128–133.

25. *Taihai shichalu*, p. 21. The calculation of quantities carried is based on the carrying capacity of the ships as suggested by Ng Chin-keong, *Trade and Society*, p. 133, n. 163.

26. *Xiamen zhi*, p. 166.

27. Ng Chin-keong, *Trade and Society*, pp. 140–142.

28. Fan I-chun, "Long-Distance Trade," p. 258.

29. Ng Chin-keong, *Trade and Society*, p. 134.

30. *Chinese Repository* 2:290 (1833).

31. Ibid., p. 134.

32. *Taihai shichalu*, pp. 47–48.

33. Hummel, vol. 2, p. 877.

34. Ye Xian'en, *Guangdong hangyun shi*, pp. 189–190.

35. *Guangzhou fuzhi* (1758), juan 47, 12a.

36. *Guangdong xinyu*, juan 14, p. 383.

37. Liang Jiabin, p. 59.

38. Ng Chin-keong, *Trade and Society*, pp. 178–183, has sketched out the transprovincial connections of the Fujian merchants, but this is a topic that awaits a full-length monograph.

39. Morse, *Chronicles*, vol. 1, p. 176.

40. Fairbank, *Trade and Diplomacy*, p. 50; Wu Ren'an, "Mingdai Guangdong sanshiliu hang chutan," *Xueqiu yanjiu* 2:18–23 (1980).

41. Katō Shigeshi, "On the Hong or the Associations of Merchants in China," *Memoirs of the Research Department of the Tōyō Bunko* 8:45–83 (1936); Shiba, *Commerce and Society*; Fujii, "Shin'an shōnin," pp. 80–82; and Rowe, pp. 70–71.

42. I am translating *hang* as "guild" only where the organizational structure was loose, as proposed by Yang Lien-sheng for the period prior to 1840, when these organizations engaged in trade but typically did not have guild rules and guild halls: Yang Lien-sheng, "Government Control of Urban Merchants in Traditional China," *Tsing-hua Journal of Chinese Studies*, n.s. 8.1–2:195 (1970). As discussed below, I have tried to distinguish between *yahang* (brokerage house) and *qihang* as well as *bang*, though on occasion terms such as *bang* and *huiguan* have an overlap in meaning in the original source; I have followed Rowe, pp. 254–255, for the distinctions between these various types of trade and commercial organizations.

43. Fujii, "Shin'an shōnin," p. 55; Liang Jiabin p. 22; Peng Zeyi, "Qingdai Guangdong yanghang zhidu de qiyuan," *Lishi yanjiu* 1:15–17 (1957).

44. Fu Yiling, *Ming Qing shidai shangren* (Beijing: Renmin chubanshe, 1956), pp. 132–133.

45. Ibid., pp. 200–201, 205; Ye Xian'en, *Guangdong haiyun shi*, pp. 149–150.

46. Mundy, p. 272.

47. Ng Chin-keong, *Trade and Society*, p. 168.

48. Fu Yiling, *Ming Qing shidai shangren*, p. 201.

49. Peng Zeyi, "Qingdai Guangdong yanghang," p. 16.

50. Ng Chin-keong, *Trade and Society*, pp. 167–177, has discussed the various dimensions of these activities as well as some of the differences in the way the systems operated in Guangdong versus Fujian.

51. Peng Zeyi, "Guangzhou shisan hang xutan," *Lishi yanjiu* 4:110–125 (1981).

52. Wang Zongyan, *Guangdong wenwu congtan* (Hong Kong: Zhonghua shuju, 1974), p. 179. See Chapter Two for details regarding Wang Po.

53. Greenberg, p. 53.

54. Hummel, vol. 1, p. 482.

55. Hao Yen-ping, *Commercial Revolution*, p. 16, has pointed out that by the 1830s the growing volume of the illegal trade in opium was such that its value constituted more than half the value of the legally imported goods at Guangzhou.

56. The term "Hoppo" is attributed to this connection the representative had with the *hubu*: Lawrence Kesseler, *Kang-hsi and the Consolidation of Ch'ing Rule* (Chicago: University of Chicago Press, 1976), p. 96; Fairbank, *Trade and Diplo-*

macy, pp. 48–49; Torbet, pp. 97–103. Torbet suggests that during the Kangxi and Yongzheng periods *neiwufu* personnel did not serve as superintendents of the Guangzhou bureau, though later appointments were primarily Manchu and linked to the Imperial Household Department.

57. Torbet, p. 103.

58. See, for example, the machinations of the governor of Liang-Guang in 1806 and 1809 regarding the rice trade from Siam and the close support of the Hong merchants: Viraphol, pp. 109–111.

59. Phipps, p. 148; Morse, *Chronicles*, vol. 4, p. 172.

60. Henri Cordier, "Les marchands hanistes de canton," *TP* 2e série, 3:282–315 (1902).

61. This dual level of merchants allowed to trade with foreigners was also common in Fujian: Ng Chin-keong, *Trade and Society*, pp. 173–174.

62. Phipps, p. 148.

63. Ibid.

64. Hunter, *The Fan Kwae*, provides much insight into the dealings of the shopmen.

65. Hao Yen-p'ing, *Commercial Revolution*, pp. 17–20, has also shown how even Jardine and Matheson bought more goods from the shopmen than from the *hong* merchants.

66. Morse, *Chronicles*, vol. 1, p. 135; Greenberg, p. 148.

67. Morse, *Chronicles*, vol. 1, p. 80.

68. Ibid., vol. 2, pp. 89–90.

69. Susan Mann, *Local Merchants and the Chinese Bureaucracy, 1750–1950* (Stanford: Stanford University Press, 1987), p. 41.

70. Katō Shigeshi, *Shina keizaishi*, vol. 2, pp. 545–549.

71. Arthur H. Smith, p. 151; Skinner, "Marketing," p. 21.

72. Rowe, p. 254.

73. Ibid., pp. 254–255. There is an extensive and complex literature on guilds and guild structures and regional merchant associations in China, and not all authors use the terms in an identical manner. While I have drawn on the works of Fujii Hiroshi, Niida Noboru, Negishi Tadashi, Liu Yongcheng, Katō Shigeshi, MacGowan, Morse, and Golas here, I have either retained the Chinese term or translated it in accordance with Rowe's translation.

74. Fang Hao, "Tainan zhi 'jiao,'" *Dalu zazhi* 44.4:177–199 (1962), has argued that the Native Guild (Kangjiao) and the Sugar Guild were one and the same from their inception, which he dates to 1780 on the basis of a stone inscription.

75. Rinji Taiwan kyūkan chōsakai, comp., *Taiwan tōgyō*, pp. 75–76; Inō Kanori, *Taiwan bunkashi* (rpt. Tokyo: Tōkōshoin, 1965), vol. 3, p. 4.

76. D. J. MacGowan, "Chinese Guilds or Chambers of Commerce and

Trade Unions," *Journal of the North China Branch of the Royal Asiatic Society*, n.s. 21:138, 146 (1886). See also K., "Chinese Guilds and Their Rules," *China Review* 12.1:5–9 (1883–1884).

77. *Dongguan xianzhi* (1797), juan 12, p. 9a.

78. Ye Xian'en, *Guangdong hangyun shi*, p. 190.

79. *Ming Qing Foshan beike wenxian jingji ziliao*, Guangdong sheng shehui kexue yuan, Lishi yanjiusuo and Zhongshan daxue, Lishixi, eds. (Guangzhou: Guangdong renmin chubanshe, 1987), pp. 341–342; Rinji Taiwan kyūkan chōsakai, comp., *Taiwan shihō furoku sankōsho* (Tokyo: Rinji Taiwan kyūkan chōsakai, 1910), supplementary vol. 3, part 1, pp. 75–76.

80. Negishi Tadashi, *Chūgoku no girudo* (Tokyo: Nippon hyōron shinsha, 1953), p. 317. Rinji Taiwan kyūkan chōsakai, comp., *Taiwan tōgyō*, pp. 121–125. The activities of the "bank" seem to have been similar to those of the *qian zhuang*, or the Chinese commercial bank, but the Japanese text uses the modern term *ginkō/yinhang*. This type of credit structure was also noted in Ningbo by Shiba Yoshinobu, "Ningpo," pp. 430, 436.

81. Rinji Taiwan kyūkan chōsakai, comp., *Taiwan tōgyō*, p. 76. The investigator points out this practice was common prior to the mid-nineteenth century, presumably when the guilds had greater power.

82. Rinji Taiwan kyūkan chōsakai, comp., *Taiwan shihō*, supplementary vol. 3, part 1, p. 76.

83. See discussion of this in Peter J. Golas, "Early Ch'ing Guilds," in Skinner, ed., p. 571.

84. Rowe, p. 187.

85. Golas, p. 571; MacGowan, "Chinese Guilds," p. 175; Shiba, "Ningpo," p. 432. Jing Junjian, "Legislation Related," p. 61, points out very clearly that it was well known that prices were fixed by brokers, official law codes notwithstanding.

86. E.g., the tong-oil dealers in 1880, the bronzeware dealers in 1879, and the Tea Guild in 1887: Rowe, p. 296,

87. Hayashi Kazuo, "Min Shin jidai Kanton no kyo to shi dentōteki ichiba no keitai to kinō ni kansuru ichi kōsatsu," *Shirin* 63:70 (1980); Ye Xian'en and Tan Dihua, "Ming Qing Zhujiang sanjiaozhou nongye shangyehua yu xushi de fazhan," in Ye Xian'en et al., eds., *Ming Qing Guangdong shehui jingji yanjiu*, pp. 93–96; and Masui Tsuneo, "Kanton no kyoshi," *Tōa ronsō* 4:263–283 (1941).

88. *Chu-lo xianzhi*, pp. 127–133. The early editions of the gazetteers contain scant information on the rural standard or local markets, and list markets under *jie shi*, or marketplaces of urban townships. See Lian, pp. 43–65, for the history of military garrisons functioning in multiple capacities.

89. *Taiwan fuzhi* (1694), Gao Gongqian, ed., rpt. in *Taiwan wenxian congkan*, pp. 46–48; *Chongxiu Fujian Taiwan fuzhi* (1740), Liu Liangbi, ed., rpt. in *Taiwan*

wenxian congkan, pp. 83–85; *Xuxiu Taiwan fuzhi* (1768), pp. 84–90, 251–252; *Changhua xianzhi*, pp. 39–42; *Chu-lo xianzhi*, pp. 28–32. However, as noted above, since these early gazetteers often just listed all Han settlements as markets, we have no way of knowing the real extent of economic activity at these markets.

90. Donald R. DeGlopper, "Lu-kang and Its Trading System," in Knapp, ed., *China's Island Frontier*, pp. 146–147, 154; Johanna Meskill, p. 54.

91. Hayashi Kazuo, pp. 3, 94–95.

92. Arthur H. Smith, p. 150.

93. *Guangdong xinyu*, juan 2, p. 47.

94. *Dongguan xianzhi* (1797), juan 9, pp. 7b–8a.

95. *Xin'an xianzhi*, juan 22, p. 560.

96. As Freedman writes, "It would seem, therefore, that control of the lowest level market town characteristically gave the controllers the dominant voice in the area served by the market, and that where there were two or more local lineages of the same higher-order lineage in this area, the ownership of the market by one of them (or by one of its segments) gave it undisputed precedence": Maurice Freedman, *Chinese Lineage and Society* (London: Athlone Press, 1971), pp. 91–92.

97. Eberhard, pp. 174–176.

98. Details based on Robert G. Groves, "Militia, Market and Lineage: Chinese Resistance to the Occupation of Hong Kong's New Territories," *JHKBRAS* 9:31–64 (1969); Baker, "The Five Great Clans," p. 31; and Rubie Watson, *Inequality*, pp. 74; 82.

99. Faure, "Lineage," p. 25.

100. Rubie Watson, *Inequality*, p. 73.

101. *Guangdong tushuo*, Mao Hongbin et al., comps. (Guangzhou: Cuiwen tang, 1879), juan 1, pp. 116–120.

102. Woon, pp. 26–27.

103. Robert Groves, "The Origins of Two Market Towns in the New Territories," in Marjorie Topley, ed., *Aspects of Social Organization in the New Territories* (Hong Kong: Hong Kong Branch of the Royal Asiatic Society, 1965), p. 18. The Wen later set up another market, called the New Tai Po market.

104. Freedman, *Chinese Lineage*, p. 82.

105. Hayashi Kazuo, p. 98.

106. Ashmore, p. 214.

107. *Chinese Repository* 3:283–84 (1865), cited in Hsiao, p. 423.

108. Kulp, pp. 13, 22.

109. Rubie Watson, *Inequality*, pp. 72–75.

110. Arthur H. Smith, p. 148.

111. Johanna Meskill, p. 60.

112. Both Myron Cohen, *House United*, and Burton Pasternak, *Kinship and Community in Two Chinese Villages*, have looked at this.

113. *Changhua xianzhi*, p. 363; Shepherd, *Statecraft*, p. 319.

114. Hsu Wen-hsiung, "Frontier Social Organization," p. 102.

115. Ibid., p. 98.

116. Lawrence W. Crissman, "Marketing on the Changhua Plain, Taiwan," in Willmott, ed., p. 254.

117. *Taiwan nanbu beiwen jicheng*, rpt. in *Taiwan wenxian congkan*, no. 218, pp. 412–417.

118. Hsu Wen-hsiung, "Frontier Social Organization," p. 100.

119. Hayashi Kazuo, p. 97.

120. Mann, pp. 41–42, has discussed the details of this case.

121. Guan Xiekuang, "Jiefangqian Xinhui kuiye jingying gaikuang," *Guangdong wenshi ziliao* 28:187–214 (1980).

122. Ibid., pp. 206–208.

123. *Ming Qing Foshan beike wenxian*, pp. 87–89. This incident has been discussed by Faure, cited below.

124. David Faure, "What Made Foshan a Town?" *Late Imperial China* 11.2:20–21 (1990).

125. Elvin, *Pattern*, p. 297; Marks, *Rural Revolution*, pp. 44–45. Elvin goes as far as to say, "There had even been a revolution in the relations between social classes, at least in the countryside." He assigns too little importance to the continued ownership of land by the elite and errs in equating the legal end of serfdom with a transformation in the social relations of production.

126. Academies, in or near commercial centers, tended to be funded primarily from commercial capital: Grimm, pp. 492–3. See also DeGlopper, pp. 648–649. Both city god temples (such as the Beidi in Foshan) and temples to popular gods were sites of markets.

127. The *Nanyue biji* repeats the *Guangdong xinyu* on this point without additional comment, suggesting this was also the case in the eighteenth century: *Nanyue biji*, juan 16, p. 206.

128. Cited in *Zhujiang sanjiaozhou*, vol. 3, p. 18.

129. Li Min (pseudonym of Li Wenzhi), "Qianlong xingke tiben zhong you guan nongye ziben zhuyi mengya de cailiao," *Wenwu* 9.72 (1975). For an abbreviated translation of this essay with commentary, see Ramon Myers, "The 'Sprouts of Capitalism' in Agricultural Development during the Mid-Ch'ing Period," *Ch'ing-shih Wen-t'i* 3.6:84–89 (1976). See also Zhongguo renmin daxue, Zhongguo lishi jiaoyanshi, ed., *Zhongguo ziben*, vol. 1, p. 250.

130. Peng, ed., *Zhongguo jindai*, vol. 1, pp. 250–256.

131. I was not able to examine the original of this contract and have relied on

Li Min's precis of its contents. The amount of sugar discussed in the transaction is given in a somewhat curious manner, for usually such contracts stipulated total weight rather than the number of pieces. The "slabs" of sugar may have referred to the common *pian tang*, 4–6-ounce slabs of light brown sugar that one can still buy in Guangdong.

132. Li Min, pp. 72–73.

133. *Guangdong xinyu*, juan 14, p. 389; *Nanyue biji*, juan 16 p. 206.

134. Zhongguo renmin daxue, Zhongguo lishi jiaoyanshi, ed., *Zhongguo ziben*, pp. 39–40.

135. Kulp, pp. 91–92.

136. This is taking into account that the *Nanyu biji* is merely a copy of the *Guangdong xinyu* text in this section.

137. Ye Xian'en and Tan Dihua, "Lun Zhujiang sanjiaozhou de zutian," p. 16.

138. Ibid.

139. Ibid. Ye and Tan have argued that this example represents a managerial enterprise and was suggestive of the incipient development of capitalism, but I disagree.

140. Staunton, vol. 2, p. 461.

141. Ibid., p. 462.

142. Eckeberg, p. 296.

143. Hommel, p. 114.

144. James Hayes, "Itinerant Hakka Weavers," *JHKBRAS* 8:162–165 (1968). Such weavers and skilled artisans were known also in Sichuan.

145. Rinji Taiwan kyūkan chōsakai, comp., *Taiwan tōgyō*. The following discussion of cane cultivation in Taiwan and its various organizations is based on this work, pp. 1–125.

146. Ibid., pp. 66–67.

147. Ibid., pp. 61–63.

148. Ibid.

149. Jiang Jiajin, "Jiawu zhanyi yiqian zhi Taiwan tangye," *Tainan wenhua* 5.2:72 (1956). I am indebted to Harry Lambley for helping me locate this. See Myers, "Taiwan under Ch'ing," pp. 389–390, for other similar contracts.

150. Rinji Taiwan kyūkan chōsakai, comp., *Taiwan tōgyō*, p. 85.

151. Ibid., p. 62.

152. Wykeham Myers, p. 449.

153. Rinji Taiwan kyūkan chōsakai, comp., *Taiwan tōgyō*, p. 65.

154. The estimates are approximate, but Lin Manhong, p. 29, has tabulated the number of cane crushers in Taiwan mentioned in all sources prior to the

nineteenth century. This shows some 738 cane crushers operating in 1764. For the nineteenth century, see Davidson, p. 448.

155. Guan, p. 212.

156. Biographical sketch from Fairbank, *Trade and Diplomacy*, p. 406.

157. Frederic Wakeman, "The Secret Societies of Kwangtung, 1800–1856," in Jean Chesneaux, ed., *Popular Movements and Secret Societies in China, 1840–1950* (Stanford: Stanford University Press, 1972), pp. 29–47.

158. Peng, ed., *Zhongguo jindai*, vol. 2, pp. 324, 529.

159. Ibid., vol. 2, p. 529.

160. Rinji Taiwan kyūkan chōsakai, comp., *Taiwan tōgyō*, p. 123. Price reduction given as 0.5–2.0 *jiao*, converted assuming 10 *jiao* or 1,000 *li* to 1 *liang*.

161. Shih, *The Silk Industry*, p. 102.

162. Mayers, pp. 52, 184.

163. Peng, ed., *Zhongguo jindai*, vol 2, p. 325.

164. Guan, p. 208.

165. Lillian Li, p. 52.

166. Ibid., p. 54.

167. Chen Han-seng, p. 93.

168. Ibid.

169. Yang Lien-sheng, *Money and Credit in China* (Cambridge: Harvard University Press, 1971), p. 100.

170. Ibid.

171. E.g., Marks, *Rural Revolution*, p. 104; Chao, *The Development of Cotton*, pp. 53–54; Elvin, *Pattern*, pp. 275–276.

172. Maurice Dobb, *Studies in the Development of Capitalism* (New York: International Publishers, 1975), p. 18. See Lillian Li, pp. 57–61, for an extended discussion of the putting-out system and scholarship on China.

173. Marx, *Capital* (1894), David Fernbach, tr. (New York: Vintage Books, 1981), vol. 3, pp. 452–453.

174. Imperial Maritime Customs, *Decennial Reports, 1892–1901*, Second issue, (Shanghai: Inspectorate General of Customs, 1904), vol. 2, p. 155.

175. Kulp, emphasis mine, pp. 91–92.

176. Faure, *The Rural Economy*, p. 111, posits that this type of switch was a profit calculation on the part of the peasant. But Faure does not look at how merchants may have influenced peasant decision-making.

177. Guoli Guangdong daxue, Nongke xueyuan, *Panyu, Zengcheng, Dongguan, Zhongshan tangye diaocha baogaoshu* (Guangzhou, 1925), pp. 7–8.

178. *Zhujiang sanjiaozhou*, vol. 5, pp. 39–40; Imperial Maritime Customs, *Reports on the Trade of the Treaty Ports of China: Shantou* (Shanghai: Inspectorate

General of Customs, 1878), p. 246; Robert Eng, *Economic Imperialism in China* (Berkeley: Institute of East Asian Studies, University of California, 1986), p. 159; Chen Han-seng, pp. 68–69.

179. Takekoshi, p. 243. Takekoshi, a stalwart supporter of all efforts to develop capitalism and an apologist for Japanese colonization of Taiwan, is of course particularly critical of all pre-capitalist relations of production.

180. Faure, *The Rural Economy*, p. 159, emphasis mine. In this respect Faure is much closer to the optimism expressed by Ramon Myers and others regarding the role of the market, with the market and its operations understood in the abstract, stripped of their social and historical context.

181. A classic example is the wool industry, see Kriedte, p. 36.

182. In fact in many cases the monopsonies remained intact well into the 1930s and 1940s; for the Palm Fan Guild, see Helen Siu, pp. 64–65.

183. Wykeham Myers, in Davidson, p. 450.

184. See the Appendix for conversion rates of currencies. Unless otherwise stated, all dollar signs used in this book refer to the Mexican silver coin that was used as bullion.

Chapter 7

1. Ch'en Cheng-hsiang, p. 315.

2. Kulp, pp. 88–89.

3. Manuel Moreno Fraginals, "Plantations in the Caribbean: Cuba, Puerto Rico and the Dominican Republic in the Late Nineteenth Century," in Manuel Moreno Fraginals, Frank Moya Pons, and Stanley Engerman, eds., *Between Slavery and Free Labor* (Baltimore: Johns Hopkins University Press, 1985), p.3.

4. Tomich, p. 154. See also Francisco López Segera, "Cuba: Dependence, Plantation Economy and Social Classes, 1762–1902" in Moreno Fraginals et al., eds., pp. 77–93; and Andrés A. Ramos Mattei, "Technical Innovations and Social Change in the Sugar Industry of Puerto Rico, 1870–1880," in Moreno Fraginals et al., eds.

5. Sidney Mintz, *Caribbean Transformation* (Baltimore: John Hopkins University Press, 1984), pp. 82–94, on the role of sugar as a major demographic force.

6. Deerr, vol. 2, p. 537.

7. John Stewart, *A Description of a Machine or Invention . . .* (London, 1767), p. 1.

8. Moreno Fraginals, *The Sugarmill*, p. 101, whom I am following here, attributes this design to Smeaton. Deerr, vol. 2, p. 537, on the other hand suggests that it was developed by John Collinge of Lambeth in 1794. But given that commercial manufacture of the design was already under way in the 1790s, I am inclined to accept Moreno Fraginals's authority on this point.

9. Deerr, vol. 2, p. 537; Moreno Fraginals, *The Sugarmill*, p. 101.

10. This section on the various advantages of the horizontal mill is based on Moreno Fraginals, *The Sugarmill*, pp. 101–102. The accident of slaves' getting their hands caught in the cane crusher was so common that most cane mills kept a cutlass next to the crusher to sever the arm.

11. Stewart, pp. 5–26.

12. See, for example, the situation in Martinique discussed in Tomich, pp. 160–163.

13. Moreno Fraginals, *The Sugarmill*, p. 103.

14. Tomich, p. 160.

15. Carlyle J. Sitterson, *Sugar Country* (Lexington: University of Kentucky Press, 1953), p. 138. In Louisiana already by 1840 there were more steam-driven mills than animal-powered ones. See also Tomich, pp. 204–213.

16. Moreno Fraginals, *The Sugarmill*, pp. 85, 127. An ironic historical footnote: the large mechanized mills of Cuba from the 1860s onwards used almost entirely immigrant Chinese labor.

17. Landes, p. 195.

18. Prinsen Geerligs, *The World's Cane Sugar*, pp. 13–21.

19. Landes's phrase, p. 323, sums up the distinctive feature of the nineteenth-century Industrial Revolution. According to Deerr, vol. 2, p. 584, the Society of West Indian Planters and Merchants was the first to employ an in-house chemist as early as 1796.

20. Deerr, vol. 2, p. 556.

21. Moreno Fraginals, *The Sugarmill*, pp. 111–112; Deerr, vol. 2, p. 560; Sitterson, p. 147.

22. Deerr, vol. 2, p. 564.

23. Eisenberg, p. 40.

24. Pol. 95 refers to the sucrose purity of the crystals as measured by the polarization of light on a saccharimeter and a polariscope.

25. Moreno Fraginals, "Plantations in the Caribbean," p. 8.

26. Much of the following discussion of ships and shipping is based on Daniel R. Headrick, *The Tentacles of Progress* (New York: Oxford University Press, 1988), pp. 18–48. Discussion of the changes in the agricultural economy based on E. J. Hobsbawm, *The Age of Capital, 1848–1875* (New York: New American Library, 1979), particularly chapter 10.

27. Moreno Fraginals, "Plantations in the Caribbean," p. 9.

28. Hobsbawm, *The Age of Capital*, p. 191.

29. Moreno Fraginals, "Plantations in the Caribbean" p. 9; Prinsen Geerligs, *The World's Cane Sugar*, p. 26.

30. Mintz, *Sweetness*, p. 144; Deerr, vol. 2, p. 531; Eisenberg, p. 19.

31. Greenberg, p. 85.

32. Morse, *The International Relations*, vol. 1, pp. 363–366.

33. Ibid., p. 243.

34. Imperial Maritime Customs, *Decennial Reports, 1922–31*, vol. 1, p. 16.

35. British Parliamentary Papers, *Commercial Reports*, vol. 13, pp. 120, 545–548.

36. Imperial Maritime Customs, *Decennial Reports, 1922–31*, vol. 1, p. 17. Very little quantitative information is available on the arms trade to China in the nineteenth century. The increase in the opium trade was spectacular: in 1844 a record 40,000 chests of opium were sold, bringing in U.S.$20 million.

37. See, for example, Wakeman, *Strangers*; Hao, *Commercial Revolution*; Fairbank, *Trade and Diplomacy*; and Chang Hsin-pao.

38. Imperial Maritime Customs, *Decennial Reports, 1922–31*, vol. 1, p. 33.

39. Ibid., pp. 33–34; Benjamin Couch Henry, *Ling-nan or Interior Views* (London: Partridge, 1886), p. 28.

40. Imperial Maritime Customs, *Decennial Reports, 1922–31*, vol. 1, pp. 54–55; G. B. Endacott, *A History of Hong Kong* (Oxford: Oxford University Press, 1958), pp. 194–195; British Parliamentary Papers, *Commercial Reports*, pp. 86, 508; vol. 13, pp. 546, 547.

41. Hobsbawm, *The Age of Capital*, pp. 27–28.

42. Ibid., p. 50.

43. Imperial Maritime Customs, *Decennial Reports, 1922–31*, vol. 1, pp. 66, 97, 105–106.

44. Donald Headrick, *The Tools of Empire* (Oxford: Oxford University Press, 1981), pp. 157–163.

45. Hobsbawn, *The Age of Capital*, p. 61.

46. Imperial Maritime Customs, *Decennial Reports, 1922–31*, vol. 1, pp. 73, 79.

47. Ibid., p. 96.

48. Hao, *The Comprador in Nineteenth Century China* (Cambridge: Harvard University Press, 1970), pp. 20–21, discusses the impact of these changes on the Western trading firms.

49. Kuo Ting-yee, "Internal Development and Modernization of Taiwan, 1683–1891," in Paul Sih, ed., *Taiwan in Modern Times* (New York: St. John's University Press, 1973), p. 230.

50. See, for example, the diverse range of investments of Jardine and Matheson and Company listed in Hao, *The Comprador*, p. 23; Hou Chi-ming, *Foreign Investment and Economic Development in China, 1840–1937* (Cambridge: Harvard University Press, 1965).

51. Deerr, vol. 1, p. 56; G. R. Knight, "From Plantation to Padi Field," *Mod-*

ern Asian Studies 14.2:184–185 (1980). The investments in India have been discussed here in Chapter Two.

52. Sheila Marriner and Francis Hyde, *The Senior John Samuel Swire* (Liverpool: Liverpool University Press, 1967), pp. 98–99. Swire's wife was from the Farrie family, one of the largest sugar refiners in Scotland and England with refineries in Greenock, Liverpool, and London: Deerr, vol. 2, p. 460.

53. Wang Jingyu, "Shijiu shiji waiguo qin Hua qiyezhongde Huashang fugu huodong," *Lishi yanjiu* 4:60 (1965). Surprisingly little information is available on the participants who organized this opposition. The only mention of the factory comes from a brief news item in the *North China Herald*, September 29, 1870, p. 23.

54. Wang Jingyu, p. 60. Such instances of Luddism also occurred elsewhere in the Delta. In 1881 the weavers in Nanhai county burned down the Yuhouchang filature: Eng, *Economic Imperialism*, p. 1. Nor were such activities limited to Guangdong. A soybean oil refinery started in Newchwang (Niuzhuang) met a similar fate in 1873.

55. Imperial Maritime Customs, *Decennial Reports, 1922–31*, vol. 1, pp. 100, 101, 108.

56. Imperial Maritime Customs, *Decennial Report, Shantou*, First Issue, 1882–1891 (Shanghai: Inspectorate General of Customs, 1893), p. 253; Fan I-chun, "Guangdong Han-Mei liuyu de tangye jingji," *Zhongyang yanjiuyuan, Jindaishi yanjiusuo jikan* 12:150 (1983). See also Liu Tsui-jung, *Trade on the Han River and Its Impact on Economic Development, 1800–1911* (Taipei: Academia Sinica, 1980).

57. Henry Lethbridge, *Hong Kong, Stability and Change* (Hong Kong: Oxford University Press, 1978), p. 58; Endacott, p. 195. In 1881, of the eighteen ratepayers listed in Hong Kong who owned property rated at or over $1,000 per quarter, seventeen were Chinese; Jardine and Matheson was the only foreigner.

58. Fairbank, *Trade and Diplomacy*, chapters 16 and 21; Hao, *The Comprador*; Wellington Chan, *Merchants, Mandarins, and Modern Enterprise in Late Ch'ing China* (Cambridge: East Asia Research Center, Harvard University, 1977). The attempts at retaining monopolies are discussed in detail in John Davis Francis, *China, during the War and since the Peace* (London: Longman, Brown, Green and Longmans, 1852), vol. 2, pp. 48–109.

59. Hao, *Commercial Revolution*, p. 235.

60. Wang Jingyu, pp. 39–74. These companies have also been discussed in Hao, *Commercial Revolution*, chapter 9.

61. Wang Jingyu, p. 60; Hao, *Commercial Revolution*, p. 255.

62. Hao, *Commercial Revolution*, p. 240; Hao, *The Comprador*, p. 100.

63. Imperial Maritime Customs, *Decennial Reports, 1922–31*, vol. 1, p. 130; Marriner and Hyde, pp. 102–104.

64. Jardine and Matheson did much better on the Japan market than their rival; by 1895 the China Sugar Refinery controlled 71 percent of the imports into Japan, and Taikoo only 29 percent: Marriner and Hyde, p. 103.

65. Letter reproduced in Drake and Eberhard, eds., pp. 104–105. Competition between the various western companies in Japan is discussed in George C. Allen and A. G. Donnithorne, *Western Enterprise in Far Eastern Economic Development: China and Japan* (London: Allen and Unwin, 1954).

66. Charles. W. Legendre, *Amoy and the Island of Formosa* (Washington, D.C.: U.S. Government Printing Office, 1871), p. 7. Legendre was the U.S. consul at Amoy, and his detailed compilation of trade and other data on Taiwan reflected the continuing competition between British and American interests vis-à-vis Taiwan.

67. Davidson, pp. 445–446.

68. Deerr, vol. 2, pp. 553–554.

69. The reason these sugars were cheaper and the social arrangements that permitted the colonial states in both instances to develop monocrop agriculture cannot be entered into here. But some of the causes are discussed in Robert Van Niel, "The Effect of Export Cultivations in 19th Century Java," *Modern Asian Studies* 15.1:25–58 (1981); Knight, pp. 177–204; and Benito F. Legarda y Fernandez, "Foreign Trade, Economic Change and Entrepreneurship in Nineteenth Century Philippines" (Ph.D. dissertation, Harvard Universtiy, 1955).

70. Yan Zhongpin et al., eds., *Zhongguo jindai jingjishi tongji ziliao xuanji* (Beijing: Kexue chubanshe, 1955), pp. 120, 258.

71. Data for 1838–1842 based on Morse, *The International Relations*, vol. 1, p. 366, Table F; data for 1859 from Imperial Maritime Customs, *Decennial Reports, 1922–31*, vol. 1, p. 91. The figure given is 6,984,920 pounds.

72. These issues have been dealt with in detail in Eng, *Economic Imperialism*, especially chapter 2.

73. Henry, p. 66.

74. *Dongguan xianzhi* (1911) juan 13, p. 348.

75. Imperial Maritime Customs, *Decennial Reports, 1922–31*, vol. 1, p. 68.

76. Lillian Li, p. 72.

77. *Dongguan xianzhi* (1911) juan 13, pp. 354–374.

78. Imperial Maritime Customs, *Decennial Reports, 1922–31*, vol. 1, p. 130.

79. Fan, "Guangdong Han-Mei," pp. 135, 138. The fact that a relatively small portion of the sugar was bought by the British refineries in Hong Kong makes it difficult to argue, as Marks has done, that the demise of the Chinese domestic sugar industry can be traced to the decision of the refineries to purchase cheaper Javanese sugars after 1907: Marks, *Rural Revolution*, p. 100.

80. Negishi Tadashi, p. 317; Fan, "Guangdong Han-Mei," p. 144.

81. Imperial Maritime Customs, *Decennial Reports, 1922–31*, vol. 1, p. 108.

82. Fan, "Guangdong Han-Mei," p. 141.

83. Fielde, *A Corner of Cathay*, pp. 110–111.

84. Philip Kuhn, p. 210.

85. This has been explored in detail in Sasaki Masaya, "Juntoku ken (Shunde xian) kyōshin to Tōkai jurokusa," in Tōyō bunko, Kindai Chūgoku kenkyū iinkai, ed., *Kindai Chūgoku kenkyū*, vol. 3 (Tokyo: Tōkyō daigaku shuppankai, 1959), pp. 161–232.

86. See Helen Siu, particularly chapter 5, and Philip Kuhn for elucidation of these topics. See also Duara, who has discussed the predation of bureaucratic and military functionaries in his book.

87. Lin Datian, "Sanjiang Longquan xiedou de qianyin," *Xinhui wenshi ziliao xuanji* 13:39–40 (1984).

88. John Thomson, *The Chinese* (Indianapolis: Bobbs Merrill, 1909), p. 107; passage also cited in Janice Stockard, *Daughters of the Canton Delta* (Stanford: Stanford University Press, 1989), p. 140.

89. Negishi Tadashi, p. 316, points to these armed mercantile conflicts in Shantou. See Marks, *Rural Revolution*, chapter 3, for a discussion of villages that lay outside the ambit of major lineages, and organized marketing and militia under the Black Flag Society and Red Flag Society, which were coalitions of weaker lineages.

90. The increased use of mercenaries in the nineteenth century has been noted by Ashmore, p. 216. The growth of mercenaries and their organization into "banner societies" has also been examined by Harry Lambley, "Lineage Feuding in Southern Fujian and Eastern Guangdong," in Jonathan N. Lipman and Stevan Harrell, eds., *Violence in China* (Albany: State University of New York Press, 1990), pp. 50–52. The unsettled rural conditions and the problems of travel in the region are graphically described in Henry A. Giles, *From Swatow to Canton Overland* (Shanghai: Kelly and Walsh, 1877) and J. R. Supercargo, *Diary of a Journey Overland through the Maritime Provinces of China (in the Years 1819 and 1820)* (London: Sir Richard Phillips and Co., 1822).

91. Ashmore, p. 214.

92. Ibid., pp. 215, 217.

93. *Shunde xianzhi* (1929), Feng Baoxi et al., eds. (rpt. Taipei: Chengwen chubanshe, 1966), juan 32, pp. 25–28.

94. Niida Noboru, *Chūgoku no nōson kazoku* (Tokyo: Tōkyō daigaku, Tōyō bunka kenkyūjo, 1952), p. 386, discusses the use of cannon and cannon emplacements in lineage villages.

95. Howard and Buswell, p. 62.

96. *Huangchao jingshi*, p. 619.

97. The Deng mobilized to resist British occupation of the New Territories in 1898: Robert Groves, "Militia, Market and Lineage." Various lineages could also join together against a common enemy: Woon, p. 38.

98. For example, Marks, *Rural Revolution*, p. 106, counts thirteen new markets developing in the Haifeng area between 1872 and 1908. Kulp, p. 22, noted during his field study in 1923 that the Phenix village market was of recent origin, set up in competition with the Tan village market.

99. Both Nanhai and Panyu Tongzhi-period editions of gazetteers show 40 additional markets over the total recorded for the Jiaqing and Daoguang editions.

100. *Shunde xianzhi* (1929), juan 3, p. 20.

101. Woon, p. 27.

102. Kulp, pp. 94–95, 120. Several such examples from the Pearl River Delta and Hong Kong have been cited and need not be repeated here.

103. Shih, p. 52. Alvin So, pp. 112–113, has also discussed the various types of silk filatures used in Guangdong and he puts the cost of the equipment at 20,000 taels.

104. Eng, *Economic Imperialism*, p. 48.

105. Ibid., pp. 1–3; Peng, ed., *Zhongguo jindai*, vol. 2, pp. 45–50.

106. Chen Tianjie and Chen Qiutong, "Guangdong diyijian zhengqi saosichang Jichanglong jiqi chuangbanren Chen Qiyuan," *Guangzhou wenshi ziliao* 8:69 (1963).

107. Ibid., p. 61.

108. Chen Qiyuan, *Cansang pu* (Guangzhou: Jihe tang, 1903), preface.

109. Ibid., 5a.

110. *Zhujiang sanjiaozhou*, vol. 4, p. 29.

111. Chen Qiyuan, preface, pp. 4b-5a

112. Lei Yue-wai and Lei Hei-kit, "Report on a Steam Filature in Kwangtung," *Lingnam Agricultural Review* 3.2:123 (1926).

113. Stockard, p. 152.

114. Lei and Lei, p. 123. See also Alvin So, pp. 108–109.

115. Eng, *Economic Imperialism*, pp. 66–67.

116. Alvin So, p. 130.

117. Jamieson et al., p. 95.

118. Chen Da, *Emigrant Communities in South China* (Shanghai: Kelly and Walsh, 1939); Kulp, pp. 47–50.

119. Chen Han-seng, pp. 63; 69;

120. Marks, *Rural Revolution*, p. 102. A similar tendency can be observed in sericulture: Eng, *Economic Imperialism*, p. 144.

121. Fielde, *A Corner of Cathay*, pp. 110, 115.

122. Fan, "Guangdong Han-Mei," p. 144.

123. Wang Yeh-chien, "The Secular Trend," pp. 360, 366. Faure argues that there was an improvement of farm income from rising prices. But I find his data unconvincing, particularly because his "estimated profits" from sugarcane and sugar in Jieyang county, Guangdong, in 1921 leave out the costs of rent, seedlings, and food for workmen in estimating the "profits": Faure, *The Rural Economy*, pp. 148–163, 157.

124. Guoli Guangdong daxue, Nongke xueyuan, pp. 7–8.

125. *Zhujiang sanjiaozhou*, vol. 5, p. 98.

126. *Shunde xianzhi* (1929), juan 20, p. 8.

127. Faure, *The Rural Economy*, p. 207. After having championed trade in his introduction, p. 21, Faure concedes in his conclusion, p. 204, that trade failed to act as a solvent of old relations of production and that non-wage arrangements persisted in work relationships.

128. *Dongguan xian Wanqingsha diaocha baogao*, p. 2.

129. Chen Han-seng, p. 58. James Watson, Helen Siu, and Woon Yuen-fong have all noted similar use of *danmin*.

130. Howard and Buswell, p. 119.

131. Ibid., p. 118.

132. Lillian Li, p. 79.

133. Stockard, pp. 150–151.

134. This theme has been dealt with at length by Stockard, chapter 8. See also Marjorie Topley, "Marriage Resistance in Rural Kwangtung," in Margery Wolf and Roxane Witke, eds., *Women in Chinese Society* (Stanford: Stanford University Press, 1975). Although Topley's work is an important contribution, I agree with Stockard's significant reinterpretation of the institution of delayed transfer marriage as the normative form of marriage in the region, and the caution with which she reads the concept of resistance into this practice.

135. Howard and Buswell, p. 143.

136. Stockard, p. 76.

137. Alvin So, pp. 119–134. While So is very aware of the connections between the women workers and the lineage elites, he nevertheless discusses the women workers under the rubric of proletarianization.

138. Stockard., chapter 4, "Becoming a Sworn Spinster," contains several oral histories of such cases. This is an important correction to the commonly held interpretation that the women became more independent as a result of wage labor.

139. The war between the Guans and the Situ lineages in 1886, for example: Woon, pp. 37–39.

140. See Headrick, *The Tentacles*, pp. 209–258, for a discussion of tropical plantations and imperialism.

141. Beaud, p. 117.

142. Hobsbawm, *The Age of Capital*, p. 48.

143. Hobsbawm, *Industry*, pp. 36–46; see Prinsen Geerligs, *The World's Cane Sugar*, pp. 25–37, for details on the sugar cartels.

144. Deerr, vol. 2, p. 504.

145. Ibid., pp. 507–508.

146. This section is based on B. C. Swerling, *The International Control of Sugar, 1918–1941*, Commodity Policy Studies, no. 7 (Stanford: Stanford University Press, 1949), p. 19.

147. Christian Daniels, "Chūgoku satō no kokusaiteki ichi" *Shakai keizai shigaku* 50.4:21–54 (1984) has looked at this question of the continued production of brown sugar in the 1870–1900 period. Taste may have been a factor in the mainland markets and some niches in Japan, where there was a marked preference for brown sugar. Although there was some difference in the quality of sugar produced in the Taiwan and Kaohsiung districts, by international standards they were both muscovado.

148. Prinsen Geerligs, *The World's Cane Sugar*, p. 89.

149. Negishi Tadashi, p. 53.

150. Samuel Ho, p. 14.

151. Lin Manhong, pp. 7–10.

152. Davidson, p. 446; Imperial Maritime Customs, *Returns of Trade at the Treaty Ports*, Statistical Series, no. 1 (Shanghai: Statistical Department of the Inspectorate General, 1859–1886).

153. Imperial Maritime Customs, *Returns of Trade at the Treaty Ports*, various years. See Table 17 above.

154. Samuel Chu, "Liu Ming-ch'uan and the Modernization of Taiwan," *JAS* 23.1:53 (1963).

155. Taiwan yinhang, ed., *Taiwan jingji shi* 4:97–98 (1956). See also Chan Lien, "Taiwan in China's External Relations, 1683–1874," in Sih, ed.

156. Lian, p. 363; Kuo Ting-yee, p. 234.

157. The *dazu hu*, or those who had undertaken the project of opening the lands in the seventeenth and eighteenth centuries, were no longer responsible for paying the land tax and therefore no longer had to be paid that portion of the rent by the *xiaozu hu*. The latter were declared the technical owners of the land and became responsible for the tax payments: Okamatsu, pp. 51–52.

158. Dai Yanhui, "Qingdai Taiwan zhi da xiao zu ye," *Taipei wenxian* 4:9–12 (1963); Edgar Wickberg, "Late Nineteenth Century Land Tenure in North

Taiwan," in Leonard Gordon, ed., *Taiwan* (New York: Columbia University Press, 1970), p. 82.

159. Okamatsu, p. 88; Wickberg, "Late Nineteenth Century Land," pp. 81–82.

160. Dai, "Qingdai Taiwan zhi da xiao zuye," p. 12.

161. Davidson, p. 395; Takekoshi, p. 239.

162. Peng, ed., *Zhongguo jindai*, vol. 2, p. 109. Gardella, pp. 54–63, has looked at the Taiwan tea industry in some detail.

163. Davidson, p. 377.

164. Rinji Taiwan kyūkan chōsakai, comp., *Taiwan tōgyō*, pp. 80–82.

165. Ibid., p. 78. Ramon Myers, "Taiwan under Ch'ing," p. 391.

166. Zhang Hanyu, "Riju shidai Taiwan jingji zhi yanbian," *Taiwan jingji shi* 2:84 (1955).

167. Rinji Taiwan kyūkan chōsakai, comp. *Taiwan tōgyō*, appendix, pp. 197–198.

168. Ibid., pp. 122–123; a merchant named Sim Chum, for example, lent the German company Lauts and Haeslop almost 8,000 Mexican dollars at 10 percent interest per annum in 1884–1885.

169. The road from Taipei to I-lan was opened in 1885–1887; the major towns on the western coast were linked by telegraph in 1888; and a postal service was also set up in the same decade: see Kuo Ting-yee, pp. 224–233.

170. Rinji Taiwan kyūkan chōsakai, *Taiwan tōgyō*, p. 125.

171. Ibid., p. 71.

172. Mikio Kuwayama, "Sogo-shosha and the Economic Development of Pre-War Japan" (Ph.D. disseratation, University of Toronto, 1982), p. 415; Kerr, *Okinawa*, pp. 406–407.

173. Marriner and Hyde, p. 103.

174. Kuwayama, p. 415.

175. Takekoshi, p. 203.

176. Prinsen Geerligs, *The World's Cane Sugar*, p. 89; Imperial Maritime Customs, *Decennial Reports, 1902–1911*, Third Issue, 2 vols. (Shanghai: Inspectorate General of Customs, 1904).

177. Takekoshi, pp. 129–131; Rinji Taiwan tochi chōsakyoku, ed., *Taiwan tochi chōsa jigyō gaiyō* (Taipei: Rinji Taiwan tochi chōsakyoku, 1905), pp. 16, 37.

178. Ramon Myers, "Taiwan's Agrarian Economy under Japanese Rule," *JCICUHK* 7.2:456–457 (1974); Edgar Wickberg, "Japanese Land Policies in Taiwan," *Agricultural History* 43:371 (1969). Wickberg believes that "the reform had little social significance." Myers argues otherwise, and I concur with Myers's interpretation, which tallies with the impression of contemporary observers such as Takekoshi and Davidson.

179. Takekoshi, p. 132.

180. Wickberg, "Continuities," p. 237.

181. Zhang Hanyu, p. 75.

182. George Barclay, *Colonial Development and Population in Taiwan* (Princeton: Princeton University Press, 1954), p. 7.

183. Ibid., pp. 78–79.

184. Samuel Ho, p. 42. This can be compared with the average farm size of 2.47 acres in the double-cropping rice region of the mainland. There is considerable evidence that a process of land concentration also occurrèd in Taiwan starting in 1900, particularly in the newly reclaimed areas: see Wickberg, "Japanese Land Policies," p. 372; and Yanaihara Tadao, *Teikoku shugika no Taiwan*, Zhou Xianwen, tr. (Taipei: Taiwan yinhang, 1956), pp. 12–13.

185. Samuel Ho, p. 43.

186. Davidson, p. 453.

187. Prinsen Geerlings, *The World's Cane Sugar*, p. 83. The output was 20,000 piculs.

188. Zhang Hanyu, p. 75.

189. Kuwayama, p. 419.

190. Yanaihara, pp. 107–108.

191. Jack F. Williams, "Sugar: The Sweetener in Taiwan's Development," in Knapp, ed., p. 236.

192. Takekoshi, p. 244.

193. George Kerr, *Formosa* (Honolulu: University of Hawaii Press, 1974), p. 91.

194. *Japonica* varieties of rice were tested in Taiwan in the early 1900s, but it was not until the 1920s that the early ripening varieties called *ponlai* replaced the *Indica* varieties, commonly called *chailai* varieties: Randolph Barker, Robert W. Herdt, and Beth Rose, eds., *The Rice Economy of Asia* (Washington, D.C.: Resources for the Future, 1985), pp. 56–60.

195. Prinsen Geerligs, *The World's Cane Sugar*, p. 82. As Kerr notes in *Okinawa*, p. 431, there was considerable competition between the agricultural experts of Sapporo Agricultural College, who were proponents of the expansion of sugar cultivation in Taiwan, and the experts from the Komaba Agricultural Department of Tokyo Imperial University, who supported the development of the industry in Okinawa. Eventually in 1915 the Taiwan Sugar Corporation was to absorb the Okinawa Sugar Company.

196. Prinsen Geerligs, *The World's Cane Sugar*, p. 83.

197. Ibid., p. 86. As in the case of rice, the major improvements in yield-output per acre were to be achieved only with continued experimentation in the 1920s.

198. Samuel Ho, p. 62, n. 48.

199. Zhang Hanyu, p. 78–79.

200. Prinsen Geerligs, *The World's Cane Sugar*, pp. 85–90.

201. In the decade of the 1910s as many as twenty-two Japanese sugar companies were absorbed by the "Big Six." The two factories of Bain and Company were also forced to close down: Kuwayama, p. 418.

202. Rinji Taiwan kyūkan chōsakai, comp., *Taiwan tōgyō*, pp. 153–163.

203. Taiwan yinhang, Jinrong yanjiushi, ed., *Taiwan zhi tang* (Taipei: Taiwan yinhang, 1949), pp. 15–16. Prinsen Geerlings, *The World's Cane Sugar*, p. 85, gives an even lower figure of only two old-style mills surviving by 1908, but this seems to be too rapid a decline to be credible.

204. Kerr, *Formosa*, p. 93.

205. Ibid., p. 101.

206. Prinsen Geerligs, *The World's Cane Sugar*, pp. 70, 115.

207. Geoffrey Masefield, *A Short History of Agriculture in the British Colonies* (New York: Greenwood Press, 1950), p. 51.

208. International Sugar Council, p. 24.

209. Imperial Maritime Customs, *Decennial Reports, 1922–31*, vol. 1, p. 131.

210. Tōa dōbunkai, vol. 1, p. 274.

211. Imperial Maritime Customs, *Decennial Reports, 1902–1911*, vol. 2, p. 583. Faure, who has also cited this passage, *The Rural Economy*, p. 110, reads it as evidence that "the collapse of the export market for sugar was, by then, a foregone conclusion." But the question here is why was China unable to even hold on to the domestic market and had to start *importing* sugar?

212. Marriner and Hyde, pp. 109–112.

213. Peng, ed., *Zhongguo jindai*, vol. 2, p. 287; vol. 3, p. 45.

214. Ibid., vol. 2, pp. 165, 471, 472.

215. Ibid., vol. 2, p. 287; Imperial Maritime Customs, *Decennial Reports, 1922–31*, vol. 2, p. 154.

216. Imperial Maritime Customs, *Decennial Reports, 1902–1911*, p. 520.

217. *Dongguan xianzhi* (1911) juan 15, p. 13.

218. Peng, ed., *Zhongguo jindai*, vol. 2, p. 442; Buck, *Land Utilization*, p. 217.

219. Dwight Perkins, *Agricultural Development*, p. 134, n. 54.

220. Deerr, vol. 1, p. 37. Feng Rui, a proponent of reviving the sugar industry of Guangdong, estimated that the total value of sugar imports to China exceeded 200 million dollars [*yuan*]: *Guangzhou Sanjiaozhou zhi ganzhe zaipei* (Guangzhou: Guangdong sheng zhengfu ju, 1935), pp. 4–5.

221. Tea exported from Guangzhou declined from 118,000 piculs in 1877–1881 to less than 20,000 piculs by 1927–1929: see Faure, *The Rural Economy*, p. 109.

222. Imperial Maritime Customs, *Decennial Reports, 1922–31*, vol. 1, p. 124.

223. Ibid.; see also Gardella, p. 57.

224. Faure, *The Rural Economy*, pp. 122–126, has tabulated rice prices.

Conclusion

1. Although drawing on earlier Sinological traditions, emphasizing the "uniqueness" of "China," the call for "a China-centered history" has been most fully articulated recently by Paul A. Cohen, *Discovering History in China: American Historical Writing on the Recent Chinese Past* (New York: Columbia University Press, 1984).

2. In addition to Guangdong and Taiwan studied here, Li Wenzhi et al., pp. 174–198, has tracked this trend in several provinces. See also Evelyn S. Rawski, *Agricultural Change*, pp. 168–163. Philip Huang also documents this, as well as the obverse impact of the market, in *The Peasant Economy*, pp. 111–137.

3. For example, David Faure, *The Structure*; Ramon Myers also has several articles on this topic including "How Did the Modern Chinese Economy Develop—A Review Essay," *JAS* 50.3: 604–628 (1991), see esp. pp. 614–617; Lloyd Eastman, *Family, Field and Ancestors* (New York: Oxford University Press, 1988); Loren Brandt, *Commercialization and Agricultural Development: Central and Eastern China, 1870–1937* (Cambridge: Cambridge University Press, 1989); Loren Brandt and Barbara Sands, "Beyond Malthus and Ricardo: Economic Growth, Land Concentration and Income Distribution in Early Twentieth Century Rural China," *Journal of Economic History* 50.3:1–30 (1990); and Thomas Rawski, *Economic Growth in Prewar China* (Berkeley: University of California Press, 1989).

4. As McCloskey, p. 146, writes: "But a world in which neoclassical economics is supposed *not* to work at all would be a paradise for the stray wise man. . . . An economy filled with people as irrational as some historians have believed, under the baleful influence of Karl Polanyi and A. V. Chayanov and James C. Scott, would be filled with opportunities to buy low from one set of fools in order to sell high to another."

5. Douglass North, "Markets and Other Allocation Systems in History: The Challenge of Karl Polanyi," *Journal of European Economic History* 6.3:706 (1977).

6. Karl Polanyi, C. M. Arensberg, and H. W. Pearson, *Trade and Market in Early Empires* (Glencoe, Ill.: Free Press, 1957), p. 357.

7. Thomas Rawski, "Economics and the Historian," in Thomas Rawski et al., eds., p. 5.

8. Polanyi et al., p. 364.

9. Ramon Myers and Chen Fumei, "Rural Production and Distribution in Late Imperial China," *Chinese Studies* 3.2:657–658 (1985).

10. Faure, "The Plight of the Farmers," p. 9. Faure cites the work of Robert Groves for evidence of competition. However, as Groves, "The Origins," p. 18, tells the story: in the Tai Po Old Market, one day a Man [rivals of the Deng] wanted to buy a particularly fine fish, but was "struck to the ground" by a member of the Deng lineage who owned the market and declared "the first choice was always the privilege of the Tangs [Dengs]." It is unclear how Faure sees this as "market competition" or what his own definition of competition implies.

11. David Harvey, *The Limits to Capital* (Chicago: University of Chicago Press, 1982), p. 74.

12. Barbara Sands and Ramon Myers, "Economics and Macroregions: A Reply to Our Critics," *JAS* 49.2:346 (1990).

13. Ramon Myers, "How Did the Modern Chinese Economy Develop," p. 616 n. 7. Moreover, endemic violence was not just a feature of South China; see, for example, Elizabeth J. Perry, *Rebels and Revolutionaries in North China* (Stanford: Stanford University Press, 1980).

14. Myers, "How Did the Modern Chinese Economy Develop," p. 614. There has been considerable interest in price history among economic historians of China; in addition to Ch'üan and Kraus's classic study there is Endymion Wilkinson, "Studies in Chinese Price History" (Ph.D. dissertation, Princeton University, 1970); and more recently, Robert Marks, "Rice Prices, Food Supply and Market Structure in Eighteenth Century South China," *Late Imperial China* 12.2:64–116 (1991); Chen Chunsheng, *Shichang jizhi yu shehui bianqian* (Guangzhou: Zhongshan daxue chubanshe, 1992); and Wu Chengming.

15. Witold Kula, *An Economic Theory of the Feudal System* (London: New Left Books, 1976), p. 109.

16. Robert C. Allen, p. 291.

17. Kula, pp. 93–99.

18. Faure, "The Plight of the Farmers," p. 9, notes this and cites his earlier work to substantiate the point. And, as my research also shows, indeed this was the case. Faure is, however, seemingly unaware of the contradiction of premising his argument for unfettered market transactions on the basis of the grain market sustained by landlords selling grain collected as rent. Marks, "Rice Prices, Food Supply," also ignores the dynamics of how and why China's market in grain so closely paralleled world-market prices. Loren Brandt, "Chinese Agriculture," pp. 168–193, also extrapolates resource allocation, productivity, and income from the data on market integration without considering social and political constraints which may have led to the uniformity in price in the first place.

19. Kula, pp. 92–93.

20. Elvin, *Pattern*, p. 284.

21. Joseph Needham, *The Grand Titration* (London: Allen and Unwin, 1969),

pp. 147–150. Elvin, writing almost thirty years after Needham first posed the question, apparently did not want to associate the genesis of his own project with that of Needham's and refers to Needham only in passing in his own work. See Nathan Sivin, "Does China's Past Have a Future?" *HJAS* 38.2:449–480 (1978), for a discussion of this in his review of Elvin's work.

22. A. C. Graham, "China, Europe and the Origins of Modern Science: Joseph Needham's *The Grand Titration*," in Shigeru Nakayama and Nathan Sivin, eds., *Chinese Science: Explorations of an Ancient Tradition* (Cambridge: M.I.T. Press, 1973), p. 45.

23. Needham, *The Grand Titration*, p. 150.

24. Elvin, *Pattern*, pp. 203–204, 303. The assumed unavailability of investable resources proposed by Elvin has been questioned by so many scholars that their comments scarcely need iterating here. See in particular Carl Riskin, "Surplus and Stagnation in Modern China," in Dwight Perkins, ed., *China's Modern Economy in Historical Perspective*, pp. 62–64; and Victor D. Lippit, "The Development of Underdevelopment in China," *Modern China* 4.3:86–93 (1978). These arguments have also been summarized by Philip Huang in *The Peasant Economy*, pp. 19–20.

25. Needham, *The Grand Titration*, p. 153.

26. Marx, *Capital*, vol. 1, p. 372.

27. Needham, *Science and Civilisation in China*, vol. 1 in Joseph Needham, gen. ed., *Science and Civilisation in China* (Cambridge: University of Cambridge Press, 1954), p. 10.

28. Needham makes a clear distinction between the earlier writings of Wittfogel and later works such as *Oriental Despotism* and points out that the earlier writings did have rather interesting notions: Needham, *The Grand Titration*, pp. 192–194, 203–204.

29. It is not relevant here to enter into a discussion of the other problems that have been identified with Needham's work, such as particular attachments to Whiteheadian metaphysics: see Shigeru Nakayama, "Joseph Needham, Organic Philosopher" in Nakayama and Sivin, eds., pp. 23–43. See also Sal P. Restivo, "Joseph Needham and the Comparative Sociology of Chinese and Modern Science," *Research in Sociology of Knowledge, Sciences and Art* 2:25–51 (1979).

30. For example, one of the standard textbooks produced by the Chinese Academy of Sciences, Institute of the History of Natural Sciences, comp., *Ancient China's Technology and Science* (Beijing: Foreign Languages Press, 1983), p. 1, starts out with a preface positing an unbroken illustrious history of 4,000 years, cites Needham's claim that China was "far in advance of contemporary Europe up to the 15th century," and concludes with "China now can and will reach or even surpass certain advanced world levels in the not too distant future."

31. Elvin, *Pattern*, p. 199.

32. Landes, p. 105. See also Jeffrey G. Williamson, pp. 687–712. For a discussion by Marx of this technological continuity with previous modes of production, see Jairus Banaji, "Capitalist Domination and the Small Peasantry," *Studies in the Development of Capitalism* (Lahore: Vanguard Publishers, 1978), pp. 354–355.

33. See Harvey, pp. 98–136, for a particularly accessible discussion of the role of technology under capitalism.

34. Samuel Lilley, "Technological Progress and the Industrial Revolution, 1700–1914" in Cippola, ed. *The Industrial Revolution*, pp. 191–193. Both Lilley's essay and Landes's *Unbound Prometheus* provide numerous examples of earlier technologies applied in novel ways during the early part of the Industrial Revolution.

35. Lilley, p. 145.

36. Tribe, pp. 10–11.

37. Graham, p. 45.

38. Indian Ocean Studies, at the forefront of efforts to delineate a history of "Asia" by stepping beyond the intellectual divides imposed through area studies, is best exemplified by Kirti Narayan Chaudhuri, *Asia before Europe* (Cambridge: Cambridge University Press, 1990). However, by ignoring Asia after the arrival of the British, the epistemological fragmentation of Asia remains implicitly unaddressed.

39. In addition to Elvin, *Pattern*, pp. 311–313, see also major proponents of this view: Chao, *Man and Land*; and John Fei and Liu Tsui-jung, "Population Dynamics of Agrarianism in Traditional China," in Hou Chi-ming and Yu Tzong-shian, eds.; and Paul K. C. Liu and Hwang Kuo-shu, "Population Change and Economic Development in Mainland China since 1400," in Hou Chi-ming and Yu Tzong-shian, eds.

40. Ji Zhuge, "The Sino-American Symposium on Chinese Socioeconomic History from the Song Dynasty to 1900," in Feuerwerker, ed., *Chinese Social and Economic History from Song to 1900*, p. 149.

41. For a very insightful critique of the Marxist counterpositioning of the socioeconomic to the demographic, see Wally Seccombe, "Marxism and Demography," *New Left Review* 137:22–47 (1983).

42. Ho Ping-ti, *Studies on the Population*, p. 270.

43. Andre Armengaud, "Population in Europe, 1700–1944," in Cipolla, ed., *The Industrial Revolution*, pp. 28–30.

44. See Brenner, "The Agrarian Roots," for an extended critique of the "demographic model" and interpretations which give primacy to demographic change alone as causal factors in historical evolution.

45. As Harvey describes the process, "None of the various forms of capital, rent on land, merchants' capital and money capital were *subservient* to a circulation process dominated by the production of surplus value by wage labor: Harvey, p. 73.

46. Dwight Perkins, *Agricultural Development.*

47. Benjamin White, "Agricultural Involution and Its Critics: Twenty Years After," *Bulletin of Concerned Asian Scholars* 15.2:18 (1983).

48. Ronald Walters, "Signs of the Times: Clifford Geertz and Historians," *Social Research* 47.3:537–556 (1980), has tabulated the increased frequency of references to Geertz in various periodical indexes as well as in conference presentations and has attempted to analyze the root causes of this interest in Geertz's recent writings. For historians and anthropologists of China using the term "involution," in addition to Bray; and Philip Huang, *The Peasant Family*, as well as *The Peasant Economy*; see Duara; and Eugene Anderson, *The Food.*

49. Bray, p. 608.

50. Imahori Seiji's classic study "Chūgoku no okeru kaikyū kubunron no seisei," *Shakai keizai shigaku* 29.6:1–25, (1964) and 30.1:39–51 (1964), has a very full commentary on how the concept of community itself was used to maintain class hegemony.

51. Bray, p. 613.

52. For Japan, see the standard classic, Thomas C. Smith, *The Agrarian Origins of Modern Japan* (Stanford: Stanford University Press, 1959). Richard Lachmann has condensed much of the existing literature on these changes in England in *From Manor to Market.*

53. Paul Bairoch, "Agriculture and the Industrial Revolution, 1700–1914," in Cipolla, ed., *The Industrial Revolution*, p. 460. For techniques adopted by the enclosed field farmers, see also Robert C. Allen, esp. chapters 6 and 7.

54. Bairoch, pp. 463–466.

55. Robert C. Allen has laid out the details of both the yeomen's revolution of the seventeenth and early eighteenth century and the more famous landlords' revolution that followed.

56. Philip Huang, *The Peasant Family*, pp. 12–13.

57. Alexander V. Chayanov, *The Theory of the Peasant Economy*, D. Thorner, B. Kerblay, and R. E. F. Smith, trs. and eds. (Homewood, Ill.: Richard D. Irwin, 1966), pp. 113ff. For a powerful critique of the Chayanovian model, see Utsa Patnaik, "Neo-Populism and Marxism: The Chayanovian View of the Agrarian Question and Its Fundamental Fallacy," *Journal of Peasant Studies* 6.4: 375–420 (1979).

58. Geertz, pp. 97–102; for a critique, see Benjamin White, pp. 26–29.

59. Philip Huang, *The Peasant Family*, pp. 11–12.

60. David Levine, *Reproducing Families* (Cambridge: Cambridge University Press, 1987); David Levine, "Proto-Industrialization and Demographic Upheaval," in L. P. Moch and G. D. Stark, eds., *Essays on the Family and Historical Change* (College Station: University of Texas at Arlington Press, 1983), pp. 9–34.

61. Robert C. Allen, pp. 235–237.

62. Ho Ping-ti, *Studies on the Population*, p. 246; R. Bin Wong, "The Development of China's Peasant Economy: A New Formulation of Old Problems," *Journal of Peasant Studies* 18.1:18 (1990), has discussed further examples of depopulation in the Yangzi Delta region.

63. For example, both Philip Huang in *The Peasant Family* and Dwight Perkins, *Agricultural Development*, suggest a seamless continuity between 1368 and the twentieth century.

64. The evocative phrase is from Beaud, p. 17.

65. Ota, p. 462; see also Chapter Three.

Appendix

1. Ch'üan and Kraus, pp. 79–98.

2. Dwight Perkins, *Agricultural Development*, p. 298.

3. Based on Wu Chengluo, *Zhongguo du liang heng shi* (Shanghai: Shangwu yinshuguan, 1934).

4. Morse, *The Trade and Administration of China*, p. 174.

5. Ch'üan and Kraus, pp. 81, 93.

6. Yule and Burnel, eds. and trans., *Hobson-Jobson*, s.v.

7. Boxer, *The Great Ship*, p. 22.

8. Chang Hsin-pao, p. 39.

9. Ibid.

10. Morse, *The Trade and Administration of China*, p. 157.

11. Ibid., pp. 117–170.

12. Davidson, p. 618.

13. Furber, *John Company at Work*.

WORKS CITED

Note: If a Chinese author has never published in English, then I have romanized the name according to the *pinyin* system. However, if an author has published in English and has chosen to romanize his or her name in either Wade-Giles or some system other than *pinyin*, I have followed the author's preference. In the text, and in the list of references, standard international postal spellings are used for place-names.

Abbreviations

AHR	*American Historical Review*
JAS	*Journal of Asian Studies*
JHKBRAS	*Journal of the Hong Kong Branch of the Royal Asiatic Society*
JCICUHK	*Journal of the Chinese Institute of the Chinese University of Hong Kong*
HJAS	*Harvard Journal of Asiatic Studies*
TP	*T'oung Pao*

Acharya, Nagendra Nath. "Trade Routes and Means of Transport in Ancient India with Special Reference to Assam," in Dineschandra Sircar, ed., *Early Indian Trade and Industry* (q.v.).

Adachi Kenji 足立啓二. "Daizu kasu ryūtsū to Shindai no shōgyōteki nōgyō" 大豆粕流通と清代の商業的農業. *Tōyōshi kenkyū* 37.3:35–63 (1978).

———. "Minmatsu Shinsho no ichi nōgyō keiei" 明末清初の一農業経営. *Shirin* 61.1:40–69 (1978).

Ahern, Emily Martin. "The Thai Ti Kong Festival," in Emily Martin Ahern and Hill Gates, eds., *The Anthropology of Taiwanese Society* (q.v.).

———. *The Cult of the Dead in a Chinese Village*. Stanford: Stanford University Press, 1973.

Ahern, Emily Martin, and Hill Gates, eds. *The Anthropology of Taiwanese Society*. Stanford: Stanford University Press, 1981.

Aizawa Takushi 会沢卓司 "Sōdai kansho tōgyō no kōsatsu" 宋代甘蔗糖業の考察. *Bunka* 34.4:364–382 (1971).

Alam, Ishrat. "Textile Tools as Depicted in Ajanta and Mughal Paintings," in Anniruddha Roy and S. K. Bagchi, eds., *Technology in Ancient and Medieval India* (q.v.).

al Baghdadi. *Kitab al-Tabikh*. Arthur J. Arberry, tr., "A Baghdad Cookery Book." *Islamic Culture* 13.1–2:21–47, 189–214 (1939).

al-Hassan, Ahmad Y., and Donald R. Hill. *Islamic Technology*. Cambridge: Cambridge University Press, 1986.

Allen, George C., and A. G. Donnithorne. *Western Enterprise in Far Eastern Economic Development: China and Japan*. London: Allen and Unwin, 1954.

Allen, Robert C. *Enclosure and the Yeoman*. Oxford: Clarendon Press, 1992.

Amano Motonosuke 天野元之助. *Chūgoku ko nōshō kō* 中国古農書考. Tokyo: Ryukei, 1975.

———. *Chūgoku nōgyōshi kenkyū* 中国農業史研究. Tokyo: Nōgyō sogo kenkyūjo, 1962.

Amin, Shahid. *Sugar and Sugarcane in Gorakpur: An Inquiry into Peasant Production for Capitalist Enterprise in Colonial India*. Delhi: Oxford University Press, 1984.

Anderson, Eugene. *The Food of China*. New Haven: Yale University Press, 1988.

———. *Essays on South China's Boat People*. Taipei: Oriental Cultural Service, 1972.

Anderson, Eugene, and Marja Anderson. "Modern China: South," in K. C. Chang, ed., *Food in Chinese Culture* (q.v.).

———. *Mountains and Water: The Cultural Ecology of South Coastal China*. Taipei: Oriental Cultural Service, 1973.

Anderson, Perry. *Lineages of the Absolutist State*. London: Verso, 1974.

Antonil, André João. *Cultura e opulencia do Brasil por suas drogas e minas*. André Mansuy, ed. Paris: Institute des Hautes Etudes de l'Amérique Latine, 1968. First published in 1711.

Arasaratnam, Sinnappah. "India and the Indian Ocean in the Seventeenth Century," in Ashin K. Das Gupta and Michael N. Pearson, eds., *India and the Indian Ocean, 1500–1800* (q.v.).

Armengaud, Andre. "Population in Europe, 1700–1944," in Carlo M. Cipolla, ed., *The Fontana Economic History of Europe, The Industrial Revolution* (q.v.).

Arthashāstra. Attibuted to Kautilya. Rudrapatna Shamasastry, tr. Rpt. Mysore: Mysore Print and Publication House, 1961. Comp. ca. 350 B.C.

Ashmore, William. "A Clan Feud near Swatou." *Chinese Recorder* 28.5: 214–223 (1897).

Ashtor, Eliyahu. "Levantine Sugar Industry in the Late Middle Ages," in G. L.

Udovitch, ed., *The Islamic Middle East, 700–1900.* Princeton: Princeton University Press, 1981.

———. *A Social and Economic History of the Near East in the Middle Ages.* Berkeley: University of California Press, 1976.

Asvaghosa. *Saundarānanda.* E. H. Johnstone, ed. and tr. Rpt. Delhi: Motilal Banarasidass, 1975.

Atwell, William S. "International Bullion Flows and the Chinese Economy circa 1530–1650." *Past and Present* 95:68–90 (1982).

———. "Notes on Silver, Foreign Trade and the Late Ming Economy." *Ch'ing-shih wen t'i* 3.8:1–33 (1977).

Aykroyd, William. *Sweet Malefactor.* London: Heinemann, 1967.

Bagchi, Prabodh C. *India and China: A Thousand Years of Cultural Relations.* Bombay: Hind Kitabs, 1950.

———. "Political Relations between Bengal and China." *Vishva Bharati Annals* 1:96–134 (1945).

———. *Deux Lexiques Sanskrit-Chinois.* 2 vols. Paris: Librarie Orientalist Paul Geuthner, 1929.

Bairoch, Paul. "Agriculture and the Industrial Revolution, 1700–1914," in Carlo Cipolla, ed., *The Fontana Economic History of Europe: The Industrial Revolution* (q.v.).

Baker, Hugh. "Extended Kinship in the Traditional City," in G. William Skinner, ed., *The City in Late Imperial China* (q.v.).

———. *A Chinese Lineage Village, Sheung Shui.* London: Frank Cass and Co., 1968.

———. "The Five Great Clans of the New Territories." *JHKBRAS* 6:25–48 (1966).

Banaji, Jairus. "Capitalist Domination and the Small Peasantry." *Studies in the Development of Capitalism.* Lahore: Vanguard Publishers, 1978.

———. "Modes of Production in a Materialist Conception of History." *Capital and Class* 3:1–44 (1977).

———. "Chayanov, Kautsky, Lenin: Considerations towards a Synthesis." *Economic and Political Weekly* 11:1594–1607 (1976).

Banno, Masataka. *China and the West, 1858–1861.* Cambridge: Harvard University Press, 1964.

Barber, William. *A History of Economic Thought.* Harmondsworth, Eng.: Penguin Books, 1967.

Barclay, George. *Colonial Development and Population in Taiwan.* Princeton: Princeton University Press, 1954.

Barker, Randolph, Robert W. Herdt, and Beth Rose. *The Rice Economy of Asia.* Washington, D.C.: Resources for the Future, 1985.

Barrow, John. *Travels in China*. London: T. Cadell and W. Davies in the Strand, 1806.

Basalla, George. *The Evolution of Technology*. Cambridge: Cambridge University Press, 1988.

Basu, Dilip. "The Peripherialization of China," in Walter Goldfrank, ed., *The World-System of Capitalism: Past and Present*. Beverly Hills, Calif.: Sage Press, 1979.

Beal, Samuel, ed. and tr. *Si-yu-ki: Buddhist Records of the Western World Translated from the Chinese of Hiuen Tsang (A.D. 629)*. London: Trübner & Co., 1884.

Beattie, Hilary. *Land and Lineage in China*. Cambridge: Cambridge University Press, 1979.

Beaud, Michel. *A History of Capitalism, 1500–1980*. Tom Dickman and Anny Lefebvre, trs. New York: Monthly Review Press, 1983.

Bencao gangmu 本草綱目. Li Shizhen 李時珍. Rpt. Beijing: Hongbaoji lithograph, 1885. First published in 1596.

Bencao qiuzhen 本草求眞. Huang Gongxiu 黃宮繡. Rpt. Shanghai: Kexue jixu chubanshe, 1959. First published in 1773.

Benjamin Shreve Letters. Canton Brig, 1816–1817. Manuscript Collection, Peabody Museum, Salem, Mass.

Bernhardt, Kathryn, and Philip C. C. Huang, eds. *Civil Law in Qing and Republican China*. Stanford: Stanford University Press, 1994.

Bernier, François. *Travels in the Mughal Empire, 1656–1668*. A. Constable, ed. Rpt. New Delhi: S. Chand, 1891.

Berridge, Virginia, and Griffith Edwards. *Opium and the People*. New Haven: Yale University Press, 1987.

Berthe, Jean-Pierre. "Sur l'histoire sucrière Américaine." *Annales, Economies, Sociétés, Civilisation* 14.1: 135–141 (1959).

Berthier, Paul. *Un épisode de l'histoire de la canne à sucre: Les anciennes suceries du Maroc et leurs réseaux hydrauliques*. Rabat: Imprimeries Françaises et Marocaines, 1966.

Bhaisajyavastu. Nalinaksha Dutta, ed. *Gilgit Manuscripts*. vol. 3. Srinagar: n.p., 1941.

Bhattacharya, Surendramohan. *Purohit Darpan*. Rpt. Calcutta: n.p., 1976. First published 1906.

Blair, Emma, and James Robertson, eds. and trs. *The Philippine Islands, 1493–1898: Explorations by Early Navigators, Descriptions of the Islands and Their Peoples, Their History and Records of the Catholic Missions, as Related in Contemporaneous Books and Manuscripts*, vol. 6 (1583–1588) and vol. 7 (1588–1591). Cleveland: Arthur H. Clark Company, 1953.

Blussé, Leonard. *Strange Company, Chinese Settlers, Mestizo Women and the Dutch in VOC Batavia*. Dordrecht: Foris Publications, 1986.

Blussé, Leonard, and Femme Gaastra, eds. *Companies and Trade*. Leiden: Leiden University Press, 1981.

Bose, D. M., et al., eds. *A Concise History of Science in India*. New Delhi: Indian National Science Academy, 1971.

Boserup, Ester. *Population and Technological Change*. Chicago: University of Chicago Press, 1973.

———. *The Conditions of Agricultural Growth*. Chicago: University of Chicago Press, 1965.

Boxer, Charles R. *Papers on Portuguese, Dutch and Jesuit Influences in 16th and 17th Century Japan*. In Michael Moscato, comp., *Writings of C. R. Boxer*. Washington, D.C.: University Publications of America, 1979.

———. *Fidalgos in the Far East, 1550–1770*. Rpt. Hong Kong: Oxford University Press, 1968.

———. *The Great Ship from Amacon: Annals of Macao and the Old Japan Trade, 1555–1640*. Lisbon: Centro de Estudos Históricos Ultramarinos, 1959.

———. *The Dutch in Brazil, 1624–1654*. Oxford: Oxford University Press, 1957.

———. *South China in the Sixteenth Century*. Hakluyt Society Publication, 2nd ser., vol. 106. London, 1953.

———. *Jan Compagnie in Japan, 1600–1850*. The Hague: Nijhoff, 1950.

———. "Notes on Chinese Abroad in the Late Ming and Early Manchu Periods from Contemporary European Sources (1500–1750)." *Tien Hsia Monthly* 9.5:447–468 (1939).

Brandt, Loren. *Commercialization and Agricultural Development: Central and Eastern China, 1870–1937*. Cambridge: Cambridge University Press, 1989.

———. "Chinese Agriculture and the International Economy, 1870–1930s: A Reassessment." *Explorations in Economic History* 22:168–193 (1985).

Brandt, Loren, and Barbara Sands. "Beyond Malthus and Ricardo: Economic Growth, Land Concentration and Income Distribution in Early Twentieth Century Rural China." *Journal of Economic History* 50.3:1–30 (1990).

Braudel, Fernand. *Perspective of the World*. Sian Reynolds, tr. New York: Harper and Row, 1984.

———. *The Structures of Everyday Life*. Sian Reynolds, tr. New York: Harper and Row, 1982.

———. *The Wheels of Commerce*. Sian Reynolds, tr. New York: Harper and Row, 1982.

Bray, Francesca. *Agriculture*. Vol. 6, part 2, of Joseph Needham, gen. ed., *Science and Civilisation in China* (q.v.).

Brenner, Robert. *Merchants and Revolution: Commercial Change, Political Conflict and London's Overseas Traders, 1550–1653*. Princeton: Princeton University Press, 1993.

———. "The Social Basis of Economic Development," in John Roemer, ed., *Analytical Marxism*. Cambridge: Cambridge University Press, 1986.

———. "The Agrarian Roots of European Capitalism," in symposium on "Agrarian Class Structure and Economic Development in Pre-Industrial Europe." *Past and Present* 97:16–113 (1982).

———. "Agrarian Class Structure and Economic Development in Pre-industrial Europe." *Past and Present* 70:30–75 (1976).

British Parliamentary Papers. *Commercial Reports Session, 1867–69*. Area Studies Series, China, vols. 8 and 13. Shannon: Irish University Press, 1972.

———. *Select Committee Report of the House of Commons on the Affairs of the East India Company and Trade with China, 1821–31*. Area Studies Series, China, vol. 36. Shannon: Irish University Press, 1972.

———. *Report from the Select Committee on the Affairs of the East India Company and Trade between Great Britain, the East Indies and China, 1830*. Area Studies Series, China, vol. 37. Shannon: Irish University Press, 1972.

———. *General Correspondence, Dispatches and Reports Relating to the Rules, Regulations, and Other Aspects of the Trade between Great Britain and China, 1831–99*. Area Studies Series, China, vol. 39. Shannon: Irish University Press, 1972.

Buck, John Lossing. *Land Utilization in China*. Shanghai: Commercial Press, 1937.

———. *China's Farm Economy*. Chicago: University of Chicago Press, 1930.

Bunong shu 補農書. Zhang Luxiang 張履祥, comp. Repr. as *Shen shi nong shu* 沈氏農書. Rpt. Beijing: Zhonghua shuju, 1956. First published in 1658. Preface dated 1620.

Buoye, Thomas. "From Patrimony to Commodity: Changing Concepts of Land and Social Conflict in Guangdong Province during the Qianlong Reign (1736–1795)." *Late Imperial China* 14.2:33–59 (1993).

———. "Violent Disputes over Property Rights in Guangdong during the Qianlong Reign." Ph.D. dissertation, University of Michigan, 1991.

Burnett, John. *A History of the Cost of Living*. Harmondsworth, Eng.: Penguin Books, 1969.

———. *Plenty and Want: A Social History of Diet in England from 1815 to the Present*. London: Thomas Nelson and Sons, 1966.

Butsurui hinshitsu 物類品隲. Hiaraga Gennai 平賀源内. Rpt. Tokyo: Nihon kōten zenshō, 1928. First published in 1763.

Buxbaum, David, ed. *Chinese Family Law and Social Change*. Seattle: University of Washington Press, 1978.

Campbell, William, ed. *Formosa under the Dutch, Described from Contemporary Records*. Rpt. Taipei: Chengwen, 1967. First published in 1903.

Candidus, George. "Account of the Inhabitants," rpt. in William Campbell, ed., *Formosa under the Dutch, Described from Contemporary Records* (q.v.). First published in 1744.

Canton, China Collection, Foreign Marketing, "Houqua Letters." MSS: 766, 1841–1843, Baker Library, Harvard University.

Cantor, S., and M. Cantor. "Socioeconomic Factors in Fat and Sugar Consumption," in M. Kare and O. Maller, eds., *The Chemical Senses and Nutrition*. New York: Academic Press, 1977.

Cao Xueqin. *The Story of the Stone*. David Hawkes, tr. Harmondsworth, Eng.: Penguin Books, 1977.

Cardwell, D. S. L. "Power Technologies and the Advance of Science, 1700–1825." *Technology and Culture* 6.2:188–207 (1965).

Casola, Canon Pietro. *Canon Pietro Casola's Pilgrimage to Jerusalem in 1494*. M. Margaret Newett, tr. Manchester: University Press, 1907.

Cefu yuangui 冊府元龜. Wang Qinruo 王欽若 et al., eds. Rpt. Beijing: Zhonghua shuju, 1960. Completed in 1013.

Chakravarti, A. K. "Some Aspects of India-China Maritime Trade (A.D. 250–1200)," in *India History Congress Proceedings, 1961*. Calcutta: University of Calcutta, 1963.

———. "Early Sino-Indian Maritime Trade and Funan," in D. C. Sircar, ed., *Early Indian Trade and Industry* (q.v.).

Chan, Lien. "Taiwan in China's External Relations, 1683–1874," in Paul K. T. Sih, ed., *Taiwan in Modern Times* (q.v.).

Chan, Wellington. *Merchants, Mandarins, and Modern Enterprise in Late Ch'ing China*. Cambridge: East Asian Research Center, Harvard University, 1977.

Chang Chun-shu. "Emperorship in Eighteenth Century China." *JCICUHK* 7.2:551–570 (1974).

Chang Chung-li. *The Income of the Chinese Gentry*. Seattle: University of Washington Press, 1962.

———. *The Chinese Gentry*. Seattle: University of Washington Press, 1955.

Chang Han-yu and Ramon Myers. "Japanese Colonial Development Policy in Taiwan, 1895–1906." *JAS* 22.4:433–449 (1963).

Chang, Hsin-pao. *Commissioner Lin and the Opium War*. Cambridge: Harvard University Press, 1964.

Chang, K. C. (Kwang-chih), ed. *Food in Chinese History*. New Haven: Yale University Press, 1977.

Chang Peng. "Distribution and Relative Strength of Merchant Groups in China, 1842–1911." Ph.D. dissertation, University of Washington, 1958.

Chang Pin-tsun. "The First Chinese Diaspora in Southeast Asia," in Roderich Ptak and Dietmar Rothermund, eds., *Emporia, Commodities and Entrepreneurs in Asian Maritime Trade, C1400–1750* (q.v.).

———. "Chinese Maritime Trade: The Case of Sixteenth Century Fu-chien (Fukien)." Ph.D. dissertation, Princeton University, 1983.

Chang Teh-ch'ang. "Maritime Trade at Canton during the Ming Dynasty." *Chinese Social and Political Science Review* 17.2:264–282 (1933).

Chang T'ien-tse. *Sino-Portuguese Trade from 1514 to 1644. A Synthesis of Portuguese and Chinese Sources*. Leiden: E. J. Brill, 1934.

Changhua xianzhi 彰化縣志. Zhou Xi 周璽, ed. Rpt. in *Taiwan wenxian congkan* (q.v.). Comp. in 1830.

Chao, Kang. *Man and Land in Chinese History: An Economic Analysis*. Stanford: Stanford University Press, 1986.

———. "New Data on Land Ownership Patterns in Ming-Ch'ing China—A Research Note." *JAS* 40.4:719–734 (1981).

———. *The Development of Cotton Textile Production in China*. Cambridge: Council on East Asian Studies, Harvard University, 1977.

Chaudhuri, Kirti Narayan. *Asia before Europe: Economy and Civilization of the Indian Ocean from the Rise of Islam to 1750*. Cambridge: Cambridge University Press, 1990.

———. *Trade and Civilization in the Indian Ocean*. Cambridge: Cambridge University Press, 1985.

———. *The Trading World of Asia and the English East India Company, 1660–1760*. Cambridge: Cambridge University Press, 1978.

———. *The English East India Company: The Study of an Early Joint-Stock Company, 1600–1640*. London: Frank Cass, 1965.

Chaunu, Pierre. *Les Philippines et le Pacifique des Iberiques (XVIe, XVIIe, XVIIIe siècles)*. Paris: Service d' Editions de Vente des Publication Educations National, 1960.

Chayanov, Alexander V. *The Theory of the Peasant Economy*. D. Thorner, B. Kerblay and R. E. F. Smith, trs. and eds. Homewood, Ill.: Richard D. Irwin, 1966.

Ch'en Cheng-hsiang. *Taiwan: An Economic and Social Geography*. Taipei: Fu-min Geographical Institute of Economic Development, 1963.

Ch'en Ch'iu-k'un 陳秋坤. *Qingdai Taiwan tuzhu diquan* 清代台灣土著地權. Taipei: Zhongyang yanjiu yuan, 1994.

Chen, Chung-min. *Upper Camp: A Study of a Chinese Mixed Cropping Village in Taiwan*. Nangang: Institute of Ethnology, Academia Sinica, 1977.

Chen Chunsheng 陈春声. *Shichang jizhi yu shehui bianqian* 市场机制与社会变迁. Guangzhou: Zhongshan daxue chubanshe, 1992.

———. "Qingdai Qianlong nianjian Guangdong de mijia he miliang maoyi" 清代乾隆年间广东的米价和米粮贸易. M.A. thesis, Zhongshan University, 1984.

Chen Da. *Emigrant Communities in South China*. Shanghai: Kelly and Walsh, 1939.

Ch'en, Fu-mei, and Ramon H. Myers. "Customary Law and the Economic Growth of China during the Ch'ing Period." *Ch'ing-shih Wen-*ti 3.5:1–32 (1976), 3.10:4–27 (1978).

Chen Han-seng. *Agrarian Problems in Southernmost China*. Guangzhou: Lingnan University, 1936.

Chen Hengli 陳恒力 and Wang Dacan 王達參. *Bunongshu yanjiu* 補農書研究. Beijing: Zhonghua shuju, 1958.

Ch'en, Jerome, and Nicholas Tarling, eds. *Studies in the Social History of China and South-east Asia*. Cambridge: Cambridge University Press, 1970.

Chen Kenneth. *Buddhism in China*. Princeton: Princeton University Press, 1964.

Chen Qian 陳茜. "Chuan, Dian, Mian, Yin, gudao chukao" 川滇緬印古道初考. *Zhongguo shehui kexue* 1:161–180 (1981).

Chen Qiyuan 陳啓沅. *Cansang pu* 蠶桑譜. Guangzhou: Jihe tang, 1903.

Chen, Shao-hsing. "The Migration of Chinese from Fukien to the Philippines under the Spanish Colonization and to Taiwan under the Dutch: An Analysis of Their Pattern of Development and Correspondences." *International Association of Historians of Asia, Second Biennial Conference Proceedings*. Taipei, 1962.

Chen Shaoxing 陳紹馨. *Renkou bian* 人口篇, in *Taiwan sheng tongzhi gao: "Renmin zhi"* 台灣省通志稿人民志, vol. 2, part 1. Taipei: Taiwan sheng wenxian weiyuanhui, 1950–1952.

Chen Tianjie 陈天杰 and Chen Qiutong 陈秋桐. "Guangdong diyijian zhengqi saosichang Jichanglong jiqi chuangbanren Chen Qiyuan" 广东第一间蒸汽缫丝厂继昌隆及其创办人陈启沅. *Guangzhou wenshi ziliao* 8:58–71 (1963).

Chen Xuewen 陳學文. "Zhongguo gudai zhetang gongye de fazhan" 中國古代蔗糖工業的發展. *Shixue yuekan* 25–28 (1965).

Chen Zhen 陈真 and Yao Luo 姚洛. *Zhongguo jindai shougongye shi ziliao* 中国近代手工业史资料. 6 vols. Beijing: Sanlian shudian, 1957–61.

Chen Zhengxiang 陳正祥. *Guangdong dizhi* 廣東地誌. Hong Kong: Tiandi tushu, 1978.

———. *Guangdong de tangye* 廣東的糖業. Hong Kong: Xianggang Zhongwen Daxue Yanjiu Yuan, 1970.

Chenghai xianzhi 澄海縣志. Jin Tinglie 金廷烈, ed. First published in 1764.

Cheong, W. M. "Canton and Manila in the Eighteenth Century," in Jerome Chen and Nicholas Tarling, eds., *Studies in the Social History of China and Southeast Asia* (q.v.).

The China Trade, 1600–1860. Catalogue of the exhibit by Patrick Conner, ed. Brighton: Royal Pavilion, Art Gallery and Museums, and the J. Paul Getty Trust, 1986.

Chinese Academy of Sciences, Institute of the History of Natural Sciences, comp. *Ancient China's Technology and Science*. Beijing: Foreign Languages Press, 1983.

Chinese Repository. Canton. May 1835–December 1851. Vols. 1–20.

Chongxiu Fujian Taiwan fuzhi 重修福建臺灣府志. Liu Liangbi 劉良璧, ed. Rpt. in *Taiwan wenxian congkan* (q.v.). Comp. in 1740.

Christie, Anthony. "Ta-Ch'in P'o-Lo-Men." *Bulletin of the School of Oriental and African Studies* 20:159–166 (1957).

Chu ci 楚辭. Attibuted to Qu Yuan 屈原. Wang Yi 王逸, comp. and annot. Rpt. in *Sibu congkan* (q.v.). Composed ca. 240 B.C.

Chu Mi (Wiens). "Lord and Peasant: The Sixteenth to the Eighteenth Centuries." *Modern China* 6.1:3–40 (1980).

Chu, Samuel. "Liu Ming-ch'uan and the Modernization of Taiwan." *JAS* 23.1:37–53 (1963).

Ch'ü T'ung-tsu. *Han Social Structure*. Seattle: University of Washington Press, 1972.

———. *Local Government in China under the Ching*. Cambridge: Harvard University Press, 1962.

Ch'üan Han-sheng 全漢昇. *Zhongguo hanghui zhihdu shi* 中國行會制度史. Rpt. Taipei: Shihuo chubanshe, 1978.

———. *Zhongguo jingjishi luncong* 中國經濟史論叢. Hong Kong: Xianggang Zhongwen daxue, 1972.

———. "Production and Distribution of Rice in Southern Song." E-Tu Zen Sun and John De Francis, eds. and trs., *Chinese Social History* (q.v.).

Ch'üan Han-sheng and Richard Kraus. *Mid-Ch'ing Rice Markets and Trade*. Cambridge: Harvard University Press, 1975.

Chu-lo xianzhi 諸羅縣志. Chen Menglin 陳夢林 and Zhou Zhongxuan 周鍾瑄, ed. Rpt. in *Taiwan wenxian congkan* (q.v.). First published in 1717.

Cipolla, Carlo M. *Before the Industrial Revolution*. New York: W. W. Norton, 1976.

———. *Guns and Sails in the Early Phase of European Expansion, 1400–1700*. London: William Collins, 1965.

———, ed. *The Industrial Revolution*. Vol. 3 of Carlo M. Cipolla, ed. *The Fontana Economic History of Europe*. Glasgow: William Collins Sons and Co., 1977.

Cobley, Leslie S. *Introduction to the Botany of Tropical Crops*. London: Longman, 1976.

Coedès, George. *Les états hindouises d'Indochine et l'Indonesie.* Paris: E. de Boccard, 1948.
Cohen, Myron. "Shared Beliefs: Corporations, Community and Religion among the South Taiwan Hakka." *Late Imperial China* 14.1:1–33 (1993).
———. *House United, House Divided.* New York: Columbia University Press, 1976.
———. "Developmental Process in the Chinese Domestic Group," in Maurice Freedman, ed., *Family and Kinship in Chinese Society* (q.v.).
———. "Agnatic Kinship in South Taiwan." *Ethnology* 8.2:167–182 (1969).
Cohen, Paul A. *Discovering History in China: American Historical Writing on the Recent Chinese Past.* New York: Columbia University Press, 1984.
Conghua xianzhi 從化縣志. Guo Yuxi 郭遇熙, ed. Rpt. Taipei: Chengwen chubanshe, 1974. First published in 1730.
Congshu jicheng 叢書集成. Wang Yunwu 王雲五, ed. Shanghai: Shangwu yinshuguan, 1935–1937.
Connell, K. H. "The Potato in Ireland." *Past and Present* 23:57–71 (1962).
Cordier, Henri. "Les marchands hanistes de Canton." *TP*, 2e série 3:282–315 (1902).
Couling, Samuel. *The Encyclopaedia Sinica.* Shanghai: Kelly and Walsh, 1917.
Crawfurd, John. *Journal of an Embassy from the Governor-General of India to the Courts of Siam and Cochin China.* 2nd ed. London: Henry Colburn and Richard Bentley, 1830.
Crissman, Lawrence W. "Marketing on the Changhua Plain, Taiwan," in W. E. Willmott, ed., *Economic Organization in Chinese Society* (q.v.).
Crooke, William. *A Glossary of North Indian Peasant Life and Materials for a Rural and Agricultural Glossary of the North-Western Provinces and Oudh.* Shahid Amin, ed. Rpt. Delhi: Oxford University Press, 1989. First published in 1879.
Curtin, Philip. *Cross-cultural Trade in World History.* Cambridge: Cambridge University Press, 1984.
Cushman, Jennifer. *Fields from the Sea.* Ithaca: Cornell University Press, 1990.
Cushner, Nicholas P. *Lords of the Land: Sugar, Wine and Jesuit Estates of Coastal Peru, 1600–1767.* Albany: State University of New York Press, 1980.
da Cruz, Gaspar. *South China in the Sixteenth Century.* C. R. Boxer, ed. and tr. London: Hakluyt Society, 1953. Compl. ca. 1570.
Dai Guohui 戴国煇. *Chūgoku kansho tōgyō no tenkai* 中国甘蔗糖業の展開. Tokyo: Asia keizai kenkyūsho, 1967.
Dai Yanhui 戴炎輝. "Qingdai Taiwan zhi da xiao zu ye" 清代臺灣之大小租業. *Taipei wenxian* 4:1–47 (1963).
———. "Qingdai Taiwan zhi jiazhi ji jiachan" 清代臺灣之家制及家產. *Taiwan wenxian* 14.3:1–19 (1963).

Da Ming huidian Wanli 大明會典萬曆. 5 vols. Rpt. Taipei: Dongnan shubao she, 1963. Comp. in 1587.

Daniels, Christian. *Biology and Biological Technology, Agro-Industries: Sugarcane Technology*, vol. 6, part 3, of Joseph Needham, gen. ed., *Science and Civilisation in China* (q.v.).

——— クリスチャン・ダニエルス. "Chūgoku satō no kokusaiteki ichi" 中国砂糖の国際的位置. *Shakai keizai shigaku* 50.4:21–54 (1984).

Daniels, John, and Christian Daniels. "The Origin of the Sugarcane Roller Mill." *Technology and Culture* 29.3:493–535 (1988).

Da Qing huidian shili 大清會典事例. Rpt. Shanghai: Shangwu yinshuguan, 1908. Comp. in 1899.

Da Qing lichao shilu, Sheng Zu 大清歷朝實錄聖祖. Nos. 7–15. Fac. Rpt. Taipei: Huawen shuju, 1964.

Das Gupta, Arun. "The Maritime Trade of Indonesia, 1500–1800," in Ashin K. Das Gupta and Michael N. Pearson, eds., *India and the Indian Ocean, 1500–1800* (q.v.).

Das Gupta, Ashin K. *Malabar in Asian Trade, 1740–1800*. Cambridge: Cambridge University Press, 1967.

Das Gupta, Ashin K., and Michael N. Pearson, eds. *India and the Indian Ocean, 1500–1800*. Calcutta: Oxford University Press, 1987.

Davidson, J. W. *The Island of Formosa: History, People, Resources and Commercial Prospects*. London: Macmillan, 1903.

Davis, John. "Diaries," in Samuel Purchas, comp., *Purchas His Pilgrimes: or, Hakluytus Posthumus: contayning a history of the world in sea voyages and lande travells by Englishman and others*. Vol. 2. Rpt. Glasgow: James MacLehose and Sons, 1905–1907. First published in 1625.

Davis, Ralph. *The Rise of the Atlantic Economies*. Ithaca: Cornell University Press, 1973.

de Candolle, A. *Origins of Cultivated Plants*. New York: D. Appleton, 1885.

de Cora, Fr. John. "Notices," in Henry Yule and Henri Cordier, eds. and tr., *Cathay and the Way Thither, Being a Collection of Medieval Notices of China* (q.v.). vol. 3 . Comp. in 1330.

Deerr, Noel. *The History of Sugar*. 2 vols. London: Chapman and Hall, 1949–1950.

DeGlopper, Donald R. "Lu-kang and Its Trading System," in Ronald Knapp, ed., *China's Island Frontier* (q.v.).

de Guines, Chrétien Louis Joseph. *Voyages à Pékin, Manille et l'Ile de France faits dans l'intervale des années 1784 à 1801*. 3 vols. Paris: Imprimerie Imperial, 1808.

Delano, Edward. Diaries. Entry dated August 9, 1841. Franklin D. Roosevelt Library, Hyde Park, New York.

Demiéville, Paul, Jun'ichirō Takakusu, et al., eds. *Hōbōgirin*. Tokyo: Maison Franco-Japonaise, 1931.

Dennerline, Jerry. "Fiscal Reform and Local Control," in Frederic Wakeman and Carolyn Grant, eds., *Conflict and Control in Late Imperial China* (q.v.).

Dennett, Tyler. *Americans in Eastern Asia*. New York: Barnes and Noble, 1922.

de Pantoia, Diego. "Notes," in Samuel Purchas, comp., *Purchas His Pilgrimes, Or, Relations of the religions observed in all ages and places discouered* (q.v.). First published in 1602.

de Rada, Martin. "Kingdome of China," in Juan Gonzalez de Mendosa, ed. and comp., Richard Hakluyt, tr., *The History of the Great and Mighty Kingdome of China*. 2 vols. Rpt. New York: Hakluyt Society, 1853. First published in 1588.

Dermigny, Louis. *La Chine et l'Occident: Le commerce à Canton au XVIIIe siècle, 1719–1833*. 4 vols. Paris: Service d'Editions de Vente des Publication Educations National, 1964.

de San Buena Ventura, Pedro. *Vocabulario de Lengua Tagala*. Pila: Thomas Pinpin et Domingo Loag, 1613.

de Solla Price, Derek J. "Joseph Needham and the Science of China," in Shigeru Nakayama and Nathan Sivin, eds., *Chinese Science: Explorations of an Ancient Tradition* (q.v.).

de Vries, Jan. *The Economy of Europe in an Age of Crisis, 1600–1750*. Cambridge: Cambridge University Press, 1976.

Dietrich, Craig. "Cotton Culture and Manufacture in Early Ch'ing China," in W. E. Willmott, ed., *Economic Organization in Chinese Society* (q.v.).

Dirlik, Arif. "Technological Determinism and the Materialist Conception of History." *Modern China* 7.4:483–497 (1981).

———. *Revolution and History: The Origins of Marxist Historiography in China, 1919–1937*. Berkeley: University of California Press, 1978.

Dobb, Maurice. *Studies in the Development of Capitalism*. New York: International Publishers, 1975.

Dong Jiasheng 東嘉生. "Qingdai Taiwan zhi dizu guanxi" 清代臺灣之地租關係, in *Taiwan jingji shi (erji)*. Taipei: Taiwan yinhang, 1955.

Dongguan xian Wanqingsha diaocha baogao 東莞縣萬頃沙調查報告, in *Guangdong sheng difang diaocha baogao ji* 廣東省地方調查報告集. Stenciled mimeo. Guangzhou: 1943.

Dongguan xianzhi 東莞縣志. Peng Renjie 彭人傑 et al., eds. 1797.

Dongguan xianzhi 東莞縣志. Chen Botao 陳伯陶 et al., eds. Rpt. Taipei: Xuesheng shuju, 1968. Comp. in 1911. First published in 1921.

Dongjing menghua lu 東京夢華錄. Meng Yuanlao 孟元老. Deng Zhicheng 登之誠, annot. and punct. Rpt. Beijing: Zhonghua shuju, 1959. First published in 1187.

Dong-Xi yangkao 東西洋考. Zhang Xie 張燮. Vols. 163–164. Rpt. Taipei: Siku quanshu zhenben jiuji, 1979. Preface dated 1617.

Drachmann, A. G. *Ancient Oil Mills and Presses*. Copenhagen: Levin and Munksgaard, 1932.

Drake, Frederick S., and Wolfram Eberhard, eds. *South-east Asia and the Hong Kong Region*. Hong Kong: Hong Kong University Press, 1967.

du Caillard, M. Romanet. *La colonization espagnole dans le nord de l'île de Formose, 1626–1642*. Paris: Association Française pour l'Advancement des Sciences, 1890.

Duara, Prasenjit. *Culture, Power and the State*. Stanford: Stanford University Press, 1988.

Duyvendak, J. J. L. "The True Dates of the Chinese Maritime Expeditions in the Early Fifteenth Century." *TP* 34:341–412 (1939).

Eastman, Lloyd E. *Family, Field and Ancestors*. New York: Oxford University Press, 1988.

Eberhard, Wolfram. *Social Mobility in South China*. Leiden: E. J. Brill, 1962.

Ebrey, Patricia B., and James Watson, eds. *Kinship Organization in Late Imperial China*. Berkeley: University of California Press, 1986.

Eckeberg, Charles Gustavus. "A Short Account of the Chinese Husbandry," in Pehr Osbeck, comp., *A Voyage to China and the East Indies* (q.v.).

Eisenberg, Peter L. *The Sugar Industry in Pernambuco, 1840–1910*. Berkeley: University of California Press, 1974.

Ellis, Henry. *Journal of the Proceedings of the Late Embassy to China*. Philadelphia: A. Small, 1818.

Elvin, Mark. "Skills and Resources in Late Traditonal China," in Dwight Perkins, ed., *China's Modern Economy in Historical Perspective* (q.v.).

———. *Pattern of the Chinese Past*. Stanford: Stanford University Press, 1973.

———. "The High-Level Equilibrium Trap," in W. E. Willmott, ed., *Economic Organization in Chinese Society* (q.v.).

Elvin, Mark, and G. William Skinner, eds. *The Chinese City between Two Worlds*. Stanford: Stanford University Press, 1974.

Endacott, G. B. *A History of Hong Kong*. Oxford: Oxford University Press, 1958.

Eng, Robert. *Economic Imperialism in China*. Berkeley: Institute of East Asian Studies, University of California, 1986.

———. "Institutional and Secondary Landlordism in the Pearl River Delta, 1600–1949." *Modern China* 12.1:3–38 (1986).

Englehardt, Zephyrin. *The Missions and Missionaries of California*. Vol. 1. Santa Barbara: Mission Santa Barbara, 1929.

Er ya 爾雅. Guo Pu 郭璞, annot. Rpt. in *Sibu congkan* (q.v.). Comp. in ca. 300.

Fa Xian (Fa Hien). *A Record of Buddhistic Kingdom.* James Legge, tr. and annot. Rpt. New York: Paragon, 1965. First printed in 1886.

Fairbank, John K. *Trade and Diplomacy on the China Coast.* 1953. Rpt. Stanford: Stanford University Press, 1969.

Fairbank, John K., ed. *Late Ch'ing, 1800–1911*; vol. 10 in John K. Fairbank, gen. ed., *The Cambridge History of China.* Cambridge: Cambridge University Press, 1978–1985.

———. *The Chinese World Order.* Cambridge: Harvard University Press, 1968.

Fairbank, John K., and Liu Kwang-ching, eds. *Late Ch'ing, 1800–1911,* vol. 11 in John K. Fairbank, gen. ed., *The Cambridge History of China.* Cambridge: Cambridge University Press, 1978–1985.

Fan I-chun. "Long-Distance Trade and Market Integration in the Ming-Ch'ing Period, 1400–1850." Ph.D. dissertation, Stanford University, 1992.

——— 范毅軍. "Guangdong Han-Mei liuyu de tangye jingji" 廣東韓梅流域的糖業經濟. *Zhongyang yanjiuyuan, Jindaishi yanjiusuo jikan* 12:127–161 (1983).

Fang Hao 方豪. "Tainan zhi 'jiao'" 臺南之「郊」. *Dalu zazhi* 44.4:177–199 (1962).

———. *Zhong-Xi jiaotong shi* 中西交通史. 5 vols. Taipei: Zhonghua wenhua chuban, 1954.

Fang Xianting (H. D. Fong) 方顯廷. *Zhongguo zhi mianfangzhi ye* 中國之棉紡織業. Shanghai: Shangwu yinshuguan, 1934.

Faure, David. "What Made Foshan a Town?" *Late Imperial China* 11.2:1–31 (1990).

———. *The Rural Economy of Pre-Liberation China.* Hong Kong: Oxford University Press, 1989.

———. "Lineage as a Cultural Invention: The Case of the Pearl River Delta." *Modern China* 15.1:4 36 (1989).

———. *The Structure of Chinese Rural Society.* Hong Kong: Oxford University Press, 1986.

———. "The Plight of the Farmers." *Modern China* 11.1:2–38 (1985).

———. "Neglected Historical Sources on the Late Ch'ing and Early Republican Rural Economy." *Ch'ing-shih wen-t'i* 4.1:58–93 (1979).

———. "The Rural Economy of Kiangsu Province." *JCICUHK* 9.2:365–469 (1978).

———. "Landlords and Farm Management: Comments on Jing Su and Lo Lun: *Qingdai Shandong jingying dizhu de shehui xingzhi.*" *JCICUHK* 11:303–311 (1978).

Faure, David, James Hayes, and Alan Birch, eds. *From Village to City.* Hong Kong: Hong Kong University, Asian Studies Center, 1984.

Faure, David (Ke Dawei) 科大衛, Wong Wing-ho 黃永豪, and Hamashita

Takeshi 濱下武志 et al., eds. *Guangdong zongzu qiju huilu* 廣東宗族契據彙錄. Tokyo: Tōkyō daigaku, Tōyō bunka kenkyūjo, 1988.

Fei, John H. "The 'Standard Market' of Traditional China," in Dwight Perkins, ed., *China's Modern Economy in Historical Perspective* (q.v.).

Fei, John H., and Liu Tsui-jung. "Population Dynamics of Agrarianism in Traditonal China," in Hou Chi-ming and Yu Tzong-shian, eds., *Modern Chinese Economic History* (q.v.).

Feng Chengjun 馮承鈞. *Zhongguo Nanyang jiaotong shi* 中國南洋交通史. Shanghai: Shangwu yinshuguan, 1937.

Feuerwerker, Albert. "From 'Feudalism' to 'Capitalism' in Recent Historical Writings from Mainland China." *JAS* 18.1:107–115 (1958).

Feuerwerker, Albert, ed. *Chinese Social and Economic History from the Song to 1900 (Report of the American Delegation to a Sino-American Symposium).* Ann Arbor: Center for Chinese Studies, University of Michigan, 1982.

Feuerwerker, Albert, and S. Chang. *Chinese Communist Studies of Modern Chinese History*. Cambridge: Council on East Asian Studies, Harvard University, 1961.

Fielde, Adele M. *A Corner of Cathay: Studies from Life among the Chinese*. New York: Macmillan, 1894.

———. "Report from the American Baptist Mission, Swatou, Guangdong," in George Jamieson et al., "Tenure of Land in China and the Condition of the Rural Population." *Journal of the North China Branch of the Royal Asiatic Society of Great Britain and Ireland* 23:110–116 (1888).

Flecknoe, Richard. *A True and Faithful Account of What was observed in Ten Years Travells into the principal places of Europe, Asia, Africa and America, written in several Letters to Noble Personages*. London: William Crook, 1665.

Fogel, Joshua A. "Debates over the Asiatic Mode of Production in the Soviet Union, China and Japan." *AHR* 93.1:56–79 (1988).

Forbes, John Murray. Letterbooks and Journals. "History of Business Done by John Forbes for Houqua." Letter dated 29 Dec. 1832. Forbes Collection, Baker Library, Harvard University.

———. Letterbooks and Journals. "American Stock Investment Company Account Journals." Forbes Collection, Baker Library, Harvard University.

Forbes, R. J. "Food and Drink," in Charles Singer, E. J. Holmyard, A. R. Hall, and Trevor I. Williams, eds., *A History of Technology*. Oxford: Clarendon Press, 1957.

Fortune, Robert. *Two Visits to the Tea Countries of China and the British Tea Plantations of the Himalayas*. 2 vols. London: Murray, 1853.

Francis, John Davis. *China, during the War and since the Peace*. Vol. 2. London: Longman, Brown, Green and Longmans, 1852.

Freedman, Maurice. *Chinese Lineage and Society: Fukien and Kwangtung*. London: Athlone Press, 1971.
———. *Lineage Organization in Southeastern China*. London School of Economics Monographs on Social Anthropology. London, 1958.
Freedman, Maurice, ed. *Family and Kinship in Chinese Society*. Stanford: Stanford University Press, 1970.
Freeman, Michael. "Sung," in K. C. Chang, ed., *Food in Chinese Culture* (q.v.).
Fried, Morton. *The Fabric of Chinese Society*. New York: Octagon Books, 1969.
Fu, Lo-shu. *A Documentary Chronicle of Sino-Western Relations (1644–1820)*. 2 vols. Tucson: University of Arizona Press, 1966.
Fu Yiling 傅衣凌. "Ming Qing shidai jieji guanxi de xintansuo" 明清时代阶级关系的新探索. *Zhongguoshi yanjiu* 4:65–74 (1979).
———. *Mingdai Jiangnan shimin jingji shitan* 明代江南市民经济试探. Shanghai: Shanghai renmin chubanshe, 1963.
———. *Ming Qing nongcun shehui jingji* 明清农村社会经济. Beijing: Xinhua shudian, 1961.
———. *Ming Qing shidai shangren ji shangye ziben* 明清时代商人及商业资本. Beijing: Renmin chubanshe, 1956.
Fu Zhufu 傅筑夫 and Li Jingneng 李竞能. *Zhongguo fengjian shehui nei ziben zhuyi yinsu de mengya* 中国封建社会内资本主义因素的萌芽. Shanghai: Shanghai renmin chubanshe, 1956.
Fujian tongzhi 福建通志. Sun Erzhun 孫爾準 et al., comps. 1871.
Fujii Hiroshi 藤井宏. "Ichiden ryōshu sei no kihon kōzō" 一田兩主制の基本構造, *Kindai Chūgoku* 5.10:67–134 (1979).
———. "Shin'an shōnin no kenkyū" 新安商人の研究. *Tōyō gakuhō* 36.1:1–44, 36.2:32–60, 36.3:65–118, 36.4:115–145 (1953–1954).
———. "Chūgokushi ni okeru shin to kyū, 'Shokkōtai' no bunseki o meguru shomondai" 中国史に於ける新と旧「織工対」の分析をめぐる諸問題. *Tōyō bunka* 9:21–40 (1952).
Furber, Holden. *Rival Empires of Trade*. Minneapolis: University of Minnesota Press, 1976.
———. *John Company at Work*. Cambridge: Cambridge University Press, 1951.
Gaastra, Femme. "The Shifting Balance of Trade in the Dutch East India Company," in Leonard Blussé and Femmme Gaastra, eds., *Companies and Trade* (q.v.).
Gallin, Bernard. *Hsin Hsing, Taiwan: A Chinese Village in Change*. Berkeley: University of California Press, 1966.
Galloway, J. H. *The Sugar Cane Industry : An Historical Geography from Its Origins to 1914*. Cambridge: Cambridge University Press, 1989.

Gamble, Sidney. "Wages of Unskilled Chinese Laborers, 1807–1902." *Far Eastern Quarterly* 3.1:41–73 (1943).

Gaoseng zhuan, Taishō shinshū Daizōkyō 高僧傳大正新修大藏經. Takakusu Jun'ichirō 高楠順次郎 et al., eds. Vol. 50. Tokyo: Taishō issaikyō kankōkai, 1922–1933.

Gardella, Robert. "The Boom Years of the Fujian Tea Trade," in Ernest R. May and John K. Fairbank, eds., *America's China Trade in Historical Perspective: The Chinese and American Performances* (q.v.).

Geertz, Clifford. *Agricultural Involution: The Process of Ecological Change in Indonesia*. Rpt. Berkeley: University of California Press, 1968.

Generale Missiven van Gouverneurs-Generaal en Raden aan Heren XVII der Verenigde Oost-Indische Compagnie (1610–1725). W. Ph. Coolhaas, ed. 7 vols. The Hague: Nijhoff, 1960–1979.

Gerard, John. *The Herball or Generall Historie of Plants*. Enlarged and revised by Thomas Johnson, 1633. Rpt. New York: Dover Publications, 1974. First published in 1597.

Gernet, Jacques. *Daily Life in China on the Eve of the Mongol Invasion, 1270–1276*. H. M. Wright, tr. Stanford: Stanford University Press, 1970.

———. *Les Aspects Economiques du Bouddhisme*. Saigon: Ecole Française d'Extrème-Orient, 1956.

Gezhi jingyuan 格致鏡原. Chen Yuanlong 陳元龍, ed. and comp. Rpt. Taipei: Shangwu shudian, 1972. First published in 1735.

Giles, Henry A. *From Swatow to Canton Overland*. Shanghai: Kelly and Walsh, 1877.

Glamann, Kristof. *Dutch Asiatic Trade, 1620–1740*. The Hague: Nijhoff, 1958.

Golas, Peter J. "Early Ch'ing Guilds," in G. William Skinner, ed., *The City in Late Imperial China* (q.v.).

The Golden Lotus (*Jin ping mei*). Clement Egerton, tr. 4 vols. London: Routeledge and Kegan Paul, 1939. Written ca. 1619.

Gongzhongdang Kangxi chao zouzhe 宮中檔康熙朝奏摺. 9 vols. Taipei: Guoli gugong bowuyuan, 1976.

Gongzhongdang Yongzheng chao zouzhe 宮中檔雍正朝奏摺. 32 vols. Taipei: Guoli gugong bowuyuan, 1977.

Gonzalez de Mendoza, Fr. Juan. *The History of the Great and Mighty Kingdome of China*. 2 vols. George Staunton, ed. Rpt. London: Hakluyt Society, 1853. First published in 1588.

Goodman, Grant K. *Japan: The Dutch Experience*. London: Athlone Press, 1986.

Goodrich, L. Carrington. "Trade Routes to China," in J. Labatut and H. J. Lane, eds., *Highways in Our National Life*. Princeton: Princeton University Press, 1950.

———. "Brief Communications." *Journal of the American Oriental Society* 60:258–260 (1940).

Goodrich, L. Carrington, and Chaoyang Fang, eds. *Dictionary of Ming Biography, 1368–1644*. 2 vols. New York: Columbia University Press, 1976.

Gopal, Lallanji. *Aspects of History of Agriculture in Ancient India*. Varanasi: Bharati Prakashan, 1980.

———. "Sugar Making in Ancient India." *Journal of the Economic and Social History of the Orient* 7:57–72 (1964).

Gourbert, Pierre. *The Ancien Regime*. New York: Harper and Row, 1969.

Graham, A. C. "China, Europe and the Origins of Modern Science: Needham's *The Grand Titration*," in Shigeru Nakayama and Nathan Sivin, eds., *Chinese Science: Explorations of an Ancient Tradition* (q.v.).

Grant, Frederic D. "Litigation Brought by and against Hong Merchants in the American Courts, 1800–1825." Paper presented at Association of Asian Studies, April 12, 1987.

Greenberg, Michael. *British Trade and the Opening of China, 1800–1842*. New York: Monthly Review Press, 1951.

Grimm, Thomas. "Academies and Urban Systems in Guangdong," in G. William Skinner, ed., *The City in Late Imperial China* (q.v.).

Grove, Linda, and Joseph Esherick. "From Feudalism to Capitalism: Japanese Scholarship on the Transformation of Chinese Rural Society." *Modern China* 6.4:397–438 (1980).

Grove, Linda, and Christian Daniels, eds. *State and Society in China: Japanese Perspectives on Ming Qing Social and Economic History*. Tokyo: University of Tokyo Press, 1984.

Groves, Robert G. "Militia, Market and Lineage: Chinese Resistance to the Occupation of Hong Kong's New Territories." *JHKBRAS* 9:31–64 (1969).

———. "The Origins of Two Market Towns in the New Territories," in Marjorie Topley, ed., *Aspects of Social Organization in the New Territories*. Hong Kong: Hong Kong Branch of the Royal Asiatic Society, 1965.

Guan Xiekuang 关协况. "Jiefangqian Xinhui kuiye jingying gaikuang" 解放前新会葵业经营概况. *Guangdong wenshi ziliao* 28:187–214 (1980).

Guangdong jingji nianjian bianzhuan weiyuanhui 廣東經濟年鑑編纂委員會, comp. *Ershijiu niandu Guangdong jingji nianjian* 二十九年度廣東經濟年鑑. Guangzhou: Guangdong sheng yinhang jinji yanjiushi, 1941.

Guangdong lishi xuehui 广东历史学会, ed. *Ming Qing Guangdong shehui jingji xingtai yanjiu* 明清广东社会经济形态研究. Guangzhou: Guangdong renmin chubanshe, 1985.

Guangdong sheng canye diaocha baogaoshu 廣東省蠶業調查報告書. Guangzhou: Guangdong sheng difang nonglin shixianchang, 1922.

Guangdong sheng difang diaocha baogao ji 廣東省地方調查報告集. Guangzhou, 1943.

Guangdong Taijingtouxiang Lishi puxi 廣東台逕頭鄉李氏譜系. Last preface dated 1975.

Guangdong tongzhi 廣東通志. Ruan Yuan 阮元, ed. Rpt. Taipei: Huawen shuju, 1968. First published in 1864.

Guangdong tushuo 廣東圖說. Mao Hongbin 毛鴻賓 et al., comps. Guangzhou: Cuiwen tang, 1879.

Guangdong Xiangshan Xushi zongpu 廣東香山徐氏宗譜. Preface dated 1882.

Guangdong xinyu 廣東新語. Qu Dajun 屈大均. Rpt. Hong Kong: Zhonghua shuju, 1974. Preface dated 1700.

Guanglusi zeli 光祿寺則例. Beijing: (*Qinding*) Neibu, 1839.

Guangyang zaji 廣陽雜記. Liu Xianting 劉獻廷. In Huang Hu 黃瑚, comp. *Zhifu congshu*. Rpt. in *Congshu jicheng* (q.v.). Comp. in ca. 1650.

Guangzhou fuzhi 廣州府志. Dai Zhaochen 戴肇辰 et al., eds. Rpt. Taipei: Chengwen chubanshe, 1966. First published in 1879.

Guangzhou Sanjiaozhou zhi ganzhe zaipei 廣州三角洲之甘蔗栽培. Preface by Feng Rui 馮銳. Guangzhou: Guangdong sheng zhengfu ju, 1935.

Gujin tushu jicheng 古今圖書集成. Chen Menglei 陳夢雷 et al., eds. Rpt. Shanghai: Zhonghua shuju, 1934. First published in 1725.

Guo Moruo 郭沫若. *Shi pipan shu* 十批判書. Chongqing: Qunyi shushe, 1945.

Guoli Guangdong daxue, Nongke xueyuan 國立廣東大學農科學院. *Panyu, Zengcheng, Dongguan, Zhongshan tangye diaocha baogaoshu* 番禺增城東莞中山糖業調查報告書. Guangzhou, 1925.

Guoli Zhongshan daxue, Nongke xueyuan 國立中山大學農科學院. *Guangdong nongye gaikuang diaocha baogaoshu* 廣東農業概況調查報告書. 3 vols. Guangzhou, 1925–1933.

Habib, Irfan. "Capacity of Technological Change in Mughal India," in Anniruddha Roy and S. K. Bagchi, eds., *Technology in Ancient and Medieval India* (q.v.).

———. "Technology and Barriers to Social Change in Mughal India." *Indian Historical Review* 5.1–2:152–174 (1978–1979).

———. *The Agrarian System of Mughal India*. Bombay: Asia Publication House, 1963.

Haguenauer, M. C. "Formose depuis les origines jusqu'a son annexion par le Japon." *Bulletin de la Maison Franco-Japonaise* 2.3–4:37–92 (1930).

Haiguo tuzhi 海國圖志. Wei Yuan 魏源. Yangzhou: Guweitang, 1898. Preface dated 1842.

Han Hengyu 韩恒煜. "Shilun Qingdai qianqi diannong yongdian quan de youlai jiqi xingzhi" 试论清代前期佃农永佃权的由来及其性质, in *Qingshi luncong* (q.v.). vol 1.

Hao Yen-p'ing. *The Commercial Revolution in Nineteenth Century China*. Berkeley: University of California Press, 1986.

———. "Chinese Teas to America—A Synopsis," in Ernest R. Mays and John K. Fairbank, eds., *America's China Trade in Historical Perspective* (q.v.).

———. *The Comprador in Nineteenth Century China: Bridge between East and West*. Cambridge: Harvard University Press, 1970.

Harrell, Stevan. "Social Organization in Hai-shan," in Emily Martin Ahern and Hill Gates, eds., *The Anthropology of Taiwanese Society* (q.v.).

Hartwell, Robert. "Demographic, Political, and Social Transformations of China, 750–1550." *HJAS* 42.2:365–442 (1982).

Harvey, David. *The Limits to Capital*. Chicago: University of Chicago Press, 1982.

Hawkes, David. *Ch'u Tz'u, The Songs of the South*. Oxford: Oxford University Press, 1959.

Hayashi Kazuo 林和生. "Min Shin jidai Kanton no kyo to shi dentōteki ichiba no keitai to kinō ni kansuru ichi kōsatsu" 明清時代広東の墟と市伝統的市場の形態と機能に関する一考察. *Shirin* 63:69–105 (1980).

Hayashi Shunsai 林春勝 and Hayashi Nobuatsu 林信篤, eds. *Ka-i-hentai* 華夷變態. 4 vols. Ura Ren'ichi 浦廉一, annot. Tokyo: Tōyō Bunko, 1958–1959.

Hayes, James. "Itinerant Hakka Weavers." *JHKBRAS* 8:162–165 (1968).

———. "Land and Leadership in the Hong Kong Region of Kwangtung in the Nineteenth Century." *JHKBRAS* 7:91–103 (1967).

He Zhuojian 何卓坚. "Xinhui kuiye shilue" 新会葵业史略. *Guangdong wenshi ziliao* 15:132–151 (1965).

———. "Jiefang qian de Xinhui chenpiye" 解放前的新会陈皮业. *Guangdong wenshi ziliao* 20:111–121 (1965).

Headrick, Daniel R. *The Tentacles of Progress*. New York: Oxford University Press, 1988.

———. *The Tools of Empire: Technology and European Imperialism in the Nineteenth Century*. Oxford: Oxford University Press, 1981.

Hedges, William. *The Diary of William Hedges, Esq*. Henry Yule, ed. Hakluyt Society Publications, 1st series. London, 1888–1889.

Henry, Benjamin Couch. *Ling-nan or Interior Views of Southern China, Including Explorations in the Hitherto Untraversed Island of Hainan*. London: Partridge, 1886.

Higuchi Hiroshi 弘子郎. *Nihon tōgyō shi* 日本糖業史. Tokyo: Naigai keizaisha, 1956.

Hirase Minokichi 平瀬巳之吉. *Kindai Shina keizaishi* 近代支那經濟史. Tokyo: Chūō Kōronsha, 1942.

Hilton, Rodney. "Towns in English Feudal Society." *Review: A Journal of the Fernand Braudel Center* 3.1:3–20 (1979).

Hilton, Rodney, ed. *The Transition from Feudalism to Capitalism*. Rpt. London: Verso, 1978.

Ho Ke-en. "The Origins of the *Dan jia* or Boat People of South China," in Frederick S. Drake and Wolfram Eberhard, eds., *Symposium on Historical, Archaeological and Linguistic Studies on Southern China* (q.v.).

Ho Ping-ti. *The Ladder of Success in Imperial China*. New York: Columbia University Press, 1962.

———. *Studies on the Population of China*. Cambridge: Harvard University Press, 1959.

———. "Early Ripening Rice in Chinese History." *Economic History Review*, 2nd ser. 9.2:200–218 (1956).

———. "The Introduction of American Food Plants into China." *American Anthropologist* 57.2:191–201 (1955).

Ho, Samuel. *Economic Development of Taiwan, 1860–1970*. New Haven: Yale University Press, 1978.

Hoang, Peter. "A Practical Treatise on Legal Ownership," in George Jamieson et al., eds., "Tenure of Land in China and the Condition of the Rural Population" (q.v.).

Hobsbawm, Eric J. *The Age of Capital, 1848–1875*. New York: New American Library, 1979.

———. *Industry and Empire*. Harmondsworth, Eng.: Penguin Books, 1968.

———. *The Age of Revolution, 1789–1848*. New York: New American Library, 1962.

Homans, Issac Smith. *A Historical and Statistical Account of the Foreign Commerce of the United States*. New York: Putnams, 1857.

Hommel, Rudolph. *China at Work: An Illustrated Record of the Primitive Industries of China's Masses, Whose Life Is Toil, and Thus an Account of Chinese Civilization*. Rpt. Cambridge: MIT Press, 1969. First published in 1937.

Honey, David. "Liturgy or Literature." *Journal of Asian Culture* 5:76–106 (1981).

Hooper, M. S. "Papers and Journal, 1840–1842." Special Collections, Duke University Library.

Hou Chi-ming. *Foreign Investment and Economic Development in China, 1840–1937*. Cambridge: Harvard University Press, 1965.

Hou Chi-ming and Yu Tzong-shian, eds. *Modern Chinese Economic History*. Taipei: Institute of Economics, Academia Sinica, 1979.

Hou Xueying 侯雪鶯. "Luetan Qingdai Chaozhou de zhetangye" 略談清代潮州的蔗糖業. Senior thesis, Zhongshan University. 1981.

Howard, C. W. *The Sericulture Industry of South China*. Guangzhou: Canton Christian College, 1923.

Howard, C. W, and K. P. Buswell. *A Survey of the Silk Industry of South China*. Hong Kong: Commercial Press, 1925.

Hsiao Kung-chuan. *Rural China*. Seattle: University of Washington Press, 1962.

Hsieh, Winston. "Peasant Insurrection and the Marketing Hierarchy in the Canton Delta 1911," in Mark Elvin and G. William Skinner, eds.; *The Chinese City between Two Worlds* (q.v.).

Hsu Cho-yun. "The Chinese Settlement of the I-lan Plain," in Ronald Knapp, ed., *China's Island Frontier* (q.v.).

Hsu, Immanuel. *China's Entry into the Family of Nations*. Cambridge: Harvard University Press, 1960.

Hsu, Vera Y. N., and Francis L. K. Hsu. "Modern China: North," in K. C. Chang, ed., *Food in Chinese Culture* (q.v.).

Hsu Wen-hsiung. "From Aboriginal Island to Chinese Frontier: The Development of Taiwan before 1683," in Ronald Knapp, ed., *China's Island Frontier* (q.v.).

———. "Frontier Social Organization and Social Disorder in Ch'ing Taiwan," in Ronald Knapp, ed., *China's Island Frontier* (q.v.).

Hu Hsien-chin. *The Common Descent Group in China and Its Functions*. New York: Viking Fund Publications in Anthropology, 1948.

Hu Shiu-ying. *An Enumeration of Chinese Materia Medica*. Hong Kong: Chinese University Press, 1980.

Huang Juezi zousu 黄爵滋奏疏. Xu Naiji 許乃濟, comp. Rpt. Beijing: Zhonghua shuju, 1959. Publ. ca. 1850.

Huang Peijing 黄佩瑾. "Guanyu Mingdai guonei shichang wenti de kaocha" 关于明代国内市场问题的考察, in Shang Yue 尚钺 et al., eds., *Ming Qing shehui jingji xingtai de yanjiu* 明清社会经济形态的研究. Shanghai: Renmin chubanshe, 1957.

Huang, Philip. "The Paradigmatic Crisis in Chinese History." *Modern China* 17.3:299–341 (1991).

———. *The Peasant Family and Rural Development in the Yangzi Delta, 1350–1988*. Stanford: Stanford University Press, 1990.

———. *The Peasant Economy and Social Change in North China*. Stanford: Stanford University Press, 1985.

Huang Qichen 黄启臣. "Ming Qing Zhujiang sanjiaozhou de shangye yu shangye ziben chutan" 明清珠江三角洲的商业与商业资本初探, in

Guangdong lishi xuehui, eds., *Ming Qing Guangdong shehui jingji xingtai yanjiu* (q.v.).

Huang Yungwu 黃永武, ed. *Dunhuang baocang* 敦煌寶藏. Vol. 127. Taipei: Xinwenfeng chuban gongsi, 1986.

Huangchao jingshi wen bian 皇朝經世文編. He Changling 賀長齡, comp. Rpt. Taipei: Guofeng chubanshe, 1963. Preface dated 1826.

Hucker, Charles O. *A Dictionary of Official Titles in Imperial China*. Stanford: Stanford University Press, 1985.

Hummel, Arthur W. *Eminent Chinese of the Ch'ing Period*. Washington, D.C.: U.S. Government Printing Office, 1943–1944.

Hunan sheng bowuguan 湖南省博物馆 and Zhongguo kexueyuan, Kaogu yanjiu suo 中国科学院考古研究所, eds. *Changsha Mawangdui yihao hanmu* 长沙马王堆一号汉墓. Beijing: Wenwu chubanshe, 1973.

Hunter, William. *The Fan Kwae at Canton*. London: Kegan Paul, Trench and Co., 1882.

I-Tsing. *A Record of the Buddhist Kingdom*. Takakusu Junichirō, tr. Oxford: Clarendon Press, 1876.

Ibn Battūta. *The Travels of Ibn Battūta, A.D. 1325–1354*. From the Arabic text edited by C. Defrémery and B. R. Sanguinetti, tr., H. A. R. Gibb and C. F. Beckingham. Vol. 4. London: Hakluyt Society, 1994.

———. "Travels in Asia and Africa," in Henry Yule and Henri Cordier, eds. and trs., *Cathay and the Way Thither, Being a Collection of Medieval Notices of China* (q.v.), vol. 4. Comp. ca. fourteenth century.

Imahori Seiji 今堀誠二. "Chūgoku ni okeru kaikyū kubunron no seisei" 中国における階級区分論の生成. *Shakai keizai shigaku* 29.6:1–25, 30.1:39–59 (1964).

———. "Chūgoku ni okeru hōkenteki shōkōgyō no kikō seisan kankei yori mitaru Naimōko no toshi to nōson" 中国における封建的商工業の機構生産關係より見たる内蒙古の 都市と農村. *Tōyō bunka* 3:1–54 (1950).

Imperial Maritime Customs. *Decennial Reports, 1922–31*. Fifth issue. 2 vols. Shanghai: Inspectorate General of Customs, 1935.

———. *Decennial Reports, 1902–1911*. Third issue. 2 vols. Shanghai: Inspectorate General of Customs, 1914.

———. *Decennial Reports, 1892–1901*. Second issue. 2 vols. Shanghai: Inspectorate General of Customs, 1904.

———. *Decennial Report, Shantou*. First issue. 1882–1891. Shanghai: Inspectorate General of Customs, 1893.

———. *Reports on the Trade of the Treaty Ports of China: Shantou*. Shanghai: Inspectorate General of Customs, 1878.

———. *Returns of Trade at the Treaty Ports*. Statistical series, no. 1. Shanghai: Statistical Department of the Inspectorate General of Customs, 1859–1886.

Innes, Robert LeRoy. "The Door Ajar: Japan's Foreign Trade in the Seventeenth Century." Ph.D. dissertation, University of Michigan, 1980.

Inō Kanori 伊能嘉矩. *Taiwan bunkashi* 臺灣文化史. 3 vols. Rpt. Tokyo: Tōkōshoin, 1965.

International Sugar Council. *The World's Sugar Economy: Structure and Policies*. London: Brown, Wright and Tuscott, 1963.

Israel, Jonathan I. *Dutch Primacy in World Trade*. Oxford: Clarendon Press, 1989.

Iwao Seiichi. "Japanese Foreign Trade in the 16th and 17th Centuries." *Acta Asiatica* 30:1–18 (1976).

——— 岩生成一. "Edo jidai no satō bōeki ni tsuite" 江戸時代の砂糖貿易について. *Nihon Gakushūin kiyō* 31.1:1–33 (1973).

———. "Reopening of the Diplomatic and Commercial Relations between Japan and Siam during the Tokugawa Period." *Acta Asiatica* 14:1–31 (1963).

———. "Kindai Nisshi bōeki ni kansuru sūryōteki kōsatsu" 近代日支貿易に関する数量的考察. *Shigaku zasshi* 62:1–39 (1953).

Jamieson, George, et al. "Tenure of Land in China and the Condition of the Rural Population." *Journal of the North China Branch of the Royal Asiatic Society of Great Britain and Ireland* 23:59–174 (1888).

Jerome, Norge W. "Taste Experience and the Development of a Dietary Preference for Sweet in Humans," in J. M. Wiffenbach, ed., *Taste and Development: The Genesis of Sweet Preference*. Bethesda: U.S. Department of Health, Education and Welfare, 1977.

Ji Cheng 集成. "Dongguan Minglun Tang shilue" 東莞明倫堂史略. *Guangdong wenshi ziliao* 16:22–32 (1964).

"Ji wen" 祭文. Xie Huilian 謝惠連. In Xiao Tong 蕭統, comp., *Wen xuan* 文選. Rpt. Hong Kong: Shangwu shudian, 1960. Comp. in 501–531.

Ji Xianlin 季羡林. "Yizhang youguan Yindu zhitang fa chuanru Zhongguo de Dunhuang canjuan" 一张有关印度制糖法传入中国的敦煌残卷. *Lishi yanjiu* 1:124–136 (1982).

Ji Zhuge. "The Sino-American Symposium on Chinese Socioeconomic History from the Song Dynasty to 1900," in Albert Feuerwerker, ed., *Chinese Social and Economic History from the Song to 1900* (q.v.).

Jiang Jiajin 江家錦. "Jiawu zhanyi yiqian zhi Taiwan tangye" 甲午戰役以前之臺灣糖業. *Tainan wenhua* 5.1:19–22 (1956), 5.2:69–74 (1956).

Jing Junjian. "Legislation Related to the Civil Economy in the Qing Dynasty," Matthew H. Sommer, tr., in Kathryn Bernhardt and Philip C. C. Huang, eds., *Civil Law in Qing and Republican China* (q.v.).

——— 经君健. "Ming Qing liangdai 'gugong ren' de falü diwei wenti" 明清两代「雇工人」的法律地位问题, in Li Wenzhi, Wei Jinyu, and Jing Junjian, eds., *Ming Qing shidai de nongye ziben zhuyi mengya wenti* (q.v.).

Jing Su 景甦 and Luo Lun 羅崙. *Qingdai Shandong jingying dizhu di shehui xingzhi* 清代山東經營地主底社會性質. Shandong: Renmin chubanshe, 1959. Tr. Endymion Wilkinson as *Landlord and Labor in Late Imperial China*. Cambridge: Council on East Asian Studies, Harvard University, 1978.

Jiu Tang shu 舊唐書. Liu Xu 劉昫 et al., eds. Rpt. Beijing: Zhonghua shuju, 1975. Comp. in 887–946.

Jorg, C. J. A. *Porcelain and the Dutch China Trade*. The Hague: Nijhoff, 1982.

Juvaini Atā Malik al-Din. *The History of the World Conqueror*. John Andrew Boyle, tr. 2 vols. Manchester: Manchester University Press, 1958.

K. "Chinese Guilds and Their Rules." *China Review* 12.1:5–9 (1883–1884).

Kahn, Harold. *Monarchy in the Emperor's Eyes*. Cambridge: Harvard University Press, 1971.

Kamm, John. "Two Essays on the Ch'ing Economy of Hsin-an Kwangtung." *JHKBRAS* 17:55–84 (1977).

Kang Yong Qian shiqi chengxiang renmin fankang douzheng ziliao 康雍乾时期城乡人民反抗斗争资料. Zhongguo renmin daxue, Qingshi yanjiusuo 中国人民大学清史研究所, comp. Beijing: Xinhua shuju, 1979.

Kanton Nihon Sōryōjikan 廣東日本總領事館. *Kantonshō nōson chōsa shiryō* 廣東省農村調查資料. Guangzhou: Nihon Sōryōjikan, 1944.

Kaogong ji 考工記. Compiler unknown. Incorporated as a section into *Zhouli* (q.v.). Comp. in ca. 400–300 B.C.

Kataoka Shibako 片岡芝子. "Minmatsu Shinsho no Kahoku ni okeru nōka keiei" 明末清初の華北における農家經營. *Shakai keizai shigaku* 25.3:77–100 (1959).

Katayama Tsuyoshi 片山剛. "Shindai Kanton-shō Jukō deruta no tokōsei ni tsuite" 清代広東省珠江デリタの図甲制について. *Tōyō gakuhō* 63.3–4:233–266 (1982).

Katō Eiichi. "The Japan Dutch Trade in the Formative Period of the Seclusion Policy—Particularly on the Raw Silk Trade by the Dutch Factory at Hirado, 1620–1640." *Acta Asiatica* 30:34–84 (1976).

Katō Shigeshi 加藤繁. "Zhongguo de ganzhe yu shatang de qiyuan" 中國的甘蔗與沙糖的起源. Yu Jingrang 于景讓, tr. *Dalu zazhi* 9.11:337–340 (1954).

———. *Shina keizaishi kōshō* 支那經濟史考證. Vol. 2. Tokyo:Tōyō Bunko, 1953.

———. "On the Hong or the Associations of Merchants in China." *Memoirs of the Research Department of the Tōyō Bunko* 8:45–83 (1936).

———. "Shindai ni okeru sonchin no teiki ichi" 清代における村鎮の定期市. *Tōyō gakuhō* 23.2:1–52 (1936).

Kerr, George. *Formosa: A Licensed Revolution and the Home Rule Movement.* Honolulu: University of Hawaii Press, 1974.

———. *Okinawa: The History of an Island People.* Tokyo: Tuttle, 1964.

Kessler, Lawrence D. *Kang-hsi and the Consolidation of Ch'ing Rule, 1661–1684.* Chicago: University of Chicago Press, 1976.

King, Franklin H. *Farmers of Forty Centuries.* Rpt. New York: St. Martin's Press, 1988. First published in 1911.

Kinjō Isao 金城功. *Kindai Okinawa no tōgyō* 近代沖縄の糖業. Naha: Hirugisha, 1985.

Kiselev, Sergei V. *Derevnii Mongolskii goroda.* Moscow: Akademia nauk SSSR, 1965.

Kishimoto, Mio (Nakayama). "On the Fluctuation of the Price of Rice in the Chiang-nan Region during the First Half of the Ch'ing Period (1644–1795)." *Memoirs of the Research Department of the Tōyō Bunko* 37:55–90 (1979).

Knapp, Ronald, ed. *China's Island Frontier: Studies in the Historical Geography of Taiwan.* Honolulu: University of Hawaii Press, 1980.

Knight, G. R. "From Plantation to Padi Field." *Modern Asian Studies* 14.2:177–204 (1980).

Kō-a-in Kanton hakenin jimusho 興亞院廣東派遣員事務所. *Kanton shō nōson chōsa hōkoku* 廣東省農村調查報告. Guangdong: Nihon sōryōjikan, 1943.

Kong Qinglai 孔慶萊, ed. *Zhiwuxue da cidian* 植物學大辭典. Shanghai: Shangwu shudian, 1918.

Kriedte, Peter. *Peasants, Landlords, Merchants and Capitalists.* Cambridge: Cambridge University Press, 1983.

Krone, Rev. "A Notice of the San On District." *Transactions of the China Branch of the Royal Asiatic Society* as rpt. in *JHKBRAS* 7:104–137 (1967). First published in 1859.

Kuhn, Dieter. *Textile Technology: Spinning and Reeling.* Vol. 5, part 9, of Joseph Needham, gen. ed., *Science and Civilisation in China* (q.v.).

Kuhn, Philip. *Rebellion and Its Enemies in Late Imperial China.* Cambridge: Harvard University Press, 1970.

Kula, Witold. *An Economic Theory of the Feudal System.* London: New Left Books, 1976.

Kulp, Daniel. *Country Life in South China: The Sociology of Familism.* New York: Columbia University Press, 1925.

Kuo Ting-yee. "Internal Development and Modernization of Taiwan, 1683–1891," in Paul Sih, ed., *Taiwan in Modern Times* (q.v.).

Kuwabara, Jitsuzo. "On Pu Shou-keng, a Man of the Western Regions." *Memoirs of the Research Department of the Tōyō Bunko* 2:1–79 (1928), 7:1–104 (1935).

Kuwayama, Mikio. "Sogo-shosha and the Economic Development of Pre-War Japan." Ph.D. dissertation, University of Toronto, 1982.

Labat, Jean Baptiste. *Nouveau voyage aux isles de l'Amerique*. 2 vols. Paris: P. Husson, 1724.

Lach, Donald. *China in the Eyes of Europe in the Sixteenth Century*. Chicago: University of Chicago Press, 1968.

Lachmann, Richard. *From Manor to Market*. Madison: University of Wisconsin Press, 1987.

Lahiri, Latika. *Chinese Monks in India*. New Delhi: Motilal Banarsidass, 1986.

Lambley, Harry. "Lineage Feuding in Southern Fujian and Eastern Guangdong Under Qing Rule," in Jonathan N. Lipman and Stevan Harrell, eds., *Violence in China*. Albany: State University of New York Press, 1990.

———. "Subethnic Rivalry in the Ch'ing Period," in Emily Martin Ahern and Hill Gates, eds., *The Anthropology of Taiwanese Society* (q.v.).

Landes, David. *The Unbound Prometheus*. Cambridge: Cambridge University Press, 1969.

Lane, Frederic C. *Venice, a Maritime Republic*. Baltimore: Johns Hopkins University Press, 1973.

Langland, William. *Piers the Ploughman*. J. F. Goodridge, tr. Rpt. Harmondsworth, Eng.: Penguin Books, 1959. Comp. ca. 1390.

Larson, Henrietta. "A China Trader Turns Investor—A Biographical Chapter in American Business History." *Harvard Business Review* 12.2:345–358 (1933–1934).

Legarda y Fernandez, Benito F. "Foreign Trade, Economic Change and Entrepreneurship in Nineteenth Century Philippines." Ph.D. dissertation, Harvard University, 1955.

Legazpi, Miguel López de. "Notices," in Samuel Purchas, comp., *Purchas His Pilgrimes, Or, Relations of the religions observed in all ages and places discouered* (q.v.). First published in 1575.

Legendre, Charles W. *Amoy and the Island of Formosa*. Washington, D.C.: U.S. Government Printing Office, 1871.

Lei Yue-wai and Lei Hei-kit. "Report on a Steam Filature in Kwangtung." *Lingnam Agricultural Review* 3.2:109–50 (1926).

Lenin, V. I. *The Development of Capitalism in Russia*. Rpt. Moscow: Foreign Languages Publication House, 1974.

Leonard, Jane. *Wei Yuan and China's Rediscovery of the Maritime World*. Cambridge: Council on East Asian Studies, Harvard University, 1984.

Lethbridge, Henry. *Hong Kong, Stability and Change: A Collection of Essays*. Hong Kong: Oxford University Press, 1978.

Levine, David. *Reproducing Families: The Political Economy of English Population History*. Cambridge: Cambridge University Press, 1987.

———. "Proto-Industrialization and Demographic Upheaval," in L. P. Moch and G. D. Stark, eds., *Essays on the Family and Historical Change*. College Station: University of Texas at Arlington Press, 1983.

Li Ding 李鼎. "Li Zhangqing ji" 李長卿集, in Xie Guozhen, ed. and comp., *Mingdai shehui jingji shiliao xuanbian* (q.v.).

Li Donghua 李東華. "Song, Yuan shidai Quanzhou haiwai jiaotongde shengkuang" 宋元時代泉州海外交通的盛況, in *Zhongguo haiyang fazhanshi lunwenji* 中國海洋發展史論文集. Taipei: Zhongyang yanjiu yuan, 1984.

Li, Lillian. *China's Silk Trade*. Cambridge: Harvard University Press, 1981.

Li Min (Li Wenzhi) 黎民. "Qianlong xingke tiben zhong you guan nongye ziben zhuyi mengya de cailiao" 乾隆刑科题本中有关农业资本主义萌芽的材料. *Wenwu* 9:69–75 (1975).

Li Qiaoping 李喬苹. *Zhongguo huaxue shi* 中國化學史. Taipei: Taiwan shangwu yinshuguan, 1955.

Li Weishi 李威士. "Guangdong sheng cansiye de maoyi jiqi shuailuo" 广东省蚕丝业的贸易及其衰落. *Guangdong wenshi ziliao* 16:7–78 (1964).

Li Wenzhi 李文治. "Lun Ming Qing shidai de zongzu zhi" 论明清时代的宗族制. *Jingji yanjiu suo jikan* 4:278–338 (1983).

———. "Ming Qing shidai Zhongguo nongye ziben zhuyi mengya" 明清时代中国农业资本主义萌芽, in Li Wenzhi, Wei Jinyu and Jing Junjian, eds., *Ming Qing shidai de nongye ziben zhuyi mengya wenti* (q.v.).

———. "Lun Zhongguo dizhu jingjizhi yu nongye ziben zhuyi mengya" 论中国地主经济制与农业资本主义萌芽. *Zhongguo shehui kexue* 1:143–160 (1981).

———. "Qingdai qianqi de tudi zhanyou guanxi" 清代前期的土地占有关系. *Lishi yanjiu* 5:75–109 (1963).

Li Wenzhi 李文治, ed. *Zhongguo jindai nongyeshi ziliao* 中国近代农业史资料. 4 vols. Beijing: Sanlian shudian, 1957.

Li Wenzhi 李文治, Wei Jinyu 魏金玉, and Jing Junjian 经君健, eds. *Ming Qing shidai de nongye ziben zhuyi mengya wenti* 明清时代的农业资本主义萌芽问题. Beijing: Zhongguo shehui kexue chubanshe, 1983.

Li Zhihuan 李治寰. "Cong zhitangshi tan shimi yu bingtang" 从制糖史谈石蜜与冰糖. *Lishi yanjiu* 2:146–154 (1981).

Lian Heng 連横. *Taiwan tongshi* 臺灣通史. Rpt. *Taiwan shiji congshu*. Taipei: Yushi wenhua shiye gongsi, 1977. First published in 1916.

Liang Fangzhong 梁方仲. "Fanshu shuru Zhongguo kao" 番薯输入中国考, in *Liang Fangzhong jingji shi lunwenji bubian* 梁方仲经济史论文集补编. Henan: Zhongguo guji chubanshe, 1984.

———. *Zhongguo lidai hukou, diandi, tianfu tongji* 中国历代户口、佃地、田赋统计. Shanghai: Renmin chubanshe, 1980.

———. *The Single-Whip Method of Taxation in China*. Cambridge: East Asian Research Center, Harvard University, 1956.

Liang Jiabin 梁嘉彬. *Guangdong shisanhang kao* 廣東十三行考. Shanghai: Guoli bianyiguan, 1937.

Liang Jiamian 梁家勉. *Zhongguo zhetang shi zheng* 中国蔗糖史证. Stenciled mimeo. Guangzhou: Huanan nongxue yuan, 1980.

Liang Jiamian 梁家勉 and Qi Jingwen 戚经文. "Fanshu yin zhong kao" 番薯引种考. *Huanan nongxue yuan xuebao* 1.3:74–78 (1980).

Liang Qichao 梁啓超. *Yinbingshi wenji* 飲冰室文集, in *Yinbingshi heji* 飲冰室合集. Rpt. in *Zhongguo wenhuashi* 中國文化史. Shanghai: Zhonghua shuju, 1937.

Lien, Chan. "Taiwan in China's External Relations, 1683–1874," in Paul K. T. Sih, ed., *Taiwan in Modern Times* (q.v.).

Lilley, Samuel. "Technological Progress and the Industrial Revolution, 1700–1914," in Carlo M. Cippola, ed., *The Industrial Revolution* (q.v.).

Lin Datian 林达天. "Sanjiang Longquan xiedou de qianyin" 三江龙泉械斗的前因. *Xinhui wenshi ziliao xuanji* 13:39–40 (1984).

Lin Manhong 林滿紅. *Cha, tang, zhangnaoye yu wan Qing Taiwan jingji shehui zhi bianqian* 茶、糖、樟腦業與晚清台灣經濟社會之變遷. Taipei: Taiwan yinhang, 1978.

Lin Renchuan 林仁川. "Ming dai siren haishang maoyi shangren yu 'wokou'" 明代私人海上貿易商人與「倭寇」. *Zhongguo shi yanjiu* 1:1–19 (1981).

Lingnan congshu 嶺南叢述. Deng Chun 鄧淳, comp. Guangzhou: Yangzhuo shanfang cangban, 1830.

Lingnan yishu 嶺南遺書. Wu Chongyue 伍崇曜, comp. Guangzhou: Yueya tang, 1831.

Lingnan zaji 嶺南雜記. Wu Zhenfang 吳震方. Rpt. in *Congshu jicheng* (q.v.). First published ca. 1702–1705. Rpt. as the collectanea *Shuo ling* 說鈴, in 1810.

Lippit, Victor D. "The Development of Underdevelopment in China." *Modern China* 4.3:86–93 (1978).

Lippmann, von, Edmund O. *Geschichte des Zuckers*. Berlin: Julius Springer, 1929.

Liu, Paul K. C., and Hwang Kuo-shu. "Population Change and Economic Development in Mainland China since 1400," in Hou Chi-ming and Yu Tzong-shian, eds., *Modern Chinese Economic History Proceedings of the Conference on Modern Chinese Economic History* (q.v.).

Liu Shiji 劉石吉. "Ming Qing shidai Jiangnan diqu de zhuanye shizhen" 明清時代江南地區的專業市鎮. *Shihuo* 8.6:274–291, 8.7:326–337, 8.8:365–380 (1978).

Liu Tsui-jung. *Trade on the Han River and Its Impact on Economic Development, 1800–1911*. Taipei: Academia Sinica, 1980.

Liu Yongcheng. "The Handicraft Guilds in Suzhou during the Qing Dynasty." *Chinese Studies in History, Translations of Selected Studies* (1982).

——— 刘永成. "Qianlong xingke tiben yu Qingdai qianqi nongcun shehui jingji yanjiu" 乾隆刑科题本与清代前期农村社会经济研究. *Lishi dang-an* 2:87–92 (1981).

———. "Qingdai qianqi diannong kangzu touzheng de xinfazhan" 清代前期佃农抗租斗争的新发展, in *Qingshi luncong* (q.v.), vol. 1.

———. "Shilun Qingdai Suzhou shougongye hanghui" 試論清代蘇州手工業行會. *Lishi yanjiu* 11:21–46 (1959).

Liubu chufen zeli 六部處分則例. Beijing: (*Qinding*) Jindong shu hang, 1877.

Lo Hsiang-lin. *Hong Kong and Its External Communications before 1842*. Hong Kong: Institute of Chinese Culture, 1963.

Lo Jung-pang. "The Emergence of China as a Sea Power during the Late Sung and the Early Yuan Periods." *Far Eastern Quarterly* 14.4:489–503 (1955).

Lock, C. G. W.; B. E. R. Newlands; and J. A. R. Newlands. *Sugar: A Handbook for Planters and Refiners*. London: E. & F. N. Spoon, 1888.

Lockhart, James. *Spanish Peru*. Madison: University of Wisconsin Press, 1994.

López Piñero, José M.; Thomas F. Glick; Víctor Navarro Brotóns; and Eugenio Portela Marco, eds., *Diccionario histórico de la ciencia moderna en España*. 2 vols. Barcelona: Ediciones Península, 1983.

López Segera, Francisco. "Cuba: Dependence, Plantation Economy and Social Classes, 1762–1902," in Manuel Moreno Fraginals, Frank Moya Pons, and Stanley Engerman, eds., *Between Slavery and Free Labor* (q.v.).

Lowe, Hsing-yuan. *The Adventures of Wu: The Life Cycle of a Peking Man*. Rpt. Princeton: Princeton University Press, 1983. First published in 1940.

Lu Gwei-djen and Joseph Needham. "A Contribution to Chinese Dietetics." *ISIS* 42:13–20 (1951).

Lu Nien-tsing, ed. *Statistics of Crop Cultivation Survey in Taiwan*. Taipei: Taiwan tudi yinhang, 1962.

Lu Yu. *Ru Shu ji, South China in the Twelfth Century*, Chang Chun-shu and Joan Smythe, trs. and annots. Hong Kong: Chinese University Press, 1977. Written ca. 1170.

Lu Yu. *The Classic of Tea* (*Cha jing*). Francis Ross Carpenter, tr. Boston: Little Brown and Co., 1974. Written ca. late eighth century.

Luk, Bernard H. K. 陸鴻基, and David Faure 科大衛. "Xiangdongcun Dushi diqi jianjie" 向東村杜氏地契簡介. *JCICUHK* 11:141–161 (1978).

Ma Huan. *The Overall Survey of the Ocean's Shores* (*Yingyai shenglan*). J. V. G. Mills, tr. Cambridge: Cambridge University Press, 1970. Written in 1433.

Ma Tai-loi. "The Authenticity of the *Nanfang ts'ao mu zhuang*." *TP* 64:218–252 (1978).

Macartney, George. *An Embassy to China, Being the Journal Kept by Lord Macartney during his Embassy to the Emperor Ch'ien-lung, 1793–1794*. J. L. Cranmer-Byng, ed. Rpt. Hamden, Conn.: Archon Books, 1963. First published in 1807.

Macauley, Melissa A. "Civil and Uncivil Disputes in Southeast Coastal China, 1723– 1820," in Kathryn Bernhardt and Philip Huang, eds., *Civil Law in Qing and Republican China* (q.v.).

McCloskey, Donald N. "The Economics of Choice: Neoclassical Supply and Demand," in Thomas G. Rawski et al., eds., *Economics and the Historian* (q.v.).

McDermott, Joseph. "Bondservants in the T'ai-hu Basin during the Late Ming: A Case of Mistaken Identities." *JAS* 40:675–702 (1981).

MacGowan, D. J. *Sidelights on Chinese Life*. London: Kegan Paul, 1907.

———. "Chinese Guilds or Chambers of Commerce and Trade Unions." *Journal of the North China Branch of the Royal Asiatic Society*, n.s. 21:133–192 (1886).

Maeda Katsutarō 前田勝太郎. "Shindai no Kanton ni okeru nōmin no tōsō no kiban" 清代の広東における農民の闘争の其盤. *Tōyō gakuhō* 51.4: 457–494 (1969).

Majumdar, R. C. "Medicine," in D. M. Bose et al., eds., *A Concise History of Science in India* (q.v.).

Mancall, Mark. "The Ch'ing Tribute System: An Interpretive Essay," in John K. Fairbank, ed., *The Chinese World Order* (q.v.).

Mann, Susan. *Local Merchants and the Chinese Bureaucracy, 1750–1950*. Stanford: Stanford University Press, 1987.

Markham, Gervase. *The English Hus-Wife Contayning, the inward and outward vertues which ought to be in a compleate woman*. Michael R. Best, ed. Rpt. Montreal: McGill Queen's University Press, 1994. First published in 1615.

Marks, Robert. "Rice Prices, Food Supply and Market Structure in Eighteenth Century South China." *Late Imperial China* 12.2:64–116 (1991).

———. *Rural Revolution in South China: Peasants and the Making of History in Haifeng County*. Madison: University of Wisconsin Press, 1984.

Marriner, Sheila, and Francis Hyde. *The Senior John Samuel Swire*. Liverpool: Liverpool University Press, 1967.

Marshall, P. J. "Private British Trade in the Indian Ocean before 1800," in Ashin K. Das Gupta and Michael N. Pearson, eds., *India and the Indian Ocean* (q.v.).

———. *East Indian Fortunes*. Oxford: Oxford University Press, 1976.

Marx, Karl. *Capital*. Vol. 1. Ben Fowles, tr. Rpt. New York: Vintage Books, 1977. First published in 1867.

———. *Capital*. Vol. 3. David Fernbach, tr. Rpt. New York: Vintage Books, 1981. First published 1894.

———. *Grundrisse*. Martin Nicolaus, tr. Rpt. New York: First Vintage Books, 1973. First published in 1939.

Masefield, Geoffrey. *A Short History of Agriculture in the British Colonies*. New York: Greenwood Press, 1950.

Masui Tsuneo 增井經夫. "Kanton no kyoshi" 広東の墟市. *Tōa ronsō* 4:263–283 (1941).

Matsuda Yoshirō 松田吉郎. "Minmatsu Shinsho Kanton Jukō deruta no saden kaihatsu to kyōshin shihai no keisei katei" 明末清初広東珠江デルタの沙田開発と郷紳支配の形成過程. *Shakai keizai shigaku* 46.6:55–81 (1981).

Matsushita Shirō 松下四郎. *Kinsei amami no shihai to shakai* 近世奄美の支配と社会. Tokyo: Daicihi shobō, 1983.

Mauro, Frédéric. *Le Portugal et l'Atlantique au XVIIe siècle (1570–1670)*. Paris: Service d'Editions de Vente des Publication Educations National, 1960.

May, Ernest R., and John K. Fairbank, eds. *America's China Trade in Historical Perspective*. Cambridge: Harvard University Press, 1986.

Mayers, William F., et al. *The Treaty Ports of China and Japan*. London: Trubner and Co., 1867.

Mazumdar, Sucheta (Mu Sujie) 穆素洁. "Shangpinxing nongye yu bianhuade xiandu: 1644–1834 nian Zhujiang sanjiaozhou de ganzhe zhongzhiye" 商品性农业与变化的限度: 1644–1834 年珠江三角洲的甘蔗种植业. *Guangdong shehui kexue* 1.1:44–51 (1989).

———. "A History of the Sugar Industry in China: The Political Economy of a Cash Crop in Guangdong, 1644–1834." Ph.D. dissertation, UCLA, 1984.

———. "Qaraqorum: The Capital of the Mongols." M.A. field paper, UCLA, 1977.

Mazzaoui, Maureen Fennell. *The Italian Cotton Industry in the Later Middle Ages, 1100–1600*. Cambridge: Cambridge University Press, 1981.

Medick, Hans. "The Proto-Industrial Family." *Social History* 1.3:291–315 (1976).

Meilink-Roelofz, M. A. P. *Asian Trade and European Influence*. The Hague: Nijhoff, 1962.

Meishu congshu 美術叢書. Shanghai: Shenzhou guoguangshe, 1928–1937.

Meng liang lu 夢梁錄. Wu Zimu 吳自牧. Rpt. Taipei: Xuesheng shuju, 1966. First published in 1275.

Meng Siming 蒙思明. *Yuandai shehui jieji zhidu* 元代社會階級制度. Rpt. Hong Kong: Longmen shudian, 1967. First published in 1938.

Mennell, Stephen. *All Manners of Food*. New York: Basil Blackwell, 1985.

Meskill, Johanna. *A Chinese Pioneer Family*. Princeton: Princeton University Press, 1979.

Meskill, John. *Ch'oe Pu's Diary: A Record of Drifting across the Sea*. Tucson: University of Arizona Press, 1964.

Metzger, Thomas A. "On the Historical Roots of Economic Modernization in China," in Hou Chi-ming and Yu Tzong-shian, eds., *Modern Chinese Economic History* (q.v.).

Milburn, William. *Oriental Commerce*. London: Black, Parry and Co., 1813.

Min bu shu 閩部疏. Wang Shimao 王世懋. Rpt. in *Congshu jicheng* (q.v.). First published in 1580.

Minchinson, Walter. "Patterns of Demand, 1750–1914," in Carlo M. Cipolla, ed., *The Industrial Revolution* (q.v.).

Mingji yiwen 明季遺聞. Zou Yi 鄒漪. Rpt. in *Taiwan wenxian congkan* (q.v.). Preface dated 1657.

Ming Qing Foshan beike wenxian jingji ziliao 明清佛山碑刻文献经济资料. Guangdong sheng shehui kexue yuan, Lishi yanjiusuo 广东省社会科学院历史研究所 and Zhongshan daxue, Lishixi 中山大学历史系, eds. Guangzhou: Guangdong renmin chubanshe, 1987.

Ming Qing qiyue 明清契約. Manuscript collection. Guangdong shehui kexue yuan, Guangzhou.

Ming Qing shiliao ding bian 明清史料丁編. Series D. Taipei: Zhongyang yanjiu yuan, 1972.

Ming shi shihuozhi 明史食貨志. Li Xun 李洵, annot. Beijing: Zhonghua shuju, 1982.

Ming shilu, Chengzu 明實錄成祖. Yao Guangxiao 姚廣孝 et al., eds. Rpt. Zhongyang yanjiu yuan, 1940. Comp. in 1430.

Ming shilu, Taizu 明實錄太祖. Zhongyang yanjiu yuan, Lishi yuyan yanjiu suo 中央研究院歷史語言研究所, ed. Vol. 6. Rpt. Taipei: Zhongyang yanjiu yuan, 1962–1967. Comp. in 1418.

Mingyi bielu 名醫別錄. Tao Hongjing 陶弘景. Rpt. in *Congshu jicheng* (q.v.). Comp. ca. sixth century.

Mintz, Sidney. *Sweetness and Power*. New York: Viking, 1985.

———. *Caribbean Transformation*. Baltimore: Johns Hopkins University Press, 1984.

———. "Was the Plantation Slave a Proletarian?" *Review: A Journal of the Fernand Braudel Center* 2.1:81–98 (1978).

Miyazaki Ichisada 宮崎市定. "Mindai So-Shō chihō no shidaifu minshū" 明代蘇松 地方の士大夫民衆. *Shirin* 37:1–33 (1954).

———. "Shinsho bōeki ni kansuru ichi shiryō" 清初貿易に関する一資料. *Tōa keizai kenkyū* 25.6:426–446 (1941).

Monier-Williams, M. *Sanskrit-English Dictionary*. Rpt. Delhi: Motilal Banarsidass, 1970. First published in 1899.

Moreland, William. *From Akbar to Aurangzeb: A Study in Indian Economic History*. Rpt. Delhi: Atma Ram, 1962. First published in 1923.

Moreno Fraginals, Manuel. "Plantations in the Caribbean: Cuba, Puerto Rico and the Dominican Republic in the Late Nineteenth Century," in Manuel Moreno Fraginals, Frank Moya Pons, and Stanley Engerman, eds., *Between Slavery and Free Labor* (q.v.).

———. *The Sugarmill: The Socioeconomic Complex of Sugar in Cuba*. New York: Monthly Review Press, 1976.

Moreno Fraginals, Manuel, Frank Moya Pons, and Stanley Engerman, eds. *Between Slavery and Free Labor*. Baltimore: Johns Hopkins University Press, 1985.

Mori Katsumi. "The Beginning of Overseas Advance of Japanese Merchant Ships." *Acta Asiatica* 23:1–24 (1972).

Morita Akira 森田明. *Shindai suirishi kenkyū* 清代水利史研究. Tokyo: Aki shobo, 1974.

Morohashi Tetsuji 諸橋轍次. *Dai kanwa jiten* 大漢和典. 13 vols. Tokyo: Taishukan, 1955–1960.

Morse, Hosea B. *The Chronicles of the East India Company Trading to China, 1635–1834*. 5 vols. Oxford: Oxford University Press, 1926–1929.

———. *The Trade and Administration of China*. New York: Kelly and Walsh, 1921.

———. *The International Relations of the Chinese Empire*, vol. 1, *The Period of Conflict, 1834–1860*. Shanghai: Longmans, Green and Co., 1910.

———. *The Gilds of China with an Account of the Gild Merchant or Cohong of Canton*. London: Longmans, Green, 1909.

Mote, Frederick. "Yuan and Ming," in K. C. Chang, ed., *Food in Chinese Culture* (q.v.).

Moulder, Francis. *China, Japan and the Modern World Economy*. Cambridge: Cambridge University Press, 1977.

Mousnier, Roland. *Peasant Uprisings in the Seventeenth Century: France, Russia and China*. Brian Pearce, tr. New York: Harper and Row, 1970.

Mukherjee, Rudrangshu. "Trade and Empire in Awadh." *Past and Present* 94:85–102 (1982).

Mu mian pu 木棉譜. Chu Hua 褚華. Rpt. in *Congshu jicheng* (q.v.). First published ca. 1800.

Mundy, Peter. *Travels of Peter Mundy in Europe and Asia, 1608–1667*. R. C. Temple and L. Anstey, eds. 5 vols. London: Hakluyt Society Publications, 1919.

Muramatsu Yuji. "A Documentary Study of Chinese Landlordism in Late Ch'ing and Early Republican Kiangnan." *Bulletin of the School of Oriental and African Studies* 29.3:566–599 (1966).

Murphey, Rhoads. *The Outsiders: The Western Experience in India and China*. Ann Arbor: University of Michigan, Center for Chinese Studies, 1977.

———. "The Treaty Ports and China's Modernization," in Mark Elvin and G. William Skinner, eds., *The Chinese City between Two Worlds* (q.v.).

Murray, Diane. *Fields from the Sea*. Stanford: Stanford University Press, 1987.

Murray, Laura May Kaplan. "New World Food Crops in China: Farms Food and Families in the Wei River Valley, 1650–1910." Ph.D. dissertation, University of Pennsylvania, 1985.

Myers, Ramon. "How Did the Modern Chinese Economy Develop—A Review Article." *JAS* 50.3:604–628 (1991).

———. "Customary Law, Markets and Resource Transactions in Late Imperial China," in R. L. Ransom, R. Sutch, and G. M. Walton, eds., *Explorations in the New Economic History*. New York: Academic Press, 1982.

———. *The Chinese Economy: Past and Present*. Belmont, Calif.: Wadsworth, 1980.

———. "The 'Sprouts of Capitalism' in Agricultural Development during the Mid-Ch'ing Period." *Ch'ing-shih Wen-t'i* 3.6:84–89 (1976).

———. "Taiwan's Agrarian Economy under Japanese Rule." *JCICUHK* 7.2:451–475 (1974).

———. "Taiwan under Ch'ing Imperial Rule, 1684–1895." *JCICUHK* 5.2:373–409 (1972).

———. "Agrarian Policy and Agricultural Transformation: Mainland China and Taiwan, 1895–1945." *JCICUHK* 3.2:521–542 (1970).

———. *The Chinese Peasant Economy, Agricultural Development in Hopei and Shandong, 1890–1949*. Cambridge: Harvard University Press, 1970.

Myers, Ramon, and (Chang) Chen Fu-mei. "Rural Production and Distribution in Late Imperial China." *Chinese Studies* 3.2:657–706 (1985).

———. "Customary Law and the Economic Growth of China during the Ch'ing Period." *Ch'ing-shih wen-ti* 3.5:1–32 (1976).

Myers, Wykeham. *British Consular Report for Tainan, 1890*. In J. W. Davidson, *The Island of Formosa: History, People, Resources and Commercial Prospects* (q.v.).

Nagazumi Yōko 永積洋子. *Tōsen yushutsu nyuhin sūryō ichiran, 1637 nen–1833 nen* 唐船 輸出 品 数量一覽. Tokyo: Sōbunsha, 1987.

Nakayama, Shigeru. "Joseph Needham, Organic Philosopher," in Shigeru Nakayama and Nathan Sivin, eds., *Chinese Science: Explorations of an Ancient Tradition* (q.v.).

Nakayama, Shigeru, and Nathan Sivin, eds. *Chinese Science: Explorations of an Ancient Tradition*. Cambridge: M. I. T. Press, 1973.

Nan Qi 南棲. "Taiwan Zhengshi wushang zhi yanjiu" 臺灣鄭氏五商之研究. *Taiwan yanjiu congkan* 90:43–51 (1966).

Nanfang caomu zhuang 南方草木狀. Attrib. to Ji Han 嵇含. Rpt. in *Congshu jicheng* (q.v.). Comp. in ca. 304.

Nan-fang ts'ao-mu chuang: A Fourth Century Flora of Southeast Asia. Li Hui-lin, tr. Hong Kong: Chinese University Press, 1979.

Nanhai xianzhi 南海縣志. Zhu Tian 柱坫, comp. 1911.

Nanhai Xuezheng Huangshi jiapu jieben 南海學正黃氏家譜節本. Private printing, 1910.

Nanjing daxue, Lishixi, Zhongguo gudaishi jiaoyanjiushi 南京大学历史系中国古代史教研究室. *Zhongguo ziben zhuyi mengya wenti taolunji* 中国资本主义萌芽问题讨论集. 2 vols. Beijing: Sanlian shudian, 1960.

Nanyue biji 南越筆記. Li Diaoyuan 李調元. Rpt. in *Congshu jicheng* (q.v.). First published in 1778.

Naquin, Susan. *Millenarian Rebellion in China*. New Haven: Yale University Press, 1976.

Naquin, Susan, and Evelyn Rawski. *Chinese Society in the Eighteenth Century*. New Haven: Yale University Press, 1987.

Needham, Joseph. *The Grand Titration: Science and Society in East and West*. London: Allen and Unwin, 1969.

———. *Mechanical Engineering*. Vol. 4, part 2, of Joseph Needham, gen. ed., *Science and Civilisation in China* (q.v.).

Needham, Joseph, gen. ed. *Science and Civilisation in China*. Cambridge: Cambridge University Press, 1954–

Needham, Joseph; Lu Gwei-djen; and Huang Hsing-Tsung. *Biology and Biological Technology: Botany, Science and Civilisation in China*. Vol. 6, part 1, of Joseph Needham, gen. ed., *Science and Civilization in China* (q.v.).

Negishi Benji 根岸勉治. *Minami Shina nōgyō keizairon* 南支那農業經濟論. Taipei: Noda shobō, 1940.

Negishi Tadashi 根岸佶. *Chūgoku no girudo* 中国のギルド. Tokyo: Nippon hyōron shinsha, 1953.

Ng, Alice N. H.; Bernard H. K. Luk; and David Faure. "Notes and Queries." *JHKBRAS* 19:192–194 (1979).

Ng Chin-keong. "The Case of Ch'en I-lao: Maritime Trade and Overseas Chinese in Ch'ing Policies, 1717–1754," in Roderich Ptak and Dietmar Rothermund, eds., *Emporia, Commodities and Entrepreneurs in Asian Maritime Trade, C 1400–1750* (q.v.).

———. *Trade and Society: The Amoy Network on the China Coast, 1683–1735.* Singapore: Singapore University Press, 1983.

Ng, Peter Y. L., and Hugh Baker, trs. *New Peace County: A Chinese Gazetteer of the Hong Kong Region.* Hong Kong: Hong Kong University Press, 1983.

Niida Noboru. "State Power and Serfdom in China." *Acta Asiatica* 8:65–73 (1965).

——— 仁井田陞. Chūgoku hōsei shi 中国法制史. Iwanami zensho series. Tokyo: Iwanami shoten, 1952.

———. *Chūgoku no nōson kazoku* 中国の農村家族. Tokyo: Tōkyō daigaku, Tōyō bunka kenkyūjo, 1952.

———. "The Industrial and Commercial Guilds of Peking and Religion and Fellow Countrymanship as Elements of Their Coherence." *Folklore Studies* 9:179–206 (1950).

———. "Shina kinsei no ichiden ryōshu kankō to sono seiritsu" 支那近世の一田兩主慣行と其成立. *Hōgaku kyōkai zasshi* 64.3:129–154, 64.4:241–261 (1946).

———. *Tō Sō hōritsu bunka no kenkyū* 唐宋法律文書の研究. Tokyo: Tōhō bunka gakuin, Tokyo kenkyūjo, 1937.

Nishijima Sadao 西嶋定生. *Chūgoku keizai shi kenkyū* 中国経済史研究. Tokyo: Tōkyō daigaku shuppankai, 1966.

———. "Shina shoki mengyō no seiritsu to sono kōzō" 支那初期棉業の成立とその構造. *Orientalica* 2:88–141 (1949).

———. "Shina shoki mengyō shijō no kōsatsu" 支那初期棉業市場の考察. *Tōyō gakuhō* 31.2:262–288 (1947).

Nishikawa Kikuko 西川喜久子. "Shindai Shukō karyū shaden ni tsuite" 清代珠江下流域沙田について. *Tōyō gakuhō* 63.1–2:93–135 (1981).

Nongsang jiyao 農桑輯要. Rpt. in *Congshu jicheng* (q.v.). First published in 1286.

Nongsang yishi cuoyao 農桑衣食撮要. Lu Mingshan 魯明善, comp. Rpt. in *Congshu jicheng* (q.v.). First published ca. 1314.

Nongshu 農書. Chen Fu 陳旉, comp. Rpt. in *Congshu jicheng* (q.v.). First published in 1149.

Nongshu 農書. Wang Zhen 王禎, comp. Rpt. Beijing: Zhonghua shuju, 1975. First published in 1313.

Nongzheng quanshu 農正全書. Xu Guangqi 徐光啓. Xibei nongxue yuan, Gunongshu yanjiusuo 西北農學院古農書研究所, annot. Shanghai: Guji chubanshe, 1979. First published in 1639.

North China Herald. 1870.

North, Douglass. "Markets and Other Allocation Systems in History: The Challenge of Karl Polanyi." *Journal of European Economic History* 6.3:703–716 (1977).

Oba Osamu. "Nagasaki and the Importation of Chinese Books to Japan in the Edo Period." *Sino-Japanese Studies Newsletter* 1.1:24–32 (1988).

Okamatsu Santaro. *Provisional Report on Investigations of Laws and Customs in the Island of Formosa*. Rpt. Taipei: Chengwen, 1971. First published in 1900.

"On the Tenure and Transfer of Real Property in China and the Mode of Succession To Land," in George Jamieson et al., "Tenure of Land in China and the Condition of the Rural Population" (q.v.). Report dated 1868.

Osbeck, Pehr. *A Voyage to China and the East Indies, by Peter Osbeck. Together with A Voyage to Seratte by Olof Toreen, and An Account of the Chinese Husbandry by Captain Charles Gustavus Eckeberg*. J. R. Forester, tr., from the German. London: B. White, 1771. First published in 1757.

Ota, K. "Manufacture of Sugar in Japan." *Transactions of the Asiatic Society of Japan* 8:462–472 (1880).

Oxford English Dictionary. Philological Society. Oxford: Oxford University Press, 1933– .

Oyama Masaaki. "Large Landownership in the Jiangnan Delta Region During the Late Ming–Early Qing Period," Christian Daniels, tr., in Linda Grove and Christian Daniels, eds., *State and Society in China: Japanese Perspectives on Ming Qing Social and Economic History* (q.v.).

Palmer, Michael J. E. "The Surface-Subsoil Form of Divided Ownership in Late Imperial China: Some Examples from the New Territories of Hong Kong." *Modern Asian Studies* 22.1:1–119 (1987).

Pang shi jiaxun 龐氏家訓. Pang Shangpeng 龐尚鵬. Rpt. in *Lingnan gui shu* 嶺南貴書. Guangzhou: n.p., 1849. First publ. 1572.

Panikkar, Kavalam M. *Asia and Western Dominance: A Survey of the Vasco da Gama Epoch of Asian History*. London: Allen and Unwin, 1953.

Panyu xianzhi 番禺縣志. Li Futai 李福泰, ed. Rpt. Taipei: Chengwen chubanshe, 1967. Comp. in 1871.

Parker, E. H. *Up the Yangtze*. Shanghai: Kelly and Walsh, 1899.

Parker, Geoffrey, and Lesley Smith, eds. *The General Crisis of the Seventeenth Century*. London: Routledge and Kegan Paul, 1978.

Parsons, James. *Peasant Rebellions of the Late Ming Dynasty*. Tucson: University of Arizona Press, 1970.

Paske-Smith, M. T. "The Japanese Trade and Residence in the Philippines before and during the Spanish Occupation." *Transactions of the Asiatic Society of Japan* 42.2:683–710 (1914).

Pasternak, Burton. *Guests in the Dragon: Social Demography of a Chinese District, 1895–1946*. New York: Columbia University Press, 1983.
———. "Economics and Ecology," in Emily Ahern and Hill Gates, eds., *The Anthropology of Taiwanese Society* (q.v.).
———. *Kinship and Community in Two Chinese Villages*. Stanford: Stanford University Press, 1972.
———. "The Role of the Frontier in Chinese Lineage Development." *JAS* 28.3:551–561 (1969).
———. "Agnatic Atrophy in a Formosan Village." *American Anthropologist* 70:93–96 (1968).
Patil, P. C. *Sugarcane Mills and Small Power Crushers in the Bombay Presidency*. Bombay Bulletin, no. 139. Poona: Department of Agriculture, 1927.
Patnaik, Utsa. "Neo-Populism and Marxism: The Chyanovian View of the Agrarian Question and Its Fundamental Fallacy." *Journal of Peasant Studies* 6.4:375–420 (1979).
Pearson, Michael N. "India and the Indian Ocean in the Sixteenth Century," in Ashin Das Gupta and Michael N. Pearson, eds., *India and the Indian Ocean, 1500–1800* (q.v.).
Pelliot Dunhuang Collection. Manuscript no. P3303. Bibliothèque National.
Pelliot, Paul. *Notes on Marco Polo*. 2 vols. Paris: Imprimerie National, 1959.
———. "Deux Itinéraires de Chine en Inde a la fin du VIIIe Siècle." *Bulletin de l'Ecole Française d'Extrème Orient* 4:131–413 (1904).
Peng Zeyi 彭泽益. "Guangzhou shisan hang xutan" 广州十三行续探. *Lishi yanjiu* 4:110–125 (1981).
———. "Qingdai Guangdong yanghang zhidu de qiyuan" 清代广东洋行制度的 起源. *Lishi yanjiu* 1:1–21 (1957).
Peng Zeyi 彭泽益, ed. *Zhongguo jindai shougongye shi ziliao* 中国近代手工业史资料. 4 vols. Beijing: Zhonghua shuju, 1957.
Perdue, Peter. *Exhausting the Earth: State and Peasant in Hunan, 1500–1850*. Cambridge: Council on East Asian Studies, Harvard University 1987.
Perkins, Dwight. "Discussion of Liu-Hwang and Fei-Liu," in Hou Chi-ming and Yu Tzong-shian, eds., *Modern Chinese Economic History* (q.v.).
———. *Agricultural Development in China, 1368–1968*. Chicago: University of Chicago Press, 1969.
Perkins, Dwight, ed. *China's Modern Economy in Historical Perspective*. Stanford: Stanford University Press, 1975.
Perkins, Thomas Handasyd. Papers. Massachusetts Historical Society, Boston.
Perry, Elizabeth J. *Rebels and Revolutionaries in North China*. Stanford: Stanford University Press, 1980.

Perry, Lily. *Medicinal Plants of East and Southeast Asia.* Cambridge: Cambridge University Press, 1980.

Phipps, John. *A Practical Treatise on the China and Eastern Trade.* Calcutta: Baptist Mission Press, 1835.

Pirenne, Henri. *Economic and Social History of Medieval Europe.* London: Kegan Paul, Trench, Trubner, 1936.

Pires, Tomé. *The Suma Oriental of Tomé Pires: An Account of the East, From the Red Sea to Japan, Written in Malacca and India in 1512–1515.* Armando Cortesao, ed. and tr. Hakluyt Society Publications, vols. 89–90. London: 1944.

Pittenger, P. S. *Sugars and Sugar Derivatives in Pharmacy.* Scientific Report Series no. 5. New York: Sugar Research Foundation, 1947.

Platts, John T. *A Dictionary of Urdu, Classical Hindi and English.* London: W. H. Allen, 1884 .

Polanyi, Karl; C. M. Arensberg; and H. W. Pearson. *Trade and Market in Early Empires.* Glencoe, N.Y.: Free Press, 1957.

Polo, Marco. *The Book of Ser Marco Polo.* Henry Yule, tr. and annot. Published in 1871, 3rd. ed. rev. by Henri Cordier. 2 vols. London: John Murray, 1903.

———. *The Description of the World.* A. C. Moule and P. Pelliot, eds. and trs. 2 vols. London: George Routledge and Sons, 1938.

Pomet, Pierre. *Histoire générale des drogues.* Paris: J. B. Loyson, 1694.

Popkin, Samuel L. *The Rational Peasant: The Political Economy of Rural Society in Vietnam.* Berkeley: University of California Press, 1979.

Potter, Jack. "Land and Lineage in Traditonal China," in Maurice Freedman, ed., *Family and Kinship in Chinese Society* (q.v).

———. *Capitalism and the Chinese Peasant: Social and Economic Change in a Hong Kong Village.* Berkeley: University of California Press, 1968.

Pottinger, Henry. *Travels in Beloochistan and Sinde.* Rpt. Karachi: Indus Publications, 1976. First published in 1816.

Prakash, Om. *Economy and Food in Ancient India.* Rpt. Delhi: Bharatiya Vidya Prakashan, 1987. First published in 1953.

———. "The Dutch East India Company in the Trade of the Indian Ocean," in Ashin Das Gupta and Michael N. Pearson, eds., *India and the Indian Ocean, 1500–1800* (q.v.).

———. *The Dutch East India Company and the Economy of Bengal, 1630–1720.* Princeton: Princeton University Press, 1985.

Prinsen Geerligs, Hendrik Coenraad. *Cane Sugar and Its Manufacture.* London: Norman Rodger, 1924.

———. *The World's Cane Sugar Industry, Past and Present.* Manchester: Norman Rodger, 1912.

Pritchard, E. H. "Private Trade between England and China in the Eighteenth Century (1680–1833)." *Journal of the Economic and Social History of the Orient* 1.1:108–256 (1957).

Ptak, Roderich, and Dietmar Rothermund, eds. *Emporia, Commodities and Entrepreneurs in Asian Maritime Trade, C 1400–1750*. Stuttgart: Franz Steiner Verlag, 1991.

Purchas, Samuel, comp. *Purchas His Pilgrimes: or, Hakluytus Posthumus: contayning a history of the world in sea voyages and lande travells by Englishman and others*. Rpt. Glasgow: James MacLehose and Sons, 1905–1907. First published in 1625.

———, comp. *Purchas His Pilgrimes, Or, Relations of the religions observed in all ages and places discouered . . . contianeth a theologicall and geographicall historie of Asia, Africa and America with the islands adiacent*. Rpt. Glasgow: James MacLehose and Sons, 1905–1907. First published in 1613.

Purseglove, J. W. *Tropical Crops: Monocotyledons*. 2 vols. New York: Halstead Press Division, 1972.

Qimin yaoshu 齊民要術. Jia Sixie 賈思勰. Rpt. in *Sibu congkan* (q.v.). Comp. ca. 535.

Qimin yaoshu jinshi 齊民要術今釋. Shi Shenghan 石聲漢, ed. and annot. Beijing: Kexue qubanshe, 1957.

Qin Jisi 金济思. "Shiqi shiji mo dao shijiu shiji chuqi Zhongguo shehui de ji zhong shougongye he shougongchang de shiliao" 十七世纪末到十九世纪初期中国社会的几种手工业和手工场的史料. *Jingji yanjiu* 5:105–107 (1955).

Qingdai dang'an shiliao congbian 清代檔案史料叢編. No. 1 Historical Archives, ed. Beijing: Zhonghua shuju, 1980.

Qingshi luncong 清史論叢. Zhongguo shehui kexueyuan, Lishi yanjiusuo, Qingshi yanjiushi 中国社会科学院历史研究所清史研究室, ed. 4 vols. Beijing: Zhonghua shuju, 1979–1982.

Qing shilu jingji ziliao jiyao 清實錄經濟資料輯要. Nankai daxue, Lishixi 南開大學歷史系, comp. Beijing: Zhonghua shuju, 1959.

Ramelli, Agostino. *The Various and Ingenious Machines of Agostino Ramelli (1588)*. Martha Teach Gnudi and Eugene S. Ferguson, trs. and annots. Baltimore: Johns Hopkins Press, 1976.

Ramos Mattei, Andrés A. "Technical Innovations and Social Change in the Sugar Industry of Puerto Rico, 1870–1880," in Manuel Moreno Franginals, Frank Moya Pons, and Stanley Engerman, eds., *Between Slavery and Free Labor* (q.v.)

Ratekin, Mervyn. "The Early Sugar Industry in Española." *Hispanic American Historical Review* 34.1:1–19 (1954).

Rawski, Evelyn Sakakida. *Education and Popular Literacy in Ch'ing China*. Ann Arbor: University of Michigan Press, 1979.

———. *Agricultural Change and the Peasant Economy of South China*. Cambridge: Harvard University Press, 1972.

Rawski, Thomas. *Economic Growth in Prewar China*. Berkeley: University of California Press, 1989.

Rawski, Thomas G., et al., eds., *Economics and the Historian*. Berkeley: University of California Press, 1996.

Ray, Haraprasad. "Bengal's Textile Products Involved in Ming Trade during Cheng Ho's Voyages to the Indian Ocean and Identification of the Hitherto Undeciphered Textiles," in Roderich Ptak and Dietmar Rothermund, eds., *Emporia, Commodities and Entrepreneurs in Asian Maritime Trade, C 1400–1750* (q.v.).

Ray, Himanshu. *The Winds of Change: Buddhism and the Maritime Links of Early South Asia*. Delhi: Oxford University Press, 1994.

Raychaudhuri, S. P.; L. Gopal; and B. V. Subbarayappa. "Agriculture," in D. M. Bose, ed., *A Concise History of Science in India* (q.v.).

Raychaudhuri, Tapan, and Irfan Habib, eds. *The Cambridge Economic History of India, 1200–1750*. Vol. 1. Cambridge: Cambridge University Press, 1982.

Rechung Rinpoche, ed. and tr. *Tibetan Medicine*. Berkeley: University of California Press, 1976.

Reesse, J. J. *De suikerhandle van Amsterdam van het begin der 17de eeuw tot 1813*. Haarlem: J. L. E. I. Kleynenberg, 1908.

Reid, Anthony. *Southeast Asia in the Age of Commerce, 1450–1680*. New Haven: Yale University Press, 1988.

Reischauer, Edwin O. *Ennin's Diary: The Record of a Pilgrimage to China in Search of the Law*. New York: Ronald Press, 1955.

———. *Ennin's Travels in Tang China*. New York: Ronald Press, 1955.

Renou, Louis, and Jean Filliozat. *L'Inde classique*. Hanoi: Ecole Française d'Extrème Orient, 1953.

Restivo, Sal P. "Joseph Needham and the Comparative Sociology of Chinese and Modern Science." *Research in Sociology of Knowledge, Sciences and Art* 2:25–51 (1979).

Rhoads, Edward J. M. "Merchant Associations in Canton, 1895–1911," in Mark Elvin and G. William Skinner, eds., *The Chinese City between Two Worlds* (q.v.).

Rhys Davids, T. W., and W. Stede. *Pali-English Dictionary*. Rpt. New Delhi: Oriental Books Reprint Corporation, 1975. First published in 1921.

Ricci, Matteo. *The Journals of Matteo Ricci, 1583–1610: China in the XVIth Century*. J. L. Gallagher, ed. and tr. Cambridge: Cambridge University Press, 1959.

Rinji Taiwan kyūkan chōsakai 臨時臺灣旧慣調査會, comp. *Taiwan tōgyō kyūkan ippan* 臺灣糖業旧慣一斑. Tokyo: Rinji Taiwan kyūkan chōsakai, 1909.

———. *Taiwan shihō furoku sankōsho* 臺灣私法附錄參考書. Supplementary volume, no. 3. Tokyo: Rinji Taiwan kyūkan chōsakai, 1910.

Rinji Taiwan tochi chōsakyoku 臨時臺灣土地調査局, ed. *Taiwan tochi chōsa jigyō gaiyō* 臺灣土地調査事業概要. Taipei: Rinji Taiwan tochi chōsakyoku, 1905.

Riskin, Carl. "Surplus and Stagnation in Modern China," in Dwight Perkins, ed., *China's Modern Economy in Historical Perspective* (q.v.).

Robertson, James A. "Spaniards Brought Animals, Fruits, Vegetables and All Manner of Plants," in Lewis Hanke, ed., *History of Latin American Civilization.* Boston: Little, Brown, 1973.

Rockhill, William W. "Notes on the Relations and Trade of China with the Eastern Archipelago and the Coasts of the Indian Ocean during the Fourteenth century." 2 parts. *TP* 15:419–447 (1914), 16:61–159, 236–271, 374–392, 435–467, 604–626 (1915).

———. *The Life of the Buddha and the Early History of His Order Derived from Tibetian Works in the Bkah-hgyur and Bstan-hygur*. London: Trubner, 1884.

Rongzhai suibi 容齋隨筆. Hong Mai 洪邁. Rpt. in *Congshu jicheng* (q.v.). First published ca. 1180–1202.

Roseberry, William. *Anthropologies and Histories: Essays in Culture, History and Political Economy*. New Brunswick: Rutgers University Press, 1989.

Roth, Gustav. *Viksuni Vinaya*. Patna: K. P. Jayaswal Research Institute, 1970.

Rowe, William. *Hankow: Commerce and Society in a Chinese City*. Stanford: Stanford University Press, 1984.

Roy, Anniruddha, and S. K. Bagchi, eds. *Technology in Ancient and Medieval India.* New Delhi: Sundeep Prakashan, 1986.

Rozman, Gilbert. *Urban Networks in Ch'ing China and Tokugawa Japan*. Princeton: Princeton University Press, 1973.

Rozman, Gilbert, et al. *The Modernization of China*. New York: Free Press, 1981.

Sabban, Françoise. "L'industrie sucrière, le moulin a sucre et les relations Sino-Portugaises aux XVIe–XVIIIe siècles." *Annales, Economies, Sociètès, Civilisation* 49.4:817–861 (1994).

———. "Sucre candi et confiseries de Quinsai: l'essor de sucre de canne dans la Chine des Song (X^{e}–XIIIe siècle)." *Journal d'Agriculture Traditionelle et de Botanique Appliquèe* 35:195–213 (1988).

Sakai, Robert. "The Ryukyu (Liu-Ch'iu) Islands as a Fief of Satsuma," in John K. Fairbank, ed., *The Chinese World Order* (q.v.).

———. "Satsuma, Ryukyu Trade and the Tokugawa Seclusion Policy." *JAS* 23.3:391–403 (1964).

Sakamaki, Shunzo. "Ryukyu and Southeast Asia." *JAS* 23.3:383–389 (1964).

Salaman, Redcliffe. *The History and Social Influence of the Potato*. Rpt. Cambridge: Cambridge University Press, 1987. First published in 1949.

San cai tuhui 三才圖會. Wang Zhi 王圻, comp. Rpt. Taipei: Chengwen chubanshe, 1970. First published in 1609.

Sands, Barbara, and Ramon Myers. "Economics and Macroregions: A Reply to Our Critics." *JAS* 49.2:44–346 (1990).

Sanguo zhi 三國志. Chen Shou 陳壽. Rpt. Beijing: Zhonghua shuju, 1962. Comp. in ca. 233–297.

Sanmin zhuyi yanjiu suo 三民主義研究所, ed. *Zhongguo haiyang fazhanshi lunwenji* 中國海洋發展史論文集. Taipei: Zhongyang yanjiu yuan, 1984.

San nong ji 三農紀. Zhang Zongfa 張宗法, comp. Preface dated 1760.

Saris, John. "English Voyages beyond the East-Indies, to the Ilands of Japan, Cauchin-China, the Philipinæ with others and the Indian Navigations further prosecuted," in Samuel Purchas, comp., *Purchas His Pilgrimes: or, Hakluytus Posthumus: contayning a history of the world in sea voyages and lande travells by Englishman and others* (q.v.).

Sasaki Masaya 佐々木正哉. "Juntoku ken kyōshin to Tōkai jurokusa" 順德縣郷紳と東海十六沙, in Tōyō bunko, Kindai Chūgoku kenkyū iinkai 東洋文庫近代中国研究委員会, ed., *Kindai Chūgoku kenkyū* 近代中国研究, vol. 3. Tokyo: Tōkyō daigaku shuppankai, 1959.

Sasamoto Shigemi 笹本重巳. "Kanton no tetsunabe ni tsuite" 広東の鉄鍋について. *Tōyōshi kenkyū* 12.2:35–48 (1952).

Satō seikakuki 砂糖製作記. Kimura Yoshiyuki (Matasuki) 木村喜之. Edo, 1797.

Savary des Bruslon, Jacques, and Philemon-Louis Savary des Bruslon. *A Dissertation on the Plan, Use and Importance of the Universal Dictionary of Trade and Commerce Translated from the French of the late Celebrated Mons. Savary, with such considerable Additions and Improvements, for the Trade and Navigation of the British Empire*. Malachy Postlewayt, tr. London: John and Paul Knapton, 1749. Comp. ca. 1686–1715.

Schafer, Edward H. "Tang," in K. C. Chang, ed., *Food in Chinese Culture* (q.v.).

———. *The Vermilion Bird*. Berkeley: University of California Press, 1967.

———. *Golden Peaches of Samarkand*. Berkeley: University of California Press, 1963.

Schlingloff, D. "Cotton Manufacture in Ancient India." *Journal of the Economic and Social History of the Orient* 17:81–90 (1974).

Schurmann, H. F. *Economic Structure of the Yuan Dynasty*. Cambridge: Harvard University Press, 1956.

———. "Traditional Property Concepts in China." *Far Eastern Quarterly* 15:507–516 (1956).

Schurz, William Lytle. *The Manila Galleon*. New York: E. P. Dutton, 1939.

Seccombe, Wally. "Marxism and Demography." *New Left Review* 137:22–47 (1983).

Sen, S. N. "A Survey of Source Materials," in D. M. Bose et al., eds., *A Concise History of Science in India* (q.v.).

Sen, Surendranath. *Indian Travels of Thevenot and Careri*. New Delhi: National Archives of India, 1949.

Sha Ding 沙丁 and Yang Dianqiu 杨典求. "Zhongguo he Lading Meizhou de zaoqi maoyi guanxi" 中国和拉丁美洲的早期贸易关系. *Lishi yanjiu* 4:107–127 (1984).

Shammas, Carole. *The Pre-Industrial Consumer in England and America*. Oxford: Clarendon Press, 1990.

Shang Yue 尚鉞, ed. Zhongguo renmin daxue, Qingshi yanjiuso 中国人民大学清史研究所, comp. *Ming Qing shehui jingji xingtai de yanjiu* 明清社会经济形态的研究. Shanghai: Renmin chubanshe, 1957.

Shen Fu. *Six Records of a Floating Life*. Leonard Pratt and Chiang Su-hui, trs. Harmondsworth, Eng.: Penguin Books, 1983. Written in 1809.

Shennong bencao 神農本草. Writers unknown. Reconstruction of text in *Xinxiu bencao* (q.v.). Late first or second century A.D.

Shepherd, John Robert. *Statecraft and Political Economy on the Taiwan Frontier, 1600–1800*. Stanford: Stanford University Press, 1993.

———. "Rethinking Tenancy: Explaining Spatial and Temporal Variation in Late Imperial and Republican China." *Comparative Studies in Society and History* 30.3:403–431 (1988).

———. "Plains Aborigines and Chinese Settlers on the Taiwan Frontier in the Seventeenth and Eighteenth Centuries." Ph.D. dissertation, Stanford University, 1981.

Shi Shenghan. *A Preliminary Survey of the Book "Qimin yaoshu," an Agricultural Encyclopedia of the Sixth Century*. Beijing: Kexue chubanshe, 1958.

Shiba Yoshinobu. "Ningpo and Its Hinterland," in G. William Skinner, ed., *The City in Late Imperial China* (q.v.).

———. *Commerce and Society in Sung China*. Mark Elvin, tr. Ann Arbor: Center for Chinese Studies, University of Michigan, 1970.

———. "Commercialization of Farm Products in the Sung Period." *Acta Asiatica* 19:77–96 (1970).

——— 斯波義信. *Sōdai shōgyōshi kenkyū* 宋代商業史研究. Tokyo: Kazama shobō, 1968.

Shiga Shūzō. "Family Property and the Law of Inheritance in Traditional China," in D. Buxbaum, ed., *Chinese Family Law and Social Change* (q.v.).

Shigeta Atsushi. "The Origins and Structure of Gentry Rule," Christian Daniels, tr., in Linda Grove and Christian Daniels, eds., *State and Society in China: Japanese Perspectives on Ming Qing Social and Economic History* (q.v.).

——— 重田德. *Shindai shakai keizaishi kenkyū* 清代社會經濟史研究. Tokyo: Iwanami shoten, 1975.

Shih Min-hsiung (Shih Min-shong). "Production and the Trade of Silk in the Late Ch'ing Period," in Hou Chi-ming and Yu Tzong-shian, eds., *Modern Chinese Economic History* (q.v.).

———. *The Silk Industry in China*. E-tu Zen Sun, tr. Ann Arbor: Center for Chinese Studies, University of Michigan, 1976.

Shinoda Osamu 篠田統. *Chūgoku shokumotsu shi* 中国食物史. Tokyo: Shibata shoten, 1974.

———. "Mindai no shoku seikatsu" 明代の食生活, in Yabuuchi Kiyoshi, ed., *Tenkō kaibutsu no kenkyū* (q.v.).

Shinzoku kibun 清俗紀聞. Nakagawa Shundai 中川忠英. Rpt. Tokyo: Tōyō bunko, 1965. First published in 1799.

Shlomowitz, Ralph. "Plantations and Smallholdings: Comparative Perspectives from the World Cotton and Sugarcane Economies, 1865–1939." *Agricultural History* 58:1–16 (1984).

Shou shi tong kao 授時通考. Ou Ertai 鄂爾泰 et al., comps. Rpt. Beijing: Imperially sponsored publication, 1847. Comp. in 1742.

Shun An 舜盦. "Baming chaoben *Tangshuang pu*" 跋明抄本糖霜譜. *Tushu jikan*, n.s. 3:59–62 (1941).

Shunde xianzhi 順德縣志. Guo Rucheng 郭汝誠. Rpt. Taipei: Chengwen chubanshe, 1974. Comp. in 1853.

Shunde xianzhi 順德縣志. Feng Baoxi 馮葆熙 et al., eds. Rpt. Taipei: Chengwen chubanshe, 1966. Compl., 1929.

Shuowen jiezi 說文解字. Xu Shen 許慎. Rpt. Shanghai: Shangwu shudian, 1935. Comp. ca. 120.

Sibu congkan 四部叢刊. Rpt. Shanghai: Shangwu yinshuguan, 1919–1937.

Siddiqi, Asiya. "The Business World of Jamsetjee Jejeebhoy." *Indian Economic and Social History Review* 19:3–4:301–324 (1982).

Sih, Paul K. T. (Hsueh Kuang-ch'ien), ed. *Taiwan in Modern Times*. New York: St. John's University Press, 1973.

Siku quanshu zongmu tiyao 四庫全書總目提要. Ji Yun 紀昀, ed. Rpt. Shanghai: Shangwu yinshuguan, 1933. Comp. in 1782.

Si min yueling 四民月令. Cui Shi 崔寔. Shi Shenghan 石聲漢, ed. and annot. Beijing: Zhonghua shuju, 1965. Comp. ca. 160.

Sinha, N. K. *Economic History of Bengal from Plassey to the Permanent Settlement.* Calcutta: University of Calcutta Press, 1956–1962.

Sircar D. C., ed. *Early Indian Trade and Industry.* Calcutta: University of Calcutta Press, 1972.

Sitterson, Carlyle J. *Sugar Country: The Cane Industry in the South, 1753–1950.* Lexington: University of Kentucky Press, 1953.

Situ Xiangji 司徒尚纪. "Mingdai Guangdong jingji dili qutan" 明代广东经济地理初探. M.A. thesis, Zhongshan University, 1981.

Siu, Helen. *Agents and Victims in South China.* New Haven: Yale University Press, 1989.

Siu, Kwok-kin (Anthony). "The Hong Kong Region before and after the Coastal Evacuation in the Early Ch'ing Dynasty," in David Faure, James Hayes, and Alan Birch, eds., *From Village to City: Studies in the Traditional Roots of Hong Kong Society* (q.v.).

Siu, Kwok-kin 蕭國鈞 and Siu Kwok-kwan 蕭國健. *Zupu yu Xianggang difang-shi yanjiu* 族譜與香港地方史研究. Hong Kong: Xianchao shushi chuban, 1982.

Sivin, Nathan. *Traditional Medicine in Contemporary China.* Ann Arbor: University of Michigan Press, 1987.

———. "Does China's Past Have a Future?" *HJAS* 38.2:449–480 (1978).

———. *Chinese Alchemy: Preliminary Studies.* Cambridge: Harvard University Press, 1968.

Skinner, G. William. "Marketing and Social Structure in Rural China." *JAS* 24.1:3–43 (1964), 24.2:195–228 (1965), 24.3:363–399 (1965).

Skinner, G. William, ed. *The City in Late Imperial China.* Stanford: Stanford University Press, 1977.

Smith, Adam. *An Inquiry into the Nature and Causes of the Wealth of Nations.* Edwin Cannan, ed. Rpt. New York: Modern Library, 1937. First published in 1776.

Smith, Arthur H. *Village Life in China: A Study in Sociology.* New York: F. H. Revell, 1899.

Smith, Carl T. "Early American Trade in China and Hong Kong, Russell and Company and the Howqua Family." *Hong Kong Amcham* 7:14–17 (1976).

Smith, Thomas C. *The Agrarian Origins of Modern Japan.* Stanford: Stanford University Press, 1959.

So, Alvin. *The South China Silk District: Local Historical Transformation and World-System Theory.* Albany: State University of New York Press, 1986.

So, Kwan-wai. *Japanese Piracy in Ming China during the 16th Century*. East Lansing: Michigan State University Press, 1975.

Souza, George Bryan. *The Survival of Empire*. Cambridge: Cambridge University Press, 1986.

Spence, Jonathan. "Ch'ing," in K. C. Chang, ed., *Food in Chinese Culture* (q.v.).

———. *Emperor of China: Self Portrait of K'ang Hsi*. New York: Knopf, 1974.

Spence, Jonathan, and John Wills, eds. *From Ming to Ch'ing*. New Haven: Yale University Press, 1979.

Spinks, Charles N. *The Ceramic Wares of Siam*. Bangkok: Siam Society, 1965.

Statistical Yearbook of China, Sample Survey. Hong Kong: Oxford University Press, 1985.

Staunton, George. *An Authentic Account of an Embassy from the King of Great Britain to China to the Emperor of China*. 2 vols. London: W. Blumer and Co., 1798.

Steinberg, David Joel, et al., eds. *In Search of Southeast Asia*. New York: Praeger Publishers, 1971.

Stewart, John Millhouse. *A Description of a Machine or Invention To Work Mills by the Power of a Fire-Engine, But particularly useful and profitable in Grinding Sugar-Canes*. New York Public Library, pamphlet collection (London: 1767).

Stockard, Janice. *Daughters of the Canton Delta*. Stanford: Stanford University Press, 1989.

Struve, Lynn A. *Voices from the Ming-Qing Cataclysm*. New Haven: Yale University Press, 1993.

———. "A Sketch of Southern Ming Events Affecting the Canton Delta Area." Paper given at Canton Delta Seminar, University of Washington, April 1973.

Su Shi shiji 蘇軾詩集. Wang Wen'gao 王文誥, ed. Rpt. Beijing: Zhonghua shuju, 1982.

Sudō Yoshiyuki 周藤吉之. "Nan-Sō inasaku no chi-iku" 南宋稲作の地域. *Shigaku zasshi* 70.6:1–53 (1961).

———. Chūgoku tochi seidoshi kenkyū 中国土地制度史研究. Tokyo: Tōkyō daigaku shuppankai, 1954.

Sui shu 隋書. Wei Zheng 魏徵 et al., eds. Rpt. Beijing: Zhonghua shuju, 1975. Comp. ca. A.D. 656.

Suiyuan shidan 隋園食單. Yuan Mei 袁枚. Rpt. Shanghai: Xiaocang shanfang wenji, 1824. First published in 1797.

Sun, E-tu Zen. "Sericulture and Silk Textile Production in Ch'ing China," in W. E. Willmott, ed., *Economic Organization in Chinese Society* (q.v.).

Sun, E-tu Zen, and John De Francis, eds. and trs. *Chinese Social History: Translations of Selected Studies*. Washington, D.C.: American Council of Learned Societies, 1956.

Sung Hok-p'ang. "Legends and Stories of the New Territories, Kam T'in." *JHKBRAS* 13:111–132 (1973), 14:160–85 (1974).

Supercargo, J. R. *Diary of a Journey Overland through the Maritime Provinces of China (in the Years 1819 and 1820)*. London: published for Sir Richard Phillips and Co., 1822.

Susruta Samhitā. K. L. Bhishagaratna, tr. 3 vols. Calcutta: private printing, 1907–1916. Comp. ca. 300–400.

Suzuki Seiichirō 鈴木清一郎. *Taiwan kyūkan kankon sōsai to nenjū gyōji* 臺灣旧慣冠婚葬祭と年中行事. Feng Zuomin 馮作民, tr. Rpt. Taipei: Zhongwen tushu, 1981. First printed in 1934.

Suzuki Shun 鈴木淳 and Nishijima Sadao 西嶋定生, eds. *Chūgokushi no jidai kubun* 中国史の時代區分. Tokyo: Tōkyō daigaku shuppankai, 1957.

Swann, Nancy Lee. *Food and Money in Ancient China*. Princeton: Princeton University Press, 1950.

Sweezy, Paul. "A Critique," in Rodney Hilton, ed., *The Transition from Feudalism to Capitalism* (q.v.).

Swerling, B. C. *The International Control of Sugar, 1918–1941*. Commodity Policy Studies, no. 7. Stanford: Stanford University Press, 1949.

Taihai jianwen lu 臺海見聞錄. Dong Tiangong 董天工. Rpt. in *Taiwan wenxian congkan* (q.v.). Preface dated 1751.

Taihai shichalu 臺海使槎錄. Huang Shujing 黃淑璥. *Taiwan wenxian congkan* (q.v.). First published in 1736.

Taiping guangji 太平廣記. Li Fang 李昉, ed. Rpt. Beijing: Zhonghua shuju, 1960. Comp. ca. 925–996.

Taiping yulan 太平御覽. Li Fang 李昉, comp. Rpt. 4 vols. Shanghai: Zhonghua shuju, 1960. Comp. in 983.

Taiwan fuzhi 台灣府志. Gao Gongqian 高拱乾, ed. Rpt. in *Taiwan wenxian congkan* (q.v.). Comp. in 1694.

Taiwan gong si cang gu wenshu ying ben 臺灣公私藏古文書影本. Fac. Taipei Palace Museum manuscript collection of land deeds. Vol. 2. Taipei: Palace Museum, 1977–1984.

Taiwan jishi 臺灣紀事. Wu Ziguang 吳子光. Rpt. in *Taiwan wenxian congkan* (q.v.). First published in 1875.

Taiwan nanbu beiwen jicheng 臺灣南部碑文集成. Rpt. in *Taiwan wenxian congkan* (q.v.).

Taiwan sheng tongzhi gao 臺灣省通誌稿. Li Ruhe 李汝和 et al., eds. *Renwu zhi* 人物志. Taipei: Taiwan wenxian weiyuan hui, 1962.

Taiwan wenxian congkan 臺灣文獻叢刊. Taiwan yinhang, Jingji yanjiushi 臺灣銀行經濟研究室, eds. Taipei: Taiwan yinhang, 1957–1972.

Taiwan xianzhi 臺灣縣志. Chen Wenda 陳文達, comp. Rpt. in *Taiwan wenxian congkan* (q.v.). Preface dated 1720.

Taiwan yinhang 臺灣銀行, ed. *Taiwan jingji shi* 臺灣經濟史. Taiwan yinhang jingji yanjiu congkan. Taipei, 1954– .

Taiwan yinhang, Jinrong yanjiushi 臺灣銀行金融研究室, ed. *Taiwan zhi tang* 臺灣之糖. Taipei: Taiwan yinhang, 1949.

Takekoshi Yosaburo. *Japanese Rule in Formosa*. George Braithwaite, tr. London: Longmans, Green, 1907.

Tan Chung. "The British-China-India Trade Triangle, 1771–1840." *India Economic and Social History Review* 11.4:411–31 (1974).

Tan Danjiong 譚旦冏. *Zhonghua minjian gongyi tushuo* 中華民間工藝圖說. Taipei: Zhonghua congshu weiyuan hui, 1956.

———. "Sichuan Neijiang de jiufa zaotang" 四川內江的舊法造糖. *Dalu zazhi* 12.6:176–183 (1953).

Tan Dihua 谭棣华 and Ye Xian'en 叶显恩. "Fengjian zongfa shili dui Foshan jingji de kongzhi jiqi chansheng de yingxiang" 封建宗法势力对佛山经济的控制及其产生的影响, in Guangdong lishi xuehui et al., eds., *Ming Qing Guangdong shehui jingji xingtai yanjiu* (q.v.).

Tanaka Masatoshi. "Rural Handicraft in Jiangnan in the Sixteenth and Seventeenth Centuries," Linda Grove, tr., in Linda Grove and Christian Daniels, eds., *State and Society in China: Japanese Perspectives on Ming Qing Social and Economic History* (q.v.).

——— 田中正俊. *Chūgoku kindai keizaishi kenkyū josetsu* 中国近代經濟史研究序說. Tokyo: Tōkyō daigaku shuppankai, 1973.

Tangshuang pu 糖霜譜. Wang Zhuo 王灼. Rpt. in *Congshu jicheng* (q.v.). First published in 1142.

Tannahill, Reay. *Food in History*. Rev. ed. New York: Stein and Day, 1988.

Tashiro Kazui. "Foreign Relations during the Edo Period: *Sakoku* Reexamined." *Journal of Japanese Studies* 8.2:283–306 (1982).

———. "Tsushima-han's Korean Trade, 1684–1710." *Acta Asiatica* 30:85–105 (1976).

Tax, Sol. *Penny Capitalism: A Guatemalan Indian Economy*. Chicago: University of Chicago Press, 1963.

Tepaske, John J. "New World Silver, Castile and the Philippines, 1590–1800," in J. F. Richards, ed., *Precious Metals in the Later Medieval and Early Modern Worlds*. Durham: Carolina Academic Press, 1983.

Thompson, Edward P. *The Poverty of Theory and Other Essays*. New York: Monthly Review Press, 1978.

Thompson, Laurence C. "The Junk Passage across the Taiwan Strait." *HJAS* 28:170–194 (1968).

Thomson, John. *The Chinese*. Indianapolis: Bobbs Merrill, 1909.

Tian Rukang 田汝康. "Shiqi shiji zhi shijiu shiji zhongye Zhongguo fanchuan zai Dongnanyazhou hangyun he shangye shangde diwei" 十七世纪至十九世纪中叶中国帆船在东南亚洲航运和商业上的地位. *Lishi yanjiu* 8:1–21 (1956).

Tiangong kaiwu 天工開物. Song Yingxing 宋應星. Rpt. in Tao Xiang 陶湘, comp. *Xiyongxian congshu* 喜咏軒叢書. 3 *juan*. Shanghai: n.p., 1929. First published 1637.

Tiangong kaiwu zhushi 天工开物注释. Zhong Guangyan 钟广言, ed. and annot. Guangzhou: Guangdong renmin chubanshe, 1976.

Tianxia junguo libing shu 天下郡國利病書. Gu Yanwu 顧炎武. Rpt. in *Sibu congkan* (q.v.). Preface dated 1662.

T'ien-kung k'ai-wu: Chinese Technology in the Seventeenth Century. E-tu Zen Sun and Sun Shiou-chuan, tr. University Park: Pennsylvania State University Press, 1966.

Tōa dōbunkai 東亞同文會. *Shina keizai zensho* 支那經濟全書. Vol. 1. Osaka: Maruzen, 1907.

Toby, Ronald. *State and Diplomacy in Early Modern Japan: Asia in the Development of the Tokugawa Bakufu*. Princeton: Princeton University Press, 1984.

Tomich, Dale W. *Slavery in the Circuit of Sugar: Martinique and the World Economy, 1830–1848*. Baltimore: Johns Hopkins University Press, 1990.

Tong, James W. *Disorder under Heaven: Collective Violence in the Ming Dynasty*. Stanford: Stanford University Press, 1991.

Topley, Marjorie. "Marriage Resistance in Rural Kwangtung," in Margery Wolf and Roxane Witke, eds., *Women in Chinese Society*. Stanford: Stanford University Press, 1975.

Torbet, Preston. *The Ch'ing Imperial Household Department*. Cambridge: Council on East Asian Studies, Harvard University 1977.

Trasselli, Carmelo. *Storia dello zucchero siciliano*. Caltanisseta: S. Sicascia, 1982.

Trewartha, George. "Field Observations on the Canton Delta of South China." *Economic Geography* 15.1:1–10 (1939).

Tribe, Keith. *Land, Labor and Economic Discourse*. London: Routledge S. K. Paul, 1978.

Ts'ao Yung-ho 曹永和. "Ming Hongwu chao de Zhong Liu guanxi" 明洪武朝的中琉關係, in Zhang Yanxian, ed., *Zhongguo haiyang fazhanshi lunwenji* (q.v.), vol. 3.

———. "Shilun Ming Taizu de haiyang jiaotong zhengce" 試論明太祖的海洋交通政策, in Sanmin zhuyi yanjiu suo, eds., *Zhongguo haiyang fazhanshi lunwenji* (q.v.), vol. 1.

———. "Pepper Trade in East Asia." *TP* 68.4–5:221–247 (1982).

———. "Chinese Overseas Trade in the Late Ming Period," in *International Association of Historians of Asia, Biennial Conference Proceedings*. Taipei: Academia Sinica, 1962.

Ts'ao Yung-ho, Lai Yung-hsiang 賴永祥, and Chou Hsueh-p'u 周學譜, comps. *Shiqi shiji Taiwan Yingguo maoyi shiliao* 十七世紀台灣英國貿易史料. *Taiwan yanjiu congkan*, no. 57. Taipei: Taiwan yinhang, 1959.

Tuan Yi-fu. *The World's Landscapes: China*. Chicago: University of Chicago Press, 1969.

Tudi weiyuanhui 土地委員會. *Quanguo tudi diaocha baogao gangyao* 全國土地調查報告綱要. Nanjing: 1937.

Twitchett, Denis. "James L. Watson, Chinese Kinship Reconsidered: Anthropological Perspectives on Historical Research." *China Quarterly* 92:623–627 (1982).

———. *Land Tenure and the Social Order in T'ang and Sung China: An Inaugural Lecture Delivered on 28 November 1961*. London: School of Oriental and African Studies, University of London, 1962.

———. "The Monasteries and China's Economy in Medieval Times." *Bulletin of the School of Oriental and African Studies* 19.3:526–549 (1957).

———. "Monastic Estates in Tang China." *Asia Major*, n.s. 5.2:123–146 (1956).

Uemura Yasuo 植村泰夫. "Tōgyō pulanteshyon to Zuyawa nōson sakai" 糖業プランテーションとヅヤワ農村社会. *Shirin* 61.3:47–74 (1978).

Umehara Kaoru 梅原郁. "Sōdai chihō shōtoshi no ichimen" 宋代地方小都の一面. *Shirin* 41.6:35–51 (1958).

United States Department of Agriculture (USDA), Foreign Agricultural Service. *Report on World Sugar Supply and Demand, 1980–1985*. Washington, D.C.: U.S. Government Printing Office, 1987.

Unschuld, Paul. *Medicine in China*. Berkeley: University of California Press, 1985.

Upasak, C. S. *Dictionary of Early Buddhist Monastic Terms*. Index to *Vinaya Pitaka*. Varanasi: Bharati Prakashan, 1975.

Van den Berg, N. P. *Uit De Dagen Der Compagnie: Geschiedkundige Schetsen*. Haarlem: H. D. Tjeenk Willink and Zoon, 1904.

van der Sprenkle, Sybille. *Legal Institutions in Manchu China*. London: Althone Press, 1962.

Van Leur, J. C. *Indonesian Trade and Society: Essays in Asian Social and Economic History*. The Hague: W. Van Hoeve, 1955.

Van Niel, Robert. "The Effect of Export Cultivations in 19th Century Java." *Modern Asian Studies* 15.1:25–58 (1981).

Viraphol, Sarasin. *Tribute and Profit: Sino-Siamese Trade, 1652–1853*. Cambridge: Council on East Asian Studies, Harvard University, 1977.

Volker, T. *Porcelain and the Dutch East India Company*. Mededelingen van het Rijks-museum voor Volkenkunde, no. 11. Leiden: E. J. Brill, 1954.

Voltaire, François M. A. de. *Essai sur les moeurs*. 2 vols. Paris: Editions Garnier Frères, 1963.

von Glahn, Richard. *The Country of Streams and Grottoes*. Cambridge: Council on East Asian Studies, Harvard University, 1987.

von Lippmann, Edmund O. *Geschichte des Zuckers: Seit den ältesten Zeiten bis zum Beginn der Rübenzucker-Fabrikation. Ein Beitrag zur Kulturgeschichte*. Rev. ed. Berlin: Julius Springer, 1929. First published 1890.

Wada Sei. "The Philippine Islands as Known to the Chinese before the Ming Period." *Memoirs of the Research Department of the Tōyō Bunko* 4:121–166 (1929).

Wakeman, Frederic. *The Great Enterprise*. 2 vols. Berkeley: University of California Press, 1985.

———. *Ming Qing Historical Studies in the People's Republic of China*. Berkeley: Institute of East Asian Studies, 1980.

———. "The Shun Interregnum of 1644," in Jonathan Spence and John Wills, eds., *From Ming to Ch'ing* (q.v.).

———. "The Secret Societies of Kwangtung, 1800–1856," in Jean Chesneaux, ed., *Popular Movements and Secret Societies in China, 1840–1950*. Stanford: Stanford University Press, 1972.

———. *Strangers at the Gate*. Berkeley: University of California Press, 1966.

Wakeman, Frederic, and Carolyn Grant, eds. *Conflict and Control in Late Imperial China*. Berkeley: University of California Press, 1975.

Waley, Arthur. *Yuan Mei, Eighteenth Century Chinese Poet*. London: George Allen and Unwin, 1956.

Wallerstein, Immanuel. *The Modern World-System*, vol. 1, *Capitalist Agriculture and the Origins of the European World Economy*. New York: Academic Press, 1976.

———. *The Modern World-System*, vol. 2, *Mercantilism and the European World Economy, 1600–1750*. New York: Academic Press, 1980.

———. *The Modern World-System*, vol. 3, *The Second Era of Great Expansion of the Capitalist World Economy, 1750–1840*. New York: Academic Press, 1974.

Walters, Ronald. "Signs of the Times: Clifford Geertz and Historians." *Social Research* 47.3:537–556 (1980).

Wan shu zaji 宛署雜記. Shen Bang 沈榜. Rpt. Beijing: Xinhua shuju, 1961. First published 1593.

Wang Gungwu. "China and South-East Asia, 1402–1424," in Jerome Ch'en and Nicholas Tarling, eds., *Studies in the Social History of China and Southeast Asia* (q.v.).

———. "Early Ming Relations with Southeast Asia: A Background Essay," in John Fairbank, ed., *The Chinese World Order* (q.v.).

———. "The Nanhai Trade." *Journal of the Malayan Branch of the Royal Asiatic Society* 31.2:1–135 (1958).

Wang I-shou. "Cultural Contact and the Migration of Taiwan's Aborigines: A Historical Perspective," in Ronald Knapp, ed., *China's Island Frontier* (q.v.).

Wang Jingyu 汪敬虞. "Shijiu shiji waiguo qin Hua qiyezhongde Huashang fugu huodong" 十九世纪外国侵华企业中的华商附股活动. *Lishi yanjiu* 4:39–74 (1965).

Wang Yeh-chien. *Land Taxation in Imperial China*. Cambridge: Harvard University Press, 1973.

———. "The Secular Trend of Prices during the Ch'ing Period (1644–1911)." *JCICUHK* 5.2:347–372 (1972).

Wang Yi-t'ung. *Official Relations between China and Japan, 1368–1549*. Cambridge: Harvard University Press, 1953.

Wang Yuhu 王毓瑚. *Zhongguo nongxue shulu* 中国农学书录. Beijing: Nongye chubanshe, 1964.

Wang Zongyan 汪宗衍. *Guangdong wenwu congtan* 廣東文物叢談. Hong Kong: Zhonghua shuju, 1974.

Warmington, E. H. *The Commerce between the Roman Empire and India*. Cambridge: Cambridge University Press, 1928.

Watson, Andrew M. *Agricultural Innovation in the Early Islamic World*. Cambridge: Cambridge University Press, 1983.

———. "The Arab Agricultural Revolution and Its Diffusion, 700–1100." *Journal of Economic History* 34.1:8–35 (1974).

Watson, James. "Anthropological Overview: The Development of Chinese Descent Groups," in Patricia B. Ebrey and James Watson, eds., *Kinship Organization in Late Imperial China* (q.v.).

———. "Chinese Kinship Reconsidered: Anthropological Perspectives on Historical Research." *China Quarterly* 92:589–622 (1982).

———. "Transactions in People: The Chinese Market in Slaves, Servants and Heirs," in James Watson, ed., *Asian and African Systems of Slavery* (q.v.).

———. "Hereditary Tenancy and Corporate Landlordism in Traditional China: A Case Study." *Modern Asian Studies* 11.2:161–182 (1977).

———. *Emigration and the Chinese Lineage*. Berkeley: University of California Press, 1975.

Watson, James, ed. *Asian and African Systems of Slavery*. Berkeley: University of California Press, 1980.

Watson, Rubie. *Inequality among Brothers*. Cambridge: Cambridge University Press, 1985.

———. "The Creation of a Chinese Lineage: The Teng of Ha Tsuen, 1669–1751." *Modern Asian Studies* 16:69–100 (1982).

Watt, George. *The Commercial Products of India*. London: John Murray, 1908.

———. *Dictionary of the Economic Products of India*. Calcutta: Office of the Superintendent of Government Printing India, 1893.

Watters, Thomas. *On Yuan Chwang's Travels in India, 629–645 A.D.* Rpt. New York: AMS Press, 1971. First published in 1905.

Wei Qingyuan 韦庆元 and Wu Qiyan 吴奇衍. "Qingdai zhuming huang Fan shi de xingshuai" 清代著名皇范氏的兴衰. *Lishi yanjiu* 3:127–144 (1981).

Wen xuan 文選. Xiao Tong 蕭統 (Prince Zhao Ming 昭明太子), ed. Rpt. Hong Kong: Shangwu yinshuguan, 1960. Comp. ca. 501–531.

Wheatley, Paul. "Geographical Notes on Some Commodities Involved in Sung Maritime Trade." *Journal of the Malayan Branch of the Royal Asiatic Society* 32.2:5–139 (1961).

White, Benjamin. "Agricultural Involution and Its Critics: Twenty Years After." *Bulletin of Concerned Asian Scholars* 15.2:18–31 (1983).

White, Lynn. *Medieval Technology and Social Change*. Oxford: Oxford University Press, 1962.

———. "Tibet, India and Malaya as Sources of Western Mediaeval Technology." *American Historical Review* 65:515–526 (1960).

Wickberg, Edgar. "Continuities in Land Tenure," in Emily Martin Ahern and Hill Gates, eds., *The Anthropology of Taiwanese Society* (q.v.).

———. "Late Nineteenth Century Land Tenure in North Taiwan," in Leonard Gordon, ed., *Taiwan: Studies in Local History*. New York: Columbia University Press, 1970.

———. "Japanese Land Policies in Taiwan." *Agricultural History* 43:369–378 (1969).

Wiens, Herold J. *Han Chinese Expansion in South China*. 2nd. ed. Hamden, Conn.: Shoe String Press, 1967.

Wilkinson, Endymion. "Studies in Chinese Price History." Ph.D. dissertation, Princeton University, 1970.

Will, Pierre-Etienne. *Bureaucracy and Famine in Eighteenth Century China*. Elborg Foster, tr. Stanford: Stanford University Press, 1990.

Williams, C. N. *The Agronomy of the Major Tropical Crops*. Kuala Lumpur: Oxford University Press, 1975.

Williams, Jack F. "Sugar: The Sweetner in Taiwan's Development," in Ronald Knapp, ed., *China's Island Frontier* (q.v.).

Williams, S. Wells. *The Middle Kingdom*. 2 vols. New York: Scribner's, 1883.

Williamson, Jeffrey G. "Why Was British Growth So Slow during the Industrial Revolution?" *Journal of Economic History* 44:687–712 (1984).

Williamson, Thomas. *The East India Vadomocum; or Complete guide to gentlemen intended for the civil, military service of the East India Company*. 2 vols. London: Parry and Kingsbury, 1810.

Willmott, W. E., ed. *Economic Organization in Chinese Society*. Stanford: Stanford University Press, 1972.

Wills, John E. "Maritime Asia, 1500–1800: The Interactive Emergence of European Domination." *AHR* 98.1:83–105 (1993).

———."Asian Maritime History, 1498–1815: The Drift to European Hegemony." Paper presented at the Conference of United States Japanese Historians, Los Angeles, August 1987.

———. *Embassies and Illusions*. Cambridge: Council on East Asian Studies, Harvard University, 1984.

———. "Maritime China from Wang Chih to Shih Lang," in Jonathan Spence and John Wills, eds., *From Ming to Ch'ing* (q.v.).

———. *Pepper, Guns and Parleys*. Cambridge: Harvard University Press, 1974.

Wittfogel, Karl, and Feng Chia-sheng. *The History of Chinese Society: Liao*. Philadelphia: American Philosophical Society, 1949.

Wolf, Arthur, and Huang Chieh-shan. *Marriage and Adoption in China, 1845–1945*. Stanford: Stanford University Press, 1980.

Wong, R. Bin. "The Development of China's Peasant Economy: A New Formulation of Old Problems." *Journal of Peasant Studies* 18.1:5–26 (1990).

Woon Yuen-fong. *Social Organization in South China, 1911–1940*. Ann Arbor: Center for Chinese Studies, University of Michigan, 1984.

Wright, Irene. "History of Sugar." *Louisiana Planter and Sugar Manufacturer* 55:174–176 (1915).

Wu Cheng-lo 吳丞洛. *Zhongguo du liang heng shi* 中國度量衡史. Shanghai: Shangwu yinshuguan, 1934.

Wu Chengming 吴承明. *Zhongguo ziben zhuyi yu guonei shichang* 中国资本主义与国内市场. Beijing: Zhongguo shehui kexue chubanshe, 1985.

Wu Ching-hong, "The Rise and Decline of Chuanzhou's International Trade and Its Relation to the Philippine Islands," in *International Association of Historians of Asia, Second Biennial Conference Proceedings*. Taipei: 1962.

Wu Han 吳晗. "Yuan diguo zhi bengkui yu Ming zhi jianguo" 元帝國之崩潰與明之建國. *Qinghua xuebao* 9.2:359–423 (1936).

Wu Jingzi. *The Scholars*. Yang Hsien-yi and Gladys Yang, trs. Beijing: Foreign Language Press, 1957. Written in 1745.

Wu Liangkai 吴量恺. "Qingdai Qianlong shiqi nongye jingji guanxi de yanbian he fazhan" 清代乾隆时期农业经济关系的演变和发展, in *Qingshi luncong* (q.v.), vol. 1.

———. "Qingdai qianqi nongye gugong de gongjie" 清代前期农业雇工的工价. *Zhongguo shehui jingjishi yanjiu* 2:17–30 (1983).

Wu Ren'an 吴仁安. "Mingdai Guangdong sanshiliu hang chutan" 明代广东三十六行初探. *Xueqiu yanjiu* 2:18–23 (1980).

Wuli xiaoshi 物理小識. Fang Yizhi 方以智. Rpt. in *Congshu jicheng* (q.v.). First published in 1664.

Xiamen zhi 廈門志. Zhou Kai 周凱, comp. 1839.

Xie Guozhen (Hsieh Kuo-ching). "Removal of Coastal Population in the Early Tsing Period." *Chinese Social and Political Science Review* 15.4:559–596 (1932).

——— 謝國楨. *Wan Ming shiji kao* 晚明史籍考. Beijing: Beijing daxue tushu guan, 1932.

Xie Guozhen (Hsieh Kuo-ching) 謝國楨, ed. *Mingdai shehui jingji shiliao xuanbian* 明代社会经济史料选编. 3 vols. Fuzhou: Renmin chubanshe, 1980.

———. *Ming Qing biji tancong* 明清笔记谈丛. Rpt. Hong Kong: Huaxia chubanshe, 1967.

———. *Qingchu nongmin qiyi ziliao jilu* 清初農民起義資料輯錄. Shanghai: Xin zhishi chubanshe, 1956.

Xie Guozhen (Hsieh Kuo-ching) 謝國楨, ed. and comp. *Mingdai nongmin qiyi shiliao xuanbian* 明代农民起义史料选编. Fuzhou: Fujian renmin chubanshe, 1981.

Xin'an xianzhi 新安縣志. Wang Chongxi 王崇熙 et al., eds. Rpt. Taipei: Chengwen chubanshe, 1974. Comp. in 1819.

Xinhui Chaolian Lubian Lushi zupu 新會潮連蘆鞭盧氏族譜. Hong Kong: private printing, 1947.

Xinhui xian Xinhui shuyuan, Xi'nan shuyuan, Dongbei gongju changtian cehuitu 新會縣新會書院西南書院東北公局常田測繪圖. Xinhui: Changchan zhengli weiyuanhui, 1946.

Xinhui xiangtu zhi 新會鄉土志. Tan Piao 譚鑣 et al., eds. Rpt. Hong Kong: Gangzhou xuehui, 1970. First published in 1908.

Xin Tang shu 新唐書. Ouyang Xiu 歐陽修 and Song Qi 宋祁 et al., eds. Rpt. Beijing: Zhonghua shuju, 1975. Comp. in 1007–1072.

Xinxiu bencao 新修本草. Su Gong (Su Jing) 蘇敬 and Li Ji 李勣 et al., eds. and comps. Rpt. Shanghai: Shanghai hengsheng chubanshe, 1959. Compl. 650–659. Based on Dunhuang fragments and Japanese copy of ca. 731.

Xuxiu Taiwan fuzhi 續修臺灣府志. Yu Wenyi 余文儀, ed. Rpt. in *Taiwan wenxian congkan* (q.v.). Preface dated 1774.

Yabuuchi Kiyoshi 薮内清. *Tenkō kaibutsu no kenkyū* 天工開物の研究. Tokyo: Kōseisha, 1953.

Yamawaki Tejirō. "The Great Trading Merchants, Cocksinja and His Son." *Acta Asiatica* 30:106–116 (1976).

——— 山脇悌二郎. "Shindai enshō to Nagasaki bōeki no dokusen" 清代塩商と長崎貿易の獨占. *Shigaku zasshi* 67.8:63–80 (1958).

Yan Zhongpin 嚴中平 et al., eds. *Zhongguo jindai jingjishi tongji ziliao xuanji* 中國近代 經濟史統計資料選集. Beijing: Kexue chubanshe, 1955.

Yanaihara Tadao 矢内原忠雄. *Teikoku shugika no Taiwan* 帝國主義下の臺灣. Zhou Xianwen 周憲文, tr. Taipei: Taiwan yinhang, 1956.

Yang, C. K. (Ch'ing-k'un). *Chinese Communist Society: The Family and the Village*. Cambridge: M.I.T. Press, 1965.

Yang Lien-sheng. *Money and Credit in China*. Cambridge: Harvard University Press, 1971.

———. "Government Control of Urban Merchants in Traditional China." *Tsing-hua Journal of Chinese Studies*, n.s. 8.1–2:186–206 (1970).

———. *Studies in Chinese Institutional History*. Harvard-Yenching Studies. Cambridge: Harvard University Press, 1961.

Yang, Martin C. (Yang Mou-ch'un). *A Chinese Village: Taitou, Shantung Province*. New York: Columbia University Press, 1945.

Ye Shaohua 叶少华. "Wo suozhidao de Dongguan Minglun Tang" 我所知道的东莞明伦堂. *Guangdong wenshi ziliao* 16:1–21 (1964).

Ye Xian'en 叶显恩. *Ming Qing Huizhou nongcun shehui yu dianpu zhi* 明清徽州农村社会与佃仆制. Anhui: Anhui renmin chubanshe, 1983.

Ye Xian'en 叶显恩, ed. *Guangdong hangyun shi (gudai bufen)* 广东航运史(古代部分). Beijing: Renmin jiaotong chubanshe, 1989.

Ye Xian'en 叶显恩 and Tan Dihua 谭棣华. "Luelun Ming Qing Zhujiang sanjiaozhou de gaolidai ziben" 略论明清珠江三角洲的高利贷资本, in Ye Xian'en et al., eds., *Ming Qing Guangdong shehui jingji yanjiu* (q.v.).

———. "Lun Zhujiang sanjiaozhou de zutian" 论珠江三角洲的族田, in Guangdong lishi xuehui, ed., *Ming Qing Guangdong shehui jingji xingtai yanjiu* (q.v.).

———. "Ming Qing Zhujiang sanjiaozhou nongye shangyehua yu xushi de fazhan" 明清珠江三角洲农业商业化与圩市的发展, in Ye Xian'en et al., eds, *Ming Qing Guangdong shehui jingji yanjiu* (q.v.)

Ye Xian'en 叶显恩, Li Longqian 李龙潜, Huang Qichen 黄启臣, and Tan Dihua 谭棣华, eds. Ming Qing Guangdong sheng shehui jingji yanjiuhui 明清广东省社会经济研究会, comp. *Ming Qing Guangdong shehui jingji yanjiu* 明清广东社会经济研究. Guangzhou: Guangdong renmin chubanshe, 1987.

Yinshan zheng yao 飲膳正要. Hu Sihui (Hoshoi) 忽思慧. Rpt. Shanghai: Shangwu yinshuguan, 1935. First published in 1330.

Yongzheng zhupi zouzhe xuanji 雍正硃批奏摺選集. Rpt. in *Taiwan wenxuan congkan* (q.v.).

Yoshida Mikutuni. "The Chinese Concept of Technology: A Historical Approach." *Acta Asiatica* 36:49–66 (1979).

Yu Ying-shih. "Han," in K. C. Chang, ed., *Food in Chinese Culture* (q.v.).

Yuan Hanqing 袁翰青. "Wo guo zhitangye de lishi" 我國製糖業的歷史, in Yuan Hanqing, ed., *Zhongguo huaxue shi lunwenji* 中國化學史論文集. Beijing: Sanlian shudian chubanshe, 1956.

Yuan, Tsing. "Urban Riots and Disturbances," in Jonathan Spence and John Wills, eds., *From Ming to Ch'ing* (q.v.).

Yuehaiguan zhi 粵海關志. Liang Tingnan 梁廷枏 and Fang Dongshu 方東樹. Rpt. Taipei: Wenhai chubanshe, n.d. First published in 1838.

Yule, Henry, and Arthur C. Burnel, eds. *Hobson-Jobson: A Glossary of Colloquial Anglo-Indian Words and Phrases*. London: J. Murray, 1903.

Yule, Henry, and Henri Cordier, eds. and trs. *Cathay and the Way Thither, Being a Collection of Medieval Notices of China*. Rev. ed. Henri Cordier, ed. Hakluyt Society Publications, 2nd ser., vols. 38–41. London: 1916.

Zavala, Silvio. *The Colonial Period in the History of the New World*. Max Savelle, tr. Abridged. Westport: Greenwood Press, 1983.

Zelin, Madeline. *The Magistrate's Tael: Rationalizing Fiscal Reform in Eighteenth Century Ch'ing China*. Berkeley: University of California Press, 1984.

Zeng Huaman 曾華滿. *Tangdai Lingnan fazhande hexinxing* 唐代嶺南發展的核心性. Hong Kong: Zhongwen daxue chubanshe, 1973.

Zhang Hanyu 張漢裕. "Riju shidai Taiwan jingji zhi yanbian" 日據時代臺灣經濟之演變. *Taiwan jingji shi* 2:74–128 (1955).

Zhang Runsheng 张润生, Chen Shijun 陈士俊, and Cheng Huifang 程蕙芳. *Zhongguo gudai keji mingren zhuan* 中国古代科技名人传. Beijing: Zhongguo qingnian chubanshe, 1981.

Zhang Weihua 張維華. *Mingdai haiwai maoyi jianlun* 明代海外貿易簡論. Shanghai: Renmin chubanshe, 1956.

Zhang Xinglan 張星烺. *Zhong-Xi jiaotong shiliao huibian* 中西交通史料匯編. Beijing: Xinmin yinshuguan, 1930.

Zhang Yanxian 張炎憲, ed. *Zhongguo haiyang fazhanshi lunwenji* 中國海洋發展史論文集. Taipei: Zhongyang yanjiu yuan, 1988.

Zhang Youyi 章有義, ed. *Zhongguo jindai nongyeshi ziliao* 中國近代農業史資料. 3 vols. Beijing: Sanlian shudian, 1957.

Zhao Rugua. *Zhufan ji*. Frederich Hirth and William W. Rockhill, trs. and annots. *Chau Ju-kua: His Work on Chinese and Arab Trade in the Twelfth and Thirteenth Centuries, Entitled Chu-fan-chi*. St. Petersburg: Printing Office of the Imperial Academy of Sciences, 1911.

Zhongguo diyi lishi dang'an guan 中国第一历史档案馆. "Qingdai chakan Taiwan guanzhuang mindi dianzu shiliao" 清代查勘台湾官庄民地佃租史料. *Lishi dang'an* 1:28–35 (1987).

Zhongguo jin sanbai nian shehui jingji taolunji 中国近三百年社会经济讨论集. Cuncui xueshe 存萃学社, comp. Vol. 1. Hong Kong: Congwen shudian, 1972.

Zhongguo renmin daxue, Zhongguo lishi jiaoyanshi 中国人民大学中国历史教研室, ed. *Ming Qing shehui jingji xingtai de yanjiu* 明清社会经济形态的研究. Shanghai, 1957.

———. *Zhongguo ziben zhuyi mengya wenti taolunji* 中国资本主义萌芽问题讨论集. 2 vols. Beijing: Sanlian shudian, 1957.

Zhongshan xianzhi chugao 中山縣志初稿. Zhongshan xian wenxian weiyuanhui 中山縣 文獻委員會, ed. Rpt. Taipei: 1968. First published in 1947.

Zhongyang yanjiuyuan, Sanmin zhuyi yanjiu suo 中央研究院三民主義研究所, ed. *Zhongguo haiyang fazhanshi lunwenji* 中國海洋發展史論文集. 2 vols. Taipei: Zhongyang yanjiu yuan, 1984–1986.

Zhou Jinsheng 周金聲. *Zhongguo jingji shi* 中國經濟史. Taipei: Zhongyang tushu chubanshe, 1959.

Zhou Xianwen 周憲文. *Qingdai Taiwan jingji shi* 清代臺灣經濟史. Taipei: Taiwan yinhang, 1957.

Zhouli 周禮. Comps. unknown. *Le Tcheou-li*. E. Biot, tr. 2 vols. Rpt. Beijing: Wentiange, 1930. Comp. in B.C. 140. Translation first published in 1851.

Zhujiang sanjiaozhou nongyezhi 珠江三角洲农业志. Foshan dichu geming weiyuan hui 佛山地区革命委员会, ed. 6 vols. (neibu), 1976.

Zurndorfer, Harriet T. *Change and Continuity in Chinese Local History*. Leiden: E. J. Brill, 1989.

GLOSSARY

Entries are arranged by the *putonghua pinyin* spellings, in a strict letter-by-letter fashion, ignoring word and syllable breaks. Cantonese and Taiwanese pronounciations of terms and proper names are placed in parentheses. Only *zi* and *kanji* for names and book titles not given in the Works Cited are listed in the Glossary.

ai di yin 碍地銀
anmole 菴摩勒
Arai Hakuseki 新井白石

bai 稗
baicha 白茶
baiqi 白契
baitang 白糖
baixian 白蜆
baizhe 白蔗
bang 幫
banmi 半蜜
Bao'an xian 寶安縣
baojia 保甲
baolan 包攬
baoren 保人
baoshou 包收
baozheng 保正
beibu 卑布
beicao 北艚
Beidi Miao 北帝廟
Beijiao 北郊
Beijiao zhen 北郊鎮
bendi 本地
bi 婢
bing 餅
bingtang 冰糖
bo 伯
bohe ye 薄荷葉
Bolomen yaofang 波羅門藥方
bujiao 布蕉

ca dou 擦斗
Chakeng 茶坑
changgong 長工
changzu 常租
Chao Guan 鈔關
Chaoyang 潮陽
chaozhe 潮蔗
cha yuan 茶園
Chen (xing) 陳姓
Chen cun 陳村
Chen Daheng 陳大恒
cheng 鐺
Chen Gongyin 陳恭尹
chenpi 陳皮
Chenshikang 赼石康
chi 尺

Chia-i 嘉義
Chikan bitan 赤崁筆談
Chu 楚
chui tang 吹糖
cun 寸

dabu 大布
dafang 大房
da fangche 大紡車
Dali Si 大理寺
Danmaxi 淡馬錫
Danmin 蛋民
Dao Xuan 道宣
Daoyi zhilue 島夷志略
Da Qing yi tongzhi 大清一統志
Daxia 大夏
Daxing xian 大興縣
dazu hu 大租戶
Deng (Tang) (xing) 鄧姓
Deng Baosheng 鄧豹生
Deng Wenwei 鄧文蔚
di 荻
Dianbai xian 電百縣
dianbian 佃變
dianhu 佃戶
diannong 佃農
dianpu 佃僕
dianqi 典契
di ding 地丁
di gu 地骨
ding 丁
dingjiao 頂郊
Ding Wenjiang 丁文江
ding xin tang 定心湯
di pi 地皮
dizhe 荻蔗
Dongben dao 東本島
dou 斗
Du (xing) 杜姓
du 都
duangong 短工
Duanwu 端午
dui 碓

Enping xian 恩平縣

fan che 翻車
fang 房
Fang Yan 方言
fangzu yin 防租銀
fan mai 番麥
fan shang 番商
fanshu (ganshu) 蕃薯
fantang shengli 販糖生理
Fan Yubin 范毓馪
Fa Xian 法顯
fen 分
Fengtai zhen 鳳臺鎮
Fengxian Dian 奉先殿
Fengxi xian 逢溪縣
Folangji 佛郎機
fudu yushi 副都御史
fugu 附股
Fulao [Hoklo] 福佬
funong jingji 富農經濟
fuyu diannong 富裕佃農

gan chuqu 趕出去
Gangjiao 港郊
gan qing 感情
Ganshu su 甘藷疏
ganzhe 甘蔗
gaoliang 高粱
ge 葛
ge 合
gonghang (Cohong) 公行
gongjia bu 公家廍
gongming 功名
gongren 工人
gongsi bu 公司廍

gongsuo 公所
Gongtong ti 共同體
gōnō 豪農
Gotō Rishun 後藤梨春
Gotō Shimpei 後藤新平
Guan (qua) 官
guan shang 官商
guan zhuang 官庄
gu gongren 僱工人
gun nian 輥輾
guzhu 僱主

haidao fushi 海道副使
hang (hong) 行
hang shang 行商
haomin 豪民
hao ren 豪人
haozu 豪族
He (zu) 何族
heisha 黑沙
heizao 黑棗
He Liangjun 何良俊
He Shide Tang 何世德堂
He Taixiang 何態祥
He Zhen 何眞
I Iong (xing) 洪姓
Hong lou meng 紅樓夢
Hou (Hau) (xing) 侯姓
hu 戶
huai 淮
huaji 花機
huan 鯇
Huang ce 黃册
huang ni shui 黃泥水
Huang Shujing 黃叔儆
hubu (Hoppo) 戶部
hufang 戶房
hui 會
Huicheng 會城
huiguan 會館
huitian 會田
Huizhou (Guangdong) 惠州
hun 圂
huo 鑊
huofa mo 活法磨
huohao 火耗
Huo Tao 霍韜

Ikegami Tarōzaemon 池上太郎左衛門

jia 甲
jia miao 家廟
jiang 醬
Jiangdong 江東
jiansheng 監生
jian shengzi 姦生子
jian tang 繭糖
jiaoche 攪車
jia shu 家塾
Jia Sidao 賈似道
jie shi 街市
Jieyang 揭陽
Jifu cong shu 畿輔叢書
jin 觔／斤
jing 精
Jingde xian 旌德縣
jingji 經紀
jing ying di zhu 經營地主
Jinrong Tang 錦榮堂
jinshi 進士
jiu 臼
Jiuzisha 九子沙
Ji Wen 祭文
Jujia biyong shilei quanji 居家必用事類全集
juren 舉人

kang 炕

Kansha ki 甘蔗記
Kao Gong Ji 考工記
kegang 客綱
kejia 客家
kenhu 墾戶
kenhu guanshi 墾戶管事
kenshou 墾首
keshang 客商
kesi tang 窠絲糖
kezi 客子
Kibi Kenja 黍檢者
kou 口
kunlun 崑崙
kunlunzhe 崑崙蔗

Lan Dingyuan 藍鼎元
lazhe 蠟蔗
Leizhou 雷州
lengbu 棱布
li 里
liang 兩
liang cong zu chu 糧從租出
Liang Jingguo (Kingqua I) 梁經國
Liang Lunshu (Kingqua II) 梁綸樞
liangmin 良民
liangtian 糧田
lianmo 連磨
Liao (xing) 廖姓
Li Cai 李材
Li Changqing ji 李長卿集
Li Dan 李旦
lijia zhi 里甲制
Lin Ben Tang 林本堂
Lingwai daida 嶺外代答
Lin Hong 林洪
Lin Shi 林石
Lin Xiyuan 林希元
Lin Zhifan 林之藩
Li Shiyao 李侍堯
Li Shizhen 李士楨
lishu 里書
Liudui 六堆
Liu Mingzhuan 劉銘傳
Li Yiguan 李一官
Li Zicheng 李自成
long gu che 龍骨車
long jiang ge 龍江葛
longyan 龍眼
Lu Dazhen 盧大振
lülong 驢礱
luohuasheng 落花生

Ma Huan 馬歡
maiban 買辦
maishen 賣身
maiya tang 麥芽糖
Makiya Sanekiyo 眞喜屋實清
manjū 饅頭
Manlajia 滿刺加
Mei (xing) 梅姓
meixi 每席
Meng Shen 孟詵
mianyi qian 免役錢
Min 閩
Minglun Tang 明倫堂
Miyazaki Antei 宮崎安貞
mu 畝
mu mian kuang chuang 木棉軖床

nancao 南艚
nan geng nü fang 男耕女紡
Nanjiao 南郊
Nanxiong 南雄
Nanyi yiwu zhi 南裔異物志
nanzhe 南蔗
neiting 內廷
neiwufu 內務府

nian 碾
Nitobe Inazō 新渡戶稻造
niuben bu 牛犇廍
niu nian 牛碾
niupi tang 牛皮糖
Nōgyō zenshō 農業全書
nongjia 農家
nongyede shangpinhua 農業的商品化
nu 奴
nüge 女葛
nupu 奴僕

pai 排
Pan (Poon) (xing) 潘姓
Pan Kun (guan) (Consequa) 潘崑官
Pan Qi (guan) (Puankequa) 潘啓官
Pan Zhencheng 潘振承
pian 片
pian tang 片糖
ping bu fan 平埔蕃
Posi 波斯
pu 僕
Pudulijia 蒲都麗家
pu zei 僕賊

Qi 齊
qian li cha 千里茶
Qianshou, qianyan Guanshiyin pusa zhibing he yaojing 千手千眼觀世音菩薩治病和藥經
qian zhuang 錢莊
qihang 齊行
qihui 旗會
qilao huiyi 耆老會議
qing 頃
qingma 清麻
Qiqi tushou 奇器圖說
Qu Shisi 瞿式耜
Qu Yuan 屈原

reizoku suru 隷屬する
Rong (xing) 容姓
ruji (yap tsik) 入籍
Rulin waishi 儒林外史

Sai On 蔡溫
Sanhe hui 三和會
Sanjiao 三郊
satō-za 糖行
Sengjia Bamo 僧迦跋摩
shanghang 商行
shang hu 上戶
shang nong 上農
Shang Shui (Sheung Shui) 上水
Shanjia qinggong 山家清供
Shaowu 紹武
shatang 沙糖
Shen Baozhen 沈葆楨
sheng 升
Shen Nong bencao jing 神農本草經
shengyuan 生員
shenshang 紳商
shenshi 紳士
shezei 社賊
Shi (xing) 石姓
shi/dan 石
shibo shi 市舶使
shibo si 市舶司
Shi Changling 施長齡
Shi Hu Xu 石湖墟
shijia 時價
Shi Lang (Shilong) 施琅
shimi 石蜜
shi nian 石碾
shipu 世僕
Shisanhang 十三行

Shōtoku shinrei 正德新例
Shouhuangtian Miao 壽皇天廟
Shou shi tong kao 授時通考
shoushi hangzhong 首事行總
shui 稅
shui dui 水碓
shuinjō 朱印狀
shui zhuan da fang che 水轉大紡車
shumin dizhu 庶民地主
Shuo Ling 說鈴
Shuowen Xinfu 說文新附
shusuan 書算
shuyuan 書院
Sima Xiangru 司馬相如
Sirong 西戎
Siyouzhai congshuo 四友齋叢說
Sō-shōkyaku 宋商客
Suining xian 遂寧縣
Sumendala guo 蘇門答刺國
Su Minggang 蘇鳴崗
Sumkon (Jan Con; Xin Gan) 心肝
Sunchang 順昌

Tabata Sabuni 田畑佐文仁
Taifan tushuo 臺番圖說
Taihai shicha lu 太海使槎錄
Tai Miao 太廟
Tamura Gen'yū 田村元雄
tangbing 糖餅
tang che 糖車
tangchuan 糖船
tangfang 糖房
tanghang 糖行
Tangjiao 糖郊
tangjiu 糖酒
tangju 糖居
tang ren 糖人
tangshuang 糖霜
Tang Gaozong 唐高宗
Tang Taizong 唐太宗
Tan Run 曇潤
tian di 田底
tian gu 田骨
tian mian 田面
tian pi 田皮
Tianzhu 天竺
ting zuo 停胙
Tokugawa Mitsukuni 德川光圀
Tongcheng 垌城
tongpu 僮僕
tongshi 童試
Tongwen hang 同文行
tongxianghui 同鄉會
tongxinghui 同姓會
Tōsen 唐船
toufen 頭分
toujia 頭家
toujia bu 頭家廍
touxian 投獻
tsūhō 通寶
tu 圖
tuan ding 團丁
tu hao 土豪
tuijia 退價
tujia 圖甲
tunzhuang 屯莊
Tu Zemin 塗澤民

wan dian kangzu 頑佃抗租
Wang Anguo 王安國
Wang Bo 汪柏
Wang Dayuan 汪大淵
Wang Fu 王黼
Wang gang 魍港
Wang Jiazhen 王家禎
Wang Yuance 王元策
Wanping xian 宛平縣
Wanqing sha 萬頃沙

wei chuan 磑船
weidui 衛隊
Wen (Man) (xing) 文姓
wo 窩
wokou 倭寇
wo zhu 窩主
Wu (xing) 吳姓
Wuben tang 務本堂
Wu Bingjian (Howqua II) 伍秉鑑
Wu Chongyue (Howqua IV) 伍崇曜
Wu Guoying (Howqua I) 伍國瑩
Wu Haoguan 伍浩官
Wu Jianzhang 吳健章
Wu Shaorong 伍紹榮
wu wei zi 五味子
Wu Xingzuo 吳興祚

xi 席
Xia cun (Ha Hsuen) 廈村
xiafu (hafu) 下夫
xia hu 下戶
xiajiao 下郊
xiang (hiang) 鄉
xian geng dian ren 現耕佃人
xiangshen 鄉紳
xiangtuan 鄉團
xiangyue 鄉約
xia nong 下農
xian zhao fangqin ren deng 先招房親人等
Xiaoguan 小關
xiaoli 校例
Xiaoxi 小溪
xiaozu hu 小租戶
xiedou 械鬥
Xie Huilian 謝惠連
Xi Jiang 西江
ximin 細戶
Xingcha shenglan 星槎勝覽
Xinghua xian 興化縣
Xin Tian (San Tin) 新田
xiucai 秀才
xiyang bing 西洋餅
xu 墟
Xuan Zang 玄奘
Xuan Zhao 玄照
Xuehai Tang 學海堂
xue yu 血瘀
Xu Guoxiang 徐國相
Xu Run 徐潤
Xuwen xian 徐聞縣

yache 軋車
yahang 牙行
Yan 燕
yangbing 洋餅
Yang Fu 楊孚
yanghang 洋行
yanghuo hang 洋貨行
yangtang 洋糖
yangyu 洋芋
Yantang jianwen zalu 研堂見聞雜錄
Yan ping 延平
Yao ge 樂歌
yaoji 腰機
yaozhe 藥蔗
yashang 牙商
Yasuda Tai 安田泰
yazhe qujiang 軋蔗取漿
yazui 鴨嘴
yi 邑
yimin 義民
Yingyai shenglan 瀛涯勝覽
yinhang 銀行
Yinshi xuzhi 飲食須知
yinzi qian 印子錢

yitian 義田
yitian liang zhu 一田兩主
yitian san zhu 一田三主
yitiao bianfa 一條鞭法
Yizhou 益州
yōkan 羊羹
yongbu jiafu 永不加賦
Yongle dadian 永樂大典
Yongning Si 永寧寺
Yoshimune 吉宗
You Gong Tang 友恭堂
Yue 粤
yu Fo shui 浴佛水
yu huang 鵌鰉
Yulin tuce 魚鱗圖册
Yu Yongho 郁永河

za 拶
za shui 雜稅
Zengcheng 增城
zhang 丈
Zhang Dajing 張達京
zhang fang 賬房
Zhang Lüxiang 張履祥
zhangmu cao 樟木槽
Zhang Xianzhong 張獻忠
zhansha 占沙
Zhao 趙
zhao hun 招魂
Zhao Rugua 趙汝适
zhaoshu 找贖
zhaotie 找貼
Zheng Chenggong 鄭成功
Zheng He 鄭和
Zheng Jing 鄭經
Zheng Tai 鄭泰
Zheng Zhilong 鄭芝龍
zhe nian 蔗碾
zhe xiao 蔗削
zhima tang 芝麻糖
zhong bao 中飽
zhong baoren 中保人
Zhongguo neiluan waihuo lishi congshu 中國内亂外禍歷史叢書
zhong hu 中戶
Zhongkui lu 中饋錄
zhong nong 中農
Zhou Mi 周密
Zhou Qufei 周去非
zhou tong 州同
Zhufan Zhi 諸蕃志
zhu pu zhi fen 主僕之分
Zhu Wan 朱紈
Zhu Yigui 朱一貴
zhu zhe 竹蔗
Zhu Zhenheng 朱震亨
zhuzhe 諸蔗
ziben zhuyi mengya 資本主義萌芽
zigeng nong 自耕農
zongqinhui 宗親會
zu 族
zumiao 族廟
zuoshang 坐商
zupu 祖譜

INDEX

HARVARD-YENCHING INSTITUTE

MONOGRAPH SERIES

(titles now in print)

11. *Han Shi Wai Chuan: Han Ying's Illustrations of the Didactic Application of the* Classic of Songs, translated and annotated by James Robert Hightower
21. *The Chinese Short Story: Studies in Dating, Authorship, and Composition*, by Patrick Hanan
22. *Songs of Flying Dragons: A Critical Reading*, by Peter H. Lee
23. *Early Chinese Civilization: Anthropological Perspectives*, by K. C. Chang
24. *Population, Disease, and Land in Early Japan, 645–900*, by William Wayne Farris
25. *Shikitei Sanba and the Comic Tradition in Edo Fiction*, by Robert W. Leutner
26. *Washing Silk: The Life and Selected Poetry of Wei Chuang (834?–910)*, by Robin D. S. Yates
27. *National Polity and Local Power: The Transformation of Late Imperial China*, by Min Tu-ki
28. *Tang Transformation Texts: A Study of the Buddhist Contribution to the Rise of Vernacular Fiction and Drama in China*, by Victor H. Mair
29. *Mongolian Rule in China: Local Administration in the Yuan Dynasty*, by Elizabeth Endicott-West
30. *Readings in Chinese Literary Thought*, by Stephen Owen
31. *Remembering Paradise: Nativism and Nostalgia in Eighteenth-Century Japan*, by Peter Nosco
32. *Taxing Heaven's Storehouse: Horses, Bureaucrats, and the Destruction of the Sichuan Tea Industry, 1074–1224*, by Paul J. Smith
33. *Escape from the Wasteland: Romanticism and Realism in the Fiction of Mishima Yukio and Oe Kenzaburo*, by Susan Jolliffe Napier
34. *Inside a Service Trade: Studies in Contemporary Chinese Prose*, by Rudolf G. Wagner

35. *The Willow in Autumn: Ryūtei Tanehiko, 1783–1842,* by Andrew Lawrence Markus
36. *The Confucian Transformation of Korea: A Study of Society and Ideology,* by Martina Deuchler
37. *The Korean Singer of Tales,* by Marshall R. Pihl
38. *Praying for Power: Buddhism and the Formation of Gentry Society in Late-Ming China,* by Timothy Brook
39. *Word, Image, and Deed in the Life of Su Shi,* by Ronald C. Egan
40. *The Chinese Virago: A Literary Theme,* by Yenna Wu
41. *Studies in the Comic Spirit in Modern Japanese Fiction,* by Joel R. Cohn
42. *Wind against the Mountain: The Crisis of Politics and Culture in Thirteenth-Century China,* by Richard L. Davis
43. *Powerful Relations: Kinship, Status, and the State in Sung China (960–1279),* by Beverly Bossler
44. *Limited Views: Essays on Ideas and Letters,* by Qian Zhongshu; selected and translated by Ronald Egan
45. *Sugar and Society in China: Peasants, Technology, and the World Market,* by Sucheta Mazumdar